Communities and Conservation

Histories and Politics of Community-Based Natural Resource Management

Edited by
J. Peter Brosius, Anna Lowenhaupt Tsing, and Charles Zerner

ALTAMIRA PRESS

A Division of
ROWMAN & LITTLEFIELD PUBLISHERS, INC.
Lanham • Boulder • New York • Toronto • Plymouth, UK

ALTAMIRA PRESS
A division of Rowman & Littlefield Publishers, Inc.
4501 Forbes Boulevard, Suite 200
Lanham, MD 20706

Estover Road
Plymouth PL6 7PY
United Kingdon

British Library Cataloguing in Publication Information Available

Library of Congress Cataloging-in-Publication Data

Communities and conservation : histories and politics of community-based natural resource management / edited by J. Peter Brosius, Anna Lowenhaupt Tsing, and Charles Zerner.
p. cm. — (Globalization and the environment)
Includes bibliographical references and index.
ISBN 0-7591-0505-7 (cloth : alk. paper) —
ISBN 0-7591-0506-5 (pbk. : alk. paper)
1. Conservation of natural resources—Citizen participation. 2. Natural resources—Citizen participation—Management. 3. Environmental management. I. Brosius, J. Peter. II. Tsing, Anna Lowenhaupt. III. Zerner, Charles. IV. Series.
S928.C65 2005
333.72—dc22 2004022202

Printed in the United States of America

™ The paper used in this publication meets the minimum requirements of American National Standard for Information Sciences—Permanence of Paper for Printed Library Materials, ANSI/NISO Z39.48–1992.

Contents

Acknowledgments

We wish to acknowledge the generous support of the Ford Foundation. Our project was made possible by a collaboration between Ford's Rural Poverty and Resources Program and their Education and Culture Program. We are especially grateful to Walter Coward and Ken Wilson of the Rural Poverty and Resources Program and Alison Bernstein and Toby Alice Volkman of the Education and Culture Program. Their enthusiasm and advice in developing and implementing this project was invaluable. We gratefully acknowledge the contributions of Janis B. Alcorn, Marcus Colchester, Margaret Keck, Pauline Peters, and Richard Schroeder, who offered advice and insight as members of the working group that convened, in 1996, to plan the Representing Communities conference that resulted in this volume. We've also benefited from the important insights of Pauline Gardner Barber, Mark Freudenberger, Robert Hitchcock, Margaret Keck, Joseph Matowanyika, Augusta Molnar, Nancy Peluso, Steven Sanderson, and Jim Spenser, all of whom thoughtfully contributed to the conference on "Representing Communities" from which this volume grew. The University of Georgia, Department of Anthropology, offered support and facilities for both the working group and the conference and we are grateful for its support. Finally, we wish to thank all the UGA graduate students who provided logistical support during the workshop and conference. David Elkin helped with the editing process. Ellen Walker made the final versions of the maps. Jeremy Campbell and Rachel Dvoskin checked the final proofs. Jeremy Campbell created the index.

The chapters in this book were written in the late 1990s. Publication delays have postponed the appearance of the collection, which reflects the situation at the period of writing. Debates about both conservation and community continue to evolve, but we believe the situations discussed in this book continue to be relevant to the present.

Introduction: Raising Questions about Communities and Conservation

Anna Lowenhaupt Tsing, J. Peter Brosius, and Charles Zerner

REPRESENTING COMMUNITIES

For more than a decade many people have been talking about the idea that communities might manage their own natural resources for conservation. It did not seem that communities could do a worse job than corporations, states, multilateral agencies, and development experts, who after all, have caused an extraordinary amount of human and environmental damage. Perhaps, advocates argued, communities could do something right: begin to redress the theft of land from indigenous peoples; offer local people control over environments they helped make; conserve a few forests and coral reefs. Thus began the effort—simultaneously diffuse and transnational—to build and extend new versions of environmental and social advocacy that link social justice and environmental management agendas under the rubric of community-based natural-resource management.

Community-based natural resource management (CBNRM) is based on several premises: that local populations have a greater interest in the sustainable use of resources than does the state or distant corporate managers, that local communities are more cognizant of the intricacies of local ecological processes and practices, and that communities are more able to effectively manage those resources through local or traditional forms of access. In insisting on the link between environmental degradation and social inequity and by providing a concrete scheme for action in the CBNRM model, nongovernmental organizations (NGOs) and their allies have sought to bring about a fundamental rethinking of how the goals of conservation and effective resource management can be linked to the search for social justice for historically marginalized peoples.

As this agenda gained momentum, more questions were raised: What is a community? What is natural resource management? Community for whom and management for what? The successes of disseminating and implementing the CBNRM model raised new challenges and dilemmas as the concepts of community, territory, locality, conservation, and customary law were worked into politically varied plans and programs in disparate sites. The rhetoric of community control has been taken up not only by grassroots organizers, but also by development agencies and conservation organizations, foundations, and the World Bank. In the confluence of these different streams, key concepts—local initiatives and international mandates, economic development, environmental protection, local rights, empowerment, and coercion—are being reshaped to mean new things. We believe the time is ripe for focused discussion about the historical development and political shape of CBNRM.

This volume has its origins in a June 1997 conference sponsored by the Ford Foundation. The impetus for the conference was an extended series of conversations between us, the three co-organizers, over a series of issues related to tensions that exist in the encounter between scholarship and advocacy. In our own work, each of us had observed slippage between generic, model-type ideas of community, common-property rules, and resource management practices as they are applied in development circles and the culturally distinctive, historically conditioned, and changing practices we had seen among the Southeast Asian communities in which we work. As scholars, we were aware of the idealized and ultimately inadequate nature of the terms we saw being employed. At the same time, we were concerned that the CBNRM movement was being used by global financial and development institutions to further their own agendas, to circulate capital through their institutional networks, and to rationalize national governments' environmental policies. The intellectual problems and ethical tensions of employing discourses that were simultaneously emancipatory and ahistorical or generic led us to a heightened awareness of the critical need to form new languages of advocacy and for discussion between advocates, donors, and scholars, based on real histories of CBNRM in situ.

To the 1997 conference we invited CBNRM advocates, engaged scholars, and foundation program officers. Within the compass of those committed to the alliance triad of social justice, cultural respect, and environmental conservation, we wanted to bring together a diversity of voices and seek clarification through debate. We hoped to tap into a particular conjuncture in which engaged scholars and informed advocates continued to differ on questions regarding the reification of tradition, community, and culturally distinctive lifeways. Since the 1980s, progressive and reflective anthropologists had been criticizing their own disciplinary practices, which through the twentieth century had convinced metropolitan publics that there were exotic primitives doing strange things out there in the jungle. These scholarly representations, the critics said, demeaned the people being represented, many of whom were also part of cosmopolitan conversations, even as they might take their cosmopolitanism with a sense of difference. Meanwhile, a growing momentum of indigenous people's movements had reintroduced the notion of culturally distinctive tribes into the calculus of metropolitan justice advocacy, producing a florescence of new organizations, publications, and political strategies. Like two waves arriving from different directions, scholars and activists met and generated a mutually critical exchange. Scholars said the activists were reproducing pernicious stereotypes, while activists replied that scholars were too busy self-indulgently advancing their own careers to notice urgent dilemmas. The conference participants hoped that somewhere in this interchange important insights might be found. Might we be able to draw upon the new criticisms of representational practices to broaden and sharpen the practical tools of CBNRM? Could we use the experiences of advocates working with marginal groups to produce a critique of representation that was more concrete and meaningful? Our hope in convening the conversation was that it would generate new, creative possibilities for social justice, cultural respect, and conservation through a blend of reflection and engagement.

We asked what, exactly, CBNRM has come to mean. Our starting point was a recognition that CBNRM is imagined differently by different actors. Populist activists hope to empower local communities in their conflicts with state resource-management agencies and national and transnational capital. Indigenous people's spokespersons argue for a new respect for local rights, knowledge, and cultures. Development organizations, driven in part by vigorous criticism of socially and economically oppressive resource-development projects that they have supported, aim to promote local participation in conservation and development. Some conservationists hope to involve local people in pursuing transnational conservation and resource-management goals as a means of protecting biological diversity and habitat integrity. Other conservationists have begun to challenge the basic premise that conservation based on the idea of CBNRM can be successful, and new larger-scale models of conservation are emerging. We hoped to examine how the histories of struggles, networks, foundation connections, and national and transnational political cultures have shaped CBNRM programs, and to gain from this a distinctive vantage from which to approach particular cases of community-management claims. We wanted to bring together case studies of advocacy and contestation and to critically reflect on some of the assumptions held by those involved.

This concern for dialogue has carried over into this volume. Most edited volumes bring together a set of independent chapters, but here we have assembled a conversation in which participants address each other to amplify each other's points, offer contrasting cases, and agree or disagree. Scholars bring to the volume concerns about essentializing discourses of community and tradition, about potential dangers of linking ethnicity and territory, and about the problematic relationship between legal pluralism and citizenship. Advocates, for their part, bring concerns that CBNRM may be co-opted by multilateral banks. And members of the donor community bring their concerns about the implications of scaling up particular models of CBNRM that have so far been successful only in specific contexts.

Information sharing, program assessment, personal reflection, critical scholarship, strategic planning, and networking are genres that do not always fit together neatly. But here we use them to create a lively dialogue, and sometimes debate, about the politics of community-based conservation and resource management. Whatever our differences, the scholars, advocates, and donors who have contributed to this volume agree that we have common interests in understanding the histories and politics of varied projects intended to promote CBNRM in specific sites and historical contexts. Only through the explication of specific histories and political dynamics can we begin to address the problems and prospects of CBNRM. For the movement to flourish, both advocates and analysts must remain alert to the contested, varied, and changing cultural and political agendas and contexts in which these programs are being implemented.

* * *

The book is divided into two parts. The chapters in part 1, *Mobilizations and Models,* offer detailed examinations of the histories and politics of specific CBNRM initiatives. They are divided into three sections: *Institutional Mandates* considers the history of institutional commitments to CBNRM; *Defining Community in National and Transnational Contexts* focuses on the specificity and spread of one rather successful model, CAMPFIRE, for representing communities; and *Empowerment or Coercion?* addresses cases where CBNRM has gained a footing in particular contexts, both as part of a broader emancipatory struggle and as a coercive instrument of state power. The chapters in part 2, *Stealing the Master's Tools: Mapping and Law in Community-Based Natural-Resource Management*, discuss the politics of the central technologies of CBNRM: mapping and legal advocacy. Mapping and law carry some of the central dilemmas of representing communities. Part 2 is divided into two sections: *Mapping against Power* examines cases where communities have challenged the spatial hegemonies of state and corporate land-use practices through countermapping projects. *Legal Strategies for the Disenfranchised* focuses on the possibilities and the perils of legal strategies for the assertion of rights to community land.

* * *

PART 1: MOBILIZATIONS AND MODELS

The conversations in this volume revolve around a number of shared questions, each of which can be asked in different ways depending on the personae we adopt. Participants switch between and translate across their roles as activists, scholars, and program builders. The questions they ask thus reverberate, shift, and talk back to each other across these roles.

How can we tell the promising programs for community control of natural-resource management from the damaging ones?

Sometimes international agencies offer prepackaged and closely supervised community forest management as a condition for local people to use forest resources. This can appear to be yet another heavy-handed type of development intervention. (See, for example, Schroeder's chapter on the Gambian-German Forestry Project.) In contrast, community rights over land and resources may be the key demand of rural people struggling against authoritarian rule. National activism for community rights over forests, in some cases, sits at the center of struggles for responsible democracy. (See Hafild's chapter on Indonesian mobilizations.) These are only two of many variants. In sorting out the very different kinds of CBNRM programs found around the world today, we discuss the multiple valences generated by the charisma of the rhetoric of CBNRM. To follow the rhetoric is not always a reliable guide to the project's promise.

When programs are formed, as they must be, around political negotiations and compromises, are there fundamental principles that should be saved at all costs?

A detailed history of the political negotiations that brought to life the much-heralded Zimbabwean program called CAMPFIRE offers a case study for thinking about the promises and perils of strategic compromise. As program founder Marshall Murphree observes, the program was in some places successful in creating community income and conserving wildlife, whereas in others it was less successful. As for the original goal of strengthening communal land tenure, the issue remains unsettled. Was it worth it? Our commentators disagree.

What happens when charismatic programs are used as inspiration in new places? How nationally specific must a good program be? What are the effects of using successful programs as models in transnational networking?

In common with the domains of development and conservation, CBNRM was created in an institutional context that placed a premium on replicability as the measure of a program's worth. The discussion of CAMPFIRE leads us into the question of the international proliferation and reception of CBNRM programs. How has CAMPFIRE stimulated and inspired other programs, in southern Africa and beyond? Our commentators agree that no program is ever imported unchanged; in programs for community empowerment the negotiations over what should count as local control are always intense and themselves local. Yet the charisma and practical example of a successful program are important stimuli for struggles over locality. Meanwhile, too, regional historical legacies work themselves out in these struggles, sometimes to community disadvantage. As critic Rod Neumann asks, "Cannot one see the shadow of colonial rule in community conservation programs?"

Why did conservation and development organizations, foundations, and agencies come to embrace CBNRM?

In considering the question of the charisma of CBNRM programs, we are brought back to why they have become so popular among NGOs and foundations. This question is important for both scholarly and practical reasons: The scholar asks, How do ideas and movements travel? and looks to see how the cultural content of charismatic packages such as CBNRM both transforms the world and is itself transformed in global movement. Activists ask, Under what circumstances does advocacy for communities succeed in influencing conservation and development policy? and look within organizational histories for winning strategies of social justice advocacy. Program builders want to know, Why do we care about collaboration and locality anyway? and take a moment for reflection. Each of these questions is relevant in recounting the histories through which organizations such as the Ford Foundation, the World Wide Fund for Nature, and the World Conservation Union (IUCN) have considered promoting policies of community resource management.

These kinds of questions—argued around very particular programs, organizations, and settings—carry us into some of the biggest debates of our times.

Are NGOs and international foundations key participants in a new imperial disciplinary regime, working in the service of capitalist globalization, or are they agents for new projects of democratization and grassroots mobilization?

Some observers see only a new, transnational empire (e.g., Hardt and Negri 2000). As Wolfgang Sachs asks, is conservation "about to transform itself from a knowledge of opposition to a knowledge of domination . . . reshaped as expert neutral knowledge, until it can be wedded to the dominating world view?" (Sachs 1993, xv). Can conservation continue to open more inclusive visions of social justice, cultural diversity, and environmental protection (e.g., Ghai and Vivian 1992)? On the one hand, international organizations have increasing power to supervise everyday life even in remote villages; on the other, exhilarating new alliances among environmentalists, indigenous rights advocates, populists, and even labor, with their ability to disrupt taken-for-granted hegemonies, offer new sources of hope. Our focused discussion of CBNRM moves beyond the abstract debate about the possibilities and dangers of NGO politics to suggest how participants have viewed power and empowerment in the making of particular, historically situated programs.

Is the concept of community the bedrock of social justice or a misleading rhetoric of rural romanticism, ethnic chauvinism, or imperial control?

The debate here is heated. Critics worry about the fetishization of pastoralist ideals of rural cultural harmony. Advocates are excited by the possibility of moving beyond the more fetishized individualist ideals of capitalism and modernization, with their naturalization of Euro-American bourgeois norms. Critics worry about the ethnic violence that might arise when a cultural group is offered control of a territory. Advocates point to the sheer, outright theft that occurs as indigenous peoples are dispossessed of their last ancestral places. Critics remind us of more widespread inequalities. Advocates argue that communities have knowledge that the world needs. Critics reply that indigenous knowledge is already a product of capitalism; communities are defined and controlled by more-powerful actors. These debates will not be settled in the abstract. Our attention to advocacy programs in which communities have been identified provides one forum for the ongoing discussion.

How should we shape human relationships to nature to create a world in which many species can live? Should we make nature a valued commodity, expanding capitalist markets to make conservation a better source of income, or should we work to maintain pockets of noncapitalist social and human–nature relations? Should we see nature as resources or as species with lives, and perhaps rights, of their own? Should we segregate nature from human endeavors—or promote development within it?

One way our contributors engage this thorny set of questions, albeit indirectly, is through struggles over terminology. Consider the discussion among the editors about what to call this mouthful—CBNRM. Brosius and Zerner like the term *natural-resource management* because it foregrounds human endeavors, escaping the problems of an environmentalist tradition that has sometimes privileged preservation over human livelihood. Tsing prefers *conservation* because it reaches out to include nonhumans and at least occasionally refers to a social movement, rather than bureaucratic practices of management over instrumentally imagined resources. All three agreed to highlight the term *community* as much as a provocation to discussion as a principle of advocacy. Other contributors have felt less comfortable using community. Borrini-Feyerabend, for example, speaks of "collaborative management" and avoids issues of communal ties to focus on the alliance among individual "stakeholders." The negotiation of terms also brings in the jargon of development, used by both critics and promoters to extend natural-resource management into modernization frames. Thus, for example, Neumann writes of CBNRM-ICDP, where the second acronym stands for integrated conservation and development project, because he wants to stress the continuity between conservation and development planning assumptions. The editors have purposely left a certain looseness to the volume's use of terms to reflect these kinds of discussions. At the same time, however, our focus on the representation of communities has pressed questions of the representation of nature, much debated elsewhere (Adams and McShane 1992; Cronon 1995; Proctor and Pincetl 1996; Slater 2000, 67–82; 2003; Zerner 1995, 2000, 2003), into a secondary place in this volume.

Institutional Mandates

Why, despite megascale development remaining the prevailing framework for internationally planned social change, has CBNRM become a hot item for many conservation organizations, development agencies, and foundations? This section asks how groups within these institutions came to endorse and propagate community-based models of conservation and resource management. In the process, we learn about the possibilities—and limitations—of the CBNRM ideal.

Janis Alcorn, formerly with the Biodiversity Support Program and the World Wildlife Fund, begins our discussion with a masterful review of the position of conservation organizations in regard to communities. To consider this issue, we must begin, she argues, by differentiating Big Conservation—the programs of big northern conservation groups—and Little Conservation—the conservation activities of ordinary people, North and South. It is only in considering Little Conservation that conservation organizations take a closer look at cultural habits and attitudes toward nature, social conventions of access, and the function and shape of communities. One goal of CBNRM, she suggests, is to make sure Big Conservation does not wipe out Little Conservation by ignoring and undermining it. As the weaknesses of Big Conservation have become clearer, a number of conservation organizations have looked toward strategies to strengthen and legitimate Little Conservation. Alcorn lays out a number of different conservation stances in regard to this issue, ranging from park-centric protectionist approaches, through sustainable development resource management approaches, to advocacy campaigns that support the rights of traditional communities. She traces the different assumptions in each of these positions, showing where they overlap and where they contradict each other. One important but often neglected divergence, for example, separates approaches that advocate for the livelihood needs of communities from those that advocate for community rights. The implications for the organization of both community and nature are quite different in each model.

Alcorn uses the example of the World Wildlife Fund-US to trace how community-oriented thinking arose in a particular conservation organization. She points to the importance of the endorsement of articulate leaders, the success of model projects, the pressures from donors, and the possibility of new kinds of conservation alliances created by community-oriented approaches. Indeed, the importance of considering the politics of these alliances frames her discussion: must conservationists, she asks, dance with national elites, corporations, and multilateral aid agencies, or might they turn to other partners, such as threatened communities? Her analysis brings us beyond the false neutrality of programs that purport to include all stakeholders as equal partners: Partnerships are always a form of political mobilization, and the choices we make about whom to include as our most important partners shape the politics of our programs, for better and for worse.

The question of partnerships also forms the focus of Grazia Borrini-Feyerabend and Christopher Tarnowski's discussion of the "collaborative management" programs endorsed by the IUCN. Their chapter offers an insightful set of reflections about the importance and limitations of collaboration. After introducing us to the history of IUCN's attraction to collaborative management programs, Borrini-Feyerabend and Tarnowski walk us through the arguments for and against collaboration. Advocates argue that collaboration allows the expression of complementary abilities, such that, for example, states and communities might work together in conservation. Yet, as opponents note, collaboration often links actors with opposing rather than complementary views; conservation's objectives are in danger of being watered down by other goals, such as profit making. Collaborative management offers the possibility that responsibilities in resource management will be widely discussed and shared among many parties. Yet conservation organizations also fear that by giving up full responsibility for projects they will lose control of their direction. Furthermore, it is possible, Borrini-Feyerabend and Tarnowski note, that collaboration may favor the powerful, rather than the weak, who are unable to set the terms of the collaboration. And yet, they argue, it is important to remember that collaboration is already the way both scientists and communities operate. Scientists transform knowledge through collaborative networks and negotiations. Communities transform the landscape through collaborative networks and negotiations. Collaborative management programs do a service if they recognize these already existing networks and negotiations in building formal models to advantage both conservation and communities.

Walter Coward, former director of the Rural Poverty and Resources Program of the Ford Foundation, moves the discussion from the philosophy of collaboration to the cultural and political content of community-based resource-management models. After all, even collaborations as specific as those between conservationists and communities can lead to many different kinds of dreams and plans. Which ones have seemed right? Which ones have become influential and spread? There is nothing self-evident about the packages that have come to be known as CBNRM programs. Only some acquire the charisma to influence policy. What makes a collaborative idea linking communities and policy makers work?

Coward is in a good position to consider these questions because of his involvement with the CBNRM programs of the Ford Foundation, which has been a major promoter of CBNRM through its regional offices around the world. His narrative is extraordinarily suggestive of how CBNRM became a charismatic package at Ford and among those they have influenced. Two conjunctures have been key. The first is the discovery of small-scale, community-based irrigation at precisely that moment that development agencies were obsessed with large-scale irrigation. Coward relates how he stumbled on small-scale irrigation in Southeast Asia in a context where international developers, unaware of or ignoring its existence, were preparing to invest major sums in building big dams. By doing local research, he found that both technical knowledge and social organization for irrigation already existed! At that period, big dams were the favored type of development—both the symbol of the possibility of national modernization and a major sink for international development funding. Small-scale irrigation was the perfect symbol for the alternative: not big dams, but small dams; not Big Development, but community-based development. The political will to support local forms of resource management owes a great deal to small-scale irrigation being such an apt carrier for the idea of community.

The second conjuncture was the extension of the promotion of community-based irrigation to the promotion of community-based forestry. At the 1997 conference, Coward discussed how he took ideas he had developed in the Philippines about small-scale irrigation and used them in building Ford's programs in Indonesia. There he met foresters who were worried about massive forest destruction and the linked loss of rural livelihoods. From their discussions, a larger domain of CBNRM emerged: community irrigation models could help reorganize forestry. Two kinds of charisma were gained in this coming together. First, CBNRM became a general resource-management model: soon, for example, Ford was thinking about community-based fisheries. Second, a whole new set of allies was acquired through the choice of community-based forestry. Conservationists were worried about forests;

indigenous rights groups were worried about forest communities. The Ford Foundation was not ready to endorse either conservation or indigenous rights; however, both their local and international programs gained momentum from the impetus of these overlapping causes.

Coward's history of CBNRM at the Ford Foundation offers a useful guide to the making of a charismatic package. This discussion is extended in the next section, which examines one particular CBNRM program, in all its specificity, to understand both its charisma and the limits of what it can do. After all, charisma requires cultural specificity to convince a particular constituency—whether international developers, conservationists, national policy makers, donors, social movement activists, or local folks. Specificity is the source of the strength, and the limits, of any particular program, because it defines community, conservation, or anything else.

Defining Community in National and Transnational Contexts

One of the best-known CBNRM programs internationally is CAMPFIRE, a government-, an NGO-, and an international-agency-supported initiative in Zimbabwe that offers rural communities a share of the income gained from international big-game hunting if they conserve local wildlife. Unlike many of the most advocacy-oriented CBNRM campaigns, CAMPFIRE does not argue for the conservation of resources for the community's own use and because of the community's traditional knowledge. Rather, it conserves resources for other people's use and appreciation in exchange for some of the substantial revenue gained from this. The local people did not really like the wildlife, which interfered with their crops, but they were willing to reconsider this position when CAMPFIRE offered them money, clinics, and schools from wildlife revenue. CAMPFIRE thus embodies an awkward compromise between two visions: one of wildlife conservation and one of income generation and community development. These visions are often stereotyped as characterizing the privileged North, on the one hand, and the underprivileged South, on the other. In fact, this stereotype is far from correct, and it would be at least as useful to argue that both visions are northern models imposed on the South or, alternately, that both are formed in complex, heterogeneous, and hybrid global conversations. Yet its popular cachet draws us into some of the central contradictions and debates surrounding conservation and development. CAMPFIRE's ability to forge an uneasy alliance between conservation and development dreams has made it "good to think with" for those engaged in imagining CBNRM.

Although CAMPFIRE has been noted and discussed a great deal internationally, no detailed account of its history had been written; thus we asked Marshall Murphree, the program's founder, to tell us how the program came to its current shape. Murphree's chapter not only makes this important history available but also offers us a model of how to think about the national specificity of advocacy programs. At the heart of building a program, Murphree shows, lie three dynamic forces, which he calls "congruent objectives," "competing interests," and "strategic compromise." Each of these requires program builders to be flexible enough to forge an effective national specificity, that is, one that will convince enough people at national, international, and subnational levels to give the program the power of institutionalization. An effective program requires the bringing together of allies and the forging of congruent objectives. For CAMPFIRE, these allies included an academic research unit, an NGO, and a government department. Together, they were able to argue for a conceptual core for the program—ecological sustainability, economic efficiency, and institutional effectiveness and acceptability—that seemed reasonable for the Zimbabwean context. The program was then able to mount a kind of political campaign within the competing interests of Zimbabwean public culture: program designers wanted to offer small farmers stronger control over land and resources. The only way to gain even partial success, however, was to engage in strategic compromise. Thus, for example, CAMPFIRE's communities were defined in relation to preexisting political structures rather than ecological or social affinities because this allowed the program to pass through government hurdles. And these national compromises were only the prelude to further negotiations at the district level. The unevenness of the program's success in various districts reflects the heterogeneous results of such negotiations.

Murphree stresses the specificity, and even the exceptionalness, of CAMPFIRE. His emphasis on this point is particularly strong because of a question raised in the 1997 conference for which the chapter was first written: has CAMPFIRE been a model for CBNRM? The conference organizers asked other advocates, scholars, and program designers to comment on CAMPFIRE under the title "Proliferating Models": had the international, high profile of CAMPFIRE allowed it to form a template for other programs? And while Murphree as well as all the commentators answered no, these answers took very different positions. Wilson: CAMPFIRE has been a positive stimulus to the making of other CBNRM programs in the region, but never as a cookie-cutter-type model. Neumann: Far from being an original creation, CAMPFIRE draws on regional colonial logics of administration and authority. Fortmann's paper title described her position: "Some Folks Don't Want No Proliferating Models Nohow." The divergence of perspectives here offers a clear indication of the transnational influence of CAMPFIRE, as well as a rather more nuanced sense than the original question of proliferating models of just how transnational influence is variously expressed.

Ken Wilson, formerly a Ford Foundation program officer in Mozambique, salutes Murphree's personal dedication and insight in the forging of CAMPFIRE's effectiveness in Zimbabwe even as he shows how the program could not be transferred in any direct way into the politically quite different Mozambique. In Zimbabwe, Wilson argues, it makes sense to make the strategic compromises that lend institutional effectiveness to a program at the national center and then transfer projects to the countryside; in Mozambique, in contrast, national political culture encourages a "bubbling up" of community initiatives from the countryside. In the 1990s the Mozambican national elite became excited about supporting community-based approaches; the example of CAMPFIRE was a stimulus to create their own regionally and nationally distinctive kinds of CBNRM programs. Wilson describes in particular the Tchuma Tchato program, which was, indeed, influenced by the example of CAMPFIRE but went through a full panoply of negotiations between the community and national and international players before assuming its local shape. Wilson stresses the importance of gifted leaders who are able to take advantage of—and make—openings to make social justice dreams begin to become real.

Geographer Rod Neumann expands on these same themes, offering them a regional and historical dimension. It is difficult for CBNRM programs in Africa, he argues, to divorce themselves from the colonial heritage of dispossession of African people from their land and resources. CBNRM programs draw on this heritage to the extent that they segregate human settlement and nature conservation. Furthermore, there is direct colonial precedent for programs that use the idea of community control to keep Africans away from state-protected natural resources. Neumann stresses the importance of voluntary, self-defined community participation in CBNRM projects, and he notes that this is an ideal rarely achieved; he worries, for example, about CAMPFIRE's compromises, particularly in allowing the state to define communities. He also outlines the mix of forces that influence decisions about the structure and definition of community approaches: local resistance to state natural-resource laws; neoliberal reforms that impoverish the state, necessitating community self-sufficiency; democratization movements; and land-reform policies. Neumann argues that we need to be alert to the dangers as well as the possibilities of the mix and tension among these forces in the creation of CBNRM.

Rural sociologist Louise Fortmann provides an almost comic relief to this serious deliberation by explaining what happens to understandings of CAMPFIRE in the animal-loving public culture of the United States. The Humane Society-US mounted a campaign against U.S. Agency for International Development (USAID) funding for CAMPFIRE in 1997 on the grounds that CAMPFIRE promoted the slaughter of elephants by allowing hunting. Fortmann's attempts to talk to advocates of this campaign about the importance of empowering communities in Africa were met with stereotypes of dangerous African savages; many people in the United States seem to have a lot more empathy for elephants than for Africans. Fortmann reminds us that CBNRM advocates may share a common vocabulary and set of assumptions that are little known in wider public contexts. The work of building and evaluating community-based programs requires reaching out to culturally diverse audiences, both in the North and in the South, and in cities as well as in forest villages.

Empowerment or Coercion?

Are CBNRM programs a good thing? Participants in the 1997 conference agreed that the rhetoric of CBNRM can lead in very different political directions: on the one hand, international agencies and national bureaucracies may encourage CBNRM as a way of cutting costs and increasing supervision over poor people's daily routines; on the other hand, CBNRM may form an aspect of emancipatory political struggles. It seems important to disentangle different varieties of CBNRM to be clearer about the political alliances and compromises we are willing to choose. To do this, we need to trace the local and global political histories in which CBNRM initiatives are embedded.

Geographer Richard Schroeder offers a cautionary tale in the case of a German-funded community-forestry project in The Gambia. The expatriate staff of the project have supported community management as a way of giving local people responsibility for the tasks of forestry management without giving up any control. The Gambian Forestry Department, describing itself as "conscious of the economic and man-power constraints that the government faces, and the availability of a large pool of cheap labor in the form of village community labor force" (Bojang 1994: 2), has promoted this plan for cost cutting. Thus communities were offered rights only on the condition that they fulfill the tasks mandated by project personnel. No attempts were made to learn about preexisting forms of common property or natural-resource management. Instead, project personnel saw their role as teaching people to be proper resource managers. Negotiating through formal contracts, they forced people to agree to the finely articulated technical requirements of the program. In most cases, the community had to fulfill program conditions for three years before even being considered for local resource rights. Here, he argues, CBNRM is a tool of structural adjustment, not social-justice advocacy.

Richard Chase Smith of Oxfam America pursues a related set of cautions but from the perspective of community organizers who have worked for many years to advocate for community control. This is "ant's labor," he points out; it takes much longer than the funding cycle at foundations or the attention span of media campaigns permits. And it is always in danger of being interrupted by community plans imposed from above. Smith describes the social movement among indigenous communities in the Peruvian Amazon for land and resource rights, with its obstacles and its small successes.

Centro para el Desarrollo del Indígena Amazónico (CEDIA), an NGO working with the Machiguenga people, has been working on community-rights issues since the early 1980s. In 1996, however, the Peruvian government signed a contract with a Shell-Mobil consortium to develop gas fields. Hoping for good public relations internationally, Shell agreed to put in place social and environmental programs. However, they consulted neither the NGOs nor the local people about these programs; instead, they started their own process. As a community advocate, Smith points to the importance of retaining some optimism in these circumstances that an opportunity for something useful can be found. However, he is also properly concerned about the unevenness of the negotiation between community Davids and corporate Goliaths. This kind of situation, in which community rights depend on finding openings in corporate plans, is increasingly important in even the most grassroots-oriented CBNRM plans.

A contrasting case is offered by Emmy Hafild's discussion of advocacy for community land and resource rights in late New Order Indonesia, where this advocacy not only addressed rural communities but simultaneously informed the national democratic opposition to authoritarian rule as well as the socially and environmentally destructive power of capital. Hafild is the former director of the Indonesian environmentalist group Wahana Lingkungan Hidup Indonesia (WALHI), or Friends of the Earth Indonesia, which gathers NGOs from around the nation to fight simultaneously at local, national, and international levels of advocacy. Under the authoritarian New Order regime (1966–1998), the central government annexed forests and other natural resources and handed them out to foreign and domestic corporations in exchange for support for the regime and its elite. Rural people lost rights to the environments that had been the source of their livelihood for generations. In these circumstances, the struggle for community control of resources was crucial, but very difficult. Protest was limited by military rule. Information was censored. Beginning in the 1980s, WALHI formed to offer a national umbrella to varied local mobilizations and campaigns. By the 1990s WALHI was able to join a growing democratic opposition to authoritarian rule, which in 1998 succeeded in ending the regime. Throughout this process, WALHI was a key voice for the marginalized communities of the countryside who were otherwise made invisible by the rhetoric of the regime or presented as happy clients of government beneficence.

Hafild's chapter offers four cases in which WALHI played a role in advocacy for particular community struggles for resource control. In each case, the community had helped to create natural resources, such as rattan gardens, dammar resin forests, and generally livable landscapes. In each case, the government had given the community-created landscape to a corporation to destroy for corporate profits. Such cases proliferated in late New Order Indonesia because the regime and its booming economy depended on such nonsustainable and unjust corporate gifts. Most rural communities were unable to mount protests against such expropriations. Those that did depended on the support of national organizations such as WALHI, with their ability to bring international attention, legal arguments, and national elite support to bear on particular abuses. As Hafild explained at the 1997 conference, WALHI imagined its role as offering communities support rather than trying to fit them into predesigned programs. Sometimes they were able to arrange negotiations with sympathetic government officials or to make use of disagreements between bureaus to carve out spaces of community advantage. But they never imagined their role at that time as more than amplifying community voices. Although Indonesian national politics has been transformed since the fall of the New Order regime in 1998, it is important to consider the late New Order period as an example of how particular community struggles for resource control can form part of a national democratic movement. The promise of this mobilization continues to inform the best possibilities of the still rather-hard-to-call resource politics of the present.

Each of the contributors, then, stresses the need to contextualize CBNRM programs—whether advocacy or development interventions—in larger political histories. CBNRM never creates an autonomous political space; it is a part of larger movements, whether of structural adjustment, corporate public relations, NGO community advocacy, or democratic struggle. The first step in assessing a CBNRM program must be to consider the alliances and mobilizations on which it depends. This returns us to Janis Alcorn's concern with the "dancing partners" of conservation programs: just whom are they dancing with? Corporate officials, government cost cutters, political movements, regional bureaucrats, village heads, local religious leaders, farmers' organizations, or school teachers? In considering the field of alliance and mobilization that CBNRM enters, it may be possible to glimpse the political potential of the program for empowering communities.

PART 2: STEALING THE MASTER'S TOOLS

In the last few decades of the twentieth century, environmentally destructive natural-resource exploitation took a new leap—into the globe's most marginal places. Miners, dam builders, loggers, ranchers, fishing consortiums, and plantation developers scrambled to take control of the last places where nature could be stolen for free with the permission of the state and the international business community. The rich countries of the North encouraged their businesspeople to turn over every rock, at home and abroad, to reap these cheap harvests. The Third World nations that had emerged from colonial rule after World War II vied with each other to sell their resources to extractive industries in the name of modernization and development. National elites found it easy to dispose of the people and environments of marginal places: no one they had to listen to lived there.

Why, at least until recently, have there been so many resources remaining in these marginal places? And why have they been free for the taking? From the perspective of corporate and national elites, these are wastelands—jungles, mountains, rivers, coral reefs, tundras, and so forth—that have been lying around unused; no one has cared about them enough to claim them except the state. But from the perspective of people who have been living in these places for generations, these resources are only there because they have exercised stewardship over them. They only seem free because national policy makers and transnational corporations have no respect for their land and resource claims. The windfall is really a rip-off.

The rip-off has not gone unnoticed. It has brought to life new political voices and, in particular, alliances of angry inhabitants of appropriated and damaged places and social-justice-oriented environmental and indigenous rights activists. Working through the transnational NGO movement, they have gathered the funding and support of a number of international foundations and agencies. In conferences and workshops, they have forged ties across ethnic and national differences. They have supported each other in protests. They exchange information. They invent practical programs that offer a start in fighting against land and resource expropriation.

One of these programs is CBNRM. What if the inhabitants of these resource-rich marginal places were to manage their own environments? Although until very recently it flew in the face of conventional international-development wisdom that dubs all rural people too ignorant and poor to manage resources properly, this idea even so has appeal. It is undeniable that there is more biodiversity precisely in the places where those people called indigenous, tribal, traditional, customary, or just plain backward live. It is also undeniable that these people are being cheated out of their inheritance. Would it not be both more just and more environmentally sound to allow these marginal people to defend their rich environments rather than giving them away to profiteering corporations?

By the end of the twentieth century, both conservationists and social-justice activists were eager for such a program, with its interlinked defense not just of minority rights but also of cultural and biological diversity. Many conservationists were realizing that top-down, coercive conservation was not working very well; they were ready to explore community-oriented alternatives. Meanwhile, a number of social-justice activists were discouraged with nationalist and class-based models that assumed that all disadvantaged people wanted was a better share of the wealth, because these models had allowed the environmental and human-rights disasters of postcolonial national development. They became open to the idea that culturally distinctive and marginalized people—once seen by the progressive left as archaically irrelevant—might have something to contribute to a social-justice agenda. For the sake of the hope embedded in the revitalization of marginalized cultures, a significant group of activists was willing to foreground the communal and cultural aspects of rural life. In this context, a variety of activists, foundation personnel, and policy makers endorsed the idea of CBNRM.

From the first, it was clear to CBNRM advocates that maps and laws were central challenges. Maps and laws had been used by both colonial and national regimes to deny the existence and criminalize the livelihoods of the marginal people who were demanding their inheritance. These were people who had been consistently and carefully left off official maps. Their lands had been declared uninhabited and visually displayed as empty, wild. Their lands had also been declared to have no owners other than the state: this was the law. When the inhabitants were noticed at all, they were often called trespassers on the lands they had occupied for centuries. They were illegal occupants, their status lower than the frontiersmen and settlers who came to reap the treasures freed by the state guarantee of open-access, unowned land.

Could maps and laws be turned around for the advocacy of community-based claims over land and resources? CBNRM advocates were willing to try. And, indeed, with the development of community countermapping and counterlaw claims, the CBNRM movement took off. It seemed possible that alternative mapping and law tools might give embattled marginal groups something to work with in national and international fora. At the same time, as geographer Dianne Rocheleau reminds us in her chapter, echoing feminist theorist Audre Lorde, the master's tools cannot dismantle the master's house (Lorde 1984). Yet it seems impossible to avoid the master's tools completely. If those of us who want to see justice, multicultural respect, and a healthy environment plan to use the master's tools, including law and mapping, we had better remain self-reflective, open to new ideas, and alert to the nuances of good as well as bad compromises. Maps and laws encode so many assumptions about power—the power of the state, of territory, of property, of prisons—that we need to be careful and creative to avoid biting off our nose to spite our face. A CBNRM program worth fighting for needs a critical, self-conscious awareness.

This kind of advocacy cannot avoid the master's tools. From the perspective of advocacy, law and mapping as strategies for community empowerment are necessary even as they are problematic. However, even the most impassioned activists agree that sometimes well-intentioned projects fail to work out very well for the communities they were supposed to empower. This is where critical reflection on the tools can be helpful. Rather than treating our tools as if they were devoid of political content or consequences, we need to consider how they carry powerful legacies, how they create new frameworks and distinctions, and how they can be used by state bureaucrats and corporations as well as community members. Just what kind of reflection and how much of it we need is obviously a subject of debate and discussion among the contributors. And the discussion is the point: through it we clarify our stakes and goals, we consider contrasting cases, and we stimulate our creativity.

Mapping against Power

What rural sociologist Nancy Peluso has called "countermapping" (Peluso 1995) has caught on like wildfire as a technique for facilitating the land and resource claims of marginalized groups around the world. Native North Americans were using the technique by the 1970s to establish their presence in areas where they had been imagined as only a distant memory by the white settler majority and the state (Brody 1981). Indigenous people in Latin America and Australia borrowed these ideas and developed their own approaches in the 1980s to respond to the possibility of indigenous land titling as it arose in various national contexts. By the 1990s community mapping projects were widespread, too, in Africa and Asia, used variously to establish a minority presence, to legitimize land rights, to negotiate boundary disputes, and to make the case for unrecognized forms of property and resource management (Aberly 1993; Alcorn 2000; Eghenter 2000; Poole 1995a, 1995b; Sirait et al. 1994; Vandergeest 1996).

Countermapping projects, under the best of circumstances, bring a community to life. Peter Poole spoke at the conference of the vitality of the project he advised on among the Ye'kuana people of Venezuela. Young people, instead of talking of migrating to town, joined in elders' excitement about defining and maintaining something that might count as community. They formed teams to hike borders. They planned clearings and gardens for definitionally important sites along the sides, imagining a new external recognition and internal pride. They produced listings of named places and resources and combined them in cunning visual representations. Roem Topatimasang also spoke of participants' excitement in seeing the visual representation of place; the striking aesthetic of this picture of their home carried people away. Seeing the map emerge, one villager said, "Only now can I see the whole of my *negeri* [country], and realize that we have been harmed by the actions of outsiders for a long time." The map depicts a community that never existed in that form before, and it can be thrilling to imagine the new possibilities of this community.

The map offers possibilities in part because it is made through conventions that can be recognized by authorities. Community organizers hope, in particular, that the map will bring recognition from those state authorities that can offer citizenship rights and communal benefits such as police protection to those making community claims. Even when state authorities are not quick to recognize the countermappers, the maps offer the possibility of being recognized by international agencies and NGOs, potential advocates. The countermap has charisma for these new, self-consciously transnational cosmopolitans. It combines the high breathlessness of satellite and computer technology, which they imagine as symbols of the coming globalization of knowledge, and the down-to-earth sagacity of village elders, which they imagine as the age-old wisdom of the people. The charisma of the map makes it a banner of hope and opportunity.

At the same time, the very conventions that make the map recognizable to state authorities and transnational organizations carry with them political histories that can be dangerous to the hopes and dreams of grassroots countermappers. The marking of boundaries, the simplification of land use and property, the necessity of fitting the newly reimagined community onto a long-established and generally disadvantageous grid: each of these carries political and cultural costs. Whose idea of community will be mapped? Which authorities will the map appeal to and what will they do with the map? And why must the community be visualized at all as a mappable, territorial unit? These questions haunt the making of maps, even as mapmakers find new, creative ways to defeat entrenched political disadvantages.

We asked Marcus Colchester to open our discussion of mapping by presenting a case study that might show why local groups and their advocates are so excited about mapping. As director of the Forest Peoples Programme of the World Rainforest Movement, Colchester has considered the question of strategies for the empowerment of disadvantaged forest peoples around the world. He explains here the dilemma of native Americans (known nationally as Amerindians) in Guyana. Rather than focusing on the process of mapping per se, he explores the larger situation in which mapping has become an urgent need. His argument about mapping, in short, is that Guyanese Amerindians cannot afford to do without it; it is essential to their struggle for basic rights.

In Guyana, British colonial claims of sovereignty in the nineteenth century curtailed the rights of the Amerindians, offering them only fragile privileges. Twentieth-century colonial policy stressed the importance of economic development in the interior, with or without the consent of local inhabitants. National independence in 1966 did not facilitate a break with colonial policy toward Amerindians; the new government stressed integration of Amerindians into national development standards. Furthermore, gold miners continued to have free rein to exploit Amerindian areas for ore. A national land commission formed in 1966 recommended that Amerindian communities receive land titles; however, titles were assigned only in 1991, and these covered small, inadequate areas with great gaps in between that could be claimed by logging and mining companies. Meanwhile, however, community leaders had gained new experience in arguing for Amerindian rights in a 1970s struggle against a dam project that would have forced many people off their lands. By 1994 they had recruited international support for making more adequate land claims than the 1991 titles allowed. Both legal experts and mappers were brought in to help train community members. The maps were completed in 1997 and immediately became cause for national debate. In this context, then, mapping is one aspect of a struggle for basic rights in the face of resource expropriations and accompanying environmental destruction.

Colchester's paper highlights problems that are common in many parts of the world. What happens to those native inhabitants at the very edges of colonial dreams of civilization and settlement as well as national schemes of development? Colonial and national maps and legal policies disenfranchise them on paper; the scramble for natural resources disenfranchises them practically by taking everything they have. Mapping in this context can be part of a self-conscious effort to restore places—to put them back into the care of long-standing inhabitants. But like all projects of restoration, mapping raises both political and technical questions: restore what to whom, and how?

The four chapters following Colchester's discuss these questions. Peter Poole, an important designer of indigenous countermapping techniques worldwide, describes technical features of countermapping projects. Technology is never neutral; it carries the traces of the previous political uses and cultural frameworks through which it was made, even as it allows new translations and manipulations. Poole offers an illuminating glimpse into the cultural history of indigenous countermapping: we begin to see the chain of transfers through which mapping projects travel, in the process combining political meaning and technical sophistication, so that techniques are always materialized networks. Thus, for example, Poole notes that the mapping of indigenous people's detailed knowledge of natural resources appeared as an urgent necessity when an Inuit group of Arctic Quebec was legally disenfranchised for supposed lack of knowledge; this kind of mapping proved its importance when deployed by the James Bay Cree (also in Canada); when the Amazonian Ye'kuana decided to use this technique it was a decision, too, to tie themselves to this North American heritage. Computer-based geographic information systems (GISs) were used to good effect by U.S. Native Americans for making land claims; other deployments of GISs incorporate this precedent. And the use of community fieldworkers to make the maps was pioneered in Central America before it spread like wildfire and was used, among other places and other peoples, by the Ye'kuana.

Poole also highlights mapping as process. The Ye'kuana want maps, they explain to Poole, in part to make community. They want to involve people in self-consciously local affairs. Mapping is one project for community building. Community building, by definition, requires a series of negotiations about authority, both within and beyond the bounds of what is being claimed. Compromise, Poole explains, is as much a part of the process as are strident demands. He discusses the group's decision to make local maps that can be read together with official cartography, even at the sacrifice of accuracy; without this consistency, the maps would be less useful to negotiate community rights. The technical aesthetics of the map are also a strategy for making claims. Ye'kuana efforts to represent the depth of local knowledge of resources—filling expansive pages with tiny drawings and symbols—are important here because the map must be complex enough to convince participants as well as outsiders that something valuable is being reconstituted here. Poole hopes that the map can be made rich enough to offer a visual representation of something one might want to call "indigenous knowledge." To take this seriously requires a major commitment to figuring out how to represent complexity—never an easy choice.

Rocheleau takes up just this challenge. Maps not only simplify, she explains; they also push us into political conventions that almost always work against already disadvantaged people. Maps are always selective. They make some people's visions more powerful by showing them as the visually obvious truth; they erase what other people know and see. This is true at the village level as much as it is at the level of empires and nation states: Even in a relatively egalitarian community, we might consider how women's ways of understanding and using space may be different from men's, or stock raisers' different from farmers'. Whenever we offer the one true map, we make it harder to access all the other possible maps.

Rocheleau does not stop at this critical reflection, however. She shows us how reflection can revitalize countermapping, allowing us to produce better maps. The first step is for mapmakers to open themselves to questions about the micropolitics of representation: how might the scale of the map, the natural and cultural features it emphasizes, the categories for land use and land cover, and the marking of boundaries give advantage to some local visions over others? What alternatives are there for representation? Rocheleau suggests that mapmakers commit themselves to "multimapping," that is, the making of many maps that show alternative representations and thus make discussion of the community and its representation possible. Her examples stretch mapmaking, allowing us to see its creative political possibilities.

Roem Topatimasang provides the perspective of a community organizer in eastern Indonesia. Topatimasang, like Colchester, argues that the situation is too critical to ignore the possible benefits of community mapping. Under the New Order regime in Indonesia, the state became an enemy of village people, expropriating their resources to give away to multinational corporations that, in turn, supported state elites and the mechanism of repressive control. Village livelihoods were deeply threatened. In this context, he suggests, it was important to make even small statements for village survival.

Thus, for example, in 1993 when the livelihood of the people of the island of Yamdena was threatened by logging operations, community organizers convinced the Ministry of Forestry to declare a three-year moratorium on logging. By 1996 the same ministry introduced plans to replace the forest with commercial tree plantations controlled by the government bureaucracy. While it was not clear that this new plan was much good for villagers, Topatimasang argues that the campaign must still be considered in the most hopeful light—as an example of a symbolic victory against powerful corporations and as a chance to learn more about political mobilization.

It is in this context of urgency that he feels the excitement of countermapping. The maps create the possibility for the survival of the complex indigenous notions of property that characterize the Moluccas—by giving them the protection of authoritative, modern representations. Compromises are always necessary to political work, he explains. At least sometimes, they can produce results. Topatimasang describes how on one occasion villagers surprised Department of Fisheries officials with a professional-looking map to make their claim for traditional territories; the officials, taken off balance, conceded to the technical prowess of the villagers. Perhaps it is useful to think of the best victories of countermaps as involving the joy of finding stolen political opportunities rather than the routine expectation of bureaucratic authority.

Legal Strategies for the Disenfranchised

Many of the chapters on mapping also discuss the use of legal specialists and legal reform to help fight for community rights. Like mapping, law is powerful and dangerous. Historically the legal system has been used to disinherit rural people who do not claim privileged legal identities—whether because they operate outside the colonial or national legal system or because they are within it as the underclass. Most of the kinds of communities discussed in this book are defined in part by their criminalization in colonial and national law: the law defined them in such as way as to take away their rights to the land and resources their forebears have been using for generations. In this context, to use law for community empowerment is a counterlegal strategy of reading and writing law against the grain.

Law offers many of the same pitfalls as mapping. Legal categories carry with them political and cultural legacies that encode the very histories of power and exclusion that disinherited these communities in the first place. The question of whether one can defend community cultural standards not supported by the national legal system by using the national legal system is always in the air. Do the necessary compromises force the community to shape itself to national codes, even as they may be dressed up with the rhetoric of tradition? What happens when locally particular understandings of rights and responsibilities are codified and simplified to fit into the legal code: what new hierarchies and systems of exclusion are created?

Yet the law is so important as an arena of struggle that activists cannot afford to ignore it (Fox 1993; Lynch and Talbot 1995). The law is the site within state rule where contestants, ideally, can make a bid for fairness and predictability. If activists want to argue for social justice as a state principle, they are unlikely to be able to avoid the legal system as one place to make the argument: that is where social justice belongs, according to the state. It is not surprising, then, that radical lawyers have been important to many social-justice struggles, and that legal reform, like countermapping, inspires utopian visions and makes it possible to imagine mobilized and empowered communities.

We asked Owen Lynch, a major architect of CBNRM law, to open the conversation on legal strategies. We asked him to begin with his experience of legal work in the Philippines, which was influential in not only forging his personal commitment to legal rights for rural communities but also shaping the particular cultural politics through which the legal reforms he has promoted have emerged into transnational influence. In his chapter he points to two major features of the 1980s Philippines scene that may have shaped the power and direction of CBNRM legal advocacy. First, the flourishing of the legal profession in the Philippines allowed Lynch to mentor a group of public-interest lawyers who pioneered a new legal orientation aiming for rural and minority group empowerment. Second, after the fall of the Marcos regime in 1986, NGOs blossomed in the Philippines, and became a major feature of national politics. By taking advantage of this organizational culture, legal reform moved forward, bypassing government bureaucracy in its formative initiatives. The Philippines was a fertile environment for the development of justice-oriented legal initiatives, and thus, too, CBNRM law developed in the Philippines forms a charismatic package for NGOs in other countries. Legal reform seems possible to activists in many national contexts because of the example of Philippine initiatives.

Lynch then explains the steps involved in legal strategies for CBNRM advocacy. First, legal workers must demystify the powerful and often unquestioned laws that disinherit rural and indigenous communities. In the Philippines, for example, the Regalian Doctrine holds that the Spanish Crown somehow magically gained all rights over Philippine land in 1521; the inhabitants of the Philippines are merely squatters. In a similar vein, the Maura Law of 1894 negates all customary property rights. The legal advocate must show the limits and irrationalities of these kinds of laws. At the same time, he or she works to uncover promising legal precedent. In the Philippines, Lynch points to the Cariño decision of 1909, which lays a legal foundation for native title. But it is not enough to list these promising legal decisions. The advocate must explore and explain why these good decisions have been kept buried; otherwise, they will continue to be powerless. Thus the import of the Cariño decision, he argues, was buried by low official estimates of the indigenous population as well as the exorbitant bureaucratic hurdles of land titling. These obstacles must be cleared to make use of this legal precedent. But this too is not enough. Lynch suggests that the legal advocate must help to build a national political climate in which legal reform has a chance. This is not a one-person job, and the best strategy is to make good use of opportunities when promising moments arise, as when a more open civil society emerged in the post-Marcos Philippines. The CBNRM-oriented Philippine legislation he describes was only possible because of this political moment. In the meantime, too, the legal advocate should share legal strategies both within and beyond the country in which reform is being conducted. The resultant networks are necessary to build and maintain the impetus of legal reform.

Lynch's chapter is followed by two replies, both of which raise critical challenges for the further development of CBNRM-oriented legal reforms. Anthropologist Tania Li offers a strong cautionary statement, objecting particularly to Lynch's invocation of a "generic," transferable set of legal initiatives that might empower rural people. She is particularly critical of the fact that Lynch privileges isolated, culturally distinctive, and strongly communal groups of rural people. These kinds of communities are hardly the majority of rural residents, she points out. She describes for us, instead, two other kinds of rural settlements. In one, migrants to the countryside are clustered in space but not in communal sociality. They are politically and economically disadvantaged: some are wage laborers, many are poor. Yet their referent for authority and political culture is the nation-state, not the community. They are in no sense traditional, but advocates might want to think about how to protect their livelihoods and guard them against discrimination. In another kind of settlement, rural people, although long-settled and even indigenous, may have rejected sustainable resource development—whether because they cannot support themselves and the environment at the same time or because they prefer the unsustainable models promoted by national authorities. To assume that rural people want to maintain biologically diverse environments is to ignore their dilemmas and their choices, she argues.

Li usefully draws our attention to the wide range of rural conditions and perspectives that inform natural resource management in the countryside. Furthermore, if legal reforms that privilege isolated tribes become state policies, rural people will have to scramble—often with great difficulty—to look as tribelike as possible; this is not necessarily the best agenda to promote rural social justice. Instead, Li argues, it is important to pay close attention to the specific complaints and desires of particular groups of people, and these may not make a neatly generic legal package. Indeed, without this attention, legal strategies for rural empowerment could instead become state strategies for rural control. The state is a dangerous ally, and legal advocates need to take seriously the possibility of their laws being used against, instead of for, the disadvantaged.

Legal advocate Gus Gatmaytan offers a different critical approach: how are CBNRM laws being used and interpreted on the ground? This approach, indeed, forms an important response to both legal modeling and academic criticism: Both could be more attentive to the social processes that laws put into motion in particular places. Gatmaytan stresses the interactive process that links legal advocates and community members. The law he describes is a strategy for political mobilization, rather than an abstract text. This approach allows him to see that even well-conceived laws might cause inequalities and hardships, and too, even flawed, incomplete legal frameworks might have politically productive uses.

Gatmaytan begins with the observation that legal advocacy is always a process of translation: Advocates strive to turn some part of community claims and understandings of the environment into a language that national bureaucrats and judges can understand. Translation necessarily changes the text; no legal advocacy offers an unadulterated indigenous consciousness. But some translations offer more political possibilities than others. The advocate must be careful with his or her translations. In fighting for legal recognition of customary ownership rights, can the advocate get across enough of the indigenous meaning of property? This is not an easily settled problem. Who speaks for the community? What is the relationship between traditional ideas of place and state-legitimated territories? These are questions that must be raised and raised again.

In the Philippines, the passing of laws allowing cultural communities to get certificates of ancestral domain claims at first seems to have solved the problem of resource expropriation. But the closer one looks, the more injustices appear. In some areas, degraded lands have been granted to communities, while healthy forests are kept for corporate exploitation. In other cases, responsibility for community management is given to officials with no everyday connection to the people they supposedly represent. These problems show that the passing of CBNRM laws is only the beginning of political mobilization, not the desired end.

Perhaps the single most important translation problem Gatmaytan raises involves traditional resource management. Advocates hope that community titles will allow the continuation of environment-friendly forms of natural-resource management; but too often the title only facilitates the making of a contract with a corporation to destroy the resources. This is due to the new laws not even trying to translate traditional resource-management practices. These practices remain unspeakable at the national level—and may become more and more silent locally as well. As Gatmaytan argues, a legal personality has been created for the community, but no other more meaningful form of recognition. Community leaders, unable to articulate alternatives, are drawn into the market subjectivities promoted by the laws they hoped to make their own. This is a key point. Critics of CBNRM like to point out that indigenous people, given the opportunity, often work hand in hand with environmentally destructive capitalist development. Gatmaytan's analysis takes this question out of ideologically overcharged debates about human nature (rational or spiritual?): laws facilitate particular kinds of social practices; if the law does not recognize alternative resource-management practices, its framework is likely to draw its users into existing hegemonies and, particularly, the legally privileged contracts of transnational capitalism. The struggle for advocates, then, is to devise new forms of translation that address the problem he calls "recognition" even more seriously.

COMMUNITY AND CONSERVATION IN AN ERA OF MILITARIZATION AND MARKET TRIUMPHALISM

The detailed case histories of CBNRM presented here, from particular social, political, and environmental contexts in Asia, Latin America, and Africa, illuminate how CBNRM was invented, borrowed, or shaped. These cases illustrate how, and in what ways, CBNRM became an inspiration, model, tool, and catalyst in diverse political contexts. By focusing on the historical specificity of these cases, we challenge the widely held notion that there is a single generalizable *model* of CBNRM that can be refined, exported, and inserted throughout the globe. For many conservation practitioners and donors, the value of any model lies in its standardization and replicability; this is most clearly evident in the emphasis placed on scaling up or moving to scale.

The cases brought together in this volume alert students, scholars, advocates, and members of the donor community to the dangers of imagining, inserting, and enforcing top down solutions to particular problems in specific contexts. We focus attention on the contexts of implementation: where, how, and in what forms this turn toward community took shape. We have flagged the problems of co-optation and manipulation posed by the global and bilateral financial and development communities deploying community-based rhetorics and instituting specific projects. We assert that model-driven programs of CBNRM are emphatically not the kinds of projects that need to be promoted. It is only when specific histories and political situations are taken into account that CBNRM offers the possibility of being productively implemented or assessed.

Now, more than ever before, it is crucial to address the concerns raised in this volume. The prospects for CBNRM are uncertain at present. This is a period that offers promise and danger, a landscape of shifting priorities and risks for the possibilities of socially just conservation, democracy, nonviolent political action, and transnational social movements.

Conservation has never been a static body of practices. CBNRM itself proliferated in the 1990s following an extended critique of traditional fortress conservation. Most early attempts at CBNRM were efforts to imagine and embody a new model of conservation incorporating ideals of democratic governance, social and economic equity, sustainable environmental management, and nature conservation (Agrawal and Gibson 1999; Berkes 1989; Brosius, Tsing, and Zerner 1998; Clay 1988; Kemf 1993; Korten 1986; McNeely 1995; Poffenberger 1990; Pye-Smith, Borrini-Feyerabend, and Sandbrook 1994; Stevens 1997; Western and Wright 1994; Zerner 2000). These appeared at a time when the primary challenge was to demonstrate the fundamental validity of community-based approaches to resource management against a long-entrenched tradition of top-down management. Soon CBNRM was embraced by a number of major organizations and institutions. We witnessed the proliferation of different models of community-based natural resource management: ICDPs, adaptive management, co-management, collaborative management, joint forest management, and more (Brick, Snow, and Van de Wetering 2000; Brown and Wyckoff-Baird 1992; Newmark and Hough 2000; Pimbert and Pretty 1997; Sivaramakrishnan 1996; White et al. 1994; Wondolleck and Yaffee 2000).

Recent years have witnessed even more dramatic changes. Among the most striking has been the emergence of a strong backlash against community-based approaches to conservation (Brechin et al. 2002; Oates 1999; Soulé 2000/2001; Terborgh 1999; Wilshusen 2002). Critics such as John Terborgh are unsparing in their condemnation of conservation organizations that have embraced community-based conservation. He argues that "when conservation organizations begin to advocate sustainable use of tropical forests, it is a signal that conservation is on the run. Starting down the slippery road to sustainable use is stepping back from that crucial line in the sand that defines one's beliefs and principles. Sustainable use represents a gray zone where politics, economics, and social pressures, not science, decide what is good for humans, with scarcely a nod to nature" (1999, 140).

Soulé and Terborgh assert that "today it is evident that the effort to protect life on earth is failing—despite all the outpouring of feel-good news releases about sustainable development, integrated conservation and development, community-based conservation, ecosystem management, and sustainable forest management" (Soulé and Terborgh 1999, 4). Oates describes community-based approaches as an "alternative romantic myth" (1999, xi), and argues that "there are serious flaws in the theory that wildlife can best be conserved through promoting human economic development. It is a powerful myth that has made all those involved in its formulation feel good" (p. xv).

With this "requiem for nature" critique have come calls for a return to more authoritarian, top-down approaches to conservation. Terborgh, for instance, advocates "building a bulwark of security around the last remnants of tropical nature" (1999, 17) and believes that "a national parks agency with the best of intentions remains powerless without the backing of those who carry the guns" (p. 163). According to Terborgh, "The focus of conservation must therefore return to the make-it-or-break-it issue of actively protecting parks, a matter that hinges above all on the quality of enforcement. Active protection of parks requires a top-down approach because enforcement is invariably in the hands of police and other armed forces that respond only to orders from their commanders" (p. 170). We ask, are these calls for security-based approaches to conservation a reveille for the militarization of conservation?

Another key development in the last few years has been the widespread adoption of cartographically driven ecoregional planning approaches by major conservation organizations. The ecoregional paradigm envisions conservation at a larger scale than before, rather than focusing on discrete protected areas, and it relies on powerful cartographic technologies to establish priorities for future conservation investments and to develop comprehensive conservation plans. A key characteristic of ecoregional conservation is the degree to which the production of maps is guided by biological rather than political criteria. Ecoregional initiatives are proliferating rapidly and reshaping the strategic visions of major conservation organizations. Examples include WWF's *Global 200* (Olson et al. 2000, 2001) and The Nature Conservancy's (2000, 2001) *Conservation by Design*. What ecoregional conservation is really good for is attracting donor support. Conservation organizations need to show that they are guided by a strategic vision and can provide both structures of accountability and ways to measure success. Ecoregional conservation provides all these in a complete, marketable package. What are the implications of a paradigm that obliterates or peripheralizes the significance of cultural claims to territory, property, and values, not to mention local and national political boundaries? Who is drawing the maps? What kinds of entities are on the map? Whose targets and goals are underwriting the cartographic surface and programmatic goals of ecoregional planning?

In conjunction with the rise of ecoregional conservation, we have also witnessed the proliferation of conservation finance initiatives. Major conservation organizations have increasingly turned to recruiting personnel from major Wall Street investment firms, and they have established formal partnerships with the Global Environmental Facility (GEF) and the World Bank. An exemplar of this trend is the Center for Conservation Finance, founded by World Wildlife Fund in June 2000 and dedicated to building "the next generation of conservation-finance models—models that can be replicated in every corner of the world" (World Wildlife Fund 2002). Other examples include the Conservation Finance Alliance, a partnership between the Wildlife Conservation Society (WCS), The Nature Conservancy (TNC), Conservation International (CI), IUCN, Ramsar, and the World Bank (Conservation Finance Alliance 2002), and Conservation International's Critical Ecosystem Partnership Fund (Conservation International 2004). One of the most significant aspects of conservation finance is that it represents an attempt to shift conservation toward a discourse of *investment.*

As conservation organizations (and the donors who fund them) have increasingly embraced more strategic approaches to conservation, we have witnessed an ever-greater insistence on the imposition of rigorous standards of accountability, most conspicuously in the form of tools to monitor project outcomes under the rubric of monitoring and evaluation, or M&E (Margoluis and Salafsky 1998). When applied to people, these frameworks rely heavily on the use of formalistic social science metrics and models to provide measurable results or manage outcomes (Brosius and Russell 2003). Several features distinguish this approach. First, there is a strong emphasis on, and valorization of, rapidity, achieved mostly through the use of survey-based approaches to data collection (Blumenthal and Jannink 2000; Chambers 1994a, 1994b, 1994c; Margoluis and Salafsky 1998; Sayre et al. 2000; Stocking and Murnaghan 2001). Equally conspicuous is an emphasis on replicability: the value of these models, in the eyes of practitioners, is a function of their ability to provide measurable results wherever they are applied. Third, such methods "focus primarily on data concerning proximate threats—that is to say, actions by local communities—rather than on the broader contexts in which those threats occur" (Brosius and Russell 2003). As local human communities are converted into "rapidly assessed" data for inclusion in ecoregional plans, they are increasingly at risk.

All of these features are closely tied to the imperatives of short funding cycles and accountability to donors. What are the implications for local communities when conservation organizations must provide measures of the success of their investments over three-year funding cycles? When conservation organizations must be more accountable to investors, do they not become less accountable to local communities? As this heavy pall of business-based managerialism descends over conservation, and as major conservation organizations move to consolidate their authority over global conservation practices, we ask, what are the implications of these trends for local communities and CBNRM? Although initially a vigorous experiment in democratic governance and nature conservation, an emancipatory enterprise, CBNRM is increasingly incorporated into the managerial apparatus of conservation and tied to the imperatives of funding cycles, replicability, metric accountability to donors, and more.

Militarization and market triumphalism, the notion that market-based models and values necessarily trump other values and principles of world making, were already becoming increasingly the norm before the 9/11 debacle in the United States. In a world in which terror is part of the "new normal," to borrow a phrase from the New York Lawyer's Committee for Human Rights, military solutions applied to a variety of realms, including conservation, just seem more natural. CBNRM was, at its inception, a vision in which forms of decentralized environmental management, or co-management, would offer the possibility of democratic local governance and social justice. CBNRM advocates attempted to imagine and implement projects in which the bases for social, cultural, and economic justice were indelibly written into the constitution of nature management and conservation programs.

All conservation programs are necessarily projects in politics and governance. The key questions have always been what kinds of politics and what forms of governance should legitimately prevail. All the changes we have observed in conservation and natural-resource-management regimes in the last decade make the questions raised in this volume more relevant than ever before.

REFERENCES

Aberly, Doug, ed. 1993. *Boundaries of Home: Mapping for Local Empowerment.* Gabriola Island, B.C.: New Society Publishers.

Adams, J., and T. McShane. 1992. *The Myth of Wild Africa.* Berkeley: Univ. of California Press.

Agrawal, Arun, and C. C. Gibson. 1999. Enchantment and Disenchantment: The Role of Community in Natural Resource Conservation. *World Development* 27(4): 629–49.

Alcorn, Janis. 2000. *Borders, Rules and Governance: Mapping to Catalyse Changes in Policy and Management.* IIED Gatekeeper Series No. 91. London: International Institute for Environment and Development.

Berkes, Fikret, ed. 1989. *Common Property Resources: Ecology and Community-Based Sustainable Development.* London: Belhaven.

Blumenthal, D., and J. Jannink. 2000. A Classification of Collaborative Management Methods. *Conservation Ecology* 4(2): 17–26.

Bojang, F. 1994. Application of Community Forest Management Agreement: The Gambian Experience. Paper presented at the third RPTES workshop, Dakar, Senegal.

Brechin, S., Peter R. Wilshusen, Crystal L. Fortwangler, and Patrick C. West. 2002. Beyond the Square Wheel: Toward a More Comprehensive Understanding of Biodiversity Conservation as Social and Political Process. *Society and Natural Resources* 15(1): 41–64.

Brick, Philip, D. Snow, and S. Van de Wetering. 2000. *Across the Great Divide: Explorations in Collaborative Conservation and the American West*. Washington, D.C.: Island Press.

Brody, Hugh. 1981. *Maps and Dreams: Indians and the British Columbia Frontier*. Prospect Heights, Ill.: Waveland.

Brosius, J. P., and D. Russell. 2003. Conservation from Above: An Anthropological Perspective on Transboundary Protected Areas and Ecoregional Planning. *Journal of Sustainable Forestry* 17(1–2): 39–65.

Brosius, J. P., A. L. Tsing, and C. Zerner. 1998. Representing Communities: Histories and Politics of Community-Based Natural Resource Management. *Society and Natural Resources* 11(2): 157–68.

Brown, Michael, and Barbara Wyckoff-Baird. 1992. *Designing Integrated Conservation and Development Projects*. Washington, D.C.: World Wildlife Fund Biodiversity Support Program.

Chambers, R. 1994a. The Origins and Practice of Participatory Rural Appraisal. *World Development* 22:953–69.

———. 1994b. Participatory Rural Appraisal (PRA): Analysis of Experience. *World Development* 22:1253–68.

———. 1994c. Participatory Rural Appraisal (PRA): Challenges, Potentials, and Paradigm. *World Development* 22:1437–54.

Clay, Jason. 1988. *Indigenous Peoples and Tropical Forests: Models of Land Use and Management from Latin America*. Cambridge, Mass.: Cultural Survival.

Conservation Finance Alliance. 2002. Conservation Finance Alliance. www.conservationfinance.org.

Conservation International. 2004. Critical Ecosystem Partnership Fund. www.cepf.net/xp/cepf/.

Cronon, W. 1995. The Trouble with Wilderness, or Getting Back to the Wrong Nature. In *Uncommon Ground: Toward Reinventing Nature*, ed. W. Cronon. New York: W.W. Norton.

Eghenter, Cristina. 2000. *Mapping Peoples' Forests: The Role of Mapping in Planning Community-Based Management of Conservation Areas in Indonesia*. Washington, D.C.: Biodiversity Support Program.

Ghai, D., and J. Vivian, eds. 1992. *Grassroots Environmental Action: People's Participation in Sustainable Development*. London: Routledge.

Hardt, Michael, and Antonio Negri. 2000. *Empire*. Cambridge, Mass.: Harvard Univ. Press.

Kemf, Elizabeth. 1993. *Indigenous Peoples and Protected Areas: The Law of Mother Earth*. London: Earthscan.

Korten, David, ed. 1986. *Community Management: Asian Experience and Perspectives*. West Hartford, Conn.: Kumarian Press.

Lorde, Audre. 1984. The Master's Tools Will Never Dismantle the Master's House. *Sister Outsider: Essays and Speeches*, ed. Audre Lord. Trumansburg, N.Y.: Crossing Press.

Lynch, Owen J., and Kirk Talbott. 1995. *Balancing Acts: Community-Based Forest Management and National Law in Asia and the Pacific*. Washington, D.C.: World Resources Institute.

Margoluis, R. and N. Salafsky. 1998. *Measures of Success: Designing, Managing, and Monitoring Conservation and Development Projects*. Washington, D.C.: Island Press.

McNeely, Jeffrey, ed. 1995. *Expanding Partnerships in Conservation*. Washington, D.C.: Island Press.

Nature Conservancy. 2000. *Designing a Geography of Hope: A Practitioners Handbook to Ecoregional Conservation Planning*, vols. 1 and 2. Washington, D.C.: The Nature Conservancy.

———. 2001. *Conservation by Design: A Framework for Mission Success*. Washington, D.C.: The Nature Conservancy.

Newmark, W., and J. Hough. 2000. Conserving Wildlife in Africa: Integrated Conservation and Development Projects and Beyond. *BioScience* 50(7): 585–92.

Oates, John. 1999. *Myth and Reality in the Rain Forest: How Conservation Strategies Are Failing in West Africa*. Berkeley: Univ. of California Press.

Olson, D. M., et al. 2000. *The Global 200: A Representation Approach to Preserving the Earth's Distinctive Ecosystems*. Washington, D.C.: World Wildlife Fund. http://panda.org/livingplanet/global200.cfm.

Olson, D. M., Eric Dinerstein, Eric D. Wikramanayake, Neil D. Burgess, George V. N. Powell, Emma C. Underwood, Jennifer A. D'amico, et al. 2001. Terrestrial Ecoregions of the World: A New Map of Life on Earth. *BioScience* 51(11): 933–38.

Peluso, N. 1995. Whose Woods Are These? Counter-Mapping Forest Territories in Kalimantan, Indonesia. *Antipode* 27(4): 383–406.

Pimbert, M., and J. Pretty. 1997. Parks, People and Professionals: Putting "Participation" into Protected Area Management. In *Social Change and Conservation: Environmental Politics and Impacts of National Parks and Protected Areas*, ed. K. Ghimire and M. Pimbert. London: Earthscan.

Poffenberger, Mark, ed. 1990. *Keepers of the Forest: Land Management Alternatives in Southeast Asia*. West Hartford, Conn.: Kumarian Press.

Poole, Peter, ed. 1995a. *Geomatics: Who Needs It?* Special issue of Poole, Peter, ed. 1995b. *Indigenous Peoples, Mapping and Biodiversity Conservation: An Analysis of Current Activities and Opportunities for Applying Geomatics Technologies*. Washington, D.C.: Biodiversity Support Program.

———. 1995b. *Indigenous Peoples, Mapping and Biodiversity Conservation: An Analysis of Current Activities and Opportunities for Applying Geomatics Technologies.* Washington, D.C.: Biodiversity Support Program.

Proctor, J., and S. Pincetl. 1996. Nature and the Reproduction of Endangered Space: The Spotted Owl in the Pacific Northwest and Southern California. *Environment and Planning D: Society and Space* 14:683–708.

Pye-Smith, Charlie, G. Borrini-Feyerabend, and R. Sandbrook, eds. 1994. *The Wealth of Communities: Stories of Success in Local Environmental Management*. West Hartford, Conn.: Kumarian Press.

Sachs, W., ed. 1993. *Global Ecology: A New Arena of Political Conflict*. London: Zed Books.

Sayre, R., E. Roca, G. Sedaghatkish, B. Young, S. Keel, P. Roca, and S. Sheppard. 2000. *Nature in Focus: Rapid Ecological Assessment*. Washington, D.C.: Island Press.

Sirait, M., et al. 1994. Mapping Customary Land in East Kalimantan, Indonesia: A Tool in Forest Management. *Ambio* 23(7): 411–17.

Sivaramakrishnan, K. 1996. Participatory Forestry in Bengal: Competing Narratives, Statemaking, and Development. *Cultural Survival Quarterly* 20(3): 35–39.

Slater, Candace. 2000. Justice for Whom? Contemporary Images of Amazonia. In *People, Plants and Justice: The Politics of Nature Conservation*, ed. Charles Zerner. New York: Columbia Univ. Press.

———, ed. 2003. *In Search of the Rainforest*. Durham, N.C.: Duke Univ. Press.

Soulé, M. 2000/2001. Does Sustainable Development Help Nature? *Wild Earth*, Winter 2000/2001: 56–64.

Soulé, M., and J. Terbough, eds. 1999. *Continental Conservatism: Scientific Foundations of Regional Reserve Networks*. Washington, D.C.: Island Press.

Stevens, Stan. 1997. *Conservation through Cultural Survival: Indigenous Peoples and Protected Areas*. Washington, D.C.: Island Press.

Stocking, M., and N. Murnaghan. 2001. *A Handbook for the Field Assessment of Land Degradation*. London: Earthscan.

Terborgh, J. 1999. *Requiem for Nature*. Washington, D.C.: Island Press.

Vandergeest, P. 1996. Mapping Nature: Territorialization of Forest Rights in Thailand. *Society and Natural Resources* 9(2): 159–75.

Western, D., R. Wright, and S. Strum, eds. 1994. *Natural Connections: Perspectives in Community-Based Conservation*. Washington, D.C.: Island Press.

White, A. T., L. Zeitlin Hale, Y. Renard, and L. Cortesi, eds. 1994. *Collaborative and Community-Based Management of Coral Reefs: Lessons from Experience*. West Hartford, Conn.: Kumarian Press.

Wilshusen, P. R., et al. 2002. Reinventing a Square Wheel: Critique of a Resurgent "Protection Paradigm" in International Biodiversity Conservation. *Society and Natural Resources* 15(1): 17–40.

Wondolleck, Julia, and S. Yaffee. 2000. *Making Collaboration Work: Lesson from Innovation in Natural Resource Management*. Washington, D.C.: Island Press.

World Wildlife Fund. 2002. What the Center for Conservation Finance Does. www.worldwildlife.org/conservationfinance/does.cfm.

Zerner, Charles. 1995. Telling Stories about Biodiversity. In *Valuing Local Knowledge: Indigenous People and Intellectual Property Rights*, ed. Stephen Brush and Doreen Stabinsky. Washington, D.C.: Island Press.

———. 2000. *People, Plants, and Justice: The Politics of Nature Conservation*. New York: Columbia Univ. Press.

———. 2003. *Culture and the Question of Rights: Forests, Coasts, and Seas in Southeast Asia*. Durham, N.C.: Duke Univ. Press

I

MOBILIZATIONS AND MODELS

1

Dances around the Fire: Conservation Organizations and Community-Based Natural Resource Management

Janis B. Alcorn

Conservation organizations and local communities have common interests that bring them to dance together. They have danced for decades, but with other partners more than each other. Their ballroom circles a fire in the forest—one that glows brightly with promises but can also flare up with conflicts that damage the partners or the forest itself.

Conservation organizations come to the ball with prior commitments to donors and national governments—their regular partners whose steps they follow almost unconsciously. Both communities and organizations wear

This paper was written in 1997 while I was working for the Biodiversity Support Program at the World Wildlife Fund (WWF) in Washington, D.C. Trends and situations have changed since that time, but the issues and analysis remain current. I thank Barbara Wyckoff-Baird, Michael Wright, Kate Newman, John Magistro, Michael Brown, David Wilke, Mark Freudenberger, Frances Seymour, Patty Larson, Meg Symington, and Nonette Royo for offering their insights on community-based conservation or commenting on earlier drafts of this manuscript. Parts of this paper were published in the Yale School of Forestry and Environmental Studies Bulletin Series (Alcorn 1995). I retain sole responsibility for the opinions expressed herein. The findings, interpretations, and conclusions expressed in this paper should not be attributed in any manner to WWF-US, The Nature Conservancy (TNC), World Resources Institute (WRI), or the U.S. Agency for International Development (USAID).

masks, and it is often unclear which—community or organization—the masked dancer represents. But it is obvious that the conservation organizations help governments and donors choose the music, and then they lead the steps. Each dancer is self-absorbed, always thinking about their regular partners on the sidelines, and they seldom take time to reflect on where their dance might be leading them. A single organization may wear different masks and follow different steps around assorted local fires, adapting itself so as to advance its agenda in diverse circumstances. Outside researchers occasionally pass by in the shadows to observe the dance and then proclaim global conclusions to the donors at the party. Their critical proclamations may fan the fire or douse the glowing promises, but rarely do they truly alter the music or otherwise change the party.

In this chapter I examine the ground tread by other researchers in this book and offer a broader context within which to read their chapters. I begin with a reflection on conservation—its meaning and its means. I highlight conflicting visions of community-based conservation (CBC) and then analyze the history of the interests, words, and actions of conservation organizations (COs) related to CBC, using the World Wildlife Fund-U.S. (WWF-US) as one example. I reflect on lessons learned from COs' experiences with CBC and close with a few recommendations.

WHAT IS CONSERVATION?

Conservation is a human enterprise and as such there is political debate over its ultimate goals. Some who place maximum value on species' rights hold the line at total preservation of all species and habitats, but most accept the goal of maintaining acceptable levels of species and habitats to ensure biodiversity for the future well-being of our planet. Conservation can be viewed as an overarching goal of resource management. Conservation is a social and political process aimed at maintaining biological diversity, and thus both biological and sociopolitical information are important for conservation decision making. Conservationists do not necessarily see the pursuit of social justice as part of their enterprise.

Who uses social and biological information to make decisions about conservation, and what values are applied to make them? Probably the first decision makers we think of are governments and international conservation organizations, such as WWF-US, because we tend to view biodiversity as a public good to be globally maintained for future generations. But in fact, many more conservation decisions are made at the local level where indigenous values and needs are the primary consideration. I would like to challenge preconceptions about conservation and conservation decision making by sketching a heuristic contrast between Big Conservation and Little Conservation (see Alcorn 1995, 13–30).

Big Conservation is global. It is big organizations and institutions run from large urban offices, as are the Global Environmental Facility (GEF), WWF-US, the international network of the World Wide Fund for Nature, Conservation International (CI), IUCN–The World Conservation Union, African Wildlife Foundation (AWF), and The Nature Conservancy (TNC). Big Conservation is the concern of international nongovernmental organizations (NGOs) and their local partner NGOs, and also of government forest ministries and park departments. Big conservation operates with big money, funded by multilateral development banks, bilateral donors, and wealthy foundations. For example, WWF-US had operating revenues of seventy-two million dollars in 1996, and GEF projects in the World Bank and United Nations Development Program (UNDP) run from one million to twenty million dollars each. Big Conservation entities are dominated by people with interests in global heritage, and they work for the preservation of habitats and ecosystems in areas far from their homes. Big Conservation depends on funding and political commitment from bureaucracies and foreign interests distant from the field sites where projects—and biodiversity—are located. Big Conservation is what most people think of when they think of conservation, and when most people think about CBC projects, they envision extensions of Big Conservation projects. They view it as a management issue unrelated to the agenda of rights and responsibilities that centers the environmental justice movement.

Little Conservation occurs when individuals make choices in their day-to-day lives, in the places where they live. On the one hand, those decisions depend on individuals' ecological knowledge and their skills in applying patterns established by traditional resource-management systems. On the other, their decisions are made within the opportunities and constraints imposed by employment options and their communities' tenurial institutions—the rules that control resource access and use. For example, sacred areas and common forests, waters, and grasslands are managed by traditional rules. Traditional systems of agriculture manage ecological processes through rituals, rules about land allocation, time limits on land use, and the maintenance of proper social relationships both within the community and between the community and supernatural powers.

Little Conservation is a largely invisible influence on those who carry it out. It is embedded in local dress and metaphors, in the "right way" to do agriculture, and in ethical relationships with ancestors. It passed on to children in songs, dances, and histories. It is part of local cultural heritage.

Little Conservation is little because globally it has been invisible, because it is carried out by politically weak groups, and because most outsiders who work with marginal groups do not look for conservation there and so do not see it. Outsiders often see the natural environment as a mere background to what interests them. The institutions that support Little Conservation have no office buildings or letterheads. A village organization may meet under trees to make its decisions, including those related to conservation. Outside its meetings, the organization is unseen—a spot under a tree or empty stools or mats in the corner of a communal house. These spaces look unimportant, and it is easy for outsiders to miss them and the institutions they house, but the political discussions here are as tightly argued and carefully watched as those heard within any national parliament building.

Little Conservation is seldom noticed because of the common view of conservation as forgoing use or setting aside areas as off limits to use, through parks or government wildlife regulations. Such protections are also found at the community level, though they are rarely documented. For example, an environmental impact team evaluating a logging concession near Madang, Papua New Guinea, found rare, endemic fish in a small area of a river and learned that local people were hand feeding the fish and limiting their take to a few individuals eaten ceremoniously in an annual ritual (Christiansen Research Institute 1991). But other types of Little Conservation are more prevalent at this same site. The community had been petitioning the government for years to grant it conservation-area status so their forests and waters would not be logged under a concession granted by the government to an outside logging company. They also use traditional agricultural and agroforestry methods that maintain forests. Although Little Conservation is holistic, it can be dissected into components by researchers, as I have done here with the Madang case.

Researchers encounter pieces of Little Conservation when they find a local farmer or housewife who maintains on their property plants that are becoming rare or argues in community meetings that everyone should spare the plants when clearing garden land. Little Conservation also occurs when village elders restrict access to certain forests or order that agricultural land lie fallow when forests dwindle. Over the past decade, research on common property management regimes (see Hess 1996) has raised the profile of Little Conservation and given us insights into its successes and failures.

Little Conservation is little because it is local. Its vision is limited to the local situation, to a small area. There are no grand designs for, or assessments of, others' situations. Little Conservation strategies and methods generally do not reflect an appreciation for regional or global trends, and the impacts of modernization are rarely foreseen.

Little Conservation is little because its budget is tiny. It is a nonentity on the global-donor screen—there is virtually no funding for Little Conservation. But Little Conservation does not require large sums; it is locally supported by cultural values, community-based institutions, and traditional resource-management systems adapted to local conditions. And yet, Little

Conservation *needs* funding to make it visible and to then develop appropriate policies that will enable local mechanisms to continue to evolve and function under changing circumstances. For example, policies are needed that recognize and support local authorities instead of imposing local government units that undermine them.

The CBC embedded in the Little Conservation tradition faces many stresses and threats. These include escalating threats from outsiders who are logging, extracting other resources, or settling on community lands; the state expropriation of lands and resources; demographic changes; cultural change; failure to educate young people in traditional ecological knowledge; missionaries; community institutions that are unable to interface effectively with outsiders; technological changes; and crop changes.

Little Conservation is also threatened by Big Conservation when (1) local institutions' conservation traditions and local knowledge are ignored or undermined, (2) local people's traditional rights are ignored and they are excluded from newly declared protected areas, and (3) Big Conservation allies itself with national elites who share interests with loggers and other resource miners. Such alliances have sometimes been criticized as "getting in bed with the enemy" (e.g., Lohmann 1991). These alliances have generated what might be called unconscious acts that, to go back to my introductory metaphor, might be captured in the phrase "dancing with the gal that brung ya."

Over the past decade, Little Conservation has become more visible on the world stage. Community groups have increasingly joined in federations, unions, and other "people's organizations" to assert their rights. These groups have sometimes sought assistance from Big Conservation when pursuing what they perceive to be a shared agenda. Nonetheless, they have on occasion fought conservationists who would throw them out of protected areas or otherwise threaten their traditional rights. For example, in Bolivia indigenous peoples (Moje–o, Yaracar, and Chimane) with territories inside the Parque Nacional Isiboro Secure (declared in 1965) fought a long battle to gain recognition of their lands, and in 1990 the area was recognized as the Territorio Indigena Parque Nacional Isiboro Secure (TIPNIS). A territory-wide community-based organization created in the process of their struggle is affiliated with several national and regional federations and has legitimately represented the groups' interests in negotiations with government. The organization has zoned the TIPNIS, developed management plans, and appointed park and border guards. But the people of the TIPNIS suffered a recent setback when laws governing protected areas were applied with precedence over laws protecting indigenous rights. Their local organizations and government are now ignored as new state-based administrative units are created to manage the area as a protected area rather than an indigenous territory (Lehm 1997).

In Colombia, indigenous peoples have rights over *resguardos* (indigenous territories) and have developed plans for protecting biodiversity, but they now find themselves fighting declarations of protected areas that overlap their *resguardos*, declarations supported by conservationist organizations (Forero and Laborde 1997).

In Thailand a conservative, well-organized Karen community has been fighting resettlement away from their forests in Thung Yai, which have been declared a World Heritage site. One Karen woman characterized their situation as "trying to stand up in a waterfall" that is pushing them out of the way (Breslin, personal communication, 1997). Despite scientific documentation of the Karen community's good track record in managing their forests, maintaining wildlife, and regulating forest use, international organizations are working with government to wrest authority over the area away from them.

DESIGN OR DISCOVERY?

Frances Seymour, recognizing the opportunities presented by Little Conservation, has laid out a continuum between "design" and "discovery" of CBC (1994, 472–96). "Design mode" refers to situations where outsiders identify a problem and design a solution. This mode is common in Big Conservation and results in the typical CBC project supported by COs. As several chapters in this book illustrate, designed CBC can lead to co-option and destruction of Little Conservation. "Discovery mode," on the other hand, refers to situations where outsiders discover that local people have identified a problem and designed a solution, and subsequently assist local communities to legitimate that solution.

The discovery mode is most frequently adopted by national or local environmentalist NGOs that seek to give local people a voice. Rather than assuming their own agenda, they take as their task representing communities to whom they are held accountable. Sometimes the discovery mode is a form of self-discovery; a community, through leaders or facilitated discussions, discovers the Little Conservation hidden in their own traditions.

Over the past decade, Big Conservation has occasionally discovered the music for Little Conservation in the pocket of its community dance partners and begun to try dancing to this different tune, letting the community lead and learning to follow. But more often Big Conservation fails to notice that local environmental NGOs are playing Little Conservation music with different instruments around a different fire. The international COs' big dances sometimes draw government, donor sponsors, and local leaders away from the local dances. The simple "save the species" tune played to the beat of project-based assistance, harmonizing with the clinking and crinkling of cash, often sounds more attractive to government and donors than does the complex rights-linked music of local NGOs amplifying local community voices.

CONSERVATION ORGANIZATIONS' APPROACHES

In an interesting 1996 paper, Piers Blaikie and Sally Jeanrenaud attempted to sort the sometimes confusing biodiversity conservation sector by classifying conservation approaches into three types: classical, neopopulist, and neoliberal. All three are defended by their proponents with ideological fervor. The classical approach is the historically dominant, bullets-and-barbed-wire protected-areas approach, in which government agents remove people from remote undeveloped areas and then use armed force to keep out anything but research and tourist activities. The neopopulist approach encompasses a variety of people-oriented approaches that seek participatory, sociopolitical solutions to conservation problems. The neoliberal approach attempts to harness enlightened market policies and economic solutions to achieve conservation goals.

Although it is useful to recognize these three distinct threads within Big Conservation, in fact most international COs support projects using all three. WWF-US, in particular, carries out a wide range of projects, owing in part to its size and also to its philosophy of adapting projects to local conditions. To better generalize about conservation organizations and their varying mandates for CBC, we can construct a continuum along which organizations supporting CBC are found: park-centric at the left end, sustainable development-centric in the middle, and advocacy campaign-centric at the right end.

Typology of Conservation Organizations Supporting CBC

Not all international campaign-centric organizations support CBC nor do all sustainable-development-centric or park-centric organizations. Among international conservation organizations, WWF-US's mix of projects, campaigns, and policy work over the past decade puts it somewhere between park-centric and sustainable development-centric. TNC and Wildlife Conservation Society (WCS) have narrower mixes, generally lying to the left of WWF-US on the continuum. The major organizations lying toward the right are Greenpeace, Rainforest Foundation, Environmental Defense Fund (EDF), and World Rainforest Movement. Local and national grassroots NGOs who are active in conservation tend to be campaign centric and particularly conscious of CBC because they often respond to communities as active agents. By contrast, local and national NGOs that have grown under donor funding tend to be service providers that implement donor projects, and they tend to be toward the left end of the continuum.

Different types of CBC are associated with this CO continuum. Although there is no perfect match, recognizing the visible patterns of association that do emerge is useful for thinking about the issues.

Organizational Types and CBC

Park-centric organizations are generally associated with Big Conservation types of CBC, especially the integrated conservation and development projects (ICDPs) found in buffer zones or otherwise associated with protected areas. Sustainable-development organizations (often coastal- or wildlife-conservation groups) are more likely to be associated with comanagement in the broader landscape (discussed later in this chapter), whereas park-centric types are involved in co-management of protected areas. Although co-management usually has evolved through decentralization of limited management rights from the state to more local government bodies, other types of CBC are best described as decentralized and discovered (i.e., decentralized through local emergence, not through processes of decentralization from the center). The campaign type of organizations who recognize CBC are most likely to be associated with these latter decentralized Little Conservation sorts of CBC (figure 1.1).

Park-Centric Organizations' Approaches to CBC

The park-centric organizations' efforts to save protected areas are often linked to ICDPs or other projects designed to include development benefits as incentives for conservation or to prevent or ameliorate negative impacts on residents. This addition of ICDPs to strictly protected areas has come about because bullets and barbed wire were failing to protect wildlife and parks were increasingly coming under siege (Adams and McShane 1992; Lewis and Carter 1993; Western, Wright, and Strum 1994). Most ICDPs are

Figure 1.1 Association of Organizational Types with CBC Type, Method, Concerns, and Agents

Org. Type:	Park-centric——Sustainable Development-centric——Advocacy Campaign-centric
CBC Type:	"Big C" CBC——"Little C" CBC
Method:	Strict Protection——ICDPs——Comanagement——Decentralized discovered——*Undiscovered*
Primary Social Concern:	Livelihoods——Rights
Agency:	CO as Agent——Community as Agent

in or border buffer zones around parks and protected areas—a sort of no man's land or minimal-use area. Although there is controversy over the definition and effectiveness of buffer zones (e.g., Brown 1992), they are still being created and demarcated. In some cases, local communities are consulted during demarcation of buffer zones and land-use zones are created to follow traditional boundaries of resource access by local people (e.g., WWF-US-Indonesia's work with the Indonesian government in Kayan Mentarang National Park, East Kalimantan).

Only rarely, however, do these efforts include activities that support local CBC. In one example of an exception to the pattern, World Wildlife Fund–Thailand staff discovered that local communities in Huay Kha Khaeng-Thung Yai have strong conservation institutions and supported them in resisting resettlement by the state (Kemf 1993). Opportunities for community-based monitoring to hold government accountable for protected-area and buffer-zone management have generally not been supported (e.g., Kothari, Suri, and Singh 1995). Instead, the trend is for ICDPs to include compacts, or covenants, that bind communities to conservation performance goals. Although COs' support for compacts may force autocratic governments to make more transparent policies, they also coerce local compliance with rules in return for promises of project benefits. The compacts are not legally binding; communities cannot seek recourse for broken promises or hold governments accountable for failing to counter threats from loggers or other extractive interests. Yet community members may be evicted from their lands if conservation goals are not met. Compacts can reduce local rights to mere privileges.

ICDPs are based on the premise that unless people affected by the establishment of protected areas feel that they benefit from protected areas they will not be deterred from unsustainable resource extraction in those areas. Most ICDPs are very local and seek the one or two incentives that will keep people out of the park, or they try to find cash replacements for resources people have lost to the park.

Park managers sometimes allow residents from outside the park to benefit by harvesting specific resources. For example, residents outside several protected areas in India and Nepal are allowed to cut grass inside the protected area for a short period each year. In addition, parks or associated NGOs offer tree seedlings for planting on private land to replace wood lost when villagers are denied access to firewood inside the park. ICDPs may promote cottage industries such as beekeeping, distribute hybrid seeds, improve water supplies, or initiate ecotourism to generate local revenue. What they have seldom done is build on Little Conservation practices and traditions.

Comanagement lies somewhere between the park-centric and sustainable development-centric nodes, because the definition of comanagement is very broad. It is sometimes applied to situations where people are allowed to harvest (not really a form of management) but also applied to situations like those in York, England, or Kakadu, Australia (Western, Wright, and Strum 1994), where park authorities and local authorities share decision-making power. Most comanagement depends on individual park or reserve managers who see the value of recognizing the rights of local, traditional owners of the resources and who are committed to developing ways to integrate them into park management decision making. These are generally ad hoc local efforts that are not official or legal policy and thus they may not be stable or sustainable.

Sustainable Development-Centric Organizations' Approach to CBC

The stated purpose of the sustainable development-centric approach is development with conservation benefits. Conservation organizations are increasingly concerned with conservation in a larger landscape as means for supporting conservation and long-term human development. In some cases, the ecoregional approach is primarily concerned with development and in others it is allied with the Deep Ecology movement, which would remove towns and cities to reconstitute wild corridors to maintain threatened ecosystems (e.g., the U.S. Wildlands Project). This approach offers an alternative to standard development that destroys biodiversity everywhere and eats away at protected areas.

The sustainable-development approach is most frequently applied by COs in areas where protected areas cannot be instituted or where the biota are migratory, for example, marine and coastal areas, wetlands, rangelands, and degraded production forests. Compared with development organizations, with which they share certain interests, COs measure their success by reversals in degradation trends, not by increasing incomes, which can be a means to reverse degradation trends. Likewise, COs do not, by and large, seek the same goals as those concerned with social justice, unless they recognize that social justice contributes to reaching conservation goals.

One marker for this approach is recognition of people's rights, in this case rights over economically valuable species and habitats, where COs feel that these rights will serve as an incentive for improved management. Examples of this type of effort include the CAMPFIRE program in Zimbabwe, ecolabeling efforts, and butterfly harvesting. Some conservation groups are involved in the sustainable-use movement, whereas others oppose it for various reasons. Sustainable use is not the same as sustainable development, but it is often discussed as though it were. COs often find themselves in conflict with animal rights groups who oppose sustainable use, one example being the current acrimonious battle over downlisting ivory under the Convention on International Trade in Endangered Species (CITES).

Less commonly, we find grassroots organizations seeking social justice and self-determination with alternative models of development linked to conservation. This is particularly common in indigenous people's community-based groups that are grappling with rapid change due to outside development pressures (e.g., Yayasan Pancur Kasih, a Dayak organization in Indonesia).

In another alternative model, COs offer technical assistance to strengthen local people's capacity to monitor and manage the biodiversity on their lands. For example, the Xavante in Brazil requested that WWF-US assist them in developing ways to survey and monitor game populations. In these cases, communities are not forced to follow the advice given—the decision is left to them. Technical assistance may also be provided in terms of legal assistance to fight illegal logging or encroachment on indigenous territories. This may take the form of direct legal assistance, background legal research, or providing them with satellite imagery to use as evidence.

The last, and perhaps largest, subtype supported by sustainable development-centric organizations is comanagement. Here COs are working to join the interests of the state and local people to work on specific management problems, an example being the joint forest-management strategies being pursued in India and elsewhere. Efforts to support joint coastal-management approaches are also widespread. The comanagement type of CBC can be undermined by tendencies toward blueprint and bureaucracy and failure to discover and build on existing community-based natural resource management (CBNRM) (Chapeskie 1995). While many comanagement projects for communities are designed to implement outsiders' projects, others are more joint ventures. Community organizing is an issue—at times the purpose appears to be more oriented toward organizing groups to perform labor for projects rather than organizing them to plan and manage activities. Social forestry and community forestry projects sometimes masquerade as CBC. The differences between forest management by forest communities and community forest plantations tended by communities have been highlighted in this decade's debates, for example, over a new community-forestry law in Thailand.

Campaign-Centric Organizations' Approaches to CBC

In the campaign-centric subtype the stated purpose is to support CBC with a goal of stopping activities that have negative impacts on biodiversity. It is something of a surprise that the organizations who most actively support the Little Conservation type of CBC tend to be campaign-centric COs. Campaigners fighting against destruction of remote forests and waters discover CBC among the local people at the sites where confrontation is occurring. In some cases, individual researchers in remote areas have discovered

CBC and go on to join or form campaign-type COs. In the case of national COs, commitment to communities and CBC is enduring, and COs stand ready to assist with renewed campaigns when requested by community organizations. In other cases, however, campaigners use local communities to further their own agenda and then simply move on, leaving the local community to face the consequences of the campaigner's activities alone.

Advocacy campaigns supporting CBC can have the greatest positive impacts beyond the local site. This is because they support policies that recognize the customary rights that underpin discovered CBC. Campaign-centric organizations generally do not actively nurture CBC, but this is not necessarily a bad thing because, unlike park-centric COs, they are less likely to create dependencies or often intervene in local political processes. Sometimes, however, these organizations have developed their own projects to support CBC in particular locations. For example, Greenpeace in the South Pacific supports site-based community forest and coastal management projects as part of its long-term campaign strategy.

Campaigns by COs do not necessarily support CBC. They have frequently ignored local rights, silenced local voices with high-profile campaigns in distant capitals of the North, and claimed the priority of global or national interests as moral vindication for their actions. COs sometimes claim the high moral ground by claiming that they are not representing themselves but rather speaking on behalf of biodiversity, representing the interests of wild animals who have no voice. Similar claims are sometimes made by indigenous people's organizations in efforts to maintain their rights over territory in the face of threatening extractive enterprises that operate in collusion with the state. CO campaigns often play to moral allegiances that are sometimes simplified into two camps, as in the propark versus antipark movements in India, which have even become associated with particular political parties. Campaigns often appeal to emotions, to feelings of justice and "what's right." They can be effective in supporting CBC, but they can also create a climate where empirical evaluations of CBC approaches are brushed aside in blind allegiance to an ideological perspective.

Agency Subtext

Another way to examine the relationship between organizations and CBC is to focus on agency. Those to the left of our continuum see themselves and government as the agents of conservation. Those on the right view communities as the agents that make the decisions. Those in the middle tend to recognize the agency of all stakeholders but to privilege government and commercial private sector agency over that of communities. Most conservationists continue to see local people as one weak stakeholder group among many. As Henry Lickers, a Mohawk scientist, once noted at a meeting related to the Convention on Biological Diversity, a stakeholder is anyone who shows up carrying a T-bone steak in each hand—in other words, anyone powerful enough to claim rights can be a stakeholder.

The critical point here is that although indigenous peoples and other long-standing communities are stakeholders with prior rights, the mandate for ICDPs seems to arise primarily from concern for the *livelihoods*, not the rights, of community members who have been denied access to resources. Evidence for this perception can be found in the words of analysts and in CO documents. For example, Wells and Brandon (1992, 2), writing about the history of ICDPs, state that "recognition thus is growing that . . . it is often neither politically feasible nor ethically justifiable to exclude the poor—who have limited access to resources—from parks and reserves without providing them alternative means of livelihood. This has led to increasing efforts by protected area managers and conservation organizations to obtain local cooperation via ICDPs." Here the purpose of ICDPs is to provide people with alternative means of livelihood to obtain their cooperation. The focus is on livelihoods as employment, not as linked to people's rights over the means of production. Wells and Brandon further note that, "balancing participation with enforcement activities is essential" (p. x). Implicit in this statement is the idea that participation does not include enforcement but rather leaves enforcement as a responsibility of the state. This problem of conflating rights and welfare to trump the rights issue is not limited to COs; many analysts have identified these same problems in social forestry and other environmental management programs, where local rights and responsibilities are often ignored.

CBC projects of the Little Conservation type, where agency for enforcement rests with local communities, are widespread, but they are often left out of discussions of CBC because the stereotypic CBC is the ICDP. Kuna Yala in Panama is one famous example of indigenous conservation, an autonomous region with its own system of government (Howe 1988). The government is based on local congresses in each of some fifty villages, and these control affairs and enforce their own laws within their respective territories. From these congresses are drawn three regional leaders who in turn give their allegiance to a single chief who heads the Kuna General Congress, a body drawn from the fifty village congresses. The chief's primary duty is not to issue edicts to his own people but rather to represent the community's voice in negotiations with the national government and other outside forces. Similar local governments exist around the world, but in most cases they are archaic remnants of traditional governments that have been undermined by colonial and neocolonial state governments. In Panama, however, traditional tribal governments have regional autonomy under the Panamanian legal structure for making and enforcing their own decisions about conservation and other sectors.

From Zaire (since 1997 the Democratic Republic of Congo) come reports of local governments establishing their own rules and tax systems to support wildlife protection in the absence of state action. In this case, there is no particular coordination with the state—an extreme example of decentralized conservation. In other cases, CBC might best be recognized as a type of common-property resource management, particularly in cases where the state has asserted its ownership over community property (lands or resources) in opposition to traditional local rights. In Ethiopia local communities have protected and managed grasslands for centuries under community laws that have evolved over time and continue to protect wildlife to the present day, and they are now seeking state recognition (Tefera 1996). In Thailand local communities have forest protection rules (Lynch and Alcorn 1994, 373–92) and enforce them locally, although the state generally ignores them and denies their right to make such rules in forests claimed by the state.

INCORPORATING CBC: THE WWF-US CASE

The WWF (also known as the World Wide Fund for Nature and widely recognized by its familiar panda logo) is similar to other COs in that it is not a monolithic entity following a narrow mandate. Conservation is a broad concept, and the work of WWF-US reflects this breadth. WWF-US's large, heterogeneous staff has diverse ideas about how conservation should be done.

WWF is the largest CO in the world, with international headquarters in Gland, Switzerland, and national organizations headquartered in twenty-five countries—collectively known as the WWF network. Special committees coordinate the work of network members, and fund-raising is a shared task. The host country governments set the stage for what is possible in any given country, but WWF and its partner organization IUCN often have the opportunity to influence what those governments view as the proper approach to conservation.

Within WWF-US, as in the WWF network generally, one can find the full range of projects, from classical strictly protected area and endangered species projects to neopopulist-type sustainable development projects, buffer-zone ICDPs, sustainable use programs, and joint management agreements. WWF-US also houses the WWF-TNC-WRI consortium's Biodiversity Support Program (BSP), funded by the U.S. Agency for International Development (USAID), which supports projects linking conservation and development around the world.

Programming choices are driven by opportunities, lessons learned, scientific analyses, and the personal interests of program officers. In addition, donors' mandates influence what COs do. Although there is a general mission statement, programs tend to coalesce around projects with captivating pictures and stories that can mobilize donor interest. In the case of WWF-US, 40 percent of the annual operating revenues come from members who are drawn from the general public; WWF-US has more than one million members (WWF 1996a). The attitudes of the general public influence fund-raising strategies that create the public image of the organization. But these unrestricted funds are largely used for core support, campaigns, educational activities, and matches for donor funds. Another 40 percent of WWF-US's operating revenues come from corporations, foundations, and the U.S. government to support particular projects. These restricted funds are the primary source for field project support. Since the mid-1980s, USAID has increasingly expanded support to WWF-US for projects that include CBC and CBNRM. Yet as WWF's representative in Cameroon stated, "One of the problems that conservation faces is 'short-termism.' This is partly a result of the fickleness of aid agencies whose development objectives, driven by their constituencies' policy agendas, constantly change—from the environment one year to poverty alleviation the next. . . . But real success is usually slow and often difficult to measure. Longterm commitment is . . . essential" (WWF 1996b, 79).

In 1996 WWF-International published a thirty-five-year historical overview beginning with its founding in 1961. Histories, of course, are interpretations of the past, and in the preface the editor notes that the historical account is not a statement of WWF-US's official policy but rather reflects "the diversity of views and characters that give WWF its strength" (WWF 1996b, 5). Claude Martin, WWF's director general, maintains that WWF's founders had a broad vision of a future world that would be better for all people and still have room left for wildlife and wild places (WWF 1996b, 11). He stresses that WWF has always been concerned about global poverty and people's well-being, that it was not founded for the narrow purpose of protecting wildlife. The book is replete with examples of WWF-International projects that lie within what Blaikie and Jeanrenaud call "neopopulist" projects that focus on locales beyond protected areas. For example, WWF-US supports river management, fisheries management, forest certification, and sustainable-use programs. But I could not find the term "community-based conservation" in this historical overview book. As far as I could ascertain, the term "integrated conservation and development projects," also known as integrated conservation and development (ICAD), has been preferred in global use until very recently. The term "community-based conservation" seems to have its origins in southern Africa and has spread globally only since 1993.

From the perspective of Little Conservation, CBC has been part of human history for thousands of years, but from a CO perspective, Raymond Dasmann was arguably the first vocal proponent of CBC. Dasmann worked with IUCN and, as a Fulbright scholar in the late 1960s and early 1970s, studied wildlife management in Rhodesia (now Zimbabwe), where he learned firsthand the linkages between local people and conservation. For nearly thirty years he has promoted a "different way" to protect biodiversity.

> People who once did a reasonable job of protecting nature on their own are driven away from the areas that are set aside for nature protection, and naturally enough take to poaching on lands that they once considered their own. It is usually a fairly brutal, insensitive approach to conservation that takes little account of the needs or wishes of those people who ultimately will be responsible for deciding whether the system will continue. (1977, 16)

In 1987 Dasmann reflected on efforts to support the different way he promoted.

> It involves learning the native language of the people who live in the areas that require long-term protection. It involves spending a lot of time talking with them, telling them your concerns, goals, and objectives, and listening to theirs. It means seeking with them ways in which these goals can be jointly achieved . . . this approach takes time and patience. For the most part, we have gone ahead, producing new generations of poachers, surrounding nature reserves with alienated people and generations, instead of embedding them within such reserves and encouraging the development of a friendly human environment of stewards and protectors. But we are finally beginning to change our ways. (1991, 11)

Managers of conservation projects began the first prototype ICDPs in the middle to late 1970s as they sought ways to work with people in and around protected areas. In the 1980s a cadre of people drawn from field projects around the world drafted the World Conservation Strategy (IUCN/UNEP/WWF 1980). This became the legitimating document for what is now known as CBC. The process of drafting the document was overtly consultative and, because the writers reached out to confer with people around the world, it well represented conservation thinking at that time.

The World Parks Congress in Bali in 1982 was also a major turning point for COs. There was a strong representation from what we now call the South. They did not reject parks as an elitist Northern idea but agreed that parks needed to be placed in a different sort of social context to make them work. In the case of Chitwan National Park in Nepal, it was proposed that the needs of local people be met by allowing them to harvest grass there. The Indonesians, on the other hand, advocated the hard-edge view—that maintaining a clear hard edge is better than confusing park boundaries through conditional-use policies that arbitrarily take and give rights. They argued that, in terms of community relations, this was worse than allowing no use at all.

Also in the mid-1980s, the Man and the Biosphere Program (MAB) of the United Nations Educational, Scientific and Cultural Organization (UNESCO) developed guidelines for integrating conservation and development in protected areas participating in the biosphere reserve program (Batisse 1986; UNESCO 1984). The ideal biosphere reserve was a core area surrounded by a buffer zone where uses were managed to protect the core. The buffer zone in turn was to be embedded in a "transitional zone of cooperation" that was to be "the principal area for involving local people in improving their own well-being through culturally and ecologically sustainable types and patterns of development and for implementing educational and training programs which help develop an enthusiastic constituency for the reserve" (Gregg 1991, 282).

It was in this mid-1980s context that WWF-US developed the Wildlands and Human Needs Program (WHNP). It was initiated when R. Michael Wright followed up a lead that the Private Voluntary Organization (PVO) Office at USAID was interested in supporting conservation that was linked to benefits to human well-being. When Wright contacted the field projects funded by WWF-US in Latin America to discuss the idea, he discovered that approximately 10 percent of WWF-US-funded projects were already working with local people but were not telling WWF-US headquarters about it because it was seen to be insignificant.

So it was not donor money that drove WWF-US to ICDPs, but donor interest did lead WWF-US top management to look more closely at field operations and recognize, and then promote, what was already happening. This generated internal discussions of existing programs and the realization that the World Conservation Strategy legitimated an effort to expand local project teams' existing initiatives.

According to Wright, the original ICDPs started as part of WWF-US projects (before WHNP) because project managers wanted to work well with their neighbors, not because they thought the parks would fail if they did not. As Wright has noted (Stone 1991, 151), ICDPs were initiated with a vision of working with local partners to create a "harmony between man and land," an approach "for which there is no moral or practical alternative." Wright believes that "conservation is about people," and "to be effective, it must address both the needs of nature and the needs of the poor and the dispossessed who ironically share their rural frontier with the Earth's biological wealth." Wright asserts that "we cannot, we must not, choose between protecting the wild beauty of a tropical jungle and allaying the suffering of a malnourished child."

In 1985 Wright pulled the preexisting projects together into a program and proposed WHNP to USAID. At that time WWF-US was primarily a grant maker, and Wright originally proposed WHNP that way—a grants program for other organizations to implement. But the USAID project officer, to meet the PVO Office's mandate to build new capacity and new program areas in American NGOs, wanted WWF-US to be more hands-on and build WWF-US capacity to implement projects linking conservation with development. USAID also wanted WWF-US to run the program globally, not just in Latin America. This contributed to WWF-US's expansion in Africa and Asia, with subsequent additional USAID mission funding at the national levels.

To learn from others with experience in community development, WWF-US set up an advisory group for WHNP in 1987. The group included Save the Children, Catholic Relief Services, Cooperative for Assistance and Relief Everywhere (CARE), Pan American Development Foundation, Christian Children's Fund, International Center for Research on Women, Cultural Survival, Organization of American States, International Institute for Environment and Development, Coordination in Development Consortium (CODEL), and Interamerican Development Foundation. WWF-US staff found these to be exciting meetings where everyone benefited from the exchange of lessons learned. In particular, WWF-US learned from the advisory group about the importance of incorporating gender concerns into their projects. The advisory group recommended a reading list for conservation project staff, and about five hundred copies of *Two Ears of Corn* (Bunch 1982) were distributed by WWF-US to project implementers.

WWF-US (Larson, Freudenberger, and Wyckoff-Baird 1997) recognizes two stages of ICDPs that evolved under WHNP. The first-generation projects were piloted in the 1980s; second-generation projects, the early 1990s. WHNP was originally designed as a three-year-grant program—a sort of add-on to existing projects. During the early years, a choice was made to limit WHNP to ongoing projects that could add a component that moved them toward working with communities. By the end of the 1980s, 75 percent of WWF-US projects had a component addressing local people (Wright, personal communication, 1997). USAID extended additional funding to WHNP, and the program continued until 1996 (totaling five million dollars over eleven years).

From 1985 to 1992, WHNP clearly contributed to WWF-US's efforts, but the CBC concept remained a sideline to WWF-US's work. During this period, WWF-US underwent several restructuring events that affected the implementation of WHNP. During the 1980s, when WHNP was created, WWF-US was a matrix organization with geographic and thematic cross-responsibilities for individuals. Then when conservation money got tight in the early 1990s there were intense internal debates within WWF-US about continuing to emphasize thematic responsibilities. The decision was made to reduce the emphasis on the means of conservation and instead structure the organization by geographic areas of responsibilities, with a small unit of thematic expertise to serve the geographic teams. This was soon followed by decentralization that moved responsibilities and authority out to field offices in different countries. This process began in the early 1990s and was recently completed, leaving few technical officers at headquarters. Opinions differ as to whether these changes served to mainstream or hobble the CBC approach. There is some consensus, however, that these changes reduced the sharing of lessons and therefore slowed the advance of second-generation CBC approaches.

WHNP was evaluated at regular intervals and efforts were made to disseminate the lessons learned. In 1992 lessons learned from WHNP were integrated into a booklet on designing ICDPs written by WHNP director Barbara Wyckoff-Baird and Michael Brown, director of another USAID-funded program (PVO/NGO-NRMS) that focuses on strengthening NGO capacity to manage natural resources (Brown and Wyckoff-Baird 1992). This booklet was published in three languages and distributed to some five thousand people and organizations in more than fifty countries. In 1991 WWF-US published a book (Stone 1991) reviewing the successes and failures of WHNP. In the book's afterword, R. Michael Wright, then senior vice president at WWF-US (now director of the Conservation and Sustainable Development program at the MacArthur Foundation), described the WHNP vision of fashioning "a mixed system of shared benefits and responsibilities" whereby local and national interests could be met (Stone 1991, 150). He also reiterated, "We must not only integrate protected areas with local community development, we must also join that small-scale, grass-roots approach to larger economic and political considerations" (Stone 1991, 151).

By 1993 CBC had been consolidated within WWF-US, and the president of WWF-US, Kathryn Fuller, reached out to members to educate them that working with local communities was one of WWF-US's guiding mandates. In a video message to all WWF-US members, she explained why local communities held the key to conserving biodiversity. Also in 1993, with funding from the Liz Claiborne and Art Ortenberg Foundation, WWF-US organized a major international conference that brought together experts from COs around the world to assess progress on "community-based conservation"—indicating that use of the term was broadening beyond the ICDPs. The findings were published in two books (Claiborne and Ortenberg Foundation 1993; Western, Wright, and Strum 1994) that solidly backed a vision of CBC as decentralized and integrated into local life, something that donors supported by giving long-term support to local processes and ideas instead of short-lived projects.

Was there a model project that shaped the discourse on the subject? Yes, the Annapurna Conservation Area Project (ACAP) in Nepal has often been called a model of the WHNP approach (Wells 1994, 261–81) and has been used over the years to illustrate WWF-US's commitment to involving local communities. ACAP is not typical but more a model for what many projects are still striving to achieve, for "enlisting local communities in projects that enhance economic well-being while protecting wildlife"(WWF 1996a, 20). ACAP was initiated by WWF-US staff who started by carrying out a careful study of local problems and needs. The study resulted in a proposal to create a multiple-use conservation area so that the hundred thousand local people living in the ACAP area would have authority to manage their own natural resources. This was in contrast to the usual solution of restricting local access to the conservation project area. A decade later livelihoods are improved, ACAP is self-funding, and rare species have more habitat.

WWF-US's commitment to CBC and ICDPs is reflected in its annual reports. The 1991 *Annual Report* states, "WWF-US's experience . . . reveals that the time-honored methods of park management must evolve to meet human needs in harmony with the long-term health of the ecosystem. More than ever before, conservation techniques must include the development demands of the rural poor" (WWF 1991, 23). The 1992 *Annual Report* describes several projects that address local needs, including the Caprivi project in Namibia where WWF-US "helped government . . . design restricted-use buffer zones where people can fish, cut firewood, and use other natural resources to support their families without endangering wildlife" (WWF 1992, 17).

In 1993, the same year that she sent the CBC video message to all members, the WWF-US president's opening statement in the *Annual Report* described the reasoning behind CBC and ICDPs.

> Wherever we work, we encourage local communities to take up the threads of conservation practices and weave them into the day-to-day fabric of their lives. . . . Why do we go to these lengths? Why are we at such pains to work with local communities in all our projects? We are not, after all, a development organization. We care, first and foremost, about addressing the full panoply of threats to nature. . . . We aim to improve the economic well-being of people who live alongside natural resources while, at the same time, protecting and preserving those resources. (WWF 1993, 6–7)

The first time the term "community-based conservation" appears in a WWF-US annual report is in 1994, where it is used to refer to a project with Miskito Indians in Nicaragua (WWF 1994, 30). In 1995 WWF-US president Kathryn Fuller described the WWF-US project in Chitwan, Nepal, noting that the "locally based forest management project developed by WWF-US and its Nepalese partners has enlisted the people living near the park to become dedicated custodians of rhino habitat. . . . [A] combination of anti-poaching efforts and local community involvement has resulted in an increase in the rhino population" (WWF 1995a, 8–9). She elaborates that, to take pressure off the park, residents have set aside special plantations for fodder, fuel wood, and hardwood: "the hand cut fodder keeps livestock from grazing and denuding whole stretches of forest, and the hardwood will soon provide a lucrative new income source for financially strapped villagers. By allowing plants and trees to regenerate in these buffer zones, local people are, in essence, extending the park's boundaries and expanding wildlife habitat in the process" (WWF 1995a, 23).

Perhaps the zenith of the CBC movement within the WWF network was reached in 1994 when Michel Pimbert and Jules Pretty wrote their controversial report promoting a new paradigm of people-centered conservation for WWF-International. Their report directly addressed the management of protected areas instead of focusing on ICDPs on the periphery of protected areas. They demanded a review of WWF-US's overall approach to protected areas and argued that "conservation efforts may need to identify and promote those social processes that enable local communities to conserve and enhance biodiversity as part of their livelihood systems" (Pimbert and Pretty 1995, 24). They stressed that "all actors and stakeholders have unique perspectives on what is the problem and what is improvement" (p. 13), and they questioned "whose knowledge should count in the design of national park systems and protected areas" (p. 15). They also stressed the need to differentiate between types of participation (p. 26) for WWF to analyze its work more effectively. But their critique was not well received, and during WWF's restructuring in 1995 Pimbert's position was eliminated. But others inside WWF continue to debate the privileged place of the protected-area paradigm as it defines conservation discourse.

Just before Pimbert and Pretty's piece, IUCN had released a new World Conservation Strategy, *Caring for the Earth* (IUCN/UNEP/WWF 1991), that crossed the bounds of what many conservationists found acceptable. Many felt that *Caring for the Earth* came too close to equating development with conservation and promoting politically correct social agendas (Robinson 1993). It was also criticized for lacking legitimacy because it incorporated no voices from the field.

Nonetheless, in 1995 WWF took another step forward and developed the first policy on indigenous peoples of any CO. The policy, in *Indigenous Peoples and Conservation: WWF Statement of Principles* (WWF 1996c), was drafted by WWF-US and adopted by WWF International as a WWF-network statement. It is a quite progressive policy statement that recognizes indigenous people's rights and pledges to collaborate with them where their interests coincide with those of WWF.

The first principle of partnership states, "Whenever it promotes conservation objectives, and in the context of its involvement in conservation activities affecting indigenous peoples' lands and territories, WWF will encourage governments to take steps as necessary . . . to guarantee effective protection of [indigenous peoples'] rights of ownership and possession of those lands and territories, as determined by the International Labor Organization (ILO) Convention 169 (Article 14)." In addition, specifically related to the Little Conservation type of CBC,

> when WWF conservation activities impinge on areas where historic claims and/or current exercise of customary resource rights of indigenous peoples are present, WWF will . . . be ready to: assist indigenous peoples' organizations in the design, implementation, monitoring and evaluation of conservation activities, and to invest in strengthening such organizations and in developing relevant human resources in the respective indigenous communities [and] assist them in gaining access to other sources of technical and financial support to advance those development objectives that fall outside WWF's mission. (WWF 1996c, 7)

Although this document seems to indicate a shift toward the right of the continuum, associated with Little Conservation CBC, in practice, as of mid-1997, minimal funds and staff time have been allocated to implement the policy and to develop the promised guidelines for field-program staff. There are as yet no instances of the application of this policy. Hence it is too early to evaluate whether the policy indicates a WWF shift toward supporting existing CBC.

In WWF-US's 1996 *Annual Report*, CBC remained front and center in the presentation of WWF-US's work, despite internal concerns that ICDPs were not contributing to conservation goals. Also in 1996 WWF-US's president coauthored a paper reviewing WWF-US's efforts to incorporate sustainable-development objectives into the organization's work. "COs are gradually making the transition from an approach that emphasized enforcement of regulations and exclusion of local communities to one that recognizes local communities as essential partners in achieving conservation objectives." But they also note that the "lessons learned are only slowly being incorporated into the design and implementation of field programs and reflected in the mandates, structures, and staffing of conservation organizations" (Seymour and Fuller 1996, 259).

The three lessons they highlight are that (1) "local conservation projects must address the needs and development aspirations of local communities," (2) [they] "must provide direct incentives for conservation, and communities must be organized and empowered to act on those incentives," and (3) "local interventions and innovations must be complemented by favorable national and international policies" (1996, 259–60). Seymour and Fuller note that as a result of these lessons

> institutional capacity concentrated in field biology has been broadened—either in-house or through partnerships with other organizations—to include rural development expertise and sensitivity to the many dimensions of the new generation of ICDPs. Skills in enterprise and organizational development, resource

> rights, gender concerns, law, economics, policy analysis, and advocacy have been developed in order to complement science-based field projects with institutional and policy reform agendas. (1996, 261–62)

They close with the recognition that "the question of who it is that NGOs represent, especially Northern-based NGOs operating in developing countries, is always an important one. NGOs should be held to the same standards of transparency, accountability, and participation that they have advocated to the [World] Bank" (1996, 267).

The ICDP approach is under continued scrutiny. WWF-US has recently completed a two-year internal review that evaluates the ICDP approach (Larson, Freudenberger, and Wyckoff-Baird 1997). Eighty field staff participated in a series of focused workshops to intensively discuss and debate the lessons learned from WWF-US's fifty-three ICDP field projects around the world. TNC has also been reviewing its efforts to involve local people in their conservation projects ("participatory conservation," also known as "compatible development"). Neither evaluation is currently available in final form for public discussion, but drafts indicate that there is an emerging consensus that more effort must be made to integrate better biological and social information into the planning and evaluation of ICDPs.

One way that WWF-US will be doing better integration is through a new filter—the Global 200 initiative—under which WWF-US will primarily fund field projects only if they are located in one of the two hundred ecoregions that have been identified as biologically important. Ford Foundation is supporting the integration of social concerns into ecoregional planning under the Global 200 initiative. Ecoregional planning involves coordinated landscape-level action to secure protected areas in linked corridors. Although there is a general consensus that ICDPs have failed to fully achieve their conservation goals in the past and that the ICDP approach should be broadened to include other CBC approaches, the WWF-US commitment to continue supporting CBC remains unwavering.

In a recent critique, Brandon (1997, 90–114), a representative of the biologists' school of thought, has observed that COs have been more concerned with social issues than with environmental issues. Similar critiques have been voiced by influential conservation biologists, including Michael Soulé (Soulé and Lease 1995). These opinions indicate a fundamental disagreement with the idea that conservation is a social process—an idea that gives priority to monitoring and managing social and political processes, with biologists relegated to providing technical advice to a project. In a recent book (Kramer, van Schaik, and Johnson 1997), biologists and other analysts seek to justify a "new protection paradigm" (van Schaik and Kramer 1997, 212–30) based on four principles: (1) "law enforcement should be a fact of life for protected areas," (2) "beneficiaries elsewhere must be prepared to pay for these benefits," (3) "foreign involvement in the management of a country's biodiversity is justified," and (4) "active involvement of local communities in conservation is mandatory" (van Schaik and Kramer 1997, 215–17). Their perspective is seen as reasonable and echoed by many WWF-US staff and others in the global conservation community.

In 1997 WWF-International published a provocative piece by Sally Jeanrenaud on the different perspectives on CBC or what she refers to as "people-oriented conservation." Jeanrenaud reviews the different arguments supporting the CBC approach, ranging from pragmatic and efficiency based to human rights based and holistic. She notes that contradictions emerge from different worldviews embedded in conservation ideologies, and therefore these conflicting perspectives are not likely to be easily resolved. She further notes that, "the contrasting views create a series of challenges for policy development within COs. Whose arguments win?" (Jeanrenaud 1997, 5). Finally, she observes that the differing perspectives lead to practical dilemmas at the level of field implementation and that "the politics of policy and practice constitutes a 'struggle for meaning' as different actors seek to enroll others into their point of view." This is an open acknowledgment of the internal debates currently going on within WWF.

This type of open discussion paradoxically can serve to both strengthen and weaken the CBC movement by opening the debate further to political jockeying for position within the organization. It calls into question WWF-US's commitments to the indigenous people's policy and other social-justice concerns. Transparent internal disagreement makes it harder to persuade the "hard edgers" that CBC is the right path. On the other hand, this transparency is necessary for the political process of conservation. WWF-field-staff reaction to the WWF ICDP review (Larson, Freudenberger, and Wyckoff-Baird 1997) indicates that this open discussion has resulted in renewed commitment to CBC.

NEW CONSERVATION PARADIGM?

COs such as WWF-US are at a crossroads. ICDPs started as responses by conservation-project staff to local situations, and they were promoted without a good understanding of the level of effort that would be needed. As a result, insufficient resources and time were committed, despite Dasmann's early advice. The consensus among the social scientists I interviewed seems to be that ICDPs are not entirely successful, not because CBC is the wrong approach but rather because COs have been doing it wrong.

Next Steps

If COs want to have biologically measurable successes from ICDPs and other forms of CBC, it seems clear that more commitment must be invested in long-term dialogue between stakeholders, in the development of consensus-based strategies and tools, and in support for a learning-based approach to CBC over many years. This approach requires patience, active participation, and "action research" to test hypotheses and monitor results. It also requires acknowledging that CBC is difficult and that conflicts are inevitable (Western, Wright, and Strum 1994, 514). This approach is pragmatic—it recognizes differences of views and needs and seeks collaboration to find shared concerns, and ways to negotiate and design new options. Beyond these commitments, the key to moving forward lies in identifying and following appropriate processes that will enable COs to respond to the specificities of local situations.

The two-year, intensive WWF-US ICDP review (Larson, Freudenberger, and Wyckoff-Baird 1997) has resulted in the following recommendations for improving the performance of ICDPs:

- seek consensus on conservation agendas among key interest groups
- view ICDPs as one tool within an ecoregional conservation strategy
- ensure that ICDPs focus on biodiversity objectives
- address external factors
- support ICDPs over the long term
- plan, monitor, learn, and adapt
- build on what exists
- clarify who controls what
- work in strategic partnerships and act as a facilitator
- generate economic benefits for local people

The review's findings, reached by the consensus of field staff, affirm the recommendations made by Brown and Wyckoff-Baird's earlier analysis (1992). The rich detail of the WWF-US ICDP review workshop proceedings (WWF 1995b, 1995c, 1996d, 1996e) also reveals a growing field-based recognition that WWF-US needs to develop a more coherent international stance in relation to repressive governments and international corporations to support the policy changes needed for successful CBC.

Barriers

Many difficulties are faced by any CO attempting to do CBC—overly ambitious goals, corruption, population growth, disintegrating local traditions, rising consumerism, and lack of community-based leadership, to name a few. But other barriers are less obvious, barriers that lie within the ways that CBC is conceptualized. These barriers are reified as the same rhetoric gets reproduced.

One central problem that has not been acknowledged by top management is that COs see their mandate as flowing from a concern for local livelihoods, not local rights, and this may be the Achilles' heel that will doom COs' CBC efforts. By understanding local people's loss of rights to resources in protected areas as the loss of jobs instead of understanding it as loss of means of production, COs try to avoid discussions of justice. Many conservationists, however, do see that promoting social justice is integral to achieving conservation. As Chatrapati Singh of WWF-India has written, "The issues actually at stake in the forest question . . . are three: (a) justice to the people, forest dwellers and non-dwellers; (b) justice to nature (trees, wildlife, etc.); and (c) justice to coming generations" (Singh 1986, 7). And, "for the past two centuries or so, the consequences of such *adharma* (injustice) have been borne by the rural poor, the tribals, and the flora and fauna of India" (p. 1).

COs' growing recognition that tenure is key to achieving CBC (Western, Wright, and Strum 1994; Claiborne and Ortenberg Foundation 1993) reflects a growing understanding that rights are central to successful CBC, but the depth of the importance of rights beyond tenure is still insufficiently appreciated by many people in a hurry to secure wildlife habitats.

Rhetorical traffic raises another barrier. It obfuscates meaningful differences and slows the transition to a new and better CBC. For example, COs have joined the bandwagon in critiquing what is a community and who represents a community—sometimes aimed at making it appear that community is a fiction and that therefore COs cannot count on such nonentities to hold rights and responsibilities for conservation. Others who acknowledge that representation is a serious issue see it not as a barrier but rather as a core issue that must be addressed if CBC projects are to succeed.

Another source of confusion in the rhetorical traffic revolves around the term *involvement*. Like the term it has replaced—*participation*—involvement can really mean anything. Sometimes it seems to mean that the community serves as a source of cheap labor. In other cases, involvement appears to be coercion, where COs have created patron systems in which the CO is the patron the community depends on.

Another common term in the rhetorical traffic jam is *partnership*, which has become so widely used as to be meaningless unless it is defined. The WWF-US ICDP review has taken pains to identify the characteristics of "authentic partnerships."

The newly popular term *decentralization* is now popping up in CO rhetoric in ways that present barriers to CBC. The term might mean recognizing local rights and responsibilities for planning and managing areas. But more often decentralization either mislabels efforts to centralize state control over areas previously marginal tc state control or teeters on the verge of state abandonment of communities, leaving them powerless against local robber-baron elites to whom power is being decentralized.

A final barrier to further progress in CBC is the conflicting views of the relationship between conservation and development. Brandon (1997, 98), for example, commenting on IUCN's Caring for the Earth strategy, writes that "in proposing this strategy, the international COs have gone a long way toward promoting the myth that development and the conservation of biodiversity are compatible." She reflects the view of many biologists. But experienced, field-tested conservationists argue that unless conservation and development are or become compatible, there is no future for conservation. Most COs, including WWF-US, seek an overlap between conservation and development—a reuniting of the two into one holistic vision of a sustainable future.

The Vision

Jonah Western has summarized the vision of CBC reached by consensus at the international review of CBC held at Airlie House in 1994.

> In practical terms, community-based conservation calls for sweeping policy reforms on a grand scale. If the locus of action is to be the community, conservation policies and practices must be turned on their heads. . . . Such changes call for nothing less than a turnaround in entrenched political norms. Every aspect of conservation, from user rights to donor roles, must be rethought. Local initiatives and skills must become the driving force of conservation. The role of government must move from center stage to the periphery and change from coercive to supportive. Governments must think in terms of integrating the activities of many conservation-oriented groups and individuals and arbitrating their disputes. . . . Local communities will become the real conservation practitioners who experiment with new techniques and disseminate them by example. National and regional conservation organizations will become the partners of local communities. . . . Conservation organizations, together with bilateral and multilateral donors, will become resource brokers looking for innovative conservation enterprises to support and foster . . . (p. 553).
>
> Conservation will cease to be a singular activity based on biology and resource use. Instead, it will be the sum of many interrelated and integrated activities that contribute to the sustainability and maintenance of biological diversity. . . . Conservation will cease to be a discrete human activity. (pp. 554–55)

In his recent analysis of lessons learned regarding conservation and cultural survival, Stan Stevens has added a dimension to the vision.

> Community-based conservation shifts the focus of conservation efforts to peoples, groups, and settlements. Ideally, it is based on supporting local practices and initiative, catalyzing these with funds and, in some cases, with new information, ideas, technology, and techniques. From indigenous peoples' perspectives, community-based conservation seems to be international validation of

> approaches that they have been employing for millennia, and in situations where governments have undermined local authority, it can be a way to empower local resource management and conservation. (1997, 287)

The WWF-US ICDP review adds the pragmatic observation that, to achieve this new vision, "the challenge for Northern NGOs is to move from 'patron-client' relationships, based on control of funds, to partnerships based on the recognition of truly reciprocal needs and obligations" (Larson, Freudenberger, and Wyckoff-Baird 1997, 47).

CONCLUSION

The move to incorporate CBC approaches at WWF-US was an outgrowth of responses of individual staff members to "real world problems that seemed to require profoundly new solutions" (Coward, this volume). The growth of the CBC approach was not associated with a leader at the top but followed from a situation where donor interest led WWF-US's Washington-headquarters staff to recognize promising directions being taken by fieldworkers. A small program was established at headquarters to nurture that approach. Staff in the field were crucial to the initiation and development of this new direction. The staff who developed and piloted the growth of that small initiative have all now left WWF-US. In an organization like WWF-US, staff is critical in shaping the direction taken by the organization. Perhaps the current generation of ICDPs might have been more successful if WWF-US had made a greater effort to recruit more social scientists and biologists with field experience in CBC, committed more resources to monitoring ICDPs for lessons, taken more direction from the field, and had moved beyond reactive management toward strategically planned long-term support for key ICDP projects. In 1992 WHNP director Barbara Wyckoff-Baird recommended that WWF review the lessons learned from first-generation CBC projects (Wyckoff-Baird 1992). Yet this review was not completed until 1997. Nonetheless, despite the lack of institution-led analysis, individuals involved in ICDP projects drew their own lessons from their experiences and moved forward, as was discovered in this 1997 global review of ICDPs (Larson, Freudenberger, and Wyckoff-Baird 1997).

Looking back over the past seventeen years of COs' dances with communities (1980–1997), I close with two personal lessons that stand out in my experience and are echoed by chapters in this book. First, CBC will not survive and prosper without policy changes. The tiny flames burning through the night in a hundred lamps in communities across a landscape are more effective in creating long-term policy change than is a single bonfire in a capital city that flares bright and then dies when the donor stops feeding it.

Community leaders' initiatives feed the smaller flames that lead to enlightened policy. Second, while it is possible to learn lessons from specific cases, generalizing from case studies is a common mistake. Mass replication based on blueprints from model cases are doomed to failure unless the blueprints lay out only general processes that can be followed (for example, see the discussion on CAMPFIRE in this book). The dance steps to long-term CBC success will be created by COs that engage in collaborative situational analyses with communities, listen closely, seize opportunities where they exist, learn from their mistakes, and follow local leaders in identifying and promoting key policy reforms, as well as in designing and implementing local projects.

REFERENCES

Adams, J., and T. McShane. 1992. *The Myth of Wild Africa*. Berkeley: Univ. of California Press.

Alcorn, J. B. 1995. Big Conservation and Little Conservation: Collaboration in Managing Global and Local Heritage. In *Local Heritage in the Changing Tropics: Innovative Strategies for Natural Resource Management and Control*, ed. G. Dicum. Yale School of Forestry and Environmental Studies Bulletin Series, no. 98. New Haven, Conn.: Yale Univ.

Batisse, M. 1986. Developing and Focusing the Biosphere Reserve Concept. *Nature and Resources* 22: 1–10.

Blaikie, Piers, and Sally Jeanrenaud. 1996. *Biodiversity and Human Welfare*. Geneva: United Nations Research Institute for Social Development.

Brandon, Katrina. 1997. Policy and Practical Considerations in Land-use Strategies for Biodiversity Conservation. In *Last Stand: Protected Areas and the Defense of Tropical Biodiversity*, ed. Randall Kramer, Carel van Schaik, and Julie Johnson. New York: Oxford Univ. Press.

Brown, Michael. 1991. *Buffer Zone Management in Africa*. Washington, D.C.: PVO-NGO/NRMS.

———. 1992. *Buffer Zone Management in Africa: Searching for Innovative Ways to Satisfy Human Needs and Conservation Objectives*. Washington, D.C.: PVO-NGO / NRMS.

Brown, Michael, and Barbara Wyckoff-Baird. 1992. *Designing Integrated Conservation and Development Projects*. Washington, D.C.: World Wildlife Fund Biodiversity Support Program.

Bunch, Roland. 1982. *Two Ears of Corn: A Guide to People-Centered Agricultural Improvement*. Oklahoma City, Kans.: World Neighbors.

Chapeskie, Andrew. 1995. *Land, Landscape, Culturescape: Aboriginal Relationships to Land and the Co-Management of Natural Resources*. Ottawa: Report to the Royal Commission on Aboriginal Peoples.

Christiansen Research Institute. 1991. Environmental Assessment of the Expanded

Logging Concession, Madang. Manuscript submitted to Department of Environment and Conservation, Government of Papua New Guinea.

Claiborne and Ortenberg Foundation. 1993. *The View from Airlie: Community Based Conservation in Perspective*. New York: Liz Claiborne and Art Ortenberg Foundation.

Dasmann, Raymond F. 1977. In *World Wildlife Fund Yearbook, 1976–1977*. Morges, Switzerland: WWF. Cited in Jeanrenaud 1997, without title.

———. 1991. The Importance of Cultural and Biological Diversity. In *Biodiversity: Culture, Conservation and Ecodevelopment*, ed. M. L. Oldfield and J. B. Alcorn. Boulder, Colo.: Westview.

Forero, Oscar A., and Ramon E. Laborde. 1997. Notas Sobre el Ordenamiento Territorial Indigena: Manejo Ambiental en el Apaporis. Paper presented at Conferencia Derechos Indigenas y Conservacion de la Naturaleza, Pucallpa, Peru.

Gregg, William P., Jr. 1991. MAB Biosphere Reserves and Traditional Land Use Systems. In *Biodiversity: Culture, Conservation and Ecodevelopment*, ed. M. L. Oldfield and J. B. Alcorn. Boulder, Colo.: Westview.

Hess, Charlotte, ed. 1996. *Common Pool Resources and Collective Action: A Bibliography*. Bloomington: Workshop in Political Theory and Policy Analysis, Indiana Univ.

Howe, James. 1988. *The Kuna Gathering: Contemporary Village Politics in Panama*. Austin: Univ. of Texas Press.

IUCN/UNEP/WWF. 1980. *World Conservation Strategy, Living Resource Conservation for Sustainable Development*. Gland, Switzerland: IUCN–The World Conservation Union.

———. 1991. *Caring for the Earth: A Strategy for Sustainable Living*. Gland, Switzerland: IUCN–The World Conservation Union.

Jeanrenaud, Sally. 1997. Perspectives in People-Oriented Conservation. *Arborvitae* (suppl.), February. Gland, Switzerland: IUCN–The World Conservation Union.

Kemf, Elizabeth, ed. 1993. *The Law of the Mother: Protecting Indigenous Peoples in Protected Areas*. San Francisco: Sierra Club / Random House.

Kothari, Ashish, Saloni Suri, and Neena Singh. 1995. People and Protected Areas: Rethinking Conservation in India. *The Ecologist* 25(5): 188–94.

Kramer, Randall, Carel van Schaik, and Julie Johnson, eds. 1997. *Last Stand: Protected Areas and the Defense of Tropical Biodiversity*. New York: Oxford Univ. Press.

Larson, Patty, Mark Freudenberger, and Barbara Wyckoff-Baird. 1997. *Lessons from the Field: A Review of World Wildlife Fund's Experience with Integrated Conservation and Development Projects, 1985–1996*. Washington, D.C.: World Wildlife Fund.

Lehm, Zulema. 1997. El caso del Territorio Ind'gena Parque National Isiboro-Secure (TIPNIS). Paper presented at Conferencia Derechos Ind'genas y Conservacion de la Naturaleza, Pucallpa, Peru.

Lewis, Dale, and Nick Carter, eds. 1993. *Voices from Africa: Local Perspectives on Conservation*. Washington, D.C.: World Wildlife Fund.

Lohmann, Larry. 1991. Who Defends Biodiversity? *The Ecologist* 21(1): 5–13.

Lynch, O. J., and J. B. Alcorn. 1994. Tenurial Rights and Community-Based Conservation. In *Natural Connections: Perspectives in Community-Based Conservation*, ed. D. Western, M. W. Wright, and S. Strum. Washington, D.C.: Island Press.

Pimbert, M. P., and Jules N. Pretty. 1995. *Parks, People and Professionals: Putting "Participation" into Protected Area Management*. Gland, Switzerland: United Nations Research Institute for Social Development / International Institute for Environment and Development / World Wide Fund for Nature.

Robinson, John G. 1993. The Limits to Caring: Sustainable Living and the Loss of Biodiversity. *Conservation Biology* 7: 20–28.

Seymour, Frances. 1994. Are Successful Community-based Conservation Projects Designed or Discovered? In *Natural Connections: Perspectives in Community-Based Conservation*, ed. D. Western, M. W. Wright, and S. Strum. Washington, D.C.: Island Press.

Seymour, Frances, and Kathryn Fuller. 1996. Converging Learning: The World Wildlife Fund, World Bank, and the Challenge of Sustainable Development. *Brown Journal of World Affairs* 3(2): 257–68.

Singh, Chatrapati. 1986. *Common Property and Common Poverty: India's Forests, Forest Dwellers and the Law*. Oxford: Oxford Univ. Press.

Soulé, Michael, and Gary Lease, eds. 1995. *Reinventing Nature? Responses to Postmodern Deconstruction*. Washington, D.C.: Island Press.

Stevens, Stan. 1997. Lessons and Directions. In *Conservation through Cultural Survival: Indigenous Peoples and Protected Areas*, ed. Stan Stevens. Washington, D.C.: Island Press.

Stone, Roger. 1991. *Wildlands and Human Needs*. Washington, D.C.: World Wildlife Fund.

Tefera, Zelealem. 1996. Ethiopia: Guarding the Guassa. *Community Conservation*, theme issue jointly produced with The African Wildlife Foundation. *The Rural Extension Bulletin* 10:52–53.

UNESCO. 1984. Action Plan for Biosphere Reserves. *Nature and Resources* 20: 1–12.

van Schaik, Carel P., and Randall A. Kramer. 1997. Toward a New Protection Paradigm. In *Last Stand: Protected Areas and the Defense of Tropical Biodiversity*, ed. R. Kramer, C. P. van Schaik, and Julie Johnson. New York: Oxford Univ. Press.

Wells, Michael P. 1994. A Profile and Interim Assessment of the Annapurna Conservation Area Project, Nepal. In *Natural Connections: Perspectives in Community-Based Conservation*, ed. D. Western, M. W. Wright, and S. Strum. Washington, D.C.: Island Press.

Wells, Michael, and Katrina Brandon. 1992. *People and Parks: Linking Protected Area Management with Local Communities*. Washington, D.C.: World Bank.

Western, David. 1994. Visions of the Future: The New Focus of Conservation. In *Natural Connections: Perspectives in Community-Based Conservation*, ed. D. Western, M. W. Wright, and S. Strum. Washington, D.C.: Island Press.

Western, D., R. Wright, and S. Strum, eds. 1994. *Natural Connections: Perspectives in Community-Based Conservation*. Washington, D.C.: Island Press.

WWF. 1991. *Annual Report*. Washington, D.C.: World Wildlife Fund.

———. 1992. *Annual Report*. Washington, D.C.: World Wildlife Fund.

———. 1993. *Annual Report*. Washington, D.C.: World Wildlife Fund.

———. 1994. *Annual Report*. Washington, D.C.: World Wildlife Fund.

———. 1995a. *Annual Report*. Washington, D.C.: World Wildlife Fund.
———. 1995b. *Creating Economic Incentives. Workshop I of the ICDP Review, Bacalar, Mexico, Final Draft Report*. Washington, D.C.: World Wildlife Fund.
———. 1995c. *Local Knowledge and Social Organizations: Foundations for Biodiversity Conservation. Workshop II of the ICDP Review, Puerto Princesa, Philippines, Final Draft Report*. Washington, D.C.: World Wildlife Fund.
———. 1996a. *1996 Annual Report, Thirty-Five Years of Saving Life on Earth*. Washington, D.C.: World Wildlife Fund.
———. 1996b. *World Wildlife Fund Changing Worlds, 35 Years of Conservation Achievement*. Gland, Switzerland: World Wildlife Fund International.
———. 1996c. *Indigenous Peoples and Conservation: World Wildlife Fund Statement of Principles*. Gland, Switzerland: World Wildlife Fund.
———. 1996d. *The Enabling Environment for ICDPs: Policies, Institutions, and Ethical Dilemmas at the Local, National, and International Levels. Workshop III of the ICDP Review, Syria, Virginia, Final Draft Report*. Washington, D.C.: World Wildlife Fund.
———. 1996e. *Measuring the Conservation Impact of ICDPs. Workshop IV of the ICDP Review, Arusha, Tanzania, Final Draft Report*. Washington, D.C.: World Wildlife Fund.
Wyckoff-Baird, Barbara. 1992. What's in a Name? Discussion paper of the World Wildlife Fund-U.S. Wildlands and Human Needs Program (WHNP). Washington, D.C.: World Wildlife Fund.

2

Participatory Democracy in Natural Resource Management: A "Columbus's Egg"?

Grazia Borrini-Feyerabend, with Christopher B. Tarnowski

It is part of Italian folklore that Christopher Columbus challenged a group of colleagues to make an egg stand on one end. They tried and tried in vain. Columbus smiled and solved the conundrum by crushing the egg against the table. Since then, "Columbus's egg" is synonymous with an ingenious solution found outside the box of conventional thinking. In this chapter we set out to explore a number of key dilemmas and challenges in natural resource management. Participatory democracy may well be the "Columbus's egg" solution, but it should be understood and pursued in full awareness of the intricacies and complexities it entails.

PEOPLE: IN OR OUT OF THE ECOSYSTEM?

Sketching a broad and rather stereotypical picture of conservation constituencies, we may set at one extreme a preservationist, nearly misanthropic position—people and nature have to be kept apart for the latter to have a chance to survive. At the other end is an anthropocentric stand—nature provides the basis for human livelihoods and needs to be protected, most of all, because of that. The former position is represented by nature lovers, animal rights advocates, and highly passionate environmentalists, largely located in the industrial countries of the North. The latter is represented by individuals and groups, often located in the South, with either a direct dependence on natural resources for their own survival or with complex personal involvement in conservation. Some of these people are engaged in conservation for the sake of sustainable development, public health, indigenous people's rights, or even human rights and social justice. In turn, divergent positions about the ultimate goals of conservation have led to debates on the involvement of indigenous and local communities in its efforts. Increasingly, over the past decades, concepts such as sustainable use, adaptive and collaborative management, cultural landscape, and more recently, governance of natural resources, have brought depth and substance to these debates. Further complexity has been added by several international conventions.[1] For instance, articles 8, 10, and 11 of the Convention on Biological Diversity (Glowka et al. 1994), which became effective December 1993 and has now been ratified by 187 parties,[2] established a firm ground for the appreciation of indigenous knowledge and skills in natural resource management and provided an important entry point for arguing for the respect of customary rights and the equitable sharing of the benefits of biodiversity. In 1994, at the General Assembly in Buenos Aires, the term *equity* was incorporated into the mission statement of the IUCN–The World Conservation Union. Even with the formal recognition of indigenous and community rights in national and international political arenas, however, there remains considerable disagreement as to the importance of sociopolitical concerns and capacities compared with biological ones and whether they should be incorporated into conservation efforts. In other words, is it more important for conservation to draw from ecological indicators, for example, to assess species-habitat degradation, or to negotiate agreements with local communities whereby people benefit from the sustainable use of that species and engage in effective conservation activities?[3] And is it a better strategy to decouple the interests of nature and people, so that people leave nature alone, or to couple them, so that they coexist harmoniously (see Borrini-Feyerabend and Buchan 1997)?

Different conservation constituencies give different answers to this question. Some still advocate a guns-and-fences approach, remaining skeptical of any efforts to promote sustainable use (Brandon, Redford, and Sanderson 1998; Terborgh 1999; Oates 1999). These arguments are often accompanied by alarms regarding growth in population and consumption (Erhlich 1997) and calls for a simultaneous approach that curbs such growth and strictly protects threatened biodiversity. Others have called attention to the embedded nature of conservation within wider socioeconomic processes, such as global economic forces, especially the expansion of free-market capitalism, structural adjustment policies, and foreign aid and development, and their roles in reinforcing both environmental degradation and poverty (Ghimire and Pimbert 1997; Esteva 1992; Landell-Mills and Porras 2002). These critical assessments emphasize that human communities and nature share a common constellation of powerful enemies: big business, global trade and investment, and the kind of sweeping and careless economic development that characterizes much of today's world.[4] In this perspective the only real chance for conservation is in rights-based, enhanced control by the rural poor over natural resources (Franks 2002; Colchester 1994.).

A variant on this argument highlights the role of culturally healthy communities as natural resource managers (through mechanisms ranging from sacred prohibitions to detailed provisions for the use of commons) and maintains that the large-scale environmental degradation of the last centuries is the result of community disempowerment by waves of colonial powers and national states. In this perspective, the severing of the relationship between people and the land (including forced resettlements and forced sedentarization) is at the root of current environmental problems. Community-based natural resource management needs to be reestablished as a condition for both the protection of biodiversity and the promotion of sustainable livelihoods (Borrini-Feyerabend 2003; Borrini-Feyerabend et al. 2004) Finally, a few demand that each case be considered as a unique product of cultural and biological history and seen for its specific relevance in local, national, and global contexts (MacDonald 2003)

In a manner of speaking, in sum, people have one foot in and one out of the ecosystem. On the policy side, and among several commentators, the upper hand is still with experts and rules that advocate separation of protected areas and people (especially people who do not consider themselves tourists but inhabitants of the land and users of the resources). On the side of practice, people worldwide are dealing with environmentally devastated areas as well as cradles of well-preserved biodiversity. What conditions make the difference? Why, in certain circumstances, do people care for their environment whereas in others they exploit it in unsustainable ways? These questions can guide us further in our exploration. The world teems with a myriad of concrete situations that can be seen as test cases, as ongoing processes of trial and error where these questions' answers can be found. In many such situations, participatory management settings appear to make—indeed—a significant difference.

PARTICIPATORY MANAGEMENT

In its most generic conceptualization, *participatory management* describes a situation in which two or more social actors with specific interests and concerns about a set of natural resources (e.g., forest, water, fisheries, wildlife) are involved in its management in a substantial way. Defined in this manner, participatory management resembles collaborative (Poffenberger 1990a; Borrini-Feyerabend 1996), joint (Poffenberger 1990b; Fisher 1995; Poffenberger 1996, 205–26), and community-based management (Messerschmidt 1993; Western, Wright, and Strum 1994; White et al. 1994). Each of these approaches shares a historical trajectory that can be traced back to early community-development programs of the 1950s and 1960s, when participation arose out of a much greater concern for the rural poor and disenchantment with large-scale, top-down, centrally planned and managed development projects (Little 1994, 347–72; see also Western, Wright, and Strum 1994). Rather than attempt to provide an unnecessarily narrow definition, our aim here is to remain broad and inclusive. We understand participatory management as a partnership among the social actors with legitimate interests, capacities, and commitment regarding the natural resources at stake. The partnership specifies their management functions and guarantees their benefits and costs, rights and responsibilities. In some cases a legal jurisdiction exists that belongs to a governmental agency or some individual landowners. Only rarely have states legally recognized customary ownership by indigenous peoples or local communities. More often, the state retains ownership of the resources in question but grants some special access rights and management responsibilities to the concerned indigenous and local communities. The innovative feature of participatory management is the understanding of the advantages of going *beyond strict legal jurisdiction* as conventionally understood (such as private property or government mandate) and of recognizing the capacities and entitlements of a variety of concerned groups, individuals, and organizations on the basis of various grounds. This recognition of multiple rights and interests marks a significant departure from legalistic, top-down management. Some examples of grounds for entitlements comprising both legally recognized (legal) and socioculturally recognized (legitimate) characteristics are listed in table 2.1.[5]

In practice, participatory management entails a *process* by which the concerned organizations, groups, and individuals (often labeled *stakeholders* or *actors*) come together to discuss, agree upon, and support in practice a given course of action. Through that process, all stakeholders usually develop some comanagement plans and complementary agreements[6] and set up one or more organizations to address ongoing management decisions and take required actions. Thus in participatory management the governance of natural resources is opened up to a plurality of social actors and becomes more experimental and open-ended.

A detailed review of the existing wide spectrum of partnerships in natural resource management has recently been attempted elsewhere (see Borrini-Feyerabend et al. 2004). Briefly, these include formal, legally codified sharing of authority between government agencies and representatives of indigenous communities,[7] pilot and experimental partnerships,[8] ad hoc voluntary agreements,[9] and sophisticated, multilevel comanagement institutions.[10] Impor-

Table 2.1 Grounds for Entitlements: Conventional and Innovative Characteristics that Prompt Different Social Actors to Claim a Role in Natural Resource Management

- possessing rights to land or resources, whether by customary law or modern legislation (e.g., traditional tenure and access rights, ownership, right of use);
- having received a mandate by the state (e.g., statutory obligation of a given agency or governmental body);
- being directly dependent on the natural resources in question for subsistence and survival (e.g., for food, medicine, communication);
- being directly dependent on them for livelihood, including for gaining basic income;
- possessing historical, cultural, and spiritual relationships with the concerned territory, area, or natural resources;
- possessing unique knowledge of, and ability to manage, the concerned natural resource management unit(s);
- possessing a long-term relationship with the territory, area, or natural resources (e.g., local communities and long-time resource users distinguishing themselves from recently arrived immigrants, tourists, hunters);
- having incurred losses and damages as a result of natural resource management decisions and activities, and/or suffering or risking to suffer severe impacts because of management initiatives;
- having invested efforts and resources in natural resource management;
- claiming to represent the views of a large number of individuals or institutions sharing the same interests and concerns;
- being the bearer of a point of view or value that enjoys broad social recognition (e.g., one "based on traditional knowledge" or "based on scientific knowledge," aimed at "sustainable use," or one following the "precautionary principle," or enhancing "equity" in the management of natural resources);
- being the bearer of a point of view or value that reflects national policies;
- being the bearer of a point of view or value that reflects international conventions and agreements.

tantly, participatory management can embrace various sorts of power-sharing agreements, from the most skewed (an agency in charge, with other stakeholders in only advisory roles) to the most egalitarian (a board of directors where all stakeholders are represented). They can range from the most simple (regular, open meetings where all concerned can participate) to the most innovative (pluralist bodies in charge of developing technical proposals by consensus with ample incentives to do so; a higher body takes over if there is lack of agreement at the more local level). That participatory management processes, agreements, and institutions take such a variety of forms and are tailored to context is one of their least known and underappreciated features.

KEY FEATURES OF PARTICIPATORY MANAGEMENT

Perhaps foremost among the understandings at the roots of participatory management is that for every set of natural resources there exists a variety of social actors (stakeholders) possessing relevant and usually different interests and concerns. And, because change is always occurring in societies, the needs and interests of actors evolve, and new actors need to be continually recognized and dealt with. Unfortunately, what benefits one group and meets conservation objectives may harm another. For example, a state agency may wish to draw on a forest's timber for financial resources, whereas the local communities need it for fodder, poles, and firewood. In other cases, men may covet wildlife revenues, whereas women see more abundant wildlife as a cost, because the animals damage their crops and endanger their lives. Elsewhere, a ban on fishing may favor the tourism industry but destroy the immediate livelihood of local fishermen.

A second important recognition is that different social actors possess different capacities and comparative advantages needed to optimally manage a particular set of natural resources (Borrini-Feyerabend et al. 2000). Indeed, effective resource management requires as many capacities and inputs as possible. For instance, government bodies can provide important regulatory and coordination mechanisms; local communities can provide detailed knowledge of local conditions and the means for effective monitoring. These are complementary, not mutually exclusive, factors that ultimately enrich the participatory process. As Kothari has remarked,

> Communities lack the resources to tackle threats or ecological issues at a regional scale, and in many places have lost their traditional ethos and institutions; government agencies lack the necessary micro-knowledge, on-the-spot human power, or even often the necessary mandate when other agencies overrule them. With rare exceptions, neither local communities nor governmental agencies are able to face on their own the onslaught of commercial forces, or able to check the destruction caused by some of their own members. (Kothari 1995)

Thus agency management and community management can broaden the perspectives of each and make them stronger and more effective. In addition, participatory management may serve to reduce ineptitude and corruption—dangers of agency management—as well as parochialism and exclusion—dangers of community management (which, in extreme cases, can degenerate into intolerance, racism, or even "ethnic cleansing").

A third fact, often overlooked, is that indigenous and local communities possess *unique* capacities—knowledge, skills, institutions, and resources rooted in local history and local conditions—that can be put to use for the benefit of conservation. An illustration of this is some of the recent understandings of ecosystem science, specifically that the size and scale of habitats are essential factors for the survival of species. But apparently more important is the pattern of distribution (or *distribution matrix)* of those habitats within a territory (Franklin 1993). The traditional model of land use of indigenous communities—a mosaic of habitats related to different community needs, including sacred groves and taboo areas—begins to be seen by some ecologists as one with important advantages. In other words, in each context it is ascertained whether a conservation objective may be best served by a large, island-like protected area surrounded by a territory dedicated solely to economic and settlement purposes (the typical model of state-managed protected areas) or by a complex zoning of smaller territories devoted to mixed ends and sustainable uses (Ingram 1997). If the latter model is the choice, the different interests and needs of families and groups in society could be made to fit rather well with conservation concerns.

A fourth fact, also not always evident to people not involved in ecological sciences, is that our knowledge about the functioning of ecosystems is very limited (Wilson 1993; Ehrlich 1997). This is true of every complex system—be it the market outlook for a particular commodity or vehicle traffic in an urban environment—but it is particularly true for biological systems. Environmental scientists lack complete understanding of the interplay among ecological properties and functions, how interdependencies function at different scales, or how biodiversity is related to stability or nutrient capture. Biologists do not really know whether earth has ten million or a hundred million species, do not know the importance of diversity among bacteria, and have only a vague idea of how patterns of habitat distribution influence the survival of a given species. Adding to this complexity and uncertainty is that natural ecosystems are in a state of constant change. Change is inevitable, is all-pervasive, takes place at all ecosystem scales, and is integral to ecosystem life. Rather than representing an optimal, final state, ecosystems are dynamic, responding to continuously varying external conditions: climate, new diseases, migration and extinction of species, and other sorts of slowly building or catastrophic conditions. In a healthy ecosystem, change is frequent, as the system responds and adapts. The limitations and uncertainty of our knowledge have two main consequences. The first is that as we engage in ecosystem management our decisions must be seen as provisional. Decisions cannot be derived from only science or only by the strict application of a plan or sets of established rules. Instead we require a process of ongoing review and improvement. The second consequence is that it makes little sense to attempt to enforce strict stability on ecosystems in the name of conservation. Even a seemingly harmless decision, such as secluding an ecosystem and leaving it alone, may not deliver the desired management objectives and may even have unintended negative consequences.[11] With the tremendous variety of factors and conditions in a dynamic state throughout the world—first among them climate change and patterns of air and water pollution—*secluding* and *saving* an ecosystem are far from synonymous!

A fifth fact is that we are dealing with an extremely consequential subject. The management of natural resources involves crucial economic and livelihood decisions in every society, making it a realm of political power par excellence. Control of the land, the water, mineral and biological resources, space, and the permission to use resources is what secular power is all about. Unfortunately, we cannot say that such power is always used in fair and just ways. Decision-making authority and the sharing of benefits and responsibilities in managing natural resources are typically distributed in an inequitable manner (see Schroeder 1999; Ribot 1999; Tarnowski 2002), accountability in natural resource management is the exception rather than the rule, and violence remains a favorite means of pushing one's "entitlements" (see Peluso and Watts 2001; Verrengia 2002).

THE DEBATE

Participatory management remains a much-debated subject among a panoply of practitioners and scholars searching for the most politically and economically appropriate means of managing and conserving natural resources. Between enthusiastic proponents and skeptical opponents we find a variety of positions, or voices, generating a remarkable cacophony. In what follows we provide an overview of some divergent positions. These are of necessity overly simplified and somewhat idealized types, and we are introducing them here only to offer a broad view of the issues involved in the debate.

Some conservationists offer several powerful arguments against participatory management. These can be summarized as follows: Conservation of nature is an imperative and a duty for every country. Experiments with participatory management can water down conservation objectives and contaminate them with other aims such as economic or cultural interests of local stakeholders (see Cigler and Loomis 1998; Brockington 2002). Participatory management thus promotes minimum-common-denominator decisions that help no one. States have a clear moral obligation to future generations; they need to ensure that unique habitats and species are conserved (McCloskey 1996). Once basic decisions about conserving a territory have been taken, no compromise is possible, and local people must simply resign themselves to finding their livelihoods elsewhere.

A principal fear often expressed by government officials and conservation-agency staff remains the loss of control implied by effective participation. This loss of control occurs at two levels. The first involves immediate decisions concerning the content of management. The agencies in charge fear relinquishing even a moderate amount of control over regulations, management practices, permission to use resources, and the like, believing that such decisions must be made by experts, not lay people. This position assumes that only experts and state officials possess legitimate claims, and that they are more disinterested and knowledgeable than other actors (Blomquist and Schlager 2000). On another level, state officials and experts fear the creative social experimentation that accompanies the wide-ranging participation of other actors, because it undermines control from the top. If we take the term *anarchy* in the original Greek sense of "absence of rules," a limited space of anarchy is necessary for a partnership of social actors to create itself and develop its own rules of functioning.

A second argument against participatory management entails an economic or utilitarian cost-benefit analysis: The process of negotiating agreements around resource management among various stakeholders is expensive and time consuming (some say that its "transaction costs" are very high). It demands a variety of human and institutional capacities and investments in communication and negotiation processes that bear fruit only over the long-term. Many management interventions, however, must be made quickly, and this makes participatory management an inappropriate strategy (Wagner 2001; Brockington 2002). This argument deserves careful consideration indeed, especially when the comanagement bodies concerned are relatively inexperienced and need to find their own modus operandi through trial and error.

A third persuasive argument, one that is somewhat surprising to hear from the left, comes from indigenous people's and community-rights advocates, entities usually considered to be beneficiaries of participatory management: Participatory management is a compromise stand with respect to the goal of social recognition of exclusive indigenous or community rights over ancestral domains. National states appropriated indigenous people's claims and control over resources in a violent and unjust manner and should not now possess a right to participate in managing indigenous people's resources. The state may be in control now, but should relinquish full authority and control over the management of resources. Indigenous and community groups should not be involved in a process that, implicitly or explicitly, recognizes the rights of others over their own land.[12]

Although we have by no means exhausted opposition arguments, let us now turn to some arguments in favor of participatory management: We need to start from the status quo. Conservation of natural resources is too often based on an inequitable distribution of costs and benefits. In the case of protected areas, for instance, too many agencies have alienated resources from the poor and marginalized groups, providing no compensation, and they have paid no attention to the material and spiritual needs of local residents and resource users. They even disregard information that suggests that biodiversity has been sustained and even promoted through local indigenous use and management practices (see Brokensha, Warren, and Werner 1980; Messerschmidt 1993; Warren et al. 1995; Posey 1998). If participatory management is the policy of choice, it would give a voice to the minorities that currently have none. It would transform a situation in which, too often, only agency staff are in control and expatriate professionals prepare management plans without consulting local leaders and resource users (Gilmour and Fisher 1991). It would be a difficult process, in which underprivileged groups would need to organize and call for change, but at least there would be a forum and an avenue for them to express their views. We should promote participatory management for the sake of equity (Ghimire and Pimbert 1997) and to improve the overall governance of natural resources (Graham, Amos, and Plumptree 2003).

A pragmatic constituency offers another argument in the debate: Participatory management is nothing less than the most effective and efficient way to care for natural resources. Some stakeholders possess a wealth of local knowledge, skills, and comparative advantages that should be put to use; for example, they can survey what happens to natural resources or they can closely monitor the status of biodiversity in a timely way. Others are willing to invest in resource management, and still others can create alliances to fend off external threats, for example, expansions of business, industry, or urban sprawl—often the worst enemies of conservation (Brokensha, Warren, and Werner 1980; Warren et al. 1995). In addition, there are economies of scale in the harvesting of resources that can be reached (Hasler 1995, 2000); for instance, several landowners together can do what no one of them could alone. If the negotiation process is successful, all the parties in the participatory management agreement will benefit, including the environment (Smith Korfmacher 1998, 2000).

Regarding the uncompromising stand of some indigenous peoples (as previously mentioned), the pragmatic constituency would likely respond with something like the following: There is a hardly a region in the world where indigenous peoples do not coexist with a national state. The relationship may still be unfair and exploitative, but every step that goes in the right direction is a good step. If the negotiation is skillful, small rights may be a prelude to the recognition of larger rights (Agrawal and Gibson 2001). Furthermore, national states may have much to offer to indigenous groups, if the relationship between them is made to improve (World Bank 1996).

Yet another voice comes from advocates for social development and democracy: Participatory management integrates conservation efforts into a broader sociopolitical agenda, increasing public awareness of conservation issues, building trust among different sectors of society, and increasing a sense of political, social, and economic security and stability that is essential for long-term investments (World Bank 1996; Agrawal 1997). At a more general, societal level, it contributes to a democratic and mature society. The opportunity to participate in decision making about conservation has been an avenue through which many people have come to recognize environmental problems, as well as possible solutions and courses of action (Bruch 2002). Conservation is best served by enhancing the number of people and groups concerned about conservation issues and capable of doing something about them.

We find all of the arguments that have been set forth, both in favor and against participatory management, quite persuasive, each in their own way. We now turn to some views that are more subtle and complex. The first is a criticism from a political economic perspective: The management of natural resources is an arena wherein power struggles are continually played out. Resource management involves sharing the costs and benefits of management, and this leads to a situation where the weak and underprivileged sectors of society consistently receive a smaller share of benefits and a higher share of costs (Ribot 1999; Schroeder 1999; Brockington 2003). In an effort to challenge this state of affairs, marginalized groups have subscribed to a variety of "weapons of the weak"—noncompliance, dissimulation, lying, foot dragging, irony, and spreading ridicule (Scott 1985)—and much less often, open revolt or revolution. There is little tradition of openly expressing needs and wants in front of the powerful or negotiating with them under transparent rules. The political-economic contexts of today have not changed enough to encourage the underprivileged to adopt new strategies with confidence. Participatory management is unlikely to serve the interests of the weak any better or worse than noncompliance or all-out struggle. Even worse, participatory approaches may be co-opted by local and national elites to serve their own interests (Ribot 1999; Chase, Hancem, and Gibson 2000; Singleton 2001; Tarnowski 2002).

It seems that the term *partnership* is frequently invoked in discussions of participatory and other forms of resource management, but partnerships are seldom among equals (Rahnema 1992, 116–31; Edmunds and Wollenberg 2002). For example, a small community or indigenous group is highly unlikely to possess any real negotiating power vis-à-vis a major transnational mining or timber company. With this in mind, we must step back and ask whose interests are served by partnerships when they strive to whitewash controversies and smooth out dissent. In a parallel, skeptical vein: Participatory management presupposes a common terrain of understanding and compromise among stakeholders. The stakeholders, however, often inhabit different worlds. Take an illiterate woman in a traditional society: will she use words and concepts that mean the same thing as they do for an expatriate conservationist? Is communication even possible between such different worlds? Should we not expect that the negotiation meetings in a comanagement process will exhaust themselves in a sterile cacophony? Will not misunderstandings and deception undermine most participatory management agreements at their very roots?

Despite these compelling and unfavorable critiques, voices from ecosystem science counter with equally compelling points in favor of participatory management: An ecosystem can be assessed according to many different criteria, including its productivity for given species, its resilience after stress, and its capacity to sustain a certain quantity or quality of biodiversity (some highly sensitive, endemic species). One can highlight its functional redundancy, its wildness (for instance, as defined by a low dependence on human interaction and an extensive presence of endemic species), its structural variety, the average age and size of some important species, the distribution matrix of habitats, its vulnerability, or particular aesthetic values. Many of these properties cannot be optimized together, only one at a time or even one at the expense of another. It follows, then, that we cannot say that a given ecosystem status is better than another or that there is some optimal state in which the ecosystem could or should be. If we decide to maximize biodiversity, we may do so at the expense of the disappearance of some endemic and fragile species. If we opt to maximize productivity, we may pay a price in terms of resilience or wildness.[13]

The problem is compounded by the fact that each property of an ecosystem may favor some interests and stakeholders in a society while displeasing others. For instance, the presence of important biodiversity in a given patch of forest may gratify some university researchers or bioprospectors in search of medicinal plants for pharmaceutical companies, but a member of the local community may be more interested in earning money from an environment managed for the maximum production of coffee or cocoa. Tourists may want to spend time in an unspoiled and wild tropical watershed, whereas urban planners seek to transform it into a water reservoir for energy production. Who should decide which value is preserved or pursued? Because science offers us no unique answers to such questions of ecosystem management,[14] the decision-making process is unavoidably a political one, one that ends up reflecting the priorities of those persons with decision-making power. One option here is the oligarchic or dictatorial control of the few, be they experts, those who have guns or wealth, the conservationists, or the local community. Another option is ongoing dialogue and negotiation among the parties possessing entitlements, interests, and concerns[15] to obtain the best available information about the consequences of decisions. This is the only way that a society can generate institutions capable of developing and implementing solutions that are responsive to changing circumstances in the ecological and socioeconomic realms. Such institutions are essential for sustaining the management setting, and they are precisely what participatory management is all about.

LESSONS AND POINTERS FOR ACTION

From the complex debate simply sketched so far, one can perceive a variety of potential strengths and weaknesses of adopting a participatory, pluralistic approach to managing natural resources and thereby involving a variety of social actors in related processes, agreements, and institutions. Table 2.2 lays out some of these points.

When all the arguments summarized in table 2.2 are taken into consideration, we can see that for the concept and practice of conservation, participatory management can represent the equivalent of participatory democracy in the broader political arena. In a democratic society, all interests and viewpoints are taken into consideration and the Platonic notion that some individuals (philosophers or experts) have inherently superior capacities to manage the public domain is challenged by the notion that all humans possess an equal, basic right to influence the direction of social life. From this same position, however, a variety of forms of organized polity can be generated, including systems of delegated democracy, participatory democracy, or mixed characteristics. In a purely delegated democracy, elected politicians are assisted by technical experts and never ask their constituency directly for opinions regarding specific issues (e.g., by referendums or other direct means). In a purely participatory (or deliberative) democracy, the citizens are called upon to influence all important social decisions and actions in a direct way, expressing their opinions on specific issues and helping to formulate and support rules, incentives, disincentives, and initiatives. Both traditional and modern societies offer interesting examples of both of these systems. Some traditional societies delegate decisions entirely to their chiefs or councils of elders (see Ribot 1996, 1999), whereas others employ a variety of explicit and hidden forms of social dialogue, negotiation, and accommodation to develop a social consensus on major pronouncements. This may require time, but generally delivers results that are broadly owned and viewed as socially legitimate. Most modern societies are structured around models of delegated democracy with organized political parties, and citizens select once every few years among only the political platforms the parties offer. Only in exceptional cases is a referendum called on specific decisions. Even more rarely are citizens asked to develop specific questions or proposals of their own. There are exceptions,[16] however, and increasingly we see methods and tools of deliberative democracy being experimented with throughout the world (Pimbert and Wakeford 2001, 2002; Borrini-Feyerabend et al. 2004).

A fundamental tenet of democracy is that of equality before the law. This means that every citizen of a democratic state can be called to office and has the same right to decide through the vote. Is there a corresponding right to decide in the management of natural resources? First, not every social actor

Table 2.2 Participatory Management of Natural Resources: Perceived Strengths and Weaknesses

Strengths/opportunities (as seen by different social actors)	*Weaknesses/problems/obstacles (as seen by different social actors)*
Gives voice to a variety of stakeholders and allows them to watch over the distribution of costs and benefits of conservation and to improve overall equity.	The approach is time-consuming. Some decisions need to be made quickly and cannot wait for social actors to communicate and develop and agree on joint decisions
By making use of complementary capacities and comparative advantages for conservation, in particular the knowledge, skills, and resources of indigenous and local communities, the approach draws out tremendous new potentials for conservation.	The approach requires important initial investments. The financial and human resources to support it may simply not be available.
The approach promotes transparency in decision-making and occasions in which to discuss issues of political and economic power and accountability. It is an antidote to corruption and vested interests that may be camouflaged as "scientific imperatives."	The playing field is skewed: how can we be sure that the interests and concerns of the poor are recognized and responded to? The participatory approach may just be old wine in a new bottle. It may even co-opt and appropriate concepts, time, and good will for the sake of corporate interests.
The approach does not assume that there exists one optimal state for a given ecosystem or set of natural resources that needs to be "preserved." It rather focuses on developing institutions capable of developing and implementing solutions that are tailored to context, responsive, and capable of adapting to varying circumstances. These are essential for sustaining the management setting.	There is a risk of watering down conservation objectives and ending up with compromise, "minimum common denominator" decisions which satisfy neither the partisans of conservation, those of development, or indigenous peoples. The governmental agencies in charge fear relinquishing control over important decisions and resources. They resist the creative experimentation (the "limited space of anarchy") that is necessary for real partnerships to flourish.
The participatory approach encourages civil society to become more aware and active in conservation matters, thereby encouraging a consensus on the economic sacrifices that conservation always requires.	Different stakeholders often live in different worlds. Is real communication possible among them? If not, how can comanagement agreements be trusted?

is equally interested or concerned nor, even more importantly, does every social actor have an equal right to decide. Management claims and entitlements are usually based on drawing lines between the haves and the have-nots (see the examples of grounds for entitlements listed in table 2.1). Moreover, it is not only individuals who make claims but also state organizations, local administrations, nongovernmental organizations (NGOs), communities, businesses, representatives of indigenous peoples, and even international bodies. Can those different actors—so unequal in terms of institutional, economic, and political power—be effectively and fairly compared in terms of the relative strengths of their entitlements to manage natural resources?[17] On the basis of such a comparison, can they be placed in categories (primary stakeholders, secondary stakeholders, etc.) and assigned different management roles (e.g., decision making, advising)? Assuming the answer is yes, what criteria should be used to select priorities?

A comprehensive body of theory of natural resource comanagement has not yet been developed to answer these questions (see, however, Bruch 2002; Hemmati 2002; Borrini-Feyerabend et al. 2004). A further difficulty is that, whereas most societies exhibit a healthy level of skepticism about politicians, this is less true of their perceptions of scientists. The realm of natural resource management is currently dominated by technical experts who defend themselves behind the banner of science and who enjoy a low level of social scrutiny and criticism. These experts are backed up by journalists who vulgarize the simplest and most impressive conservation messages and back them up with teary images of baby elephants and seals while asking for donations to save nature. And yet, as mentioned in the previous summary of debates, science provides no single or definitive answer to natural resource management questions, and equitable and fair systems must recognize a variety of claims and entitlements. In this regard, participatory natural resource management systems—not unlike participatory democracy and democracy in general—are far from perfect, but we possess no superior alternative for a society that strives to be open and nonpaternalistic. Even if participatory management systems are never perfect, we cannot shy away from continually attempting to improve them. In this endeavor, extracting lessons from past experience is crucial.

Here are just a few: Effective management partnerships build on existing local and traditional knowledge, practices, and institutions (Brokensha, Warren, and Werner 1980; West and Brechin 1991; Warren et al. 1995). They maintain and strengthen what is positive but also recognize, as appropriate, the existence of new actors and interests, build on their capacities, and incorporate their languages and practices. In this way, management partnership can play an effective role in sociocultural innovation.

Effective management partnerships generally have multiple stakeholders and multiple levels and are multidisciplinary. They engage a variety of interests and entitlements within and outside local communities, but they also encompass a variety of perceptions, languages, maps of the present and the desired future and systems for generating, classifying, and using knowledge. It is crucial to promote and institutionalize multiplicity in resource management, and due attention must be paid to facilitating effective communication and dialogue. This is a crucial foundation for building participatory resource management.

Effective management partnerships strive for conditions that stimulate social communication, quality of debate, and transparency from the beginning of the partnership processes. This allows the partners to discuss alternative choices (risks and opportunities) based on sound information and a good understanding of the likely consequences. There must be no assumption that one form of knowledge (e.g., knowledge derived from scientific research) is necessarily better than another (e.g., that derived from sustained experience in a particular site). As Renn, Webler, and Wiedermann (1995) have remarked, the partnership process must be competent ("pursuit of relevant information and interpretations, allows partners to use the best procedures for resolving disputes among themselves") and produce quality results in a reasonable span of time.

Effective management partnerships are the product of a negotiation process. But we must recognize that such negotiation does not usually take place on a level playing field (Edmunds and Wollenberg 2002) and must attempt to lessen power differentials where they exist (Renn, Webler, and Wiedermann 1995). In other words, the individual interests and concerns of all affected partners should be expressed, protected, and incorporated into the development of the collective will. This is likely to include helping weaker parties to organize and attend meetings, clarifying the rules of negotiation, offering the help of facilitators and guarantors not directly involved as parties in the process, and fostering systems to ensure the respect of decisions.

Effective management partnerships are those that provide as much as possible for equity and proportionality in the sharing of costs and benefits of managing natural resources.[18] They make use of a variety of rules and incentives (from social appreciation to economic advantages), and they are supported by sensible policies. When such policies are absent, the partners strive for policy change.

To conclude, effective partnerships are vehicles that deliver the benefits of pluralism to the practice of natural resource management. By doing so, they put into new perspective all claims, views, and entitlements, including those of conservation professionals that often carry a patina of holiness. As Di Lascia (1995) has written, "Every tyranny is built on a dream of salvation." Many conservationists (and passionate humanists) have such a dream, and some believe in its holiness and try to impose it on others. Their rhetoric should not contribute to building authoritarian societies by denying others a chance to assert their rights. Perhaps it is possible for some to build a "conservation fortress" and retire inside, impervious to its human costs and lack of linkages to society (Brockington 2003). We believe, however, that all walls—between people or between people and nature—are fundamentally misguided and pernicious. Conservation dreams will more likely come true and stay true if we pursue them through sound governance, social consensus, and equity.

NOTES

1. This was accompanied by the entrée into the field of business groups and professional associations vying to establish their credentials and secure lucrative contracts in conservation and sustainable development projects.

2. A notable exception is the United States.

3. According to its mission statement, the goal of IUCN is to "influence, encourage, and assist societies throughout the world to conserve the integrity and diversity of nature and to ensure that any use of natural resources is equitable and ecologically sustainable" (www.iucn.org/about). Should IUCN be staffed by bioenvironmental scientists or social scientists? At the moment, the bioenvironmentalists have the far greater numbers. But is not this issue irrelevant? In the experience of many IUCN members, successful work depends on integrating different capacities and backgrounds. And working successfully with local communities is based more on respect, fairness, and political savvy than on the books read in graduate school.

4. Indeed, this is not a new understanding. Thirty years ago there was ample evidence that development was sacrificing both the ecological integrity of natural environments and the social integrity of local communities (e.g., Farvar and Milton 1972).

5. Modified from Borrini-Feyerabend 1996 and Borrini-Feyerabend et al. 2000; see also Leach, Mearns, and Scoones 1997.

6. These agreements can take many forms, from formal contracts with penalties for noncompliance to informal letters or memoranda of understanding.

7. The management boards of many protected areas in Australia, including the Great Barrier Reef Marine Park Authority (Smyth 2001), are examples.

8. Examples are those between local parishes and the national wildlife authority for the management of national parks in Uganda (Wild and Mutebi 1996; Chhteri, Mugisha, and White 2003).

9. The one signed by the Sustainable Forestry Roundtable in Washington State, United States, is an example in which individual landowners, conservation NGOs, and forestry agencies specify the size and type of areas to be conserved and the specific rules for timber extraction elsewhere (Franklin 1993; see also Wilson 2003).

10. An example is the Galapagos Marine Reserve (Heylings and Bravo 2001).

11. This is particularly true when such ecosystems evolved with some amount of human interference. The bird habitats of Keoladeo National Park, India, degraded when cattle were prevented from grazing in them. After local protests that left several people dead and after a one-million-dollar study, cattle were reintroduced to restore the park's original habitat quality.

12. This is frequently the underlying sentiment among indigenous groups and small local communities, but it is seldom a political platform from which such groups negotiate or the end goal they seek. However, one exception comes from a community-based coastal-resource-management project in the Philippines, where an indigenous group, the Tagbanua, sought an exclusive Ancestral Domain Claim and declined any external assistance (Ferrari and De Vera 2003).

13. Borrini-Feyerabend wishes to acknowledge here most useful conversations on this subject with Luigi Boitani, vice chair of the IUCN Commission on Species Survival.

14. Indeed, unlike what is generally believed by nonscientists, the sciences do not provide unique answers in *any* field!

15. The process of identifying the people and institutions with entitlements is often referred to as *stakeholder analysis* (see Borrini-Feyerabend et al. 2000).

16. In Switzerland the occurrence of referenda is frequent and people receive in the mail the condensed views of the proponents of different courses of action.

17. This returns us to a fundamental criticism of participatory management: in terms of power its playing fields are usually uneven.

18. Marshall Murphree (1997) recommends that balances between benefits and costs be maintained, if at all possible, down to the level of the individual.

REFERENCES

Agrawal, A. 1997. Community in Conservation: Beyond Enchantment and Disenchantment. Conservation Development Forum working paper, Gainesville, Fl., April.

Agrawal, A., and C. Gibson, eds. 2001. *Communities and the Environment*. New Brunswick, N.J.: Rutgers Univ. Press.

Blomquist, W., and E. Schlager. 2000. Political Pitfalls of Integrated Watershed Management. Paper presented at the annual meeting of the Western Political Science Association, San Jose, Calif., 24–26 March.

Borrini-Feyerabend, G. 1996. *Collaborative Management of Protected Areas: Tailoring the Approach to the Context*. Gland, Switzerland: IUCN–The World Conservation Union. Also available online at http://www.iucn.org/themes/spg/Files/tailor.html.

———. 2003. Community Conserved Areas (CCAs) and Co-Managed Protected Areas (CMPAs)—Towards Equitable and Effective Conservation in the Context of Global Change. Report of the IUCN joint CEESP/WCPA Theme on Indigenous and Local Communities, Equity, and Protected Areas (TILCEPA) for the Ecosystem, Protected Areas, and People (EPP) project. www.iucn.org/ceesp/Wkg_grp/TILCEPA/community.htm.

Borrini-Feyerabend, G., and D. Buchan, eds. 1997. *Beyond Fences: Seeking Social Sustainability in Conservation*, 2 vols. Gland, Switzerland, and Cambridge, U.K.: IUCN–The World Conservation Union. http://www.iucn.org/themes/spg/Files/beyond_fences/beyond_fences.html.

Borrini-Feyerabend, G., M. T. Farvar, J. C. Nguinguiri, and V. A. Ndangang. 2000.

Co-management of Natural Resources: Organising, Negotiating and Learning by Doing. Heidelberg, Germany: Deutsche Gesellschaft für Technische Zusammenarbeit / World Conservation Union, Kasparek Verlag.

Borrini-Feyerabend, G., M. Pimbert, M. T. Farvar, A. Kothari, and Y. Renard. 2004. *Sharing Power: Learning by Doing in Co-management on Natural Resources throughout the World.* Tehran, Iran: International Institute for Environment and Development and World Conservation Union (IUCN) / CEESP/CMWG, CENESTA.

Brandon, K., K. H. Redford, and S. E. Sanderson, eds. 1998. *Parks in Peril: People, Politics and Protected Areas*. Washington, D.C.: The Nature Conservancy, Island Press.

Brockington, Dan. 2002. *Fortress Conservation: The Preservation of the Mkomazi Game Reserve, Tanzania.* Bloomington: Indiana Univ. Press.

———. 2003. Injustice and Conservation—Is "Local Support" Necessary for Sustainable Protected Areas? *Policy Matters*, no. 12:21–30.

Brokensha, D., D. M. Warren, and O. Werner, eds. 1980. *Indigenous Knowledge Systems and Development*. Lanham, Md.: Univ. of America Press.

Bruch, C., ed. 2002. *The New Public: The Globalization of Public Participation*. Washington, D.C.: Environmental Law Institute.

Chase, C., B. J. Hancem, and G. Gibson. 2000. Adaptive Participation in Watershed Management. *Journal of Soil and Water Conservation* 55(3): 248–52.

Chhetri, P., A. Mugisha, and S. White. 2003. Communities' Resource Use in Kibale and Mount Elgon National Parks (Uganda). *Parks* 13(1): 28–38.

Cigler, A. J., and B. A. Loomis. 1998. *Interest Group Politics*. Washington, D.C.: Congressional Quarterly.

Colchester, Marcus. 1994. Salvaging Nature: Indigenous Peoples, Protected Areas and Biodiversity Conservation. Discussion Paper 55. Geneva: United Nations Research Institute for Social Development (UNRISD).

Di Lascia, M. 1995. *Passaggio in Ombra*. Milan: Feltrinelli.

Edmunds, D., and E. Wollenberg. 2002. Disadvantaged Groups in Multi-Stakeholder Negotiations. CIFOR Programme Report, Ms.

Ehrlich, P. R. 1997. *A World of Wounds: Ecologists and the Human Dilemma*. Luhe, Germany: Ecology Institute, Oldendorf.

Esteva, G. 1992. Development. In *The Development Dictionary*, ed. W. Sachs. London: Zed Books.

Farvar, M. T., and J. P. Milton, eds. 1972. *The Careless Technology: Ecology and International Development*. New York: Doubleday / Natural History Press, published for the Conservation Foundation and the Centre for the Biology of Natural Systems.

Ferrari, M., and D. De Vera. 2003. Coron Island and Rights-Based Conservation in the Philippines. *Policy Matters* 12: 166–70.

Fisher, Robert J. 1995. *Collaborative Management of Forests for Conservation and Development*. Gland, Switzerland: IUCN–The World Conservation Union.

Franklin, J. E. 1993. The Fundamentals of Ecosystem Management with Applications in the Pacific Northwest. In *Defining Sustainable Forestry*, ed. G. H. Aplet et al. Washington, D.C.: Island Press.

Franks, P. 2002. A Partnership for Social and Environmental Justice. *Policy Matters* 10: 38–39.

Ghimire, K., and M. Pimbert, eds. 1997. *Social Change and Conservation*. London: United Nations Research Institute for Social Development and Earthscan.

Gilmour, D. A., and R. J. Fisher. 1991. *Villagers, Forests and Foresters: The Philosophy, Process and Practice of Community Forestry in Nepal.* Katmandu: Sahayogi Press.

Glowka, L., et al. 1994. *A Guide to the Convention on Biological Diversity*. Gland, Switzerland, and Cambridge, U.K.: IUCN–The World Conservation Union.

Graham, J., B. Amos, and T. Plumptree. 2003. Governance Principles for Protected Areas in the 21st Century. Discussion paper, Institute on Governance in collaboration with Parks Canada and CIDA.

Hasler R. 1995. *Political Ecologies of Scale: The Multi-tiered Co-management of Zimbabwean Wildlife Resources*. Wildlife and Development Series No. 7. London: International Institute for Environment and Development.

———. 2000. Towards Political Ecologies of Scale: Conceptualizing Community-Based Coastal and Fisheries Management on the West Coast of South Africa. In *Ocean Yearbook*, no. 14, ed. E. Borgesse et al. Chicago: Univ. of Chicago Press.

Hemmati, M. 2002. *Multi-stakeholder Processes for Governance and Sustainability: Beyond Deadlock and Conflict.* London: Earthscan.

Heylings, P., and M. Bravo. 2001. Survival of the Fittest? Challenges Facing the Co-management Model for the Galapagos Marine Reserve. *CM News* 5: 10–13. http://www.iucn.org/themes/ceesp/Publications/Publications.htm#CMWG.

Ingram, B. 1997. Tradeoffs in Conservation. Ms.

Kothari, A. 1995. Protected Areas, People and Participatory Management: The Indian Experience. Paper presented at workshop on community management in protected areas in Uganda, Mbale, Uganda.

Landell-Mills, N., and Porras. 2002. Silver Bullet or Fools Gold? A Global Review of Markets for Environmental Services and their Impacts on the Poor. London: International Institute for Environment and Development.

Leach, M., R. Mearns, and I. Scoones. 1997. Environmental Entitlements: A Framework for Understanding the Institutional Dynamics of Environmental Change. Brighton, U.K.: Univ. of Sussex Institute for Development Studies, Discussion Paper 259.

Little, Peter D. 1994. The Link between Local Participation and Improved Conservation: A Review of Issues and Experiences. In *Natural Connections: Perspectives in Community-Based Conservation*, ed. D. Western, M. W. Wright, and S. Strum. Washington, D.C.: Island Press.

MacDonald, K. 2003. Community-Based Conservation: A Reflection on History. TILCEPA, http://www.iucn.org/themes/ceesp/Wkg_grp/TILCEPA/community.htm#A.

McCloskey, M. 1996. The Skeptic: Collaboration Has Its Limits. *High Country News* 28: 9–13.

Messerschmidt, D. A. 1993. Common Forest Resource Management: Annotated Bibliography of Asia, Africa and Latin America. Rome: Food and Agriculture Organization.

Murphree, M. 1997. Synergizing Conservation Incentives: Sociological and Anthropological Dimension of Sustainable Use. Paper presented at the STAP Expert Workshop on the Sustainable Use of Biodiversity, Kuala Lumpur, Malaysia, 24–26 November.

Oates, John. 1999. *Myth and Reality in the Rain Forest: How Conservation Strategies Are Failing in West Africa.* Berkeley: Univ. of California Press.

Peluso, N., and M. Watts, eds. 2001. *Violent Environments.* Ithaca, N.Y.: Cornell Univ. Press.

Pimbert, M. P., and T. Wakeford. 2001. *Deliberative Democracy and Citizen Empowerment.* PLA Notes 40. London: International Institute for Environment and Development.

———. 2002. *Prajateerpu: A Citizens Jury/Scenario Workshop on Food and Farming Futures in Andhra Pradesh, India.* London: International Institute for Environment and Development. Also available online at www.iied.org/pdf/Prajateerpu.pdf.

Poffenberger, M. 1990a. *Keepers of the Forest: Land Management Alternatives in Southeast Asia.* West Hartford, Conn.: Kumarian Press.

———. 1990b. Joint Management of Forest Land: Experiences from South Asia. New Delhi: Ford Foundation.

———. 1996. From Chipko to Uttaranchal: Development, Environment, and Social Protest in the Gharwal Himalayas, India. In *Liberation Ecologies: Environment, Development, Social Movements,* ed. R. Peet and M. Watts. London: Routledge.

Posey, D. A., ed. 1998. *Cultural and Spiritual Values of Biodiversity.* London: Intermediate Technology Publications.

Rahnema, M. 1992. Participation. In *The Development Dictionary: A Guide to Knowledge as Power,* ed. W. Sachs. London: Zed Books.

Renn, O., T. Webler, and P. Wiedermann. 1995. *Fairness and Competence in Citizen Participation.* Dordrecht, the Netherlands: Kluwer.

Ribot, J. C. 1996. Participation without Representation: Chiefs, Councils and Forestry Law in the West African Sahel. *Cultural Survival Quarterly* 20(3): 40–44.

———. 1999. Decentralization, Participation and Accountability in Sahelian Forestry: Legal Instruments of Political-Administrative Control. *Africa* 69(1): 23–65.

Schroeder, Richard. 1999. Community, Forestry, and Conditionality in the Gambia. *Africa* 69(1): 1–22.

Scott, James. 1985. *Weapons of the Weak: Everyday Forms of Peasant Resistance.* New Haven, Conn.: Yale Univ. Press.

Smith Korfmacher, K. 1998. Invisible Successes, Visible Failures: Paradoxes of Ecosystem Management in the Albermarle-Pamlico Estuarine Study. *Coastal Zone Management.* [No other publication information available].

———. 2000. What's the Point of Partnering? A Case Study of Ecosystem Management in the Darby Creek Watershed. *American Behavioral Scientist* 44(4): 548–64.

Smyth, D. 2001. Joint Management of National Parks in Australia. In *Working on Country—Contemporary Indigenous Management of Australia's Lands and Coastal Regions,* ed. R. Baker, J. Davies, and E. Young. Oxford: Oxford Univ. Press.

Tarnowski, C. 2002. Forest Places, Political Spaces: The Social Implications of Community Forestry in Nepal. Ph.D. diss., Univ. of Georgia, Athens.

Terborgh, J. 1999. *Requiem for Nature*. Washington, D.C.: Island Press.

Verrengia, J. 2002. Wyoming Doctor Recruits Army in Africa to Save Animals from Poachers. *Environmental News Network*. 17 October.

Wagner, John. 2001. The Politics of Accountability: An Institutional Analysis of the Conservation Movement in Papua New Guinea. *Social Analysis* 45(2): 78–93.

Warren, D., L. Michael, Jan Slikkerveer, and David Brokensha, eds. 1995. *The Cultural Dimension of Development: Indigenous Knowledge Systems.* London: Intermediate Technology Publications.

West, P. C., and S. R. Brechin, eds. 1991. *Resident Peoples and National Parks*. Tucson: Univ. of Arizona Press.

Western, D., R. Wright, and S. Strum, eds. 1994. *Natural Connections: Perspectives in Community-Based Conservation*. Washington, D.C.: Island Press.

White, A. T., L. Zeitlin Hale, Y. Renard, and L. Cortesi, eds. 1994. *Collaborative and Community-Based Management of Coral Reefs: Lessons from Experience*. West Hartford, Conn.: Kumarian Press.

Wild, R. G., and J. Mutebi. 1996. *Establishing Collaborative Management at Bwindi Impenetrable and Mgahenga National Parks.* People and Plants Series. Paris: UNESCO.

Wilson, E. O. 1993. Forest Ecosystems: More Complex than We Know. In *Defining Sustainable Forestry*, ed. G. H. Aplet, N. Johnson, J. T. Olson, and V. A. Sample. Washington, D.C.: Island Press.

Wilson, R. K. 2003. Community-Based Management and National Forests in the Western United States: Five Challenges. *Policy Matters* 12: 181–89.

World Bank. 1996. *The World Bank Participation Sourcebook*. Washington, D.C.: World Bank.

3

Building Models of Community-Based Natural Resource Management: A Personal Narrative

E. Walter Coward

> Our irrigation system is sick in the head but they sent us a foot doctor.
>
> —Javanese villager

My involvement with community-based natural resource management (CBNRM) has been built on a base of field research on local irrigation systems in a number of locales in Asia. Here I want to recount some of this research so that readers will understand the experiences that helped shape my engagement with this topic.

While in graduate school, I was invited to be associated with Asia Society's Mekong Project. The project was connected with the U.S. government's amorphous plan to help develop the Mekong region as part of the American deal to find an end to the war in Vietnam. The Asia Society organized a series of workshops about the Mekong region and administered a small research project fund.

The expansion of irrigation in the Mekong region was one topic being examined. Several researchers proposed to conduct survey research, mostly in northeast Thailand, to find out if local people were interested in irrigation and how much they would be willing to pay for it, contribute to its upkeep, and so on. I found this approach of only marginal interest and proposed to conduct research in western Laos where I knew that the U.S. government was already involved in an irrigation development activity—the Nam Tan project.

In any event, funding was provided and I carried out research in the villages to be served by the project. This was in the summer of 1969, and the research resulted in my first publications about local irrigation organization (Coward 1971, 1976). This initial irrigation fieldwork introduced me to a pattern that was to repeat itself many times over. One striking finding for me was that a significant number of the rice fields to be served by the Nam Tan project already were irrigated through a number of small, rudimentary irrigation structures. A second finding, profoundly interesting to me, was that institutional arrangements existed for operating, maintaining, or replacing these structures. These remote locations had what we later came to call community-based resource management. A third and very troublesome finding, again often to be repeated, was that those designing and implementing the contemporary project knew nothing about either the physical or social structures on which they were overlaying their new apparatus.

Not long after completing this fieldwork (but, as frequently occurs, before completing the writing and publishing of my results), I began an assignment in the Philippines with the International Institute for Rural Reconstruction. In preparation for going to the Philippines, I began to read the literature on the area and came across a remarkable book by Henry Lewis (1971). On the basis of field research in the province of Ilocos Norte (situated in the northern reaches of Luzon island), Lewis's book provides the reader with a stunning account of the area's rural production and an especially rich portrait of the local irrigation systems, called *zangjeras*. These local systems—likely some amalgamation of Spanish and pre-Spanish practices, techniques, and organizational arrangements—alerted me to the possibility of finding other such systems in the Philippines.

My work location was primarily in the province of Cavite, and although I soon learned that there were no *zangjeras* there, there were small irrigation systems referred to more generally by the government as *communal irrigation*. This category of communal irrigation systems, by which the government typically meant small-size systems, were operated by local groups and most often built and maintained through a combination of local and external resources and inputs. They later came to play a significant role in helping to define early thinking about community-based resource management at the Ford Foundation and elsewhere.

While living and working in the Philippines, other commitments prevented me from doing any research with *zangjeras*, but soon after I joined the faculty at Cornell I was able to return to the Philippines and conduct fieldwork in Ilocos Norte. As was increasingly becoming my methodology of choice, I chose to focus on a particular *zangjera*, while also visiting and observing a significant number of other irrigation systems. In this research I was able to uncover the considerable organizational complexities that underlie these remarkable human concoctions that blended natural phenomenon, engineered artifacts, and social organization.[1] I remember feeling like a discoverer as I went about my field studies.

Soon after returning from the Philippines and joining the faculty at Cornell, I was invited by the Ford Foundation to conduct a field-based seminar in Chiang Mai, Thailand, to begin introducing Thai researchers to the study of irrigation, particularly village irrigation. I was familiar with a somewhat obscure report on the *muang fai* irrigation systems of this area and eager to learn more about them (Frutchey 1969). Although I never directly conducted research on the *muang fai* systems, I subsequently worked with a Thai doctoral student who did a superb dissertation on this topic and who later continued a remarkable program of applied research that brought her in close contact with both *muang fai* leaders and officials of the government's irrigation department (Tan-kim-yong 1983).

Also attending this research workshop were two Filipino colleagues, one of whom, Carlos Isles, went on to work closely with the Ford Foundation–supported work of the National Irrigation Administration (NIA) with participatory communal irrigation. As that program developed, I had a rewarding experience working with the foundation's program officer responsible for this program, Frances Korten, and her many able Filipino colleagues.

There were two other important pieces of fieldwork that greatly influenced my thinking. One was my investigation of *kuhls* in Himachal Pradesh, the Himalayan state of India. I had come to know of these through involvement with a team working with U.S. Agency for International Development (USAID) to plan a hill irrigation project in this state. In my background reading of British settlement reports and other literature, I had come to learn that a large part of this state was served by so-called minor irrigation systems. As I have described elsewhere (Coward 1990), this fieldwork reinforced all that we had been seeing elsewhere about the ignorance of and disdain for local experiences and capabilities on the part of states. It also introduced me to the potential power of legal water rights, both as an asset and a limitation.

Later fieldwork on irrigation in Aceh, a northern province on the Indonesian island of Sumatra, introduced me to the idea that local irrigation is a better marker than community irrigation.[2] In Aceh, responsibility for the *seunalop* systems was an unusual blend of rural neighborhood leadership and local government—not quite community, but also not quite government. In writing about this unique arrangement, I characterized them as something like a local utility company.

My latest encounter with local irrigation has been in New Mexico. I had known about the *acequia* systems of southern Colorado and New Mexico for some years, but it was only through my work at the Ford Foundation, beginning in 1990, that I came to learn much more about these remarkable systems. Perhaps analogous to the situation in Ilocos Norte, these systems represent some blend of Spanish irrigation ideas and Native American ideas and techniques. Among the many fascinating aspects of this case is that, over time and through numerous convoluted processes, management of the irrigation facilities and the irrigated lands has become divorced from the management of the watersheds on which they depend. Many of these watersheds now are managed by public agencies such as the U.S. Forest Service or in some cases by private landowners.

Throughout these episodes of fieldwork, I was continually interested in trying to identify broad patterns or themes with which to make sense of the unique and diverse arrangements that I and others were observing and reporting. One early and useful step was to deconstruct the notion of irrigation and identify (perhaps overly rigidly at first) several subcategories. In 1980 I proposed that, "in general, existing irrigation systems approximate one of three types: they may be community systems, operated and maintained by the water users themselves and/or their representatives; they may be bureaucratically managed systems, fully administered by an agency of the government; or they many be jointly managed systems, in which some functions are performed by the irrigation agency while others are the responsibility of one or more water-user communities." As far as I can tell from the written record, and from my own recollections, this is as close as I came to using the phrase "community-managed irrigation."

So this is what I was doing to pursue my compelling urge to understand local experiences with irrigation. I also had a strong desire to have this information about local systems applied to influence the irrigation development policies and programs under way during this period. Here it is important to remind the reader that most of the work that I have just described took place in an era of very heavy investment in irrigation development around the world, especially in Asia. My colleagues and I were able to find support for our research and writing precisely because irrigation development was such a significant component of development aid. Many of us also benefited from the fact that during this period the Ford Foundation also was focused on influencing the outcomes of the enormous irrigation investments planned and under way at the time. Thus those of us interested in irrigation were supported in our research, invited to organize and attend important seminars and workshops, supplied with graduate students, and invited to collaborate with the foundation's grantees in government agencies, research organizations, and nongovernmental organizations (NGOs).

FORD FOUNDATION AND COMMUNITY MANAGEMENT

Uncovering the origins of the Ford Foundation's concerns with community-based natural resources is a complicated task. So far as I can discern, there was no specific mandate that led in this direction. Instead, I would suggest, there were two important starting points: individual foundation staff who viewed local actions as relevant and important to the foundation's work (or perhaps in some cases, who had experienced the limitations of macro work), and real-world problems that seemed to require profoundly new solutions.

One important source of these ideas was Franklin Thomas, who became president of the foundation in the summer of 1979. Before heading the foundation, Frank had been deeply involved in local community actions in the Bedford-Stuyvesant section of Brooklyn. Among the many important views that he brought to the foundation was the notion that communities counted and that a larger portion of the foundation's work ought to be aimed at supporting those closest to the problems.

Meanwhile, interesting things were happening in the foundation's work in Asia. Two projects came to have a buzz about them—the Sukamajri project in India and the Laur project in the Philippines. The Sukamajri project evolved from government concern with the siltation of the reservoir serving the city of Chandigar, located north of Delhi and near the edge of the Shawalik Hills, an outer range of the Himalayas. Through direct intervention and grants to the government's soil-conservation research unit, the foundation supported tests of various alternatives to land use in the highly erodable soils of the Shawaliks, a presumed source of the siltation in the reservoir. A project was begun in the hill village of Sukamajri where lands were being used primarily for grazing. The soil-conservation group ultimately constructed a small reservoir above the village to be used as a source of domestic, livestock, and irrigation water. This was done in exchange for an agreement by the villagers to discontinue grazing in certain highly vulnerable lands. Subsequent to the construction of the small reservoir, staff from the foundation and the soil-conservation unit began conversations with local people as to how to allocate the water for irrigation purposes—in essence, what water rights to create. A very interesting debate arose over whether to give everyone an equal water right, regardless of the amount of land they owned, or alternatively, to allocate water rights in proportion to the land owned. In the end the novel solution was rejected. This experience with local management of natural resources, land, water, and grasses, was an early example of the foundation's work that brought a natural resources agency into close contact with local people. In retrospect, what was missing was a determined effort either to organize the local community to deal effectively with the bureaucracy or to examine agency procedures and understand how they facilitated or complicated agency-community dealings.

Meanwhile, a parallel effort was beginning in the central Luzon region of the Philippines—the Laur project.[3] Here the foundation decided to provide support to the NIA to assist it in devising new ways to provide needed services to the communal irrigation sector—the many local irrigation systems largely built and operated by local people. The NIA was searching for new procedures and arrangements because a presidential decree had directed that NIA assistance to communal irrigation was to shift from being a grant to becoming (in part) a loan. The NIA realized that without community commitment and involvement in the project planning and implementation, there was little likelihood that NIA would recover its loans. The Philippines had a long tradition of community organizing, and community organizers were active in promoting change and social justice in the urban slums of Manila and elsewhere. There also was a smattering of literature on the communal irrigation sector that documented the considerable social infrastructure that existed in various locations to operate and maintain these systems.

The novel activities that the foundation funded drew on these existing lines of work. Foundation support assisted the NIA in employing a cadre of community organizers to work with the local communities participating in NIA's communal irrigation program. The strategy was to help communities organize around irrigation so that they could be more equal partners in dealing with the NIA and so that they could effectively manage and use the new facilities after the project was completed. Foundation support also allowed a talented group of social science researchers at the Institute of Philippine Culture and management experts at the Asian Institute of Management to research and document these pilot efforts, to quickly bring problems to the attention of the program managers, and later to devise a series of effective training programs for participating NIA staff. Senior NIA staff became highly committed to this approach and at a later stage helped negotiate a major World Bank loan to allow NIA to significantly expand what became known as the participatory communal irrigation program.

While this successful approach to community irrigation development was being consolidated, there was growing interest inside and outside the foundation in the deteriorating conditions in the upland communities, particularly concerning the state of forest lands. Thus the foundation decided to expand its rural activities to include an uplands program with a tight focus on community-agency interactions. Over time, this program also was constructed around the central idea that communities could and did play a much larger role in natural resource management than originally assumed by the government. This work also was greatly assisted by the growing presence of the NGO community, and many NGOs increasingly gave attention to the plight of upland people and their need to gain greater control over basic natural assets of land and forests.

In the early months of 1980, while on sabbatical from Cornell, I joined the foundation's office in Jakarta with the mandate to explore the possibility for grant making in the field of irrigation development. I began by looking at two activities that were under way in Indonesia. The first was a government program called *sederhana*—literally, "simple" (irrigation)—which provided assistance to village irrigation systems of Indonesia (what Filipinos had called *communal irrigation*). This program was jointly managed by the Department of Public Works and Agriculture. The second activity was the public works tertiary development program, whose activities were conducted within the large-scale government-managed irrigation systems. It focused on improving the irrigation facilities at the lowest level of the system so that water would reach farm fields effectively and efficiently.

I also found in my discussions with the agency staff that there was very little understanding—and sometimes profound misunderstanding—of what actually was happening in either of these large or small systems at the local level. Especially lacking was any understanding of how local people were organized to operate and maintain the irrigation apparatus or the complex roles and rules that often were in place. I also knew that there was a small handful of Indonesian social scientists already at work in this field with whom I could connect. Over a period of months, and through a series of visits around Indonesia, I was finally able to recommend a set of grants to launch our work on this topic. We began with grants to several groups of university-based researchers in critical locations around Indonesia to launch fieldwork investigating how community systems were managed and operated in several distinctive regions: Bali, central Java, west Sumatra, and Palembang. Originally I had hoped to involve two other distinctive regions—Tanah Toraja and the Batak communities of north Sumatra—but researchers in this region were not then ready to act. Later in this process my successor, Fran Korten, brought her savvy and grant-making experiences to Indonesia and used them to more effectively connect these research teams and forge links between the researchers and the irrigation staff.

With the fruitful engagement of community organizers in the Philippines in mind, I also looked for a way to make community organizing a part of the Indonesian program. As part of both the *sederhana* and tertiary-development programs, superficial attention was given to organizing so-called water-user associations. But this was not a task that most irrigation staff understood well. Through an unexpected meeting at an evening party, I conversed with the director of an Indonesian NGO who told me about their program of community organizing in the urban neighborhoods of Jakarta. From that conversation we went on to develop a long-standing grant relationship with this organization, whose staff also became deeply involved in community organizing for irrigation development.

CONTESTED TOPICS

Much of the internal discussion and debate concerning CBNRM occurred as efforts were initiated to apply these ideas to new resource situations—

from the lowland irrigated valleys to the upland forested areas, for example—or from one national setting to another. Five contested topics often arose.

One concerned the issue of staff intensity, especially the number of community organizers and the duration of their work. The early models in the Philippines, for example, assigned a community organizer to one or a few villages to help establish a community-based organization. Often this meant many months of work in a single location. The debate concerned matters such as how many villages a community organizer could serve, how much time was required to accomplish the tasks, and whether this work could be done by existing field staff of the resource agency or local people trained to act as organizers.

A related topic concerned the availability and capacity of NGOs to plan and implement such community activities. In the initial work with small-scale irrigation systems there were practically no existing NGOs with irrigation experience. In other cases, for example, Himachal Pradesh, India, there were almost no NGOs working in rural areas at all. A very large issue was the lack of NGO experience working closely with government, and the reluctance of many NGOs to do so (as well as a reluctance of government agencies to have NGOs as partners). The debate concerned the ability to assist existing NGOs in taking on these new resource-management topics and whether there was a need to establish new organizations, sometimes as intermediaries with the objective of assisting the many smaller groups in the field.

This brings us to a third contested topic: the will and ability of large and powerful natural resource agencies to reinvent themselves, to adopt new objectives and professional roles, to enter into partnerships with communities and NGOs, and to adjust their administrative procedures to accommodate new concerns, new rhythms of planning and work, and new measures of success. New grant makers needed encouragement that such bureaucratic modifications, while never simple, were at least possible over time.

Concerns about the bureaucracy commingled with concerns about efficiency—did community involvement lead to efficient procedures and processes? There was considerable debate about how best to combine the technical expertise that defined the persona of the agency staff with the everyday experience and knowledge of local people, the latter being largely unknown to the external agents. In the irrigation sector there were many existing conventions about water-use efficiency, technical standards for the size of canals, and also existing control structures and procedures for the rotation of water delivery. Although they were not always easily discernable in the simple apparatus of a community irrigation system, most such physical structures both reflected and reinforced intricate rules and rights constructed locally.

Finally, a topic of continuing debate was the character of the communities themselves, especially their fairness in allocating limited resources to community subgroups defined by gender, class, caste, or otherwise. While there was an urge to build on sometimes long-standing local institutional arrangements, there was also a recognition that often such preexisting arrangements severely disadvantaged women, the poor, ethnic minorities, or others. Indigenous and fair were not always correlated and, in equal measure, fair and effective were not always synonymous, at least in the short run.

Uncontested, however, was the concept that communities mattered. The foundation's long experience with urban neighborhoods and communities, in particular, provided an organizational context for this work and a direct connection with the experiences and values of the senior leadership of the foundation from at least 1979. Over time, this community theme was described in the Rural Poverty and Resources program as a crucial solution to rural poverty and good natural resource management. Nevertheless, we recognized that communities could not do everything and that they needed to be assisted by the NGO sector, by researchers and analysts, and by good government policies and programs.

GOVERNMENT ENTANGLEMENTS

This brings us to the role of government and to the entanglement of community-based resource management programs with government agencies. In the Ford Foundation's thinking, governments have always been prominent, because we understand that, at some point, usually sooner rather than later, government regulations and procedures will need modification and government resources will be required to reach the scale of effort ultimately intended. Although the foundation could assist with the costs of a limited number of experimental programs—for example, using community organizers to assist villages to organize to be partners with the NIA's communal-irrigation program—any significant expansion beyond the pilot areas would require government funding from the Philippines or elsewhere. Thus each foundation effort to support a community-based approach to natural resource management has included some degree of involvement by a relevant government agency.

Trade-offs are, of course, required. Typically, government actions can only reach an effective scale if some modifications are made in the procedures developed during the pilot activities. Differently trained or motivated field staff may be engaged. Fewer financial resources may be available per site. And a shortened implementation period may be imposed. All in all, there will be a tendency to move from interventions tailored to local situations to more standardized, even caricatured, styles.

Moreover, as such activities scale up, additional donors are typically engaged in the process, and each entity may have its own views about implementation, required procedures, and so on.

While such complexities cannot be entirely avoided, the foundation has found some ways to ameliorate the difficulties that arise. Usually, these actions need to be taken in concert and, to some extent, they act as checks and balances on one another. One is to help create and sustain a strong NGO presence to increase the likelihood that community concerns will continue to be considered even while implementation by the government agency advances. A second is to continue support to independent, but connected, researchers and analysts who can examine field cases and overall trends, and report problems as they emerge. A third is to foster within the agency itself a senior-level working group that is committed and is able to assess outcome and propose modifications and corrections, as needed. A fourth approach—one that is just beginning to take shape—is to support the emergence of federations of community-based organizations that are able to serve their own developmental needs and to advocate with the government for needed attention and actions. Such federations have come forward among the community forest-user groups in Nepal, tank-irrigation groups in south India, and among the CAMPFIRE associations in Zimbabwe.

In some ways, of course, the most fundamental entanglements with government concern the rhetoric and actions of those in power with regard to the rights and responsibilities of local, sometimes culturally distinct, people. Here the foundation finds itself working in vastly different contexts from Mexico to China, Mozambique to Indonesia. Although it is remarkable how widely touted the concept of CBNRM has become, one needs to recognize the enormous constraints under which such an approach is pursued in some locations as compared with others. An extreme case is the Philippines, a setting fundamentally unlike any other because of the widespread presence of NGOs, along with efforts there toward agency devolution and commitment to collaboration with NGOs and community-based organizations.

CIRCULATING IDEAS

The Ford Foundation acts in a highly decentralized manner, and thus individual staff often are the carriers of ideas such as community-based resource management. Given the foundation's preference for relatively short tenure for program officers (a policy with many exceptions), two staffing approaches have been helpful in reinforcing these ideas within the foundation. First, staff with good records of achievement have been invited to move from one field office to another (including to and from the United States) or to assume leadership positions. Second, recruitment of new staff has given preference to individuals with direct experience with or commitment to community-based approaches.

In the late 1990s, the foundation became more explicit in its intention to use the fact of its parallel work in unlike contexts to accelerate learning and the spread of good practice, both within the foundation and within the larger professional community. One means for this was the creation of an internally managed affinity group whose core members are the program staff around the world who made grants in support of CBNRM. The affinity group met annually, invited to its session selected grantees and other key resource people, monitored the state of the field, and identified unusual opportunities in, and constraints to, the field for foundation action.

In addition, the foundation teamed up with colleagues at the University of Florida to create a new international entity, the Conservation Development Forum (CDF). The mission of CDF was to help shape the emerging field of environment and development with special attention to community-based management strategies. It did do so by sponsoring state-of-the-art reviews, convening theorists and practitioners in workshops and international forums, and publishing materials on lessons learned.

SOME REFLECTIONS

We now have on our hands an emerging social movement, one covered by not only the Public Broadcasting System (PBS) but also media entities the likes of ABC News. It is no longer just a topic for academic papers or articles in the *Earth Times*, but also for articles in the *Wall Street Journal*. Is there anything we should brood about? Well, a few concerns deserve mention.

First, I want to underscore the risks associated with creeping orthodoxy—the silent, invisible, and soft ways in which concepts, assumptions, and approaches become commonplace, repeated, and unchallenged in our thinking, writing, and actions. We all need to remain vigilant for the imprudent and unreflective use of concepts like *local* and *indigenous* (fill in the blank with your choice) and conserve their value and worth through careful and appropriate use.

A second concern is to stay alert to imitations. While recognizing that CBNRM will and should come in different forms and shapes, we need to distinguish desirable variation from ersatz versions and recognize caricatures for what they are. In short, the field needs to develop standards, criteria, and best practices to inform assessments of activities emerging in the new arena.

Third, we also need to carefully examine failures: those cases that produce breakdowns or undesired, unintended outcomes. Such a large number of contingencies influence any particular case that we need to give careful attention to poor outcomes and the conditions associated with them. We are all aware of the fad phenomenon associated with development. Unexamined failures, unattended problems, and uncritical assessments could be the preconditions for abandoning commitment to communities and local involvement. We need to avoid the production of palinodes in favor of alternative hypotheses: that government could do better, that corporate involvement is needed, or that the market is the solution. All of these ideas are latent in the natural resource management debate.

A final concern to mention here is the risk of theorizing and acting in any particular community-based case, as well as the entire field, on the basis of outmoded perceptions of community realities. Theory and practice in CBNRM must emerge not from idealized notions but rather from authentic understandings of what is happening in particular communities—that political power is shifting, that money is becoming more important, that inequality is increasing, that women's roles are being altered dramatically, or that resource ownership is being concentrated. Too much of our thinking, writing, and action rests on a view of rural places as being unconnected, or only recently joined, with their regional economies or as having clear, fair, and uncontested rules for access to resources. As in all other spheres of human interaction, local groups are constantly in motion, perpetually negotiating the terms of social intercourse, and continually painting new ideas and actions with familiar colors from the palette of tradition.

POSTCLOCKWORK UNIVERSE

I want to end with a few more abstract reflections drawn from the work of my talented colleague at Cornell, Norman Uphoff. My reference is his highly original book on Gal Oya, in which he discusses the implications for social science that derive from the dilemmas of a "postclockwork universe," the discovery of a "nonlinear world," and other ideas associated with so-called chaos theory (Uphoff 1992). The challenges that he identifies for social scientists apply in equal measure to grant makers and international donors. They include a number of challenges that have direct applicability to our work with CBNRM.

- The need to move away from mechanistic and reductionist ways of thinking that attempt to identify a handful of variables that predict some future state of affairs, and instead move toward the view that much in our work is inherently and inescapably uncertain. This has direct and important implications for theory and practice in CBNRM. It reminds us that blueprint thinking will be especially stunting if used to inform scale-up and replication activities.
- The recognition that although many phenomena and relationships have

extremely high probabilities, all are contingent, is likewise of great utility to CBNRM work. At a minimum, it should keep us humble while not paralyzing either our thoughts or actions. It suggests the profound and regrettably uncommon need for policies and programs that admit contingent factors and recognize the need for in-process learning.
- The need to recall the observation that if you want to know reality you must try to change it. One of the powerful contributors to better theory in the CBNRM field is the myriad of demonstrations and actions underway around the world. We need to find productive ways for theory to both inform and be informed by this practice.

Much of the foundation's grantmaking in CBNRM, as well as in other fields, is about providing resources to people and organizations who are striving to alter what remains a probable scenario—for example, that the Forestry Department of Bihar will continue to exclude local people from forest management, or that the *acequias* of northern New Mexico will proceed to lose their water rights to others. Effective grantmaking helps by adding to the pool of alternative possibilities. Sometimes, of course, the foundation does nothing more than create new possibilities that have little probability of being realized. In other cases, foundation support helps to sharply raise the probability levels for an already possible outcome. Our work in the field of CBNRM we hope will do some of both.

NOTES

1. The principal publication reporting this research is Coward 1979. At Cornell I worked with two other students who each did important research on *zangjeras*. See Siy 1982 for Robert's report on his work. One article that I felt was important but that received little notice was Coward and Siy 1983.

2. The most detailed description of this research is found in my 1988 monograph (Coward 1988). A briefer, more accessible account is found in Coward 1991.

3. A fuller description of this starting point and the later consequences is found in Korten and Siy 1988.

REFERENCES

Coward, E. Walter, Jr. 1971. Agrarian Modernization and Village Leadership: Irrigation Leaders in Laos. *Asian Forum* 3: 158–63.

———. 1976. Indigenous Organization, Bureaucracy and Development: The Case of Irrigation. *Journal of Development Studies* 13: 92–105.

———. 1979. Principles of Social Organization in an Indigenous Irrigation System. *Human Organization* 38: 28–36.

———. 1988. Baskets of Stones: Government Assistance and Development of Local Irrigation in a District of Northern Sumatra. Water Management Synthesis Project. WMS Report no. 80.

———. 1990. Property Rights and Network Order: The Case of Irrigation Works in the Western Himalayas. *Human Organization* 49:78–88.

———. 1991. Planning Technical and Social Change in Irrigated Areas. In *Putting People First: Sociological Variable in Rural Development*, 2d ed., edited by Michael Cernea. Oxford: Oxford Univ. Press.

Coward, E. Walter, Jr., and Robert Y. Siy. 1983. Structuring Collective Action: An Irrigation Federation in the Northern Philippines. *Philippine Sociological Review* 31: 3–7.

Frutchey, Rose House. 1969. Socioeconomic Observation Study of Existing Irrigation Projects in Thailand. Prepared for the Bureau of Reclamation, U.S. Department of the Interior, Washington, D.C.

Korten, Frances F., and Robert Y. Siy, eds. 1988. *Transforming a Bureaucracy: The Experience of the Philippine National Irrigation Administration.* West Hartford, Conn.: Kumarian Press.

Lewis, Henry T. 1971. *Ilocano Rice Farmers: A Comparative Study of Two Philippine Barrios*. Honolulu: Univ. of Hawaii Press.

Siy, Robert Y. 1982. *Community Resource Management: Lessons from the Zanjera*. Manila: Univ. of the Philippines Press.

Tan-kim-yong, Uraivan. 1983. Resource Mobilization in Traditional Irrigation Systems of Northern Thailand: A Comparison between Lowland and Upland Irrigation Communities. PhD diss., Cornell Univ.

Uphoff, Norman. 1992. *Learning from Gal Oya*. Ithaca, N.Y.: Cornell Univ. Press.

4

Congruent Objectives, Competing Interests, and Strategic Compromise: Concept and Process in the Evolution of Zimbabwe's CAMPFIRE, 1984–1996

Marshall W. Murphree

The background papers for the 1997 conference this chapter was originally written for called for the presentation of CAMPFIRE as a case study of a model in community-based natural resource management (CBNRM) that has resulted in emulation and proliferation. While it is true that CAMPFIRE (the acronym is derived from the full title of the program, Communal Areas Management Programme for Indigenous Resources) has achieved a high regional and international profile and has contributed to the shape of CBNRM programs in the southern African region, there is good reason to be cautious about regarding it in its specifics as a model for the generality of CBNRM projects and programs that have proliferated over the last decade.[1] It is in fact atypical: it had a local, Zimbabwean origin and was not imported by international agencies; it was initially conceived in a government agency and not by nongovernmental organizations (NGOs) and their allies; it has never had the protected-area conservation focus characterizing integrated conservation and development projects (ICDPs)[2]; and its implementation has been quite heterogeneous.

With these caveats, CAMPFIRE does provide an instructive case study.

First, its conceptual design encompasses a broad spectrum of factors nested in the evolution of Zimbabwe's political economy, giving insights into inter-institutional linkages that are critical for such programs. In this dimension it is a design that recognizes the "intrinsic relatedness" of microlevel strategies with strategic macrolevel options for sustainable development (Moyo 1991, 130). Second, it has an extended track record, allowing analysis of process and evolution. Third, it is unusually well documented and has been subjected to professional analyses that go well beyond advocacy or consultancy evaluations. An annotated bibliography on CAMPFIRE produced by the Centre for Applied Social Sciences (CASS), University of Zimbabwe, lists 310 items for 1985–1996 alone (Dix 1996),[3] and the list is not comprehensive for the period.

Drawing on this wealth of experience, documentation, and analysis, I trace in this chapter the evolution of CAMPFIRE from its conceptual roots (the "congruent objectives" of the title), the issues it has had to face ("competing interests"), and its implementational history ("strategic compromise"). The principal themes are economic motivation under changing market and trade conditions, resource appropriation, and center-periphery relationships in governance. To maintain this focus, I underplay important dimensions, such as the role of extension and donor agencies, the importance of indigenous knowledge systems (see Matowanyika, Garibaldi, and Musima 1995), and the anthropological hermeneutics of environmental history (see Moore 1996). I explore the replicability of the program and conclude that CAMPFIRE cannot be regarded as a blueprint model. I also suggest, however, that certain generalizations that have wide salience can be drawn from CAMPFIRE's history.

BACKGROUND BASICS

For this chapter to be comprehensible, certain background factors have to be sketched. These include Zimbabwe's ecological and demographic profile, its political-economic history, its tenure system, its structures of subnational governance, and its wildlife policy.

Ecology, Political-Economic History, and Land Allocation

Zimbabwe is predominantly wooded savanna lying at altitudes between three hundred and twenty-eight hundred meters above sea level. Soil types vary, but the greatest ecological determinant of land use is rainfall, which has considerable correlation with altitude. Vincent and Thomas (1961) provided a classification of the country's land surface comprising five agroecological regions based on rainfall, altitude, and temperature criteria. Regions I–III are suitable for cropping and relatively intensive livestock production, and regions IV and V are generally unsuitable for dryland crop production and suited only to extensive livestock production. Table 4.1 provides details of this classification. Map 4.1 shows the profile of this mapping,[4] with the most viable arable areas lying in an arc from the country's center to its eastern borders. The overall area of potential arable land is estimated at 22 percent (Republic of Zimbabwe 1982) and falls largely within this arc.

Given this profile, it is not surprising that white-settler agriculture appropriated to itself land largely falling within regions I–III. The only major exception to this was the creation of extensive cattle ranches in the south and west. This appropriation was part of a racially structured system of minority dominance with coercive, ideological, economic, and political components.[5] Appropriation was effected by the removal of resident peoples to native reserves (subsequently known as tribal trust lands and then communal lands) and formalized by the granting of title deeds. By 1931 nearly 60 percent of land was private, commercial, white farm land, with black farmers confined to slightly more than 20 percent of the land. Subsequent shifts in land allocation meant that, by 1975, 40 percent of land was communal, 42 percent was commercial, and the balance of 18 percent was state land. Land redistribution since Independence in 1980 had reduced commercial land to 33 percent by 1990 (table 4.2).

Table 4.1 Agro-Ecological Regions of Zimbabwe

Region I	In the *Eastern Highlands,* covering less than 2 percent of Zimbabwe. Rainfall above 1,000 mm. High altitude and low temperatures enable afforestation and intensive diversified agriculture including tea, coffee, deciduous fruits, and intensive livestock production.
Region II	The *northeastern-highveld* covering some 16 percent of the country. Reliable rainfall of 750–1,000 mm between November and March; suitable for intensive cropping and livestock production.
Region III	Mainly in the *midlands* and covering 18 percent of the country. Rainfall between 500–750 mm but subject to mid-season dry spells and high temperatures; suitable for drought-resistant crops and livestock. Semi-intensive farming.
Region IV	*Low-lying* areas in the north and south of the country and covering 37 percent of Zimbabwe. Rainfall between 450–650 mm. Subject to periodic seasonal droughts and severe dry spells during the rainy season. Generally unsuitable for dryland cropping and suited to livestock production.
Region V	*Lowland areas* generally below 900 m and covering 27 percent of the country. Erratic rainfall usually below 650 mm. Suited to extensive livestock production or game ranching.

Source: Murphree and Cumming (1993, 149), adapted from Vincent and Thomas (1961).

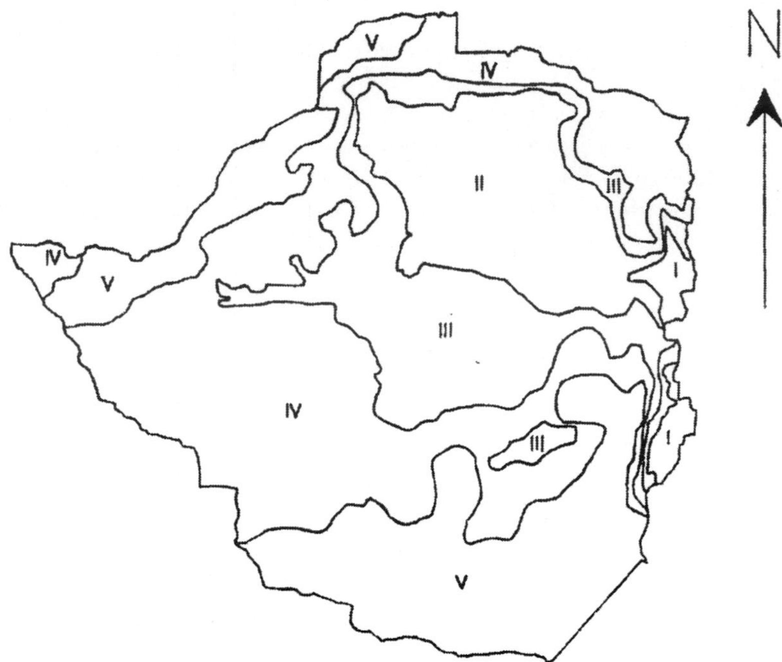

Map 4.1 Agro-Ecological Regions of Zimbabwe

Source: Murphree and Cumming (1993, 150).

Table 4.2 Summary of Changes in Statutory Land Apportionment in Zimbabwe, 1911–1990

Year	*Communal farmland*	*State land*	*Parks and wildlife*	*Forestry land*	*Commercial farmland*
1911	20	60	0	0	20
1925	20	50	0	0	30
1931	20	15	5	5	55
1961	30	4	8	3	55
1965	40	5	10	3	42
1975	40	2	13	3	42
1990	50	3	12	3	32

Note: Resettlement land is included within communal land and small-scale commercial farm land within commercial farm land.
Source: Murphree and Cumming (1993, 141), adapted from Kay (1970) and Cumming (1991).

Demography and Land Use

The statistics of the prior section do not provide the full picture of the growing pressures on land and resources in communal lands. The 1982 census indicated that 56.7 percent of the population lived in communal lands and 20.8 percent on commercial farm land (Republic of Zimbabwe 1984, 6). However, the location of communal lands is skewed toward areas less capable of intensive arable production, as table 4.3 shows. With annual population growth estimated at 3.13 percent per annum in the 1980s (Republic of Zimbabwe 1992, 10), pressure on viable land by communal-land farmers was obviously growing and had resulted in an extension of human settlement in areas of regions IV and V where arable agriculture is tenuous and erosion hazards high (CASS 1988; Derman 1990). Use of viable arable land in the commercial sector is far lower (table 4.4), and the reallocation and more effective use of much of this land is a political, economic, and ecological imperative.

Land and Resource Rights, Local Governance

The important fact to note, for the purposes of this discussion, is that communal lands are, in law, unalienated state land. This also applies to natural resources on the land. Communal-land farmers are accorded usufruct to arable land, and though they commonly use natural resources such as pasturage and wood products for firewood and building, they have no ownership status over these in law, either individually or as groups. Commercially valuable species of flora and fauna are claimed by the state.

This tenure situation is a perpetuation of the expropriations of the colonial period, when long-established populations not only lost land but also secure rights to resources on the land they were left with. After Independence, aspects of this situation were modified through amendments to the District Councils Act and the Rural District Councils Act of 1988. Although these changes did not confer ownership to individual communal-land farmers (or

Table 4.3 Land Allocated to Commercial and Communal Farming and Other Uses in Relation to Natural Region in Zimbabwe, 1980

	Large-scale commercial farms	*Small-scale commercial farms*	*Communal land*	*Parks, forests, and other land*
I & II	50	3	12	2
III	35	5	30	5
IV & V	80	5	125	49

Source: Murphree and Cumming (1983, 153).

Table 4.4 Distribution of Potential Arable Land and Areas Cultivated in 1980, in square kilometers, percentages in parentheses

			Soil		
	Arable	*Cultivated*	*Crops*	*Fallow*	*Irrigated*
Commercial farmland					
Large-scale area	48,000 (55.8)	10,200 (29.1)	6,200 (24.5)	4,000 (41.0)	1,517
Small-scale area	5,000 (5.8)	900 (2.6)	700 (2.8)	200 (2.1)	—
Communal farmland Area	33,000 (38.4)	24,000 68.4)	18,450 (72.8)	5,550 (56.9)	—
Total	86,000	35,100	25,350	9,750	1,517
Percentage of Zimbabwe	22.0	9.0	6.5	2.5	0.4

Source: Murphree and Cumming (1993, 151).

groupings of them), they did provide for the conferment to district councils of rights over communal land and natural resources on them. The specification of these rights varies, depending on the specifics of the warrant concerned (see Wood 1991). Thus under certain circumstances rural district councils (RDCs) may lease land and exploit natural resources on behalf of their communal-land constituencies.

The substructures of RDCs as set up after Independence are as follows: At the lowest tier are the village development committees (VIDCOs), putatively comprising one hundred households. The next tier is the ward development committee (WADCO), comprising six VIDCOs. Each WADCO elects a councilor to the RDC, which may also have councilors elected from commercial farm areas within the district. The size of each council will vary according to the district's population, but there are generally from ten to twenty-eight councilors. For this discussion it is important to note that (1) the delineation of VIDCOs and WADCOs was imposed and often did not follow traditionally established boundaries of territory and membership; (2) VIDCOs and WADCOs are essentially planning and administrative units, per se they do not have legal rights to ownership or exploitation of land and resources and can act in this capacity only as delegated units of RDCs; and (3) RDCs often preside over areas that are highly heterogeneous in population densities and resource endowments.

Wildlife Policy

The history of wildlife policy in Zimbabwe until the 1950s is similar to that of other territories under British colonial rule (McKenzie 1988). Government appropriated formal control over all wildlife and then, through a sequence of enactments, provided hunting rights to resident whites and visiting sport hunters. Blacks, through a combination of hunting and firearms restrictions, were almost totally excluded from any legal use of wildlife, and thus for communal-land farmers wildlife was a complete liability, except for those who were willing to risk unsanctioned exploitation as poachers.[6] Even for the white owners of farms and ranches, wildlife was often seen as competition to crops and livestock and eliminated illegally. Parallel to this alienation of wildlife from farmers, the state also created game reserves, which were to form the basis of the Parks and Wild Life Estate of today, covering 12.5 percent of the country's land surface (see table 4.2).

The early 1960s saw a radical shift in wildlife policy away from protectionist philosophy to one of conservation through sustainable use. The essence of the new approach was that proprietorship and the ability to earn direct economic benefits from wildlife would provide a more effective incentive for wildlife conservation.[7] A related hypothesis was that, in certain ecological contexts, wildlife ranching could economically outperform cattle ranching because of the ability of wild animals to make use of a greater variety of flora. Research on ranches in the southeast lowveld during the early 1960s concluded that comparative meat production in the two forms of ranching was relatively equal, with somewhat lower values for game meat because of marketing constraints. However, game ranching was found to be more environmentally friendly (see Dasmann and Mossman 1961; Cumming 1991; Mossman 1963, 247–49; Child 1988). With the introduction of the international safari industry in the mid-1960s, wildlife values rose sharply, and this tipped the economic scales dramatically toward wildlife in these ecological contexts.

These developments cumulated in a formalization of the policy shift through the promulgation of the 1975 Parks and Wild Life Act. The preamble of the act states inter alia the objective "to confer privileges on owners or occupiers of alienated land as custodians of wildlife, fish and plants" (Government of Zimbabwe 1996). The act designates these "owners or occupiers of alienated land" as "appropriate authorities" over wildlife, and this effectively made farms and ranches into proprietorial wildlife units, combining ownership, management, cost, and benefit. Certain conditions remained that allowed exempting specially protected species and preserved the government's ability to impose restriction orders in cases of flagrant abuse. Since the inception of the act, wildlife populations have increased on farms and ranches, their ecological health has improved, and the wildlife industry in Zimbabwe has boomed.

Zimbabwean wildlife policy continues to accord a place to more conventional conservation approaches. The 1989 *Policy for Wild Life* states a commitment to "preserve examples of Zimbabwe's flora and fauna in their physical environments, to protect areas of scenic beauty and of special interest," and "to preserve populations of rare, endangered and endemic species" (p. 14). However, for the purposes of this analysis, the most important statement of this policy paper is the following: "Outside the Parks and Wild Life Estate, government views wildlife as a resource capable of complementing domestic livestock and will favor neither one above the other in the development of the country. It will rather allow economic processes to determine the outcome of competition" (Government of Zimbabwe 1989, 7).

This is a bold and radical statement and places wildlife outside parks, in the realm of economics and land use rather than that of conservation per se. In effect, the statement asserts what Aldo Leopold said seventy years ago: "Game management is a form of agriculture" (Leopold 1986, 395). This is one of the fundamental conceptual roots of CAMPFIRE, to which we now return.

CONCEPTUAL GENESIS

At Independence in 1980, the demonstrated effectiveness of the new policy was still confined to the commercial, freehold sector. Enacted during the colonial era, the 1975 act conferred proprietorship (or "Appropriate Authority") over wildlife only to white farmers and ranchers. Small-scale black farmers, many of them living in the underdeveloped but wildlife-rich periphery of the country, did not receive the privileges and benefits of the act. It was clearly discriminatory, and in 1982 the government amended the act to allow the minister to appoint an RDC "to be the appropriate authority for such area of Communal Land as may be specified" (Section 95 [1]). The purpose of this amendment was to eliminate discrimination between farmers on private lands and communal-land farmers and to extend the demonstrated economic and environmental benefits of the act to communal-land farmers. The amendment, given the political climate of the day, had no difficulty in passage through parliament. Although, as shall be argued, it failed to address important issues, it was nevertheless a step forward and constituted partial legal enablement for the program that was to develop subsequently. Even at this early stage, the stochastic nature of CAMPFIRE's evolution can be seen retrospectively.

It is, however, one thing to pass enabling legislation and another to realize its intent. The Department of National Parks and Wild Life Management (DNPWLM) was aware of inherent problems in transferring success from the private to the communal-land sector and set itself to the task of creating the conceptual framework and implementational vehicle that could effect this transfer. In the interim, DNPWLM continued to implement a program it had initiated in 1978, designated WINDFALL (Wildlife Industries New

Development for All). The basic premise of WINDFALL was that human-wildlife conflicts would be reduced and attitudes to conservation improved in communal lands if the benefits of wildlife were returned to communities living with wild animals. This was to be done by making meat from culls in the adjacent national parks available to local inhabitants and by returning revenues from safari hunting to the relevant district councils.

WINDFALL largely failed to achieve its objectives. Little meat found its way back to local communities, and only a small proportion of the proceeds survived the circuitous routes of bureaucratic accountancy to return to district councils, let alone to producer communities. More fundamentally, WINDFALL failed to generate local participation in decision making or a sense of local proprietorship. The money that found its way back to source communities was seen as a government handout and conveyed little sense of the relationship between the money and the management of wildlife resources (Murphree 1993a, 135–36).

WINDFALL bore many features that characterize a plethora of CBNRM projects—oblique compensation, resource sharing, convoluted bureaucracy, tenuous linkages between costs and benefits, and nonlocal control. For peasant farmers, it meant a perpetuation of colonial alienation from resources. This was succinctly put to me by one farmer in a WINDFALL area as we discussed his frustration at not being allowed to cultivate good soils on the other side of a game fence next to his household. "Why are they protecting this land for wildlife?" I asked. His wry answer was pregnant with meaning. "Ngekuti mhuka dzinodiwa nge Council ne varungu"(Because wild animals are valued by the Council and whites).

DNPWLM strategists were well aware that WINDFALL was not the vehicle for the replication of game-ranching success in communal lands. They also recognized that the issues involved were more economic and institutional than ecological. They thus sought the advice of economists and social scientists in a dialogue that, over time, coalesced into a conceptual think tank. The discourse in this conceptualization was essentially dialectical. Although the following sequence omits significant details and does some violence to actual chronology, it gives a reasonable summary of the dialectic involved.

Core Problems

The first stage involved the identification of major impediments to the replication in communal lands of the essential institutional profile that provided success—tight proprietorial units that combined ownership, management, and costs and benefits.

- The tenure situation of communal-land farmers was less secure and they were more vulnerable to planning and regulation imposed from outside their communities.
- The appropriate proprietary units analogous to farms and ranches were communities of collective interests; management was therefore more complex. How were they to be defined, and what management structures did they require?
- Legally, these communities still did not have appropriate authority. This had been granted to councils, which are large, heterogeneous administrative units rather than units of production. Wildlife production came from their subunits (VIDCOs or wards [WADCOs]). These units paralleled farms and ranches, but they did not have the same position in law regarding the proprietorship of wildlife. Thus a legal discrimination between private farmers or ranchers and communal-land farmers persisted in regard to wildlife.

Institutional Approach

An institutional formulation was then produced that took into account the game-ranch experience and modified it for the communal-land context. Fundamental to this formulation was a tenurial assumption: it was postulated that neither the current status of state tenure nor the alternative of the individualization of tenure would viably address the requirements for the transplant. State tenure could not provide the required institutional profile, whereas individualization of communal-land holdings, extended to common-pool resources, would result in a fragmentation of management to levels where any possible benefits would be negated. The only viable alternative was a third tenurial category: a societally sanctioned communal common-pool property regime legitimated by title or lease granted to it as a corporate body.[8] Such a communal-property regime is one in which use rights to common-pool resources "are controlled by an identifiable group and are not privately owned or managed by governments; there exists rules concerning who may use the resource, who is excluded from the resource and how the resource should be used" (Berkes and Farvar 1988, 10).

This identification of a communal-property regime with strong tenurial rights as the appropriate management unit in communal-land contexts is the second fundamental conceptual root of CAMPFIRE, following from the first noted previously—the economically instrumentalist approach to wildlife resources. Informed by this perspective, the institutional formulation was shaped at an abstract level in terms of five principles for policy.

- Effective management of natural resources is best achieved by giving it focused value for those who live with them.

This principle encapsulates the propositions that people seek to manage the environment when the benefits of management are perceived to exceed its costs and that local people are the de facto managers of natural resources, whatever de jure assertions exist.

- Differential inputs must result in different benefits.
  This principle relates to the question, value for whom? The answer is those who have the resource and pay for its existence. Natural resource assets are distributed unevenly in any national context, and so too are the costs of sustaining and managing these assets. Policy must ensure therefore that benefits are directly related to inputs.
- There must be a positive correlation between quality of management and the magnitude of benefit.
  The principle that differential inputs require differential benefits not only involves the assets mentioned above but also incorporates management costs, both quantitative and qualitative. A fundamental policy objective is to provide the motivation for good management, thus policy should ensure that good management pays.
- The unit of proprietorship should be the unit of production, management, and benefit.
  Institutionally, this is the only structure that can efficiently combine the preceding principles. Proprietorship (which answers the question, who decides?) cannot be separated from production, management, and benefits and is a fundamental component in any communal-resource regime. The management prerogatives and responsibilities implied in proprietorship need not conflict with larger structures of management activity. Such structures are necessary because of the nature of natural resources, but they should be primarily coordinative and regulatory.
- The unit of proprietorship should be as small as practicable, within ecological and sociopolitical constraints.
  From a social dynamics perspective, scale is an important consideration: large-scale structures tend to be ineffective because they increase the potential for inefficiency, corruption, and the evasion of responsibility. Conversely, a communal-resource management regime is enhanced if it is small enough (in membership size) for all members to be in at least occasional face-to-face contact, to enforce conformity to rules through peer pressure, and for the regime to have a long-standing collective identity.[9]

Note that the first three principles are, in effect, a reformulation of the economically instrumentalist approach of DNPWLM. They deal with incentives and ways to institutionally capture them. The last two principles flow from the advocacy of communal-property regimes, locate them in larger context, and deal with governance.

From Policy to Program

Although the five principles addressed the three problems initially identified, they did not provide details on some of the critical issues that had to be addressed if policy was to be translated into program. They are a statement of optimal conditions not a strategy of implementation. Of particular and immediate importance were the following three questions:

- How could tenurially strong communal-property regimes be created under state tenure in communal lands?
- What were the "communities of collective interest"?
- How could appropriate authority be accorded to management entities that had no status in law?

At this stage, the process of conceptual dialectic could not ignore the imperatives of urgency. Expansion of cultivation into areas of marginal arable viability (described earlier) was proceeding at a rapid pace, foreclosing options for wildlife-production activities of greater economic benefit to the populations concerned. Expectations for the rapid introduction of a new program were high. Ideal conceptions of the future would have to accommodate themselves to the realities of the present.

The result was strategic compromise, embodied in DNPWLM's program document *Communal Areas Management Programme for Indigenous Resources (CAMPFIRE)*, published in revised version in April 1986 (Martin 1986).[10] At this point I will examine the document in respect only to the three strategic questions previously posed.

In respect to the issue of the creation of tenurially strong communal-property regimes under state tenure, the document noted that "the land tenure system may need to be modified to give group ownership of defined tracts of land to resident communities" (p. 14). However, as an immediate implementational measure, the document proposed the formation by communities of "Natural Resource Co-operatives with territorial rights over defined tracts of land called Communal Resource Areas within the Communal Lands" (p. 17). These cooperatives would be formed under the provisions of the Co-operative Societies Act, giving their membership stronger tenurial rights than those provided under the 1982 Communal Lands Act.

In respect to the second question, the identification of communities, the document proposes a strategy of self-definition through a process of dialogue and negotiation (pp. 33–35).

On the issue of the conferment of appropriate authority, the document is strangely silent, possibly because the program was meant to address the use and management of all natural resources[11] and thus could not rest solely on the Parks and Wild Life Act. However, by implication, appropriate authority would still rest with RDCs because the natural resource cooperatives would still be nested within the VIDCO and WADCO structures of local government (pp. 17, 26).

In retrospect, one can see how the document was flawed. Nevertheless, it was a landmark document, impressively detailed and sufficiently persuasive to convince the Ministry of Environment and Tourism to embark on a program with the ultimate objective, in the document's words, of "the realization of an agrarian system able to optimize land-use patterns and maximize group and individual investment and effort" (p. 19).

GAINING ACCEPTANCE: THE TACTICS OF PRAGMATISM

Ministerial endorsement of a program is of course different from support of its implementation. In 1986 DNPWLM had an approved CAMPFIRE Programme but little means of putting it in place. A CAMPFIRE agency located in DNPWLM had been projected in the 1986 document (pp. 30–31), but the cash-strapped department had no funds for it. DNPWLM thus turned for assistance to the agencies that had participated in the program's conceptual development. Among these were CASS at the University of Zimbabwe, which had been assigned a socioeconomic research and evaluative role in appendix 8 of the 1986 document (pp. 104–10). Another was the World Wildlife Fund (WWF) Multispecies Animal Production System Project in Zimbabwe, and a third was the Zimbabwe Trust, a rural-development NGO. This brought together a coalition of partners with different objectives. By their mandates DNPWLM and WWF had a primary conservation objective. The Zimbabwe Trust had an interest in facilitating rural economic and institutional development, and CASS had a mandate for the conduct and application of social science research in the fields of rural development and governance. There were thus multiple objectives in the coalition with the order of means or ends being different. Formally, DNPWLM and WWF were interested in the program as a means to the sustainable use of natural resources. The Zimbabwe Trust saw it as a means to sustainable rural development. For CASS the program provided that relatively rare opportunity in social science methodology, the chance to engage in a natural successional experiment.[12] It also offered a training ground for a new generation of young Zimbabwean social scientists. What was important was that these different formal objectives were complementary and compatible, both programmatically and conceptually.

From 1986 to 1988 DNPWLM and its partner agencies involved themselves in extensive proto-CAMPFIRE discussions with district councils and communities.[13] In part, this was to identify locations for the inception of the program using two main criteria: (1) voluntary interest in participation by communities and district councils and (2) the presence of wildlife populations capable of producing sustainable and economically significant revenues. Regarding the first criterion, the exercise involved extensive debates and meetings over many months. Given the colonial history of wildlife policy, the idea of the program met with a great deal of skepticism from hard-headed communal-land farmers. In some cases the idea was rejected categorically at communal meetings,[14] in others it was sidelined by polite prevarication. However, in certain communities the program gained provisional acceptance after much debate, with each instance having its own particular profile of decision making.[15]

The second criterion, that of the presence of wildlife at economically significant levels, clearly reflects the weight given to economic incentive by the program. Of the natural resources putatively addressed by CAMPFIRE, it was wildlife that could produce high returns with little capital investment within a short time. It followed that the initial test cases should be selected in areas with high wildlife densities. In the event, the combination of these criteria produced an initial focus on Nyaminyami District, Guruve District, and the southern tip of Chipinge District at Mahenye.

During the 1986–1988 period, DNPWLM and its CAMPFIRE partners were also involved in adjusting the program's proposals to meet the views of political and bureaucratic gatekeepers and the demands of institutional and administrative detail. I have already noted that the 1986 program document represented a strategic compromise between concept and policy. For the program to be accepted at this stage further compromises were needed, which reflects the pragmatic tactics that have been a component of CAMPFIRE's evolution. Let me mention three.

Natural Resource Cooperatives

This approach to creating tenurially strong communal regimes in the absence of any radical change in communal-land tenure status was quietly shelved. It became apparent that RDCs would not support such a development, because they saw it (rightly) as a step that would effectively remove areas of communal land from significant aspects of their authority and would appropriate significant revenues currently flowing to them. As recently established local authorities struggling to demonstrate their financial viability in the face of central government cutbacks in budgetary allocations from the central fisc, RDCs were not interested in any de jure devolvement of their control over the management and control of what was, actually or potentially, their greatest source of revenue. The compromise was that RDCs would undertake to effect a de facto devolution of management and revenue.

This rejection of a de jure tenure status for wildlife-production units in communal lands created what is the most significant current weakness of CAMPFIRE: it creates pervasive uncertainties in the perspectives of producer localities regarding the security of any of their investments in sustainability. It undermines the actualization of one of CAMPFIRE's fundamental conceptual roots. It perpetuates the legal discrimination between access rights to wildlife accorded to farmers in the commercial sector and those accorded to communal-land farmers. Finally, by placing devolution at the discretion of councils, it has led to the wide variation in the program's degree of success, because councils have responded to their commitment in different ways.

Defining the Community

The definition and delineation of the communal natural resource property-rights regime (or natural resource cooperative) was, in the program document, to be a task of a process of negotiation and self-definition. Ideally, this would take cognizance of long-established traditional jurisdictions and resource aggregations that made managerial sense, marrying social and ecological topography. Once again, this notion was quietly shelved. There were three main reasons: First, the process would be a massive and drawn-out exercise, for which neither the time nor resources were available. Second, with the scrapping of the natural resources cooperative approach, no legal imperative for delineation was now required. Third and most important, the Ministry of Local Government and the RDCs were committed to the subdistrict structures of wards and VIDCOs that had been delineated after Independence and were hostile to the proposal of a different, socioecologically derived mapping to be superimposed on the communal-land landscape with competing management structures.

The result was again a compromise: CAMPFIRE would operate within the existing subdistrict structures, and the localized unit of management and production would be the ward. Legally, the status of these wards would remain that of lower-tier structures of the RDC, which as the designated appropriate and responsible authority would delegate to wards such aspects of proprietorship as implied by their commitments to the program. This was the easy way out; ready-made structures were on the ground and both councils and the Ministry of Local Government were comfortable with the approach. However, it carried with it the possibilities of dissonance between ecological and social configurations and the seeds of intraward, ward-ward, and ward-council conflicts.

Revenue Distribution

Having won general acceptance for the program through these compromises, DNPWLM remained adamant that the cost-input-benefit linkages of its principles (the second and third principles previously listed) could not be lost, otherwise it would fail. Wards bore the costs of production and they should receive its fruits. As the legal proprietors of wildlife resources, it was the RDCs that entered into the lease arrangements that marketed wildlife and were in receipt of the checks paid out by the concessionaire.[16] They could not be allowed to appropriate such revenues for council purposes without compromising the necessary incentives to producers. RDCs countered that they also bore some of the costs of production—the provision of infrastructure, administration, and district-level wildlife management.

In this situation, DNPWLM fell back on a tactic of conditionality. Guidelines for implementation and revenue distribution would be attached to the conferment of appropriate-authority status to RDCs, and they would have to be followed, with failure penalized by withdrawal of appropriate-authority status. The guidelines for revenue distribution specified that the RDCs could keep 15 percent of revenue as a levy (or tax), and up to 35 percent for district wildlife-management costs, and would distribute not less than 50 percent of revenue to producer communities. The guidelines also specified that it was the wards who should decide how this revenue was used.[17]

With the three accommodations made, the program was now in a form that had the support of all the major gatekeepers, and CAMPFIRE was formally born in October 1988 when two RDCs—Guruve and Nyaminyami—were awarded appropriate-authority status by notice in the Government Gazette. In the process of CAMPFIRE's embryonic transition from concept to acceptance and birth, DNPWLM had conceded on two fundamental points: the legal status and the self-definition of the communal units of management and production. Because it was forced to fall back on conditionality and intent as the instruments to achieve its intended profile, it was at birth a program with inherent defects. At the same time, it gained the inception of an approach that, for all its defects, had the potential to evolve into a close approximation of its conceptual ideal. Whether the pragmatism of these negotiated compromises was appropriate is a matter for debate. It can be argued that it introduced flaws that will ultimately be fatal for the program. It can also be argued that without it CAMPFIRE would still be on the drawing board, a stillborn concept incapable of experimentation, adaptation, and growth. I will return to this theme later.

GROWING UP: THE COSTS AND BENEFITS OF SUCCESS

Overview

With the conferment of appropriate-authority status to the Nyaminyami and Guruve Districts in October 1988 came their right to be in direct receipt of 1988 hunting revenues. The deposit of these monies into the two RDC accounts had a dramatic effect. CAMPFIRE meant cash—significant cash. CAMPFIRE meant real devolution in the ownership of wildlife revenues from central government to RDCs. As a result, the historically underdeveloped but wildlife-rich districts on the periphery of the country lined up for inclusion in the program. They had little to lose and much to gain. By the end of 1989, seven additional districts had received appropriate-authority status. In the national press and in public circles, CAMPFIRE was hailed as a leap forward in rural development, and the program received the ultimate approbation when, in the lead-up to the 1990 general elections, the manifesto of the ZANU-PF ruling party stated that CAMPFIRE had been a party innovation.

By the end of 1991, twelve districts were in the program and had collectively grossed US$1,106,000 in revenue for that year. By 1995 twenty-five districts were in the program and revenues had continued to move upward, that year exceeding US$1,600,000.

This expansion in the program was paralleled by an expansion in national structures to support it. The need for extension services grew and donor moneys flowed in to support them. It is impossible in this chapter to go into the details of the expansion, but one development must be mentioned, that of the establishment and growth of the Campfire Association of District Councils. The Campfire Association was formed in April 1990, full membership being accorded to councils with appropriate authority status, although other councils could have associate membership. In addition to providing various services to its membership, its objectives included the following, which are important to this analysis and are quoted verbatim from the association's constitution: "to promote and protect the rights and interests of Appropriate Authorities and to make such representations and take such steps as may be deemed necessary or desirable in connection therewith for the common interests of the Appropriate Authorities; . . . to encourage the introduction of legislation aimed at further strengthening Appropriate Authorities to better administrate and manage their wildlife resources; . . . to promote the fundamental principle enshrined in the Campfire concept of proprietorship of wildlife resources by producer communities" (Campfire Association 1991, 2–3).

The first two objectives define lobbying functions for the association at the national political center in the interests of member councils. In this regard the record is clear that the association, over the period 1990–1995, did establish itself as a politically salient voice for an important segment of the government's constituency. The third objective introduces an incipient tension in terms of the association's identity: was it to be an association of councils or a producer association?

In summary, CAMPFIRE's growth from 1989 to 1995 can be considered a success, if the criteria used are geographical spread, RDC acceptance and participation, public and political endorsement, revenue generation, and the devolution of the control of this revenue to RDCs. To judge it a success in terms of the realization of its central conceptual objectives—the creation of economic incentives to make wildlife a competitive form of land use where this made ecological and economic sense and to create strong communal-proprietary natural resource regimes—is more problematic because the record shows a wide spectrum of result. The reasons for this I now explore, first by describing a case study of a relative success and then by looking at the factors that have made such instances relatively scarce.

Masoka: A Case Study in Relative Success

Our example of success is Kanyurira Ward, four hundred square kilometers, and its farmer population in the Dande Communal Land of the Guruve District.[18] Kanyurira Ward is the governmental administrative designation for this subunit of the Guruve RDC, which has twenty-four such wards, each with designated and mapped boundaries. Kanyurira is the name of the subchief, but the area is locally and commonly called Masoka, from the name of spirit medium Nemasoka who represents the ancestral spirit owners of the land. In local perspectives, these land spirits have a much larger territory than the ward boundaries of the council map, and their territory includes parts of the neighboring Doma and Chewore Safari areas under state control.[19]

The people of Masoka are residentially clustered along a six-kilometer stretch of the Angwa River, which flows through the ward. In 1988 the settlement was made up of sixty households, with a total population of 482 people.[20] Household subsistence came from dryland cultivation of grains, winter cultivation of riverine lands for maize and vegetables, and some remittances from the export of male labor. The one cash crop, cotton, was grown by 73 percent of households. For most households, net revenue from this source was small because their remote location posed formidable transport and marketing problems. Owing to the presence of tsetse fly, no cattle and only a few goats were present. Some of the population's protein requirements came from poultry, and a larger proportion came from poached game meat that yielded about forty kilograms per person per annum.[21] The benefits of this harvest were, however, balanced in farmers' minds against its costs. Nearly every household experienced regular crop raiding by wildlife, especially elephants, buffalo, wild pigs, baboons, and monkeys. Costs also included personal jeopardy—fourteen households (23.3 percent) reported incidents of injury or death (three deaths) from encounters with wildlife in the previous three years (Cutshall 1989, 28–31).

Modern infrastructural services were almost completely absent. Before

1988 there was no school. The few children whose parents wanted them to have schooling had to walk thirty kilometers on Sundays through the bush to the nearest primary school at Angwa Bridge, where they slept in grass shelters and cooked for themselves during the week, returning home on Fridays. No clinic existed, and the sick had to make the same journey to the clinic at Angwa Bridge.

Since Masoka was a wildlife-rich area, there was a hunting safari camp in the ward. The professional hunter, operating under a concession issued by DNPWLM in Harare, would occasionally provide transport for the seriously ill. He also provided work for five males in the settlement.

In retrospect, we can see how 1988 was a pivotal year in determining the directions the farmers of Masoka would take with their wildlife. Three events were of particular significance. The first was the erection of a two-roomed school in January 1988 by the district council, using wildlife revenues made available to it by DNPWLM through WINDFALL. Researchers from CASS and WWF had previously suggested to the people of Masoka that their wildlife had far higher values than their local takes represented. The erection of the school had a significant impact on the farmers' view of this message. "We see now that you are right," they said, "these buffalo are worth money to us."

But ambivalence remained, spurred by the second major event of 1988. This was the clearance of tsetse fly by aerial spraying in the Zambezi Valley tsetse control program of the European Economic Commission (EEC) (see Derman 1990; Derman and Murombedzi 1994). This opened the way for the introduction of cattle and the encouragement of new settlement by immigrants, who were already flooding into eastern wards of Dande. People were not blind to the fact that cattle and immigrants would over time diminish their wildlife resources, but on balance they were in favor of encouraging immigrants to settle in the ward. Three reasons were put forward: First, immigrants would be allocated lands on the periphery of the settlement and thus take the brunt of crop damage by wildlife. Second, there was plenty of land. Third, more people would mean a better case for Masoka when it appealed to the council for a school, a clinic, transport, and other facilities (Cutshall 1989, 21–23). This last reason is revealing; the farmers of Masoka were still strategizing in the extractive-dependency mode that had been created by colonialism and was still characteristic of center-periphery relationships in much of rural sub-Saharan Africa.

The third significant event was the conferment of appropriate authority status to the Guruve District in October 1988, followed by a series of debates leading to a wildlife-revenue distribution in Masoka the following March. In the council debates over the use of 1988 hunting revenue, two issues were paramount. First, should council appropriate all these revenues and use them in all wards? The ward councilors from wards with no wildlife were not surprisingly in favor of this approach, arguing for equity. Fortunately for Masoka, the council, with the insightful leadership of a council chairman, district executive officer, and district administrator, adopted the principle that "differential inputs must result in differential benefits." The decision was taken that wildlife revenues—less council levies and administrative costs—should be returned to wards in proportion to the safari hunting take (under district-wide quotas) that had been provided by these wards. As a result, Masoka received the lion's share of 1988 hunting revenues distributed to the wards, forty-seven thousand Zimbabwean dollars.

The second issue was what Masoka should do with this forty-seven thousand dollars and who should make this decision. Again, there was an element in these debates that argued that the council should make the decision and that the money should be used for community infrastructure. There were paternalistic and instrumental components to this argument. The people of Masoka were really not sophisticated enough to make decisions regarding such a large amount of money—they would squander it on beer and self-indulgence. And if the council made the allocation and built, for instance, another two classrooms for the school, it would be seen by government as having fulfilled its development responsibilities. Fortunately again for Masoka, and with the enlightened guidance of the leadership just mentioned, the council resolved to give the entire forty-seven thousand Zimbabwean dollars to Masoka and let its people decide what to do with it. Their decision was to declare a wildlife dividend of two hundred Zimbabwean dollars to each household (now numbering sixty-four) and to use the balance to improve their school.

At a ceremony in Masoka in March 1989, a representatives from each household stepped forward and received $200 in cash. The impact was profound. For all households, but particularly for the poorer ones including those headed by widows, the amount was substantial, equivalent to an additional 56 percent on average gross income from cotton. More subjectively, but no less important, perceptions of their wildlife resource were changing. "We see now," said the chief, "that these buffalo are our cattle. We are going to farm them." The resource was valuable and it was theirs to use sustainably.

If the buffalo (and other wildlife) were theirs, how should the resource be managed? CASS and WWF researchers suggested to the Masoka farmers that they needed to do some land-use planning, only to be told in response that they already had a plan "in their heads." Their plan allocated eighteen square kilometers around the settlement for residential and cropping purposes to be surrounded by an electric fence to keep out buffalo and elephant. The plan was submitted to the council for approval, assertively. Their councilor was charged with presenting the proposal to the council: "Tell them that these are our animals and these are our plans. We will not accept any changes imposed by others."

The plan was approved and the fence built during 1989, with funds obtained by WWF.[22] The one technological intervention in the Masoka case study, the fence, was significant in a number of dimensions. First, it worked in its explicit objective. Crop raiding within the fence became insignificant.[23] No deaths and only two injuries from wildlife had occurred since its erection. Second, institutionally, the fence accelerated organizational development for collective resource management because the fence had to be monitored and maintained, which Masoka's wildlife committee did by employing (from wildlife revenues) four uniformed fence minders. Finally, its subjective and attitudinal impact was profound. Wildlife, for the farmers of Masoka, was no longer an uncontrollable and amorphous asset. It was an asset that could be controlled and managed for sustainable benefit. It had, in effect, been semidomesticated and had taken on some of the characteristics of livestock.[24] Sometime after the erection of the fence I asked Masoka farmers if the fence was working. "Marvelously," was the reply. "Only we have some buffalo inside the fence at the moment which were driven in by lions." "How many?" I asked. "Six: two bulls, two cows, and two calves. But no problem, we will drop a section of the fence and drive them out." They were, in fact, living up to their resolve. They were farming their buffalo and, like any good farmer taking inventory of livestock, they were beginning to see buffalo in terms of numbers, sex, and age. Also like good farmers, they were looking after the habitat of their wildlife "livestock." By 1996 Masoka's four hundred square kilometers were under a fire-control regime. A wildlife water-point-development plan had been initiated. There were no snares, species numbers had increased, and Masoka was entering the live-sale market with the sale of roan antelope.

The development of local collective management of wildlife production is, however, only half the picture. Equally important is management of people—internal conflict and deviance—external relations, market conditions, and fiscal management and revenue allocations. In each of these aspects, the Masoka case study provides a wealth of data that cannot be fully analyzed here, but I do want to comment on certain aspects of Masoka's management regime most relevant to this chapter.

- The locus of decision making
  In Masoka the focal point for most, although not all, of this management is the Wildlife Committee, which in practice is merged with the WADCO, government's officially designated unit for local development planning. Typically, in Zimbabwe, WADCOs are weak, since they have no fiscal resources of their own and act primarily as conduits to articulate ward aspirations and requests to district councils. Masoka's relative

and conditional proprietorship of resources and revenues meant that its wildlife committee had significant finance and powers. Membership on the committee was thus important and the subject of intraward political maneuvering, drawing on traditional and modern elective legitimations. Membership has changed considerably over time, and the composition of the committee reflects an organic evolution in response to the demands for administrative and negotiation skills while maintaining its responsiveness to local consensus. There was little doubt that the committee is representative—a survey on this issue showed that 81 percent of the households were satisfied with its decisions.[25] Equally important is that its decisions were primarily responsive to its own local constituency. The committee had been given some facilitative guidance from the district council and NGO agencies, but decisions remained firmly under its control.

- Poaching
  Masoka had developed bylaws that regulated all use of the commonage and that applied to not only terrestrial wildlife but also fish and woodland resources. They had never read Ostrom's "design principles" (1990) but they had "graduated sanctions" that were progressively applied, and one household had been expelled after having been found guilty of setting veld fires three times. But the most effective instrument for bringing compliance was the peer pressure of a tightly knit social group. Poaching was no longer seen as individual and entrepreneurial defiance of state regulations; it was now theft from the community and one's neighbors because it reduced the size of household dividends and collective resources.

- Immigration
  After the 1989 dividend ceremony, attitudes toward immigration began to shift rapidly. Wildlife was valuable, and the more habitat available to it, the greater its numbers and value would be. Wild land thus became more valuable, and it had to be used parsimoniously and made available only for the "children" of Masoka. With Masoka's economic success, many of these children returned, and by 1995 there were 123 households on the dividend list. This listing, this membership in the communal regime, is a valuable economic asset. It was conferred carefully, because the farmers of Masoka could do their arithmetic and knew that the size of the denominator would influence the size of household dividends in any given year.

- Managing market relations
  The farmers of Masoka enthusiastically entered the market for wildlife resources. Their preference for subsistence usage of these resources was,

in their calculations, displaced by the realization that the safari market provided components that made the value of a gracefully bounding impala far higher than its meat value. In 1990 the district council, in an effort to sell CAMPFIRE throughout Dande, instituted a cropping program to provide wards with a limited amount of fresh meat. When the cropping team came to Masoka, it was told to leave. Farmers preferred the safari price of an impala, which would buy ten goats, the team was informed.

Masoka still does not have control of the hunting-concession lease, which under current legislation remains in the hands of the council. They are thus not ultimately responsible for negotiating with the market. But they are quickly mastering the details of their market[26] and exercise their authority to the extent permitted. Out of their wildlife revenues, they employed four game scouts who monitored all safari hunts. The records of the safari operator and district council were carefully checked against their own. A healthy realization had developed among both the farmers and the operator that success for both depended on mutual cooperation.

- Allocation of wildlife revenues

  Wildlife revenue allocations by the farmers of Masoka for the years 1990–1995 are shown in table 4.5. The table aggregates the fifteen line items of Masoka's budget prepared annually into the three categories of resource management, household dividends or food relief, and community projects. The household dividends or food relief category includes direct cash payments to households, and in some years funds are used collectively to purchase grain for distribution to households.

Table 4.5 underscores the following points:

- The value of Masoka's off-farm wildlife resource was significant and was escalating as market values rose and their resource management improved. By entering an export-oriented and foreign exchange–generating market, these farmers were capitalizing on the comparative international advantages that their large mammal populations provide.
- This exploitation of an off-farm natural resource was highly significant for the household economies involved. Per-household cash revenues from wildlife by 1995 were more than double the average household income from their other cash crop, cotton. There was, furthermore, an equity impact. Cotton production was highly uneven in Masoka, with revenues ranging from zero to forty thousand Zimbabwean dollars. Wildlife revenues were distributed equally among households on the membership list.

Table 4.5 Masoka Wildlife Revenues and Budget Allocations, 1990–1995 (in Z$)

		Budget Allocations		
Year	*Revenues (After deduction of council levies)*	*Rescurce management*	*Household dividends/ drought relief*	*Community projects*
1990	78,170	10,260 (13%)	25,200 (32%)	42,710 (55%)
1991	89,293	7,798 (8%)	69,677 (78%)	11,818 (13%)
1992	276,745	44,279 (16%)	10,640 (4%)	221,826 (80%)
1993	459,891	65,599 (14%)	127,000 (28%)	267,292 (59%)
1994	639,290[1]	138,290 (22%)	165,000 (26%)	336,000 (52%)
1995	526,593	115,200 (22%)	140,000 (26%)	271,393 (53%)

Note: 1. Includes $120,000 from one-off live sale of twelve roan antelope.
Sources: Masoka Wildlife Committee and Guruve District Council records.

- The farmers of Masoka were reinvesting a significant proportion of their wildlife revenues in the management of the revenue.
- By entering the wildlife market, these farmers were reducing their vulnerability to the vagaries of drought and growing conditions. Note that 1991 revenues were allocated at nearly 80 percent for household dividends and drought relief, because of an almost complete crop failure in the 1991–1992 growing season. By contrast, 1992 revenues were used primarily for the development of local infrastructure because of good crops from the 1992–1993 growing season. In other words, they were shrewdly using their wildlife revenues flexibly, in good crop years for collective development, in years of crop failure as food security. Their preference, when conditions permitted, was to tilt revenue allocations toward collective infrastructure, and by 1996 Masoka had a six-room school and a new Z$350,000 clinic, all planned and paid for by themselves. Not one penny of government or donor aid had gone into these buildings, and Masoka's sense of self-accomplishment was perhaps as important an output as the services these buildings provided. They were, in effect, lifting themselves out of the extractive-dependency mode mentioned earlier. This is an essential element in any program aimed at sustainability.

The Masoka case study is one of relative and conditional success in linking sustainable wildlife use and rural development through local empowerment. It is relative because Masoka's empowerment has not yet reached the stage of legally backed proprietorship. It is conditional because Masoka's empowerment remains dependent on the council's continued devolution of de facto authority and responsibility to the ward. The people of Masoka are well aware of this conditionality. In one discussion of their budget allocations, a participant commented, "In times of drought we have to use our wildlife revenues for household food needs. But when the crops are good we use as much money as possible to improve our community, because we do not know how long government will let us keep our wildlife."

Constraints to Generalized Success

As noted, instances of relative success such as Masoka are scarce. By 1996 the nationwide performance of CAMPFIRE showed a wide spectrum of approximation to its ideal, ranging from a few examples similar to Masoka to instances of almost complete negation, with most on-the-ground situations falling somewhere between and each with its own complex combination of determining variables. Of the factors that constrained success I mention seven:

- *Devolution conditionally and through persuasion rather than statutory mandate.* The delegation of proprietorship to RDCs on the basis of intent and guidelines gave them wide discretion given their statutory powers. The threat of the withdrawal of appropriate authority status in cases of nonconformity was relatively hollow, as RDCs realized. As a result some RDCs had appropriated the bulk of the revenues generated by their producer communities, made promises they had not kept, marginalized any participation in wildlife planning and management by communities, and created hypertrophic district-level wildlife management structures that served the interests of RDC bureaucracies. They had, in effect, replicated the extractive pattern of the older colonially generated policies of the state at district levels. In such instances, the decentralization of CAMPFIRE has become the recentralization of a district-level elite (Murombedzi 1992; Hill 1996). The result has been ignorance of or hostility toward CAMPFIRE, mistrust of the councils concerned, increasing intolerance of wildlife in localities, and a continued lack of communal environmental controls.
- *Imposition.* The integrity of CAMPFIRE's conceptualization rests, inter alia, on the self-definition and voluntary participation of localized natural resource-management entities. This aspect was compromised by the designation of preexisting, administratively designed wards as the

communal production units. In some instances, where the profile of socioecological topography[27] was suitable, this compromise worked, as it has at Masoka. In many instances, however, ward boundaries do not supply this profile. Wards are often internally differentiated socially and ecologically and lack the cohesion to motivate consensual entry into the program (see Moore 1996; Dzingirai 1996). This has been the case particularly in wards with histories of recent migration. Councils on the other hand have had strong economic motivations to expand wildlife land and in several instances have imposed their district versions of the program, relocating settlement to make way for contiguous wildlife areas (see Madzudzo 1997; Nabane, Dzingirai, and Madzudzo 1996). Such cases are the prescription for council wildlife-utilization programs not communal wildlife-management regimes.

- *The differential contexts of economic incentive.* A conceptual assumption of the program is that high wildlife values, combined with collective interests, can create the necessary incentives for individual or household participation. However, the program has not fully addressed intracommunal differentiation or the difference between household and communal economic strategies with their inherent implications for incentive. A community may, for instance, reach the conclusion that buffalo provide greater collective economic value for the use of their range than do cattle and have a collective incentive to move into wildlife production. This value is, however, realized through collective receipts and finds its way back to households through the filter of communal decision making. At the household level the farmer, although recognizing the higher value of buffalo compared with cattle, may nevertheless wish to opt for cattle because cattle are individually owned and the disposal of worth is at the farmer's sole discretion. Murombedzi (1994) has suggested that under small-holder agricultural conditions prevailing in communal lands cattle are a main form of household accumulation. Unless CAMPFIRE revenues at household levels are sufficient to offset the perceived loss of the accumulative potential of livestock, the program is likely to encounter opposition at these levels. His research suggests that this opposition is likely to be particularly strong in wealthier households (p. 280), a conclusion supported by Madzudzo's research (Madzudzo 1995a).
- *Resource-demand ratios.* This is an issue tightly related to the preceding factor. CAMPFIRE benefits in cash and kind (community infrastructure) at household levels are clearly related to these ratios and are highest where human population densities are low and wildlife resources high. Within the program districts these ratios differ widely. Bond's 1993 data show that all wards in the program earning more than two hundred thousand Zimbabwean dollars had population densities of less

than twenty persons per square kilometer.[28] This could lead to the conclusion that the program can truly be successful only in certain favorable demand-ratio contexts, especially if it continues to be based primarily on economic incentive.

- *Devolution in value appropriation.* The devolution of revenue appropriation from state to councils and from councils to producer communities (at various levels, see the first factor) is demonstrable in the program's history. Whether this has meant a devolution of resource value in real terms has been questioned. At the state level the state had foregone direct revenues from safari hunting but had maintained the base for a rapidly expanding taxed tourism industry, suggesting a win-win arrangement for both the state and district councils. At the council level the program has provided revenues from a commodity that previously had little financial value to councils, leading Hill to perceptively comment that CAMPFIRE "not only is a wildlife program; it is also very much a rural taxation program" (1996, 116). At the local level the possibility remains that real appropriation of value can be siphoned away. For instance, Masoka has built its own clinic in a policy climate where it assumed that this is a government council responsibility. This is in effect a government council savings, and if these savings are used to build a clinic elsewhere this is an indirect reappropriation of value. CAMPFIRE communal regimes are not unaware of this, but the inherent contradictions between the concurrent policy stances of self-reliance and government paternalism in communal lands has not as yet been resolved. In the absence of such resolution, the incentive dynamic of the program is diluted.
- *The politics of resource appropriation.* The high and escalating values of the wildlife resource have had the effect of intensifying political conflict over the appropriation of these values at community, district, and national levels. Within communities and districts the program has brought into sharper focus competing interests drawn on class, status, and ethnic lines (see Madzudzo 1995b; Dzingirai 1996). At the national level the economic performance of the industry has attracted the attention of the political elite and their private-sector allies, who seek to appropriate a higher share of its value through patronage, shrewd negotiation, or bureaucratic recentralization. CAMPFIRE, which from its initial conceptualization had profound political implications, has through its relative successes now become a high-profile arena of political maneuvering with outcomes that will remain dynamic and dependent on the strength of its constituency.
- *Vertical compartmentalization in legislation and agency responsibility.* Legislatively, CAMPFIRE has been based largely on the Parks and Wild Life Act as amended. Other resources, notably forestry and water

resources, fall under different legislation and are served by other government agencies. Beyond this a number of other government ministries have jurisdictional responsibilities relevant to the program, including the Ministry of Agriculture.

This vertical compartmentalization of resource jurisdictions is one of the reasons CAMPFIRE, in concept and name a holistic program encompassing all natural resources, has in practice been a program focused on wildlife, fisheries, and tourism. In local contexts such as Masoka, communities have ignored these divisions and have placed all natural resources under the control of the ward wildlife committees. Mineral resources constitute an important appropriation issue in some districts and wards as their constituencies watch valuable exports from their land with little or no value returned to them. The CAMPFIRE Association is now beginning to lobby for the transfer of mineral rights to their members. The Mines and Minerals Act is one of the most entrenched pieces of Zimbabwean legislation, and with the high values involved, its amendment to accommodate approaches of local proprietorship is likely to cause intense center-periphery conflict.

Devolution as conceptualized in CAMPFIRE requires a much wider legislative base than the current Parks and Wild Life Act. Strategically, the program needs to shift its government linkages to a broader spectrum of ministries. The CAMPFIRE Association is aware of this, and is attempting to form alliances with farmer associations and closer communication with the Forestry Commission and the Ministries of Agriculture and Lands.

The seven issues discussed above are among the primary factors constraining a pan-national success profile for the program. They are CAMPFIRE's clay feet, arising from conceptual gaps, implementational compromise, and paradoxically, its elements of success. They have been outlined in a form that masks the fact that the program has made progress in dealing with some of them. Particularly in regard to the first two, it should be noted that revenue retention by some councils has progressively dropped and that imposition in implementation is diminishing (see Madzudzo 1997). They nevertheless remain high on CAMPFIRE's evolutionary agenda and must inform any attempt to use the program as a model elsewhere.

PROLIFERATION OF THE MODEL

CAMPFIRE has been developed in a national context by nationals for a national objective. What has never been intended is the packaged export of the program in its specifics to other countries. It cannot be denied, however, that CAMPFIRE's core conceptual foundations have been vigorously propounded in international debates. Nor can it be denied that, within the southern African region, its principles have influenced policy directions in neighboring countries. A regional Southern Africa Development Community (SADC)[29] conference held in Botswana in April 1995 on CBNRM used CAMPFIRE's five principles as the framework for a comparative analysis of initiatives in member states. The report of this conference (Rihoy 1995) shows wide regional variation in programmatic detail and considerable variation in policy alignment with the principles. Two countries, Botswana and Namibia, came closest to Zimbabwe in policy congruence. This congruence arises in part from certain similarities in their wildlife policy histories and their land tenure situations. It also stems from conceptual discourse between their wildlife policy makers and those of Zimbabwe, which has been fairly constant and intense.[30] Thus the development of CBNRM programs in the three countries is best seen as a case of parallel evolution conceptually linked by continuous dialogue. This section briefly compares aspects of CBNRM policy and performance in Botswana and Namibia with that of Zimbabwe's CAMPFIRE. It concludes with a brief examination of a different mode of proliferation, encapsulated in a case study of communication across the Zimbabwe-Mozambique border.

Botswana

While exhibiting a significantly different ecological profile, Botswana shares with Zimbabwe a situation of significant wildlife resources located on state or communal lands. White-settler land appropriation has never had the policy prominence that it has had in Zimbabwe, and up until the 1960s low human population densities meant that little pressure was placed on wildlife populations in most of the tribal or communal lands. Competition over wildlife habitat rose sharply after Independence in 1964 as national elites rapidly expanded their land accumulation for livestock pasturage.[31] Competition over the wildlife resource itself rose sharply in the 1970s with the development of the safari industry and a rapid escalation in wildlife values. This competition was exacerbated by a rise in meat hunting by an emergent national elite equipped with modern equipment. Under the existing legislation, access to this type of hunting was relatively open, and local communities experienced the frustration of having their land base eroded and their wildlife exploited without benefit to themselves. Thus the central problem of wildlife policy strategists was similar to that faced in Zimbabwe: the loss of wildlife habitat and the potential foreclosure of a high-value land use option through a lack of incentive structures for localized sustainable management and use.

Their response was a CBNRM policy similar in its essentials to the

CAMPFIRE approach. As in Zimbabwe, the transition from policy to program and implementation underwent a long gestation period. The land tenure context for the realization of communal property-rights regimes was somewhat different. Land authorities in Botswana are the District Land Boards, whose spatial jurisdictions (in the relevant areas) are far larger than RDC jurisdictions in Zimbabwe. Their devolution of rights and responsibilities over land and wildlife to communities required extended negotiation. In the event, the Botswana version of the Zimbabwean compromise was agreement that the land boards would provide long-term (ten-year) leases of designated land to communities at nominal rates. These communities would then be legally entitled to lease tourism concessions and hunting rights to operators at market rates (Rihoy 1995, 112–13). In essence, this arrangement is remarkably similar to the natural resources cooperative approach originally proposed for CAMPFIRE. The first such entity, or community trust, was established in the Chobe enclave in 1994, comprising the five villages. Such community trusts have stronger legal proprietorship than do wards in CAMPFIRE, and in this dimension Botswana can be said to have more closely approximated the communal property-rights regime ideal than Zimbabwe.

Namibia

The evolution of Namibia's wildlife policy closely parallels that of Zimbabwe. The owners of alienated commercial farms and ranches were accorded use rights over wildlife in 1967. This devolution, reinforced by the Nature Conservation Ordinance (No. 4 of 1975), was based on the landowner meeting certain requirements, including boundary game fencing. As in Zimbabwe, the wildlife industry boomed into a multimillion-dollar game-farming, tourist, and hunting enterprise. Economic and ecological considerations dictated that collaboration between game farms and ranches was desirable, and in 1991 the Ministry of Environment and Tourism produced a policy encouraging such collaboration in voluntary units called conservancies. The ministry's policy document defined a conservancy as "a group of farms on which neighboring landowners have pooled their resources for the purpose of conserving and utilizing wildlife on their combined properties. The conservancy concept does not have to be restricted to the commercial farming areas, but can be extended to communal land as well" (Namibia 1995, 2).

The last sentence of this quote indicates the intent to transplant commercial land wildlife industry success to communal lands, in many dimensions replicating the CAMPFIRE approach. Indeed the rationalizations for this approach cite CAMPFIRE's five principles (Namibia 1975, 7).

However, Namibia's conditions are different, including the fact that to date lower-tier structures of governance in communal lands are not as clearly defined as they are in Zimbabwe. Thus policy has used the conservancy model to create the management context for wildlife and natural resources in communal lands. The promulgation of the 1996 Nature Conservation Amendment Act provides that "any group of people residing on communal land and which desires to have the area which they inhabit, or any part thereof, to be declared a conservancy shall apply to the Minister of Environment and Tourism . . . ('conservancy' means any area declared a conservancy in terms of section 24A(2) (ii)—notice in the gazette giving boundaries)" (Namibia 1996, 4).

Thus, through application to the minister to have their land designated a conservancy, a community can acquire the authority necessary under Namibian wildlife legislation to manage and utilize wildlife and natural resources within the designated conservancy area. The group's membership must be listed and must be structured as a conservancy committee, served by a conservancy constitution. The key institutional ingredients are listed membership, a constitution, designated boundaries, administrative and financial competence, sustainable management and utilization objectives, accountability, and transparency. The minister retains regulatory oversight and ultimately may use such external sanctions as withdrawal of recognition, amendment, or withdrawal of conditions.

By pushing forward this conservancy legislation in advance of any definitive legislation on lower-tier structures of local governance, Namibia has avoided the "socio-ecological topography" dissonance introduced into CAMPFIRE by its designation of wards as the collective units of wildlife proprietorship. Whether this preemption is followed by local government legislation remains to be seen. Furthermore, the conservancy legislation confers communal use rights over wildlife and tourism resources only. It does not confer communal tenure over land itself, and in this respect Namibia's CBNRM status resembles that of Zimbabwe's CAMPFIRE.

Mozambique

Botswana and Namibia are cases where conceptual cross-fertilization has taken place between CAMPFIRE and other regional CBNRM approaches at the level of agency officials, planners, and scholars. As programs have developed, exchange visits between local-level leadership have also taken place. The cross-border Zimbabwe-Mozambique example taken up here falls in a somewhat different category, in that the initiation of a pilot CBNRM project involved, at an early stage, communal leadership in the exchange of perspectives and the specifics of planning.

Mozambique, with its colonial legacy of highly centralized administration and distracted by a long civil war, did not begin to give serious policy attention to devolution issues until the beginning of the 1990s. Within the wildlife sector the government agency involved (DNFFB, the National Directorate of Forestry and Wildlife in the Ministry of Agriculture) was interested in CBNRM and, together with other agencies (in particular the Ministry of the Environment and the Institute for Rural Development, INDER) convened meetings in Maputo that solicited regional profiles of policy and experience on the approach. Political flux and capacity constraints have, however, meant that explicit national policy shifts have been slow in emerging.

In this context, government has taken a cautious, experimental approach. Legislation has been enacted allowing the decentralization of resource management and retention of benefits to provincial and district levels. The extension of this decentralization to community levels is now under pilot-project experimentation in a number of modes and sites. One example is the community of Bawa in the Tete Province, located on the border with Zimbabwe. The project, locally titled Tchuma Tchato (our wealth), is facilitated by a DNFFB officer and has been supported by the IUCN, International Development Research Centre (IDRC), and the Ford Foundation. As Cruz comments, "It is an interesting feature of evolving CBNRM in Mozambique that policy and legal changes are taking place in tandem with implementation (and sometimes led by projects) as opposed to the more usual development of policy and legal aspects prior to programs. Given the complex political, policy, and legal changes occurring in Mozambique, pilot programs will probably continue to play an important role in advancing the policy and legal framework for CBNRM in Mozambique" (1995, 207).

To return to the theme of this section, the Tchuma Tchato project provides an example of lateral cross-fertilization between communities themselves. Initiated at the end of 1994, external facilitators first encountered the mix of interest and skepticism typical of much of CAMPFIRE's experience. Community opinion oscillated between acceptance and rejection from meeting to meeting as collective and individual assessments attempted to weigh the implications of implementation. An important event leading to acceptance and participation was a three-day exchange visit between the natural resources council of Bawa and the wildlife committee of Masoka. In its first phase, the Masoka committee visited Bawa and, having introduced their approach and experience to a general meeting, answered a broad range of incisive questions with equally incisive answers. In the second phase, the Bawa council traveled to Masoka, examined their management techniques, and had another round of debate with the Masoka wildlife committee. I was privileged to attend these meetings as an observer, and what struck me was the conceptual insight and grasp of implementational detail that characterized them. Many of the issues raised in this chapter were touched on and debated in a local and experiential idiom far more powerful than the abstractions of professional intellectual discourse.

This example has profound implications for proliferation. The mode of extension it represents is the only one that has the built-in resources to comprehensively reach down to the multitude of locality contexts of the region. Beyond this, it is the most effective mode. In the rural settings of CBNRM the messenger is as important as the message. The tests required for acceptance and involvement are those of similar experience, as much emic as etic. Similarity in social location provides a communicative channel that is closed to others, however adept they may be in professional techniques.

CAMPFIRE AS A MODEL? FINAL REFLECTIONS

CAMPFIRE was conceived and has been developed in a Zimbabwean context, and its contextual specificity has been further sharpened in that it has sought to transfer a successful policy innovation in one tenure category to another. Its history thus reflects a situational focus and is inherently an argument against making it a generic approach. It cannot serve as a model in its specifics, and any attempt to have it do so would be self-contradictory. If it has value for other similar approaches, this value must be sought in some of its more general features. To comment on these, I return to the title of this chapter.

Congruent Objectives

CAMPFIRE's central objectives—ecological sustainability, economic efficiency, and institutional effectiveness and acceptability—are congruent. This congruency is not, however, unique to CAMPFIRE. This is a general configuration of compatible objectives and constitutes much of the appeal for CBNRM approaches universally.

What singles out CAMPFIRE from the generality of CBNRM approaches in this congruence is the robust form in which it has been conceptualized. This takes two forms. First, its analysis is a grounded one, taking as its starting point objective realities and constraints and then examining alternatives and seeking a direction rationalized on the basis of viability. Secondly, it takes the congruence of its objectives but prioritizes their means and sequence differently from those of most CBNRM approaches that have common currency. To date, most CBNRM approaches that have had international inception and support have been cryptoconservationist in their motivational core. A dissonance then arises in that, current state endorsements of the international prioritization of environmental concerns notwithstanding, the real priorities of these states are in the sphere of economic growth. CBNRM approaches are therefore consistently accorded second-order prioritization in the national contexts where they are implemented. A further dissonance arises in national contexts. Governments are interested in economic growth, centrally led and controlled. At local levels the priorities are the appropriation of power and value from the center. CAMPFIRE in its conceptual core prioritizes congruent objectives in terms of local appropriation as a means of economic growth and economic rationality as an incentive for ecological sustainability, thus reversing the means–end sequence implicit in many CBNRM approaches.

Competing Interests

Most if not all initiatives for change involve competing interests, but they are typically put forward in a guise that masks this. CAMPFIRE, in its conceptualization if not always in its implementation, has always recognized that it is about power, about center-periphery relationships, about resource and value allocations. It is, in other words, about politics. For the situation in which its primary constituency lives it is inherently revolutionary. This situation is one where small-scale farmers exist in fiefdoms of bureaucracy under tenurially discriminatory conditions, in a system where "title deeds are the emblems of competence, and communal land ownership the badge of incompetence" (Parker 1993, 3). CAMPFIRE contains the seeds of a change in this situation and in this dimension its implications reach far beyond its stated congruent objectives. This is both its strength, in terms of its synergy with mounting pressures for the further development of civil society in Zimbabwe, and also constitutes an obstacle to success as elite centers of power and privilege resist change.

Strategic Compromise

Conceptualized with a profile inherently political, CAMPFIRE has been implemented politically. This has involved the acceptance of strategic compromise as a political imperative in process. In this acceptance, has it introduced crippling and ultimately fatal flaws or has it provided the basis for stochastic and progressive change? Any categorical conclusion on this question is elusive but I instance one development that may indicate the latter.

From 1 November 1993 through 15 November 1994, a Presidential Commission of Inquiry into Appropriate Agricultural Land Tenure Systems under the chairmanship of Professor M. Rukuni carried out a comprehensive review of the topic, in an exercise that included hearings at more than eighty locations in communal lands. Its findings, presented to parliament in May 1994, constitute a landmark document with wide implications for Zimbabwean policy (Government of Zimbabwe 1994). For our purposes it is sufficient to note that the commission paints a dark picture of resource degradation in communal lands and singles out CAMPFIRE as the one approach that has provided the incentive for communities to "manage and use their natural resources sustainably" (vol. 1, 29). In its recommendations the commission suggests that security of tenure "should improve if the State relinquishes the *de jure* ownership of Communal Land and passes on full rights to village communities" (vol. 1, 49).

> The Commission strongly recommends that government recognize the traditional village, which should be constituted under the kraalhead as the basic unit of social organisation in Communal Areas. Members of a traditional village should be given formal perpetual rights over all land resources in each village. A schedule of rightful members of the village community needs to be maintained and regularly updated on permanent record. The village community must have the discretion to accept or reject new persons or families wishing to enter its community.
>
> The Commission recommends that the administrative functions on land and natural resources be shifted from Village Development Committees (VIDCOs) to the traditional village where the structure of a village "Dare" (Shona) "Inkundla" (Ndebele) is to be formalised to act as the local land, water and natural resources board. (vol. 1, 50–51)

Thus the conceptual foundations of CAMPFIRE reemerge, in a broader arena and a higher forum. Government has stated its acceptance of the commission's recommendations in principle. Whether they are translated into policy and legislation remains to be seen and will depend on, among other things, the assertiveness of the constituency for which they were made.

Ian Parker, with his usual pithy cynicism, wrote in 1993 a brief essay on why CAMPFIRE would fail. He found its fatal flaw to be the discrimination in ownership status of communal farmers that the program had accepted in its strategic compromises. He concluded, "Hopefully the dichotomy in policy is transient: a stepping stone to conceding the benefits of full ownership. Yet if it sticks halfway—as at present—the CAMPFIRE programs will stress to the owners what they are missing—not what they are getting. And for this reason the project will fail" (Parker 1993, 3).

I share with Parker the sentiment of his first sentence. I agree with the analysis of the second. But I part company with him on the conclusion of the third. To the farmers of communal lands, the delineation of what they are missing is a critical step in the escalation of their assertiveness. CAMPFIRE's role in raising this assertiveness and channeling its voice may, in retrospect, constitute its greatest contribution to Zimbabwe's societal progress.

AFTERWORD

Written for presentation in 1997, this chapter is an analysis of CAMPFIRE's inceptive history, 1984–1996. That history has not changed, and the validity of the analysis has, I believe, stood up to the test of subsequent developments. Where it has proved inadequate in emphasis or coverage I have avoided the temptation to massage the text to make it seem more prescient that it was.

Since 1997 Zimbabwe has experienced radical political-economic changes that have inevitably affected CAMPFIRE's profile and performance. To thoroughly review these impacts and results is beyond the scope of this afterword, but a brief summary of some critical elements may enhance our understanding of how context dependent and vulnerable programs such as CAMPFIRE are.

First, one should note that since 1997 Zimbabwe has experienced a major decline in its national economic performance. Real gross domestic product (GDP), which stood at 8.7 percent in 1996, has now fallen into negative territory. The percentage of the total population in formal employment, 18 percent in 1995, is now less than 10 percent. Annual inflation, which had reached 60 percent by 2000, has now spiraled out of control and is estimated to exceed 1,000 percent. Linked to this adverse economic shaft, and fed by perceptions of political instability, has been a sharp decline in Zimbabwe's international tourism industry, with many hotels reporting occupancy rates of less than 30 percent. Interestingly, the hunting safari tourism component has remained far more robust, and in this dimension CAMPFIRE has to an extent been insulated from the general economic turmoil. Far more seriously, for CAMPFIRE, has been its impact on household livelihood strategies. A shrinking labor market in the formal sector has led to urban–rural migration. Masoka, for instance, (see previous discussion) now has more than 400 households compared with the 123 present in 1995. This is in part due to natural population growth and the immigration of outsiders attracted by the success of Masoka's wildlife enterprise, but it is also the result of an influx of households that claim residence in Masoka on the basis of extended kinship. This has increased pressure on the natural resources and institutional controls of Masoka's program. That Masoka and a handful of other communities in the program continue to maintain successful wildlife enterprises is indicative of their resource richness and institutional resilience. More generally, however, CAMPFIRE communities are struggling to maintain their programs in a context where immediate survival needs outweigh any concerns for ecological or institutional sustainability. As Bond states, "Falling real incomes have forced, and will continue to force, both rural and urban house-holds to exploit natural resource capital as their only possible alternative. Under these conditions effective institutional change for the management of natural resources will be very difficult to achieve" (2001, 242).

A second development of particular note is land acquisition under the government's fast-track resettlement program, which started at the end of

1999. The statistics in table 4.2 are now obsolete; by the middle of 2003 most of what had formerly been classified as commercial farm land had been announced as state resettlement land. A clear profile of land- and resource-use patterns on this resettlement land has yet to evolve, and it is not certain what proportion will be managed under collective or individualized regimes. It is reasonable to predict that the exploitation of wildlife in the commoditized CAMPFIRE mode is unlikely to be an important land-use choice in resettlement lands except in regions IV and V. Here the program will face new challenges and opportunities either in its current communal form or through collaborative arrangement between different landholders.

With these all-embracing changes in the Zimbabwean economic and tenurial landscape, CAMPFIRE's road to maturity has not been straightforward or easy. Indeed it might be expected that its impact would be in decline. However, recent professional evaluations of the program's performance on ecological and economic grounds have been surprisingly positive. Wildlife populations have been stable or increasing in CAMPFIRE areas during a period when poaching has severely reduced wildlife in areas affected by the land-acquisition program. CAMPFIRE's direct contribution to national income is estimated to be at least ten million U.S. dollars annually, and when the multiplier effect on tourism, local industry, and employment is added, this figure rises to more than twenty million U.S. dollars per year.

This ecological and economic success has not, however, been matched by progress in proprietorial devolution to subdistrict communal levels in either its financial or legal dimensions. Dispersals of direct CAMPFIRE revenues to producer communities by RDCs reached a high point of 60 percent in 1996; since then this percentage has steadily declined and now stands at 38 percent. The incentives for RDC retention of CAMPFIRE revenues have been reinforced by a loss of tax revenue from commercial farms eliminated by the land-acquisition exercise, the general economic decline, and a situation in which wildlife revenues exceed all other sources of local income for many RDCs (Bond 2001, 233). At the formal and legal level, the centralist policies of government have steadfastly assisted jurisdictional devolution to levels below the RDCs, which remain essentially decentralized units of the government hierarchy. Government has thus subverted the devolutionary essence of CAMPFIRE into a recentralizing strategy where, as Murombedzi puts it, "the top-down preferences of central governments on communities have merely been replaced by the top-down preferences of local governments on communities" (Murombedzi 2001, 255).

In retrospect, it can be suggested that the chapter's analysis failed to give sufficient attention to the critical linkage between national macroeconomic health and successful community initiatives in natural resource proprietorship. The local and the national are inextricably linked in their economic fortunes, and communal enterprises cannot proceed in isolation from the environing economic climate. Where the analysis got it right, however, was in its emphasis on the pivotal importance of devolution and the formidable obstacles to its achievement (see discussion of factors constraining generalized success). At its core, CAMPFIRE is about the realignment of jurisdictional mapping in natural resource use and management in response to motivational and institutional imperatives. Currently, CAMPFIRE remains a case study in aborted devolution—a devolution that has proceeded far enough to make its retrenchment politically difficult but not far enough to fully liberate the dynamic of its potential. The jurisdictional remapping that is required remains incomplete, held in a stasis of strategic and political compromise that is likely to be broken only when macropolitical changes introduce a more participative democracy where rural peoples enjoy concrete economic rights and are empowered to shape these to local opportunities and aspirations.

NOTES

1. Originally prepared for presentation in 1997, this paper focuses on the program's first inceptive thirteen years, 1984–1996.

2. Compare with Brandon and Wells 1992.

3. Hill remarks that "indeed very little research exists on the ability of CAMPFIRE to bring about true institutional change and to facilitate local decision-making in the rural areas" (1996, 114). To anyone familiar with this research, this statement is astonishing. It may in part be a function of a protracted period between writing and publication. Hill's references include no items published after 1992.

4. This agroecological mapping has formed the basis for much of national policy and planning. Although having considerable analytic utility, its aggregated characteristics mask microecological variation and can inhibit consideration of the full range of factors necessary for adequate planning. As noted by Moyo, "In reality, numerous conflicts exist between expected and real land uses because the zones are not based as they should be, on human requirements and technological developments, reflecting a static approach to planning and little commitment for investment to change and improving the environment" (1991, 3).

5. For elaboration see Arrighi 1973; Murphree 1975, 245–76; and Palmer 1977, 221–33.

6. For a detailed analysis of this history see Murombedzi 1994, 23–50.

7. This approach was not new. It had been propounded by Aldo Leopold in the United States in the 1930s to (largely) deaf ears (Leopold 1986).

8. The analytic pedigree of this formulation in common property theory will be apparent. Note that a communal property regime is a type of common property regime. They are not synonymous, although analysis frequently conflates the two.

9. The five principles are stated, with minor modification, in Murphree 1993b, 6–7.

10. This was a revised version based on earlier drafts; see Metcalfe 1994, 164.

11. Wildlife, forestry, grazing, and water are specified (p. 12).

12. Social science generally operates under a comparative constraint in that it is not able to experimentally manipulate variables in the manner of, for example, chemistry or biology. Furthermore, its ethos is generally adverse to social manipulation for experimental purposes. Its analysis of process is thus usually retrospective. The natural successional experiment is one in which a long-term institutional development profile can reasonably be predicted, with critical variables identified at the outset and then tracked diachronically.

13. For a more detailed history, see Metcalfe 1994.

14. An instance is Simuchembu in Gokwe North (CASS 1989). For a later period, Madzudzo 1995b and Dzingirai 1997 record details of initial communal rejection. Alexander and McGregor 1996 provide an extreme instance from the 1994–1995 period in Nkayi and Lupane Districts.

15. For descriptive case studies see Child and Peterson 1991 and Peterson 1991.

16. To date, CAMPFIRE revenues have derived primarily from international sport hunting marketed by professional operators. Concession fees for the lease of nonconsumptive tourism ventures are now a growing component of total revenues in districts that have the scenic environments to attract it.

17. The guidelines also specified that DNPWLM would initially set take quotas. When RDCs and wards had attained sufficient training and experience, quota setting would then become their prerogative. Subsequently, DNPWLM issued revised guidelines that specified that 80 percent of revenues should be returned to producer wards and that councils could retain up to 20 percent of revenues, 15 percent for program management and 5 percent for general administration (Child 1995, 6).

18. Brief descriptions of Kanyurira's experience with CAMPFIRE also appear in Murphree 1993b (pp. 9–10) and Metcalfe 1994 (pp. 179–81). This account is taken, with minor alteration, from Murphree 1996 (pp. 12–20).

19. This is a highly compressed statement on the ecopolitical and ecoreligious dimensions of land and resources in Masoka, which are highly relevant but cannot be addressed here.

20. CASS at the University of Zimbabwe has been conducting research in Masoka for more than ten years. The 1988 statistics are from Cutshall 1989.

21. This estimate is based on Murindagomo's study of the neighboring ward, Chisunga, which exhibits similar conditions (Murindagomo 1988, 82).

22. The fence cost seventy thousand Zimbabwean dollars, labor being provided by Masoka farmers. This seventy thousand dollars and funding for initial two-year maintenance has been the only direct external project input into Masoka's program.

23. Some farmers plant crops on riverine alluvium outside the fence, in areas impossible to include within it because of seasonal flooding. Masoka's view is that farmers using these areas do so at their own risk and accepts no collective liability.

24. Arguably, this is the best way of ensuring the survival of a species. *Bos taurus* appears on nobody's list of threatened species. The domestication of the ostrich (*Struthio camelus*) and the Nile crocodile (*Crocodilus niloticus*) are more recent examples.

25. The specific question yielding this statistic was whether the decisions of the wildlife committee were in the interests of both men and women (Nabane 1997, 85).

26. At a wildlife committee meeting at Masoka, I was asked for the current exchange rate between Zimbabwean and U.S. dollars. When asked why they wished to know, the reply was that they knew that the safari operator's contract signed the year before stipulated Zimbabwe dollars. "But," they said, "we know that the operator receives money from his clients in U.S. dollars and that these now buy more Zimbabwe dollars. Where has the extra money gone?"

27. For a discussion of this concept see Murphree 1996 (pp. 20–22). Turner 1996 provides significant data related to the concept.

28. Ivan Bond, unpublished material, supplied by the courtesy of Ivan Bond.

29. The SADC is a formal intergovernmental consortium of southern African states for coordinated regional development, with sectoral coordinative responsibilities assigned to specific states. Malawi holds this responsibility in respect to forestry, fisheries, and wildlife.

30. The fact that Namibia, Botswana, and Zimbabwe have since 1989 been in an alliance to change the Convention on International Trade in Endangered Species (CITES) appendix I listing of their elephant populations is relevant.

31. For a much more fine-grained analysis see Werbner 1993, 101–30.

REFERENCES

Alexander, J., and J. McGregor. 1996. Our Sons Didn't Die for Animals. Attitudes to Wildlife and the Politics of Development: Campfire in the Nkayi and Lupane Districts. Paper presented at the International Conference on the Historical Dimensions of Democracy and Human Rights, Zimbabwe, Harare, 9–14 September.

Arrighi, G. 1973. The Political Economy of Rhodesia. In *Essays on the Political Economy of Africa*, ed. G. Arrighi and J. Saul. New York: Monthly Review Press.

Berkes, F., and M. Taghi Farvar. 1988. Introduction and Overview. In *Common Property Resources*, ed. F. Berkes. London: Belhaven.

Bond, I. 2001. CAMPFIRE and the Incentives for Institutional Change. In *African Wildlife and Livelihoods. The Promise and Performance of Community Conservation*, ed. D. Hulme and M. Murphree. Oxford: James Currey.

Brandon, K. E., and M. Wells. 1992. Planning for People and Parks: Design Dilemmas. *World Development* 20(4): 557–70.

Campfire Association. 1991. Campfire Association Constitution (mimeograph).

CASS (Centre for Applied Social Sciences, Univ. of Zimbabwe). 1988. A Survey of In-migration to Portions of the Guruve, Kariba and Gokwe Districts, 1981–1987. Harare: CASS, Univ. of Zimbabwe (unpub. ms.).

———. 1989. Files.

Child, B. A. 1988. *The Role of Wildlife Utilization in the Sustainable Economic Development of Semi-arid Rangelands in Zimbabwe.* PhD diss., Oxford Univ.

———. 1995. *Guidelines for Managing Communal Lands Wildlife Revenues in Accordance with Policy for Wildlife, Zimbabwe.* Harare: Department of National Parks and Wild Life Management.

Child, B., and J. H. Peterson. 1991. *CAMPFIRE in Rural Development: The Beitbridge Experience*. Harare: Centre for Applied Social Sciences, Univ. of Zimbabwe.

Cruz, E. 1995. Mozambique: Community Based Natural Resources Management Initiatives. In, L. Rihoy, ed., *The Commons without the Tragedy? Strategies for Community Based Natural Resources Management in Southern Africa.* Lilongwe, Malawi: Southern Africa Development Community.

Cumming, D. H. M. 1991. Wildlife Products and the Market Place: A View from Southern Africa. World Wide Fund for Nature Multispecies Animal Production Systems Project Paper No. 12, presented at the Second International Game Ranching Symposium, Edmonton, Canada, 4–8 June.

Cutshall, C. R. 1989. *Masoka/Kanyurira Ward. A Socio-Economic Baseline Survey of Community Households.* Harare: Centre for Applied Social Sciences (CASS), Univ. of Zimbabwe.

Dasmann, R., and A. S. Mossman. 1961. Commercial Utilization of Game Animals on a Rhodesian Ranch. *Wild Life* 3: 7–17.

Derman, W. 1990. The Unsettling of the Zambezi Valley: An Examination of the Mid-Zambezi Rural Development Project. Harare: Centre for Applied Social Sciences (CASS) Working Paper, Univ. of Zimbabwe.

Derman, W., and J. Murombedzi. 1994. Democracy, Development, and Human Rights in Zimbabwe: A Contradictory Terrain. *African Rural and Urban Studies* 1(2): 119–43.

Dix, A. 1996a. *CAMPFIRE. An Annotated Bibliography. 1985–1996*, 2d ed. Harare: Centre for Applied Social Sciences (CASS), Univ. of Zimbabwe.

———. 1996b. Every Man Must Resettle Where He Wants: The Politics of Settlement in the Context of the Community Wildlife Management Programme in Binga, Zimbabwe. *Zambezia* 23(1): 19–30.

———. 1989. *Policy for Wild Life.* Harare: Department of National Parks and Wild Life Management. Approved by the Minister of Natural Resources and Tourism, 22 September 1989.

———. 1994. *Report of the Commission of Inquiry into Appropriate Agricultural Land Tenure Systems* Harare: Government Printer, 3 vols.

———. 1996. *Parks and Wild Life Act 1975*, Rev. ed. Harare: Government Printer.

Dzingirai, V. 1995. *Take Back Your Campfire. A Study of Local Level Perceptions to Electric Fencing in the Framework of Binga's CAMPFIRE Programme.* Harare, Zimbabwe: Centre for Applied Social Sciences, University of Zimbabwe.

Hill, K. A. 1996. Zimbabwe's Wildlife Utilization Programs: Grassroots Democracy or an Extension of State Power? *African Studies Review* 39(1): 103–23.

Kay, G. 1970. *Rhodesia: A Human Geography.* London: University of London Press.

Leopold, A. 1986. *Game Management.* Madison: Univ. of Wisconsin Press. Original published 1933 by Charles Scribner's Sons.

Madzudzo, E. 1995a. *Grazing in the Bulalimamangwe Natural Resource Management Area.* Harare: Centre for Applied Social Sciences (CASS), Univ. of Zimbabwe.

———. 1995b. *A Comparative Study of the Implications of Ethnicity on CAMPFIRE in Bulalimamangwe and Binga.* Harare, Zimbabwe: Centre for Applied Social Sciences (CASS), Univ. of Zimbabwe.

———. 1997. Power and Empowerment in Community-Based Natural Resource Management. Paper presented at the conference of the Association of Social Anthropologists, Harare, Zimbabwe, January.

Martin, R. B. 1986. *Communal Areas Management Programme for Indigenous Resources (CAMPFIRE* rev. version, April). Harare, Zimbabwe: Department of National Parks and Wild Life Management.

Matowanyika, J. Z. Z., V. Garibaldi, and E. Musimwa. 1995. *Indigenous Knowledge Systems and Natural Resource Management in Southern Africa*. Harare, Zimbabwe: IUCN–The World Conservation Union.

McKenzie, J. M. 1988. *The Empire of Nature: Hunting, Conservation and British Imperialism*. Manchester, U.K.: Manchester Univ. Press.

Metcalfe, S. 1994. The Zimbabwe Communal Areas Management Programme for Indigenous Resources (CAMPFIRE). In D. Western, R. M. Wright, and S. Strum, eds., *Natural Connections: Perspectives in Community-based Conservation*. Washington, D.C.: Island Press.

Moore, D. S. 1996. *A River Runs through It: Environmental History and the Politics of Community in Zimbabwe's Eastern Highlands.* Harare: Centre for Applied Social Sciences (CASS), Univ. of Zimbabwe.

Mossman, A. S. 1963. Wildlife Ranching in Southern Rhodesia, In *Conservation of Nature and Natural Resources in Modern African States*. IUCN Publications New Series, No. 1. Salisbury: IUCN–The World Conservation Union.

Moyo, S. 1991. *Zimbabwe's Environmental Dilemma: Balancing Resource Inequities*, ed. P. Robinson, Y. Katerere, S. Stevenson, and D. Gumbo. Harare, Zimbabwe: ZERO.

Murindagomo, F. 1988. *Preliminary Investigations into Wildlife Utilization and Land Use in Angwa, Mid-Zambezi Valley, Zimbabwe*. M. Phil. thesis, Department of Agricultural Economics and Extension, Univ. of Zimbabwe.

Murombedzi, J. 1992. *Decentralization or Recentralization? Implementing CAMPFIRE in the Omay Communal Lands of the Nyaminyami District*. Harare: Centre for Applied Social Sciences (CASS), Univ. of Zimbabwe.

———. 1994. *The Dynamics of Conflict in Environmental Management Policy Making in the Context of the Communal Lands Management Programme for Indigenous Resources. CAMPFIRE.* PhD diss., Centre for Applied Social Sciences (CASS), Univ. of Zimbabwe.

———. 2001. "Committees, Rights, Costs, and Benefits: Natural Resource Stewardship and Community Benefits in Zimbabwe's CAMPFIRE Programme." In D. Hulme and M. Murphree, eds., *African Wildlife and Livelihoods: The Promise and Performance of Community Conservation*. Oxford: James Curry, 244–55.

Murphree, M. W. 1975. Race and Power in Rhodesia. In *The Politics of Race*, ed. D. Baker. Lexington, Mass.: Lexington Press.

———. 1993a. Decentralizing the Proprietorship of Wildlife Resources in Zimbabwe's Communal Lands. In *Voices from Africa: Local Perspectives on Conservation*, ed. D. Lewis and N. Carter. Washington, D.C.: World Wildlife Fund.

———. 1993b. *Communities as Resource Management Institutions*. London: International Institute for Environment and Development. Revision of a 1991 publication under the title *Communities as Institutions for Research Management*. Harare: Centre for Applied Social Sciences (CASS), Univ. of Zimbabwe.

———. 1996. Approaches to Community Conservation. In *African Wildlife Policy Consultation, Final Report.* London: ODA.

Murphree, M. W., and D. H. M. Cumming. 1993. Savanna Land Use: Policy and Practice in Zimbabwe. In *The World's Savannas. Economic Driving Forces, Ecological Constraints, and Policy Options for Sustainable Land Use,* ed. M. D. Young and O. T. Solbrig. Paris: UNESCO and Parthenon Publishing Group.

Nabane, N. 1997. *Gender Dimensions in the Communal Areas Management Programme for Indigenous Resources: A Zambezi Valley Community Case Study.* M. Phil. thesis, Centre for Applied Social Sciences (CASS), Univ. of Zimbabwe.

Nabane, N., V. Dzingirai, and E. Madzudzo. 1996. *Membership in Common Property Regimes: A Case Study of Guruve, Tsholotsho and Bulalimamangwe CAMPFIRE Programmes.* Harare: Centre for Applied Social Sciences (CASS), Univ. of Zimbabwe.

Namibia, Govt. of. 1975. *Nature Conservation Ordinance, No. 4.* Windhoek.

———. Ministry of Environment and Tourism. 1995. *Wildlife Management, Utilization and Tourism on Communal Land.* Windhoek.

———. 1996. *Nature Conservation Amendment Act.* Act No. 5, Gazette No. 133. Windhoek.

Ostrom, E. 1990. *Governing the Commons. The Evolution of Institutions for Collective Action.* Cambridge, U.K.: Cambridge Univ. Press.

Palmer, R. 1977. The Agricultural History of Rhodesia. In *The Roots of Rural Poverty in Central and Southern Africa*, ed. R. Palmer and N. Parsons. London: Heinemann.

Parker, I. 1993. Natural Justice, Ownership and the CAMPFIRE Programme. Unpub. ms.

Peterson, J. H. 1991. *A Proto-CAMPFIRE Initiative in Mahenye Ward, Chipinge District.* Harare: Centre for Applied Social Sciences (CASS), Univ. of Zimbabwe.

Republic of Zimbabwe. 1982. *Transitional National Development Plan.* Harare: Government Printers.

———. 1984. *1982 Population Census. A Preliminary Assessment.* Harare: Central Statistical Office.

———. 1992. *Census 1992. Preliminary Report.* Harare: Central Statistical Office.

Rihoy, L., ed. 1995. *The Commons without the Tragedy? Strategies for Community Based Natural Resources Management in Southern Africa.* Lilongwe, Malawi: Southern Africa Development Community.

Turner, S. D. 1996. Conservancies in Namibia: A Model for Successful Common Property Resource Management? Discussion Paper No. 13. Windhoek: Social Sciences Division, Univ. of Namibia.

Vincent, V., and R. G. Thomas. 1961. *An Agricultural Survey of Southern Rhodesia. Part 1: Agro-ecological Survey.* Salisbury: Government Printer.

Werbner, R. P. 1993. From Heartland to Hinterland: Elites and the Geopolitics of Land in Botswana. In *Land in African Agrarian Systems*, ed. T. Bassett and D. Crummey. Madison: Univ. of Wisconsin Press.

Wood, J. 1991. CAMPFIRE: The Legal Issues. Harare: unpublished paper commissioned by Zimbabwe Trust on behalf of the CAMPFIRE Collaborative Group.

Government of Zimbabwe. 1994. *Report of the Commission of Inquiry into Appropriate Land Tenure Systems.*

5

Of Diffusion and Context: The Bubbling Up of Community-Based Resource Management in Mozambique in the 1990s

Kenneth Wilson

In responding to Professor Marshall Murphree's nodal chapter in this volume from the perspective of the proliferation of the CAMPFIRE concept to Mozambique, it seems important to first make general remarks about CAMPFIRE's evolution in Zimbabwe to set the context for understanding its influence and lack of influence on the proliferation of community-based natural resource management (CBNRM) in neighboring countries.

Zimbabwe's CAMPFIRE is often seen from outside as being (1) a resounding and profound success resulting from (2) the implementation to near perfection of universal principles of CBNRM based on (3) a popular peasant movement to gain rights over wildlife and in interaction with (4) a global movement for new participatory ways to involve communities in resource management. But as Murphree's chapter succinctly—but quietly—demonstrates, the sequence is better seen in reverse. First, CAMPFIRE did not evolve in synergy with a global movement; rather its history is intimately nested in Zimbabwe's numerous peculiarities. Second, the drive for CAMPFIRE originated almost entirely from a small group within government and from national nongovernmental organizations (NGOs). This enabled the launching of an innovative program in a conservative and centrist society but also necessitated a series of compromises regarding community-resource management principles (Murphree's "fatal flaws" and "clay feet"). This has meant that the program's success has actually been mixed and that it has remained somewhat insecure. Furthermore, while CAMPFIRE is touted as transformative of political-economic relationships, it and its sister programs in the region are often better understood as creatures of a common colonial heritage of land and resource expropriation. The crux of this inheritance is that the postcolonial state finds itself perpetuating a legal defense of illicitly obtained private rights of the landed elite; the state has found that its authority over the rural population depends on its controlling rights over their land and natural resources. Thus, as Dr. James Murombedzi perceptively remarked in commenting on this chapter, a political-economic perspective is critical because, "in such a context, communal lands could not be transformed, only reformed, and consequently CBNRM offered a solution to not only extend some limited control over property rights to the residents therein, but also an opportunity for the post-colonial state to appear to be doing some meaningful land reform and thus pre-empt demands for complete land reform" (personal communication, 2002).

In appraising Murphree's chapter, one must stress that he was himself a major factor in the implementation of CAMPFIRE. Apart from doggedly plying his wisdom and charm in offices and villages for more than a decade, he also played a critical role in developing and then communicating with great clarity and persistence—both nationally and internationally, to scholars and practitioners—his well-known principles for community management. These principles—and the fact that CAMPFIRE in some locations made a lot of money for rural people while apparently driving improvements in local governance and resource stewardship—are at the core of the proliferation equation for CAMPFIRE in Southern Africa. Murphree's CAMPFIRE vision inspired many of us, though his modesty can sometimes hide his seminal importance.

Regarding CAMPFIRE's proliferation to neighboring countries, while the great Murphree principles were often honed precisely by the problems of CAMPFIRE, some have viewed them as *the* principles of the CAMPFIRE program as it was actually realized in Zimbabwe. Yet Murphree himself and the exceptional group of people attracted to CAMPFIRE never evinced this misunderstanding. His chapter masterfully demonstrates the pragmatic way they, having allied around "congruent objectives," maneuvered CAMPFIRE over, around, and through the "competing interests" of a political and institutional minefield. Through "strategic compromise" they were able to bring about realization of the program's basic elements in parts of about half the districts in Zimbabwe, with nearly three million U.S. dollars received annually in the late 1990s as local dividends.

CONCEPTUAL MODELS ADDRESSING CAMPFIRE PROLIFERATION

During the 1990s, Southern Africa became a world leader in CBNRM for local income generation, and the CAMPFIRE program has served as a flagship for this. But the actual nature of the linkages between the development of CAMPFIRE in Zimbabwe and similar programs in neighboring countries has rarely been explicitly reviewed. Murphree is undoubtedly correct in his argument that the major contribution of CAMPFIRE to the development of CBNRM in the region has not been—and could never have been—the export of an institutional blueprint. As he intimates, CAMPFIRE is so legally and institutionally rooted in Zimbabwe that neighboring countries have found it difficult to comprehend its precise nature, let alone to import it lock, stock, and barrel. Furthermore, because Zimbabwe has gained a reputation regionally for having a certain superiority complex, even well-meaning attempts by Zimbabweans to tell their neighbors how things should be done have tended to create negative reactions. Thus any cookie-cutter model for proliferation based on a straightforward replication or diffusion has not been viable.

At the other end of the spectrum is a model for developing CBNRM experiments in each country as essentially homegrown affairs, allowing in situ independent developments. This analytic approach assumes that the same economic and social dynamics that have pushed forward innovation and change in resource management in Zimbabwe have also been at work in the region's other countries—each country's move toward community-based approaches is seen as internally shaped and driven. Consequently, the particularities of political culture and institutional relationships in each country have required—to use Murphree's Zimbabwe framework—different alliances of institutions around congruent objectives, who in turn have negotiated with different sets of competing interests. Consequently, different strategic compromises have been made to generate products—CAMPFIRE analogues—each of which is basically its own progenitor and is necessarily unique. One section of this chapter will trace aspects of this independent development of in situ process in Mozambique. The in situ model of parallel evolution suggests that the similarities between the various CBNRM programs in the region reflect, not exchange or diffusion, but rather a shared political-economic heritage and similarities in rural societies and natural resource-based economies.

A third conceptual model for understanding proliferation is what we might call the stimulus model, whereby CAMPFIRE's principles challenge and inspire actors in neighboring countries to define congruent interests of the same ilk and form alliances around them, but perhaps with little reference to the concrete nature of CAMPFIRE. This model helps us to focus on a series of interactions, several of which are mentioned in Murphree's chapter. He points out, for example, how government and agency figures in both Namibia and Botswana learned about and reflected on CAMPFIRE thinking and subsequently—in countries with both parallel and divergent histories—found ways of realizing their own programs. He then contrasts this with the powerful experience of community-to-community exchange, which he illustrates with the case of the Tchuma Tchato program of the Zambezi Valley in Mozambique. I shall return to this case shortly.

At least two other aspects of the stimulus model require consideration, however. The first is the role of donors, a topic curiously, if refreshingly, absent in Murphree's chapter. Donors in Africa are typically blamed for all that is wrong or alternatively (and equally simplistically) are assumed to be capable of masterminding the continent's recovery and willing to do so. Donors are important here because their interpretations of what CAMPFIRE means have greatly shaped whether and how they have engaged with CBNRM in neighboring countries. (I myself first took a reality check by visiting the CAMPFIRE village of Masoka before I recommended approval of the first CBNRM grant for Mozambique.) Consideration of donors is also important because in Southern Africa they are the main link between global thinking and local action. Few southern Africans think they have much to learn from outsiders regarding resource management: only through money can outsiders really gain influence. Donors can also mobilize far greater resources than can governments and local NGOs in the region, so it matters what they choose to fund. The second dimension to a stimulus model is the mobile role of professionals in the field, shifting as they do between countries as well as between governments, NGOs, and research institutions. Thus, for example, the late Dr. Richard Bell, scholarly pioneer of these programs, started the work in Malawi, moved on to Luangwa in Zambia, then to Botswana, and subsequently carried out advisory work in Mozambique. Dr. Brian Child, one of CAMPFIRE's most dedicated field-workers, is now engaged in the reform of the Luangwa program in Zambia. Murombedzi, having worked on CAMPFIRE in Zimbabwe, became the Ford Foundation's program officer working on regional land and natural resource management issues. And Mike Murphree and Peter Tilley took their experiences with CAMPFIRE and with Zambia's Administrative Management Design for Game Management Areas (ADMADE) to help launch these programs in Mozambique.

Following a brief introduction to Mozambique, this chapter applies these three conceptual models first to the proliferation of CAMPFIRE-type programs in Mozambique and then to Tchuma Tchato, which during the 1990s was the most advanced pilot initiative in that country. But first it is necessary to paint a general picture of the contrasting political environment for the development of community-based management initiatives in southern Africa.

CENTRALIZED DEVELOPMENT VERSUS BUBBLING-UP

During a 1997 meeting of regional specialists in sustainable use, Simon Anstey, then an IUCN program officer for Mozambique and Angola, remarked that there are two basic contexts for the contemporary development of CBNRM in southern Africa. The first is the centralized context, characterized by a constellation of national agencies that secure legal tenure reform at a central level and then work together throughout the country to encourage projects that—while locally adapted and led—all work along similar lines to realize these new resource rights. Zimbabwe, as well as Namibia, Botswana, and to a considerable extent Zambia, is characterized by this approach.

Other countries, by contrast, display what Anstey calls a *bubbling-up* approach, one characterized by the absence of legal transformations but occurring within a general policy and political environment that enables communities to press government and the private sector for land and resource ownership and management rights and predisposes government officials to promote them. Such a policy and institutional environment means both that communities can themselves take greater initiative and that a wider range of institutions tend to become involved in nurturing such initiatives. This is coupled with a greater diversity of donors and a greater provincialization of government and NGOs in these countries, and the result is a suite of highly varied programs in different parts of the country. This model, Anstey argued, is exemplified by the new South Africa and by Mozambique.[1]

These Anstey characterizations stimulate examination of a number of teasing correlations. The first of these is that the U.S. Agency for International Development (USAID) was during the 1990s the principal funder of CBNRM in all of the countries with the centralized approach but a negligible funder in those with the bubbling-up approach. Surely, it might be argued, this is an example of bureaucratic impact: an agency with a bird's-eye view aims to get in place a tight legal and policy framework that is then implemented nationally with generous funding. Or we might hypothesize that a donor like USAID can support only programs of the scale typical of the centralized model. A brief reflection on the history of the programs in these four countries—and I am not qualified to make a more profound one—suggests both explanations have elements of truth. Zimbabwe and Namibia in particular both developed their centralist approach before or in parallel with USAID support, while in each of these countries USAID funding does appear to have consolidated a national approach with national institutions. This even though USAID actually supported CAMPFIRE in Zimbabwe as a governance exercise promoting decentralization. It is also worth noting that considerations of such a program in central Mozambique in 1995–1996 were abandoned by USAID, perhaps in part because there was no tight nexus of strong institutions and legal reforms to drive the program.

A second correlation also emerges sharply from the Anstey paradigm. The countries with centralist models are those where central government is least willing to decentralize rights to the rural people of the wilderness zones and where, concurrently, the imagination of a national culture is strongest. In these countries, the apparent irony that legislation is more progressive and government more involved than in the countries with the bubbling-up approach can obscure the actual nature of the competing interests and strategic comprises involved in promoting community initiatives in such a state. South Africa and Mozambique undoubtedly needed in the 1990s to develop more specific enabling legislation and institutional mechanisms for the realization of resource rights by rural people. Yet it has been precisely the reduced strength of hostile competing interests and the subsequent greater freedom from fatal strategic comprises that has enabled the freer emergence of more diverse and arguably more community-led processes in these countries. The local-versus-central dynamic is clearly a complex one[2]—the centralist approach is followed by those countries where local government has the highest degree of administrative and financial competence and control, not where it is weakest. And in countries such as Mozambique, the bubbling-up approach ironically left programs particularly vulnerable to unaccountable local government structures that even central government had difficulty reining in. This illuminates for us the paradox of why the most centralized states were the ones most comfortable with legally promulgating decentralized rights over land and resources.

But beyond even this, it needs to be recognized that a key feature—across the continent—of the imagined unitary and overcentralized state is a desire to strongly define communities on the ground, whether as villages, wards, party cells, chiefs, or whatever, and so to create them as the lowest tier of government or party. This means that the stronger the state, the more defined and structured (and politically weak) is the local community. Thus one reason countries like South Africa and Mozambique had such difficulties in the 1990s with developing legislative and policy mechanisms to legally enshrine community-based management is that the relatively profound nature of their political transitions meant that there were no grounds or powers for neat administrative definitions of community. One feature of the bubbling-up process, then, is that the dynamic is as much about defining the nature of local politics—the relations between individuals and communities and their horizontal and vertical linkages—as it is about what they might actually do with their wildlife and natural resources.

So it was that in the late 1990s, in an area around South Africa's Kruger National Park, the educated political generation—whose alliances spanned rural and periurban sectors and formed a bridge between provincial and national politics—challenged the Social Ecology Unit of National Parks over the latter's intent to work with defined small rural communities. They posited that this represented a desire to work "at snake level—bellies in the dust," with the implied intention of avoiding the wider socioeconomic linkages in the postapartheid era between traditional rural communities, the ethnic structures of the former homelands, the hundreds of thousands of people forced from "White Areas" into these rural peripheries, and the complex rural–urban migratory networks. National Parks staff, meanwhile, argued that the only realistic hope for success was to work with defined groups of people who actually had direct social and economic ties to the land and natural resources, and were thus able to make local, meaningful compromises.

Such dilemmas about how the state should relate to rural social structures were clear in these complex debates about the relationships between traditional authorities and local democratic government in South Africa and Mozambique. In both cases, there was a deep awareness of the manner in which traditional leaders have been compromised historically by conservative political interests. There was a sense of unease concerning the apparent antidemocratic nature of such power and the implications this had for other issues such as gender relations. But as these governments sought to develop more democratic and inclusive forms of local government, they found that these traditional-leadership institutions had considerable legitimacy in the eyes of local people, who saw them as being more accountable to them than were the externally constituted elected local and national government institutions. Indeed, they were commonly believed by rural people to possess capacities that enabled them to make sounder and more enforceable decisions about land and resources. Thus in Mozambique the government appeared in 1997 no closer to deciding for or against formally reinstituting traditional authority than it had been five years before. At national, legal, and policy levels government preferred to refer to "people of local influence" and to let local officials work out their relationships on the ground. Of course one effect of this was to perpetuate the situation where the state, the private sector, and individuals all existed in law and were able to deal in land and resource assets. Meanwhile, the community could not gain legal personality or own resources and could get to the table only through special pleading.[3] One of the main reasons communities have leaders is to facilitate relations with the outside world, and a large part of the social history of chiefs in Africa—not least in Mozambique—has been a complex negotiation of the articulation of the emergent colonial state with its citizens. Thus it is not surprising that the continuing vacuum in the definition of local leadership roles created confusion and resentment in the village political elites.

Having drawn the contrast between these two broad frameworks, with Mozambique characterized as a country where initiatives take the form of bubbling up, we now turn to seeking an explanation of the complex forces within Mozambique that facilitated experiments with CBNRM in the 1990s.

INTERNAL FACTORS STIMULATING EMERGENCE

Mozambique is more than double the size of Zimbabwe, with a much larger wilderness area, reflecting the country's long history of uneven and limited economic development. Indeed, in both absolute and proportional terms, Mozambique has larger wilderness areas than any other country in eastern and southern Africa excepting perhaps Angola. Thus, whereas a mere 10 percent of South Africa supports indigenous vegetation, only 7 percent of Mozambique is cultivated. Perhaps as much as 50 percent is inaccessible by vehicle and supports populations of less than five people per square kilometer in ecosystems that are relatively marginally altered. There are also tenure differences: in Zimbabwe, Namibia, and South Africa most land remained in private—historically, white—hands, meaning in turn that most wilderness development and wildlife management has occurred under individual and private land tenure. In Mozambique, however, the settlers and private companies were mostly stripped of their land at Independence, albeit often with the land subsequently incorporated into state farms, at least until the late 1980s. In the 1990s the country stood at a crossroads where the majority of the land ostensibly belonged in some way to the state on behalf of rural communities, but the private sector was busy securing concessions. Potentially, therefore, the areas of wilderness that might come under formal systems of CBNRM in Mozambique appeared to be one or even two orders of magnitude larger than those in neighboring states. Therefore the stakes for this approach in Mozambique were high.

Nonetheless, the explosion of interest in CBNRM approaches in Mozambique cannot be explained simply by the country being mainly wilderness with nearly all such land in the hands (albeit insecurely) of rural communities. Instead the shift has probably been due to the nature of the country's elite and their political projects. As Mozambique emerged from war in 1992 and successfully brought off the country's first-ever multiparty elections at the end of 1994, a younger generation of elites emerged, one that had forged the nation in the cauldron of state socialism in the context of forced rural modernization, external military destabilization, and locally generated rural rebellion. This new elite brought to the fore a set of values and experiences that set them apart from the elites of neighboring countries and predisposed them to search for novel approaches. Some of these attitudes reflected experiences gained after Independence, but others had been deeply shaped by the colonial experience, during which a nascent elite was forged with few roots in rural ethnicities or recent rural experiences and a strong identification with international social movements.[4]

Some of the views of this particular faction of the elite in the mid-1990s can be summarized as follows: First, there was a deep hostility toward the feasibility or desirability of state-led and top-down approaches and toward authoritarianism, megaprojects, and policing approaches to resource management. At the same time, there was a commitment to decentralization of decision making without tribalistic overtones.[5] Communities were generally viewed as natural and organic and with vital but previously oppressed indigenous leaderships, and there was a desire to see them replace or complement the central state as decision makers in rural areas. These political sentiments were complemented by economic views that had been shaped by the painful legacy of state socialism. There was a great concern that activities and projects not just sound nice but be economically sound, and although the private sector was genuinely accepted as an engine of growth, it was recognized that appropriate policies and controls would be needed if this engine was to benefit rural communities and not damage the environment. There was a great desire to generate activities that would address rural poverty in what was then the poorest country in the world and at the same time to deal with the ongoing rape of forests for tropical hardwoods and other natural resources in the situation of nearly open access that had been created by the collapse of state authority in rural areas.

Despite the ambitious nature of these concerns and the great Mozambican capacity for self-deprecation,[6] there were a number of reasons why the elite addressed this project with great energy and confidence. These included a fervent—even naive—belief in the capacity of heretofore neglected social research to identify solutions to developmental and governance issues; a strong identification with the global environmental movement and its achievements; and a positive, even romantic, idea of what rural societies are like and able to achieve (based at times on a notion of them as the mirror image of the failed central state). Finally it should be noted that the Mozambicans also brought to this project a relatively strong identification with ideas of gender equality and female participation in development. This was both a cause and consequence of the Mozambican elite being perhaps the most gender equal in the world; at that time about half the Mozambicans with degree-level training in forestry and environmental science disciplines were women.

When in 1991–1993 I first became involved with the Mozambicans who now lead the movement for CBNRM, each of the attitudes just described were well developed, if highly variable between individuals, and it was clear that it was these attitudes that had led them to CBNRM approaches. Of course, it was also true that key figures at the time were aware of what was happening in the wider world. For example, Milagre Nuvunga and António Ribeiro had studied in Australia and Oxford, respectively, and had thus already been exposed to such programs. That said, it was also clear that the strength of their commitments to these new approaches had grown out of their professional experience in Mozambique in the 1980s. It is difficult, perhaps, for people not associated with Mozambique to imagine the speed and extent of the changes that took place in the human-resource base during this period and the impact they had. In 1997, for example, perhaps three-quarters of those Mozambicans with degree or diploma training in relevant fields had graduated since 1992, and half of those had received solid training at Eduardo Mondlane University in forestry or biology (and occasionally veterinary science). The rest had been trained in Europe, Australia, Tanzania, and elsewhere. The wave of new graduates—some of whom had already had solid work experience when they left to study—brought dazzling energy and commitment to the community-based approach. In contrast with other countries, there was little old guard to fight against, and quite frankly there were no functioning institutions to create bureaucratic inertia. The impacts of the advances in training were reinforced by the gradual posting of people from this group to the provinces—former backwaters of a kind but places where dedicated staff could make huge differences given the ongoing moves toward decentralization and the determined provincialization of the funding agendas of the Ford Foundation and some other donors.

The sorts of values that motivated this diverse group of young people had increasingly become accepted within the national policy framework by the middle to late 1990s. In the new government at the end of 1994, a majority of ministers and vice ministers were appointed from this cohort—graduate-educated nonparty functionaries in their thirties and early forties—and this provided further space for such talent. This dynamic—the forming of alliances with people upward into the government hierarchy rather than within the institutions of civil society—was another interesting feature of Mozambique's reforms of the 1990s. While NGOs have been slow to gain interest in CBNRM in Mozambique, the country's arts and media institutions at local and national levels have been much quicker to the mark. Significant contributions have been made to date through dance, theater, video, and later community radio, although admittedly this partly reflects the influence of Ford Foundation grants.[7]

This picture of a dynamic, open, and forward-looking elite taking the initiative in community-based approaches has to be balanced against two points: First, intellectual honesty requires admission that the Ford Foundation did play a role in nurturing many of these individuals, funding their training and work, and bringing them together from their various institutions.[8] The right ingredients were there, but the foundation was important as a catalyst. Second, a crucial factor in the context of actually seeking to realize these programs was the extent of the chaos in postwar Mozambique. Almost the entire infrastructure had been destroyed. By the time the peace agreement was signed, almost every law, policy, and administrative procedure had been rendered irrelevant by the shattering of state presence and authority. A yawning gap between the old state socialism and the unfolding new dispensation remained in place for two long years between the signing of the peace agreement and the swearing in of the newly elected government. Even after the new government had been inaugurated, the lack of resources and administrative mechanisms, and the sheer size of the country, left the government suspended above what was essentially a self-help state, where resources were accessed at will and officials survived through petty corruption. Meanwhile, the country was divided into sectors and regions by donor agencies that in the absence of sustained state initiatives had taken over, at times almost entirely, from policy to implementation. Given the megaprograms of many of these donor agencies and the considerable resources at their disposal, the capacity Mozambique retained to absorb and overwhelm initiative of any kind was remarkable, the consequences tending toward differently rather than less chaotic. One thing that must have struck the first wave of Mozambican visitors (including President Chissano) to the Tchuma Tchato pilot program in the Zambezi Valley was that it actually existed on the ground and did in fact bring some order and direction to rural socioeconomic processes.

CAMPFIRE AS A STIMULUS

The descriptions provided earlier of the particularities of CAMPFIRE as a Zimbabwean program and then of the impossibility of creating and realizing a national program in the chaotic circumstances of postwar Mozambique are ample explanations in themselves of why a cookie-cutter approach to the proliferation of a CAMPFIRE model in Mozambique was never in the cards. On the other hand, although it is clear that diverse historical forces created an extremely intellectually fertile environment for the in situ development of such programs, it is not true that CBNRM in Mozambique is totally or even mainly homegrown. As will become clear in the case study below, the single most influential program in Mozambique—Tchuma Tchato in Tete—owes a great deal to CAMPFIRE. And though none of the other Mozambican programs show any similar degree of Zimbabwean influence, even those in other Zimbabwean border areas, such as the Chimanimani Mountains program in Manica Province, ideas about CAMPFIRE have been important in stimulating Mozambican initiative.

Thus it was that when the Commission for the Coordination of Environment Action and the National Directorate of Forestry and Wildlife became interested in community-based approaches in 1993–1995 several Zimbabweans, including in particular Marshall Murphree, Mike Murphree, Stephen Kasere, and James Murombedzi, played a direct role in introducing them to the practicalities of CAMPFIRE. Furthermore, and in support of the efforts by Mozambican professionals to experiment with these approaches, I spoke about CAMPFIRE with the majority of relevant ministers, national directors, provincial governors, researchers, and NGO leaders in Mozambique during 1993–1996. In particular, I used these discussions to make the following points: that considerable revenues could be generated for communities, that the private sector would welcome and benefit from such partnerships, that communities can manage resources effectively, and that there is a natural link between decentralization and rural democratization and community-based land management.

To convey CAMPFIRE to Mozambicans, I tended to use the example of Masoka, the village described by Murphree in this volume, which I have visited numerous times. It is worth noting that, try as I might, I could not obtain any Marshall Murphree paper or any other document that made the above general points about the benefits of CAMPFIRE and the potential revenues that could be generated. All Murphree could provide were papers, such as "Communities as Natural Resource Managers," that reviewed his principles and the challenges of their realization in Zimbabwe. It was very important that I be able to explain with concrete examples the CAMPFIRE experience in Masoka. Indeed, the existence of an up-and-running program in Mozambican border areas was key to convincing Mozambican leaders that this talk of CBNRM was not simply another piece of development propaganda and that its goals could be realized over significant areas of southern African wilderness. I think that talk of the sums of money involved had the greatest impact. Being able to discuss CAMPFIRE's weaknesses was also very helpful, because it was possible to use the example of problems in Zimbabwe to convey to Mozambicans the dangers of only partially conceding rights to Mozambican communities, and Mozambicans took comfort in the knowledge that Zimbabweans did not have all the answers.[9]

Discussion of the CAMPFIRE program was useful in introducing ideas to not only the Mozambican leadership but also to Mozambican peasant communities. I, myself, Zimbabwean collaborators (especially Marshall Murphree), and even Mozambican officials would recount elements of the CAMPFIRE experience to communities we were trying to convince to experiment with the approach. This was of course easiest in areas of the Zambezi Valley where many Mozambicans also had firsthand knowledge of these programs through life as refugees in Zimbabwe. But I was also struck that people in these villages were as likely to use the ADMADE program in Zambia as a reference point, even though this program is typically viewed as less successful and is far less-known internationally. Reference to ADMADE presumably reflected in part the greater economic integration of western Tete with Zambia.

In addition to the general diffusion of the concept of CAMPFIRE to Mozambique, a series of direct-exchange visits were of tremendous importance in helping key actors to learn concrete lessons and to begin their work. As I explain later in the case study of the Tchuma Tchato program, visits to Harare and the village of Masoka by key people from the National Directorate of Forestry and Wildlife in 1994 and the provincial government of Tete in 1996, played a key role for policy makers and program implementers, as did the presence of Zimbabweans at a policy workshop on Tchuma Tchato in Mozambique at the end of 1996. Likewise, as described by Murphree, an exchange visit between Masoka and the Mozambican village of Bawa in early 1996 was critical at the local level. These exchange visits tended to reinforce the confidence of Mozambicans in the feasibility of such programs as income-earning exercises, and they conveyed lessons about the need to protect community management from competing bureaucratic agencies of government. The existence of CAMPFIRE programs was also valuable for Mozambican officials in a psychological sense in that it strengthened their faith and aspirations in the face of the inevitable difficulties they would face. It has to be said that sometimes false beliefs in the success of CAMPFIRE were more valuable than was informed knowledge. António Serra is a dedicated action researcher of the Center for Forestry Research (CEF), a Mozambican research institute promoting community participation. He was then working in the Moribane Forest east of the Chimanimani Mountains, carved out his program single-handedly, having been encouraged by the success of a CAMPFIRE-type program in the similar forests on the mountain of Haroni-Rusitu. He was quite astonished and rather crestfallen when I had to tell him during a meeting with the chief of the area in 1997 that the program in Zimbabwe—after more than four years of discussion—had still to achieve anything concrete and that it faced multiple institutional challenges.

In short, the idea that CAMPFIRE was successfully operational played a major role in stimulating similar programs in Mozambique. However, it had little programmatic linkage or impact on the administrative and legal frameworks that unfolded in Mozambique, excepting perhaps in the principle that elected village committees are an effective tool in building responsive and legitimate local management structures (which is at least a feature of the major programs).

To illustrate further the nature and limitations of this stimulatory impact, it is interesting to reflect on the nature of the new wave of initiatives in Mozambique that emerged in 1996–1997. The scale of these developments is conveyed in an excellent 1997 review by the IUCN that describes nineteen separate such projects, with an estimated total funding of some $34.8 million, although half that funding is concentrated in two megaprojects.[10] The review also demonstrates the extraordinary diversity in these endeavors, though all are ostensibly CBNRM projects. As the authors diplomatically remark, "Some appear to be driven by donor ideology or private-sector public relations, some are led from the top, others being forced up from the local or provincial level. Some are being catalyzed by individuals concerned with resolving locally experienced conflicts or promoting social justice. Some involve conventional project systems with long development phases and major funding inputs, others are processes or adaptive experiments with minimal funds" (IUCN-Mozambique 1997).

It is also noteworthy that, as indicated in this quote, none of the projects were set up to replicate CAMPFIRE or Tchuma Tchato. Although most did refer to "applying Tchuma Tchato principles" in their public relations, with one or two exceptions the people involved in conceiving and implementing them had little knowledge or interest in what was actually happening in Tchuma Tchato. In my view, one slice of the projects had been generated on the international circuit and related to an interface between donor needs, institutional orientations, and on occasion, local realities, whereas the second group was post hoc attempts to articulate major private-sector ecotourism investments with local communities, and the third slice was tiny Mozambican attempts to collaborate with small communities with exceptional forest or other resource assets. (An amusing exception to this pattern was the Afrikaner general involved with the now failed MOSAGRIUS settlement of Afrikaner families in northern Mozambique, who confided to a senior Mozambican government official that they would not have problems with developing hunting concessions because "we have information on how Tchuma Tchato is organized at the local level in Tete.")

To further explore the diverse forces shaping these initiatives, I now briefly examine the emergence of three widely separated programs in the mid-1990s: The first involved attempts to structure a community stake in a joint venture covering more than forty thousand square kilometers of Niassa around the Mecula Reserve on Mozambique's northern frontier with Tanzania. The second program has attempted to grant communities subsistence rights and a stake in commercial resource use in northern Sofala (Gorongosa-Marromeu) on the Lower Zambezi in central Mozambique. The third entails work in the small Tanga area of the Licuati forest near the Rio Maputo in the extreme south of the country. None of these three programs make reference to CAMPFIRE, nor do they involve actors who have been significantly encouraged or informed by CAMPFIRE.

In the case of northern Sofala, the single most important reason for its success has been the presence and leadership of Baldeu Chande, and subsequently Roberto Zolho, Abdul Adamo, and other gifted and dedicated Mozambican professionals who sought ways to structure genuine community engagement. Clearly aware of the global trend toward such programs and aware and at times inspired by CAMPFIRE and Tchuma Tchato, the real origin of these initiatives to guarantee community access to the prodigious resources of the region was Chande's sense of environmental justice and his capacity for practical policy making. The subsequent program under GERFFA was able to build on resource-sharing programs with the fisheries of Gorongosa and to enable communities to gain a 25 percent gross-revenue share from logging operations in the Gorongosa buffer zone. This was the first time such a right had been granted in Mozambique, and the new initiatives that emerged in community resource management of the Marromeu flood plain, and subsequent discussions around giving communities rights in the substantial hunting concessions (*coutadas*), were all part of an increasingly systematic effort by the provincial government to turn the natural resources of northern Sofala into a real asset for community development. This group of projects is especially interesting in that it managed to apply major donor funding in a flexible and locally appropriate manner, and it also steadily won decentralized management for national parks and other major resources.

There were elements of the same human dynamic in the case of Mecula in Niassa: António Abacar, a former participant in Tchuma Tchato, became responsible for the Mecula Reserve; the provincial director for Agriculture and Fisheries brought enthusiasm for Tchuma Tchato when he was relocated to Niassa from Tete; and Hilário Akissa, formerly a researcher with the CEF became the head of the Provincial Forestry and Wildlife Service. However, on their own these individuals were unable to realize the kinds of programs in Niassa that had unfolded in northern Sofala because they completely lacked state resources and could not secure donor interest in this isolated province. The context then changed dramatically as plans to develop the area for ecotourism came to a head. The persistent presence of the IUCN (most notably in the person of Simon Anstey) and the subsequent backing of the national director for Forestry and Wildlife, Sérgio Chitará, created the means to bring ideas of community participation into the negotiations between the Mozambique government and Niassa Investimentos, Lda. Niassa was a private company backed by Norwegian millionaire and environmentalist, Halvord Alstrup, the owner of the Madal group. The outcome of this process on the ground remained, however, unclear. There were a number of potential private-sector actors, the provincial government structures took time to become closely involved, and solid community participation, too, developed only gradually. There was no government or donor funding to solidly complement the projected private-sector investments.

The application of Mozambican talent locally was another feature of the Tanga forest program, in the persons of Tereza Alves, Camila de Sousa, Esperança Chamba, Henrique Massango, and J. Halufo of the CEF. In the mid-1990s, they brought to this forest near Maputo a faith in the capacities and rights of communities to manage natural resources, along with abilities to come up with practical suggestions for joint management. They brought with them useful experience from pilot activities in the Chimanimani Mountains area of Manica Province, and an oblique knowledge of Tchuma Tchato. The real origins of the program in Tanga, however, were the extraordinary strength of organization and commitment from the local people themselves, under a charismatic healer-headman, to conserve their natural resources from external pillaging and to search for viable sustainable-use strategies. (This local strength was necessary because, for complex bureaucratic and political reasons, the project was unable to protect their resource rights and develop the promised programs.) A groundswell for new initiatives in Mozambique having originated within the community has been a feature—with varying degrees of strength—of most of the new programs or at least those actually operating to good effect.

It should be added that by the late 1990s the target for regional intellectual exchange and collaboration for most of these new Mozambican programs became South Africa (and to a lesser extent Botswana and Namibia) and no longer Zimbabwe and CAMPFIRE, due especially to a growing focus on ecotourism as the principal revenue-generating mechanism. South Africa emerged as the region's leader in the ecotourism field not because it had mature programs well funded by donors or government, but rather because of the activities of private capital in a situation of dramatic political transition and the capacity of organized communities to demand benefit from this. Spirited negotiations between communities situated in resource-rich areas and a new generation of business people have provided a laboratory for creating joint ventures between communities and the private sector that provide real income and an incentive for sound environmental management. Researchers, NGOs, or consultants got involved, usually sideways, somewhat at odds with their initial raison d'être, in brokering and facilitating these discussions, often to great effect, but they were rarely the instigators of such deals. Their expertise, and more importantly the South African companies with their capital and marketing abilities, are likely to have a big impact in Mozambique over the longer term. Likewise, Zimbabwe's engagement in Mozambique is likely to shift from collaborations with NGOs and researchers toward relations with private-sector entities, mostly small ecotourism companies run by hardy and dynamic entrepreneurs engaged in such fields as sport fishing and bird watching. The CAMPFIRE link, too, tends toward modest two-way exchange programs of parallel initiatives and the engagement of a trickle of trained Zimbabweans coming to work for Mozambican programs.

CASE STUDY

The Tchuma Tchato pilot program on the Zambezi River in Tete Province became in the 1990s the most established of Mozambique's experiments with CBNRM, and easily the best known. The factors shaping its emergence provide an interesting case study of four related processes: (1) how Zimbabweans succeeded in sharing and extending their experience with CAMPFIRE to Mozambique; (2) how Mozambicans constructed a program framework to resolve particular challenges and realize particular visions in an isolated area of the country; (3) how a Mozambican community in interaction with an exceptional wildlife-department official switched directions from passive resistance to active engagement with the initiative, becoming at once more Mozambican and more integrated with people from neighboring states and the outside world; and (4) how a program in Mozambique came to stimulate other pilot programs and national debate on the nature of the environmental and developmental challenges faced by Mozambique.

First, a brief overview of Tchuma Tchato as the realization of Zimbabwean visions and actions. It is important to make clear at the outset that this twenty-five-hundred-square-kilometer strip of land sandwiched between the Zimbabwe border and the Zambezi River in Mozambique's westernmost extension (where Tchuma Tchato first started) is in geographical terms contiguous with Zimbabwe and is seen by Zimbabweans as a natural extension of their country.[11] In one chance encounter I had with some Zimbabweans in 1995, they told me that "we are glad to see something happening there now, we always thought we should just annex the whole area directly for CAMPFIRE." Indeed, the area shares its game population, especially its elephants and buffalo, in seasonal migrations with the prime safari hunting areas for CAMPFIRE in Zimbabwe's Dande. During 1992–1993, a number of Zimbabweans, notably Marshall Murphree and his son Mike, with brokerage by the Southern African Regional Office of IUCN (IUCN-ROSA), which is located in Harare, began to explore just such an eventuality with interested Mozambican parties. Mike was posted to the Mozambican Wildlife Department by the IUCN, and from Maputo he began advocating for the establishment of a CAMPFIRE-type program in the area. Meanwhile, it was a Zimbabwean company, perhaps ironically called Mozambique Safaris, that held the concession in the area.

Key preparatory phases for the launching of the pilot project in 1994 and the subsequent establishment of the program as a provincial government priority in 1996 involved high-level visits by Mozambicans involved with CAMPFIRE. The warm reception and assistance they received during these visits to Harare, to the district capital of Guruve, and to the village of Masoka displayed the enthusiasm of Zimbabweans at governmental, nongovernmental, and village levels to see their experiences shared and disseminated. Even after the Tchuma Tchato program had been well established, the Zimbabwean perception was neatly indicated by the reaction of a Zimbabwean provincial governor who, on learning of the initiative in early 1997, responded with great enthusiasm, "Well, if they are to do that we must send our Zimbabweans to teach them CAMPFIRE from *A* to *Z*."

This well-meaning interest of Zimbabweans to see CAMPFIRE extended into this area of Mozambique was—on its own—not going to amount to much. Very few Zimbabweans understand much about Mozambique or can speak Portuguese,[12] and although this area lay within a few hundred kilometers of Zimbabwe's capital and three thousand kilometers from Maputo, whatever was to be realized there would require a commitment from the national level in Mozambique.

Three further factors are key to understanding how this commitment from the Mozambican national level was generated in the National Directorate of Forestry and Wildlife in Maputo. First, in 1992 two remarkable young Mozambicans studying wildlife management in Mweka College in Tanzania—Luís Namanha and António Abacar—were sent to the area to undertake their fieldwork because no other wilderness areas of the country were safe enough, due to the war, to conduct serious wildlife management activities. Namanha and Abacar brought an awareness of CAMPFIRE gained at their college to their fieldwork, which focused on conflicts between the Zimbabwean safari company that believed they had exclusive rights and local people who had never been consulted in the allocation of the concession and had received no benefits. The two men had even seen a film at their college about the Masoka village, described in Murphree's chapter, which Brian Child had been instrumental in making some years earlier.[13]

Namanha and Abacar's field report, written in English, revealed problems involving lack of community involvement and lack of mechanisms to deal with these problems in Mozambique. Copies of the report found their way to Maputo but generated greater resonance with officials in the IUCN office in Harare, which had provided them with logistical assistance. Although in Maputo no action was taken on the findings, the report was important because it placed the issue on the table, so that advantage could be taken of the second development, which precipitated the Tchuma Tchato program. This was that three leading figures in the national directorate, Milagre Nuvunga, Bartolomeu Soto, and Afonso Madope, determined that with peace the country must move in the direction of community programs and that a pilot program would be a key step in this policy shift. This view had its origins primarily in the negative experiences this group had seen with other approaches during the 1980s, as well as their exposure to these new ideas. Afonso Madope had even visited CAMPFIRE programs in Nyaminyami in Zimbabwe in 1993.

The Tchuma Tchato area was the obvious pilot site, given that a hunting safari company already operated there and that the area was close to the CAMPFIRE region of Zimbabwe. A third factor precipitating the project was my arrival as Mozambique program officer for the Ford Foundation. Ford had backed the action research behind CAMPFIRE in Zimbabwe and had determined that CBNRM would likely be their new focus in Mozambique. Furthermore, because its regional office was then in Harare, the foundation hoped to focus on rural areas of Mozambique that were within driving distance of Zimbabwe. The Zimbabweans at IUCN had already approached the foundation about funding this Mozambican project before my appointment. I had done my doctoral work in Zimbabwe, was close to the Centre for Applied Social Sciences (CASS) and Marshall Murphree, and was simultaneously talking to the Mozambican National Directorate of Forestry and Wildlife about their plans. The combination of these factors led to a rapid determination that the foundation would fund the Tchuma Tchato program.

Despite this collective agreement, the actual establishment of a program required a further, political insertion into the Mozambican landscape. No legal framework existed for granting community rights over land and natural resources, and the Zimbabwean company Mozambique Safaris had high-level Mozambican connections. It had gained de facto total rights over the area and was operating with apparent impunity. This was the period between peace and the elections, and the government had developed no policy framework in this area, nor did it have the desire or capacity to implement anything decisively. Furthermore, and in contrast to most of the other safari companies in the region, Mozambique Safaris was at that time hostile to CAMPFIRE approaches. It was even said that they had left Zimbabwe because no local council or community would grant them concessions, because of their poor record in this regard, and that they had been expelled from Tanzania on similar grounds. The program's Zimbabwean CAMPFIRE allies could therefore not prevail on the company to support this endeavor.

In February 1994 I arranged with Marshall Murphree and CASS for Soto and Madope to visit the area for the first time. We were accompanied by Zimbabwean Mike Murphree, who was being seconded by IUCN to Mozambique's Forestry and Wildlife Department, and another key Mozambican actor in this general field, Camila de Sousa. This field visit was a formative experience. Quite apart from being denied access to the area by the Mozambican administrator of a district who turned out to have no jurisdiction over the area, we agonized over how the process could be legalized. One idea was to create a cooperative. We listened in shock to the complaints of the local people about their treatment by the company. It was only later that year, when President Chissano announced a decentralization strategy based on local elected municipalities with legal rights to allocate resources and to levy taxes, that Soto and Madope saw a way forward. Ironically, this was announced in the Changara District of Tete, and the press cutting adorned the wall in Soto's office for many months. With this policy commitment to decentralize (its legal basis advanced little, and it was eventually abandoned entirely for the poorer and marginalized wilderness districts), it was possible to imagine the means forward, but what could motivate and justify such a step politically?

The opportunity to change the relationship of the company to the community then arose when Cadmiel Muntemba, governor of Tete, began receiving reports of company abuses of local people. Subsequently, he felt himself insulted by the proprietor of Mozambique Safaris when he convened a meeting to address these complaints and his authority to do so was challenged.[14] Discussing the issue with me in Maputo during the First National Land Conference, Muntemba decided to discipline Mozambique Safaris and gained authorization from President Chissano to suspend the company's operations and hold an inquiry into their conduct. This presented the Wildlife Department with an opportunity to propose an agreement wherein Mozambique Safaris would work with the community as a condition for their being allowed to resume operations. These changes were facilitated when, at the end of 1994, two allies of Mozambique Safaris—the prime minister and ambassador to Zimbabwe—were shuffled out or down within the new government. The opportunity was a limited one, and I suspect that their report was very gentle and careful. The minister of Agriculture and Fisheries apparently went so far as to tell them that if this attempt at community involvement did not work it would not be explored elsewhere.

Taking advantage of this political space, the Wildlife Department sent Luís Namanha—who had now graduated from Mweka and returned to Mozambique—to establish the program in the area with logistical and technical support from Mike Murphree and the IUCN regional office in Harare. Meanwhile, the Wildlife Department in Maputo set about working on how revenues could be generated for the community from safari hunting. From the outset it was clear that the CAMPFIRE mechanisms were not appropriate at this stage in Mozambique. They were based on legally and politically different local government structures and on a capacity for transparent and competitive allocation of safari-hunting tenders, with companies offering proportional shares of gross revenue. It seemed clear that in the case of Mozambique Safaris the only option was a tax-based approach.

In search of a workable tax-based approach, Madope took an imaginative line whereby revenues would be derived through setting special trophy prices for the area that were about three times higher than normal Mozambican fees but still lower than those in neighboring countries. The idea was that the difference between the normal fees and the special fees would be used as the local dividend. A fascinating period followed while Madope sought approval for this plan from his own minister of Agriculture and Fisheries, the Ministry of State Administration, the Ministry of Justice, and the Ministry of Finance. Each had a different view of what share communities should obtain and which entity of provincial or local government should get the balance (in addition to one-third for the central treasury). The initial proposals to benefit the provincial or the district forestry and wildlife service or agriculture department were replaced by an agreement to support local government to build constituency and not destabilize the local areas by having communities with far greater budgets than government. Madope decided that an even split between them would be the best way to avoid further debate. This process had, of course, all the ingredients of the kind of strategic compromise described by Murphree in his nodal chapter on CAMPFIRE (this volume).

We now turn to the local dimension of the establishment of Tchuma Tchato in the Bawa community. It is a striking and inspiring story of how a deeply alienated and hostile community, previously dependent on compromise with powerful outsiders in the pillaging of the area's natural resources, was gradually won over by Luís Namanha. In the process Luís came to be recognized as one of the continent's most gifted wildlife department officials, now celebrated across Mozambican society. But this was nevertheless a slow process with passive resistance gradually giving way to active engagement as people acquired confidence and, over time, a new sense of well-being. Luís surmounted extraordinary logistical problems, and he faced down great personal dangers as he challenged armed groups who were profiting from wildlife hunting. These groups often had links with the local military police, government, and military officials. Above all, Luís's dedicated service and scrupulous ethics gained him the trust of a series of village communities who had never encountered an outsider and government official who actually tried to empower them. This was a laborious process, creating elected and accountable village councils, establishing a locally recruited force of wildlife scouts, and securing mechanisms to control the hunting of the safari company. Without this process, however, no amount of external contact would have enabled the program to flourish. But useful external contact there was, and in truth it was a dynamic that simultaneously demonstrated that programs of this nature can succeed only when they are deeply felt to be locally owned and that people often develop, come to know, and find value in their own visions and identities through interacting with the outside world.

Probably the single most important interactions with outsiders were the exchanged visits between the community of Bawa in Mozambique and Masoka in Zimbabwe in February of 1996. As a pioneer community of the CAMPFIRE program, the Masoka wildlife committee was well placed to explain with confidence the challenges and opportunities of these programs to the assembled villagers in Bawa and then to show off their achievements on a return visit from Bawa community leaders. As Murphree argues in his chapter, this exchange was particularly powerful because it combined attention to a credible messenger with a credible message. He modestly omits that he himself was one of the credible messengers, in that Bawa village members warmed to Murphree as someone who had clearly demonstrated a capacity to care and deliver in Masoka and so, it was felt, would therefore do the same in Bawa. The second really significant external exchange, where the Bawa community felt a recognition of their achievements, was when four Bawa leaders traveled to the International Association for the Study of Common Property in Berkeley, California, in June 1996. There they gave a powerful presentation to an enraptured audience and were asked, "What made you really believe you could achieve all this?" They answered, "When Marshall Murphree came with the Masoka people to tell us about CAMPFIRE." While my own frequent visits and meetings with them were useful, I had no track record like Murphree's, with points of reference that were so meaningful for them. (However, in popular Bawa folklore my role appears to be growing.)

In addition to these important contacts with the CAMPFIRE process, and the validating experience of telling the outside world of their efforts, Bawa villagers' confidence and vision have been buttressed by a series of visits by important and appreciative outsiders, including no less than Mozambican president Joaquim Chissano, prime minister Pascoal Mocumbi, and numerous other ministers and senior officials. Other visitors have come from other provinces and donor agencies interested in replicating the program within Mozambique. The making of a film in Bawa about their experience, by the Mozambican film company Ébano, also helped structure their reflections on what they had achieved. Seeing this movie, and a subsequent film (*Mariana and the Moon*) describing the travels of perhaps their most gifted and engaged spirit medium (shaman), Mariana Mphande, also greatly increased their sense of the value of what they had achieved.

According to members of the Bawa community, this process of interacting with the outside world, with leading Mozambicans, and with neighboring Zimbabweans helped them not only to sense the value of their aims and achievements but also to become Mozambicans. This was true in both a literal sense in that community leaders who had never had Mozambican papers (let alone passports) or even visited their provincial capital had to go through these processes to partake in these exchanges. But it was even more true in the psychological sense that in the emergence of a program based on people gaining control over their land and resources—and over the direction of their socioeconomic development—Bawa people for the first time had a reason to feel Mozambican with pride and to look to Mozambique as their future. Thus even before revenues were distributed to the population, large numbers of people originally from the area returned from long economic and political exiles in Zimbabwe and Zambia, and local people began building much more beautiful homes to replace the huts of temporary sojourn used during their wanderings around neighboring countries in search of income, education, shops, or services. With the program, Mozambican currency has come into use, and the circulation of people and ideas within the Mozambican interior has reached unprecedented levels.

To mirror this sense of self-initiative at the village level, a seminar held at the provincial capital of Tete in November 1996 helped the Mozambican officials involved to feel that they were taking the policy and intellectual initiatives from outsiders and from CAMPFIRE. Brilliant presentations by Zimbabweans at this meeting, most notably from Stephen Kasere on the challenges faced by CAMPFIRE, began to be seen as exchanges between peers rather than as lessons from superior neighbors. This has been coupled with an aggressive approach to expanding and deepening Tchuma Tchato in the province, masterminded by the gifted provincial governor at the time, Virgílio Ferrão, alongside the provincial director of Agriculture and Fisheries, Sérgio Yé, and the head of the Tchuma Tchato unit, Marcelino Foloma. The combination has conveyed to the Mozambicans a sense of both ownership and the importance of their endeavor. They have brought this new sophistication and confidence to bear in their current efforts to learn from South Africa about the opportunities and mechanics of creating joint ventures between communities and the private sector in ecotourism. At the time, it was assumed that this comparative South African and Botswanan ecotourism experience would primarily be applied to partnerships with Zimbabwean companies, given positive experiences with CAMPFIRE principals like sport fishermen Tiger Odyssey and safari company Zambezi Hunters. Events in Zimbabwe, however, as well as the failure of the Mozambican authorities to create a clear legal basis for joint ventures with Tchuma Tchato communities, resulted in little action in this regard.

CONCLUSION

This chapter has sought to convey the multiple and convoluted processes through which ideas about CBNRM in Mozambique were generated and disseminated, and to demonstrate that this happened in ways that were both linked and unlinked to Zimbabwe's CAMPFIRE program. I have argued that CAMPFIRE was an important stimulus for the Mozambican initiative but that this stimulus created response—and indeed created a particular kind of response—only because of Mozambique's unique context and because of processes that generated Mozambican visions of what they needed and wanted to achieve through such programs. Indeed, it was the strength of the latter that resulted in the veritable bubbling up of such initiatives in Mozambique, compared with the systematic growth of the centrally managed CAMPFIRE program in Zimbabwe's rather different political economy. This interpretation very much chimes with the spirit and detail of Murphree's nodal chapter in its consideration of the complex sets of relations and processes that inevitably condition and drive such programs, both in terms of the endogenous nature of the process and in terms of the importance of the sharing of experiences between societies. This sharing occurs both in the realm of intellectual and government leadership and at the community grassroots level. Murphree's account represents an intriguing challenge regarding how we should conceive of intellectual and institutional histories, as we try to untangle the visions and roles of individuals and the sociopolitical contexts that create and interpret them. Writing this chapter has challenged me in similar ways. Like Murphree, I have had to try to deal with having been a central actor more than an observer. And, in case any reader could possibly imagine otherwise by now, it should be clear that in a country as wonderfully dis-integrated and creatively chaotic as Mozambique, many other versions of this process still await articulation in academic English.

But what does this process of disseminating notions of CBNRM actually mean to people? Two weeks before the June 1997 conference for which this chapter was originally written, I spent some time with the village leadership of Daque, a crowded settlement on arid soils among giant baobabs on the southern shore of the giant Cahora Bassa reservoir. The origins of Daque lie in a tangle of war and coercive development over a twenty-five-year period. It began in the early 1970s as a garrison of Portuguese troops sent to halt the guerrilla fighters of Frelimo in their successful penetration of central Mozambique across the Zambezi river through the Manherere hills. During the 1970s the population crowded into Daque as fugitives from the rising water of the reservoir and under the coercive "villagization" programs of the colonial Portuguese and independent Frelimo governments. During the 1980s, more people arrived as the notorious Renamo guerrillas spread across the area with the Frelimo, Zimbabwean troops responded with scorched-earth policies, and relief agencies focused their support on more secure population centers. After peace in 1992, the area was flooded with outsiders looting the natural resources. Portuguese engineers from the dam shot game at night with spotlights, Zimbabwean *kapenta* fishermen hauled tons of fish from the lake to Harare, and immigrant Mozambicans and other foreigners netted bream. Sports fishermen pursued tiger fish, and loggers were everywhere cutting construction timber and fuelwood. Try as they might, the local people could do nothing to deal with these invaders.

Yet the irony in recent history, explained the village Frelimo secretary, was that amid all this pain, each of the ratchets that had ground people further into social disruption, penury, and environmental degradation had been initially presented by the authorities as the beginning of a developmental utopia. Cahora Bassa was to be an engine of economic growth for the whole region. Liberation and socialism would develop Mozambique in just ten years. "Villagization" would bring services and modernize the village economy. Renamo would destroy socialism and herald the benefits of capitalism. The aid agencies would use relief to bring development. Peace would enable resource extraction and an economic boom. But, the elders lamented, none of these development processes had ever responded to the actual problems of Daque; the government would not even listen when they talked of how Cahora Bassa had destroyed their livelihoods, they explained. Asked whether the land-guardianship spirits could not step in and create a sense of community and address the environmental imbalances created by concentrated settlement, one old man quipped "the spirits have simply given up; they are waiting to hear from the government!" Meanwhile, the government had no solutions and stopped even sending administrators to Daque because "they all either died or went mad."

In this context, Marcelino Foloma and I sat with the local villagers and discussed Tchuma Tchato. The program could establish control over external resource users and demand real benefits; it could negotiate to regulate the water levels in Cahora Bassa to enable local agricultural and fisheries benefits; it could provide for realistic local resource governance with a place for the land spirits. Very good. But it was another utopia, remarked the FRELIMO secretary, who then added, "We are like the kudu, who, approached by the hunter, is startled, but then curious. It stops and cranes its neck around a trunk to see who is coming, and delays a moment too long, and catches a bullet. So that is how we see Tchuma Tchato. It could be a bullet like the other development plans. But this is the first time we were ever really asked about our problems, and heard anything meaningful in response from outside. We cannot let this chance pass." This, then, is the context in which Mozambicans try with vision, sincerity, and naïveté to reverse decades of distortions in centuries of developmental failure. And as the villagers say along the Zambezi, in the growing hope that such an approach will really be meaningful, "Viva Tchuma Tchato!"

In the years since this chapter was first written, Tchuma Tchato in Daque has taken deep root, even if the increasingly variable rainfall and the erratic management of the Cahora Bassa dam have submerged its operational headquarters and ruined Daque's agricultural economy, and even if the incomes from wildlife have been terribly delayed for legal reasons. Tchuma Tchato as a whole, meanwhile, became simultaneously more a local and community-based program and more of a government program, and despite solid advocacy from Tchuma Tchato staff and others—there being by 2001 close to fifty community-resource management programs in the country—Mozambique is more clearly on the edge than ever: either to decide to grant communities real resource rights or perhaps only to ask them to participate. A lack of clarification of resource rights has prevented the development of more than rudimentary economic activities, in turn constraining the revenues needed for actual management and community benefit. Meanwhile, Tchuma Tchato has suffered seriously from the winding down of Ford Foundation support. Links to CAMPFIRE have faded, though important lessons, especially about institutional sustainability, are still to be learned from it and though rural Zimbabweans (and rural Mozambicans) need all the friends and outside contact they can get. The situation in the region still seems to be that, despite the flow of ideas, vision, and enthusiasm and the development of working models, it has not been possible to escape a political economy where real land and resource rights for rural people are too threatening for the postcolonial state to countenance. This is the case whether they bubble up or are centrally dispersed with donor support. As Mozambicans say, sometimes wearily, "A luta continua!"

NOTES

1. Anstey also remarked on a third model—exemplified by Angola—marked by high levels of local initiative and leadership consequent on a withdrawal of the state, a policy vacuum, and the absence of NGOs and other institutions at the local level.

2. I am further grateful to Dr. James Murombedzi for his stimulating comments on this issue.

3. Particularly frustrating for the African rural populations is that they are both denied legal personality as individuals in respect to land and resource rights—being told in effect that their category of citizenship, by direct colonial inheritance, allows them to express rights only as part of a collective entity (nowadays termed *community*)—and cannot hold rights against a state, rather than being subordinate to it, because states never developed any legal framework allowing it.

4. In 1991, when Minister of Culture Dr. Mateus Katupha sought to explain the interest of his government in the research I was undertaking in rural Mozambique during the war, he remarked, "Look, we Mozambicans know all about the latest intellectual fashions of Paris, the new economic theories coming out of Washington, and the academic debates in London. But we have not the faintest idea what our own peasants are thinking about."

5. In other African states, attempts to ground resource-management and local-governance issues in local communities and cultures have tended to immediately become tangled up in the politics of essentialism and tribalism. In Mozambique the lack of tribal identifications among the elite—excepting perhaps in the cases of Ndau-Sena conflict in Sofala and Makua-Makonde conflict in Cabo Delgado—is enormously liberating for such debates and policies.

6. In a discussion with Mozambicans from the embassy in Harare of the differences between CAMPFIRE and the Tchuma Tchato program, a senior embassy offi-

cial jested, "Well, being Mozambican, Tchuma Tchato would certainly have to be more ambitious than CAMPFIRE."

7. I have said little in this description about the attitudes and internal dynamics within rural Mozambican society that are relevant to the emergence of such initiatives. This is difficult to address in a general way, the country being so large and diverse, but my omission also reflects that it was the young technicians who seized the political initiative in 1990s Mozambique. This is later discussed further regarding the case study of Tchuma Tchato.

8. The creation in 1997 of a national office for the IUCN in Mozambique, then headed by Dr. Ebenizário Chonguiça and after 2000 by Dr. Isilda Nhantumbo, enabled a change in this dynamic because the IUCN has increasingly been able to convene its member agencies and other interested parties around these agendas.

9. It is amusing to contemplate that if CAMPFIRE had been even more successful it might not have spread so quickly to Mozambique.

10. "A Review of Community Wildlife/Natural Resource Management Initiatives in Mozambique," IUCN-Mozambique, unpublished paper, 1997.

11. In point of fact, from a historical perspective, it is really the reverse: Zimbabwe and Zambia's Zambezi Valley, at least as far as Chirundu, were tightly integrated into the trading and political system centered on the Portuguese-speaking middle and lower Zambezi over several centuries before Britain's superior power in Europe saw the area annexed by Cecil John Rhodes's British South Africa Company.

12. Although the rural peoples of central Mozambique speak similar or related languages to those of Zimbabwe, the country's different social histories mean both that Zimbabweans find rural Mozambican society surprisingly alien and that it is virtually impossible for Zimbabweans to deal with Mozambican officialdom in Shona. This is in part because many officials do not speak these languages and also because the idea that official business could be conducted in such local languages is anathema for Mozambicans.

13. Ironically, the film was never used for the dissemination of CAMPFIRE within Zimbabwe as intended because of political interference. It was first seen in Masoka when taken there by the Mozambican company making the film on Tchuma Tchato. Furthermore, the cameraman for the Zimbabweans on the Masoka film, João Costa (Funcho), was then involved in making the award-winning Mozambican Tchuma Tchato film.

14. Aaron Makina, a gifted eccentric and phenomenal linguist, had drifted back and forth between Mozambican and Zimbabwean identities, spending much time in western Tete during and immediately after the war. He added to the complaints by reporting the company to the provincial attorney general in Beira, and with my brokering, he made a formal submission on the company's behavior to the National Directorate of Forestry and Wildlife.

6

Model, Panacea, or Exception? Contextualizing CAMPFIRE and Related Programs in Africa

Roderick P. Neumann

This chapter is at once a response to Marshall Murphree's richly detailed and insightful chapter on CAMPFIRE (this volume) and a reflection on my own hopes and fears for community-based natural resource management (CBNRM) and integrated conservation and development projects (ICDPs) in Africa. Many of the examples will be taken from my research experience in Tanzania. I begin with some general observations and reactions to Murphree's chapter. This is followed by an examination of the broader spatio-historical and political-economic contexts for natural resource management policies in Africa. Here I address how international and national political-economic structures and processes interact with CAMPFIRE and other CBNRM programs and ICDPs elsewhere. The chapter closes with some thoughts on future directions for research.

REACTIONS AND OBSERVATIONS

Exploring CAMPFIRE's Exceptionalism

Murphree begins with two opening caveats concerning the transferability of CAMPFIRE to other locales: first, that CAMPFIRE was not imported by international agencies and, second, that it never had the protected area conservation focus common with most ICDPs. The first point is a critical one in judging the potential of CBNRM and ICDPs to alter the relations between state and society and in particular to reduce conflicts between natural resource agencies and rural communities. The voluntary participation of communities in CAMPFIRE is rarely duplicated in interventions led by international conservation nongovernmental organizations (NGOs). In most CBNRM programs and ICDPs I know or have seen reviewed, communities are targeted for projects because of their location near protected area boundaries. Often, these are communities with histories of struggle with state conservation agencies and marked by active resistance to and protest of protected area policies. Some types of ICDPs, particularly buffer zones, constitute a geographical expansion of state and international NGO authority beyond the boundaries of protected areas and into rural communities. Communities whose participation is not voluntary but encouraged by external agents as a way of reducing historic pressures on protected areas will generally not have the same intense self-interest demonstrated by Murphree's Masoka example. Like many rural development projects, this means that success will last only as long as the inputs—be they in the form of financial, managerial, or enforcement capabilities—keep flowing.

I do not completely agree with the second caveat, which draws a distinction between CAMPFIRE and ICDPs. I expand on this later. It suffices to say here that even a quick glance at a land-use map of Zimbabwe shows a strong geographical correlation among communal lands, protected areas, and agriculturally marginal lands. Although location next to a protected area is not a criterion for participation in CAMPFIRE, it is fairly common in existing projects.

I do agree, however, that the ideological underpinnings of CAMPFIRE are quite different from the Western romanticism that has driven the creation of national parks in Africa and elsewhere. Murphree quotes Leopold on game management as a form of agriculture to emphasize the utilitarian approach to wildlife that underpins CAMPFIRE. Leopold himself was influenced by earlier developments in scientific forestry as introduced in the United States by Gifford Pinchot through the principle of sustained-yield timber harvesting. Wildlife, shorn of its romantic fleece, is thus seen as a potential source of accumulation. As such, it has played an important supporting role in the integration of the world's regions into a global capitalist economy. Particularly in European settler colonies, from North America (Wolf 1982) to Southern Africa (MacKenzie 1987, 41–61; Gordon 1992), wildlife as a source of protein for labor or as a source of income from the sale of animal products was fundamental to the advance of market relations into the hinterlands.

CAMPFIRE policies likewise recognize wildlife as a commodity but with an important difference from past conditions: they are intended to shift the locus of accumulation from the level of the global and national to one more local. Herein lies the critical defining characteristic of CAMPFIRE: the devolution of (some) ownership and control of a natural resource from the national, state, or multinational capital to more localized political entities and small-scale entrepreneurs. This characteristic is also key for developing categories of CBNRM programs such as CAMPFIRE. That is, what seems important for categorizing and differentiating these programs is not whether they are associated with protected areas (some ICDPs are, some are not; see Bergin 1995) or whether they are oriented toward conservation or production, but how they affect the distribution of power over ownership and control of land and resources between state and society.

Strategic Silences

Murphree makes two crucial observations on key areas of political struggle that were glossed over in the negotiations to create CAMPFIRE. The first is the issue of defining or conferring appropriate authority for the purposes of resource management. Rather than create new forms of political units or new political institutions for wildlife management, the CAMPFIRE document of 1986 remained silent on appropriate authority. As a consequence, this left natural resource co-ops within the administrative structure of existing Rural District Councils (RDCs) and Village Development Committees (VIDCOs). This is a critical silence for CAMPFIRE, and any attempts to emulate it elsewhere inevitably run into the same issue. If existing political institutions are undemocratic, unrepresentative, or not accountable, any CBNRM program and ICDP created within them can scarcely hope to be a source of equitably distributed benefits derived from wildlife. Thus the proposed linkage between the redistribution of benefits and an improved climate for wildlife conservation that underpins many CBNRM programs and ICDPs is far from guaranteed. This linkage can begin to be made only if relatively democratic institutions either already exist or are created as part of the CBNRM-ICDP intervention. (I think this is clearly supported by Murphree's example of the relatively successful case of Masoka.) This is one of the reasons I wish to argue for environmental interventions in Africa, particularly those led by international conservation NGOs, to take a more politically progressive approach. Institutional reform and democratization are prerequisites for successful community resource management in most rural areas of Africa.

The second observation concerns the question of what constitutes a community for the purposes of implementing CAMPFIRE. Put more generally, the meaning of *community-based* is to a large degree determined by the way communities are identified. In the case of CAMPFIRE, the original goal of having self-defined communal units of management and production was abandoned upon implementation in 1989. Although Murphree recognizes that some consider this a fatal flaw, he argues that at least the potential is there for future attainment of self-defined management units. Whichever the case for CAMPFIRE, I think that the ideal of voluntary, self-defined community participation is critical for implementing CBNRM programs and ICDPs in all cases. Yet it is rarely pursued, and this can be a deadly defect in programs with less international profile and national support than CAMPFIRE.

Even in cases where this policy is pursued, very difficult questions arise concerning the process by which communities are self-defined. Communities are defined through the narration of particular versions of history, tradition, and land claims. In Africa the process of community definition has a long and conflictual history involving questions of social identity and tenure rights (Colson 1971, 193–215; Berry 1992; Iliffe 1979). Any CBNRM- or ICDP-type intervention, then, raises the issue of who has the power to make their version the legally sanctioned one. In attempting to secure property rights for local communities, CBNRM programs and ICDPs are in danger of igniting internal power struggles and generating conflicting claims on land and resources.

LARGER SPATIO-HISTORICAL AND POLITICAL-ECONOMIC CONTEXTS FOR CBNRM PROGRAMS AND ICDPs IN AFRICA

Historical Considerations

Undoing Past Injustices?

European colonialism is everywhere inscribed upon the African landscape. In no country is it more clear than in Zimbabwe. The widespread displacements of Africans in favor of European settlers has produced a geographically based and racially determined structure of poverty. There is no need to review this here, because the story is told vividly in several of the tables and figures of Murphree's chapter. The point I wish to make is that CAMPFIRE is viewed in some circles, most notably within ZANU at the national level (see Murphree, this volume), as a way to mitigate if not correct the historical displacements of the vast majority of the country's population. This connection between the history and politics of land distribution and national-government support for CAMPFIRE will be elaborated in a later section. First, I want to address the question of mitigation of past policies in a broader geographical and historical context.

In other African countries, related CBNRM programs and ICDPs have also taken the position that, whereas colonial and postcolonial policies have ignored local interests, international conservation NGOs offer a new approach that will help rectify some of these wrongs. In many African countries, past displacements of African populations occurred not only to make room for European settlers, as in Zimbabwe, but also to create the naturalized landscapes of national parks and protected areas. These displacements produced and were produced by a fundamental opposition and antagonism between existing local meanings and uses of space and the competing meanings and uses of European colonizers. The practical outcome was a disruption of existing African spatial practices and the beginning of decades of resistance to state resource conservation practices. Resistance took many forms, from armed rebellions over wildlife laws to cattle trespass, wood theft from forest reserves, and boundary encroachment (Neumann 1998). Many actions were conducted at the community level or with widespread community acquiescence. At its most basic, whatever the form it took, it was resistance to the colonial state's reordering of social space, of its attempt to obliterate the social space of African societies.

Apropos of Murphree's observation that CAMPFIRE has "never had the protected area conservation focus" of ICDPs, the program is nevertheless relevant to protected area management and the mitigation of past conservation displacements in Zimbabwe. Child notes that Operation Windfall, the precursor to CAMPFIRE, was originally motivated by the Department of National Parks and Wild Life Management's (DNPWLM) fear that the "four protected areas in [Sebungwe] region . . . would become ecological islands threatened by settlement" (1996, 361). The western portion of Tsholotsho District—where the district planned its wildlife area as part of CAMPFIRE—borders Hwange National Park (Thomas 1995). Several of the CAMPFIRE projects involve communities displaced in the creation of protected areas or by development projects. Mukwicki Communal Land, Hurungwe District, is on the southern boundary of Mana Pools National Park. Parts of it were settled in the early 1960s by Korekore people relocated from protected areas (Bird and Metcalfe 1995, 3). Mahenye Ward, part of Ndowoyo Communal Land, is on the border of Gonarezhou National Park, and "most of the people were relocated there to make room for the national park" (Murphree 1995, 9). Omay Communal Land in Nyaminyami District surrounds the southern half of Matusadona National Park. The Tonga people were settled there in the 1950s after being displaced by the filling of Kariba Dam (Taylor 1995).

In attempting to redress past injustices and address local concerns generated by the establishment of protected areas, few of the CBNRM programs and ICDPs suggest any retreat from the spatial segregation of nature and society. Most do not allow for any sort of comanagement or selective resource harvesting within existing state-owned protected areas. In the new approach of CBNRM programs and ICDPs, mitigation is the operative word; past conservation displacements will not be undone. In many cases, the CBNRM programs and ICDPs associated with protected areas require further segregation and a rigid spatial ordering of land uses. Settlement must be removed from areas set aside for grazing, grazing from subsistence hunting areas, and hunting areas from fuelwood collecting areas. In general, this sort of segregation of land uses means somebody, or some segment of the community, has to work harder. Cattle herds must be moved greater distances from settlements, fuelwood collected farther from homesteads, and so forth.

Two questions (in the interests of prompting debate) arise from this brief examination of CBNRM and ICDP proposals. First, in attempting to distance a new approach from colonial conservation practices and from racially based land distribution systems, is it possible to alter conflictual social relations without altering spatial relations? In other words, if the displacements and colonial-implemented spatial practices remain intact, what is fundamentally new about the new approach? Second, is the approach of contemporary CBNRM programs and ICDPs fundamentally different from the ideologies that drove past interventions in community resource management? I would like to explore these questions with an example from colonial Tanganyika.

Back to the Future with CBNRM

An early example of state-led CBNRM can be observed in colonial Tanganyika's system of Native Authority Forest Reserves. The idea for the system began with Governor Donald Cameron's vision of delegating responsibility for the protection of the state's Forest Reserves to Native Authorities.[1] Cameron wanted forestry "on a shoestring" (Berry 1992), with the central government's Forest Department taking the role of expert adviser. It was in essence the extension of the principles of indirect rule to forest-reserve management. Cameron's vision of Native Authority forestry was never fulfilled at the scale he imagined, but by the end of the 1930s, a number of small Native Authority Forest Reserves had been established throughout the territory.[2] A 1938 review of the Forest Department states that in "a Territory in which indirect rule is a feature of the administrative system, it is interesting to note the [efforts] to promote an interest in forestry among the natives" (Troup 1938). In line with the principles of indirect rule, any and all benefits derived from native reserves would accrue to the Native Authority treasury.

Forest officers' interest in African forest management had much to do with finding a politically palatable way to eliminate free issue for Africans. Under the early colonial forest laws, Africans with customary claims in forest reserves were allowed to take forest products for their own use but not for sale. Many in the Forest Department saw free issue as inhibiting both scientific forest management and accumulation by the state. They saw native reserves as a source for "purely local needs" (Troup 1935, 15), that is, household consumption, that could supplant free issue from government forests. An associated program of plantation establishment on Native Authority lands was also promoted as a way to reduce free issue.[3] In one such program in the Mbulu District of the Northern Province, residents were stopped from exercising their right to free issue unless they were able to prove they had "made a genuine effort to plant trees on their own" (Moffett 1955, 661).

Forest Department staff, in sum, assumed a direct relationship between the creation of a CBNRM system and the elimination of free-use rights for Africans. The idea of native reserves was representative of the tendency in colonial resource management to spatially segregate productive activities (Beinart 1989). Recognizing that curtailing free use "would be considered a serious interference with traditional rights,"[4] the administration and Forest Department concocted a long-term spatial solution to a political problem. The Forest Department and its clientele of timber concessionaires would exploit the government reserves, and the domestic needs of African peasants would be met by gradually developing a separate forest reserve system.

Is this strategy all that different from many contemporary CBNRM and ICDP proposals in Africa? In particular, how different is it from ICDPs on the boundaries of protected areas that seek to reduce pressure on protected area resources by diverting demand? Like many CBNRM programs and ICDPs, Native Authority forests were planned and directed by the state in targeted communities that were resisting the loss of access to state-owned protected areas. Like many CBNRM programs and ICDPs, the authority over management and revenue rested with existing local political institutions. In this case, it was the individual Native Authorities that the British created to implement indirect rule and that often lacked legitimacy among their constituencies. Finally, like most CBNRM programs and ICDPs, the Native Authority reserves did not alter the pattern of the fragmenting of the African landscape into rigidly separated production, consumption, and occupation categories introduced with colonial occupation.

CONTEMPORARY POLITICAL ECONOMY

The colonial state's conceptualization of community-based management of local forest reserves as a solution to pressures on state-owned reserves can only be explained with reference to the broader policy of indirect rule. Similarly, the relatively recent adoption of CBNRM programs and ICDPs must be understood as related to larger political and economic processes now unfolding across much of the continent. References to these larger processes in Zimbabwe will also aid in assessing CAMPFIRE's transferability to other national settings. Any evaluation of transference potential must be based on a solid historical and political-economic analysis of specific places and the potential for the devolution of authority and control from the national to more local levels. In short, I would like to pursue the question of what political-economic conditions, analyzed at various geographic scales, would promote or enable the devolution of property rights in a similar manner as CAMPFIRE.

Murphree argues cogently in his chapter that, although compromises and silences on key questions of authority and property rights make CAMPFIRE less than ideal, it was probably the best outcome given the political-economic context of its implementation. It might be useful, then, to examine the structures and processes that can constrain, facilitate, and shape CBNRM programs and ICDPs. In the interest of generating debate, I suggest four interrelated political-economic phenomena that provide the context for CAMPFIRE specifically and CBNRM programs and ICDPs in other African countries. First, there is the history of local resistance to state natural resource laws and policies, particularly those related to the establishment and administration of protected areas. Second is the implementation of neoliberal economic reforms in the form of economic structural adjustment programs (SAPs) imposed by the World Bank or International Monetary Fund (IMF). Third is the uneven but promising movement toward democratizing the political process at all levels of government. Fourth is the nearly continentwide implementation of national land reform as a strategy to increase agricultural production.

Resistance to Emparkment

Local resistance to the bounding of space in Africa, specifically to the creation of vast areas of exclusion for nature conservation, is arguably the major force compelling international organizations and national governments to initiate ICDPs. Writing for IUCN, Oldfield asserted that "new ideas are needed" in biodiversity conservation because "local people all too often see parks as government-imposed restrictions on their traditional rights" (1988, 1). These imposed restrictions have been resisted by local communities in actions ranging from organized protests to violent confrontations to "everyday forms of resistance" (Scott 1985) such as poaching and wood theft. Elsewhere I have demonstrated that peasant resistance to the state's conservation policies have a long and consistent history in Africa (Neumann 1998). African peasants and pastoralists have generally resisted these policies because of the coercive and nonparticipatory way they were implemented and because they threatened local livelihoods.

The persistent conflicts between conservation advocates and managers and affected communities have revealed the limits of coercion. Communities have been known to attack natural resource officers attempting to enforce the unpopular conservation laws of the state (Adams and McShane 1992; Neumann 1998). In a worst case scenario for conservationists, national parks have been reclaimed by neighboring communities when the state's ability to make good on threats of violence is diminished (e.g., Lowry and Donahue 1994). In Zimbabwe and South Africa, struggles over park lands have been central in ongoing conflicts between the peasantry and the state and between white and black populations (Carruthers 1989, 1994; Ranger 1993; Moore 1993). Thus conservation thought in Africa shifted in the 1980s in response to the lack of support and often outright hostility among the peasantry. Currently, the notion that conservation will not succeed unless local communities participate in the management of, and receive material benefits from, protected areas drives national government and international conservation NGO initiatives, including CAMPFIRE.

Structural-Adjustment Programs

The World Bank and IMF SAPs implemented in virtually every country in sub-Saharan Africa provide both material and ideological support and motivation for the CBNRM programs and ICDPs. The influence of SAPs on conservation policies is so complex and contradictory that I can only begin to address the relationship here. First, the neoliberal philosophy of SAPs encourages the privatization of all aspects of production, beginning with land. I discuss at greater length later the issue of land tenure. Here I want to point out that in Tanzania, neoliberal reform and the privatization of property have sometimes heightened conflicts over national parks and wildlife conservation. Massive foreign investment in tourist developments (encouraged by Tanzania's liberalized investment code) has had the effect of further marginalizing local communities (Neumann 1995). There is evidence that local communities are losing their claims to land and resources as customary rights are usurped by new title deeds held by outsiders (United Republic of Tanzania 1992).

Zimbabwe has been under various SAP agreements with the IMF off and on since 1982. Like all SAPs, these agreements call for reduced state expenditures, price decontrol, and the privatization of state enterprises. SAPs put extreme political pressures on national governments in Africa whose legitimacy is linked to their ability to deliver the goods in the form of jobs and services. Under the demands of structural adjustment, African governments have drastically reduced expenditures on rural education and health care. Given these conditions, it is easy to understand why ZANU took credit for CAMPFIRE in the way that Murphree describes. The benefits to local communities have been precisely those things that the government can no longer provide, including those directly related to wildlife management: wages, revenue, and food and social services and infrastructure such as clinics, schools, and roads. Masoka is a perfect example of how income from wildlife is now used to provide rural areas with the jobs and services that were formerly the responsibility of the state.

Democratization and New Social Movements

In conjunction with structural adjustment, many African countries have begun to democratize political activities. In many cases, this has meant a movement away from single-party governments toward multiparty national elections. The process has been uneven and marked as often by increased repression and ethnic conflict as by greater mass participation in political life. Although democratization is as ill-defined and poorly understood as local participation, there are nevertheless potential political changes of great importance to CBNRM programs and ICDPs. Most important for the discussion at hand are the possibilities for grassroots political organizing, particularly around land and resource access rights.

An important consideration for proposals for local participation is the role of local institutions—particularly the rapidly proliferating indigenous NGOs—in defining and negotiating land and resource tenure for rural communities. Locally based NGOs have acquired powerful cachet among international donors and conservation NGOs. We cannot, however, assume that local NGOs, which often play a central role in the new CBNRM programs and ICDPs, represent local people's interests for the purposes of regulating land use and access.[5] By definition, NGOs are not popularly elected institutions accountable to an electorate. As Hodgson points out, in Tanzania a handful of well-educated men have positioned themselves as the representatives of Maasai interests to outside donors by virtue of their leadership of indigenous NGOs, and in the process they have marginalized the role of elders and women (1995). Similarly in Masoka, the CAMPFIRE wildlife committee is all male (Nabane 1995), raising questions concerning the extent to which women's interests are represented. In another CAMPFIRE project, Derman points out that a newly created local NGO constituted a layer of bureaucracy between the communal-land residents and their resources (1995, 207). In Zambia the Administrative Management Design for Game Management Areas (ADMADE) program identified chiefs as traditional rulers. Subsequently, "chiefs used these initiatives to secure more power for themselves rather than to facilitate local participation for wildlife" (Gibson and Marks 1995, 947). To summarize from Colchester, local elites will rarely willingly make way for local people's participation but rather will manipulate projects to advance their own political power (1994, 34).

National Land Tenure Policies

A final phenomenon affecting most African countries is the effort to convert customary land tenure to modern forms of land registration and titling.

The main impetus for tenure reform has been the stubbornly low levels of agricultural productivity. Underlying the push for tenure reform is the assumption that customary tenure systems cannot provide the basis for intensified production because they do not provide secure private property rights. Without security of tenure, the argument goes, the investments necessary to increase productivity will not be made. Without going into detail here, it should be noted that validity of this reasoning and these assumptions has been severely challenged by empirical case studies (see Bassett and Crummey 1993).

Similar reasoning has been applied in CBNRM and ICDP designs. For instance, several buffer zone projects or proposals in Tanzania have a land-titling component that overlaps with local (particularly Maasai) efforts to secure customary land rights (African Wildlife Foundation 1989; KIPOC 1992; Makombe 1993, 24; Mbano et al. 1995, 605–16; Neumann 1995; Newmark 1993). These proposals are based on the supposition that titling of land leads to greater security in property rights and greater security will create the conditions for conservation (Oldfield 1988; Cleaver 1993). Evidence from land titling and tenure reform in general does not always support the first part of the hypothesis, and some findings support its converse—that land titling may threaten the security of many customary rights holders (United Republic of Tanzania 1992; Roth 1993, 298–325; Vivian 1994).

The case of Zimbabwe is particularly interesting with regard to land-tenure reform. Ranger (1993, 354–85) details how peasant hopes for a post-unilateral-declaration-of-independence redistribution of land were never met. By the mid-1980s the focus of the land question had shifted from one of redistribution of commercial farms to one of land tenure reform in communal lands. Under this reconceptualization, land degradation, population growth, and customary tenure on communal lands rather than unequal land distribution was responsible for poor agricultural productivity and rural poverty. Given this context, it is easy to see how CAMPFIRE fits ZANU's interests in intensifying production on communal lands to reduce demands for resettlement and land redistribution.

SUGGESTED DIRECTIONS FOR RESEARCH

With the exception of CAMPFIRE, much of the writing on CBNRM programs and ICDPs has been light on analysis and evaluation. Thus ICDPs and CBNRM programs are being rapidly planned and implemented across Africa with little understanding of their effects on social welfare or their effectiveness for biodiversity conservation. There are frightfully few studies conducted that actually examine who wins and loses in the implementation of CBNRM programs and ICDPs, particularly those, like CAMPFIRE, that explicitly engage in restructuring property rights. CAMPFIRE is routinely cited as a successful model for a new approach to conservation in Africa without considering its particular context, specific objectives, and level of success. As Murphree's chapter notes, however, CAMPFIRE failures are at least as common as successes and those projects that are considered successes are highly contingent and limited.

We need to begin to understand how class, gender, ethnic, and regional interests influence the ways that property rights are defined, negotiated, and contested in settings ranging from the peasant household to the state. We need to gather the empirical evidence to show how the new CBNRM programs and ICDPs help shape and are shaped by local contestations and negotiations over the control of land and resource access. Stated differently, we need to understand how conservation interventions are incorporated into ongoing local processes of defining property rights and to investigate the degree to which they merely endorse existing claims or provide opportunities for the generation of new ones. A focus on the micropolitics of land and resource access and its relationship to environmental conservation is one of the principal areas of research that can contribute to the successful implementation of CBNRM programs and ICDPs.

Research needs to be directed toward identifying the lines of fracture in rural communities and determining how segments of the community are differentially and even adversely affected by conservation proposals. Specifically, we need to recognize that local communities are not homogeneous entities whose members share a common set of interests regarding land and resource rights and that conservation interventions, almost by definition, will produce winners and losers in struggles over access. We should use empirical case studies to theorize environmental interventions as a significant and even primary force in the process of changing property relations in parts of rural Africa. In the existing theoretical literature, explanations of change in customary property systems are focused on the role of population growth and expanding agricultural commercialization (Bassett 1993, 3–34). Environmental conservation has been overlooked as a factor in theorizing change in land tenure systems, despite conservation policies having fundamentally reshaped society–land relationships in significant portions of Africa. Most importantly, we need to conceptualize the notion of traditional or customary land tenure as a continuing process of intercommunity and intracommunity negotiation and struggle over rights, rather than a set of ancient laws frozen in time.

Research should seek to understand the effects of CBNRM- and ICDP-type interventions on customary property systems in rural Africa within the larger context of democratization and the rapid growth of new social movements. Specifically, research should address a number of empirical and theoretical questions relating to the dynamics of property rights in this context.

How do these conservation interventions alter the relationship of power between local communities and the state to control land and resource access? Do they decentralize control over land and resource access as the ICDPs intend, or do they recentralize and extend state control as some case studies have suggested (e.g., Hill 1996)? What historical, social, cultural, and political conditions are conducive to one outcome over another? How are communities mobilized politically to either resist or endorse efforts to transform customary tenure systems? Which individuals or segments of society gain and which lose in either of the outcomes?

We need further to recognize that past and present conservation policies are complicit in creating the climate of land-tenure insecurity and environmental degradation within which many rural African communities operate. The establishment of virtually every national park in sub-Saharan Africa required either the outright removal of rural communities or, at the very least, the curtailment of access to lands and resources. Research needs to be directed toward identifying and developing institutional mechanisms for controlling access and use of lands and resources that are seen as legitimate by affected communities and that have a detectable effect on conservation goals.

Finally, we need to understand how CBNRM programs and ICDPs relate to environmental conservation. Often projects are designed not to improve livelihoods but merely to defuse local opposition. This is a very short-sighted and short-lived solution and simply buys the support of (some segments of) local communities rather than integrating conservation with development. Whether the benefits from conservation are reaching the people most directly involved in activities that threaten wildlife and protected areas, and if they are, whether they have any marked effect on their land and resource decisions remain open questions. Research focused on the politics of land is needed to demonstrate the link between conservation and the improvement of local livelihoods.

Are these suggestions asking too much of CBNRM programs and ICDPs? I think not, because these programs must intersect with existing relations of power and be constrained or facilitated by political economic conditions at multiple levels of scale. In rural Africa, there is no possibility of separating environmental conservation questions from questions of property rights, social welfare, human rights, and justice. Murphree clearly recognizes this and sees hope for CAMPFIRE's success and progressive societal contribution in "the escalation of [peasants'] assertiveness" (this volume). Just as resistance to the loss of access rights to land and resources has motivated new efforts to redistribute conservation benefits and promote social welfare in communities adjoining protected areas, so will further pressure from below necessitate close attention to questions of justice and equity. Local demands can be politically radical, and most international NGOs and state authorities are reluctant to go so far as to grant sole control of forests and wildlife habitat to villages or other local political entities. Local participation and local benefit sharing, however, are not the same as local power to control use and access. Yet, in the end, this is what many communities seek. A fascinating example of one of the more radical initiatives coming from below is Murphree's reference to the CAMPFIRE Association now lobbying for the transfer of mineral rights to their members. This is an area of critical theoretical interest as well as of important policy implications for other CBNRM programs and ICDPs. It is also a clear example of why we need more careful research and analysis of the potential of CBNRM programs and ICDPs to promote progressive social change rather than further extend bureaucratic control over local resources.

NOTES

1. Chief Secretary to Conservator of Forests, 9 June 1931, Tanzania National Archive, Secretariat File 10580.
2. Governor Young to Under Secretary MacDonald, 5 July 1939, Tanzania National Archive, Secretariat File 12005.
3. Provincial Commissioner, Southern Highlands to Chief Secretary, 5 May 1939. Tanzania National Archive, Secretariat File 23259.
4. Provincial Commissioner, comments on Forest Circular No. 1, 3 Jan. 1933, Tanzania National Archive, Secretariat File 23259.
5. According to a 1994 study by Thomas-Slayter (1994), the emergence of grassroots organizations has led, in some cases, to increased equity and democratization and, in others, to increased social stratification.

REFERENCES

Adams, Jonathan S., and T. O. McShane. 1992. *The Myth of Wild Africa: Conservation without Illusion*. New York: W.W. Norton.

African Wildlife Foundation. 1989. Protected Areas: Neighbors as Partners: African Wildlife Foundation Community Conservation Projects. Paper presented at the Wildlife Resource Management with Local Participation Workshop, Harare, Zimbabwe.

Bassett, T. 1993. Introduction: The Land Question and Agricultural Transformation in Sub-Saharan Africa. In *Land in African Agrarian Systems*, ed. T. Bassett and D. Crummey. Madison: Univ. of Wisconsin Press.

Bassett, T. J., and Donald E. Crummey, eds. 1993. *Land in African Agrarian Systems*. Madison: Univ. of Wisconsin Press.

Beinart, William. 1989. Introduction: The Politics of Colonial Conservation. *Journal of Southern African Studies* 15(2): 143–62.

Bergin, Patrick. 1995. Conservation and Development: The Institutionalization of

Community Conservation in Tanzania National Parks. PhD diss., Univ. of East Anglia; Norwich, U.K.

Berry, Sara. 1992. Hegemony on a Shoestring: Indirect Rule and Access to Agricultural Land. *Africa* 62(3): 327–55.

Bird, Cherry, and Simon Metcalfe. 1995. *Two Views from CAMPFIRE in Zimbabwe's Hurungwe District: Training and Motivation, Who Benefits and Who Doesn't?* IIED Wildlife and Development Series No. 5. London: International Institute for Environment and Development.

Caruthers, Jane. 1989. Creating a National Park, 1910 to 1926. *Journal of Southern African Studies* 15(2): 188–216.

———. 1994. Dissecting the Myth: Paul Kruger and the Kruger National Park. *Journal of Southern African Studies* 20(2): 263–83.

Child, Graham. 1996. The Role of Community-based Wild Resource Management in Zimbabwe. *Biodiversity and Conservation* 5: 355–67.

Cleaver, Kevin. 1993. A Strategy to Develop Agriculture in Sub-Saharan Africa and a Focus for the World Bank. World Bank Technical Paper Number 203. Washington, D.C.: World Bank.

Colchester, Marcus. 1994. Malaysian Loggers Come Out of the Woodwork. World Rainforest Movement. Ms.

Colson, Elizabeth. 1971. The Impact of the Colonial Period on the Definition of Land Rights. In *Colonialism in Africa 1870–1960. Vol. 3, Profiles of Change: African Society and Colonial Rule*, ed. Victor Turner. Cambridge, U.K.: Cambridge Univ. Press.

Derman, B. 1995. Environmental NGOs, Dispossession, and the State: The Ideology and Praxis of African Nature and Development. *Human Ecology* 23(2): 199–215.

Gibson, C. C., and S. A. Marks. 1995. Transforming Rural Hunters into Conservationists: An Assessment of Community-based Wildlife Management Programs in Africa. *World Development* 23(6): 941–57.

Gordon, Robert. 1992. *The Bushman Myth: The Making of a Namibian Underclass.* Boulder, Colo.: Westview.

Hill, K. A. 1996. Zimbabwe's Wildlife Utilization Programs: Grassroots Democracy or an Extension of State Power? *African Studies Review* 39(1): 103–23.

Hodgson, D. 1995. Critical Interventions: The Politics of Studying "Indigenous" Development. Paper presented at the annual meeting of the American Anthropological Association, Washington, D.C.

Iliffe, John. 1979. *A Modern History of Tanganyika.* Cambridge, U.K.: Cambridge Univ. Press.

Korongoro Integrated Peoples Oriented to Conservation (KIPOC). 1992. *The Foundation Program: Program Profile and Rationale*. Principal Document No. 4. Loliondo, Tanzania: Korongoro Integrated Peoples Oriented to Conservation.

Lowry, Alma, and T. P. Donahue. 1994. Parks, Politics, and Pluralism: The Demise of National Parks in Togo. *Society and Natural Resources* 7: 321–29.

MacKenzie, John. 1987. Chivalry, Social Darwinism and Ritualized Killing: The Hunting Ethos in Central Africa up to 1914. In *Conservation in Africa: People, Policies and Practice*, ed. D. Anderson and R. Grove. Cambridge, U.K.: Cambridge Univ. Press, 41–61.

Makombe, K., ed. 1993. *Sharing the Land: Wildlife, People and Development in Africa*. IUCN/ROSA Environmental Series No. 1. Harare, Zimbabwe: IUCN–The World Conservation Union.

Mbano, B. N., R. C. Malpas, M. K. Maige, P. A. Symonds, and D. M. Thompson. 1995. The Serengeti Regional Conservation Strategy. In *Serengeti II: Dynamics, Management, and Conservation of an Ecosystem*, ed. A. R. Sinclair and P. Arcese. Chicago: Univ. of Chicago Press.

Moffett, J. P., ed. 1955. *Tanganyika: A Review of Its Resources and Their Development*. Dar es Salaam, Tanzania. Government Printers.

Moore, Donald. 1993. Contesting Terrain in Zimbabwe's Eastern Highlands: Political Ecology, Ethnography and Peasant Resource Struggles. *Economic Geography* 69: 380–401.

Murphree, Marshall. 1995. *The Lesson from Mahenye: Rural Poverty, Democracy and Wildlife Conservation*. IIED Wildlife and Development Series No. 1. London: International Institute for Environment and Development.

Nabane, Nontokozo. 1995. *Lacking Confidence? A Gender-sensitive Analysis of CAMPFIRE in Masoka Village*. IIED Wildlife and Development Series No. 3. London: International Institute for Environment and Development.

Neumann, R. 1995. Ways of Seeing Africa: Colonial Recasting of African Society and Landscape in Serengeti National Park. *Ecumene* 2: 149–69.

———. 1998. *Imposing Wilderness: Struggles Over Livelihood and Nature Preservation in Africa*. Berkeley: Univ. of California Press.

Newmark, William. 1993. The Role and Design of Wildlife Corridors with Examples from Tanzania. *Ambio* 22: 500–4.

Oldfield, Sara. 1988. *Buffer Zone Management in Tropical Moist Forests: Case Studies and Guidelines*. Gland, Switzerland: IUCN–The World Conservation Union.

Ranger, Terence. 1993. The Communal Areas of Zimbabwe. In *Land in African Agrarian Systems*, ed. Thomas J. Bassett and Donald E. Crummey. Madison: Univ. of Wisconsin Press.

Roth, Michael. 1993. Somalia Land Policies and Tenure Impacts. In *Land in African Agrarian Systems*, ed. Thomas J. Bassett and Donald E. Crummey. Madison: Univ. of Wisconsin Press.

Scott, James. 1985. *Weapons of the Weak: Everyday Forms of Peasant Resistance*. New Haven, Conn.: Yale Univ. Press.

Taylor, Russel. 1995. *From Liability to Asset: Wildlife in the Omay Communal Land of Zimbabwe*. IIED Wildlife and Development Series No. 8. London: International Institute for Environment and Development.

Thomas, Stephen. 1995. *Share and Share Alike? Equity in CAMPFIRE*. IIED Wildlife and Development Series No. 2. London: International Institute for Environment and Development.

Thomas-Slatyer, B. 1994. Structural Change, Power Politics, and Community Organizations in Africa: Challenging Patterns, Puzzles, and Paradoxes. *World Development* 22(10): 1479–90.

Troup, R. S. 1935. Report on Forestry in Tanganyika Territory, 1935. Tanzania National Archive, Secretariat File 23115.

———. 1938. Review of "Tanganyika Territory: Annual Report of the Forest Department for 1937." *Empire Forestry Review* 17: 325–26.

United Republic of Tanzania. 1992. *Report of the Presidential Committee of Inquiry into Land Matters. Vol. I.* Dar es Salaam: United Republic of Tanzania.

Vivian, Jessica. 1994. NGOs and Sustainable Development in Zimbabwe: No Magic Bullets. *Development and Change* 25: 167–93.

Wolf, Eric. 1982. *Europe and the People without History*. Berkeley: Univ. of California Press.

7

What We Need Is a Community Bambi: The Perils and Possibilities of Powerful Symbols

Louise Fortmann

While it is commonplace to talk about university professors as living in some sort of theoretical ivory tower disconnected from the real world, serious scholars of rural development actually spend a great deal of time living in the very real rural village world of maize meal, mud, and malaria. This chapter explores the perils of a different kind of disconnection—assumptions about symbols that have deep meanings in our own popular culture. This is important because the concepts and misconceptions of popular culture can and do drive political decisions.

I learned this the hard way when I was plunged into the world of congressional politics and op-ed writing after a colleague brought me a copy of an editorial from the *San Francisco Examiner* (14 April 1997) titled "Elephant Killers."[1] The editorial was the result of a Humane Society of the United States (HSUS) campaign to end United States Agency for International Development (USAID) funding for a Zimbabwean program for village control of natural resources, especially wild animals, known as CAMPFIRE (Communal Areas Management Programme for Indigenous Resources).

For me, community was a powerful symbol. When Marshall Murphree (this volume) talks about communities, I get a warm and fuzzy feeling and a picture flashes into my mind of him joking with Chief Kanyurira of the CAMPFIRE village of Masoka. I suspect that most field-oriented people also respond at some level to the invocation of community with some personal reference point—people in a place where we have lived and worked. That community matters is self-evident to people with such experience in rural communities. But assuming that communities are a similarly powerful symbol for everyone can have negative consequences for our ability to spread our models of community resource management. Nowhere has this been more clear to me than in the course of countering the HSUS campaign against CAMPFIRE.

This chapter proceeds in three parts woven around the story of my own involvement. I begin with a brief description of CAMPFIRE. Second, I present three anti-CAMPFIRE editorials and analyze the underlying stories on which they rely. Third, I explore the missing story of community and the implications of its absence.

CAMPFIRE

Starting in the late nineteenth century, European settlers in present-day Zimbabwe seized most of the best land, forcing African residents onto small patches of poor quality, poorly watered land that have been known by various names over time. They are currently called Communal Areas. In 1989 the Zimbabwean government instituted a program under which proprietary rights over wildlife that heretofore had been vested in the state were devolved to appropriate local authorities in the Communal Areas, in the same way that they had effectively been devolved to white commercial farmers under the white-settler government's 1975 Parks and Wildlife Act. Under CAMPFIRE rural villages were able to manage their own wildlife, including making arrangements with safari operators to bring in hunters and photographers. CAMPFIRE has had its ups and downs, but at its best it has provided villagers with cash income and wild animals with protection from poaching (Murphree, this volume; Murphree and Hulme 2001).

ANTI-CAMPFIRE EDITORIALS

The first anti-CAMPFIRE editorial I saw was in the 14 April 1997 issue of the *San Francisco Examiner*. It featured a drawing of a rather droopy elephant and the subhead "The U.S. spends millions of dollars to promote the hunting and slaughter of pachyderms in a corrupt program in Zimbabwe."

> When we see elephants perform in the circus or caged in the zoo, compassion for the treatment of these extraordinary beasts prompts us to ask about the conditions of their servitude and confinement.
>
> Perhaps we should begin now to ask about how millions of U.S. tax dollars

are spent on a program in Africa that promotes the ultimate form of mistreatment—the slaughter of elephants for fun and profit.

For the well-to-do elephant killers, the fun consists of arriving in Zimbabwe with the proper bush jacket and an artillery piece known as a Buffalo Hunter .458 rifle. In Matabeleland, the brave hunter stands at a prudent distance, pulls the trigger and bruises his affluent shoulder with recoil. He proudly sees a huge bullet smack into the brain of a 40-year-old bull elephant with tusks of trophy length. The hide goes to makers of briefcases and shoes; the meat, to crocodile farmers; the money, to government officials.

For Zimbabwe, the profit comes from enormous fees paid by trophy hunters and the $7 million that U.S. taxpayers have contributed since 1989 to promote the killing of elephants.

Another $20 million has been allocated in the next four years. The money from the U.S. Agency for International Development is invested in a Zimbabwe project cutely called CAMPFIRE, or Communal Areas Management Programme for Indigenous Resources. In other words, elephant killing by rich tourists.

The Humane Society of the United States went to Congress last month and begged the Senate subcommittee on foreign operations to stop spending taxpayer funds to kill elephants, which are listed as threatened by the Endangered Species Act (half of Africa's elephants have been killed in the last two decades by poachers, hunters and ivory merchants.)

Naturally, government officials in Zimbabwe regard American concern for elephants as an arrogant intrusion on the affairs of a nation with major economic problems. At the same time, however, the Humane Society points out that $600,000 in U.S. funds have financed lobbying to remove elephants from the Endangered Species Act. The lobbyists also want resumption of international trade in ivory, which has been banned since 1989.

What's more, the Humane Society presented the Senate with abundant documentation of waste, corruption and mismanagement in how the CAMPFIRE program actually operates in Zimbabwe. Although profits from trophy hunting were supposed to go to rural villagers, an audit by U.S. officials shows the local folks get about 11 percent.

We can't do much about Zimbabwe, but the Congress certainly can bring a halt to the spending of U.S. funds for the slaughter of elephants for the benefit of wealthy hunters who hope that big guns will make up for any personal shortcomings.

If you agree, send a note to Sens. Dianne Feinstein and Barbara Boxer. Tell them to douse CAMPFIRE.

This had been preceded by the following editorial, "Save the African Elephants," in the *San Francisco Chronicle* (18 April 1997)[2]:

At a time when African elephants are in precipitous decline, Congress is considering funding a foreign aid program in Zimbabwe that would encourage trophy hunting of pachyderms to provide economic benefits to rural villages.

> The U.S. Agency for International Development (AID) is seeking $21 million to fund the Zimbabwe-based Communal Area Management Program for Indigenous Resources (CAMPFIRE), an outfit that is aggressively promoting elephant hunting as it seeks to lift the ban on the ivory trade and weaken the Endangered Species Act.
>
> Because of the value of ivory tusks, poachers in the 1970s and 1980s wantonly massacred elephants, cutting the population in half from 1.3 million in 1979 to only 600,000 by 1989 when international trade in ivory was outlawed. Still, elephants continue to be hunted to the edge of extinction.
>
> The Humane Society of the United States, the nation's largest animal protection organization, opposes CAMPFIRE—arguing that American taxpayers should not pay for a mismanaged, corrupt, and cruel program that encourages even more slaughter of endangered elephants.
>
> We join the Humane Society in urging the House and Senate to withhold AID funding from CAMPFIRE, and redirect the $21 million to African villages, where the money could be invested in more humane, profitable, and environmentally sound projects.

Finally, on 8 May, columnist Peter Rowe (1997), in the *San Diego Union Tribune*, used the CAMPFIRE controversy to fire a political shot across the bow of a local congressman, in "Stampeding Toward Ivory and Irony."

> Rep. Randy "Duke" Cunningham is a crucial vote in an upcoming showdown, one heavy with irony and ivory.
>
> From where I sit, the issue before the Escondido Republican could not be simpler. Should the United States give millions to a foreign outfit that attacks U.S. policy? Of course not.
>
> No-brainers, though, often befuddle our Capitol Hill brain trust. CAMPFIRE, a Zimbabwe group dedicated to the dubious propositions that the world needs more dead elephants and rhinos, could have had Cunningham playing political Twister.
>
> CAMPFIRE has spent $7 million in U.S. foreign aid. Now, it wants $20 million more.
>
> The Duke hates foreign aid.
>
> But CAMPFIRE is backed by Safari Club International.
>
> For a while, it looked like Cunningham was caught on the horns and tusks of a dilemma. No longer.
>
> **Aid Allergy**
>
> For months, the Humane Society of the United States had tried to pin down the Duke's position. This week, I tried to do the same. Yesterday, his office made this statement:
>
> "He supports CAMPFIRE because it is a smart and effective conservation program."
>
> Much about the Communal Areas Management Programme for Indigenous Resources is open to debate, but this much is clear:

CAMPFIRE wants to overturn the global ban on ivory and rhino-horn trading.

"The CAMPFIRE Association maintains its position that marketing of our natural resources including legally obtained ivory and rhino horn should be allowed," the in-house *CAMPFIRE News* reported in June 1995.

Since 1989, Congress has opposed this trade, arguing that it nearly wiped out the rhino and African elephant. CAMPFIRE is unimpressed.

"CAMPFIRE fights to change American law," *CAMPFIRE News* editorialized in December 1995. "The United States Endangered Species Act (ESA) negatively impacts on sustainable development and conservation programs in Southern Africa."

This fight is waged by an army of lobbyists attached to a CAMPFIRE affiliate. Lobbyists that you and I hired at $635,000 last year, and $546,000 this year.

American taxpayers are funding a group that battles American interests. CAMPFIRE supporters call this "free speech."

CAMPFIRE wants to speak freely? Be my guest. But don't ask me to buy the megaphone.

Tragic Stampede

This could have been where the Duke, the Humane Society and I agreed. While he is the co-chair of the Congressional Sportman's Caucus, Cunningham is allergic to foreign aid.

The Duke has "two political agenda items in conflict," Wayne Pacelle, Humane Society vice president for government affairs, said earlier this week. "His opposition to foreign aid and his support of trophy hunting."

But that conflict is over. And the Duke may have joined the winning side. CAMPFIRE doesn't lack allies on Capitol Hill and even within environmental circles.

The World Wildlife Fund, for instance, argues that CAMPFIRE encourages the sellers of ivory and rhino horn to protect their "suppliers," the elephants and rhinos.

But we've stampeded down this path before, with tragic results. Between 1979 and 1989, the ivory trade halved the African elephant population and the rhino-horn market killed off 90 percent of the world's rhinos.

Why resume a hunt that costs so many dollars and makes so little sense?

POPULAR BELIEFS AND POWERFUL SYMBOLS: EDITORIAL STORIES THAT TELL THEMSELVES

Obviously, there is no one CAMPFIRE story. There are serious critiques of CAMPFIRE and possible CAMPFIRE futures (see Murphree, this volume; Murombedzi 1994; Hill 1996; Hughes 2001). But these thoughtful critiques were not the basis of the HSUS attack. Rather, as the previous quotes indicate, the HSUS position was based on scenarios of corruption, slaughter, and extinction. The portrayal of CAMPFIRE was so grotesque, I felt obliged to try to tell a different CAMPFIRE story to Congress and the public.

My efforts took two forms—trying to get op-ed pieces into the newspapers where hostile editorials had been printed, and mobilizing a pro-CAMPFIRE letter-writing campaign. I quickly discovered that people who had worked at the community level, particularly overseas, immediately "got it." For them the word *community* had meaning, a meaning that encompassed livelihoods and knowledge and governance. They assumed that African communities were inhabited by sentient, responsible human beings just like themselves. For others the idea was more difficult to grasp.

I came to the realization that the conflict here was not overpresentation of fact, although that was an issue.[3] Rather, the strength of all three editorials (and the campaign that begot them) lies in implicit appeals to prevailing beliefs about Africa and to powerful environmental symbols that make their message almost a foregone conclusion.

AFRICA IS AFRICA: THE POWER OF POPULAR BELIEFS

One of the first things I tell students in my freshman seminar on environment and conservation in sub-Saharan Africa is that there is no language called *African* and that there are more than fifty nation-states and at least two thousand languages on the continent.[4] This is usually a revelation to most of them. All three of the anti-CAMPFIRE editorials start from the implicit assumption, common in the United States, that Africa is a single, homogeneous, and rather dire place (see Roe 1999, 4–8). By evoking misleading prevailing beliefs about Africa, the editorial writers set the reader up to believe a negative story about CAMPFIRE.[5]

For example, these editorials tap into a common belief that most if not all African governments are shot through with corruption. So the *Examiner*'s (incorrect) statement that "the Humane Society presented the Senate with abundant documentation of waste, corruption and mismanagement in how the CAMPFIRE program actually operates in Zimbabwe," resonates with the image of corrupt Africa, even though corruption in Africa varies in its form and its intensity not only from country to country but among government departments and levels of government, just as it varies from state to state, county to county, and city to city in the United States.[6]

The assumption that Africa is Africa extends to wildlife as well. Thus, these editorial writers appear to have assumed that it is possible to talk in aggregate terms about the African elephant when there are actually several subspecies of African elephant (*Loxodonta africana*), including *L. africana africana*, the bush subspecies, and *L. a. cyclotis*, the forest subspecies. There are recognized differences among widely separated African elephant populations, from the large desert elephants of Namibia on down. In addition, the fate of one population does not necessarily reflect the fate of all (Wayne Getz, personal communication, 23 February 1998; Jeheskle 1992). Thus the *San Francisco Chronicle* editorial's 1997 statement that the total number of African elephants was halved between 1979 and 1989 does not necessarily mean that all populations were halved. While some elephant populations are clearly in danger, the Zimbabwean elephant populations are not among them. To the contrary, a study of the four main elephant regions of Zimbabwe showed that all four had experienced increases in the elephant populations between 1980 and 1995 and that the national population had increased by 2.2 percent per annum "despite population reduction exercises" (Price Waterhouse 1996, ii–iii). But the Africa-is-Africa mind-set made it easy for these editorials to mislead readers by implying that aggregate African elephant figures accurately reflect the state of elephants in Zimbabwe.

ELEPHANT AS BIG BAMBI: THE POWER OF SYMBOLS

Elephants are rapidly becoming the African equivalent of Bambi, just a lot bigger.[7] It can be argued that many Americans are moved by a discourse of nature, a set of meanings, that are exemplified by popular wildlife television shows. Their vision of Africa is a vast savanna inhabited[8] by majestic wild animals or a rain forest in whose mists gorillas frolic. We see *every* aspect of animal life—how and what they eat, their mating rituals, their incredibly cute babies (of which, the shows often suggest, there are too few)—and the intricacies of their social organization in aesthetically pleasing, sometimes breath-taking footage. That these films are positioned as apolitical educational programs adds to their power.[9]

And where is community in this elephant-as-Big-Bambi presentation of nature? Where is contemporary culture? Not on the map—literally. For example, the map of Kenya depicted on a television wild animal program is devoid of all human institutions, dotted instead with representations of animals, mountains, and lakes. Not in the films—here people serve as exotic background: dancing warrior-waiters clad in traditional dress and pastoralists drinking blood.[10] All too often villagers in these films are portrayed as not having any particular livelihood (unless they are poachers) or knowledge that should be taken seriously, nor do they make decisions, certainly not about wildlife. They do, however, the shows often imply, have too many babies.

Animal rights activists tap into this powerful discourse and turn it against our models. In this discourse CAMPFIRE is symbolized not by little children walking safely to the nearby new elementary school in Masoka (instead of walking for kilometers through a forest filled with fierce buffalo), but by the palpable horrors of a dying elephant. Its power to persuade is reflected in the vehement assertion of one very-well-educated person: "I saw a program on elephants. They are very intelligent, maybe more intelligent than we are. Killing elephants is just like Hitler's killing the Jews" (anonymous personal communication).

I must state here that I personally find trophy hunting grotesque, and I suspect that even the most avid trophy hunter would agree that a dying animal is not a pretty sight—but neither is a child gored by a buffalo or suffering from malnutrition. This brings us to the problem of the missing story.

MISSING STORY

In contrast to the richness of the portrayals of animal life, human communities and their relationship to wildlife have little symbolic or emotional impact when the topic is nature.[11] Thus these three editorials never turn their gaze toward the realities of life in many CAMPFIRE sites. Three omissions are particularly noteworthy.

The first omission is mention of the limits on the possibility of any livelihood, let alone a sustainable one, in many CAMPFIRE areas. Many CAMPFIRE villages are located on the least-fertile, most poorly watered land in remote areas where the possibility of even a subsistence livelihood from arable agriculture is often uncertain. For many households the only possibility of even a poverty-level livelihood lies in sending male members off to work as wage laborers far from home. Thus the well-intentioned suggestion of the *San Francisco Chronicle* that twenty-one million dollars should be sent "to African villages, where the money could be invested in more humane, profitable, and environmentally sound projects" reveals an ignorance of the scarcity of development projects that work anywhere, let alone in such remote, resource-poor areas.

The second part missing from the story is the human cost of wildlife. For most African villagers (and here a continentwide generalization is probably appropriate), an elephant is less like Bambi and more like an enormous hairless rat that destroys crops, raids and ruins granaries, and sometimes takes a human life. Buffalo are extremely dangerous and, like giraffes, have a fondness for cotton plants. Hippos have voracious appetites and are dangerous both in the water and on land. And so the story goes for a variety of animals. Without CAMPFIRE, villagers have every reason to kill these animals or to turn a blind eye when outside poachers do so.

The third aspect of the story that is missing is the transformation of human-wildlife interactions that a program like CAMPFIRE brings about.

CAMPFIRE transforms the villagers' pests into a source of cash, thus making it worth people's while to protect wildlife habitat and the animals themselves from poachers, both locals and outsiders.[12] It also provides a modicum of protection from elephants and other dangerous animals in the form of solar-powered electric fences. At its most successful it can make a local school, clinic, or maize mill possible.

For most audiences, the missing community story just does not tell as well as the nature story. The killing of a charismatic elephant is a clear and awful sin of commission, a clear and compelling story, whereas the omission of local people with no compelling image carries little weight on the sin scale. Their story is, at best, fuzzy.

CREATING A COMMUNITY BAMBI

Trying to spread models of community management of natural resources can catapult us into arenas (such as U.S. politics) where our story of community has no valence and where hostile counterstories of nature hold sway. If implementing our models depends on bilateral aid, the content of international treaties such as the Convention on Trade in Endangered Species, or on reining in the excesses of international capital in the ecotourism boom, we must identify both the people who influence decisions and the discourses that influence them. We must find ways to share our view of human communities. Pointing out the racist and colonialist underpinnings of much of nature discourse is not persuasive to those who would not practice overt racism in their personal interactions and who have a man-the-lifeboats sense of urgency about the fate of nature. Rather, we must find ways to make human communities and their links with wild communities compelling, appealing, and self-evident. Masoka, Zimbabwe, and Bawa, Mozambique, must evoke the same warmth and, indeed, the same powerful sentimentality as Bambi. If we cannot create a community Bambi, our chances of spreading our models of community natural resource management are going to be very slim indeed.

NOTES

1. One of the more revelatory aspects of this whole experience was my shocked realization that when a newspaper takes a stand in an editorial, it does not necessarily mean that anyone has bothered to check the facts. They certainly had not in this case.

2. Reprinted with permission.

3. The editorials suffered from too many inaccuracies and significant omissions to detail in this chapter, which is not intended to be a point-for-point rebuttal. For

just one example, the *Examiner* editorial alleges that only 11 percent of trophy hunting receipts go to villagers. There have indeed been instances (as revealed by critical research built into CAMPFIRE, conducted by Zimbabweans and acted upon by the program) in which the major share of profits were retained by the district council (Murombedzi 1994). However, aggregate figures tell a different story. Between 1989 and 1996, roughly 59 percent of the total wildlife revenue received at the district level went to the subdistrict level (Bond n.d., 1–2). Similarly, these editorials omit any discussion of the apparent decrease of elephant deaths from poaching due to the vigilance of village wildlife managers.

4. Personal communication, Larry Hyman, Department of Linguistics, University of California at Berkeley, 1998.

5. My assessment of popular beliefs about Africa comes from twenty-five years of reading the popular press and teaching about, writing about, and discussing Africa with a wide spectrum of people.

6. And one could obviously come to the conclusion that these editorial writers, too, believe in corrupt Africa even though they all live in a state known for corrupt politics.

7. What the role of Dumbo is in all this, I would not venture to guess.

8. When I gave the talk on which this chapter is based, I nearly said "peopled" instead of inhabited. The slip is instructive.

9. The power of the mass media to shape the meaning of nature can be seen in the fact that the murders of refugees in the Democratic Republic of Congo (formerly Zaire) were repeatedly reported as occurring not in the precious and pristine rain forest, but in the *jungle* (see also Slater 1994, 2000, 67–82).

10. Sometimes traditional dress is indeed traditional; sometimes it is an odd pastiche of what tourists think "Africans" should wear.

11. It is worth noting that photos of starving babies are used with powerful effect in famine and refugee stories. But these photos never appear in the context of a nature story. The symbol is powerful but it does not travel well.

12. Encouraging data suggesting that elephant deaths from poaching have declined significantly with the advent of CAMPFIRE must be viewed with caution because accurate poaching data are hard to come by.

REFERENCES

Bond, Ivan. n.d. Comments on the Rhetoric or Reality ('The Patel Report'). Harare, Zimbabwe: WWF Programme Office.

Hill, K. A. 1996. Zimbabwe's Wildlife Utilization Programs: Grassroots Democracy or an Extension of State Power? *African Studies Review* 39(1): 103–23.

Hughes, David M. 2001. Rezoned for Business: How Eco-Tourism Unlocked Black Farmland in Eastern Zimbabwe. *Journal of Agrarian Change* 1(4): 575–99.

Jeheskle, Shoshani. 1992. *Elephants: Majestic Creatures of the Wild.* Emmaus, Pa.: Rodale.

Murombedzi, J. 1994. *The Dynamics of Conflict in Environmental Management Policy Making in the Context of the Communal Lands Management Programme for*

Indigenous Resources. CAMPFIRE. PhD diss., Centre for Applied Social Sciences, Univ. of Zimbabwe.

Murphree, Marshall, and David Hulme, eds. 2001. *African Wildlife and Livelihoods: The Promise and the Performance of Community Conservation.* Oxford: James Curry.

Price Waterhouse Consultants. 1996. Elephant Census in Zimbabwe, 1980–1995: An Analysis and Review. Report to Ministry of Environment and Tourism, Zimbabwe. September.

Roe, Emery. 1999. *Except Africa: Re-making Development, Re-thinking Power.* New Brunswick, N.J.: Transaction Books.

Slater, Candace. 1994. *Dance of the Dolphin: Transformation and Disenchantment in the Amazonian Imagination.* Chicago: Univ. of Chicago Press.

Slater, Candace. 2000. Justice for Whom? Contemporary Images of Amazonia. In *People, Plants and Justice: The Politics of Nature Conservation*, ed. Charles Zerner. New York: Columbia Univ. Press.

8

Community, Forestry, and Conditionality in The Gambia

Richard Schroeder

The environmentalism of the late 1980s and early 1990s was distinguished by massive global undertakings such as the Rio Earth Summit, the proliferation of global-change studies in the academy, and development interventions carried out under the aegis of the Global Environment Facility (Sachs 1993). These multifaceted efforts, which absorbed the energies of agencies all along the local-to-global continuum, involved asserting global primacy in the construction and prioritization of specific environmental problems and invoking particular rationalities for environmental management (World Commission on Environment and Development 1987; Groombridge 1992; McNeely et al. 1990; World Bank 1995, 1996). In this regard, the global scale was wholly "produced" (Smith 1990), as multiple practices of discursive and direct material incursion combined to eclipse other-scale spaces and places and subsume the needs and desires of people in particular localities to global imperatives (see Escobar 1995).

Another version of this chapter was originally published in *Africa, Journal of the International African Institute* 69(1): 1–22 and is reprinted with the permission of the International African Institute, London. It subsequently appeared In *Contesting Forestry in West Africa*, edited by R. Cline-Cole and C. Madge (Aldershot, U.K.: Ashgate), 148–71. I would like to thank Pete Brosius, Anna Tsing, Charles Zerner, Jesse Ribot, Michael Watts, Louise Fortmann, Roderick Neumann, Dorothy Hodgson, and three anonymous reviewers for the journal *Africa* for their advice and suggestions. Finally, I gratefully acknowledge research funding from the Rutgers University Research Council.

More recently, environmentalists have been engaged in a countervailing effort to produce a more local scale. While global-change scenarios still hold tremendous sway, state governments and donors are now intensely engaged in designing environmental programs to be implemented at the *community* level. This striking shift in emphasis demands explanation. In part, the resurgence of the community scale as a central organizing principle guiding contemporary environmental initiatives (Brosius, Tsing, and Zerner 1998; McNeely 1995; Western, Wright, and Strum 1994) derives from a backlash of sorts by local polities that have been directly disenfranchised through different types of environmental intervention. In Africa repeated efforts to impose land, water, forest, and wildlife-management practices on different groups dating back to the colonial period (Beinart 1984; Peters 1987, 171–94; Anderson and Grove 1987; Neumann 1992, 1995; Bonner 1993; Bassett 1993, 3–34; Leach 1994; Hodgson 1995; Fairhead and Leach 1996) have generated a legacy of "suspicion and mistrust" toward environmental programs (Biodiversity Support Program 1993, xiv). Local groups, wielding the threat of sabotage and asserting long-standing claims to property, resources, and place-based identities, have responded to environmental initiatives with demands for greater recognition of their needs. Sympathetic allies positioned in nongovernmental organizations (NGOs) and state agencies have backed these claims for a more equitable distribution of resources and power by promoting more extensive community involvement and participation. To save face and blunt criticism, donors such as the World Bank and some of the major environmental NGOs have followed suit, embracing "the community" as a basic unit of environmental planning and project implementation.[1]

Although local groups and their political supporters working within development and environmental bureaucracies have forced the state and donors to recognize the legitimacy of local claims, the motivations behind the apparent decentralization of responsibility and authority over natural resources have not always been so populist in character. Often the move to assert the communal scale has been prompted by the donors' own economic and political interests. Bioprospectors and rent-seeking state governments, for example, promote community resource management as a means of gaining access to critical environmental knowledge held by indigenous groups, thereby opening up new frontiers for commercial exploitation of the environment (Laird, Cunningham, and Lisinge 2000, 345–73; Cunningham and Cunningham 2000, 309–29). Similarly, neoconservative politicians often emphasize community action as a means of fostering the development of civil society and consolidating political gains in the post–Cold War era (Watts 1995, 44–62).

This chapter pursues a political-economic analysis of community resource management further by setting such policies against the backdrop of the structural adjustment programs that swept the African region in the 1980s and 1990s. Structural adjustment is typically associated with the series of conditions the World Bank and the International Monetary Fund have imposed on African governments to address problems of balance of payments and debt. Related steps donors have taken to withdraw financial aid from African governments in recent years are also of crucial significance. Each of these developments has left African governments struggling to deliver even the most basic of governmental services to their respective constituencies. This has meant that state environmental managers in Africa have had to rely ever more heavily on community efforts to accomplish environmental objectives, even as the scope of those objectives as envisioned under global change scenarios has expanded. In such a political-economic context, the devolution of responsibility for environmental management to the community has become a convenient means of extending the reach of limited state resources.

The specific case I use to illustrate this argument involves the German-funded Gambian-German Forestry Project (GGFP). The GGFP has been in existence in The Gambia since 1979. Originally charged with management of several of The Gambia's national forest parks, the project, which operates wholly under the auspices of the Gambian Forestry Department but is partially staffed by expatriate personnel, has conducted a series of land-use surveys in the country. These studies purport to show progressive patterns of degradation in national forest lands (Forster 1983; Ridder 1991), and have led to calls for urgent action to reverse deforestation trends. Forestry Department officials have, however, been frustrated by a lack of central government support for their efforts. While funds allocated to the department actually increased incrementally between 1976 and 1994, for example, these allocations were primarily absorbed by the hiring of additional staff. The unit's programming budget, meanwhile, failed to keep pace with the growing demands for intervention (Bojang 1994b). Consequently, when the GGFP adopted the objective of intensifying management practices in the nation's forests, it was forced to do so under tight budgetary constraints. In this context, the promotion of community resource management was not simply a populist gesture inviting more local participation but instead formed part of a deliberate financial strategy to decentralize project costs.

A critical issue confronted by GGFP managers (and one that poses difficulties to many who seek to promote community management of natural resources) was the question of how they could devolve responsibility for many of the tasks associated with forest management without forfeiting managerial control. I demonstrate in the following how the project resolved this dilemma through the use of formal contracts that bound community groups to specific management plans. A systematic review of project planning documents reveals how Forestry Department and GGFP authorities agreed to grant communal rights to forest reserves, but only on condition that communities commit themselves to a broad range of specific labor tasks. Community control was thus acquired only in stages, provided the communities continued performing their obligations faithfully, as stipulated in their forest management contracts. In effect, the GGFP managers, motivated as they were by the need to contain the costs to the state and its donors of forest management, offered a form of graduated sovereignty to communities seeking to control local forest reserves. I argue that, in such cases, there is a need to inspect carefully the political character of community-resource-management policies and the conditions they place on community control. Participatory rhetoric notwithstanding, I contend that the idea of the community can in some circumstances serve to extend rather than devolve centralized control over resources and communities alike.

GGFP AND FOREST MANAGEMENT IN THE GAMBIA

The colonial government in The Gambia did not establish a Forestry Service until 1950. Previously, all control of forests was vested in the District Chief (*seyfo*), who issued licenses for extraction of particular forest products. It was not until 1976 that the Forest Service was formally elevated to departmental status under the Ministry of Agriculture and Natural Resources.[2] With the passage of the 1977 Forest Act and 1978 Forest Regulation, sixty-six forest parks gazetted during the colonial period were placed under the direct control of the Forestry Department. Working with limited resources, the department managed the parks and sought to protect them from conversion to agricultural or other uses. At the same time, the department ran an annual national tree-planting campaign and collaborated on projects promoting community woodlots (funded by the United States Agency for International Development [USAID] from 1980 to 1985) and orchards (funded by the European Economic Commission (EEC) 1986 to 1990).[3]

These activities notwithstanding, the Forestry Department lacked central government support for its project activities. Indeed, the forestry sector helped subsidize the government insofar as funds generated from wood-cutting licenses were absorbed by the central treasury (USAID 1992; see further discussion in Ribot 1995b). Consequently, the Forestry Department was forced to rely quite heavily on foreign assistance to sustain itself. While the USAID and EEC projects provided important financial and logistical support, the Forestry Department's primary collaborator since its establishment has been the German government, under the auspices of the GGFP. From the beginning, the GGFP involved itself in a range of activities, including fire protection, road construction, afforestation, enrichment planting, the tending and weeding of forest stands, and deadwood utilization (Foley 1994).

Twelve of The Gambia's forest parks were managed directly by the GGFP, either as plantations or as protected areas.[4] In addition, in 1980, the GGFP conducted an extensive aerial survey and inventory of The Gambia's national forest resources. This survey was intended to fill numerous data gaps: "At the beginning of the project the situation and the condition of the forests in The Gambia was unknown. The speed of degradation, the main factors of destruction, the rehabilitation capacity, standing stock, tree species and diameter distribution and the health condition, all necessary information for the development of a strategy to fight forest degradation were lacking" (Schindele and Bojang 1995, 3).

The primary conclusion drawn from this survey was that the forest resource base in The Gambia was under threat because of poor forest management practices of rural people. The survey determined that the areal extent of The Gambia's forests had in fact remained fairly constant at 45 percent of the country's land surface since 1968, when a round of devastating droughts hit the region.[5] The main concern centered around the degradation of the existing forest resources (Forster 1983; see discussion in Foley 1994).

Schindele and Bojang (1995) report that, at the time of the survey, the standing stock was of extremely low quality. Much of the closed-canopy forest had converted to open-canopy, a change, they argue, that marked the beginning of a downward spiral in the battle to control damaging bush fires.[6] Within the existing stock, there were almost no trees younger than forty years of age and very little natural regeneration of several of the more valuable tree species. Moreover, the incidence of dead (9 percent) and decayed trees (45 percent) was very high. Whereas these findings were sobering enough, a second GGFP study (Ridder 1991) drew the even more alarming conclusion that the deforestation rate in The Gambia was 6 percent per annum. (These findings have, however, been contested; see Foley 1994.) Planners argued that this pattern of degradation was of critical importance for rural Gambians, and they felt that it had profound regional implications as well.

> At present the forests of The Gambia form the last vegetative frontier towards the desert. Because of its suitable geographic location as a long belt along the River Gambia, it would be comparatively easy to finally stop desertification at this point by safeguarding and rehabilitating the still existing forest lands. If the Gambian forests can be saved not only the livelihood of the Gambian population will be maintained, but also that of the people which are living south of The Gambia. (Schindele and Bojang 1995, 7)

On the basis of the 1991 findings, GGFP managers concluded that the need for intervention in the forests was much more dire than they had previously assumed.

Most of the degradation detected in the two land-use inventories was, according to GGFP analysts, due to "bushfire and uncontrolled firewood exploitation rather than by conversion of forests into agricultural land or other land uses" (Schindele and Bojang 1995, 16). Because problems existing in The Gambia's forests were framed in terms of degradation rather than the amount of area of forest cover lost, the GGFP's approach was to design a program that would emphasize forest regeneration. As planners reasoned, "A forest area in The Gambia of 45 percent is still large enough to supply the country with sufficient forest products assuming that it is protected, rehabilitated and sustainably managed" (Schindele and Thoma 1995, 16). The emphasis on regeneration, which became known as natural forest management, had several virtues: "It is more economical to protect and rehabilitate existing natural forests than to leave them for further degradation and to start with afforestation of fast growing species elsewhere. In addition natural forests are much better adapted to the climate. The risk of failure is less and the ecological value (wildlife habitat, biodiversity etc.) is much higher than compared with those of plantations" (Schindele and Thoma 1995, 16).[7]

Ultimately, however, the tasks of fencing or maintaining firebreaks around forest parks proved untenable because of the costs involved.[8] Even with the use of food aid provided by the United Nations World Food Program, the mobilization of labor for firebreak establishment and maintenance proved problematic (Dumbuya 1994). When the recurrent costs of forest park protection proved to be beyond project means, the whole approach to forest management in The Gambia was reworked. The director of the Forestry Department summarized this conclusion quite succinctly.

> Although the management of natural forest was found to be much cheaper per [hectare] as compared to plantation establishment and management, forest parks constituted only 7 percent (in 1983) of total forest lands of the country. The environmental and socio-economic impacts of the management of these parks will be insignificant unless a much larger area could be covered. Conscious of the economic and man-power constraints that the government faces, and the availability of a large pool of cheap labour in the form of village community labour force which could be harnessed for achieving wider forest protection, provided . . . adequate empowerments and incentives could be ensured, it was decided in 1987 to venture into community forest management. (Bojang 1994a, 2; see also Bojang and Reeb 1998)

Thus it was that community involvement became a central objective of forest management along the Gambia River basin.

COMMUNITY AND FOREST MANAGEMENT

In some policy documents issued by the Forestry Department, the rationale for undertaking a policy premised on community-based forest management included the populist goals of community participation and control.

> Reversing trends of forest deterioration will be possible only if forest policies place much more emphasis, than in the past, on the immediate needs and wishes of the local people and if the policies encourage the forest administration and individual forest officers to see beyond the trees and become more concerned with people and the multiple-use potential of forest lands. The traditional approach of foresters needs to be widened in favour of involving the rural population, that stay close to the forest, in the management and rational utilization of the forest resources. (Government of The Gambia 1994, 3)

Indeed, some of the early sociological studies sponsored by the GGFP seemed quite committed to incorporating the local knowledge and full political participation of rural community members in the design and implementation of a community forestry program (Seibert 1989). As the preceding discussion has indicated, however, the switch from natural forest management to community forest management was ultimately motivated less by a concern with people who are close to the forests than by cost concerns and a desire to extend a particular model of forest management over the whole of The Gambia.

The initial efforts at community management were centered in three villages in Western Division along the south bank of the River Gambia. The forests in question were not part of forest parks but were included in a category of land use the government and the GGFP labeled open-access forest. Under the land-use agreement of 1977, these forests were designated property of the Gambian state. Use of open-access areas was subject to a permitting process controlled by the Gambian government.[9] On the project's land-use maps, roughly 90 percent of Gambian national territory falls into the open-access category, but the absence of any discussion of the distinction between open-access and common-property areas in the GGFP classification system renders that claim suspect. Theorists of natural resource and forestry tenure systems define open-access goods quite specifically as resources that are not under *any* form of tenure constraint and are therefore "free goods" (see Fortmann and Bruce 1988). It seems much more likely, given that forest communities and pastoralist groups regularly use many of these forests, that what the Forestry Department and GGFP called open-access forests are often actually common-property resources, subject to rules and conditions set by community members on forest product use (see discussion in Freudenberger, Carney, and Lebbie 1997). That this distinction may have been lost in the GGFP system of land-use classification is crucial, because it is precisely the perceived *lack* of management that the GGFP's community forestry project was intended to fill.

The reason project personnel did not involve communities in forest management any earlier was that certain conditions for doing so had not yet materialized. Specifically, before the mid-1980s, the possibilities for community forest management were precluded by the fact that rural production systems were still dominated by groundnut production.

> Groundnuts were the only cash crop for the local farmer. For their production, he depended on the practice of shifting cultivation using fire as a cheap and easy tool for clearing. The production of groundnuts competed directly with the forest cover. Forests had always been there and were not used by anybody and did not produce anything valuable for the farmer except for the subsistence use of fuel and minor products. At that time these forest products were still available in abundance and the rural as well as the urban societies did not suffer as yet from any shortages. (Forestry Department and GGFP 1995, 6)

Thus it was determined that "the general attitude of the local population towards the forest was quite *negative*. . . . It was clear from the very beginning that the Gambian forests could only be conserved if the local population would support forest conservation and protection efforts actively. But for this the negative attitude of the people towards the forest had to be changed. The problem was how to make out of present users future managers of the forest" (Schindele and Bojang 1995, 4).

Key Forestry Department and GGFP project documents enumerate several changes in rural livelihood systems that favored the eventual adoption of community-based forest management. First, the market price for groundnuts fell and the IMF-sponsored structural adjustment program removed all subsidies favoring groundnut farmers. The net effect, according to project managers, was that "there was *no more competition for land*" (Schindele and Thoma 1995, 25). Second, the supply of rhun palm splits, a key forest product used for roof beams in construction projects, "dropped to almost nil because of excessive over exploitation" (Forestry Department and GGFP 1995, 6). Third, firewood prices rose significantly. Fourth, a generalized decline of climate conditions contributed to crop production shortfalls and rural water shortages. Fifth, the documents claim that the successes of "natural forest management" in forest parks had a kind of demonstration effect: communities surrounding the Forestry Department and GGFP field stations recognized the benefits of forest management seen in the field station trial plots, and sought to replicate them in their own forests. Finally, in 1991, the national government adopted a natural resources-management plan that made "community resource management" official policy by calling for "the involvement of the local people in managing the forest resources . . . [and] transfer[ing] . . . management responsibilities and even ownership" (Forestry Department and GGFP 1995, 6). Thus when the Gambian government prepared a full-scale National Environmental Action Plan, the role of communal involvement in forest management was prominently featured.

> A forest policy exists for the sector but is generally regarded inadequate as it puts too much emphasis on the role of the state in the development of the sec-

> tor. Although this policy recognizes the need for the promotion of the private sector's involvement in forest enterprise it falls short of recognizing the important role public participation and involvement has to play. The policy does not provide for private or community tree tenure. Consequently the prospect for active community and private/individual participation in forestry activities has been largely compromised. *The public sector's limited human and financial resources became overstretched in its attempt to ensure forest protection and development* [my emphasis]. This has lead to the creation of a rift between the government service and the local communities. The latter viewed the former as having taken their "property" from them. Forest fires and illegal cutting for domestic and commercial use have therefore increased resulting in the degradation of the forest resource. (Government of The Gambia 1994, 2)

Other assertions embedded in the Forestry Department's GGFP planning documents repeated the contention that Gambian forests were unmanaged. For example, GGFP officials argued that since most agriculture in rural Gambia is "based on subsistence . . . farm development plans do not exist. Even within one cropping period, most farmers do not plan. Thus, many activities [including those that impinge on forest management] are undertaken based on ad hoc decisions" (Forestry Department and GGFP 1995, 7).[10] In terms of the forest proper, rural Gambians were not yet sufficiently attuned to "sustainable" forest management techniques (Forestry Department and GGFP 1995, 9): "The problems of desertification were unknown. Who of the local farmers had ever heard about desertification and, even if he did, did he really understand what desert meant and how his livelihood may change when the forests have disappeared?" (Schindele and Thoma 1995, 14–15). Indeed, according to this perspective, "villagers need assistance in developing a genuinely critical view of their own situation and a realistic assessment of their ability to take-up necessary steps and to implement activities according to the priorities set by them" (Forestry Department and GGFP 1995, 7).

This set of assumptions is crucially important in understanding the subsequent direction of Forestry Department and GGFP policies. The idea that rural Gambians were ignorant and inept forest managers belies the technical bias of project planners. The condescending attitude planners displayed toward rural Gambians predetermined the validity of their claim that some form of outside intervention was necessary if the forests were to be saved. Villagers in rural communities had, thus, to be trained in suitable land-use planning techniques, and they were allowed to cooperate with the state only if they first submitted a village land-use and development plan for GGFP approval. Moreover, the experience of GGFP planners led them to conclude that incentives used to entice rural people to undertake particular development projects were often counterproductive, insofar as they predisposed communities to embark on projects without genuine commitment to long-term development goals. Thus the GGFP community forestry project worked with a performance-based system of rewards. Communities had to first demonstrate their willingness and capacity to manage forests in compliance with Forestry Department and GGFP requirements before the government would grant concessions allowing them direct control.

PARTICIPATION BY CONTRACT: COMMUNITY FORESTRY-MANAGEMENT AGREEMENTS

In 1991 The Gambian government, working closely with the World Bank, USAID, and other donors, set forth several provisions that were meant to help create a suitably enabling environment and facilitate the decentralization of responsibility for environmental management to the community level. The centerpiece of the policies generated under The Gambia's action plan was a kind of contract known as the "community forest management agreement" (CFMA). This contract was described by USAID analysts as

> a formal covenant signed between a community (be it a traditional group, a Village Development Committee, or a newly-organized group of resource users) and the Government. The Agreement authorizes shared control over a natural resource previously controlled exclusively by The Government. Specifically, the Agreement sets out the rights and obligations of both parties with regard to control, management and usufruct rights related to either a particular common land area with multiple resource uses (e.g., crop/range lands), or a single resource (e.g., water, trees, forage, fish). (USAID 1992, 44)

Ideally, these arrangements "are not imposed from above" but are "negotiated agreements that rest upon a solid consensus"; they are the product of "a thorough, and often lengthy, dialogue within the community, and then between the community and government technical services" (USAID 1992, 44–45). Indeed, the emphasis on consensus and dialogue received a great deal of attention in planning documents. On closer inspection, however, the process laid out for implementing the contracts in the forestry sector effectively *reinforced* centralized control over community resources.

The basic procedure leading up to the signing of a CFMA typically began with the Forestry Department conducting a sensitization campaign at the divisional or district level. As this campaign got underway, target areas were "preselected" using available mapping instruments (Forestry Department and GGFP 1995, 13). Communities in areas deemed a high priority for either forest protection or production purposes were targeted for inclusion in the community forestry program. Thus in 1991 the first CFMAs were signed in three pilot communities, and eight other applications were submitted. In effect, two sets of management objectives were in play, one directed at protecting existing state-run forest parks and the second more particularly focused on the objective of creating community forest reserves. Wherever possible, the Forestry Department and GGFP located community forestry reserves on the outskirts of forest parks. Under these circumstances, the benefits of environmental education campaigns conducted by project personnel could accrue to both the community reserve and the forest park. At the same time, the Forestry Department was convinced that its forest parks had a demonstration effect, which could spread to surrounding areas. In effect, although not explicitly rationalized as buffer zones in project documents, the community reserves functioned as buffer zones in many cases.[11]

Once well-situated communities with appropriate resources were identified, the first round of contacts between forestry personnel and community residents was made. The purpose of these early contacts was to "assess . . . villagers' perceptions and attitudes towards forest management" (Forestry Department and GGFP 1995, 13). Following a positive assessment, a specific approach to management of the community forestry reserve had to be determined. This required demarcating the reserve, conducting an inventory of forest assets, defining specific management steps to be taken, and filing an application for a CFMA award. These steps were immediately followed by a series of meetings with each of the various groups in the village (defined as "elders, women, [and] youth"), at which forestry personnel assessed the strength of the available labor pool and other resources necessary for forest management tasks. The village elders then appointed a forest management committee, which consulted with the GGFP staff on the preparation of a forest management plan. In theory, this plan was to be generated by the community; in practice, however, it was often drafted by project personnel (Bojang 1994a). After the plan was approved locally, it was submitted for review and approval by the district chief, the Forestry Department head, and the minister of Natural Resources, at which stage a CFMA award was granted.

CFMA CONCESSIONS

At the heart of the CFMA agreement were two concessions on the part of the government: the waiver of the provisions of the land-use acts of 1990 and 1976, which awarded control of open-access forest land to the state, and the granting of forest reserve rights to individual communities for ninety-nine-year renewable terms. Of special significance to communities was the former concession, by which the state effectively declared a unilateral moratorium on awarding licenses to outsiders for extraction of timber and other forest products from the newly created community reserves. In practical terms, this meant the government—and, potentially, individual civil servants—

forgoing revenue from fees and rents generated through the permitting and licensing process. For the communities, the concession meant that for the first time their rights over their forests included exclusivity; they now had legal authority, at least in theory,[12] to prevent others from tapping local forest resources for commercial gain (compare Ribot's [2000, 134–58] analysis of similar dynamics in Senegal). And communities often welcomed the opportunity to sign CFMA agreements, at least initially. In the words of one of the local town chiefs, the cessation of outside extraction activities was "a dream come true" (Dumbuya 1994, iv).

CFMA CONDITIONALITIES

There were two sets of conditions applied to community forestry reserves under the new management approach, one embodied in the community-level forest management plan previously mentioned and a second, more stringent set of controls detailed in the Forestry Department and GGFP program documents. The management plan prepared at the community level was a precondition for the award of a CFMA to any given community. Designed by the community forestry management committee in consultation with Forestry Department and GGFP personnel, the plan was intended to "protect, manage and guide the conduct of [the forest's] utilization" (Dumbuya 1994, 35). To give one example, in the forest reserve comanaged by the communities of Brefet, Besse, and Ndemban in Kasila Forest in The Gambia's Western Division, the management plan spelled out access rights to several different commodities (firewood, bush poles, deadwood, etc.) for different classes of resource users. In particular, it rewarded participation by community members in the various work tasks entailed in forest management and developed a schedule of fees for resource extraction that outsiders were required to pay. Thus it drew a clear distinction between active participants who were residents of the contracted communities, active participants who were nonresidents, and nonparticipants, whether resident or nonresident. In the case of bush poles used for roofing and fencing, for example, these three groups were charged next to nothing: a quarter of a dalasi and one dalasi per pole, respectively.[13] A similar pricing structure was established for certain forest fruits, whereas the right to fell certain kinds of deadwood was reserved exclusively for active residents of the contracted communities.

While such community management plans were by no means inconsequential, their provisions were nonetheless subsumed under a higher order of directives written into the very structure of the CFMA agreement itself, and it is these conditions that are most interesting for my present purposes. The CFMA program, as it was called, included more than thirty-five separate conditions designed to regulate community forestry management

(Gambian-German Forestry Project n.d.). While the community management plan reflected local concerns of the individual grantee communities, the program stipulations gave voice, as it were, to the Forestry Department and GGFP. In this regard, program conditions ensured that Forestry Department and GGFP personnel would control the finest details of forest management in project communities, not despite, but *because of,* a devolution of tenure rights to the community.

The program requirements set by the Forestry Department and GGFP can be grouped into several partially overlapping categories.[14]

At a most basic level, community members in grantee communities were required to cooperate with project personnel. This meant attending all meetings and workshops the Forestry Department and GGFP set up for planning, program review, or environmental education purposes; allowing site inspection on demand by Forestry Department authorities; and even providing Forestry Department staff lodging whenever they came to the community in connection with project activities. Beyond simply maintaining a generally cooperative spirit, the community residents were required to organize a workforce and mobilize it on demand to perform a broad range of work tasks. For example, the program required all communities applying for CFMA grants to assist the Forestry Department and GGFP with the physical survey, demarcation, and inventory of the forest resources in question. This meant considerable work clearing survey lines through the forest and operating chains used for demarcation and measurement. Community residents were also expected to share their expertise in resource classification and in the design and production of roads and trails.

- *Conditions that defined the terms of community access to forest resources.*
  For the state to grant a community concession over a particular block of forest, all members of the community had to first relinquish any prior claims to the forest. Only then would the forest be reinstated to them as a community forest reserve to be managed according to a common-property regime. (This explicit requirement belies the fact, of course, that at least some parts of the forests in question were under some form of management before the introduction of community forestry practices.) This property regime was to be defined in the community management plan, and no extraction, utilization, or sale of forest products would be allowed until the management plan was approved by the Forestry Department or the minister of Natural Resources. Communities were expected to update their management plans (including a new resource inventory) every ten years. If for any reason the community grantees violated any of the provisions of their management plans

or the CFMA program itself, the CFMA was unilaterally revocable by Forestry Department officials.

- *Conditions that defined management practices the communities were required to perform in the forest.*
  In general, the management practices that communities were to follow in their forests were to remain consistent with specific legislative mandates relating to natural resource management use in the country, to the resource inventory described above, and to sustainable management principles, by which the project meant practices that were financially self-supporting. A major expectation of the project was that grantee communities would adopt some form of protection system that would insulate the forest reserve from bush fires. This system was to include a protection belt surrounding the reserve or internal fire breaks where feasible. The program also required the CFMA recipients to develop a plan for protecting the forests *surrounding* the reserve from fire damage. (All of these requirements were made despite the project's own efforts repeatedly failing to control fire by these means.) The community committees charged with preparing management plans were required by the program to set particular limits on quantities of goods extracted from the forest, the seasons in which they could be taken, and the species from which they could be drawn. Protected species could not be removed under any circumstances, and the contract documents stipulated which species fell into that category. Wood harvesting was to start with deadwood and trees felled to build firebreaks and roads. Only then could community timber harvesters move to other tree species not otherwise protected within the reserve. Wood for fuel and timber could be cut only selectively according to provisions to be outlined in the management plan.[15] All wood harvesting was to take place only during the dry season. In this way, natural regeneration was allowed to run its course during the rains. Rainy season community work was instead to focus on replanting trees to take advantage of the most opportune conditions for stand establishment. For every tree cut in the reserve for whatever purpose, ten seedlings were to be replanted in locations that the Forestry Department considered understocked. The emphasis in this effort was to be placed on indigenous species. Beyond such replacement planting, the community was expected to perform routine tasks of timber-stand improvement and weeding and tending as required by the community management plan.
- *Conditions that regulated the marketing of community forest reserve products and outlined the structure of community forest reserve finances.*
  Commercial harvesting rights were not to be granted to communities until the fire protection measures were in place. Communities also had

to demonstrate their trustworthiness in managing funds by providing quarterly reports to the Forestry Department on their forest management finances. In the early stages of project implementation, cooperating communities were subject to royalties and levies assessed by the Forestry Department against commercial producers elsewhere in the country. They were also required to obtain regular permits for transporting goods and were precluded from transporting goods at night or on holidays when their movements would be more difficult to monitor. They had to agree to site inspections by the GGFP so that yields could be calculated and proper fees and levies assessed. Wherever forest depletion or destruction occurred, communities could be held liable for the costs of restoring the forest to its prior state. Communities were blocked from subcontracting any of the labor tasks entailed in forest extraction to anyone outside the community. The sale of round wood was discouraged, and local processing of wood was encouraged. All sales of commercial products drawn from the forest were to be made to registered dealers. An exception to this rule applied to sales of small bundles of wood (no more than fifty dalasis, or roughly five U.S. dollars, in value), that could be made directly to consumers. Finally, "for the purposes of sustainability" (Bojang 1994a), the Forestry Department imposed a requirement that the community set aside roughly 40 percent of each year's earnings in a "community forestry fund" for reinvestment in the community's forest. At a later stage, an additional 15 percent was levied in the form of a payment to the National Forestry Fund, which was set up to offset government budgetary constraints and pay for the department's technical assistance in surveying, mapping, planning, and training (Bojang and Reeb 1998).

GRADUATED SOVEREIGNTY

This remarkable set of interventions reveals with stark clarity the pervasiveness of state and donor control retained under the putatively communal forest management system in The Gambia. Yet the GGFP planners remained unsatisfied with their program. While twenty-nine communities had become involved in the CFMA process by 1995, GGFP managers felt a need to extend community management more rapidly, if possible without incurring additional expense. To them, the 1991 survey of land-use conversions (Ridder 1991) demonstrated the increasing urgency to reverse environmental degradation in the river basin. Thus to "bring as much forest land as possible under villagers' control in a comparatively short time" (Forestry Department and GGFP 1995, 8) and "to see how seriously participants take up protecting 'their' forests" (Forestry Department and GGFP 1995, 7), the

Forestry Department and GGFP revamped their community-forestry policy yet again. They modified their approach by introducing a new set of contractual conditions known as the Preliminary CFMA (PCFMA). In justifying this shift, the Forestry Department and GGFP managers argued, "Inevitably, high intensity of personnel inputs provided during the [community forestry] pilot scheme cannot be maintained to introduce [community forestry] on a larger scale. . . . The approach and forest management planning procedure have to be simplified and certain services such as boundary and forest surveys, technical skills training, etc., postponed to a later stage" (Forestry Department and GGFP 1995, 7).

In essence, the PCFMA imposed a waiting period on potential CFMA recipients. These communities were required to demonstrate their "seriousness" by performing protection services and other forest management tasks outlined in the CFMA for three years without receiving full CFMA benefits.

> The PCFMA is valid for a maximum of [three] years and will then be automatically replaced by the CFMA if the community fulfilled its duties. Depending on the community's performance and capacity, the CFMA can also be granted earlier. Since with the PCFMA only temporarily defined use permits but no long-term user rights are granted to the community, PCFMAs can be issued by the director of the [Forestry Department]. Hence, the issuance procedure takes a comparatively short period of time. The PCFMA . . . is more or less designed to speed-up the transfer of *responsibility* [my emphasis] over the identified forest area to the community by promising resource ownership whenever an effective forest protection system is in place. (Forestry Department and GGFP 1995, 8)

The litmus test for the grant of sovereignty and control was thus made much more stringent, the process of granting permits was streamlined, and the service obligations borne by the project were reduced. The combined effect of these changes was to produce significant cost savings.

> By employing the PCFMA, personnel inputs are the highest in launching [community forestry] projects until the forest reserve is identified, a simple work plan prepared, and the PCFMA signed. Then personnel inputs can be reduced. Another reduction is possible whenever the community has gained enough managerial and technical skills, and a forest management plan is jointly developed. Thereafter, it is assumed that, [one] forest manager is able to supervise [a community forestry reserve] area of some 5,000 hectares. (Forestry Department and GGFP 1995, 8)

In sum, participation as defined in both the CFMA and PCFMA contracts involved the community committing itself to a broad set of interactions with project staff and opening itself up for inspection and monitoring at the government's discretion. Moreover, to ensure that they were able to maintain active participant status, individual community members were required to carry out a wide range of work tasks, corvée obligations that were in force year-round and meant to obtain in perpetuity. While much was made of the participation of a community-level forest management committee and its input into a forest management plan, it is clear that the management plan touted by the Forestry Department and GGFP was in fact so tightly circumscribed by the CFMA itself that the Forestry Department and GGFP retained de facto control over the forests. This control extended to marketing arrangements and preserved for the state important sources of income in the form of permit fees and royalties assessed upon the sale of high-value forest commodities. The terms of community access were defined in such a way that some of the most sought after benefits—the opportunities for commercial exploitation of the forest—were withheld until a long list of work tasks were performed or, in the case of a PCFMA, until a probationary period of three years had passed. In effect, both forms of contract offered communities little more than *graduated sovereignty* over their forest reserves predicated on specific plan performance.

POLITICS OF COMMUNITY RESOURCE MANAGEMENT

In conclusion, I want to first make clear what I have *not* argued in this chapter. I have not argued that we should abandon an emphasis on community-based development as a means of addressing questions of equitable access to natural resources. Nor have I claimed that we should oppose this model where it works to preserve distinctive cultures and ways of management that contribute to a healthy resource base. I have not even *categorically* rejected the GGFP's approach to community forestry. Project documents claim that by the late 1990s more than three hundred villages had agreed to participate in this project (Bojang and Reeb 1998). The question is how that response to the GGFP initiative should be interpreted. Does this fact signal that rural Gambians wholeheartedly endorsed the CFMA concept or does it simply reflect their desperation to (re)gain control over forests in search of expanded economic opportunities? Did community groups, or their leaders, willingly shoulder the burdens of decentralized forest management plans, or were the conditions imposed by the community forestry contracts simply a better alternative than having no legal access to commercial exploitation of local forests at all?

These are questions that cannot be answered without further community-level ethnographic research. It is fair to say, however, that the GGFP planning documents reviewed here do not inspire confidence. Several of these plans and reports (some of which were authored by senior Gambian civil servants) display a dismissive, condescending attitude toward rural Gambians. Their underlying assumption that the residents of The Gambia's peasant farming communities are ignorant and inept environmental managers in need of training raises serious questions concerning the essential political character of the CFMA. Other authors commenting on the burgeoning practice of introducing community-based natural resource management have argued that the participation generated by such programs is often antidemocratic (Ribot 1995a, 2000, 134–58; Peters 1996; Neumann 1997). They have, likewise, questioned the tendency displayed by proponents of community-based approaches to romanticize local politics and thereby mask social and economic hierarchies within community units (see Leach 1994; Ribot 2000, 134–58; and discussion in Brosius, Tsing, and Zerner 1998). While each of these concerns is applicable in the Gambian case, my main purpose here has been to inspect the use of participation contracts as a tool for devolving administrative responsibilities and binding communities into particular labor and management commitments.

In my view, the value of community-based management is diminished when, as in the Gambian case, contract terms (1) stipulate the form of participation each forest community is expected to enact, (2) make access to forest resources contingent on meeting specific performance goals, (3) define management criteria so tightly that very little initiative remains at the local level, and (4) force communities to assume certain costs of management while preserving for the state important sources of revenue. Such excessive use of conditionalities robs efforts to promote community-based management of their creative and productive potential (compare Cline-Cole 1997) and undermines their usefulness in addressing the need for a more equitable distribution of control over resource-management decisions.

On balance, it seems clear that, whatever else the promoters of forest concessions in The Gambia may have generated by way of benefits to local communities, they clearly succeeded in converting community-based resource management into a tool of structural adjustment. Specifically, they helped the Gambian government decentralize many of the costs of expanding the scope of Forestry Department activities while reducing the department's services during a period of general fiscal constraint. The appeal of the community-based approach to the major donors and to Forest Department planners must be understood in this light. This is particularly relevant given that aid to African countries from several key sources, notably the U.S. government (Cason 1997; USAID 1996), has been drastically curtailed in recent years. What this has meant in practical terms is that aid-granting agencies have been in the position to be much more selective in the types of projects they are willing to support and to place more stringent conditions on them (Nelson 1996). As developed in The Gambia, the notion that community-based development produces greater participation on the part of groups normally disenfranchised in the decision-making process was turned on its ear: the leverage gained through the use of contracts and conditionalities simply ensured intense levels of donor participation in the community decision-making processes; it gave them a way to retain managerial control by inserting themselves into the finest details of policy implementation.

NOTES

1. See International Institute for Environment and Development 1994 for a useful summary of the literature pertaining to these developments.

2. In 1981 the Forestry Department was transferred to the Ministry of Water Resources, Fisheries and Forestry, and in 1994 it was moved into the Ministry of Natural Resources, a new unit created as a part of the comprehensive Gambia Environmental Action Plan of 1993 (Government of The Gambia 1994, 2).

3. Schindele and Bojang 1995 and Schroeder 1995 and 1999 discuss these specific initiatives further.

4. For details on some of the controversial management practices of the GGFP, see Freudenberger and Sheehan 1994.

5. Among the less publicized results of this survey was the finding that roughly twenty-one hundred hectares of land contained within forest parks previously created by the Gambian government had been lost to encroachment by farmers. This loss was attributed in part to the failure of the Gambian government to adequately maintain the parks and to the inadvertent clearing of park lands by settlers too new to the area to have been aware of the existence of park boundaries. After determining the scope of the loss and assessing the political sensitivities attached to reclaiming the land, the government simply wrote off the losses and consolidated the remaining forest park areas behind new, fixed boundaries (Schindele and Bojang 1995).

6. "With increasing population more forest lands had to be cleared for shifting cultivation. For this purpose fire was used being the most expedient tool for clearing. Forests close to villages were used for the collection of firewood and building materials. Thus the forest cover was opened and grass growth was stimulated. While fire does not create much destruction in closed forests, the situation was quite different in more open forest with grass and woodwaste on the ground. Here, fires burn hotter and even large trees mainly of nonfire species succumb. In addition most of the natural regeneration is eradicated. This leads to a further opening of the forest, increased grass-growth, higher and hotter fires which kill more large trees. In the long run . . . all the forests are burnt every year" (Schindele and Thoma 1995, 7).

7. Schindele and Thoma (1995) describe GGFP research showing how the root structure of indigenous species, among other factors, renders them much more resilient in the face of recurrent drought conditions than fast-growing exotic species.

8. The GGFP approach to fencing is revealing: "Fencing of forest parks is in fact the most essential protection measure. Fencing has two basic effects. It is on the one hand a physical boundary against cattle (not against people, as there are gates and oversteps), on the other hand, which is of much more importance, it has *psychological* effects. In the Gambia, every valuable piece of land, which belongs to somebody and

which is managed in one or another way, is fenced. Un-fenced areas are reversely [sic] considered as *open access areas* [my emphasis]" (Schindele and Thoma 1995, 22). For a markedly different perspective, see Freudenberger, Carney, and Lebbie 1997.

9. Schindele and Bojang (1995) provide a detailed description of the permitting process for various forest products.

10. The notion that forest resources are completely unmanaged is misleading. The practice of *tongo*, which prohibits specific forms of resource extraction and types of access at certain times of the year, is but the most obvious counterexample (Freudenberger, Carney, and Lebbie 1997; Dumbuya 1994). Freudenberger (1993, 1994), Freudenberger and Sheehan (1994), and Madge (1995) provide additional information on management of forest resources. For that matter, some of the GGFP's own research provides fairly extensive details on forest management practices (Seibert 1989).

11. That this approach amounted to a buffer zone strategy is apparent from the planning document: "After having approached all villages within the catchment area of a forest station following the procedure described, the preliminary management plan for [forest parks] has to be prepared. This plan has to consider as much as possible the villagers' interests and needs identified so far. . . . For [forest park] management activities, labor is to be recruited from nearby villages and from those more remote villages which have concluded the [agreement]. . . . Great attention must be paid in recruiting laborers. Creating employment opportunities may attract many people and priority has to be given to employing local labor forces so that the multiplier effect takes place. A certain amount of vacancies has to be reserved for laborers coming from villages which have already concluded the [agreement]. Their recruitment has to be based on clear conditions and time limits so that as many villagers as possible can benefit from the employment and training opportunity" (Forestry Department–GGFP 1995, 14; compare McNeely 1995; Western, Wright, and Strum 1994).

12. Residents surrounding the Kasila community forest reserve were justifiably disappointed when permits for the commercial extraction of forest products from Kasila forest were issued to outsiders after a CFMA had supposedly been finalized (Dumbuya 1994).

13. One dalasi was roughly equivalent to twelve cents in 1995.

14. The specific conditions outlined here were expressly stated in the CFMA Award Form (Gambian-German Forestry Project n.d.), which representatives of all participating communities were required to sign.

15. In some earlier versions of the CFMA contract, even trees grown on farm lots adjacent to the community reserve were subject to the development of a farmlot management plan to be approved by the Forestry Department.

REFERENCES

Anderson, D., and R. Grove, eds. 1987. *Conservation in Africa: People, Policies and Practice.* New York: Cambridge Univ. Press.

Bassett, T. 1993. Introduction: The Land Question and Agricultural Transformation in Sub-Saharan Africa. In *Land in African Agrarian Systems*, ed. T. Bassett and D. Crummey. Madison: Univ. of Wisconsin Press.

Beinart, W. 1984. Soil Erosion, Conservationism and Ideas about Development: A Southern African Exploration, 1900–1960. *Journal of Southern African Studies* 11(1): 52–83.

Biodiversity Support Program. 1993. *African Biodiversity: Foundation for the Future.* Washington, D.C.: World Wildlife Fund, The Nature Conservancy, and World Resources Institute, with the U.S. Agency for International Development.

Bojang, F. 1994a. Application of Community Forest Management Agreement: The Gambian Experience. Paper presented at the third RPTES workshop, Dakar, Senegal.

———. 1994b. Forest History of The Gambia. Unpublished mimeograph.

Bojang, F., and D. Reeb. 1998. Community Forest Ownership: Key to Sustainable Forest Resource Management—The Gambian Experience. Paper presented at the International Workshop on Community-Based Natural Resource Management. Washington, D.C.: World Bank.

Bonner, R. 1993. *At the Hand of Man: Perils and Hope for Africa's Wildlife.* New York: Vintage Books.

Brosius, J. P., A. L. Tsing, and C. Zerner. 1998. Representing Communities: Histories and Politics of Community-Based Natural Resource Management. *Society and Natural Resources* 11(2): 157–68.

Cason, J. 1997. The U.S.: Backing out of Africa. *Review of African Political Economy* 71: 147–53.

Cline-Cole, R. 1997. Promoting (Anti-)social Forestry in Northern Nigeria? *Review of African Political Economy* 74: 515–36.

Cunningham, A., and M. Cunningham. 2000. Profits, *Prunus,* and the Prostate: International Trade in Tropical Bark. In *People, Plants and Justice: Resource Extraction and Conservation in Tropical Developing Countries*, ed. C. Zerner. New York: Columbia Univ. Press.

Dumbuya, F. 1994. *Decentralization and Natural Resource Management in The Gambia: A Case Study of the Kasila Community Forestry Programme.* Banjul, The Gambia: Ministry of Natural Resources, Policy Analysis and Planning Unit.

Escobar, A. 1995. *Encountering Development: The Making and Unmaking of the Third World.* Princeton, N.J.: Princeton Univ. Press.

Fairhead, J., and M. Leach. 1996. *Misreading the African Landscape: Society and Ecology in a Forest-Savanna Mosaic.* Cambridge, U.K.: Cambridge Univ. Press.

Foley, G. 1994. The Gambia Energy Sector Review: Woodfuels and Household Energy, New and Renewal Energy Sources, Rural Electrification. Report prepared for the Nordic Consulting Group. Copenhagen, Oslo, and Stockholm.

Forestry Department–Gambian German Forestry Project. 1995. The Gambian Forest Management Concept (GFMC). Manuscript. Banjul, The Gambia: Forestry Department/GGFP.

Forster, H. 1983. *Evaluation of the National Forest Inventory of The Gambia.* GGFP Report No. 10. Feldkirchen, Germany: Deutsche Gesellschaft für Technische Zusammenarbeit / Deutsche Forstservice.

Fortmann, L., and J. Bruce, eds. 1988. *Whose Trees? Proprietary Dimensions of Forestry.* Boulder, Colo.: Westview.

Freudenberger, M. 1993. *Institutions and Natural Resource Management in The Gambia: A Case Study of the Foni Jarrol District.* Madison: Univ. of Wisconsin Land Tenure Center.

———. 1994. *Tenure and Natural Resources in The Gambia: Summary of Research Findings and Policy Options*. Madison: Univ. of Wisconsin Land Tenure Center.

Freudenberger, M., J. Carney, and A. Lebbie. 1997. Resiliency and Change in Common Property Regimes in West Africa: The Case of the Tongo in The Gambia, Guinea, and Sierra Leone. *Society and Natural Resources* 10: 383–402.

Freudenberger, M., and N. Sheehan. 1994. *Tenure and Resource Management in The Gambia: A Case Study of the Kiang West District*. Madison: Univ. of Wisconsin Land Tenure Center.

Gambian-German Forestry Project. N.d. CFMA award form. Mimeograph.

Government of The Gambia. 1994. Forest Policy, Republic of The Gambia (1993–2003) (draft). Banjul, The Gambia: Forestry Department.

Groombridge, B., ed. 1992. *Global Biodiversity: Status of the Earth's Living Resources*. London: Chapman and Hall.

Hodgson, D. 1995. The Politics of Gender, Ethnicity and "Development": Images, Interventions and the Reconfiguration of Maasai Identities in Tanzania, 1916–1993. PhD diss., Univ. of Michigan, Ann Arbor.

International Institute for Environment and Development. 1994. *Whose Eden? An Overview of Community Approaches to Wildlife Management.* London: International Institute for Environment and Development.

Laird, S., A. Cunningham, and E. Lisinge. 2000. One in Ten Thousand? The Cameroon Case of *Ancistrocladus Korupensis*. In *People, Plants and Justice: Resource Extraction and Conservation in Tropical Developing Countries*, ed. C. Zerner. New York: Columbia Univ. Press.

Leach, M. 1994. *Rainforest Relations: Gender and Resource Use among the Mende of Gola, Sierra Leone.* Washington, D.C.: Smithsonian Institution.

Madge, Clare. 1995. Ethnography and Agroforestry Research: A Case Study of The Gambia. *Agroforestry Systems* 32: 127–46.

McNeely, Jeffrey, ed. 1995. *Expanding Partnerships in Conservation*. Washington, D.C.: Island Press.

McNeely, J., et al. 1990. *Conserving the World's Biological Diversity*. Gland, Switzerland and Washington, D.C.: IUCN–The World Conservation Union, World Resources Institute, Conservation International, World Wildlife Fund-U.S., and World Bank.

Nelson, J. 1996. Promoting Policy Reforms: The Twilight of Conditionality? *World Development* 24(9): 1551–59.

Neumann, R. 1992. The Political Ecology of Wildlife Conservation in the Mount Meru Area, Northeast Tanzania. *Land Degradation and Rehabilitation* 3(2): 85–98.

———. 1995. Ways of Seeing Africa: Colonial Recasting of African Society and Landscape in Serengeti National Park. *Ecumene* 2: 149–69.

———. 1997. Primitive Ideas: Protected Area Buffer Zones and the Politics of Land in Africa. *Development and Change* 28(3): 559–82.

Peters, P. 1987. Embedded Systems and Rooted Models: The Grazing Lands of Botswana and the "Commons" Debate. In *The Question of the Commons: The Culture and Ecology of Communal Resources*, ed. B. McCay and J. Acheson. Tucson: Univ. of Arizona Press.

———. 1996. Who's Local Here? The Politics of Participation in Development. *Cultural Survival Quarterly* 20(3): 22–25.

Ribot, J. 1995a. From Exclusion to Participation: Turning Senegal's Forest Policy Around? *World Development* 23(9): 1587–99.

———. 1995b. Local Forestry Control in Burkina Faso, Mali, Niger, Senegal and The Gambia: A Review and Critique of New Participatory Policies. Review of Policies in the Traditional Energy Sector (RPTES). Discussion Paper Series. Washington, D.C.: World Bank.

———. 2000. Rebellion, Representation and Enfranchisement in the Forest Villages of Makacoulibantang, Eastern Senegal. In *People, Plants and Justice: Resource Extraction and Conservation in Tropical Developing Countries*, ed. C. Zerner. New York: Columbia Univ. Press.

Ridder, R. 1991. *Land Use Inventory for The Gambia on the Basis of Landsat-TM Scenes Including a Comparison with Previous Investigations*. Feldkirchen, Germany: Deutsche Gesellschaft für Technische Zusammenarbeit / Deutsche Forstservice.

Sachs, W., ed. 1993. *Global Ecology: A New Arena of Political Conflict*. London: Zed Books.

Schindele, W., and F. Bojang. 1995. *Gambian Forest Management Concept, Part I: The Forest Sector of The Gambia*. GGFP Report No. 29. Feldkirchen, Germany: Deutsche Gesellschaft für Technische Zusammenarbeit / Deutsche Forstservice.

Schindele, W., and W. Thoma. 1995. *Gambian Forest Management Concept, Part II: The Development of the Gambian Forest Management Concept (GFMC)*. GGFP Report No. 30. Feldkirchen, Germany: Deutsche Gesellschaft für Technische Zusammenarbeit / Deutsche Forstservice.

Seibert, K. 1989. *Possibilities of Introducing Community Forestry in The Gambia, Part II: Gambia-German Forestry Project, Deutsche Gesellschaft für Technische Zusammenarbeit (GTZ)*. Feldkirchen, Germany: Deutsche Forstservice.

Smith, N. 1990. *Uneven Development: Nature, Capital and the Production of Space*, 2d ed. Oxford: Basil Blackwell.

United States Agency for International Development (USAID). 1992. Program Assistance Approval Document. Agriculture and Natural Resources Program and Support Project. Banjul, The Gambia: United States Agency for International Development.

———. 1996. *Making a Difference in Africa: A Report on USAID Assistance to Africa*. Washington, D.C.: United States Agency for International Development.

Watts, M. 1995. A New Deal in Emotions: Theory and Practice and the Crisis of Development. In *Power of Development*, ed. J. Crush. London: Routledge.

Western, D., R. Wright, and S. Strum, eds. 1994. *Natural Connections: Perspectives in Community-Based Conservation*. Washington, D.C.: Island Press.

World Bank. 1995. *Mainstreaming the Environment: The World Bank Group and the Environment since the Rio Earth Summit.* Washington, D.C.: World Bank.

———. 1996. *Toward Environmentally Sustainable Development in Sub-Saharan Africa: A World Bank Agenda.* Washington, D.C.: World Bank.

World Commission on Environment and Development. 1987. *Our Common Future.* Oxford: Oxford Univ. Press.

9

Can David and Goliath Have a Happy Marriage? The Machiguenga People and the Camisea Gas Project in the Peruvian Amazon

Richard Chase Smith

During the past three decades, national governments, under heavy pressure from local social movements and international institutions, have been recognizing the tenure rights of indigenous Amazonians to their traditional homelands and demarcating areas for protection and for property titles. Now that this situation is being resolved, local community organizations and the nongovernmental organizations (NGOs) working with them are moving into a new phase. The goal is now to achieve the long-term sustainable use of their common property territories and natural resources through planned management. However, as we are learning in the practice, reaching that goal is not so easy.

Resource planning and management with local communities is a slow, complex, and laborious process of conflict resolution and institution building among entangled interests and conflicting visions of a future (Mehta et al. 2000; Mehta, Leach, and Scoones 2001). Positive outcomes in this process depend to a large degree on having an effective community organization with strong institutional arrangements for establishing and implementing agreements on resource use and conservation (Agrawal 1997; Cleaver 2001; Ostrom 2001; McCay and Jentoft 1998). But both community-defense and resource-management efforts in indigenous Amazonia are part of a much broader historical process over which the local people have little understanding or control (Smith 1997). And in this historical process, community institutional arrangements have been very vulnerable to the uncertainty of extracommunity contextual factors, be they the result of natural phenomena or of human-induced situations (Cleaver 2001; Smith et al. 2001, 36–46).

In a frontier region like Amazonia, where everyday business involves opening and incorporating new regions into a dominant political and market system, political violence, instability, and economic rapaciousness are a constant. So even particularly interesting cases of community use and conservation of resources, which today are held out as hopeful models, may like the U.S. Agency for International Development (USAID) Palcazu Resource Management Project in the mid-1980s, end up being tomorrow's pariah project. In the Palcazu case, the addition of guerrilla terror and drug-dealing greed to an already politically weakened project in the late 1980s resulted in a breakdown of the institutional arrangements and abandonment of the collective management efforts. By 1994 individual community members were selling off timber from the forest plots once managed by the Yanesha Forestry Cooperative while the million-dollar investment in its infrastructure and equipment provided by the project sat idle (Benavides and Pariona 1995, 27–51; Gram, Klint, and Helles 1994).

Under such volatile conditions as we have witnessed over the past three decades in Amazonia, it is extremely difficult for indigenous Amazonians to plan from one year to the next, let alone the three or four decades needed for good forest management. And certainly this challenge is made more difficult when we add to the mix pressure to demonstrate success within the three-year time frame of a foundation funding cycle, within the budget process of the U.S. Congress as determined by electoral cycle politics, or within the time limits imposed by what theme happens to be de rigueur within the development funding world. The modern historical process does not seem to provide the time and pace required for the detailed and time-consuming efforts needed to reach the goal of community-based resource management.

In this chapter, I am interested in showing how getting to community-based resource management is part of an ongoing historical process with changing actors, context, and stakes. I focus on the impact of modern oil and gas development on the efforts the Machiguenga people of the lower Urubamba river valley in Peru tc consolidate and manage their titled territory. The main actors in this drama are the former Shell-Mobil Consortium formed to carry out the Camisea Gas Project; the Centro para el Desarrollo del Indígena Amazónico (CEDIA), the NGO with the longest history of working in the area; and the Machiguenga Council of the Urubamba River (Consejo Machiguenga del Rio Urubamba, or COMARU), the community federation promoted by CEDIA. The Machiguenga communities in the lower Urubamba watershed of southern Peru, with the support of COM-

ARU, CEDIA, and other NGOs, reached the threshold of territorial planning and management after a fifteen-year struggle to consolidate their title and control over a large portion of their traditional homeland.

In 1995–1996 three international petroleum giants—Shell, Mobil, and Chevron—entered the lower Urubamba stage: the Shell-Mobil Consortium with a multibillion-dollar, forty-year contract to exploit the Camisea gas fields[1] and Chevron with a three-year contract for petroleum exploration, all in the midst of the Machiguenga communities. With their presence, the historical development process in the lower Urubamba was suddenly pulled away from its community focus and immediately refocused on the international petroleum market. In 1998 a series of disputes between the Shell-Mobil Consortium and the Peruvian government led to a rupture of the forty-year contract and an end to Shell-Mobil presence in the Urubamba. This chapter analyzes the impact that the international business perspective of the Shell-Mobil Consortium had on the local Machiguenga process for territorial consolidation and organization building during that three-year period.

The existence of the enormous Camisea gas and oil deposits could undermine the Machiguenga's growing dream of control and sustainable development for their homeland, especially if the petroleum giants developing the deposits continue to ignore the ongoing local processes. But these deposits could also represent an opportunity. Depending on how their development unfolds, the petroleum companies could become collaborators with the Machiguenga to move the communities past the threshold and into the realm of long-term territorial planning and resource management. Or, as in the case of the Shell-Mobil Consortium, they can become an obstacle in their path.

HISTORY AND CONTEXT

Enormous Changes in the Peruvian Amazon

The changes in the Peruvian Amazon and its indigenous peoples over the past three and a half decades, resulting from geopolitical decisions made outside the basin, have produced truly new socioeconomic and biophysical realities. With help from USAID, the European Union, the World Bank, and the Inter-American Development Bank, massive investments were made by successive governments in roads and communications infrastructure, state-promoted colonization schemes, extension programs in agriculture and cattle raising, and projects for petroleum and other resource extraction.[2]

Indigenous Amazonian societies were deeply affected by the influx of new settlers into their territories, by the market pressures that came with the new highways and feeder roads built into the forest, and by the forest clearing for sprawling cattle ranches, coca fields, African palm plantations, mining centers, and oil wells promoted by subsidized credit and government services.

One result of these changes was a marked increase in conflict over ownership and usufruct to land, natural landscapes, and other resources. Initially, the fundamental rights of the indigenous inhabitants were ignored by the law and government policies and by incoming settlers, land speculators, and the extractive industry. In the late 1960s indigenous Amazonians began constructing a broad federative social movement based in their local settlements, which demanded recognition for their collective rights to land and resources (Chirif Tirado, Hierro, and Smith 1991; Smith et al. 2001). By the mid-1970s this movement brought about gradual recognition of their individual and collective rights, codified in national laws and later in the Peruvian Constitution.

Nonetheless, the years of physical displacement, tenure insecurity, pressure to join the labor force, and general conflict created an extremely unfavorable context for developing long-term plans for community-based resource management among indigenous Amazonians. Many communities were displaced and assimilated, whereas others abandoned their traditional systems for use and management of resources in exchange for cash-crop systems. For those reasons, the top priority for indigenous communities during the 1970s and 1980s was to gain government title to their land and resource base.

Tenure Security for Community Lands

In 1974 the Peruvian government enacted Law 20653, recognizing Native Communities in its Amazonia region, legalizing among other things their collective property rights to the land and forest areas they "traditionally occupied," including those used for hunting, fishing, and gathering (International Labour Organization 1997; Garcia 1995).[3] This law established that the lands of titled Native Communities cannot be alienated under any circumstances nor are they subject to a lien for unpaid debts.

In 1977, under pressure from conservationists who argued for the strict regulation of forest use as well as from resource nationalists who argued that timber should be a public resource, a new forestry and conservation law nationalized all forested lands and established a special regime for national parks and reserves. Less than a year later, the Native Communities law was modified to reflect these changes. Since then, the Peruvian state has no longer recognized indigenous property rights over forest lands; instead, the revised law granted the community the possibility of a long-term, preferential concession from the state for certain forest usufruct rights within the area demarcated for the community.

However, in partial compensation, the Forestry Law of 1977 established the possibility for creating Communal Reserves, large areas of forest designated for collective nonagricultural use and management by the communities bordering on it. Until 2001 neither the law nor government policy established how a Communal Reserves was to be governed or managed and only one had been established. Three more have been set up since 2001.

During the first decade, government officials in charge of implementing the 1974 Native Communities law, influenced by the Andean community experience, recognized and titled each indigenous settlement, no matter how reduced in size, as a Native Community. As a result, most Amazonian peoples were broken up into archipelagos of small, often isolated, communities; the lands between were opened for colonization and extractive activities by nonindigenous peoples. Many of these individual communities were too small and densely populated to permit traditional practices of extensive resource use and management.

Beginning in the mid-1980s two factors brought about a change in the patterns of land demarcation and titling for Peruvian Native Communities: (1) The Coordinating Body for Indigenous Organizations of the Amazon Basin (COICA), influenced by the proceedings of the United Nations Workgroup on Indigenous Populations, introduced its member organizations to a new discourse on aboriginal rights to a territory, that is, to a large continuous homeland, including all forest, aquatic, and subsoil resources (Chirif Tirado, Hierro, and Smith 1991; Smith 2002).[4] (2) Beginning in 1986, COICA initiated an aggressive international campaign for support and recognition of indigenous territorial rights in Amazonia. By the end of the decade, private and multilateral funding agencies, including the World Bank, the European Economic Commission, the Inter-American Development Bank, bilateral funding agencies, and the northern conservation community, began financing land demarcation efforts by NGOs in conjunction with Native Community federations and local government agencies (Smith 2002).

As a result, larger tracts of land (up to fifty thousand hectares) were titled to individual settlements in Peru, and where possible, larger territorial units were pieced together through mosaics of individual communities with common borders, proposed communal reserves, and conservation units (Chirif Tirado, Hierro, and Smith 1991; Garcia 1995).

A country's land- and resource-tenure regime greatly influences the degree of security an indigenous community feels regarding its resources and its future relationship to them; this in turn conditions community confidence in developing or continuing long-term practices in resource management. In Peru indigenous peoples in general have virtually no political clout and consequently little chance of influencing the shape of the country's tenure regime. The "Land Law" enacted by the Fujimori government in 1995 as part of a move toward privatization of the Peruvian economy, weakened collective tenure rights and produced a new wave of tenure insecurity among indigenous communities in the Peruvian Amazon.[5]

Subsoil Resources

In 1969 a tax dispute with the International Petroleum Company (IPC), a subsidiary of Standard Oil of New Jersey, triggered a military coup and a series of laws and policy decisions that declared state ownership over all subsoil resources in Peru and expropriated all outstanding and inactive subsoil concessions handed out by previous governments.

Under these laws, the Peruvian state has exclusive right to grant mineral and oil concessions under the terms and conditions it deems most advantageous for the nation. Two state corporations were established to administer Peru's subsoil resources and negotiate contracts for their exploitation: Mineroperu for mineral resources, and Petroperu for petroleum resources. Both state companies were also given the exclusive right to develop any new refineries in the country, and through their subsidiaries, to market all the production.

New mining and petroleum codes recently legislated under the Fujimori government have made foreign investment in subsoil resource extraction much more attractive in terms of repatriating profits and far less restricted by environmental and tax laws (International Labour Organization 1997). Both Petroperu and Mineroperu were stripped of their administrative functions and of their monopoly over marketing. As a result, a new oil boom began in the Peruvian Amazon; by 1996 more than twenty new petroleum companies had signed contracts for petroleum exploration in the Amazon and in Pacific coastal waters.

Under Peruvian law, a land title, whether community or individual, does not give the proprietor any claim to the subsoil resources. Article 29 of the 1974 Native Communities Law states: "The lands of the Jungle are subject to the following: free passage for oil and gas pipelines; installations for the exploration and exploitation of minerals and petroleum. . . . The establishment of such services will not require the payment of any indemnity to the property owner."

Under the legislation created by the Fujimori regime, subsoil resources remain the property of the state. Article 7 of the 1995 Land Law held out hope for just compensation to the title-holding landowners for damage caused by subsoil extractive activities. The procedural code for Article 7 (Supreme Decree No. 017-96-AG) states in its first clause that an oil company cannot use privately owned land for any of its activities without a previous agreement with the owner. Clause 3 then says that the landowner has thirty days in which to accept the company's proposal for use of the surface and compensation; clauses 4–7 establish the procedures by which the state intervenes after thirty days to decree a right of way for the company and determines the damages to be paid to the owner. The landowner has no right of appeal.

Peruvian jurisprudence in general does not recognize the concept of aboriginal rights, including rights to either forest or subsoil resources found in an indigenous people's homeland. However, by becoming a signatory to the International Labour Organization (ILO) Convention 169 in 1994, Peru committed itself to respecting a series of collective rights of its indigenous and tribal peoples. Article 15 of the convention obligates the government to determine whether the interests of an indigenous people are risked by granting subsoil extraction rights to third parties, to ensure that the affected people will share in the benefits of the extraction, and to pay compensation for any damages occurring to their homeland in the extraction process. We will return to this point.

MACHIGUENGA TERRITORY CONSOLIDATION IN THE LOWER URUBAMBA

The eight thousand or so Machiguenga, an Amazonian people of the Arawak linguistic family, live in dispersed settlements in the forested valleys of the Urubamba River and its small tributaries.[6] The area around the modern town of Quillabamba has been a coca leaf–growing colony of Andean societies for centuries, since before the Spanish arrived. During the colonial and late republican era, several enormous haciendas came to dominate the valley, producing tea, coffee, and cacao, as well as coca leaf.

Some Machiguenga were incorporated into the labor force of these haciendas where they remained generation after generation. Others fled down river, past the Pongo de Mainique—a dangerous cut through the last range of the Andes—or into the inaccessible upper reaches of the smaller tributaries where to this day some still avoid contact with outsiders. With the demise of the haciendas in the 1970s, those who had been part of the labor force continued to work small parcels in the marginal areas of the former haciendas, maintaining their sense of community and identity as Machiguenga.

The Dominican Order of the Catholic Church established three missions among the Machiguenga in the 1940s: one at Koribeni in the upper valley and two in the lower valley below the Pongo at Timpia and Kirigueti. These missions continue to exercise limited influence over the Machiguenga who live close to these centers.

In the 1950s the Wycliffe Bible Translators–Summer Institute of Linguistics (WBT-SIL) sent a missionary-linguist to work with the Machiguenga of the lower Urubamba to develop an alphabet for the Machiguenga language, translate the Bible into it, and develop a bilingual education program for the region, giving teacher training to carefully selected Machiguenga at WBT-SIL's Pucallpa base. Until the mid-1980s, the Machiguenga bilingual teachers were an influential source of news about land struggles of other indigenous Amazonians, about the new law guaranteeing the Native Communities, and about the growing movement of indigenous Amazonian organizations. In 1975, following the example of the Amuesha and Ashaninka peoples, a group of bilingual teachers established a federation, the Central de Comunidades Nativas Machiguengas (CECONAMA) among six communities where WBT-SIL worked.

The tension between the Machiguenga influenced by the Catholic missions and those under the WBT-SIL Protestant network continues to dominate the social and political dynamic of intercommunity life in the lower Urubamba today.

The Machiguenga missed out on the early government efforts (1974–1978) to recognize and title Native Communities. By the time the revised version of the Native Communities law appeared in 1978, the military government had lost interest in implementing it. In response, a group of anthropologists and lawyers involved in the earlier government efforts established an NGO, Centro de Investigación y Promoción Amazónica (CIPA), to continue the land-titling work with private-foundation funding.

In 1979 CIPA signed an agreement with the Ministry of Agriculture (Cuzco region) for a fifteen-month project to recognize, demarcate, and title the Machiguenga settlements in the Urubamba valley. This effort coincided with a renewed interest in the Cuzco region in colonizing the unoccupied lands in the upper Urubamba. After the short-lived CIPA project ended, potential colonizers organized into cooperatives and pressured government officials to ignore the Machiguenga land claims in favor of the colonists and land speculators.

In 1982 former personnel of CIPA set up a new NGO called CEDIA, which reestablished accords with the Ministry of Agriculture to finish the titling process for the Urubamba Machiguenga. By 1985, with growing resistance from the Machiguenga and the fall of coffee and cacao prices, the colonization boom had ended. This allowed CEDIA to secure twenty-one Native Community land titles for the Machiguenga, seven in the upper valley and fourteen in the lower valley, for a total demarcated area of 301,918 hectares (including both titled property and forest concession; map 9.1).

Until 1987 CEDIA worked in the upper valley with the seven small communities there to establish living boundaries as a defense measure against incursions by land-hungry colonists wanting to expand their holdings. CEDIA also initiated a series of intensive courses for community members about their legal rights as indigenous Amazonians and as Peruvian citizens and on the intensification of cash-crop farming to improve their advantage in the marketplace.

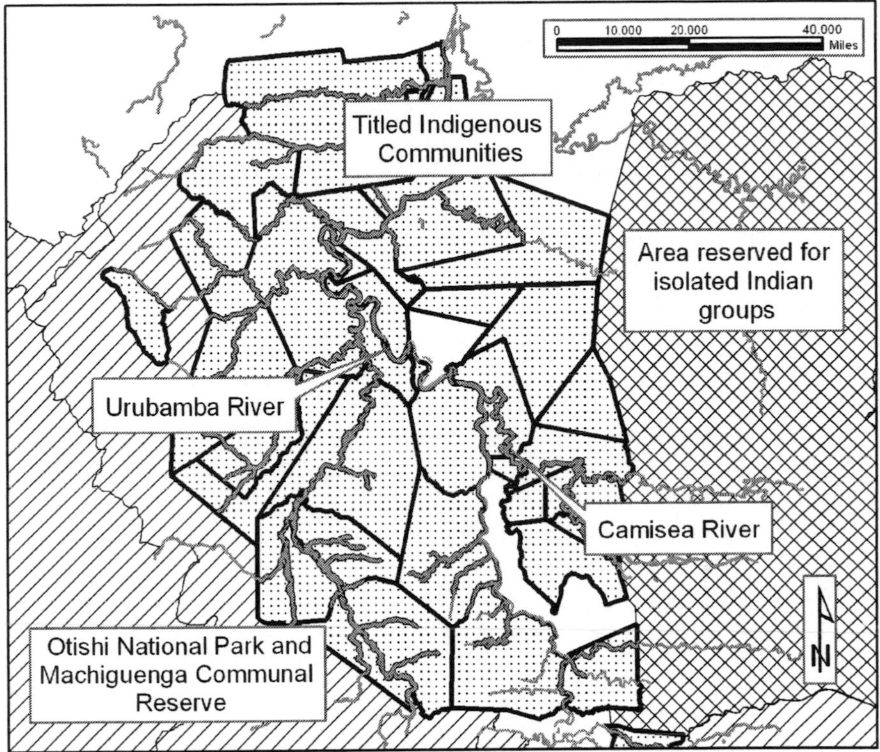

Map 9.1 Territories of Titled Indigenous Communities and Areas Reserved for Isolated Indigenous Groups, Lower Urubamba and Camisea Rivers

Source: SICNA-IBC, Ministry of Energy and Mines, INRENA.

In 1987 CEDIA opened a new program for the fourteen Machiguenga communities in the lower Urubamba. This program began with three main thrusts:

- consolidating the community land and resource base
- developing a working concept of community organization
- training on legal rights and issues

These three thrusts, redefined and expanded many times over, continue to underlie CEDIA's work with the Machiguenga today. In this chapter I will focus on the first two.

Territorial Planning and Consolidation

In line with their work in the upper Urubamba, CEDIA's concept of consolidation at first revolved around securing community boundaries from incursions by colonists as a preventive measure. They established community nurseries for propagating coffee, *Bixa orellana,* and a few exotic tree species for planting in the trails cleared along the boundaries. But because the majority of the boundaries were shared by other communities or bordered public lands with no river frontage and because there was relatively little land pressure, these efforts slowly waned over the first couple of years.

The year 1988 was one of uncertainty for the Machiguenga communities because Petroperu and Shell Oil Company were negotiating a contract for exploiting the gas deposits Shell had discovered along the Camisea River in the heart of their community territory. Because of the fears and concerns expressed by the local communities, CEDIA incorporated into its concept of land consolidation ideas of environmental impact and protection.

That year, Petroperu conducted an extensive consultation process in the lower Urubamba to determine how the gas project might affect the local population. Through the government agency responsible for community development (INDEC), a subcommission on the Camisea project was formed that included two NGOs (CIPA and the Catholic Church–sponsored CAAAP) and the two national confederations of indigenous communities (AIDESEP and CONAP), together with an ad hoc Interethnic Commission from the lower Urubamba.[7] At the end of 1988, Shell decided against signing the contract and turned its base camps over to the local communities.

Spurred by the threat represented by a possible future Camisea project and by the new ideas of indigenous territoriality that had been filtering down from the work of COICA and others, CEDIA again redefined its thrust for land consolidation. Together with COMARU, the Machiguenga community organization established in 1988, CEDIA formulated a vision of a large Machiguenga territory as a mosaic of many smaller units, each permitted by different laws and policies, neatly fitting into a single whole. CEDIA now called this programmatic thrust Territorial Planning and Consolidation.

During 1989, under agreements with the Ministry of Agriculture and the regional government, CEDIA demarcated three new Native Communities and increased the size of three existing communities. Using aerial photographs and topographic sheets, CEDIA presented a proposal for creating a special reserved area for the Kogapakori and Nahua peoples who remained uncontacted, demarcating an area bordering the Machiguenga communities to the east of the Urubamba River. At the end of that year the Ministry of Agriculture approved the creation of the Kogapakori-Nahua Reserve, with 443,000 hectares.

That same year, alluding to the need to conserve biodiversity in the region, CEDIA formally launched two new proposals: one for the creation of a National Sanctuary in the southern end of the valley focused on the Pongo de Mainique and a second for the creation of a Communal Reserve on the eastern slopes of the Vilcabamba mountain range bordering the communities to the west of the Urubamba River (see map 9.1). Work was begun to prepare the technical studies and maps to justify those conservation areas under the 1977 Forestry Law. Although the technical work has been complete for a decade, the Communal Reserve was only recently declared, in January 2003; the National Sanctuary, unfortunately, continues to await government action.

Between 1989 and 1996, CEDIA, with increasing involvement of COMARU, demarcated and coaxed out of the government bureaucracy three additional community titles plus titles for land increases for twelve of the previously titled communities (table 9.1).

Community Building and Local Organization

The Velasco government (1969–1975) promoted a vision of rural development based on a strongly ideologized notion of community as a tightly knit corporate entity seamlessly sharing resources, labor, economic initiatives, and marketing efforts. Community projects and community enterprises were encouraged around the country with government seed money and official recognition. Despite the romanticism of this vision, the government was not about to let community affairs take their natural or even traditional course. Very detailed norms were enacted dictating how communities, including very traditional pre-Colombian Andean communities, were to organize themselves and conduct their affairs. This view of community, as I said before, became very influential in the Peruvian Amazon.

CEDIA came to its work in the Urubamba after almost a decade of collaboration with government efforts to promote community in rural areas. CEDIA team members became aware that the official vision of community that they brought with them often came into conflict with the underlying

Table 9.1 Indigenous Peoples' Territory in Lower Urubamba, January 2003

	Designated Area (in hectares)
Titled property of twenty-four Native Communities	433,482
Property of 195 colonist families	23,679
Kogapakori Nahua Reserve	443,887
Machiguenga Communal Reserve	272,679
Megantoni National Sanctuary (proposed)	176,900
Total Area	**1,350,627**

Machiguenga social organization. CEDIA expressed frustration that within the new Native Communities social and political life continued to revolve around family clusters rather than the community as a whole. Yet under the law, they reasoned, the Machiguenga and their lands were now recognized as Native Communities and their best strategy to defend themselves was as Native Communities.

For this thrust, CEDIA established a goal of assuring that the Machiguenga internalize the concept of community as defined in the current legal norms. They launched an intensive effort to work with the assembly of members in each community to develop an understanding of collective responsibility and defense, to create mechanisms for making community decisions in assembly, and to develop written "statutes" for governing the community. CEDIA worked closely with elected community leaders to help them understand and carry out their new roles and responsibilities.

Although CEDIA had been instrumental in gaining titles to fourteen Native Communities in the lower Urubamba, they initiated their program there with the nine communities that accepted their institutional presence. A series of factors led some of the CECONAMA member communities to reject CEDIA's program. By the end of 1989, with three new titled communities, the CEDIA program was working with thirteen of the seventeen legally recognized communities in the lower Urubamba.

Aware of the need for the Machiguenga to find their own voice in the newly created regional government based in Cuzco, CEDIA worked with the seven communities of the upper Urubamba to develop the notion of intercommunity cooperation, defense, and organization. In November 1988 these seven communities established COMARU. All the communities of the lower Urubamba were invited to attend as observers.

By 1989 both CEDIA and some Machiguenga leaders had been influenced by the debates surrounding the identity of indigenous populations as peoples that had been widely disseminated in Peru by COICA, AIDESEP, and their collaborators. In response, CEDIA expanded its definition for the community-organization thrust of their work to include the promotion of an ethnic-based sense of people among the Machiguenga, linking this to territorial rights and to broad intercommunity cooperation and political expression. Finding broad support for this new vision among the communities, CEDIA and COMARU promoted a series of interchanges between the Machiguenga of the upper and the lower Urubamba, later reaching out to the relatively isolated Machiguenga communities in the upper Madre de Dios watershed.

At the end of 1989, leaders from twenty-one Machiguenga communities, seven from the upper and fourteen from the lower Urubamba, gathered for their first formal congress. After three days of discussion, they agreed on the following priority points: (1) The communities needed to pressure the government to finish the land-titling process and recognize the Communal Reserve and the National Sanctuary. (2) They needed to demand that Shell Oil Company and the government respect the autonomy of the communities, their customs and traditions, and the flora and fauna of their territory in any future development of the Camisea Gas Project. (3) They needed to name one representative for the regional government in Cuzco and another for the subregional government in Quillabamba.

Although these communities continued to meet for several years independently of both COMARU and CECONAMA, the underlying question—would the unaffiliated communities of the lower Urubamba join COMARU or CECONAMA or create their own organization?—was always in the air. In 1993 nine of the lower communities opted to join COMARU.[8]

Toward Territorial Zoning and Management

With the issues of tenure security and territorial consolidation nearly resolved, with the communities functioning reasonably well, and with a growing intercommunity organization, the Machiguenga of the lower Urubamba seemed in a good position to begin asking tough questions about the future of their common-property territory. For example, how would they both use and conserve the resources of their territory to satisfy their current needs as well as those of future generations?

To begin to answer that question and to develop the long-range management tools they would need, precise information about the makeup of the indigenous territory was essential. Community owners would likely have an intimate knowledge of the layout and resource base for the smaller areas of each community that they managed directly. But no single person, Machiguenga or otherwise, would have an intimate or even general picture for the entire 1.3 million hectare territory. Indeed, there are large areas that are known to no one, such as the Kogapakori-Nahua Reserve, most of the Machiguenga Communal Reserve, and parts of the national sanctuary. In such cases, it is most efficient to put together a team of technically trained field specialists working with local people to gather the necessary information with which to construct a global picture.

In 1995 CEDIA, COMARU, and Oxfam America entered into an agreement to study and map the major types of vegetative cover and their distribution throughout the lower Urubamba territory (Houghton and Hackler 1996). Under the technical direction of Woods Hole Research Center, the study combined satellite-image interpretation with fieldwork for ground truthing and species identification and with data from many other sources. The study identified two major forest types and a variety of other vegetative cover and land-use types. These results were incorporated into a geographic information system (GIS) database of the territory based on topographical sheets, satellite images, forest maps, and census and survey data.

In May 1996 preliminary results were presented to members of COMARU and CEDIA at a workshop held in Santa Cruz, Bolivia. The workshop stressed the importance of caring for an indigenous territory as the common patrimony of a people. This caring requires (1) planning for the long-term sustainable use and conservation of the resources found in the territory, (2) defense of the territorial integrity from external threats, and (3) an institutionalized consensus among those sharing the territory for governing and managing the territory well.

The workshop introduced and examined the concept of zoning as a tool for accomplishing a long-term caring relationship with a territory. Zoning, it was concluded, should be a process based on both indigenous and scientific knowledge to identify areas where use types appropriate to the biophysical and current social characteristics can be promoted and to identify areas with special problems or needs and those that require protection or conservation. Parallel to that process, the local community organizations need to establish an agreement among all the territory's inhabitants to respect the agreed-upon uses for the different zones identified.

The workshop identified and discussed the different use types that would need consideration in designing such a zoning plan for an indigenous territory. These included five general categories of areas:

- to support the indigenous economy and culture
- for productive activities directed toward the market
- for biodiversity conservation
- of "national sacrifice" (petroleum exploitation, military installations, etc.)
- for future urban-commercial expansion

The workshop organizers suggested a four-step methodology for conducting such a zoning process in indigenous territories. These included (1) systematization of all available cartographic and descriptive data using a computerized GIS, (2) prezoning activities including identification of natural territorial units based on thematic analysis of their biophysical characteristics and identification of current land-use and socioeconomic needs and perspectives for all parts of the territory, (3) zoning activities to produce a recommended zoning model based on integration of natural zones with socioeconomic conditions, and (4) a process of negotiation and management.

The results of the Oxfam-WHRC biomass study, particularly the GIS database integrating the vegetation maps with the other layers of spatial data, were presented as an important ingredient for beginning a process of ecological-economic zoning in the Machiguenga territory.

GREEN LIGHT FOR CAMISEA GAS PROJECT

On 17 May 1996, after a year of quiet negotiations, Petroperu, representing the Peruvian state, signed a contract with the Shell-Mobil Consortium for the development of the Camisea gas fields over the following forty years. The contract was divided into two phases: a two-year appraisal phase for continued exploration and analysis of the gas fields and a production phase, contingent on the results of the first, for the development and exploitation of the fields.

If the project had moved into the second stage, the Shell-Mobil Consortium would have been committed to invest at least $2.8 billion to transport the gas products to a terminal near the Lima market and to pay the Peruvian state $6 billion in rent and royalties over the lifetime of the project. As an incentive, the Peruvian state changed its tax regulations to exonerate the project from import duties, export taxes, and the sales tax on natural gas, for different periods of time.

This contract covered two small lots: no. 88-a (Mipaya gas field) and no. 88-b (San Martin and Cashiriari gas fields), where there are an estimated 11 trillion cubic feet of natural gas and 545 million barrels of liquid gas (see map 9.2; Inter-American Development Bank 2003; La Torre 1996). After further negotiations, Petroperu and the Shell-Mobil Consortium signed a second contract permitting exploration for gas and petroleum in lot no. 75, a much larger area surrounding lots 88-a and 88-b to the north and east.

The appraisal phase activities included building a base camp and airport in the Native Community of Nuevo Mundo under a three-year contract signed with leaders of the community and CECONAMA. The contract provided some protection and benefits for the community. This logistics center began handling an initial part of the estimated seven thousand tons of materials and equipment that were to be brought into the area. The Shell-Mobil Consortium redrilled one well from its 1987 explorations (San Martin 1) and developed two new wells (Cashiriari 3 and San Martin 3); plans were laid for redrilling a second existing well (San Martin 2). All four were located in lot 88-b, along the Camisea River.

Technical-financial plans were also developed for the second phase. The international consortium, led by Bechtel, a U.S. company that also built the base camp and airport at Nuevo Mundo, won the estimated three-billion-dollar contract for design and construction of the gathering station in the Camisea where the gas and its distillates were to be separated, of the trans-Andean pipeline taking the liquid gas to a point near Lima, and at the end of the pipeline, of a major installation for fractionating and distributing the gas. Separate plans were developed for a gas-driven six-hundred-megawatt power plant to be located in the upper Urubamba.

Still reeling from the market impact of its problems in Nigeria and the

North Sea, Shell invested up front in the Camisea project to "do it right" regarding the indigenous peoples in the area and the fragile tropical forest and mountain ecosystems. Six months before Shell signed the first contract with the Peruvian government, Shell hired a London consulting firm to scout out stakeholders and find out their concerns and possible pitfalls. On the basis of that study and other consultations, Shell announced it would follow an offshore strategy to minimize contact with the local ecosystem and human population. By this, Shell meant that it would not build a road into the lower Urubamba but rather would use river and air transport to bring personnel, material, equipment, and supplies into a base camp in the region and helicopters to fly these into the well sites. At the same time, it would fly out all industrial waste.

Shell then hired a health, safety, and environment (HSE) manager, who in turn hired a community liaison officer and an environmental officer plus other short-term field people, to design and implement guidelines and agreements with the local population for avoiding long-term social and environmental problems. Through the HSE office, Shell maintained a wide range of contacts with stakeholders, NGOs, and government officials, regularly informing them of planned and ongoing activities.

In September 1996, in a two-day forum held in Lima titled "Cultural and Biological Diversity in the Lower Urubamba," the Man and the Biosphere Program and the Biodiversity Program of the Smithsonian Institution presented the results of a week-long field visit by a team of scientists to the lower Urubamba (Smithsonian 1996). The participants learned later that the forum was underwritten by Shell-HSE, and this led eventually to a longer-term collaboration between Shell and the Smithsonian to conduct a baseline study of the biodiversity in the Camisea region.

Shell expressed the opinion that in the long-term the Peruvian government is responsible for local development in the lower Urubamba. However, Shell-HSE adopted the position that in the shorter term the company has a responsibility for getting a local development process off the ground. To this end, Shell-HSE created what it called a Social Capital Program and identified as its priorities addressing the need for health and educational infrastructure, promotion of agriculture, social development, and addressing the problems of women (Shell 1996, paper 4).

As a first step, Shell-HSE hired the consulting firm Pro-Natura (a Brazil-U.S. company) to develop a diagnostic study of the lower Urubamba that would be the basis for development planning. Shell-HSE negotiated the financial and operational participation of the regional government in Cuzco, along with four Cuzco-based NGOs, in the diagnostic study, which began in July 1997. Shell-HSE was hopeful that the diagnostic study would produce clear and concrete goals for the future development of the lower Urubamba.

Cuzco regional authorities have never been very sympathetic to the rights or land claims of the Machiguenga. In fact a strong lobby among Cuzco politicians for building a road into the lower Urubamba for colonization and timber extraction continues to exist. It is difficult to understand why, given this historical tension, Shell-HSE decided to bring the Cuzco regional government into the diagnostic process for the Machiguenga homeland. The HSE manager explained that the Social Capital Program required a regional focus and a long-term commitment from government authorities.

Despite Shell's intention to "do it right" in the Camisea project, by the end of 1997 there were indications that the Social Capital Program and the environmental process initiated by Shell for the region were replicating traditional top-down approaches and moving in the direction of conflict with the lower Urubamba communities, their supporters, and their long-range interests, needs, and plans. Let me summarize several reasons why this was so.

First, the lower Urubamba is the traditional homeland for the Machiguenga, who now have surface title to most of it, including most of the area over the gas fields. There was no indication that the Peruvian government or the Shell-Mobil Consortium was considering negotiating a long-term big-picture settlement with the Machiguenga over the major issues of consultation, right of way, compensation, environmental or resource use and protections, and the long-term benefits the Machiguenga would receive from the resources extracted from their homelands.

Strictly adhering to the regulations of the Land Law, Shell-HSE focused on resolving issues with those communities that were directly affected by their activities. The Shell-Mobil Consortium, through HSE, signed short-term agreements with a few communities that permitted the consortium's presence or activities on community land in exchange for a symbolic compensation.

One could argue that even in the case of CN Nuevo Mundo—the site of the main Shell-Mobil Consortium base camp and operations center, which reportedly was to receive more than one hundred thousand dollars in benefits—or that of the CN Cashiriari, which was to receive about twenty thousand dollars for the test wells being dug, the compensation remained symbolic if compared with the size of the project's investments and profits. There is no general framework or even clear precedent for establishing compensation to landowners in Peru. In the case of Chevron, which had exploratory rights to the lot on the western side of the lower Urubamba, compensation for seismic testing consisted of t-shirts, soccer balls, school notebooks, pens, and pencils.

Second, the Camisea project is an enormous business deal. During their brief period there, the Shell-Mobil Consortium was on a tight time schedule of investment and return. Reaching operational goals in a timely and efficient manner are always of utmost importance in a project of this kind. Because they have no rights to subsoil resources, the local population was viewed by both state officials and by those involved in the Shell-Mobil Consortium as an obstacle rather than as a partner in the business deal. At the same time, the Shell-Mobil Consortium, even the Shell-HSE division, had only a meager understanding of the Machiguenga and their long-term needs and little idea of how to communicate directly with them. This led to conflict over the forms and the pace of consultation between those pushing the project forward and the local communities. During the Shell-Mobil Consortium work in the Camisea region, two sets of problems arose.

No process was established for negotiating agreements about right of way and compensation. My sources indicated that the Camisea communities signed agreements under pressure and without the benefit of consultation with legal counsel.[9] Indigenous peoples like the Machiguenga are slow and deliberate in coming to decisions about allowing outsiders to use their common-property resources. After gathering the necessary information and advice from outsiders, they prefer to discuss it among themselves, and if there is a consensus, they prefer to formalize it in a general community meeting. Such a lengthy process is likely too costly for a multibillion-dollar petroleum and gas project.

The Shell-Mobil Consortium approached "doing it right" as a corporate challenge. Shell-HSE personnel and consultants were expected to produce solutions to local issues at a pace with operations. Thus ideas for solutions, like the Smithsonian baseline study or the development diagnostic study, were acted on without asking the Machiguenga whether they thought it was a good idea or whether they wanted such activities carried out within their territories. There was no process that brought the Shell-Mobil Consortium together with local people to discuss how they would live together and benefit mutually over the duration of the forty-year contract.

Third, as I have shown, most of the Machiguenga have participated in a two-decade-long process of territorial and community consolidation with the early support of CIPA and since 1983 with that of CEDIA. That process brought the Machiguenga and their territory to the threshold of a new era focused on territorial zoning and resource management. For some reason, the efforts for incorporating social and environmental concerns initiated by Shell-HSE ignored this historical process and, except in a formal sense, all but ignored the principal actors and stakeholders: COMARU, CEDIA, and Oxfam America.

Both the Smithsonian biodiversity study and the diagnostic study for long-term development could have been important complements to the Oxfam America–Woods Hole vegetative-cover study and GIS database and to the long-term work of CEDIA, forming a unified effort to help the Machiguenga plan the future use and conservation of their territory. Yet neither the communities, CECONAMA, COMARU, nor CEDIA were ever brought into the discussion about either Shell-HSE study at the idea, proposal, or implementation stages. At the same time, there was no coordination between the two Shell-HSE studies and the local organizations or CEDIA. As local people see it, the Shell-HSE studies were promoted and carried out by outsiders whose interests were likely served by the studies. Neither of the study teams had any members who had ever worked before with the Machiguenga in the lower Urubamba.

In other words, it apparently did not occur to the Shell-HSE personnel that they were establishing a parallel effort in the lower Urubamba and that their activities did not fit with local processes, decision-making patterns, current programs, or aspirations.[10] In conclusion, both of these Shell activities were divorced from the historical process in the lower Urubamba and unconnected with any ongoing COMARU, CECONAMA, or CEDIA efforts.

EPILOGUE: CAMISEA GAS PROJECT CHANGES HANDS

In 1998, after writing the original version of this chapter, a series of disputes arose between the Shell-Mobil Consortium and the Peruvian government over financing for the trans-Andean pipeline and over gas distribution rights within the Lima market. These led to a rupture of the forty-year contract and an end to the Shell-Mobil presence in the Urubamba.

In May 1999 a special governmental committee for the Camisea project opened an international public bidding process to award license agreements for two components of the project: (1) the upstream component for the exploitation of the gas fields and the separation of the gas and liquids, all carried out within the lower Urubamba valley and (2) the downstream component for the transportation of the liquids and gas to the coast via two pipelines, a fractionation plant on the coast with port facilities for exporting natural gas liquids, and a natural gas distribution network from this plant to consumers in Lima and Callao.

Eleven companies were prequalified to bid for the exploitation segment and twelve for the transportation and distribution. In February 2000 the Peruvian government awarded a forty-year license for the exploitation of the Camisea fields (the upstream component) to a consortium led by Pluspetro Perú Corporation SA (Argentina), with the participation of Hunt Oil Company of Peru LLC (United States), SK Corporation (Korea), and Tecpetrol del Perú SAC (fully owned by Techint Group of Argentina). The license was awarded based on the highest royalty rate offered.

In October 2000 Petroperu awarded contracts to Transportadora de Gas del Perú SA (TGP), a consortium led by Tecgas N.V. (fully owned by Techint

Group), with the participation of Pluspetrol Resources Corporation (Argentina), Hunt Oil Company, SK Corporation, Sonatrach Petroleum Corporation BVI (Algeria), and Graña y Montero SA (Peru) for liquid and gas transportation to the coast and gas distribution in Lima and Callao (the downstream component). TGP is a company formed by the consortium specifically for the development and operation of this downstream component of the Camisea project.

The downstream component of the project includes three different thirty-three-year contracts: one for the transportation of gas from Camisea to Lima via a 714-kilometer-long pipeline, a second contract for the transportation of natural gas liquids from Camisea to the coast via a separate 540-kilometer-long pipeline (including the fractionation plant), and a third for the distribution of gas in Lima and Callao. They were awarded on the basis of the lowest

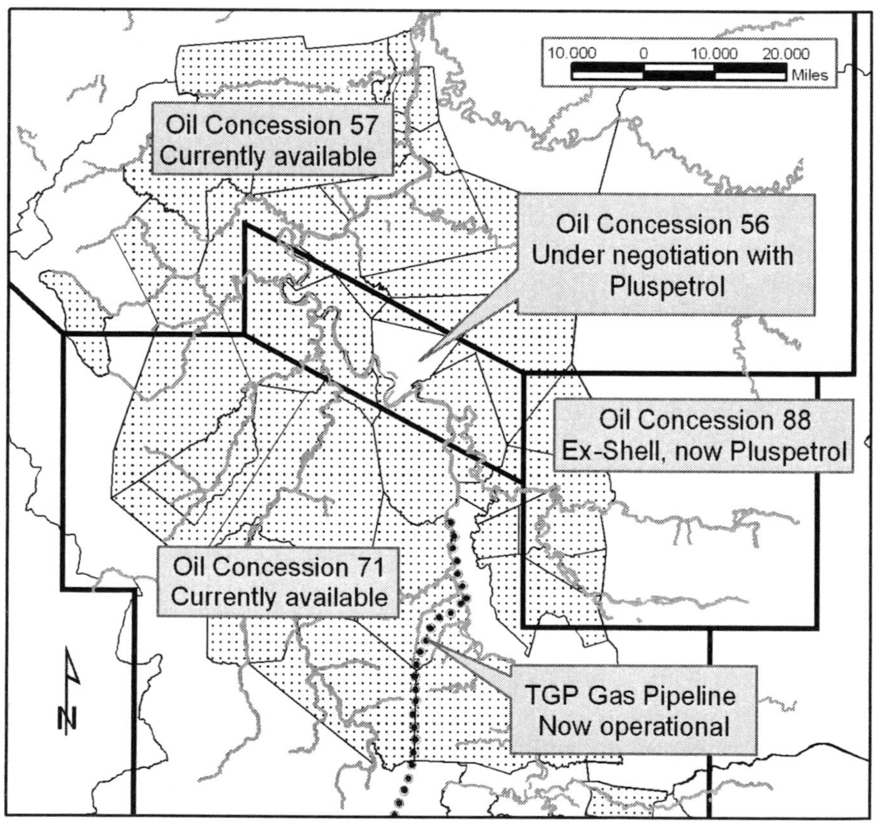

Map 9.2 Overlap of Petroleum Concessions and Territories of Indigenous Peoples, Lower Urubamba and Camisea Rivers

Source: SICNA-IBC, Ministry of Energy and Mines, INRENA.

service cost offered, which determined the natural gas transport and distribution tariffs. Early in 2002, TGP subcontracted Tractebel (France) as the developer and operator of the Peru-based company for the natural gas distribution service in Lima and Callao. The total cost of the downstream component is estimated at US$820 million. Commercial operation must start no later than August 2004.

Currently an estimated fifteen hundred workers in the upstream component live in two camps in the lower Urubamba and thirty-one hundred workers in the downstream component living in eight camps at different points along the pipeline route.

CAN DAVID AND GOLIATH HAVE A HAPPY MARRIAGE?

The presence of petroleum giants in Machiguenga territory represented an enormous threat to the territory's ecosystems and to the locally controlled processes for sustainable development. Oil companies have the resources, the political clout, and the public relations apparatus to market their own images of development and resource use, that is, their vision of what is best for the local people, whether in the Urubamba or any other area where they work. CEDIA, COMARU, and other local actors cannot compete.

But the presence of these companies did not have to result in competition with local actors; it could also have been an important opportunity for the Machiguenga. The project, if done correctly, could have turned into a long-range collaborative effort between Shell-Mobil and local actors to satisfy the Machiguenga's growing material needs through the sustainable use of the collective resource base of the entire territory. The opportunity side depended on at least five factors.

- the willingness and capacity of the Peruvian state, the Shell-Mobil Consortium, and the local actors to look at the big picture and to negotiate a long-term agreement around the big picture issues raised in this chapter
- the Peruvian state's willingness to recognize and act on the fundamental aboriginal rights and needs of the Machiguenga as part of its vision of the national interest
- the petroleum companies' willingness to approach their role in local development (1) as a trust-building exercise in which they join local organizations in their ongoing efforts, working at their pace, to build on the goals of the local peoples and their collaborators; and (2) as a joint-venture enterprise with local peoples, their organizations, and their collaborators as partners of equal standing
- the petroleum companies' willingness to invest a portion of their pro-

jected profits over the long term in underwriting some of the costs of the laborious process required for building long-term community-based resource management in the Machiguenga homeland, as well as in the prevention of and recuperation from environmental damage caused by their operations

- the abilities of the Machiguenga, CEDIA, and other local actors to seize the opportunity, to define a common agenda, to exert the necessary political pressure, and to negotiate a long-term settlement with Shell-Mobil and the Peruvian state benefiting their homeland and their future generations

The same opportunities and success factors still hold true under the new conditions in the Camisea. David's suitor, Goliath, is now an unwieldy conglomeration of smaller companies and subsidiaries of larger companies from a half dozen different countries. None of them have a well-known international face; several are not publicly traded. None have brand-name products in the marketplace. The Machiguenga's shotgun marriage to a partner who is not very accountable to the public is not particularly auspicious. The Inter-American Development Bank, which is currently considering a large private-sector loan to TGP, could serve as their marriage counselor, assuring that the wedding vows are kept. Whatever the outcome of the marriage, the social and environmental face of the lower Urubamba will change dramatically over the next decade.

NOTES

1. Shell Oil carried out exploratory work in the lower Urubamba region between 1983 and 1987 that led to the discovery of the Camisea gas fields. In 1988 Shell signed a terms of agreement with Petroperu for the exploitation of Camisea. However, the contract negotiation concluded without reaching an agreement. Again, in 1994, Shell signed a new agreement with Petroperu for the evaluation and development of the Camisea fields. After submitting a feasibility study in May 1995, Petroperu negotiated a contract with the Shell-Mobil Consortium for the exploitation of the Camisea fields that was finally signed in May 1996.

2. The impact of these policy decisions is clearly reflected in the region's changing demographics. Census figures since 1940 show that the population of the Peruvian Amazon region has more than tripled in thirty-five years (Instituto Nacional de Estadística e Información 1994; International Labour Organization 1997). According to Peru's 1993 census, the following Amazonian cities are among the urban areas of greatest growth since the 1981 census: Puerto Maldonado (ranked first, with 7.8 percent annual growth rate), Tarapoto (ranked third, with 6.9 percent) and Pucallpa (ranked forth, with 5.6 percent). Lima is ranked second (Instituto Nacional de Estadística e Información 1994).

Appendix 9.1 Acronyms of Organizations

Acronyms	*Full Name*	*Headquarters*
CEDIA	Center for the Development of the Amazonian Indigenous Peoples	Lima
COMARU	Machiguenga Council of the Urubamba River	Quillabamba
USAID	United States Agency for International Development	Washington, D.C.; Lima
COICA	Coordinating Body for Indigenous Organizations of the Amazon Basin	Quito, Ecuador
ILO	International Labour Organization	Geneva, Switzerland; Lima
WBT/SIL	Wycliffe Bible Translators/Summer Institute of Linguistics	
CECONAMA	Central Organization of Machiguenga Native Communities "Juan Santos Atahualpa"	Community of Nuevo Mundo
CIPA	Center for Amazonian Research and Promotion	Lima
CAAAP	Amazon Center for Applied Anthropology and Practical Application	Lima
AIDESEP	Interethnic Association for the Development of the Peruvian Amazon	Lima
FECONAYY	Federation of Yine Native Communities	Lower Urubamba
Shell-HSE	Health, Safety and Environment Office of Shell Petroleum Company	
GIS	Geographic Information System software	
TGP	Transportadora de Gas del Perú S.A.	

3. According to official sources, 1,175 Native Communities have been recognized and titled in Peruvian Amazonia since 1974, with collective property rights or usufruct to 10.5 million hectares (PETT 2000).

4. COICA was established in 1984 by national confederations made up of local community-based federations from five Amazonian countries: Colombia, Ecuador, Peru, Bolivia, and Brazil. As a participant in the United Nations debates, COICA played a key role in disseminating and promoting the concepts of indigenous people and territory through its member organizations around the Amazon during the 1980s. In 1992 confederations of indigenous peoples from Venezuela, Guyana, Surinam, and French Guyana joined COICA.

5. Law for Promoting Private Investment in the Development of Economic Activities in the Lands of the National Territory and of the Native and Peasant Com-

munities, No. 26570. In October 1996, Law No. 26681 added a new article to Fujimori's land law that states: "From the moment this law is enacted, the State will proceed by public auction with the sale or concession of all unclaimed lands under public domain."

6. Information for this section is taken from the CEDIA and COMARU project files (1987–1997) in Oxfam America, personal communications, personal visits and reports, and the Oxfam America–Woods Hole Research Center Biomass Study (Houghton and Hackler 1996).

7. CAAAP is a Catholic Church–sponsored NGO; AIDESEP is a national confederation of indigenous organizations founded in 1979; CONAP is a national confederation of indigenous organizations founded by CIPA in 1987, and the Interethnic Commission consisted of one representative each of CECONAMA, the non-CECONAMA communities, and the Piro communities farther down river.

8. In 2003 fifteen of the lower Urubamba communities are formally affiliated with COMARU, eight with CECONAMA, and one (a Piro ethnic group) with FECONAYY. Affiliation, however, is a rather fluid business.

9. The Shell HSE manager said that the CN Cashiriari agreement took four months to negotiate and in the end the terms were those dictated by the community. Furthermore, he claimed that when consulted, the communities emphatically rejected any intermediaries such as lawyers or NGOs negotiating on their behalf.

10. In a meeting with Shell's HSE manager, while the original version of this chapter was being written, he conceded the oversight and said it was not too late to bring CECONAMA, COMARU, and CEDIA into the studies.

REFERENCES

Agrawal, A. 1997. Community in Conservation: Beyond Enchantment and Disenchantment. Conservation Development Forum working paper, Gainesville, Fl., April.

Benavides, Margarita, and Mario Pariona. 1995. Yanesha Forestry Cooperative and Community-Based Management in the Central Peruvian Forest. In *Case Studies of Community-Based Forestry Enterprises in the Americas*, ed. Land Tenure Center; Institute for Environmental Studies. Madison: Univ. of Wisconsin Press.

Chirif Tirado, Alberto, Pedro Garcia Hierro, and Richard Chase Smith. 1991. *El indigena y su territorio son uno solo: Estrategias para la defensa de los pueblos y territorios indigenas en la cuenca amazonica.* Lima: Oxfam America and COICA.

Cleaver, Francis. 2001. Institutional Bricolage, Conflict and Cooperation in Usangu, Tanzania. In Environmental Governance in an Uncertain World. Special issue, *IDS Bulletin* 32(4): 25–37.

Garcia H., Pedro. 1995. *Territorios indígenas y la nueva legislación en el Perú*. Lima: IWGIA and Racimos de Ungurahui.

Gram, Soren, Jacob Klint, and Finn Helles. 1994. *Forestry among Indigenous People in Natural Rain Forests: A Case Study from Peru*. Copenhagen: Centre for Alternative Social Analysis.

Houghton, Richard, and Joe Hackler. 1996. Establishment and Operation of a Carbon Monitoring System to Measure and Record Changes in Carbon Sequestration in Areas of the Amazon Basin. Final Report. Woods Hole, Mass.: Woods Hole Research Center, October.

Instituto Nacional de Estadística e Información. 1994. *Censo Nacional 1993 (Tomo I)*. Lima: Instituto Nacional de Estadística e Información.

International Labour Organization. 1997. Informe Integral: Pueblos Indígenas de la Amazonía Peruana y Desarrollo Sostenible (Proyecto SAT-1). Lima: International Labour Organization.

Inter-American Development Bank. 2003. Análisis ambiental y social del Proyecto Camisea. Document circulated by the Private Sector Department, Inter-American Development Bank, Washington, D.C.

La Torre, Lily. 1996. *Camisea: El más grande yacimiento de gas de latino américa en territorio indígena*. Lima: Grupo de Trabajo Racimos de Ungurahui.

McCay, Bonnie J., and Svein Jentoft. 1998. Market or Community Failure? Critical Perspectives on Common Property Research. *Human Organization* 57(1): 21.

Mehta, Lyla, Melissa Leach, and Ian Scoones. 2001. Editorial: Environmental Governance in an Uncertain World. In Environmental Governance in an Uncertain World. Special issue, *IDS Bulletin* 32(4).

Mehta, Lyla, et al. 2000. *Exploring Understandings of Institutions and Uncertainty: New Directions in Natural Resource Management.* Univ. of Sussex, Brighton, U.K.: IDS Discussion Paper 372.

Ostrom, Elinor. 2001. Reformulating the Commons. In *Protecting the Commons: A Framework for Resource Management in the Americas*, ed. J. Burger et al. Washington, D.C.: Island Press.

PETT. 2000. *Directorio de Comunidades Nativas del Perú 1999.* Lima: Ministry of Agriculture.

Shell Prospecting and Development (Perú) B. V. 1996. Briefing Papers 2, 3, 4, and 5. Lima, 31 May–19 November.

Smith, Richard Chase. 1997. Community and Resource Management as Historical Process: Comments on Arun Agrawal's working paper, "Community in Conservation: Beyond Enchantment and Disenchantment." Conservation Development Forum working paper, Gainesville, Fl., April.

———. 2002. Los indigenas amazonicos suben al escenario internacional: Reflexiones sobre el accidentado camino recorrido. In *Lo Transnacional: Instrumento y Desafío para los Pueblos Indígenas*, ed. F. Morin and R. Santana. Quito: Abya Yala.

Smith, Richard Chase, Danny Pinedo, Percy M. Summers, and Angelica Almeyda. 2001. Tropical Rhythms and Collective Action: Community-Based Fisheries Management in the Face of Amazonian Unpredictability. In Environmental Governance in an Uncertain World. Special issue, *IDS Bulletin* 32(4).

Smithsonian Institution, Biodiversity Programs. 1996. *Proceedings from the Workshop on Biological and Cultural Diversity of the Lower Urubamba, Peru*. Lima, September.

10

Social Movements, Community-Based Natural Resource Management, and the Struggle for Democracy: Experiences from Indonesia

Emmy Hafild

I am given a difficult task to be a nodal speaker on the topic of social movements, community-based resource management, and the struggle for democracy. Because I am neither a sociologist nor a scientist, I will try to avoid presenting this chapter within a theoretical framework. Rather, I prefer to share with you my experiences as a nongovernmental organization (NGO) activist working in an undemocratic country, trying to promote community-based resource management while demanding democratic governance and attempting to build a powerful social movement. I will let you—academicians, responders, scientists—analyze my experience and place it within a broader theoretical frame. My experience is only within the territory and circumstances of Indonesia, and thus I cannot speak to circumstances elsewhere.

Because *Wahana Lingkungan Hidup Indonesia* (WALHI, or, Friends of the Earth Indonesia)—the environmental forum where I currently work—is building a popular-based environmental movement, many of our ongoing strategies cannot be shared in this chapter—our survival over the coming years depends on them. Instead, I will recount some well-known cases that I have been involved with. Specifically, I would like to tell you about four cases that I am directly engaged with: those of the Mangkiling in south Kalimantan, the Bentian in east Kalimantan, the Amungme in Timika, Irian Jaya (West Papua), and lastly the Damar garden in Krui in Lampung Province.

MANGKILING

Mangkiling is a Dayak community in south Kalimantan. We became involved there in 1987 when *Sekretariat Kerjasama Pelestarian Hutan Indonesia* (SKEPHI, or the Indonesian Network for Forest Conservation) and WALHI were hosting an international conference on people, logging, and tropical forests. We needed a field site where we could illuminate a conflict between a logging company and a local indigenous community. Our local partner, a youth nature-lover club called KOMPAS Borneo, was in contact with the Mangkiling people, who have maintained the Damar forest for generations, because they were struggling against the Lihat Papernya timber company, which was encroaching on the forest.

Because our conference was an international one, the governor and the *bupati* (district administrator) were very much involved. The governor opened the conference, and the bupati attended, giving a speech and engaging in a dialogue with participants. As part of the conference, we orchestrated a field trip to Mangkiling and arranged for the dialogue with the bupati to take place after the trip. We brought with us to the meeting the leader of the Mangkiling, and he and other conference participants confronted the bupati about the conflict. The participants also presented a statement demanding that the bupati put a stop to logging activities.

Surprisingly, the bupati responded to the demand, and in this he was supported by the governor. A few months later, he canceled the license of the logging company (in a battle with the Department of Forestry in Jakarta), and then granted recognition to Mangkiling land rights in the form of a bupati decree. For ten years, the Mangkiling have had their forest back and have been happy. However, their position is far from secure.

After ten years, we have come to realize that the bupati decree is not strong enough to stop logging, either by the old one or different companies. The bupati who recognized the Mangkiling ownership to the land has been replaced with a new one who is eager to resume logging activities. It has been rumored that Barito Pacific, the biggest logging company in Indonesia, is trying to build a road across the Mangkiling forest. The people are nervous that Barito Pacific is interested in the Damar trees that are abundant in their forest.

WALHI is trying to reintroduce these new Mangkiling problems into the agendas of NGOs in South Kalimantan. Unfortunately, the activists who were involved before are no longer active, and the current NGOs who belong to WALHI are not strong enough to take on an advocacy case and at the same time work to rebuild their alliances with the Mangkiling people. We are currently working on a new strategy to secure the forest rights of the Mangkiling people, rights that every bupati should respect.

JELMU SIBAK CASE OF THE DAYAK BENTIAN IN EAST KALIMANTAN

Bentian is subgroup of Dayak Benuaq who reside in the area of Sungai Lawa between East and Central Kalimantan. We have been in contact with this group since 1991, when one of their leaders contacted us about the problems they were facing. The Bentian territory was being carved up by at least three logging companies, and the Bentian had been in continual conflict with them. WALHI made the area our case study for understanding the economic impacts of logging activities on a local economy, and the findings were published as *The Political Economy of Logging in East Kalimantan* (Bahasa, Indonesia).

The Bentian are famous for their rattan cultivation techniques, which were introduced to the area late in the nineteenth century. They are the source of *rotan sega*, a type of rattan that demanded very high prices before the rattan trade was regulated. Rattan became the major source of cash for the Bentian after they were excluded from the timber economy when their areas were given over to logging concessions. With their income from rattan, they can send their children to the secondary school in the nearest town, visit their families in other towns, pay for hospital and medical expenses, and maintain their houses.

Nevertheless, Bentian rattan cultivation was not properly recognized, and their cane was considered to be "bird dropping" rattan, rather than planted-garden rattan. Their rattan gardens were considered to be unmanaged land (*lahan terlantar*) and therefore under the jurisdiction of the state. The Bentian form of land ownership relies on markers such as trees, hills, and rivers, markers recognized by every member of Bentian society but not by the government. Therefore when a logging company wants to expand its activities, the government gives them permits to convert the rattan gardens without bothering to gain local community permission.

In 1993 a group from the Bentian village of Jelmu Sibak again had a dispute with PT Kalhold Utama, a subsidiary of Kalimanis Group, which is the holding company of Bob Hasan, the Indonesian timber tycoon. The dispute was over Jelmu Sibak forest and rattan gardens that the company had converted into a timber plantation and transmigration settlement. The Bentian were angry because not only had thousands of their rattan vines been destroyed but also hundreds of their fruit trees, some ancestral graves, and honey trees. The Bentian tried to raise the issue with the company and the government, but they were ignored.

After their lack of success in negotiating directly with the company and the government, the people tried to make their problems public with the help of PLASMA and other NGOs in Samarinda. Local NGOs then helped with the establishment of SJR (Sempekat Jato Rempangan), a Bentian association made up of people whose lands had been taken by Kalhold Utama. Through the organization SJR the case of Jelmu Sibak was exposed to the public on both the provincial and national levels. WALHI was subsequently contacted to assist with the national and international advocacy campaign on their behalf.

The case was bound to fail from the beginning. First, the opponent was Bob Hasan, the most powerful businessmen in Indonesia and a close friend of the president. There was no way we could win the battle, because even though the Department of Forestry and the minister of Transmigration sympathized with SJR, there was little they could do against Hasan. Second, unlike the Mangkiling people, the Bentian were not well organized. Their traditional structure and leadership had already been weakened by state intervention, and their communities were divided. The Jelmu Sibak *kepala adat* (the village traditional leader) was on the side of the company because his son-in-law was one of the supervisors of the company and he had received many benefits from the company. Given this situation, the case was not supported by the whole Bentian community, and even within SJR itself there were many defections.

Although we recognized all of these problem from the start, we still took up the case. It received much attention from not only the provincial but also the national and international media. The work was divided among the different NGOs involved: the NGOs in Samarinda were responsible for the provincial advocacy activities and for assisting SJR in organizing themselves and NGOs in Jakarta—WALHI, *Lembaga Studi dan Advokasi Masyarakat* (ELSAM, or Institute for Policy Research and Advocacy), and *Yahasan Lembaga Bantuan Hukum Indonesia* (YLBHI, or the Indonesian Legal Aid Foundation) were responsible for national advocacy, lobbying, and acting as the SJR lawyers.

Yet the attention given to the case was not enough to convince Hasan to change his attitude toward SJR. SJR leaders became the target of a good deal of intimidation, verbal harassment, personal attacks, and humiliation, and one man was even formally accused of forgery and interrogated as a criminal in the East Kalimantan police headquarters. He was kidnapped twice and forced to sign agreements that he later annulled.

The untouchable Hasan, with his divide-and-bribe strategy, and weak community organization by the NGOs, left the case going nowhere. We then persuaded the director general of Forest Utilization to mediate between

SJR and the company. He was willing to instruct the company to accept his proposal, which indeed would have resulted in a win-win solution for SJR and Hasan. However, the negotiation process did not go well because of our own failure to properly organize SJR. NGO failures included a lack of communication among some of the leaders and an inability to make collective decisions fully supported by the entire community. That negotiations came to a halt was due not to the enemy's actions but rather to our own failings.

The persistence of the SJR leader, L. B. Dingit, was not matched with a well-organized community organization, and the followers left him one by one. Because of economic hardship, some accepted money from the company, and some even took jobs with the company, acting as scouts for the survey of the very forests that they had been defending. The leader was not given information on how to build a coalition among his people or on how to make important decisions collectively among all SJR members. Our most tragic failure was that we did not build SJR as an institution that represented the Bentian people. So the support base for SJR never grew, and in the end Dingit was left to fight alone with only a handful of supporters.

Then in 1997 L. B. Dingit received the Goldman Award on behalf of the Bentian people, who had struggled to maintain their community forests. The award awakened an awareness among the Bentian people that their community forest was recognized by the international community and that it was worth defending. This generated new support from other Bentian leaders, and when Dingit returned from receiving the award in San Francisco, the Bentian Brotherhood chairperson himself came to Jakarta to welcome him back. We hope that this new development will help us to rejuvenate SJR and remobilize the Bentian people.

The Bentian case has taught us that no advocacy we undertake will be successful if it is not supported by a majority of the community we represent. Learning from this, we have adopted a new approach. Before we take on advocacy of a community's case, we make sure all its members are behind it and determined to struggle for it. We make sure they have a good leader with a good understanding of collective decision-making processes who is accountable to his or her people. Thus for us community organization is now one of the key steps in our advocacy activities. The executive body has now established a program called Civic Education, which is targeted at community organizing and education. With this new awareness, we have thrown our full support behind Tom Beanal and the *Lembaga Musyawarah Adat Suku Amungme* (LEMASA, or the Amungme Tribal Council) in their case against Freeport Indonesia, Inc., in Irian Jaya.

AMUNGME VERSUS FREEPORT INDONESIA

WALHI is interested in the activities of Freeport, a U.S.-based copper and gold mining operation in Irian Jaya, Indonesia, the western part of the island of New Guinea. George Aditjondro is a member of our board and lived in Jayapura, Irian Jaya, but we had never before made a serious attempt to work on this issue because Freeport had always been a very secretive company. No one was allowed to enter their area without permission, and their concession was heavily guarded by the Indonesian army. So we rarely entered the area, never had good information about their operation, and had never made good contacts with the local people. We knew that Freeport dumped their tailings directly into the rivers, that people had repeatedly protested against Freeport, and that several violent actions had taken place in the area.

We knew, too, that since 1971 the Amungme had persistently battled Freeport. Peace protests and even protests involving bows and arrows were reported. We also knew that people had blown up a Freeport slurry pipe in 1977. Because of their resistance to Freeport, the Amungme had been subjected to human-rights abuses, and some had joined the *Organisasi Papua Merdeka* (OPM, or the Free Papua Movement) resistance movement in the mountains. But again, we never had any contact with the people.

In 1990 WALHI and other, U.S.-based NGOs published a letter to Freeport McMoran in New Orleans asking for information about their operation. Rainforest Action Network in San Francisco then published a strong action alert concerning Freeport. It was worded so strongly that the government of Indonesia was forced to react. In a conscious attempt to undermine U.S.-based NGOs, Freeport then approached WALHI to open a relationship with Indonesian NGOs. In this way, Freeport was able to refuse the U.S.-based NGOs' request to visit their mining areas by saying that they were already talking with Indonesian NGOs.

After several confrontational meetings, WALHI was invited to visit the mining area and tour it under heavy guard. To do this, WALHI made an unwritten agreement that we would not release any information collected without Freeport approval. We could not talk to journalists or publish anything about the visit, and we could not share information with our NGO friends. I personally objected to this unwritten condition, but M. S. Zulkarnaen, WALHI's director at that time, agreed to it because he felt it was the only way we could gather our own information. After a heated dispute, we in the end agreed with Zulkarnaen's idea. Indeed, without this visit we would never have had an opportunity to obtain firsthand knowledge about the problem.

An all-woman team (this was Zulkarnaen's idea)—two of WALHI's secretariat staff, two photographers, and one young activist from Jayapura NGOs—were sent to the mining town of Tembagapura. For three days we toured the mining area, fully guarded at all times by Freeport officials. Freeport, of course, spoke of and showed only good things and spared us the bad ones. But they could not fool us, and we gained firsthand proof of what they were doing. We did not meet any of the local people, however. Because Freeport had arranged meetings with only communities that had been "sterilized," we refused these encounters.

Returning from this short trip, we had two more confrontational meetings. But in the end, Freeport agreed that we should sit on the Environmental Impacts Assessment team of the Department of Mines and Energy. The environmental impact assessment took four full years to complete. Most of the time, Freeport fought with their own consultants because they did not agree with the original findings, and this resulted in the document being heavily watered down. When finally the environmental management plan was unveiled in December 1994, it was simply a legitimation of what Freeport had been doing over the previous twenty-eight years.

We were extremely disappointed, and we abrogated the unwritten agreement to not speak. We went public and released a great deal of information about Freeport through the national and international media. Freeport fought back and produced advertising intended to discredit WALHI, even trying to get WALHI's U.S. Agency for International Development (USAID) support cancelled. This was quite a hectic year for us. One heated issue surrounded the Amungme people; Freeport maintained that WALHI had no connection with the Amungme and that our information about them was wrong, that the Amungme were happy with Freeport.

At this time Tom Beanal, an Amungme leader who had been exiled from Timika in 1977 because of his alleged involvement in an explosion, returned. He now lived in Timika and had started his own organization, the Lorentz Foundation, with the help of other Amungme leaders. He then made contacts with other Irian Jaya groups, and in 1992 he was elected as a WALHI board member representing Irian Jaya. Our connection with the Amungme began with Beanal.

WALHI had learned much from the Bentian case, and we realized that we needed to solicit popular support for our advocacy campaign. During 1994 some killings took place around and within the Freeport concession, organized by army personnel in pursuit of the OPM. We found ourselves facing both environmental problems and social and human-rights problems. But before we took on the human-rights problems we needed to prepare the people and our friends in Jayapura so that we could establish a united front of groups at all levels: Jakarta, Timika, and Jayapura. We did a great deal of organizing and strategizing, and in Jakarta we cooperated with other NGOS such as YLBHI, ELSAM, International NGO Forum on Indonesian Development (INFID), and *Lembaga Penelitian dan Pembangunan Sosial* (LPPS, or Institute of Social Research and Development). In Jayapura a new network was established—the Peace and Justice Forum—to address human rights issues in Irian Jaya.

All of us—the NGOs in Jakarta and in Jayapura—were involved in the human rights investigation and exposé. With the help of friends in Jayapura,

LEMASA organized eyewitness testimony about the killings, torture, and kidnappings that had taken place from June to December of 1994. We asked the Catholic Church in Jayapura to take the case and to report the situation to the *Komisi Nasional Hak Asasi Manusia* (Komnas HAM, or the National Commission on Human Rights). The bishop agreed, and did exactly that. We then released the reports to the national and international news media. (The first report came from Australian Council for Overseas Aid [ACFOA], but we could not use it because it contained no eyewitness testimony.) Eyewitness testimony is crucial in such cases, and luckily Amungme fully cooperated, eager to report what they had seen and felt.

The national and international news media covered the report of the events that Komnas HAM investigated. Almost every important newspaper in the world carried the story, including the *Washington Post*, *Los Angeles Times*, *New York Times*, *Wall Street Journal*, *Newsweek*, *Asiaweek*, *Asian Wall Street Journal*, *International Herald Tribune*, and the Cable News Network (CNN). It was a great boost to our case.

The weakness of our organizing attempts in Bentian still haunted us, and so a conscious effort was made to build up a strong institution to represent the Amungme people. Our friend John Rumbiak was given the responsibility of doing this. Tom Beanal and his Lorentz Foundation were responsible for supporting LEMASA, which had been established in 1993. A community organizer from Jayapura was then placed with LEMASA. We raised funds to pay some of the Lorentz Foundation expenses, and we provided support for institution building and for offices, computers, telephones, faxes, and the like. Tom Beanal organized LEMASA in a transparent way and proved capable of eliciting popular support. Within a few months, LEMASA had expanded from a presence only in Timika, a village of a few hundred people, to fifty-five villages and hamlets in the highlands and fifteen thousand followers.

LEMASA is a unique organization and fully represents not only the Amungme but all the tribes who reside within their territory. The government and Freeport so fear its strength that it is subjected to government intimidation. Freeport's divide-and-conquer strategy has bedeviled LEMASA. They have thrown money to people who are willing to go along with Freeport. To weaken LEMASA, Freeport has helped in establishing seven foundations representing each tribe living within the Freeport mining concession. LEMASA has proved strong in fighting against bribery overall, but some of their people cannot resist the money. Defections such as those in the Bentian case also occurred here, but in very low numbers. Despite all of these factors threatening to weaken LEMASA, the organization has managed to pull itself together after each conflict. Indeed, LEMASA is growing stronger with each new conflict between collaborators and noncollaborators.

LEMASA, realizing that Freeport had no intention of resolving problems or dealing equitably with them, adopted a new strategy: they filed a lawsuit in the United States. The case is ongoing.

Recognizing the potential danger of bribery money coming from Freeport to their own people, LEMASA worked to establish economic opportunities for its followers. They founded a credit union, and within four months they were able to collect fifty million rupias from LEMASA members, each member, regardless of age, voluntarily donating five hundred rupias. With this initial money, LEMASA has set up some small businesses and lending schemes for their people.

Even though WALHI is not a community-development organization—in fact we are an advocacy group—we cannot ignore the potential threat of bribery. So we have connected LEMASA with other NGOs who have experience with credit unions and small community businesses. We have organized visits from LEMASA to other areas and helped connect LEMASA activists to other training activities. We hope that through this support we can sustain the Amungme's struggle through LEMASA, because we know this struggle is likely to be a long one.

At the same time, WALHI has been the target of intimidation and accusations that we support the OPM. Indeed, WALHI and Tom Beanal have been blamed for instigating several kidnappings. Beanal is continually badmouthed by the government, the military, and of course by Freeport itself. The LEMASA office is constantly watched and monitored by government intelligence people, and our telephones are continuously bugged. WALHI has now been labeled as a "radical and problematic" NGO. Because of this, we have faced difficulties in pursuing a dialogue with government officials who are sympathetic to us. We are banned altogether from the Ministry of Mining and Energy, and Beanal's U.S. lawyer has been deported twice from Indonesia.

Of course, the environmental and related problems themselves have not been resolved. Freeport still discharges tailings into the Ajkwa river, the acid mine drainage continues, and Freeport still refuses to negotiate with the people on an equal basis. Nevertheless, Freeport is now more sensitive to environmental and social issues. They have done more regarding the environment in the last five years than in the previous twenty-five years. But this is not enough, and we need to go further to reach a just and fair solution for the Amungme and maximum protection for their environment.

DAMAR GARDEN

The Krui people have maintained their Damar garden for generations. They do not cut the Damar trees, which are a valuable hardwood, but rather harvest their resin. The Damar garden has become a research target for many scientists. It covers five *kecamatan* (subdistricts) and encompasses several thousand people. The Department of Forestry morally recognizes the Krui people's ownership of the Damar garden, and yet several parts of the garden are still included in the *Tata Guna Hutan Kesepakatan* (TGHK, or Forestry Land-Use System), which means it is under the ownership of the Indonesian government. However, the Department of Forestry has never touched these areas or granted licenses to logging companies to work there. According to the director general of Forestry Land Use, the department has no intention of doing so, even though it is categorized as Limited Production Forest.

In late 1996, we received a letter from one community reporting that their Damar garden had been given up by the governor to a palm oil plantation. This community came to *Lembaga Bantuan Hukum Lampung* (LBH Lampung, or Lampung Legal Aid Institute) and a local NGO, a member of WALHI named *Wahana Pecinta Alam Lampung* (WATALA, or Lampung Friends of Nature Group), who referred them to us in Jakarta and advised the people to write a letter to the minister of Forestry and to WALHI. Responding to this letter, we wrote to the minister of Forestry to report the case and to urge him to instruct the governor to cancel the license. A similar letter was also sent by WALHI Lampung to the governor of Lampung. In response, the minister wrote to the governor informing him of the importance of the Damar garden, that it was under the jurisdiction of Department of Forestry, and that its conversion to a palm oil plantation needed his approval, which he would never give.

At this point we organized a meeting in Jakarta between the director general of the Forestry Land-Use System and representatives of Krui communities. In this meeting the director general assured the community that the conversion of Damar garden into a palm oil plantation would never take place, because the Department of Forestry would never give its approval. In this meeting the director general also mentioned that the Department of Forestry had no intention of licensing Damar garden to any logging company. He assured the people that they would be allowed to harvest resin so long as people did not cut the trees.

There are several national and international NGOs and research institutions working in Krui. All are very concerned about the problems, but they have different opinions on how to solve them. Some disagree with the advocacy approach that WALHI is taking and argue for a low-profile lobbying approach. We even had a dispute over what type of recognition to demand for the Damar garden. There are two opinions: complete ownership, which under the TGHK is considered people's forest (*Hutan Rakyat*), or management rights—a community forest. More complicated is that these different NGOs work with different Krui communities, and all try to influence their partner communities to take their advice. Communities are caught in the middle and divided by the different options, a handicap when the goal is to maintain a united front to defend the Damar garden. Despite the disputes, all of us agree that the state of the garden is in danger because land rights over it have not been secured. The state considers this to be state-owned land.

Recognizing that the disputes dividing NGOs hampered the advocacy efforts—which need to be sped up because some Damar trees have been cut—WALHI Lampung organized a strategic meeting with all communities to develop a collective strategy. In this meeting we discussed the issues and all the options of recognition available under the circumstances, so the people could themselves choose one option that best suited their interests. The other NGOs and research institutes also organized a seminar in Lampung about Damar garden, as part of the implementation of their lobbying approach. However, WALHI has taken a different path: community organizing and high-profile advocacy. Our first and immediate goal has been to revoke the palm oil license, the second to gain recognition of local land rights and the community-based forest management system. In the end, I think those two approaches have been mutually reinforcing. In March the governor of Lampung finally invited the people and WALHI Lampung to a meeting, where a heated debate took place between the Krui people and the governor. The governor agreed to revoke the license that he had already granted, and he then wrote a decree to preserve the Damar garden. The immediate problem has thus been at least temporarily solved. However, because land rights over the Damar garden have not yet been secured, problems could resurface if the governor is replaced.

Anticipating this possibility, WALHI continues its work to organize the Krui people to become a united power to demand recognition of their land rights and that their Damar garden be recognized as a people's forest. (After the pros and cons were discussed in WALHI's strategic meeting, the people chose people's forest as their option.) The executive body, which is organizing the national-level advocacy, worked closely with WALHI Lampung, which organized provincial-level advocacy and community organizations in collaboration with WATALA. The community is already quite organized, however. As a result of the strategic meeting in Lampung before the meeting with the governor, they formed an association of Damar farmers, which united farmers from different villages and NGO alliances. We are working with this newly formed association to further the second goal—the recognition of Damar garden as a people's forest and the securing of local land ownership.

CONCLUSION

Drawing on these four cases we can make several observations:

- There is no recognition of community-based resource management within the Indonesian government's current political stance, even though it is acknowledged by the Indonesian constitution, by agrarian law, and by forestry law (though in the latter only vaguely).

- The absence of a democratic system creates a situation in which there is no clear mechanism for advocating for the recognition of community-based resource management. Such recognition depends on the goodwill of the highest-level officials in charge of an area. Elite political interests play the key role in deciding whether community-based resource management will be recognized.
- Constant abuse has been directed at community leaders (except in the Krui case) who struggle for the recognition of their traditional rights to resources.
- NGOs at all political levels need to cooperate fully and have definite and clear roles that are mutually agreed upon in advance.
- Strong community organization is crucial. In the case of Mangkiling, our involvement in organizing local people was minimal. Most of the organization has been done by KOMPAS Borneo. Luckily, Mangkiling is a well-organized community where the traditional leaders are still respected. They are very solid, and the women are quite active. Indeed, the head of the village is a woman, and it was she who visited the *kecamatan* and the bupati and who first contacted the NGOs to ask them to fight for their case. There have been no institution-building efforts directed at the Mangkiling structure, and no new organization has been established.

Editor's note: At the time of writing, Emmy Hafild was the director of Friends of the Earth Indonesia (WALHI). For updates on the Indonesian situation, readers may want to consult the WALHI web page; the English version's address is www.eng.walhi.or.id/.

II

STEALING THE MASTER'S TOOLS: MAPPING AND LAW IN COMMUNITY-BASED NATURAL RESOURCE MANAGEMENT

11

Maps, Power, and the Defense of Territory: The Upper Mazaruni Land Claim in Guyana

Marcus Colchester

Maps are an assertion of power—a means of projecting perceptions and policies, laws, and institutional relations onto natural environments and human landscapes. Power—the ability to influence the allocation of scarce resources with alternative ends—shifts. It may be imposed by conquering armies and assertive governments, but it may equally be expressed by local communities: by villagers, tribal peoples, and by nongovernmental organizations (NGOs) that try to support them (see Topatimasang, this volume). Maps may be tools in the hands of the rulers but may also be tools through which local peoples contest government impositions and project their own countervailing visions of how land should be held, used, and managed.

This chapter summarizes the way maps are now being used by Amazonian Indian groups in one part of Guyana to assert rights to their lands in the face of pressure first from colonial powers and now the modern State of Guyana to annex and administer the area and make it available to outside interests.

The area now known as Guyana was originally the homeland of numerous American Indian peoples—*Amerindians* as they are known in Guyana. In the seventeenth century the area became a trading enclave of the Dutch, who established forts on the coast and ranged through the interior in search of forest products and cheap labor and thereby stimulated the evolution of a predatory trading network based on the sale and exchange of slaves. In this commercial exchange the Amerindians were crucial trading partners who held the balance of power between the Dutch and the Spanish. The establishment of plantations on the coast shifted the center of the political economy away from the interior, and by the time the area was ceded to the British in the early nineteenth century, as a result of wars in far-off Europe, the Amerindians were reduced to players of only slight significance to the Europeans.

Since the 1950s, new mining and logging techniques have changed this situation of political isolation. The interior is again coveted as a supplier of valuable commodities for the international market. The collapse of the coastal economy during the first two decades of independence under a one-party dictatorship has intensified pressure on the interior as a source of government revenue. Since the mid-1980s, the International Monetary Fund (IMF) and World Bank have imposed a structural adjustment program on the country that has opened the interior to transnational logging and mining companies, and the country is on the way to becoming a major gold and diamond producer.

The boundaries of the area were hazy and undefined in the colonial mind until the mid-nineteenth century. Dutch and Spanish traders and missions jockeyed for control of the Amerindian communities and sought to expand their areas of influence. However, it was only from the mid-nineteenth century that the borders were actually mapped, contested, negotiated, and agreed upon through treaty.

During all these centuries the Amerindians have pursued their own political trajectories, although power in their relations with the colonial state was eased from their grasp once their role in the trading and plantation economy became marginal. A paternalist and then integrationist colonial state further eroded the Amerindians' independent political voice. Following independence, two decades of cooperative socialism further quashed the Amerindians' independence. However, the political liberalization and the restoration of electoral politics that accompanied structural adjustment in the late 1980s has allowed the reemergence of Amerindian organizations and community leaders empowered by their own people to question government impositions. Amerindians have begun to speak out with increasing authority against mining and logging companies granted concessions by government to exploit their lands. Maps of their land claims are a tool in this new dialogue with government as they contest the rights of these outside interests to invade their ancestral domains.

ORIENTATION: GUYANA AND THE PEOPLES OF THE UPPER MAZARUNI

Approached from the sea, the coast of Guyana is not obviously welcoming. Muddy beaches extend along the forested coast where powerful silty rivers debouch through slack tidal mudflats. Westward, the coast is heavily covered by mangrove swamps, behind which flooded wet savannas and coastal forests are cut through by a maze of narrow channels as sluggish waters from the interior meander seaward. Protected only by the mangroves and beaches, the extensive inland forests and swamps are for much of the time below sea level and for long were considered uncultivable wastelands. Inland from the swampy coastal forests, the interior is more open. Patches of savanna on famously infertile white sands alternate with forests whose tannin-rich leaves stain the clear river waters a brackish brown. Farther inland again the ground rises slightly and here extensive rain forests cover the entire width of the country, stretching away in an almost continuous carpet to the Brazilian frontier 650 kilometers due south.

Yet it is only after traveling some 150 kilometers inland that the relief changes. Travelers voyaging up the lower rivers sooner or later run up against spectacular falls, where the rain-charged rivers spill over the outer edges of the Guyana Highlands. These are the outermost defenses of the country's mountainous interior, a vast eroded tableland established on ancient rocks dating back to the continent's creation. Known by geologists as the Guyana Shield, the Precambrian crystalline rocks that underlie the hinterland are still capped in places by Cretaceous sandstones, the eroded remnants of which stand as spectacular mesas—huge cliff-edged massifs that rise into the clouds. Greatest of these, tucked into the corner of the country, is Mount Roraima, which at twenty-seven hundred meters is one of the continent's highest mountains east of the Andes and whose inaccessible heights gave rise to Sir Arthur Conan Doyle's vision of the *Lost World*.

Here, on the Brazilian and Venezuelan border, are large swathes of grassland that extend from the Gran Sabana in Venezuela, east into the Rupununi savannas and south down to the Rio Branco in Brazil. Under a wide sky and across rolling hills and plains, the landscape offers sweeping vistas interrupted near and far by forested watercourses that wend their way down to the Amazon and the high sandstone mesas that tower over all.

Nestled in this corner of Guyana are the Pakaraima Mountains, which extend from south Venezuela, through Mount Roraima, into central Guyana. Long protected from outside intrusion by its remoteness and inaccessibility, the area has also long been the home to a scattering of Amerindian settlements of peoples known by their neighbors as Arekuna, Akawaio, and Patamona, whom anthropologists now recognize as speaking languages of the Carib family. They call themselves *kapon* and *pemon* (human beings) and, so far as we know, have traditionally lived in widely dispersed homesteads that move frequently from place to place to make the most of the weak soils, which they cultivate by swidden agriculture, and of the scarce game, which provides crucial protein supplements to the nutritionally poor vegetable diet.

The Akawaio were renowned as traders, notably of cassava graters, labori-

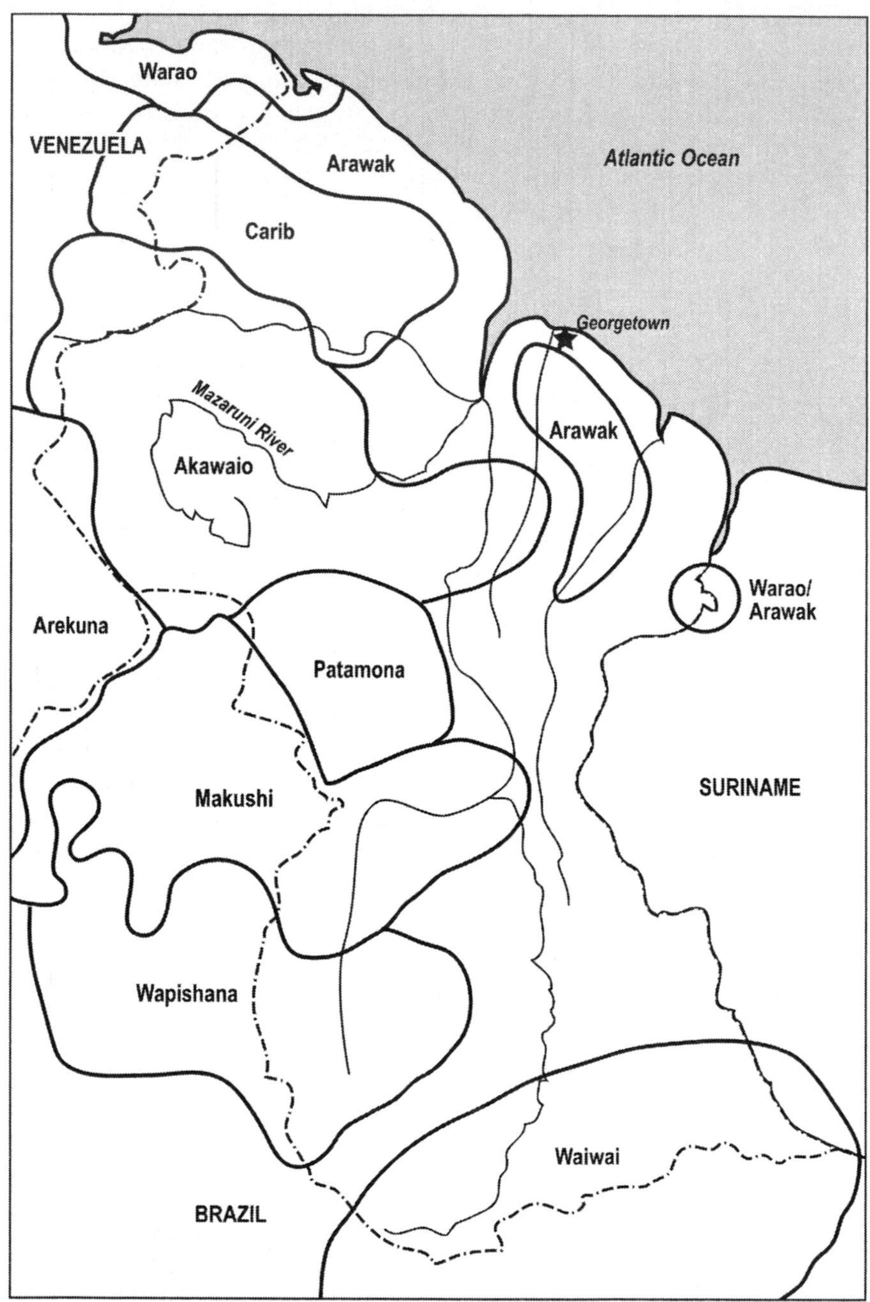

Map 11.1 The Amerindian Peoples of Guyana: Generalized Distribution

ously made by inland tribes by hammering narrow chips of jasper into a wooden board. They also specialize in making wood-skins, delicate river craft made by cutting off the strong, curved bark of the purpleheart tree. Heavier than water and thus perilous to the inexperienced if they ship water, the little boats are ideal for navigating the narrow creeks of their mountain territory. Akawaio also live downstream, at one time populating the upper reaches of the Berbice, Demerara, and Cuyuni as well as the middle Essequibo (Butt Colson 1983–1984).

All these communities were, and still are, woven together by an intimate network of intermarriage and trading alliances, in which foodstuffs, tools, poisons, drugs, resins, dyes, magical objects, and a host of other forest products were exchanged. Communications were maintained along the maze of waterways and across portages, around falls and rapids, and over low watersheds, which reached right up into the highlands. Where water connections became impossible, they were complemented by an intricate network of forest trails (Butt Colson 1973; Coppens 1971).

Both the Kapon and Pemon peoples are noted by anthropologists for their acephalous social structure. Like other Guyanese societies—as in the Piaroa (Kaplan 1975) and Carib groups such as the Maroni River Caribs (Kloos 1971), the Trio (Riviére 1969; 1984), the Yekuana (Arvelo-Jimenez 1971) and the Panare (Henley 1982), and the Pemon and Kapon (Butt Colson 1983–1984)—they order their social relations through a Dravidian relationship terminology in which terms relating to cousins are of the Iroquois type. The system is prescriptive in that marriage is always reckoned to have taken place between a male ego and a woman in the category *wife*, which includes female cross-cousins. However, they lack "any type of formal social grouping and, with the exception of the relationship terminology, any verbal categories which have absolute rather than relative value with which to differentiate members of society" (Riviére 1969, 61). In these systems, relations are recognized cognatically—equally through male and female lines. The characteristic Guyanese social system may be summarized thus: "instead of two groups exchanging wives, the model is that of a group which maintains itself through time as a consanguineal unit by restricting exchange to within itself" (Kaplan 1975, 2). Central to this system is the sense of unity of the cognatic kindred.

Power within these societies is diffuse and leadership weak and contested. Hereditary chieftains are unknown, hierarchy is absent, and centralized decision making not observed. As Thomas has put it, they maintain "order without Government" (1982).

The lack of formal polities and centralized authorities, widely dispersed homesteads, and raiding between villages being common until the nineteenth century do not imply that they lack identity or any sense of cultural cohesion. As Butt Colson has documented, both the Pemon and Kapon do have a sense of cultural unity and relatedness expressed through their shared language, marriage ties, and trading links: "The network of trading relationships and the paths along which goods are carried, have served to knot together the territories and inhabitants of the Guiana Highlands into a mutually obligated association of Peoples . . . myths, tales, songs, dances, news and exchanges of knowledge and experience, all pass via the same links and create an overarching cultural unity" (Butt Colson 1983–1984, 84–85).

Butt Colson has noted that, in addition, dispersed homesteads within a river system shared a sense of common identity expressed as "the people of such and such a creek." As outside societies began to put increasing pressure on these areas, these forms of cultural unity have been reinforced through common opposition to imposed values, through exploitation and the alienation of land, and as a result of government efforts to resettle the people into larger centralized villages with defined captains and councilors. Such unification has been expressed through religious revival, a broader sense of ethnic unity, a formalization of leadership structures, and more recently, though identity with the struggles of indigenous peoples worldwide.

BOUNDARY ISSUES

As Thongchai Winichakul has noted with reference to Siam, the notion of the "bounded" nation is a modern one (1993). Until the mid-nineteenth century, Dutch and British administrative capacity extended only weakly into the interior and commercial interests focused on the plantation economy on the coast. The exact line of the boundaries between Dutch, Portuguese, Spanish, and British colonial possessions was largely irrelevant.

However, as the legal justifications of colonial control became increasingly subject to international negotiations during the nineteenth century, the practice of mapping and demarcating boundaries became more expedient, and the vexed question of where indeed the colony's boundaries lay began to exercise the minds of the British administrators. The Amerindians in the interior, though still largely forgotten, found their rights being asserted by the British as a means of defending the colony's boundaries against others (Menezes 1977, 17).

The eastern boundary, it was agreed, lay along the Corentyne, and the matter came into dispute with Suriname in the twentieth century only as a result of conflicting surveys identifying different headwater streams as the real Corentyne.

The border to the west was far less clear. Dutch trading posts had certainly been established far up into the hills now known as the Sierra Imataca, but as Spanish power had grown and trade with the Caribs had shifted inland, the Capuchin missionaries had moved in. These mission stations had, in turn, collapsed during the wars of Independence from Spain, and many of the Amerindians had moved east to make the most of British protection and trading opportunities. In an attempt to settle the matter, in 1844 the British government offered the coast to the newly independent state of Greater Colombia as far east as Moruca on condition that Amerindian rights were protected. Receiving no reply and having discovered gold in the area, the British then decided instead to assert a line recently surveyed by the colonial geographers Robert and Richard Schomburgk, who had trudged and canoed their way along virtually the whole frontier between 1839 and 1842 (Burnett 2000). The decision remains contentious, however, and Venezuela continues to claim all of Guyana up to the Essequibo River.

Responsibility for the Amerindians of the interior was increasingly considered the duty of the Christian missions. As Governor Light wrote in the 1830s, "The only chance of making the rising generation of Aborigines permanently useful to the colony is by religious and moral instruction" (in Menezes 1977, 246).

The Dutch, who had at first been highly suspicious of missionaries, had later allowed them to take over in certain areas some of the duties of the post holders, or authorized traders sponsored by the administration to maintain trading links between the Amerindians in the interior and the coastal settlements and also charged with keeping the peace and maintaining good relations (Whitehead 1988). Moravian missions, first founded in Suriname in 1735, had been opened on the Berbice, Corentyne, and at Hope between 1738 and 1821 but moved back to Suriname with the transfer of power. The first Anglican missionaries started to operate in Bartica in 1831 and gradually expanded to include the Berbice, Waraputa, the Pomeroon, Moruca, and Demerara by the 1860s. A Roman Catholic mission was allowed to establish itself in Santa Rosa in Moruca 1837, to cater to the Amerindian fugitives from Venezuela who had fled the collapse of loyalist missions during the war of independence.

The expansion of British missionary efforts into the Rupununi savannas also led to the definition of the southern frontier with Brazil. In 1838 a zealous young missionary originally stationed at Bartica had moved by stages, and without official authorization, to an old Brazilian cattle station at Pirara on the upper Rupununi. The Brazilian authorities strenuously objected to his presence there and this, combined with reports of continued Brazilian slaving raids across the Tacutu, embroiled a reluctant British government in the dispute.

As the anthropologist Peter Riviére has documented in detail, the plantocracy in Guyana gave very low priority to the frontier. They refused to allocate local revenues either for mapping and demarcating the border or for the establishment of religious missions. And once the governor decided that the British would have to assert control of the frontier and rescue the mission, they likewise refused to fund the necessary military expedition (Riviére 1995; see Menezes 1977, 166).

After protracted negotiations, mutual denunciations, and flag waving at the frontier, the Brazilian government, fearful that the British might use the incident as an excuse to expand their claim south to the Amazon, acceded to British demands, and the present line of the frontier, formally agreed upon only in 1904, was defined.

All these frontier agreements were made without any reference to the indigenous peoples. As Audrey Butt Colson has noted,

> From the point of view of the indigenous occupants of these territories, the treaties represent an international carve up, in that national sovereignty was assigned in distant capitals of the world, principally in other continents, and boundaries were created without reference to the traditional rights of the occupants. These superimpositions could make no sense in terms of local structures, for they cut across and divided geographical, ecological, social and cultural unities, placing in separate political areas populations which conceived themselves to have been in possession of the land "from the beginning of time" and as being far more closely interrelated amongst themselves than the peoples and cultures of the nation states which were engulfing them. (Butt Colson 1983)

However, the direct influence of westerners on the residents of the Upper Mazaruni was not really felt until the 1930s, when missionaries began to establish a permanent presence in the area. Seventh Day Adventists founded their first missions in the Kamarang valley in the 1930s, the Anglican Church began to establish its missions among the Akawaio in the 1950s, and evangelical Baptists established far-flung missions among the Akawaio of the upper Kako in the 1960s. At the same time, the Akawaio themselves evolved their own syncretic religion, a prophetic cult merging Christian and indigenous traditions (Butt Colson 1960). At first condemned by the colonial administration as an expression of rebelliousness (Myers 1993), the Hallelujah Church was later strongly supported by the Anglican missionaries and was accepted into the Guyana Council of Churches.

OFFICIAL POLICY TOWARD THE AMERINDIANS

Unlike other British colonies, where the land rights of native peoples were expressly recognized by treaty and became a basis for subsequent national laws, no such clarity exists for Guyana. In Guyana the colonial regime could not claim rights either of sovereignty or land ownership, based on conquest or cession by treaty or papal bull, yet it asserted sovereignty nonetheless. Nor has the Amerindians' status ever been tested in Guyanese law since, either with respect to their land rights or to self-determination. Instead, the colonial state had stealthily assimilated the Amerindians as its subjects and then claimed frontiers against other colonial states, on the basis of extending the protections of British law and order over them.

British law, as it was developed in the colony, assumed—not necessarily correctly—that all lands not already allocated to settlers could be treated as Crown lands, owned and administered by the colonial power. However, the emerging laws at first conceded a special status to the "Aboriginal Indians of the colony" by recognizing their "traditional rights and privileges" to hunt, fish, gather, and cultivate wherever they wished on Crown lands, without need for a special permit (Benjamin and Pierre 1995). However, as competing interests began to move into the interior, these rights were progressively curtailed, and reflecting similar legal changes taking place in India (Gadgil and Guha 1992), Amerindians were instead accorded privileges, defined by regulations, to continue their subsistence activities. From 1887 Amerindians were expressly prohibited from cultivating Crown lands granted to other parties for logging, mining, balata collection, or ranching (Benjamin and Pierre 1995).

Worldwide, government policies toward indigenous peoples have varied widely. On the one hand, some state policies, like those pursued until then in Guyana, seek to isolate indigenous people and keep them apart from the national majority, treating them as legal minors and wards of the state to be protected from outsiders by a paternalist administration. On the other, in a pattern that became prevalent in the 1930s and 1940s, states developed policies that sought to eradicate indigenous people's lifestyles and cultures and integrate them into the national mainstream. In both cases the underlying prejudice is that indigenous peoples are inferior and must either be elevated to a more modern cultural level or kept apart from their superiors. Policies of integration received the sanction of international law in 1957, with the promulgation of the International Labour Organization's Convention 107 on Tribal and Indigenous Populations. The conventional wisdom behind this approach was that indigenous peoples were doomed to extinction if they clung to their outmoded ways. They needed to be encouraged to change their ways so that they could join the national mainstream and, in the meantime, remain protected from exploitation (Bodley 1982).

Oxford anthropologist Audrey Butt Colson, who has made a careful study of policy toward the Amerindians, argues that integration became the keynote of British Guiana government policy in the postwar years. The recommendation of an influential government report circulated in 1948 was that "a long range Amerindian Policy be adopted based on the assumption that it is necessary and desirable for these people to gradually achieve Western Civilization, and that accordingly all planning should be directed with this object in view" (Gregory-Smith 1948, 3, in Butt Colson 1983).

The policy recognized that it would take time to prepare the "widely dispersed" groups with "semi-nomadic tendencies" for civilization, and in the meantime certain areas should be set aside for their use, while development schemes were promoted to hasten their integration into the market. The reservations were there to buffer the Amerindians against the rougher side of development. The colonial policy stressed, "There must be no question of the permanent segregation of these people, and reservations should be looked upon as temporary sanctuaries and Tribal Amerindians should be left alone only until such time as it is considered that they have reached a standard of civilisation which will enable them to take their place in the general life of the colony" (Gregory-Smith 1948, 10, in Butt Colson 1983).

The policy formally adopted by the colony emphasized that the idea was "to cease mollycoddling the Amerindians as though they were Museum Pieces and to give those who so desire the full privileges and responsibilities of citizenship so that they may take their proper place as an equal partner with the other communities in the economic and cultural life of the colony" (Legislative Council debate 1944, in Butt Colson 1983).

The colonial government also had other plans for the interior, however. Mining, logging, and cattle ranching were expanding and the government was also considering developing intensive agriculture in the interior. Fruit plantations and agricultural settlements were proposed for the lowlands, while the Pakaraima highlands were considered very suitable for temperate vegetable crops, in high demand in Georgetown and the Caribbean. To fit into this scheme of accelerated interior development, the Amerindians would need to be encouraged to abandon their dispersed residence patterns and concentrate about the new administrative centers, so that they could be easily reached by agricultural extension officers and more easily offered health and educational services. The concentration of the Amerindians around the new centers would also free up land for other interests such as logging, mining, and even hill resorts where coastal residents could travel for holidays.

The colonial administrators felt that the interior was underpopulated and proposed encouraging migration, particularly into the highlands. At various times, areas like the Upper Mazaruni were proposed as locations for settling migrants from St. Lucia, Jews from Europe, and even "Assyrians."

To achieve these ends, a new emphasis was placed on building up an administrative structure in the Amerindian areas. Under revised legislation passed in 1951, reservations were renamed Amerindian Districts, to be run by the Department of the Interior, with the commissioner in Georgetown supported by district commissioners and district officers who would live and work in the Amerindian districts (Butt Colson 1983). At the same time, in line with Britain's preferred policy of administering native people by indirect rule, the authorities sought to impose a more democratic system of governance on the Amerindian villages. The new centralized settlements were encouraged to elect their captains, previously appointed by the administration, and they were to be supported in their work by district councils, also of elected members. The captains continued to receive a small stipend, a uniform, and a staff of office and were vested with the powers and immunities of a rural constable. According to the Amerindian Ordinance of 1951, it was "the duty of every captain to carry out such instructions as may be issued to him by the Commissioner or District Commissioner" and to maintain law and order in his area. The net effect of all these interventions was that the "Amerindians were to become part of an administrative uniformity in which, it transpired, national development was to be paramount" (Butt Colson 1983).

The result was what Butt Colson has called the "administrative annexation" of the Amerindian peoples and their territories (see Ferguson 1994), which had the express aim of "merging the remaining Amerindians with the other inhabitants of the country" (Gregory-Smith 1949, 11, in Butt Colson 1983).

ESTABLISHMENT OF UPPER MAZARUNI DISTRICT

The consequences of these policies were soon to be felt. The entire Upper Mazaruni basin, for example, was designated as an Amerindian district in 1945 and six years later a District Officer was posted to the region to implement the new policy. During the 1950s and 1960s the administration pursued a vigorous policy of voluntary resettlement, encouraging the then highly dispersed Akawaio and Arekuna, whose small mobile homesteads were spread across the region up to the very headwaters, to descend to the lower reaches of their creeks and rivers to the new centers, where they could be effectively administered and provided with government services. Administration was shifted from Imbaimadai to Kamarang as a more central and convenient marketing and communications point, with a river stretch suitable for landing amphibious Grumman aircraft and soils considered more suitable for intensive farming and cash crops.

In the Imbaimadai area of the Upper Mazaruni, where villages and homesteads were widely scattered through the savanna, the Akawaio were persuaded that, as the poor soils of the area would not allow for the intensive agriculture and peanut farming advocated by the District Officer, they should remove themselves from the region down to a new centralized village. The move was agreed to after the headman of one of the Imbaimadai villages died, and a site for a new community was selected at Jawalla. As the District Officer remarked, this consolidation of population "would be a great help to the administration" (Seggar 1954). The removal was also convenient because the British colonial administration was at the time considering settling the area upstream of Imbaimadai with refugees and opening the Imbaimadai area itself as a holiday resort.

Many Akawaio feel today that they were unfairly tricked into abandoning their ancestral lands to allow others access to the area. Some also feel that their old dispersed residence pattern was more ecologically sound than the present concentrated pattern, which places heavy pressure on local resources.

A remarkable aspect of Guyana's gaining of independence in 1966 was the extent to which the colonial state's integrationist policies went unquestioned and were even reinforced. Indeed, the Independence Agreement itself stated that: "It is the policy of the government to assist the Amerindians to the stage where they can, without disadvantage to themselves, be integrated with the rest of the community." The Forbes Burnham government duly went further than the British in pushing an assimilationist policy. In 1969 the new government did away with the Amerindian Development Committee and replaced it with an Interior Development Committee, which aimed at creating a sense of national unity and national integration in the interior. It was time for the Amerindians to stop feeling Amerindian and start identifying themselves as Guyanese.

EXCISION OF THE LOWER AND MIDDLE MAZARUNI FOR MINING

The successive changes in Amerindian policy corresponded to important shifts in the interior economy. In the late nineteenth century the interior began to be opened up—to logging, to balata bleeding, and above all to mining. Pressure on Amerindian lands intensified dramatically. The rush to exploit the gold of the region was triggered by lucrative finds in western Guyana in the 1840s and eastern Venezuela in the 1860s. Panners, using techniques refined in the gold rushes of North America, had found rich auriferous deposits in the Sierra Imataca and upper Cuyuni. The boom refocused Venezuelan interest in the region and fomented their territorial claims to the whole of the Cuyuni basin and all the lands west of the Essequibo. Meanwhile, a major gold rush got underway in Guyana. A first concerted attempt to mine gold was made by a local syndicate on the Mazaruni in 1863 and 1864. By the 1880s a boom took off and declared production soared from 40 ounces in 1882 to 11,906 ounces in 1887. Partly to fend off Venezuela's territorial claim and partly to bring order to the uncontrolled frontier mining camps that mushroomed through the region, the British Guiana administration opened the northwest to mining claims in 1887, and three years later the North West District, with its boundary along the Schomburgk line, was formally declared (Daly 1975, 275–76; Menezes 1977, 234).

Mining, which offered wealth and an escape from the plantations to the poor, was viewed with alarm by the colonial planters, since they feared losing their captive labor force. But despite trying to hobble small-scale miners with red tape, the plantocracy was unable to resist the gold rush. By the turn of the century an estimated six thousand black pork knockers (so-called because of the barrels of pork they used as a staple food) were at work in the interior, and gold production reached 138,000 ounces in 1893. Diamond production peaked somewhat later, reaching a record 214,000 carats in 1923 (Daly 1975, 276; World Bank 1993, 35). Although such high levels of production could not be maintained for long and soon declined once the easiest deposits were worked out, the mining way of life established in the late nineteenth century became an integral part of the Guyana hinterland.

The North West District remained the main focus for mining in Guyana until the 1930s, but restless gold seekers spread throughout the interior from the earliest years of the century. This trend was encouraged by the discovery of diamonds in the Mazaruni in 1887 and later in the upper Cotingo just over the border in Brazil in 1912 (MacMillan 1995, 24; Cleary 1990). Mining spread south, up the Puruni, Barima, and Barama in the 1880s; up the Cuyuni in the 1890s; up the Demerara in the 1900s; and into the Middle Mazaruni by 1920.

Given mining's increasingly important role in the economy, the administration became keen to promote it in ways that reduced conflicts between those making claims and to ensure that revenues accrued to the exchequer. They gave little heed to the needs or rights of the original owners of the land, the Amerindians. As Anna Benjamin and Laureen Pierre of the Amerindian Research Unit have remarked, "Mining traditionally has been given precedence over all other economic activities in the interior. From the beginning, mining districts were declared . . . wherever a gold strike occurred, and usually with scant reference to any other consideration. The presence of indigenous communities in a given locale, therefore was no bar to the declaration of a mining district, once it was known to be auriferous or diamantiferous" (Benjamin and Pierre 1995).

Although colonial laws designed to protect Amerindians prevented mining districts from being set up within Amerindian reserves, the legislation was easily circumvented. Amerindian reserved areas could be abolished at the stroke of a pen and then gazetted as a mining district. The Mazaruni is a case in point. In the 1930s, the pressure on the Middle Mazaruni became so intense that the area, previously reserved to Amerindians, was opened as a mining district and the Akawaio were exposed to thousands of pork knockers who streamed into their territory to search for the gold and diamonds in the river banks. What weak protections that the colonial state had afforded to the Akawaio communities of the middle and lower river were swept aside so that only the Upper Mazaruni remained as a reserve for exclusive Amerindian occupation. As noted, the area was reclassified as the Upper Mazaruni Amerindian District in 1945. However, the district was not to endure intact for long. In 1959, following the program of resettlement and after a major diamond find near Imbaimadai, the very same area that the Amerindians had been encouraged to abandon, was abolished on the grounds of being unused and unoccupied and was gazetted as a mining district.

AMERINDIAN LANDS COMMISSION

As Independence approached, and partly as a result of a growing understanding among the colonial officers posted to Amerindian Districts of the importance of land security to the future of the Amerindians, the British administration belatedly moved to provide secure land rights to Amerindian villages. Under the provisions of the Independence Agreement, by which sovereignty was transferred from Britain to the newly independent government of Guyana, it was stipulated that the Amerindians should be granted legal ownership to the lands where they were "ordinarily resident or settled": "The Government of British Guiana has decided that the Amerindian should be granted legal ownership or rights of occupancy over areas or reservations or parts thereof where any tribe or community of Amerindians is now ordinarily resident or settled and other legal rights, such as rights of passage, in respect of other lands they now by tradition or custom de facto enjoy freedoms and permissions corresponding to rights of that nature. In this context, it is intended that legal ownership shall comprise all rights normally attaching to such ownership" (Annex C, Section L of 1965 Guyana Independence Agreement).

In fulfillment of this legal obligation, an Amerindian Lands Commission was established in 1966 and made a comprehensive, but not exhaustive, review of the Amerindians' land situation and documented indigenous land claims. In the Upper Mazaruni, the commission took note of the land claims made by each village and also recorded being handed a petition in the name of all the captains of the Upper Mazaruni communities that requested legal recognition of their rights to the ownership of the full extent of the Upper Mazaruni Amerindian District as defined in 1959.

The report of the commission was published in 1969 and recommended the provision of community titles to the majority of Amerindian communities in the country. There were some notable exceptions: land titling was not recommended for a scattering of communities on the lower rivers (Mazaruni, Cuyuni, and Demerara) and in the mining districts such as the Middle Mazaruni and the Barama-Kaituma areas. Moreover, in a number of cases—

notably in the North West District (Arawak and Warao), the Upper Mazaruni (Akawaio and Arekuna), the South Rupununi (Wapishana) and the North Rupununi (Makushi)—the commission recommended community titling of areas substantially smaller than the territorial claims made by the Amerindians to the commission (Amerindian Lands Commission 1969). Exactly these areas have now become the subjects of land disputes: between Amerindians and logging companies (North West District), miners (Upper Mazaruni), ranchers (South Rupununi), and conservationists (North Rupununi–Iwokrama project).

Having received the report, the government prevaricated in applying its recommendations. It was not until international controversy about a proposed hydropower project on the Upper Mazaruni focused attention on the government's failure to abide by its commitment at independence to secure Amerindian land rights that it passed the Amerindian (Amendment) Act No. 6 of 1976, providing Amerindians with community title and the right to administer their areas through their captains and councils.

The act was not comprehensive and there were some notable exceptions where the government chose not to follow the commission's recommendations. A number of communities in the lowlands, like the Akawaio of the Demerara, did not get the titles that the commission had recommended (Fox and Danns 1993), probably because logging was given priority. The Amerindians of the Upper Mazaruni, where the government still planned a big dam that would displace some forty-five hundred Akawaio, were also left without land title. The Caribs of the upper Barama, where the government was encouraging foreign mining investments, were similarly excluded. In the extreme south the Waiwai were ignored (Colchester 1991).

MAPS AND SURVEYS

Until the mid-nineteenth century no formal maps based on surveys had ever been made of the Upper Mazaruni District. Indeed more or less accurate sketch maps locating the major rivers and tributaries, with rough stippling to mark mountains and highlands, continued to be the main tools used to orient government administration until the 1970s. The exceptions were the actual boundaries with Suriname, Venezuela, and Brazil, first formally surveyed by Schomburgk in 1839–1842. Additional surveying was carried out by the colonial administration in certain areas of importance, notably to fix the sites of the rough airfields that started to be cut in the region during the 1950s. The Amerindian Lands Commission had only these rough maps to work with, and as a result, the errors in these unsurveyed sketch maps crept into the descriptions of proposed title boundaries recommended by the commissioners. The widespread application of modern surveying and mapping techniques was carried out only in the 1970s when the need for accurate information was stimulated by renewed interest in the interior and plans for large-scale development projects. In the Upper Mazaruni, detailed aerial surveys were carried out by the Ottawa-based TERRA surveys, and this information was turned into a set of generally accurate 1:50,000 maps through photointerpretation and a very limited amount of ground truthing. With the exception of some larger-scale technical drawings made for the hydro project and the new maps now generated by the Amerindian Peoples Association (APA), these 1:50,000 maps made in the 1970s remain the only modern maps of the Upper Mazaruni region.

HYDROPOWER PROJECT AND THE CAMPAIGN TO STOP IT

In 1973 the Guyanese government announced its intention to build a major hydropower project at Sand Landing in the Upper Mazaruni. The project, which came with a price tag of some $3 billion U.S. dollars, was designed to generated three thousand megawatts of electricity for national consumption and proposed bauxite smelters. The project was also aimed at securing Guyana's claim to the western part of the country, over which Venezuela has asserted ownership (Bennett, Butt Colson, and Wavell 1978; Henningsgaard 1981).

The dam would have created an extensive reservoir that would have flooded almost all the forty-five hundred Akawaio of the Upper Mazaruni off of their lands. To overcome Amerindian resistance to the project, the Minister of Energy and Natural Resources called five community captains to Georgetown where they were presented with the plans as a fait accompli and encouraged to sign a letter accepting them. Fearing a loss of government assistance if they refused to cooperate, all but one signed. However, on returning to their villages, they encountered dismay and widespread opposition and were obliged to retract their support for the project (Bennett, Butt Colson, and Wavell 1978, 4; Henningsgaard 1981, 14).

For the whole of the following decade, the Amerindians of the Upper Mazaruni lived with the knowledge that the government planned to forcibly relocate them. They were unanimous in their opposition and were supported by concerned anthropologists, church leaders, and international human rights organizations such as Survival International and Cultural Survival, which energetically campaigned for a recognition of Amerindian land rights and pressured international financial institutions such as the World Bank not to support the project.

The Akawaio were outspoken in their opposition to the project and petitioned the government repeatedly to respect their right to continue to live on their lands.

> Why We Don't Want to Move
>
> This land is where we belong—it is God's gift to us and has made us who we are.
>
> This land is where we are at home, we know its ways: and the things that happened here are known and remembered, so that the stories the old people told are still alive here.
>
> This land is needed for those who come after—we are becoming more and more than before, and we must start new settlements, with new farms around them. If we have to move, it is likely that there will be other people there and we shall not be free to spread out as we need to: and the land will not be enough for our people, so that we will grow poor.
>
> This land is the place where we know where to find all that it provides for us—food from hunting and fishing, and farms, buildings and tool materials, medicines. Also the spirits around us know us and are friendly and helpful.
>
> This land keep (*sic*) us together within its mountains—we come to understand that we are not just a few people or separate villages, but one people belonging to a homeland. If we had to move, we would be lost to those that remain in the other villages. This would be a sadness to us all, like the sadness of death. Those who moved would be strangers to the people and spirits and places where they are made to go. (The Akawaio Indians, Upper Mazaruni District, Guyana, 1977, in Bennett, Butt Colson, and Wavell 1978, 9)

While the project was gradually developed and a new road was thrust up toward the upper river from the Middle Mazaruni, the government also opened the upper river to mining with the aim of dredging out the diamonds from the river beds before they were more deeply submerged. In the event, international financial support for the hydropower project was not forthcoming. The mining economy, however, was to transform the lives of the Upper Mazaruni communities.

MINING AND ITS IMPACTS

As noted, in 1959, immediately after a major diamond strike was reported, one-third of the Upper Mazaruni Amerindian District around Imbaimadai was excised and gazetted as a mining district. In 1977 the government passed regulations opening the rivers of the Upper Mazaruni to diamond mining using pumps and divers. The following year the whole of the Upper Mazaruni was declared a mining area (Butt Colson 1983). It was only in 1991, after the hydropower project had been dropped, that the Amerindians were granted titles to a small part of the original Upper Mazaruni Amerindian District, but mining was still permitted along the rivers and in the gaps between the community titles. Today multinational companies have secured exploration rights to search the entire area, including titled lands. When it comes to mining, the Amerindians find they have no protection.

Not surprisingly, these mining invasions and laissez faire policies have had a devastating impact on the Amerindians. As in many other parts of Amazonia, the gold rush has brought a host of problems to their communities. Most obviously, the miners have introduced new diseases to which the Amerindians have little resistance, and very high mortality rates have resulted. Anopheline mosquitoes thrive in the braided streambeds and pools left in the wake of mining, and miners themselves restlessly move about the country serving as vectors to the malaria they carry. A study in 1992 revealed that nearly all the forty thousand people associated with small-scale mining in the interior tested positive for malaria (Sassoon 1993, 7). Tuberculosis, so prevalent in mining areas where lack of hygiene, poor nutrition, and ill health provide perfect conditions for its propagation, has also become a major problem among the Amerindians of the Pakaraimas. Venereal diseases have become a problem in many areas, and gonorrhea is rife, reducing fertility in Amerindian women. Recently, even AIDS cases have begun to be reported (ARU n.d. a–d).

Traveling about the interior, one encounters two main responses from the Amerindians to the invasion of their areas by miners. Some groups—and this applies even to some Carib communities with the longest experience of mining—have sought to move away from the destructive cultural influences of the mines, establishing new settlements up small creeks or in interfluves where they can redevelop autonomous communities and subsistence economies. It is a hard choice, however, for it may mean moving out of a titled area, leaving behind the minimal educational and medical services provided by the government while still being exposed to the infectious diseases that enter the population through occasional trading.

More commonly, Amerindian communities have themselves been caught up in the mining fever. Amerindian labor has long been integral to the mining economy as mine workers, porters, and providers of river transport. Some Amerindians have adopted the pork-knocker way of life and opened their own mines, and indeed some Amerindians have become quite wealthy from mining. Yet the costs to communities and cultures have been severe.

In the Middle Mazaruni, which was opened to mining in the 1930s, the Akawaio have been denied rights to land or any protections. As a result they are in crisis. When they demand land, the pork knockers object and tell them to move to areas where Amerindians already have title. Amerindians who have spoken out against the mining on their lands have been threatened by drunk pork knockers with cutlasses. In early 1994 a man was killed in Oranapai in a land dispute. As Celian Roland, elected captain of Kurupung told me in 1994,

> Now they are saying we must move to the Upper Mazaruni. That makes their heart ache. They'll get no big fish up there. They are all getting this confusion but I say that we should not listen to all confusion but settle and develop our own communities. . . . They are really aching these Indians, really aching themselves. They say they'll take up their bamboos [arrows]. I think war will break out with the negroes because they cut our farms.

In a detailed and disturbing record of the impact of mining on the Akawaio and Arekuna of the Upper Mazaruni, Butt Colson shows how the very presence of mining has seriously undermined traditional Amerindian life. Mining, she writes, has provoked a collapse of the subsistence economy. Not only has game been reduced by overhunting to provide meat for the miners, but the involvement of the menfolk in mining leads to a steady decline in food production. New garden plots are not cut, production declines, and expensive store-bought food from the coast comes to replace local food, which grows scarce and expensive. The result is the classic development paradox, where rising incomes lead to falling standards of living. Observes Butt-Colson (1983), "Despite an apparent prosperity from the sale of diamonds, there was a fall in real income though an ever-rising cost of living, affecting in particular those unable to mine through age, sex and opportunity." As early as 1977 malnutrition was identified as a major health problem at Kamarang, and exploitative labor relations also began to develop, with poor Amerindians yoked into debt bondage to coastal miners who ran the dredges and stores. The overall results are increasing dependence on mining and permanent wealth differentiation.

Since the 1970s, with the opening of the whole area to river dredges, the government station of Kamarang has been transformed from a calm and well-ordered administrative center, with a religious mission and active Amerindian community, into a tawdry tinsel town of grog shops, brothels, and discos along one side of the airstrip. Red Light City, as it is known, has had a sad effect on Amerindian social life, generating what Butt Colson refers to as the typical "pork-knocker syndrome of drink, gambling, sex, conspicuous consumption and, from time to time, violence" (1983).

Deprived of effective legal protections, village captains have been unable to expel miners from their areas and are instead obliged to negotiate the best deals they can with them. Corruption of community leaders is undermining village politics and fragmenting villages. Traditions of cooperation and communal living are being replaced by self-interest and mistrust.

Many young Indians have found jobs in the mines, and they are often assigned the dangerous task of diving to direct pumps and dredges along the river beds. These mine workers say that there have been numerous fatal accidents that have not been reported in the national press. They also complain that the companies do not compensate injured workers or the families of workers killed in accidents (Colchester 1991).

Mining has had a disproportionate impact on women and children. With the men often absent, sometimes for long periods, in the mining camps, women have had to shoulder a heavy burden of domestic duties: farming, fishing, and gathering to feed and maintain their families. But with male labor absent, new gardens cannot be cleared, obliging women to seek alternative sources of income (Butt Colson 1983; Fox and Danns 1993; Forte 1995). Inevitably, these long absences and separations have increased family tensions. Prostitution and promiscuity have flourished: "Coastland miners are mostly young men, unattached, frequenting Kamarang at weekends to sell their diamonds, collect fuel and buy food. They are a source of attraction for Akawaio women, who trek to 'Red Light City' in order to 'sport with the pork-knockers.' Apart from some seductions and rapes, most deliberately embark on a prostitute's career to obtain money, as no other employment is available, and to enjoy life" (Butt Colson 1983).

The effects of these changes in lifestyle on Amerindian cultures have been marked. Old values of sharing and cooperation have been replaced by cash values and monetary exchange. Traditional beliefs and knowledge of the environment have been eroded and sophisticated arts and crafts have fallen into disuse, thereby increasing dependency on mining as a mainstay of the economy. Moreover, as mining technology has become increasingly sophisticated and expensive, control of the local economies has become concentrated in fewer and fewer hands. It is often outsiders and Georgetown-based syndicates that have the capital and connections required for successful mining ventures.

New lightweight portable engines have greatly extended the range of mining operations, with pumps providing water to mine old river terraces and water courses now far from the streams and rivers that deposited them. These so-called land dredges, sometimes supplied with water by hundreds of yards of plastic piping, depend on powerful hoses that flush out alluvial beds. The liquefied soil is then sucked up by pumps for processing. Land dredging is a relatively new trend in Guyanese mining, and according to the World Bank, is likely to favor the emergence of larger, more highly capitalized companies that can afford the costly overhead of prospecting (World Bank 1993, 37).

Georgetown-based companies have also developed so-called missile dredges, huge remote-controlled vacuum cleaners shaped like torpedoes and mounted on river dredges, which pump water into alluvial deposits and suck them up to process the minerals. These dredges can dig deep into the river banks, sometimes as far as seventy meters, liquefying mud and gravel as they go.

Flights over the mining areas reveal the obvious environmental impact of mining. What were once clear rivers flowing between forested banks have become wide washes of mud and debris, crisscrossed by meandering red-brown streams of water and slurry searching for a way through the tailings, with stagnant pools and a moonscape of spoil heaps and sandbanks along the banks. Navigation has been seriously impeded in some rivers and the turbid waters have caused fish stocks to crash, further affecting the Amerindian diet. The Mazaruni Christian Council complains that the Upper Mazaruni "may soon be a mud-choked gutter almost cleared of fauna and flora and the rainforest at its most magnificent" (Colchester 1991, 11). The situation on the Middle Mazaruni is worse. Says Celian Roland, elected captain of Kurupung, "There are pork-knockers all along the river with their dredges. You see the condition of the river, it is all choked with big banks of sand. The river is all choked up. You have to be a river captain to pick your way through the shallows in a boat."

Mining sites are almost never reclaimed and there is considerable concern that the abandoned pits may be producing acid mine drainage, which finds its way into waters used for fishing and human consumption (Moody 1994).

The problem is that not only does the Guyana Geology and Mines Commission (GGMC) lack the biologists, toxicologists, and laboratories needed to carry out a proper study of these environmental problems, but no regulations control the environmental impacts of mining anyway. Indeed, so feeble is the outreach of the commission that even the regulations regarding filing claims, staking out concessions, declaring finds, and paying royalties are regularly evaded.

The headwater mining camps, in particular, are almost completely beyond government control. According to the Amerindians, mine officers are rarely able to visit their settlements and as a result no regulations are enforced. As the Akawaio community of Jawalla pointed out in a public presentation in 1994, "We in the Upper Mazaruni solely live by way of fishing and hunting. We have experienced that there is no longer fishes in any great amount as before, as a result of miners destroying the river banks and creeks on which we tremendously depend and live on. We set fish traps to catch fish but in vain. . . . There is a serious water pollution existing in the Upper Mazaruni. The miners top-side destroy the rivers, causing the residents to suffer. The water we use for domestic purposes is no good right now. We feel the pollution is against health regulations" (quoted in Forte 1994, 223).

THE 1991 TITLES

It was not until 1991 that the Akawaio and Arekuna of the Upper Mazaruni and Wenamu were finally granted land titles by the government. They were issued—many said as an electoral ploy—in the run-up to the first relatively free election since Independence. Hurriedly rushed through without any new consultation or survey, the titles followed almost verbatim the text prepared by the Amerindian Lands Commission fifteen years before. The titling thus ignored the fact that villages had moved and subdivided in the intervening period and also ignored the improved maps made in the 1970s. The descriptions of the boundaries of the titles, based on the flawed maps made in the 1950s, could not be easily reconciled with the real geography. The titles also implied a rejection of the petition made by the captains of the Upper Mazaruni for ownership of the entire Upper Mazaruni Amerindian District as defined in 1959.

The issuance of the titles and the election of a new government prompted the communities to take stock of their new situation. They noted that their new titles granted them considerably less territory than the area they had repeatedly claimed, and moreover, that the titles were not contiguous but rather left substantial areas of apparently vacant Crown lands in the gaps between the village areas. More educated members of the villages studied the land laws to ascertain their rights under Guyanese laws and realized that even within their titled areas, they were not secure against expropriation or the issuance of mining licenses to third parties. As Lawrence Anselmo, captain of the Arekuna community of Paruima noted: "These laws were made by Colonial people in a language not fully understood by the Amerindians. As Amerindians learnt the English language, they realized that certain laws

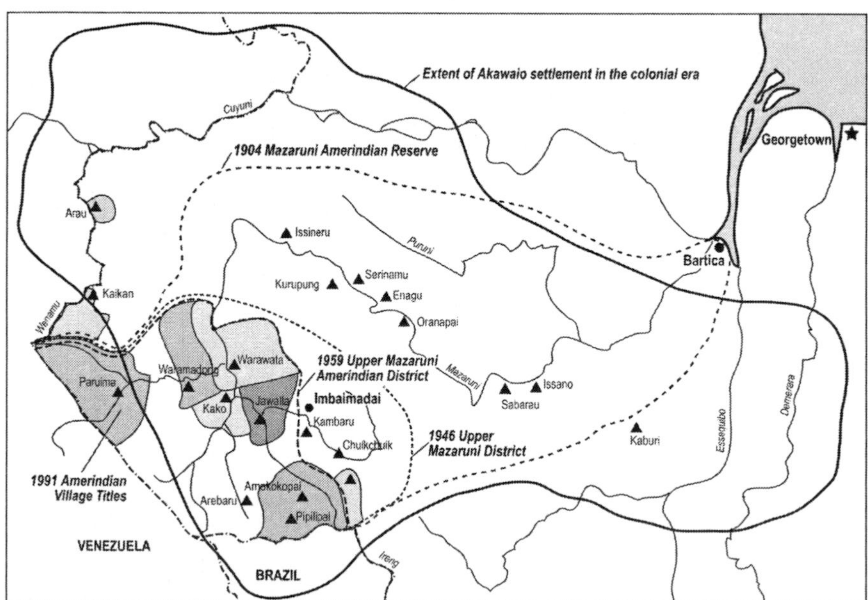

Map 11.2 The Shrinking Land Base of the Akawaio

were not suited to Amerindian needs. Some of these laws make our living in our homelands very uncomfortable" (quoted in Forte 1994, 13).

A number of smaller homesteads such as Waramabia and others in the upper Arebaru and Kwiara, and also one substantial village, Kambaru, found themselves provided with no land rights whatsoever. The community of Chinowieng found that its land area was very small, being limited to a narrow strip of savanna that in no way encompassed the area the villagers used for farming, much less the extensive territory they ranged over in hunting and fishing. The community of Chinowieng was indignant at this unilateral expropriation of their lands and noted in a public appeal,

> We were told that this was not Amerindian land but Crown land, but by what right our ancestral lands were removed from our ancient homeland we do not know. We are an unconquered people and have never heard that our forefathers signed away their rights by any treaty with the colonial riders. Today the miners dominate and despoil a large area as if it were their own, and at Imbaimadai we are often treated as if we are strangers, in the place that was, not long ago, a strong and revered village with its central church and extensive farmlands. By what right? What is our offence? (quoted in Forte 1994, 221)

Having determined that the land titles that they had been granted were inadequate for their needs, the communities resolved to press their claim for an extension of their territory and they sent a petition to Georgetown demanding a recognition of their land rights.

They were encouraged to take this course by the election manifesto of the new government (PPP-Civic) that criticized the previous administration (PNC) for electioneering. The PPP-Civic manifesto of 1992 noted,

> The PNC is now using the distribution of land titles to Amerindians as a political gimmick. In fact, Amerindians are complaining that they are not receiving titles to all the lands they occupy. The PPP-Civic will ensure that titles are given to Amerindians to all the lands they occupy. Communal titles will be given to all Amerindian villages/settlements through their genuine elected councils. The boundaries of villages and settlements will be clearly defined and demarcated. Amerindians will be consulted on development projects which are likely to affect their rights and interests. The new government will work towards the allocation of part of the proceeds from the extraction of minerals and precious stones within the boundaries of any settlement, which is carried out with the consent of the Amerindian council, to be given to the settlement as development revenue. (*Time for Change. Time to Rebuild*, PPP-Civic Manifesto, 1992)

Probably the most encouraging aspect of the Amerindians' situation in Guyana today is their increasingly vocal and self-assured presence in the national arena. The political liberalization of Guyana with the ending of socialist dictatorship has seen an indigenous resurgence, as Amerindians have taken advantage of the new political space to assert their own views. The first to emerge on the national scene was the APA, which was set up in 1991 to push for Amerindian land rights and to ensure that the Amerindians' voices were heard in policy making at the national level. Its structure is designed to ensure that the Amerindians of the interior control the organization's advocacy while being directly represented in Georgetown.

Accordingly, the APA draws its authority from its general assembly, which meets every two years and which elects an executive committee with at least one member representing each region, including a chairperson, vice-chair, treasurer, secretary, and women's representative. The assembly also elects a programs administrator who is authorized by the committee to pursue the goals of the association between assemblies in coordination with the committee. This administrator and other support staff maintain a small office in Georgetown. None of the committee members is normally resident in Georgetown, all being from interior communities.

The assembly comprises representatives of units established in some seventy Amerindian communities throughout the country. Each unit, made up of at least ten Amerindians but often of whole villages, has its own committee and office holders, elected by its membership in its respective areas. Each unit sends two representatives to the general assemblies. The APA has carried out vigorous campaigns against logging, mining, and road building in the interior and has energetically denounced what it sees as government attempts to sell off Amerindian lands.

The APA is firmly in support of self-determination for its peoples, by which it means that Amerindian territorial rights should be recognized and legally secured and they should be empowered to take charge of their own affairs in their own areas. The APA argues that development in Amerindian territories should be under community control and subject to their free and informed consent. It has urged the government to revise the outdated Amerindian Act and adopt the International Labour Organization's Convention 169 (Amerindian Peoples Association 1994).

The APA thus rejects the government's current policy of integration and, in line with indigenous people's aspirations at the international level, insists that Amerindians should be in charge of their own destinies. As a past APA coordinator, Gerald McIntyre, told me,

> We are not ready for "integration" yet. If you haven't got education or land title, you're done. You're politically weak. You're nothing. Integration just means your women become call-girls, waitresses, and bar girls. Your men are just laborers. And you get taken over all around—they take your forests and your mines. They take everything off you and you're nothing. The time is past when they told us what is good for us and what is bad for us. It is time we decided for ourselves. (personal communication, 1 November 1994)

BUFFER ZONES AND MULTINATIONAL MINING

Meanwhile, the Upper Mazaruni communities got further evidence of the precarious nature of their land situation as the government, far from prioritizing the titling of Amerindian lands, accelerated the process of handing out logging and mining concessions to foreign companies (Colchester 1991, 1994, 1997). The government also entered into intensive negotiations with international mining companies interested in the Upper Mazaruni, and small-scale mining licenses were also granted to coastal miners in the gaps between the community titles.

In June 1994, therefore, the captains of the Upper Mazaruni again descended to Georgetown to discuss their land situation with the head of the GGMC and were afforded assurances that the government would proceed cautiously with the hand out of claims in these areas.

The promises again proved worthless. The same year, the Denver-based mining transnational, Golden Star Resources Limited (GSRL), was granted a license to nearly the whole of the Upper Mazaruni basin for exploratory prospecting by remote sensing and spot surveys.

These allocations gave rise to great concern in the affected communities, especially since they had been not been consulted before the claims were registered and no information was provided to the communities thereafter by the GGMC. Remonstrations by the community leaders with GSRL led the company to promise to consult with the communities in the future before developing their operations.

As a result, there was a heightened concern in the Upper Mazaruni about their land situation, which led the Amerindians to send another delegation to visit the president in September and seek assurances that their land claim would be recognized. The president was not able to provide these assurances or promise that GSRL would not get mining rights in their area. At the same time, the delegation suffered the further indignity of being told they would not be permitted to represent themselves through the APA, and other members of their delegation who were not captains were also excluded. In addition to their land claim, therefore, a second petition was thus handed to the president protesting this political manipulation.

MAPPING THE LAND CLAIM

Denied government support, the Upper Mazaruni captains appealed to the APA to seek other means of bolstering their land claims. Therefore in November 1994 I, who had worked with the APA since shortly after its foundation, was asked to carry out a survey of the Upper Mazaruni to clarify the nature of the land claim and explore means of supporting the communities in natural resource management.

The village leadership was quite clear, however, that talk about community development was premature until the land issue was first settled. One captain, Czar Henry, told me that "the main issue is the question of land. If this could be settled to our satisfaction, we could think about progress and our future development. But though we have plans for developing our community, we find it hard to concentrate on this while our land tights are so uncertain" (personal communication, 7 November 1994).

The communities were also unanimously clear about the importance of the land claim. As one resident, Derrick Krammer, eloquently told me during a village meeting in Kako,

> We use the lands for hunting, mining, fishing and farming and also to get things that are important to our lives like materials for baskets, timber for housing and canoes and many other things. We will run short of these things locally if we do not have an area which we can expand into.
>
> Up until now, we have only asked for rights to land and not for forestry and mineral rights. But now we are seeking control of the sub-soil too. Even if we don't own the sub-surface resources we need to benefit from the use of the minerals. To get a share, we need to be able to negotiate terms.
>
> The main reason we are claiming back this land is that we know that in future our way of life will be different. Our children will be educated and will live differently from the way we do today. Just twenty years ago we were very different to the way we are today and in another twenty years we will be able to manage our own businesses for our future benefit.
>
> Today the government emphasizes the need for self-development. We therefore feel that we should control all our land and that it is right that we should also control the minerals so we can have our own development based on our own initiatives and resources. That is the reason we are asking for additional lands. And we are increasing in numbers. When this village was founded there were only three families, now we are nearly six hundred. How many more will we be in the future? So we need our land for our future development. That is our dream, and that is our future.
>
> Development is a big word which needs defining more clearly. Even though we may not have big buildings we are also developed. You cannot look at only one aspect. You can destroy both the culture and the environment by just focusing on money and that is what we are trying to avoid.
>
> This territory is rich but we need to develop it carefully. If we get rights to this land, we can develop it by ourselves. We have to go ahead and develop our own community. It is not that we are selfish; we are self-employed and believe development means becoming self-sufficient. (Personal communication, 16 November 1994)

During the course of this consultation the communities made two main requests for support with their land claim. They requested the advice of a lawyer and they asked for maps to clarify the extent of their titles and the boundaries of their claim. In the conventional NGO manner, two projects were thus devised to fulfill these needs and money was sought from funding agencies to cover project costs.

Conceptually, the legal project was a simple one. It involved recruiting an expert in aboriginal rights in international, British, and Dutch-Roman law to carry out a comprehensive review of the legal basis for making a land claim in the Upper Mazaruni, in Guyana. The aim was to develop a legal argument for backing the land claim after a detailed process of consultation with the concerned communities. Because there was no precedent in Guyanese law for filing such a claim, it was necessary to research the full complexity of Guyanese property and common law to establish the possibilities for making a claim.

Funds for the project were obtained from the Rainforest Foundation, and the lawyer, a British barrister versed in all three of the relevant bodies of law, researched the legal material. He then traveled to Guyana in October 1995 and with the APA programs administrator visited the Upper Mazaruni to discuss the legal case with the community leaders. After running through several drafts that were circulated to the communities for discussion, comment, and amendment, a final text was completed in late 1996. The study concluded that there was a firm legal basis for mounting a land claim to the Upper Mazaruni basin on the grounds of immemorial possession, and it outlined the possible procedures to be used to advance the claim, either through the courts or through direct appeal to the government. The study also concurred that a detailed mapping of the territory and the boundaries would help to justify the claim, legally and politically.

Accordingly, a second, mapping project was also written up and circulated to funding agencies. It was noted that the total area of the land claim was estimated to be some forty-five hundred square miles and included an upland area of varied terrain covered by very diverse vegetation types. Corresponding to very ancient and weathered rocks that underlie the area, the soils and rivers are typically nutrient poor and acidic. Rivers are clear or black-water types, high in tannin. The forests range from dry-ground rain forests and small localized areas of swamp forest, to montane forests on the higher ground. There are also extensive areas of savanna, with characteristic stands of palms in wet areas, and highly specialized vegetation types on the summits of some of the *tepui* (sandstone inselbergs). The corner of the area includes Mount Roraima on the border of Brazil and Venezuela, the highest point in the Guyana Highlands. Although comprehensive surveys of the vegetation and fauna have not been carried out and the limnology little studied, local biologists have noted the very high levels of species endemism in the Upper Mazaruni and have registered the area near Roraima as one of priority for conservation efforts in Guyana.

Given the biological importance of the area, IUCN–Netherlands agreed to fund the second project, to be carried out by the APA with the help of the Forest Peoples Programme, with the aim of mapping the full extent of the land claim. The aim was to map not only the boundaries of the existing titles and land claim but also, as fully as possible, the people's own vision of their territory, by recording all named features of the landscape, new and old village sites, hunting, fishing, and other resource areas, sites of religious significance, trails, portages, and any other important features of the area.

TECHNIQUES AND RESULTS

What was innovative about the project was not that it aimed to end with a detailed map of the land use of the Upper Mazaruni based on indigenous knowledge, but that this was achieved by a team of indigenous technicians from the area itself. This team was provided with training by outside experts but then left to carry out the actual data gathering themselves, in their own languages, without external technical assistance until it came to the last stage of entering the field data into computers and generating the final maps.

In preparation for the field project, the lines of the rivers and creeks of the twenty-nine relevant 1:50,000 maps were scanned onto two large one-by-two-meter base maps, using standard layout software. The maps show rivers and creeks, airstrips, named mountain peaks, villages, and some creek and river names. Fifty sets of these working maps were then printed up for field use, as were several sets of the government's 1:50,000 topographical maps. One set of 1:100,000 topographical maps were also carried into the field. Geomatic and mapping technology was also acquired for the project; these included, crucially, a number of small handheld global-positioning-system (GPS) devices.

The team from the Forest Peoples Programme and the APA then traveled to the Upper Mazaruni and spent five weeks carrying out on-site training of the four APA members from the Upper Mazaruni. In intensive training workshops, trainees learned about the points of the compass, how to read a compass, taking a bearing, plotting a bearing, and triangulation. They studied the meaning of grids, latitude and longitude, coordinates, plotting coordinates, scale, legends and symbols, reading contours, identifying river sources and watersheds, the keeping of map inventories, and the recording of boundaries. They also learned to use the geomatic devices, including taking a position, recording coordinates, using the devices' mapping and tracking functions, and taking bearings. Instruction continued in the means of recording indigenous knowledge through interviews; making sketches of land use, rivers, and trails; and through hiring guides and relating this knowledge to georeferenced locations. Finally, they learned how to enter this information onto the base maps. Boundaries, information on land use, and toponymy were all entered onto the 1:50,000 topographical maps.

A legend and set of symbols was developed for recording land-use information and a standard orthography was elaborated to try to ensure consistent spelling of features. A format for carrying out a census in each community was also developed. Standard travel logs to record named features and corresponding GPS-derived coordinates were also prepared.

After this training, the field team spent the following six months traversing the entire territory, spending an average of three weeks in each community trekking and canoeing about the village lands to record as much as possible of the local knowledge of the landscape.

In November 1996 the Forest Peoples Programme returned to Guyana for an evaluation workshop to assess the results and learn lessons from the experience for future exercises of the same kind. The final map was then prepared after it was again checked by the community representatives. Then in June 1997 the APA presented the map at a public meeting in Georgetown, which was boycotted by the government.

The Upper Mazaruni residents take a long-term view of the process. As the secretary of the APA, Lawrence Anselmo, who is captain of the Arekuna community of Paruima, stressed to a district council meeting in the Upper Mazaruni in January 1996 that

> We can't make decisions in haste, as these will have consequences for five or six generations. . . . We need to carefully weigh up what kind of development we really want. Already we are seeing the negative effects of development on our people—you all know what I mean. Our culture has been affected. Our way of life will be confused by development. We welcome it because we do not know what it means, what it leads to. We need to be careful to ensure that we get the kind of development that we really want. Our future generations, our little ones who are coming up, they will get better education in the future and they will look back at the decisions we make now. They will be sorry if they realize we have not made the right decisions for the futures of our peoples. . . . We must not think only in terms of ourselves or our immediate grandchildren but in terms of seven generations. We want them to enjoy the same privileges that we do.

RECENT DEVELOPMENTS

In December 1998 the captains of the Upper Mazaruni submitted a statement of claim to the High Court in Guyana, suing the government to recognize their rights to their lands. The lawsuit, based on the common-law doctrine of aboriginal title, seeks a judicial declaration that the indigenous peoples of Guyana are entitled to full and equal protection under the provisions of the Guyana constitution; large parts of the Amerindian Act are unconstitutional because they violate the constitutional prohibition of racial discrimination; they have unextinguished title to the whole of the area known as the 1959 Upper Mazaruni Amerindian District; and freehold title to this area must be vested in the captains on behalf of the communities (UMADC, APA, and FPP 2000, 56). The case builds on the legal advances achieved by indigenous peoples in international law and in a number of Commonwealth countries, where it is now accepted that indigenous peoples retain radical title to their lands based on immemorial possession and according to their own laws and customs (Colchester 2001, 17). However, if the Amerindians expected a quick resolution of the conflict, they have been disappointed. The government took more than a year even to respond to the Statement of Claim, and more than three years later no date for a court hearing has been set.

Meanwhile, access to the area by mining companies has continued. In July 1999 the government of Guyana signed an agreement with a South African mining consortium called Migrate Mining, Ltd., granting it mineral exploration rights over 3.3 million hectares in the Pakaraima Mountains. The area encloses every single Amerindian community of the Upper Mazaruni and upper Wenamu. There was no prior consultation or notification of the communities, and the communities found out about this agreement only when it was announced in the newspapers (UMADC, APA, and FPP 2000, 89). However, as a concession to the communities, the government did require that the company gain community consent before carrying out exploration work on titled lands (Colchester, La Rose, and James 2001).

Small-scale mining has also continued in the area, leading to a series of complaints by Amerindians. Heavy-handed police actions against resentful Amerindian residents have worsened relations between Amerindians and pork knockers, and despite halfhearted efforts by the GGMC to prevent miners from discharging soiled waters directly into the river, the practice continues unchecked (Colchester, La Rose, and James 2001). Indeed, recently, the mining commission has granted further small-scale mining permits in areas that the Amerindians claim overlap their titles.

The government's unilateral actions to permit mining in disputed areas have only stiffened the Amerindians' resolve to defend their lands. At the first Amerindian-organized National Conference of Amerindian Captains, held in April 1999, the following resolution was passed: "We demand that the Government stop granting concessions to mining and logging companies in and around Amerindian lands. And all mining and logging operations be suspended immediately, until all Amerindian land rights issues are settled" (quoted in UMADC, APA, and FPP 2000, 90).

REFERENCES

Amerindian Lands Commission. 1969. Report. Georgetown, Guyana.

Amerindian Peoples Association. 1994. Report on the Situation in the Upper Mazaruni. Georgetown, Guyana. Ms.

ARU. N.d.a. Background Paper on Amerindian Population and Health. Georgetown, Guyana: UNDP Consultation on Indigenous Peoples.

———.b. Background Paper on Mining and Amerindians. Georgetown, Guyana: UNDP Consultation on Indigenous Peoples.

———.c. Background Paper on Forestry and Amerindians. Georgetown, Guyana: UNDP Consultation on Indigenous Peoples.

———.d. Background Paper on Amerindian Land Issues. Georgetown, Guyana: UNDP Consultation on Indigenous Peoples.

Arvelo-Jimenez, Nelly. 1971. *Political Relations in a Tribal Society*. Ithaca, N.Y.: Cornell Univ., Latin America Studies Program, No. 31.

Benjamin, Anna, and Laureen Pierre. 1995. Review of Legislation in Relation to Land, Forestry and Mining. Annex I in *Report of the UNDP Consultation on Indigenous Peoples and National Development held at Beterverwagting Guyana on February 14–15, 1995*, ed. Janette Forte. Georgetown, Guyana: Amerindian Research Unit.

Bennett, Gordon, Audrey Butt Colson, and Stuart Wavell. 1978. *The Damned*. London: Survival International.

Bodley, John. 1982. *Victims of Progress*: Mountain View, Calif.: Mayfield.

Burnett, D. Graham. 2000. *Masters of All They Surveyed: Exploration, Geography and a British El Dorado*. Chicago: Univ. of Chicago Press.

Butt Colson, Audrey. 1960. The Birth of a Religion: The Origins of a Semi-Christian Religion among the Akawaio. *Journal of the Royal Anthropological Institute* 90(1): 66–106.

———. 1973. Inter-tribal Trade in the Guiana Highlands. *Antropologica* 34: 1–70.

———. 1983. National Development and the Upper Mazaruni Akawaio and Pemon. Ms.

———. 1983–1984. The Spatial Component in the Political Structure of the Carib Speakers of the Guiana Highlands: Kapon and Pemon. *Antropologica* 59–62: 73–124.

Cleary, David. 1990. *Anatomy of the Amazon Gold Rush*. London: Macmillan.

Colchester, Marcus. 1991. Sacking Guyana. *Multinational Monitor*, September: 8–14.

———. 1994. Malaysian Loggers Come out of the Woodwork. World Rainforest Movement. Ms.

———. 1997. *Guyana: Fragile Frontier. Loggers, Miners and Forest Peoples*. London: World Rainforest Movement and Latin America Bureau.

Colchester, Marcus, ed. 2001. *A Survey of Indigenous Land Tenure*. A Report for the Land Tenure Service of the Food and Agriculture Organisation, Rome.

Colchester, Marcus, Jean La Rose, and Kid James. 2001. *Mining and Amerindians in Guyana*. Georgetown, Guyana and Ottawa: Amerindian Peoples Association and the North-South Institute of Canada.

Coppens, Walter. 1971. Las Relaciones Comerciales de los Yekuana del Canza. Paragua. *Antropologica* 30: 28–59.
Daly, Vere T. 1975. *A Short History of the Guyanese People*. London: Macmillan.
Ferguson, James. 1994. *The Anti-Politics Machine. "Development," Depoliticization, and Bureaucratic Power in Lesotho*. Minneapolis: Univ. of Minnesota Press.
Forte, Janette, ed. 1994. *Proceedings of the Amirang. National Conference of Amerindian Representatives: Amerindians in Tomorrow's Guyana*, 11–14 April. Georgetown, Guyana: Amerindian Research Unit, Univ. of Guyana.
———, ed. 1995. *Situation Analysis of Indigenous Use of the Forest with Emphasis on Region 1.* Georgetown, Guyana: Univ. of Guyana Amerindian Research Unit.
Fox, Desrey, and George K. Danns. 1993. *The Indigenous Condition in Guyana: A Situation Analysis of the Mabura Great Falls Community*. Georgetown, Guyana: Univ. of Guyana.
Gadgil, Madhav, and Ramachandra Guha. 1992. *This Fissured Land. An Ecological History of India*. Oxford: Oxford Univ. Press.
Henley, Paul. 1982. *The Panare: Tradition and Change on the Amazonian Frontier*. New Haven, Conn.: Yale Univ. Press.
Henningsgaard, William. 1981. The Akawaio, the Upper Mazaruni Hydroelectric Project and National Development in Guyana. Harvard: Cultural Survival Occasional Paper No. 4.
Kaplan, Joanna. 1975. *The Piaroa*. Oxford: Clarendon.
Kloos, Peter. 1971. *The Maroni River Caribs of Surinam*. Assen, the Netherlands: Van Gorcum.
MacMillan, Gordon. 1995. *At the End of the Rainbow? Gold, Land and People in the Brazilian Amazon*. London: Earthscan.
Menezes, M. N. 1977. *British Policy towards the Amerindian in British Guiana, 1903–1873*. Oxford: Clarendon.
Moody, Roger. 1994. The Ugly Canadian. Robert Friedland and the Poisoning of the Americas. *Multinational Monitor* November: 21–23.
Myers, Iris. 1993. The Makushi of the Guiana–Brazilian Frontier in 1944: A Study of Culture Contact. *Antropologica* 80: 3–99.
PPP-Civic Manifesto. 1992. *Time for Change. Time to Rebuild.*
Riviére, Peter. 1969. *Marriage among the Trio*. Oxford: Clarendon.
———. 1984. *Individual and Society in Guiana: A Comparative Study of Amerindian Social Organization*. Cambridge: Cambridge Univ. Press.
———. 1995. *Absent-Minded Imperialism. Britain and the Expansion of Empire in Nineteenth-century Brazil.* London and New York: Tauris Academic Studies, I. B. Tauris Publishers.
Sassoon, Meredith. 1993. Guyana: Minerals and the Environment: Working Paper for the National Environment Action Plan. Ms.
Seggar, W. H. 1954. Some Aspects of Development of a Remote Interior District. *Timehri* 33: 30–40.
UMADC, APA, and FPP. 2000. *Indigenous Peoples, Land Rights and Mining in the Upper Mazaruni. A Report by the Upper Mazaruni District Council, the Amerindian Peoples Association of Guyana and the Forest Peoples Programme*. Nijmegen, the Netherlands: Global Law Association.

Whitehead, Neil L. 1988. *Lords of the Tiger Spirit. A History of the Caribs in Colonial Venezuela and Guyana, 1498–1820*. Dordrecht, the Netherlands: Foris Publications.

Winichakul, Thongchai. 1993. *Siam Mapped: A History of a Geo-body of a Nation*. Chiang Mai, Thailand: Silkworm Books.

World Bank. 1993. *Guyana: Private Sector Development*. Washington, D.C.: World Bank.

12

Ye'kuana Mapping Project

Peter Poole

In the absence of an effective legal framework or a serious government commitment to negotiate recognized title to their traditional territory, fifteen Ye'kuana communities in the upper Orinoco river basin of Venezuela have adopted a strategy aimed at inducing such negotiations by a preemptive demarcation of their lands.

The mapping was a collaborative effort involving Ye'kuana ground teams and financial-technical support from Canada. Once the boundary had been demarcated and delineated on a geographically correct map, the communities expanded the project to map Ye'kuana names, resources, and places and are now contemplating a further phase: the preparation of an integrated management plan for the future of their lands.

In addition, the project has quickened local interest in sustainable development and two local projects have begun. These extra phases were not initially contemplated by the communities but seem to have been precipitated by the success of the demarcation phase and facilitated by the training and technology process required for the mapping.

This chapter describes the mapping methodology that evolved for the project and goes on to describe the expanded activities that the mapping played a role in precipitating. Finally, I look at the Ye'kuana project in relation to other indigenous mapping efforts and to mainstream conservation.

BACKGROUND

Territory and Community

There are 2.2 million hectares of demarcated Ye'kuana territory, located in Venezuela's state of Amazonas, and fifteen Ye'kuana communities, whose combined population is thought to be around twenty-three hundred people, are participating in this project.

The Ye'kuana landscape is characteristic of the Guyana Shield. In the north, massive plateaus and outcrops rise above upland rainforest. In the south, humid lowlands are found alongside the Orinoco River. The forested areas have not yet been seriously affected by logging, commercial fishing is limited to the Orinoco, and mining is theoretically prohibited. Nonetheless, illegal mining is progressively affecting Ye'kuana in the form of malaria contracted when villagers travel to the regional logistics center, La Esmeralda.

Although the physical impacts of industrial-scale resource development within Ye'kuana territory are minimal at present, this could change swiftly and radically if the national government elects to subject Amazonas to development on the Brazilian model. This has happened once already as a result of activities by the parastatal Corporacion Venezolana de Guayana (CVG) in Bolivar State. For a recent election campaign, CVG disseminated to the public a map depicting a future Amazonas transformed by industrial infrastructure (Colchester 1993).

Ye'kuana depend heavily on forest resources for building materials, canoes, food, and medicines. Until recently, villages would move every few years, but now there is a tendency to consolidate around schools, transport, and energy facilities. This has caused local fishing intensity to increase. Families are now obliged to either travel farther to develop new garden plots or to shorten the fallow period for older gardens. Conscious of these trends, communities are seeking to resolve these local problems by devising alternative strategies for future settlements and the logistics of resource utilization.

A local problem of considerable concern to the communities is the rate at which family life is changing, as children spend more time in community schools and parents spend more time traveling to Puerto Ayacucho for short-term labor. The Ye'kuana feel that there *should* be ways to use the large resource base accessible to them in such a way as to create a local economy that would keep families together. A settlement of the land issue is seen as an essential step in reversing this trend toward reduced family cohesion.

National Parks and Biosphere Reserves

About two-thirds of traditional Ye'kuana territory falls within Duida-Marahuaca National Park. So far, relations between the communities and the national parks agency have not been constructive. The park was established without local consultation. After two field seasons of residence, national park staff declined to live any longer within the community and left their Culebra office for Caracas. When applying for a license for ecotourism, the community-based group Empressa Waana was told that it would not automatically obtain one, even though other tourist operators run regular tours in the park. Ye'kuana were offended when a parks field team landed its helicopter on their sacred mountain, Marahuaca, which is forbidden to Ye'kuanas. They find the rules on traditional resource use to be capricious. The park boundary, originally limited to the 1,000-meter contour, was without explanation, lowered to the 300-meter contour, encompassing areas regularly used for gardening, hunting, and gathering. Yet even this 300-meter contour rule cannot be enforced because the current topographic maps depict contours only at 250 and 500 meters.

Understandably, these experiences have not disposed the affected communities to look favorably upon the national park. However, the picture is more ambiguous and complex at the institutional level. Duida-Marahuaca National Park is but one of a complex of conservation and protected areas, including forest and hydraulic reserves, that have been recently designated within the state. The largest is the Reserva de Biosfera Orinoco-Casiquiare. Collectively, these belong to the 55 percent of Amazonas that is defined as ABRAE (Areas Bajo Regimen de Administration Especial), areas administered by special decree (Colchester 1993).

Throughout Amazonia, relations between parks and resident communities have always been at best ambivalent. Industrial resource exploitation may be prohibited but indigenous settlement and resource uses may also be excluded or circumscribed to the extent that these activities are traditional. The Biosphere Reserve idea was conceived in the 1970s as a means of accommodating a complex of conservation areas, harmonized by buffer zones: strict nature reserves, national parks, traditional land-use areas, and so forth. Biosphere Reserves do not categorically prohibit human settlement and resource use; they only require that it be "sustainable." Thus there may be scope for Ye'kuana to request changes in designation, consistent with their traditional practice, or to use such designated protected areas to forestall the industrial-scale resource development that they ostensibly prohibit.

Municipalization of Amazonas State

In the early 1990s steps were taken to make the State of Amazonas into a municipality. Indigenous communities were apprehensive about this on the grounds that it could preempt settlement of outstanding land-tenure issues. In 1994 the Organizacion Regional de los Pueblos de Amazonas (ORPIA) filed against the process on grounds that there had been no consultation with indigenous communities. The Supreme Court finally heard the case in December 1996 and ruled for ORPIA, giving them ninety days in which to devise an alternative legal regime. Toward that end, ORPIA organized extensive community consultations throughout Amazonas early in 1997. One of the options discussed during these meetings was the possibility of ethnic municipalities—a possibility opposed by many nonindigenous people and interest groups in the state.

Legal Status of Ye'kuana Territory

In Venezuela there is no legal framework, specific to indigenous peoples, within which to negotiate recognition of ancestral land rights. The existing law, applied by the National Institute for Agrarian Reform, categorizes indigenous peoples along with rural peasants, qualified to obtain title to small patches of forest, so long as they convert these for agricultural purposes. During the 1960s, as part of its Conquest of the South program, the government offered communities legal title to small patches of their traditional lands. Those communities that elected to join the program were given Provisional Titles of Possession—promissory notes that have yet to be honored.

CHRONICLE

Early Discussions

In 1993 with support from the GAIA Foundation, a series of community assemblies were convened to discuss the issue. Otro Futuro, a Caracas-based nongovernmental organization (NGO), was asked to commission a lawyer to research and prepare a brief. Eventually, the lawyer reported to assembled community representatives that there was virtually no law available to them. Instead, he could do no more than counsel a "political act."

With little prospect of building a strong legal case and in the absence of a legal framework for negotiations, the Ye'kuana decided upon a preemptive political strategy. They would unilaterally demarcate their lands, support this by their historical account, and present the result to the government, along with whatever legal arguments they could muster.

Project Support

Shortly after that meeting, in July 1993, Simeone Jimenez, from Culebra, and Nelly Arvelo-Jimenez attended a workshop on indigenous peoples and conservation sponsored by IUCN–Zuni, New Mexico. The Local Earth Observation (LEO) Project and the Environmental Division of the Assembly of First Nations (AFN) were asked to help in gaining external support.

This support was later gained from the Environment and Development Support Programme (EDSP) of the Canadian International Development Agency (CIDA). The funding strategy included emphasis on the project as one in which a northern-based indigenous people's organization assumed the responsibility to deliver development assistance to a southern-based indigenous group, a currently popular idea among donors.

Phase I

In February 1994 representatives from the fifteen Ye'kuana communities met for ten days with Otro Futuro, AFN, and LEO in Culebra. They first decided on the demarcation method: to cut trails from the villages to strategic entry points to Ye'kuana territory and to then cut twenty or more thirty-meter-diameter circles to mark those points. Intervening boundary markers were either rivers or straight lines. To accomplish this, they formed six teams, of thirty men and women each, that would cover agreed border segments in two months.

In response to donor guidelines calling for 25 percent cash or in-kind contributions from participants, the Ye'kuana then estimated their sweat-equity (twelve thousand days) and food contribution at sixty thousand dollars, based on replacement costs for food and labor at Puerto Ayacucho. This Ye'kuana contribution was in fact 20 percent more than the fifty thousand dollars provided by CIDA and EDSP.

The LEO Project was asked to make a "white man's map" (explicated as the kind with straight lines and numbers) of the boundary that would be presented to the government. A year later, the fifteen communities had cut trails to the boundaries of their lands and carved thirty-meter circles at critical entry points to their lands. A light aircraft was used to locate the circles and geocode their positions with a handheld global positioning system (GPS) receiver.

In Ottawa three versions of the map were produced: three thousand copies for distribution to each Ye'kuana, several glossy enlargements for officials, and fifty 1:250,000 scale no-name work maps with all place names deleted save those of the communities (map 12.1). This phase of the map production was accomplished using a standard graphics program rather than geographic information system (GIS) software.

Phase II

With the demarcation phase completed according to plan, CIDA and EDSP agreed to support a subsequent phase. In this, the work maps are being used by the communities to map Ye'kuana names for streams and places, their traditional resources, and the places that are special for spiritual reasons. Table 12.1 shows the provisional legend worked out during the March 1997 GPS training session.

The mapping is about what people do as much as what they know. The Ye'kuana take the position that knowledge in the form of named places and

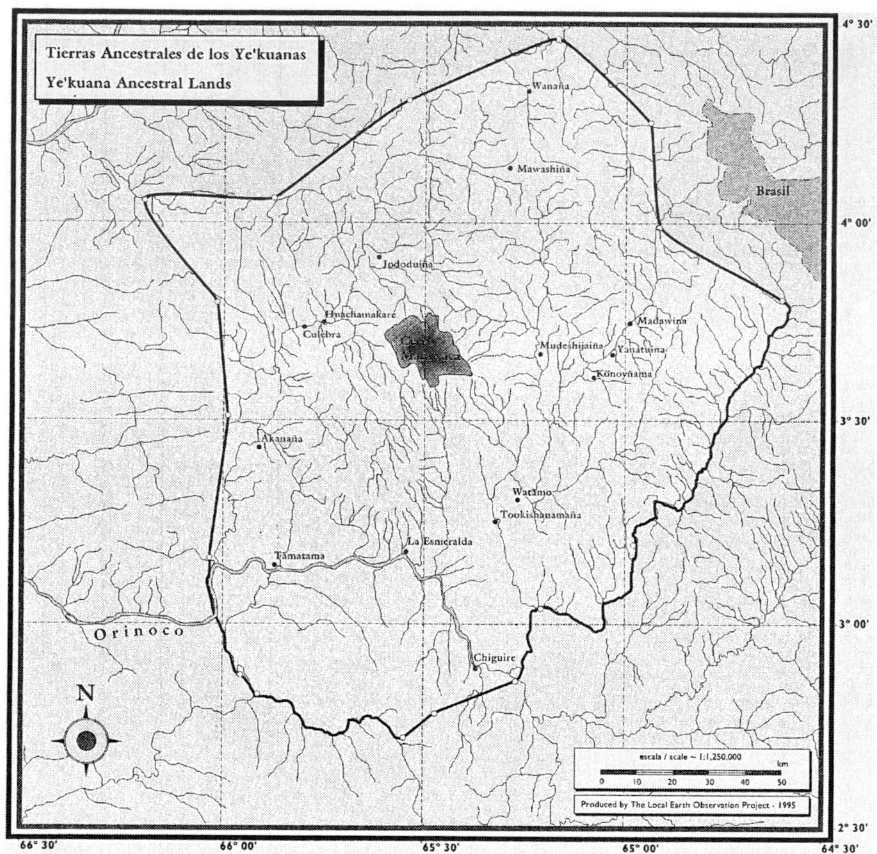

Map 12.1 1995 Project Map of Ye'kuana Ancestral Lands

resources indicates regular use of the land, which is in turn tantamount to ownership. This employs an argument that has been used elsewhere in its reverse mode: to deny indigenous ownership of resources.

When deployed by mining interests during the Nunavut negotiations, this argument held that Inuit do not qualify for ownership on the grounds that they lack the technical capacity to divine the presence of mineral resources or to mine them; they could not own them because they could not know them. The mineral companies qualify for ownership by virtue of their capacity both to know where minerals are and to exploit these resources.

The Grand Council of the Crees demonstrated the importance not only of using the land but of being able tc prove that use in their case against the hydro project James Bay II. The Cree disputed the claim that the land to be flooded was unoccupied with heavily documented evidence—tabular, carto-

Table 12.1 Ye'kuana Knowledge and Resources Map: Provisional Legend

Ye'kuana	**Spanish**	**English**
shodu	*raudal*	rapids
joo	*montana*	mountain
ama	*trocha*	trail
tunacaca	*cano*	stream
dhantado	*isla*	island
taju	*piedra*	rocks
iija	*pozo*	pond
wa'shadi	*tapir o danto*	tapir
kana	*peces*	fish
wata	*puerto*	landing
munuwaca wotatojo		hunting camp
cudieda ditojo		canoe-building camp
audaja jatado		garden camp
ma amaaja	*campamento turista*	tourist camp
audaja	*conuco*	garden
audaja	*conuco*	new
audaja	*conuco*	active
audaja	*conuco*	fallow
tadaude dheedo	*piedras para rallo*	stones for manioc grater
toncoi	*sebucan*	material for manioc squeezer
curiera	*caura o curiara*	canoe wood
cudeata	*cerbontana*	blowpipe material
wowa	*cesta mujeres*	women's basket material
jena	*canalete*	paddle material
amoi	*sagrado*	sacred
maka	*zanado*	high malaria risk

Seven Kinds of Palm

Ye'kuana	**Spanish**
kujaka	*macanilla*
madamachigui	*chiqui*
waaju	*manaca*
washi	*temiche*
kujedi	*seje chiquito*
kudai	*seje grande*
maijaduiwaru	*waru*

SPECIAL AREAS

Special areas of known abundance are to act as reservoirs within which no one would be allowed to hunt.

Zona reserva fauna
Zona reserva de los aves birds

graphic, and computerized—of the intensive and extensive land-based activities of the Cree communities in the twenty years following the James Bay I land settlement. The records had been accumulated in a GIS as part of the Cree Hunter Support Programme, funded with compensation monies from that settlement.

The Ye'kuana are aware of this, and one community at least is planning on its next visit to maintain its boundary circle to establish a camp and garden nearby. This demarcation strategy, to show evidence of use at strategic entry points by cutting a *manga*, was used by the Awa in the early 1980s in demarcating the Awa Ethnic Forest Reserve in Ecuador.

The knowledge mapping is intended to serve two purposes: to reinforce their negotiating position and to gather and share the information needed to plan a Ye'kuana future. This in turn will lead to the final phase of the project: creation of a long-term environmental protection and sustainability plan, designed to feature in their negotiations as evidence that they are capable of managing such a large territory.

The results of phase II will be depicted on a single map of 1:250,000 scale that encompasses Ye'kuana territory on a sheet of roughly one square meter.

Phase III

Once the mapping of names and resources is complete, the Ye'kuana plan to map out their ideas about the future in the form of long-term sustainable resource development plan. Elements of the plan and map discussed so far include:

- conservation of resources close to communities
- inventory of plant uses
- domestication of new plant varieties
- location of protected habitats
- future renewable energy resources
- potential new village and camp sites
- location and control of tourism

The Ye'kuana are conscious of how ten thousand hectares per person might be portrayed by opposing interests to the Venezuelan public, and they are taking steps to convince both the public and officialdom that they are best qualified to look after their territory. When a project coordinator, Simeone Jimenez, had his seven minutes on Venezuelan national television, he used them to reassure viewers about Ye'kuana intentions. He referred to pressure from intrusions of *garimpeiro* gold-miners from Brazil, and he cited incursions of Colombian narcoguerrillas across the Orinoco—the most recent involving fourteen Venezuelans and their arsenal. He proposed that the public think of the Ye'kuana as guardians of the national forest patrimony, acting on their behalf.

LOCALIZING GEOMATIC TECHNOLOGY FOR MAPPING

Geomatics has emerged as a useful term to refer to a blend of traditional surveying and cartography with digital, imaging, navigation, and communications technologies. Technology for the project was selected according to its cost, simplicity, durability, ease of operation, energy consumption, and survivability in hot humid zones.

Conventional Topographic Maps and Satellite Imagery

The official maps available to the Ye'kuana are small scale (1:500,000) and show only major streams, communities, and some contour lines. At this scale, the 100-meter variability of the civilian GPS units is negligible, 0.2 millimeter.

An alternative would have been to use satellite imagery. But this presents drawbacks of its own: the imagery is expensive, rainforest imagery is often partially cloud covered, and specialized skills and equipment are needed to convert the image into a usable base map. Finally, it made sense to present the demarcated Ye'kuana territory on the official map, however inaccurate.

Global Positioning System

The GPS is a net of twenty-four satellites originally positioned for military purposes. A GPS receiver can indicate its own position (latitude and longitude) and can also be used to navigate to other positions. When taken along a trail or river, a GPS receiver will maintain a record of its track that can later be retrieved from the receiver's memory and entered into a computer.

GPS operations have two limitations. The first is that GPS receivers need sufficient exposure to the sky to lock on to a minimum of three satellites to calculate a position and will not function consistently under a dense forest canopy or when the canopy bordering a stream narrows to a certain point. The second limitation is imposed by the military authorities operating the GPS. The satellite signal accessible to civilian receivers is scrambled to reduce accuracy from a potential of about fifteen to twenty meters to one hundred meters. However, the U.S. Pentagon is under constant pressure to improve the accuracy of these receivers.

Even without this indulgence, advanced geomatics companies have already devised a method for improving positioning accuracy. This is known as differential GPS (D-GPS) and requires two receivers. One, the base unit, is placed at a site with known coordinates. The other, the rover unit, can be deployed at distances up to three hundred kilometers from the base unit.

When the rover unit is in use, the base unit records the minute fluctuations in the GPS satellite net. Afterward these are downloaded from the rover-unit track record, which improves the accuracy of the track-record positions to equal the known accuracy of the base-unit position. In many parts of North America, D-GPS accuracy can now be obtained without recourse to a second unit. For example, the U.S. Coast Guard monitors deviations in the satellite and broadcasts these on a signal that can be received by a simple radio receiver attached to the GPS unit, and this will correct its readings in real time.

Such a facility is contemplated for Caracas, and it is likely that D-GPS accuracy will be available to the Ye'kuana within a year. Equally likely, it is possible that civilian access will improve to the fifteen to twenty meter accuracy that handheld units are theoretically capable of. In either case, current trends indicate that Ye'kuana will enjoy increasing accuracy without comparable price increases. The GPS units now used by the Ye'kuana cost about two hundred dollars each. Their operating costs are negligible; they operate for twenty-four hours on four AA batteries.

Geographic Information Systems

A GIS is a powerful analytic technology capable of storing large volumes of geocoded data (data tagged with geographic coordinates) in the form of multiple layers. It is the digital equivalent of a set of overlying transparent maps. Data in each layer can be measured, manipulated, and compared with data from other layers. GISs can create three-dimensional models of landscapes and inspect them from all angles.

Until a few years ago, most of the GISs available were complex and expensive and required sophisticated workstations and the attention of full-time and fully trained operators who needed to be in regular communication with the GIS producer.

Now, lower-cost systems are available that are suitable for mapmaking and are compatible with desktop and laptop computers. These cannot perform complex data analyses, but they can store large volumes of data in layers and compile maps from these.

Despite this, many GIS users have gone into technological overload. It was recently estimated that 80 percent of the GISs acquired by First Nations resource groups in Canada were not operating to capacity, for one reason or another: systems were too complex for local needs, systems didn't perform as the user manual promised, operator skills were inadequate, manufacturer support was lacking, or consumer education or preparation was insufficient.

A Biodiversity Support Program survey of more than sixty projects in which indigenous groups used geomatics suggested that the main local information need was for maps, not complex interrogations of information layers

(Poole 1995). There are several computer-based mapping systems that rate low in GIS prestige but are potentially well suited to most local needs.

However, advanced GISs are proving useful at the association level and have been put to effective use by many tribal resource groups in the western United States—Apache, Zuni, Yakima, and Navajo—for the management of reserve lands and in transactions with neighboring resource agencies. It has been put to similar uses following land settlements in northern Canada. Following the James Bay Agreement, Makivik generated the first of these GIS databases, for Nunavik. The GIS installation now being established by Inuit for Nunavut is as capable as are most academic or agency systems.

One imperative affects all GISs: the initial GIS base map, to which all subsequent layers must fit, must be geographically exact. In North America this is not a problem, because digitized versions of the familiar 1:50,000 scale topographic maps are available to use as the base layer and can be interfaced with any GIS. But such digitized maps are not usually available elsewhere. In this case we were obliged to manually digitize 1:500,000 maps, which we had already confirmed to be inaccurate to several kilometers.

Amerindian Peoples Association Mapping Project in Guyana

An effective series of local community mapping projects in Central America (Chapin, Gonzalez, and Threlkeld 1995) have relied on community-based field-workers, who use interviews and sketch maps on blank paper for initial data gathering and then work with staff from cartographic agencies to transfer field data to topographic maps.

The Amerindian Peoples Association (APA) Mapping Project uses a similar method for data gathering but has developed a different approach in the final mapping of the data. The data are placed on maps derived from existing topographic coverage but depicting only those features relevant to the exercise; thus the working base map compiled for the APA project showed only the drainage pattern, communities, lines of longitude and latitude, and as a background line, the boundaries of village lands assigned in 1991. This no-name map is similar to the Ye'kuana boundary map.

The APA base map excluded the names and the contour lines. At the specified scale of 1:100,000, contour lines on the base map would simply have been too congested to allow the placement of the Amerindian data. The 1:50,000 topographic map series for Guyana was produced in the 1970s and is geographically accurate. However, the original color plates for printing these maps have been allowed to deteriorate, and the maps are now available only in blurred black and white copies, several generations from the originals and stretched by repeated copying.

The area covered by the APA mapping team used seventeen 1:50,000 topographic map sheets. The 1:100,000 working base map covers 150-by-150 centimeters, printed in two halves. The team had two options at their disposal for presenting their data for computer-mapping: it could be placed on the base map or on the topographic maps. Initially, they chose the base map; it is easier to read and handle. But as they became more accustomed to reading the topographic maps, the team elected to place their field data directly upon these maps. These along with the GPS-coded field logs comprise the basic data set used for compiling the final map on a computer.

By June 1996, three months into the data gathering, it became clear that the team was collecting far more data than expected. Early estimates of GPS observations were that they would number from eight hundred to twelve hundred; the final number is between four thousand and five thousand. To accommodate these greater numbers and to set up a database for the long term, it was decided to change from the current program, Adobe Illustrator, to an entry-level GIS, Map Maker.

This transition proved to be difficult, because of software failure or its incompatibility with the format that the APA data were then in. This problem was aggravated by an obvious difference between the original cartographic system employed in the 1:50,000 topographic maps and those that the GIS could accommodate.

In January 1997 the data were converted to another GIS, ArcView 3. Initially, this worked well, although the program has certain structural limitations. ArcView favors the analysis of existing data sets rather than the incorporation of new data sets and creative cartography. Its large reservoir of legend symbols is exclusively oriented toward business, municipal, or military affairs. Contrary to the assertion in the manual and despite hours on the company's telephone help line, it will not accept scanned versions of the legend symbols drawn by the Ye'kuana to represent the legend features listed in table 12.1.

Despite this, about half the data set was entered over several weeks. Then, in the course of routine manipulations, the file of mapped names was corrupted. The software producer, Environmental Systems Research Institute, diagnosed the problem but could not resolve it. The symbols file then became corrupted.

In the face of these setbacks, it was decided that rather than reconstituting what had been saved to that point, it was preferable to revert to another layout program, a new version of CorelDRAW 7, which promised to be compatible with the formatting of the APA data. The results proved accurate, and the layout method was learned in a day. One hundred computer hours were required to map the data set of four thousand to five thousand names and symbols.

There are several advantages to using such layout software rather than GIS-specific software. The program is more robust and easier to use, and it has greater versatility in manipulating the appearance of the final map. Moreover, the original legend symbols devised by the APA mapping team could be drawn in the map legend.

The principal advantage of GIS—the precision of geocoded data—can be enjoyed only if a precise digital database is accessible. Geocoded field data are then positioned automatically once entered in the GIS. Where the digital base is imprecise, a final edit is required to correctly place the data. Such an edit is also needed when compiling maps with a layout program, but the results here are superior.

In cases where is it possible to obtain a well-mapped drainage system, it is possible to circumvent the problems posed by inaccurate GIS base maps. Field data are still gathered with GPS but the data are used as a form of data logging and storing rather than precise positioning. The GPS-based data collected by the APA team are oriented along rivers, and all that is needed when entering data into CorelDRAW 7 is to exactly place the name or symbol in relation to others.

As a result of this experience with the APA, the Ye'kuana mapping methodology will compare both approaches. A digital ArcView database will be maintained, and a comparable CorelDRAW 7 data compilation will run in parallel.

Map Production

Map production is done using either an expensive large-format plotter or by using a regular printer to produce the map in sections, or tiles. For the Ye'kuana project, the territory base map was first stored in ArcView 3, on a color laptop, and then printed locally on a portable color printer. This was used to print out color tile maps from geocoded data collected along the rivers, to locally demonstrate the entire information-generation process, from data to map.

Localizing Geomatic Technology

Problems in the mapping process have been related to software rather than hardware. In operational terms, the equipment demonstrated in Culebra proved sufficient to gather local data, analyze it, compile maps and reports, and print them. Using solar power, this full process was demonstrated at the community level. A storage cabinet and gel-based method for humidity control are being tested by the Ye'kuana. However, GIS technology will not be left in the community until users are trained and a communication link is established for operator support.

Ye'kuana Approach to Mapmaking

Venezuela does not have 1:50,000 topographic maps of the kind that are used by the APA mapping team for plotting field data. In the absence of these, the Ye'kuana were left with two choices: to use blank paper or working base maps derived from the existing, small-scale 1:500,000 coverage. A GIS-produced base map was derived by manually digitizing 1:500,000 topographic maps into ArcView 3. From this, a series of local base maps for the Culebra area were printed at a scale of 1:50,000, showing only the drainage patterns, the contours, and the communities.

For the first field exercise, the mapping teams traveled by river from Culebra to Huachamacare. They were not given the 1:50,000 work maps, only a blank coordinate-grid map of the area at the same scale. Upstream, the teams were asked to take GPS readings at each significant bend in the Cunacunuma River and to make a general sketch of the river course as they progressed. Downstream, they were asked to take GPS readings for any feature or name that they wished to map.

Afterward, the teams created an original map by plotting the Cunacunuma River course on the blank coordinate-grid map and then plotted the features. They subsequently plotted the same GPS data on the 1:50,000 work map, which displayed the Cunacunuma River course as depicted on the 1:500,000 maps.

There were immediately obvious discrepancies between the two versions: the GPS-based river course was consistently displaced by up to two kilometers—significantly beyond the predictable GPS error of one hundred meters. As with many GIS base map problems, it was impossible to discover whether the differences reflected inconsistencies in the map projections used or the accuracy of the data used in the 1:500,000 maps.

The Ye'kuana then had two choices: compromise or correction. That is, to fudge GPS readings to fit the most likely corresponding position on the river course as shown on the official map or to insist on a corrected river alignment as indicated by their GPS readings. The compromise choice would not necessarily dilute the potency of the maps as negotiating material, because official negotiators would not have access to the improved GPS data.

To insist on a corrected river course would, in the final map, introduce discontinuities at the points where tributary streams flow into the surveyed river. Unless all tributaries were also surveyed by the Ye'kuana, the final map would appear confused, or else another kind of fudging would be needed to reconnect the tributaries.

Faced with a choice between the compromised but proper-looking map and the accurate but unfinished-looking map, the Ye'kuana at first elected to produce the accurate version. Later this decision was amended to one where compromise maps, consistent with official cartography, would be produced to support negotiations, and the communities would reserve the GPS-correct data for their own purposes.

To do this, the teams will first gather field data using GPS and blank sheets of paper marked only with lines of latitude and longitude. They will produce

GPS-based sketch maps of the river course and trails surveyed, together with the locations of the features recorded with GPS.

The mappers will then transfer these features from the sketch maps to the 1:50,000 work maps. Because these are derived from the base map now entered into the computer, final plotting will reflect more accurately the positioning of features by the team. This exercise in transfer—from sketch map to work map—will also equip the Ye'kuana mappers to later undertake final map compilation on the computer.

Projected Results of Phase III

- A 1:250,000 territory map will be built up from four ArcView 3 or CorelDRAW 7 layers, including physical map (rivers, contours, mountains, rapids, and so on), human map (communities, camps, trails, boundaries, and so on), and traditional-resources map (fish, palms, woods, and so on).
- A future-prospects map will include energy, resources, tourism, and so on.
- Community maps will be as detailed as possible, showing local gardens and resources, layout, and some demographics. They will be shown as large-scale inserts around the margins of the territory.
- The legend was discussed at length, in terms of symbols, detail, and relation to map scale. A freehand list of legend features was drawn up in Ye'kuana, Spanish, and English (see table 12.1) and provisional symbols were depicted. These will be reviewed in relation to ArcView capacities.

EXPANDED EFFECTS

Expanded Interests and Activities

In the three years since the inception of this project, progress on the legal side seems to have stagnated, whereas the communities have become progressively more engaged and proficient in its mapping elements. Initially compelled to rely on outside help to produce a "white man's map," the Ye'kuana have since developed the capacity to detect and rectify positional errors in the official maps of their territory and will soon be able to generate detailed local maps to internationally accepted standards of accuracy.

To that extent, the project has progressed well beyond the geomatic objectives of phase I: demarcation and a relatively simple map. Without abandoning their legal strategy, the Ye'kuana have equipped themselves to fashion a complementary strategy around the proposition that they are the people best qualified, by tradition, knowledge, intentions, and capacity, to look after their traditional territory.

The expanded interests and activities precipitated by the initial demarcation phase serve two purposes: to reinforce the Ye'kuana case for legal recognition of their lands and to address present social and economic issues confronting the communities. Quite apart from mapping, the project is increasingly being used as a medium for exploring new ways to utilize the traditional resource base. These are seen to have survival value and would probably continue even if the Ye'kuana case for their land were eventually to fail.

Although this local development trajectory was subsequent to the demarcation exercise, it would not have emerged without the five conditions described in the following being in place.

Community Engagement and Control

The maps are useful in their way, but equally valuable is the way that the *mapping process* has provided opportunities for communities and individuals to become directly engaged in generating the case for their land—to a depth that would not be possible were their case to be conducted by proxy—and to gradually assume command of the process. This was especially noticeable during the GPS training. The project came to be seen as more than a mapping exercise. It is a vehicle that could be redirected to work for them in addressing other local issues. Project continuity is valued on its own account; to signify its interest, the three communities of Culebra, Akanana, and Huachamacare are combining their resources to construct a building to house the project in Culebra.

Technical Capacity Building

The local technical capacities being generated go beyond those needed to reach its initial objective. After the recent training, a group of twelve to fourteen people, representing three neighboring communities, have the competence needed to complete phase II. This expertise will be passed on to three or four more communities while the mapping is in progress.

During the GPS training, we were able in one day to demonstrate to community representatives the complete information cycle: gathering geocoded data on the river in the morning and entering it into a GIS and printing out a final map in the afternoon using laptops and solar power.

It will take one to two years to establish local mapmaking as a routine operation in Culebra. The Ye'kuana have made a start on this by experimenting with humidity-control methods to keep equipment dry through the rains. The results will be incorporated into the project house, which is to be built in 1997.

Intercommunity Relations

At the meeting to start the demarcation project, early in 1994, the first few hours were devoted to discussions on how the process had drawn together communities that had been out of contact for more than thirty years. People expressed the view that this renewed solidarity was worth preserving, whatever the outcome of the project.

This is reflected in the composition of the project maps. Although communities accepted local responsibilities for demarcation and they have agreed among themselves on the limits of community lands with respect to each other, there is no interest in placing community boundaries on any of the project maps. Not only might these precipitate dispute in the future, but it would compartmentalize the process by which the maps are made. This collective approach implies an obligation to ensure contributions from all communities.

However, not all communities have maintained this momentum. There is concern about three small, remote communities in the upper Padamo that have not participated in activities since the demarcation was completed. These communities did not take part in either of the two training sessions. Those that did, the villages along the Cunacunuma, have since decided to complete the knowledge map of the Cunacunuma watershed independently and disseminate the results to these other communities, with an invitation to rejoin the process.

Safeguarding Indigenous Knowledge

Two IUCN publications (Posey and Dutfield 1996; Posey 1996) present exhaustive accounts of various manifestations of the "indigenous knowledge issue." These fall loosely into two opposing categories. First are those cases where outside interests want to obtain or exploit indigenous knowledge in one of its manifestations, exemplified by the attentions of medical industries and the activities of bioprospectors. Second are those cases where outside interests ignore, discount, or delete indigenous knowledge, exemplified by disputes between biologists and hunters over the impacts of hunting or the abundance of fish, whales, and deer.

In dealing with indigenous knowledge issues of the first category, that of appropriation, the authors consider two courses of action open to knowledge holders: local and global. Local actions control or deny access to traditional knowledge at its source and are largely preventive. Global actions, on the other hand, aim for compensation or some other form of recourse to knowledge holders. Such actions are generally remedial and rely on advocacy in distant political or legal spaces.

The books propose to clarify these spaces by adopting the collective term *traditional resource rights* (TRR), which envisions the emergence or generation of a body of hard and soft law covering all the forms of external use of local resources and which provides for global protection and compensation and mechanisms for legal recourse. However intellectually and morally compelling this concept may be, the authors are not optimistic that it can galvanize equivalent political or legal force among global institutions.

The alternative, local strategy aims to protect knowledge at its source. Tactics range from "just don't tell anyone" to community-based mechanisms for gathering and consolidating knowledge and advising individuals on the issues and how to recognize and treat overtures from bioprospectors. Such a method requires a high degree of local cohesion, access to external information, and means to disseminate local information. The direction taken by the Ye'kuana should equip them to put the second strategy into effect. They have started a systematic collection of local plant uses, and they are developing means of external access to the information needed to identify and anticipate bioprospectors.

In many cases, knowledge conflicts of the second kind have been resolved by the indigenous protagonists assuming responsibilities for conducting their own surveys or for devising their own protective measures. These strategies have worked for Inupiut as regards bowhead whale hunting, for Inuit regarding caribou hunting, and for Yakima regarding forestry (Poole 1993). In those cases, communities have devised local institutions that take account of traditional knowledge but also make selective, pragmatic use of other knowledge systems. In action, in response to resource-management problems, they effect the integration of the two knowledge systems so often called for in conference halls. A similar, utilitarian interest in information is motivating Ye'kuana to develop a database and methodology that conserves traditional ecological knowledge in the most effective way possible: by using it.

Access to Information and Support

As the knowledge mapping has proceeded, community members are taking increasing advantage of the presumed contacts and information sources of the AFN and LEO group to pursue other lines of inquiry and of development of local interest, such as the possibility of minihydro and solar fruit dryers. Their support has also been enlisted in developing a proposal for a pilot project in ecological tourism.

Increasingly, the community is treating the project as a channel for gaining information and technical advice, a useful asset in the communities' continuing inquiries into ways of addressing their economic and social problems.

LARGER PERSPECTIVE

Continuity

There is a continuity between the content and purpose of the Ye'kuana mapping project and the methods that evolved in the Canadian north in the 1970s. In response to a readiness by government to negotiate, Inuit organizations in Arctic Quebec (Nunavik) and the Northwest Territories (Nunavut) evolved what have come to be called Land Use and Occupancy Studies, usually combining maps with supporting text.

These studies were the results of community-based research in the form of interviews with elders, hunters, and fishers. Each interview led to a personal or family map biography. Using traditional cartographical methods, these were then assembled to produce a comprehensive geographic statement about the areas and resources traditionally used by Inuit.

In northern Canada, negotiated land settlements have acted as a threshold beyond which the information and experience acquired through land-use and occupancy research is applied to a different set of problems and responsibilities, those precipitated by the settlement itself: resource inventories and management plans, environmental protection and impact management, and negotiations with external agencies.

As part of their strategy, the Ye'kuana communities have compressed this evolutionary process. They are already engaging in these kinds of postsettlement activities, combining evidence of historical occupancy and use with a demonstrated capacity to manage resources in the future.

Relations with Conservation Organizations

Given the large areas of land that may eventually revert to some measure of indigenous control, the question of whether conservation-oriented organizations and land-based peoples could ever work well together becomes significant. Recent estimates from the World Watch Institute (Durning, personal communication) suggest that the current round of land negotiations in the Americas may result in about 13 percent of the continent reverting to some measure of indigenous control, including one-third of the Amazon Basin. This is roughly double the area currently designated as protected areas in the Americas. Moreover, it is widely accepted that 70 to 80 percent of those protected areas are occupied by land-based peoples.

The realignment of external resource interests and agencies that confront indigenous peoples after a land settlement increasingly comes to resemble those regularly addressed by conservation organizations. In the early 1980s, this resemblance led some observers to postulate or advocate a "convergence" between the interests of land-based peoples and conservation groups

(Clad 1985, 45–62), one that could lead to "co-managed" projects and "integrated" indigenous knowledge.

This trend coincided with a growing recognition within the mainstream conservation community that a global strategy dominated by protected areas and species was reaching its limits and that the expansion of conservation practice into other areas would call for some form of accommodation with land-based peoples already living there. This has served to revive the Biosphere Reserve idea, moribund since its conception in the early 1970s. Out of necessity, global conservation is gradually becoming people centered.

Within the rhetoric of global conservation—the language of Agenda 21 and the Biodiversity Convention—indigenous people and their knowledge and practices occupy a prominent position. But this is rarely reflected in local realities. In South and Central America, relationships between protected-area authorities and local indigenous peoples are often strained by mutual distrust and ignorance. If conservationists and indigenous peoples are in fact converging, it appears to be solely regarding the last parts of the Americas to have so far escaped some form of designation.

The Ye'kuana project is one of many local efforts driven by the logic that the people who have always lived in a place are best placed to continue looking after it. In the absence of external pressures, traditional skills and practices would no doubt continue to accomplish this, but they would not necessarily enable the Ye'kuana to handle a constantly shifting array of new pressures. This project has demonstrated that certain technologies can be localized to contend with such contingencies. It is also evolving as a vehicle for the Ye'kuana to express their own specific ideas and agenda on environmental conservation.

The first sketches of the long-term management plan for the Culebra watershed set aside several protected areas for specific animals and plants. Most communities already apply local rules to deal with increased fishing intensities. The resource development plans envisioned by the Ye'kuana employ renewable energy and are properly sustainable. It is clear that they are not in principle opposed to environmental conservation, as that notion has evolved within industrialized societies. The issue is not so much what the rules say as it is who sets them.

REFERENCES

Chapin, M., N. Gonzalez, and B. Threlkeld. 1995. Participatory Land Use Mapping: Case Studies from Honduras and Panama. Centre for the Support of Native Lands. Ms.

Clad, J. C. 1985. Conservation and Indigenous Peoples: A Study of Convergent Interests. In *Culture and Conservation: The Human Dimension in Environmental*

Planning, ed. J. McNeely and D. C. Pitt. London: Croom Helm / International Union for the Conservation of Nature.

Colchester, M. 1993. *Trip Report: Venezuelan Amazonas, 1993*. Oxford: World Rainforest Movement, Forest Peoples Programme.

Poole, P. 1993. *Indigenous Agendas for Conservation: A Directory of Indigenous Peoples' Projects in Environmental Protection and Resource Management in the Americas*. Katlodeeche First Nation, Northwest Territories, Canada: Dene Cultural Institute.

———. 1995. *Indigenous Peoples, Mapping and Biodiversity Conservation: An Analysis of Current Activities and Opportunities for Applying Geomatics Technologies*. Washington, D.C.: Biodiversity Support Program.

Posey, D. A. 1996. *Traditional Resource Rights*. Gland, Switzerland: IUCN–The World Conservation Union.

Posey, D. A., and G. Dutfield. 1996. *Beyond Intellectual Property: Toward Traditional Resource Rights for Indigenous People and Local Communities*. Ottawa: International Development Research Centre.

13

Maps as Power Tools: Locating Communities in Space or Situating People and Ecologies in Place?

Dianne Rocheleau

> A whole history remains to be written of spaces . . . from the great strategies of geopolitics to the little tactics of habitat.
>
> —Michel Foucault 1980

> The master's tools will never dismantle the master's house.
>
> —Audre Lorde 1984

TO MAP, TO COUNTER-MAP, OR NOT TO MAP: IS THERE AN OPTION?

The current race to map the planet (and our places on it) from above and from below raises the question of how we can make maps that reflect the complex relations and separate realities of diverse peoples and ecologies in place. The new wave of community-based resource mapping and counter-mapping risks using the master's (blunt) tools to frame the infinite complexity of local places and peoples on the planet within a two-dimensional global grid of property rights and political authority. The making of a map by, with, or for any given local group is not just a map *against* power, it is an exercise *of* power by, within, and between units such as communities. Mapping projects also implicate cultural and environmental mapping advocates, including researchers, in complex relations of power between men and women within communities; between different occupational, ethnic, and class groups; between different communities; between local and larger systems; and between entire communities and those of us engaged in this activity as professionals, advocates, and academics. This does not suggest that we shrink from dealing with power but rather that we must address it with care and skill.

Like many others, I have fanned the flames and fueled the fire of participatory mapping (Rocheleau et al. 1989, 14–23; Rocheleau and Edmunds 1997; Slocum et al. 1995) and countermapping (Peluso 1995; Wood). Maps of the usual sort (property, terrain, and administrative maps) might at first glance seem an ideal way to portray the land and related resources of critical importance to people at risk of losing their living space, livelihoods, and way of life. Many of us have used such maps to make visible and legitimate the invisible and complex environmental needs, knowledge, uses, and claims of people disenfranchised and misrepresented in maps made by powerful state and commercial interests. In the absence of mapping initiatives in their *own* interests, many people may otherwise be evicted from their homes (whether ancestral or recently acquired) or they may find themselves transformed into squatters or refugees in their own homelands, trapped in a degraded and depleted environment under the control of state or corporate extractive industries. There is a clear case for maps that can buy time and secure people's spaces against outright seizure or ruin by powerful external interests or local elites. Mapping projects tied to land survey and land-tenure reform can also provide new resources with legal and practical protection for people who would otherwise be landless or live as trespassers, their very homes and livelihoods criminalized (Peluso 1992; Lynch, this volume).

However, I am troubled by some elements of the recent rush to locate everyone and everything, once and for all, on simple maps that project complex and separate realities onto a single two-dimensional surface. This leaves people, their resources, their homes, and their habitats fixed in the Cartesian grid, what I like to call the iron grid of Descartes, reduced to a two-dimensional picture that, in any given place, can only "see" and display one thing at a time on a flat surface (Roth 2003).

If there is a basic assumption that runs silent and deep in mapping practice, from the halls of the U.S. Defense Mapping Agency to the legal offices of environmental and social movement advocates (mapping in self-defense), it is the efficacy of the Cartesian grid, the system of x and y coordinates that allows us to depict the world in two dimensions on conventional maps. While this has proven invaluable for many purposes, the overreliance on the iron grid of Descartes reduces dynamic, complex, n-dimensional realities to static, simple, two-dimensional constructions. Cartesian space undergirds the dominant mapping practices that facilitate control of land and resources and that so often function as both the tools and the alibis of powerful political and commercial interests. Yet many efforts to protect particularly vulnerable people and places have globally positioned them on this grid, treating it as a bedrock of security in geopolitical, strategic space. These efforts often leave "the little tactics of habitat" (Foucault 1980, 149) out of the picture, off the map. Yet what is to be done? Should we abandon the global positioning system (GPS), the flat-earth map, and all hope of legitimating property, or do we resort to maps that reduce the separate realities of complex communities to two-dimensional tracts of real estate?

Pragmatically, one might argue that we could raise the same problems with the use of paper money, yet few of us would eschew daily use of the dollar, the pound, the euro, and the yen for our payments and purchases pending the transformation of an admittedly distorted and dysfunctional global economy. But many of us can and do question or oppose the use of this currency to represent the value of life (individual and collective, human and otherwise) or to price everything from cultures to creatures as shadow commodities in a marketplace model of the universe.

Mapping poses a similar challenge—to live with, and work within, a dominant framework to effect change. The experience of mapmaking and social movements suggests that advocates of community-based resource management should not abandon maps nor should we go blindly into the mapping enterprise. Rather, we need to be clear-eyed and open to multiple visions and ask ourselves a few basic questions: Who are we putting on the map? Who is left out? What are we putting on the map? Who is mapping? And whose mapping practice will we follow? What will result? Will we make one true map, the other map, or a variety of maps from different perspectives and for distinct purposes? Will our maps be mere tools of struggle, or will they also represent terrains of struggle and tools of ongoing negotiation, within the boundaries as well as beyond them?

We should ask several questions of any given map (our own or others): What is the authority and the power from which it derives and to which it appeals? What determines the standing of a given person or entity as a mapper and the legitimacy of the unit or entity mapped? Who does the mapper represent and with what mandate? Each map or mapping project may derive from a wide range of imperatives, from military to moral, including legal, economic, scientific, and identity (race, culture, class, gender, religion) criteria, with appeals ranging from history to necessity to destiny.

Mapping, including countermapping, is a practice, not a discovery or an exposition of a fixed reality. Mapping as an activity brings with it the power to name, to define, to locate, and to situate. The intent also matters, and mappers may harbor wishes to simplify, to obscure, or to clarify an issue in a given place. Maps can be made through presence, practice, words, paper, or code, but always they depend on and facilitate the exercise of and recognition of power. That power may be distant or proximate, and it may be deployed to invade, to evict, to exclude, to contain, to conserve, to remain, to resist, to protect, to persist, to extract, to retain, to transform, or to pass through. While maps alone are not sufficient to change the course of history and the shape of regional geographies, they are often necessary preconditions, and they can facilitate destructive, creative, and protective outcomes.

Maps are made by many kinds of actors, from empires (past, present, and emergent), states (from national to local), international agencies, commercial interests (from global to local), and environmentalists (from preservation to conservation) to nongovernmental organizations (NGOs) and social movements of all stripes (from forest protection and human-rights advocates to fundamentalist religious groups and racial supremacists). All or some of these groups may operate in isolation, competition, conflict, or solidarity. Maps are also inscribed on the face of the planet and in the imaginations of ordinary people through presence, through precedent, and by their daily practices in home, workplace, marketplace, sacred space, and habitat. Practice makes common-law property maps and simultaneously creates new ecological properties in the landscape, shaping the land and complex ecologies with signs of human life, social relations between people, and their connections to a multitude of beings-in-relation in place.

Bruno Latour (1987) refers to maps as immutable mobiles, an innovation that allowed European explorers to carry the knowledge of prior expeditions in a fixed form. The combination of GPS and geographic information system (GIS) technology has now produced infinitely mutable mobiles (multiple maps and digital data sets in GIS format) that still fix each data point and often a final map in Cartesian space through GPS (the immutable, mobilized eye). GIS embodies a potential liberation of maps from the fixity of a single paper image and implies the possibility of a recombinant freedom to restructure the data into a myriad of maps as contingent products. However, under current practice, most mappers employ the multiple images synthesized from the data sets to derive a final product that still purports to be the single best summary map or to represent an optimum solution derived from overlays. Despite current practice, the potential remains, however, to use GIS and even the apparent fixity of GPS within a paradigm that nests mapping in a broader context of conflict resolution and negotiation—across scales, from individual to international levels (Roth 2003; Rocheleau et al. 1995).

UNWRITTEN AND INVISIBLE MAPS

Not all maps appear on paper or computer screens. There are a number of ways to make maps and many distinct kinds of maps. Some of the most powerful are the seemingly private mental maps that derive from cultural and political terrains and often reflect highly uneven power relations. The maps we cannot see, the ones that lie behind the eyes, can hurt people and other living things—they can also nurture, inspire, and protect. Invisible maps are applied and simultaneously rewritten through the movement of large military forces, local militias, and laborers; through the application of state subsidies, punitive regulations, and corporate investments; and through employment practices, sacred rites, culturally significant artistic performances, and daily practices of resource use and management in particular places. Hugh Brody (1981) and Woodward and Lewis (1998) have made eminently clear to us the importance of dreams in the maps of indigenous peoples in the Arctic, the Australian outback, Africa, and the Pacific Islands. However, the dreams of generals, priests, fashion designers, corporate executives, stockholders, diamond miners, warlords, safari hunters, animal rights activists, television producers, and their audiences have also marked the maps of ecological properties etched on the face of the planet.

Sometimes the legends behind these mental maps are more powerful than the more openly acknowledged calculus of economic or biological inventories. This is particularly dramatic in the case of North American visions of Africa. Half a century of Tarzan movies and other popular films (*The African Queen, The Snows of Kilimanjaro*, *Out of Africa*, *Black Hawk Down*), decades of television news shows, and a continuing stream of wildlife documentaries has shaped the invisible maps of Africa behind the eyes of most people in the United States. These internalized maps affect their reading of the current armed clashes, environmental conflicts, cultural and artistic contributions, droughts, famines, coups, plagues, peace treaties, and economic success or failure of Africa. Emory Roe (1999) describes the creation of a fictional continent that he calls "Except Africa," defined by narratives of predestined failure and immunity to positive development trends elsewhere.

Exaggerated and polarized narratives of Africa's natural splendor and political carnage have etched a compelling (albeit fictional) picture in the popular imagination as well as in the minds of policy makers in North America. While the evidence may often contradict or at least complicate these mental maps, the broad outlines of the narrative have inscribed a very fixed focus on political hot spots in some countries (wars in Somalia, Liberia, Rwanda, Burundi, Zaire; AIDS in southern Africa; land clashes in Zimbabwe) and environmental riches at risk in others (the primate habitat in the forests of Madagascar and Uganda, the vast herds in the Rift Valley savannas of Kenya and Tanzania, the rainforests of west and central Africa, the elephants of Zimbabwe). International conservation and development policy and funding decisions reflect seemingly opposite but entwined stories of paradise at risk (for example, *The Sinking Ark*, by Norman Myers) and unfolding chaos (for example, "The Coming Anarchy," by Robert Kaplan).

In his evocative descriptions of a coming apocalypse, Robert Kaplan's deeply pessimistic (and arguably racist) vision of Africa extends to an explicit reference to maps, the dissolution of states as territorial entities, and a deep distrust of multiplicity and fluidity: "To appreciate fully the political and cartographic implications of postmodernism—an epoch of themeless juxtapositions, in which the classificatory grid of nation-states is going to be replaced by a jagged-glass pattern of city-states, shanty-states, nebulous and anarchic regionalisms—it is necessary to consider, finally, the whole question of war." In Kaplan's view, the blurring of boundaries and the acknowledgement of multiple claims is synonymous with apocalyptic scenarios of chaos, "barbarism," brutality, and warfare.

Interestingly enough, much of the brutality and warfare of the last century in Africa could just as easily be traced to the very fixed maps of colonial conquests and conflicts in the Victorian era. Half a century later, Cold War conflicts between superpowers played out in surrogate wars in nation-states carved and mapped into existence in the infamous scramble for Africa in 1918. Environmental, linguistic, and cultural maps (especially of valuable resources and the people attached to them) have played a role in these conflicts and also reflect the outcomes of various wars. Yet these very fixed maps, for better or for worse, originally derived from much broader and internalized invisible maps of local and global order. Whether we find that the mapped units are too fixed or not fixed enough, we still need to question and make visible the visions behind the eyes (including our own) that make and use maps.

VARIETY OF MAPS AS USUAL

Four types of maps are commonly used for political, military, and economic purposes: topographic (terrain) maps, thematic (special topic) maps,[1] cadastral maps denoting property boundaries, and political maps with a focus on administrative units. These all have in common the reduction of multidimensional realities to two-dimensional surfaces, each map with an emphasis on particular characteristics of the landscape, social relations, population distributions, natural resources, and infrastructure. Cartesian space is assumed in each of these, and in all but the topographic maps the emphasis is on the demarcation of boundaries between mutually exclusive categories, as, for example, forest and not-forest or between territories and parcels of land held by different owners or managed by different political authorities.

In thematic maps the categories are usually taken as a given, not as contested (a subject of give-and-take), and the end product is usually a single map, presented as an objective rendering of a selected category and its distribution over an area, by subunits. Such maps (for example, color-coded land-use types) are often used as the one true map for that particular topic in a given place. The interpretive function of the mapmaker is submerged, relative to the implied authority of the map itself. As map users we rarely question whether each point on the map has one and only one value as noted by the mapmaker. The official (legally recognized) maps of property and political and administrative units are usually constructed by national and local state agencies and, in some cases, international agencies or their private contractors. The creation of maps by state and commercial agencies has a history spanning millennia (Karrow 1997), but the invention and adoption of the Cartesian grid intersected with the rise of European colonialism to provide a major impetus to mapping of colonial territories over the last four hundred years (Demeritt 2001a, 2001b).

Colonial maps were used to name peoples and put them in their places, from the first Spanish and Portuguese linguistic and ethnographic maps of the Americas and the Vatican's lines of demarcation between Spanish and Portuguese domains, to the colonial boundaries established in the post–World War I scramble for Africa. In the British Colony of Kenya in east Africa, early twentieth-century thematic maps reflected zoning of colonial space through designation of native reserves, Crown lands, settler and commercial lands, and towns, as well as agrozones and ecozones. The latter were broad land-capability maps that determined the legal limits of designated areas for growing coffee, cotton, and other cash crops and named entire regions for the commercial crops they were meant to produce: tea, coffee, cotton, livestock, and millet. The most productive areas for commercial farming were alienated from farming and agropastoral and pastoral people and reallocated to European settlers, resulting in a correspondence between maps of agrozones and ecozones, property regimes, and ethnic groups. The colonial town plans (as in the case of Kitui in the semiarid southeastern district of Kenya) extended to the mapping of ethnic zones such as Swahili villages that set aside separate residential areas for merchants (Swahili-speaking coastal peoples or immigrants from South Asia), European settlers, and the Akamba (local Africans) in one provincial town.

Although the maps did not cause the separation—at regional or local levels—the dominant mapping practice both encouraged and entrenched zonal classification of crops, racial and ethnic groups, types of markets, and land-tenure categories in two-dimensional models of inclusion and exclusion. Many of these zones outlasted the colonial administrations that created them, and to this repertoire the newly independent states and international development agencies added maps of land-tenure reform (regional, local, and plot specific), combined with maps of drought, famine, productivity, population, desertification, deforestation, biodiversity and erosion of genetic resources, land-use intensification, and land degradation, as well as "environmental recovery" (Rocheleau et al. 1995).

In the colonial context, as well as in twentieth-century states in North America and Europe, even many seemingly neutral maps of soil type, rainfall, topography, or flora and fauna became the basis for derivative classification schemes such as land-capability maps. Depending on the political context, the latter can translate readily into exclusive or hierarchical zones of land use and management, with related regulation (and sometimes prohibition) of farming, forestry, livestock management, and residential use. The standard land-capability classification (LCC) used by the U.S. Soil Conservation Service groups land into eight categories, "according to its ability to support a range of crops on a long-term sustainable basis. The evaluation is based on the degree of limitation imposed on that land by a variety of physical factors which include erosion, soils, wetness and climate" (Helms 1992, 60–73).[2]

The classification is used to guide conservation and resource management as well as agricultural development. Land that is deemed capable of supporting commercial farming could also be used for forest (under conservation guidelines) but would be deemed by economic development analysts to be underutilized. By the same token, on land areas designated as forest, farming would not be allowed, because the classification allows less-intensive but not more-intensive uses than the designated category. Underutilization is allowed, though not encouraged, whereas overutilization is not allowed. The scale of mapping matters in this case, as well as the overall logic. For example, a class VIII designation would allow forest cover but not agriculture, even though small patches of highly productive and less fragile land within the area might be intensively cultivated by small farmers or gardeners without risk of land degradation.

The LCC and similar mapping and zoning schemes in many areas have created templates for land alienation based on high potential for commercial agriculture (zones of economic opportunity for colonial, state, or commercial interests) and, conversely, low potential for farming and high potential for conservation (Roth 2003; Vandergeest 1996, 2003; Lynch 1996). This system was centered on agricultural potential under a series of assumptions about technology and scale of production, as well as regionally specific conditions of climate and soil. In this case a counter-map is more about contesting the system of land evaluation rather than the specific lines on the maps themselves. The use of maps as power tools to demarcate fixed regions in two-dimensional space always carries a risk. As noted by Willems-Braun regarding the Pacific Coast and island forests of Canada, maps (two-dimensional maps) make nature visible and also make nature available to particular modes of economic and political (and scientific) calculus. The global positioning of regional and local resources, including land, in two-dimensional Cartesian space does not necessarily lead to destruction and displacement, but it does prepare them for legal designation as units of property (state, community, or private). This in turn renders them interchangeable and exchangeable in both global and local land and commodity markets.

During the 1980s and 1990s, international and national environmental interventions under the auspices of sustainable development increasingly shaped the landscapes and economies of people in contested forest and savanna regions (Schroeder 1993; Neumann 1995; Neumann and Schroeder 1995; Peluso 1995; Rangan 1995; Rocheleau and Ross 1995). Maps of ecological properties have been translated into global and national real estate in the form of parks, reserves, and target areas for conservation and reforestation programs or agricultural development and settlement (Lynch 1996; Rocheleau 1997). In particular, forest maps have often served as green umbrellas for land alienation by state timber and conservation interests. Forest maps in some cases have provided an alibi for de facto and de jure redistribution of land and resources projected through the lens of environmental and ecological maps. Reference to ecological value and its fragility, damage, and potential (intrinsic, commercial, utilitarian, and symbolic) can mask very different intentions by powerful state agencies and corporations within maps of reserves, settlements, and areas shared by multiple users.[3]

Likewise, land-tenure reform that both creates and maps fixed holdings at household scale among formerly mobile people can work against ecologically attuned land-use and production strategies and can eventually function more to contain than to enable smallholders. I still clearly remember being taught about the meaning of grids by a group of elders in Machakos District, Kenya, when I explained my concerns that land use was being homogenized across very distinct ecozones, from the slopes of the nearby range that rises three hundred meters to the valley below and the banks of the Athi River. I proposed the complicated ecological zoning map of my simplified dreams, that is, a map of locally diversified land use that would work from the comparative ecological advantage of each ecological niche at mesoscale, differentiated by slope, aspect, soil type, and access to water.

"That would have been the best way to [intensify farming]," they said, but "the survey has been here and these [little boxes on the grid] are all that we have." They noted that it could be done differently elsewhere, "but now, with separate small plots of private property, each family must have something to eat, some animals, and some cash crops. There is no room to leave a large part of the land in forest or bush or pasture. How can we do that when some children have no land to make a farm, to build a house? So we must each try to put everything useful that we can from the larger land[scapes] and fit it into our plots. That is what we can do now." The people in the group were quite aware that ecosystems are not scale neutral and that some species and some ecosystem functions cannot be replicated at plot scale, squeezed into small blocks in a forest farm mosaic, or a farm patchwork. The group invoked the example of Iveti, a place where people are very densely settled, packed into small plots where they have houses and gardens with small plots of tomatoes, onions, and cabbage and with no space for maize, beans, and pigeon peas. For some in the group this example represented a nightmare; for others, a constrained but promising dream of progress. For all of them it seemed the most likely outcome of current trends in this post-privatization, postcadastral-map landscape.

VARIETIES OF COUNTER-MAPS

We have abundant examples of official state or commercial maps and local counter-maps of contested spaces, in struggles ranging from culturally based land claims to citizen investigations of environmental contamination and health hazards, to terrains of deforestation and reforestation and refuges of biodiversity (Eghenter 2000; Dana 1998; authors in this volume). During the last two decades, dueling groups have brandished different maps with distinct, overlapping, and often conflicting claims. These close encounters between separate realities have often pitted glossy high-tech maps and land-use plans against locally produced sketches and testimony about long histories of access, use, knowledge, management, and cultural and religious significance of specific species and particular places. This dramatic contrast between formal and informal maps and modern versus traditional values has increasingly given way to glossy maps and sophisticated scientific and legal arguments (about ecology, ethics, identity, and tradition) on all sides. Nation-states, corporations, and many popular social movements now have access to electronic and software technologies (GIS, GPS, and remote-sensing imagery) as mapping power tools.

Counter-maps come in many forms (table 13.1); the presentation may be quite distinct from or parallel to official maps. Where the format is the same as official maps, the difference is in the mappers and their interpretations of the facts. Various kinds of contrasting or conflicting information may be presented, particularly with respect to claims of ownership, sovereignty, and land or resource use (actual or potential). In legal and policy forums, the object is often to portray the counter-map as the true map, as opposed to an erroneous or incomplete official map. Counter-maps can resemble official maps, with contested claims about the location of boundaries or the authority over various units pictured.

In addition to drawing different boundaries on cadastral and political maps or attributing authority and ownership of mapped territories to different groups, it is possible to develop more complex maps and mapping strategies (Roth 2002). To respond to the dominant narratives implicit in both mental maps and official maps of contested lands and resources, we can make visible the visions that guide them, forcing a discussion of the interests and

Table 13.1 The Varieties of Countermapping

1. Cadastral Maps
   With indigenous groups, communities, cross-cutting groups,* or households
   - to claim collective or communal property not yet surveyed
   - to contest boundaries and content of state surveys and maps
   - to contest boundaries and content of commercial surveys and maps
2. Political/Administrative Maps
   With indigenous groups or communities
   - to claim or clarify zones of authority for various local and regional entities
   - to clarify zones of common, public, and private property
   - to contest or clarify zones of authority claimed/mapped by nation-states
3. Thematic Maps
   With indigenous groups, communities, or cross-cutting groups
   - to contest the extent and distribution of categories in official maps
   - to map distributions of new categories that contradict prior maps
   - to map new categories and their juxtaposition with others already mapped
   - to compare the distinct maps of the same variables by different groups
4. Sketch Maps
   With indigenous groups, communities, cross-cutting groups, or households
   - to illustrate locations of significant local and regional features
   - to document co-occurrence of particular species, people, and artifacts
   - to illustrate patterns and placement of various elements in landscape
   - to illustrate the range of significant resources and their distribution
   - to illustrate the nesting of various features across different scales
   - to compare past, present, and future conditions in a given place or region
   - to create alternative scenarios of possible futures
5. GIS-Generated Geo-Referenced Maps of Land Use and Cover, Resources, Demography
   With indigenous groups, communities, cross-cutting groups, or households
   - to map evidence of use and occupancy from survey data
   - to overlay locations or distributions of cultural and ecological features
   - to overlay multiple claims to identify areas of conflict and competition
   - to document environmental threats through overlays of ecology and use
   - to identify alternate routes or sites for proposed developments
6. Integrated and Expanded GIS
   With indigenous groups, communities, cross-cutting groups, or households
   - to combine multimedia records** with geo-referenced maps
   - to combine qualitative and quantitative data on culture and ecology
   - to illustrate the range of circumstances within single categories of land use, land tenure, or ecological zones
   - to link voices of multiple and complex groups to landscape and land use
   - to link livelihood with landscape and land use in geo-referenced maps
   - to build scenarios in broadly intelligible formats
   - to enable informed negotiations through data analysis and mapping

Notes:
*Cross-cutting groups can include gender, ethnic group, race, class, religion, or occupation.
**Multimedia records could include digitized photographs; music or art relevant to specific places or types of features or categories of land; community or life histories in digitized versions of text, photo, audio, or video format; local expert knowledge in same formats; testimony relevant to land and resource claims, cultural status claims or stewardship claims; scanned versions of sketch maps; and alternative maps of landscape, land use, land condition, resources, ecology, and the distribution/subdivisions of authority, control, access, labor, and responsibility in various land units.

values at stake. In the case of LCC, a counter-map is more about contesting the system of land evaluation than about redrawing the specific lines on the maps themselves. We can also present revised thematic maps as counter-evidence, for example, about the distribution and relation of people, trees, crops, and wildlife. We can produce radically reversed thematic maps as counternarratives, that is, by changing and redefining the categories to be mapped. A group defending their rainforest home could present a map of homelessness and predicted evictions in juxtaposition to an official map of enterprise zones, parks, forest concessions, or other state and commercial designations. We might also create multiple local maps, pictures, and stories as an alternative narrative in both content and form.

TRAPS IN THE MAPS

Mapping by any group, for any purpose, can fall prey to unintended consequences, and counter-mappers will need to consider these traps to avoid them. As more groups rush to put themselves on the map, literally to position themselves for community-based resource management, it is crucial to explore and complicate the meaning and the practice of mapping. Maps derive from particular practices, within specific cultural, economic, and ecological contexts. While the mapping process can be fun, instructive, and may seem intrinsically liberating, the resulting maps can have serious and often distinct consequences for various groups of humans and other beings, as well as the rivers, oceans, coastlines, mountains, plains, soils, and the very air of their surroundings.

To make a place your own (in terms of legal rights to own, use, or sell and otherwise transfer it) may indeed be liberating and secure people's homes and whole ecosystems against commercial or state intervention. However, some mapping and even associated tenure-reform projects may be part of a larger process that lifts whole groups of people (one by one, household by household through the land market) off ancestral lands and into a state of homelessness. The same kind of process, in a different context, can also serve to make a new home for entire groups of landless and near-landless people, by constructing new community territories, one plot, one grid square at a time, through land-tenure reform.

In other cases, the mapping and registration of boundaries may strengthen some groups and disenfranchise others within preexisting communities. For example, in some cases land-tenure-reform maps can strengthen men's land rights through freehold title deeds to household lands and erase women's terrains of use and access rights in household plots and formerly common lands. One group's homemade map may secure their ancestral gathering and residential sites at the expense of a neighboring group's seasonal fishing and hunting grounds. Mapping individual property and administrative territories may be only one part of a process that allocates large areas of indigenous forest people's lands to industrial agriculture or mining. Such dramatic transformations of the regional landscape can, by default, banish many species from the area, change local livelihoods, pollute air and water, and modify local diet and nutrition.

When we study indigenous maps and territories we may make visible the metamap, the scaffolding or dreamlines of the mapping practice, yet when we take maps as power tools to the people, we do not seem to take the trouble to explore and understand the meaning of grids. Silent as well as spoken assumptions of the dominant mapping practice are embodied in topographic, cadastral (property survey), environmental, and political maps. For example, the mapping authority and criteria of many peoples derive from the standing of the land itself and other species or communities and the role of those elements in creating and maintaining them as a people (Woodward and Lewis 1998; Walker and Peters 2001; Rundstrom 1995). This contrasts with a logic that would map the same elements based on the authority of states, which appeals to the superiority of social construction of territory on a formless or disordered nature. It behooves us, when mapping, to become grid smart and to bring the same insights to participatory mapping projects.

Maps of land claims, whether official, counter-maps, or alternative forms, embody the fractal properties of power and the fractal powers of property. Good mapping may, but does not necessarily, lead to good results, and even good process may not lead to positive results for all concerned. Like most tools, maps may be mobilized in both creative or destructive acts of transformation; they can be wielded with either malice or compassion. And like any power tool (a chain saw, for example), computer-generated maps may yield better results with less labor, or they may wreak severe damage even through naive carelessness. To avoid cartographic chainsaw massacres we need to stop, look, listen, think, and then map carefully.

Several choices that usually occur by default may build in serious errors and render maps useless or even counterproductive:

- The scale of the map, if biased entirely toward villages or communities or watershed units, may conceal major differences within and between households or between age, gender, or occupational groups across households.
- Property survey maps, and especially regional land-claim maps, tend to demarcate external boundaries at the expense of attention to internal patterns, contents, and characteristics.
- Most mapping efforts tend to fix boundaries and features, rather than seeing them as floating, and therefore map their relation to each other or their current status, pattern, and location. The delineation of single

boundaries in areas where land use, tenure, and management actually overlap can lead to conflict between social groups that previously worked in cooperation.

- Mappers draw hard, firm lines around items and regional constructs that are permeable and malleable.
- Categories mapped are taken as given rather than as contested products of give-and-take.
- Maps tend to picture structures rather than processes, although processes of change can be mapped in thematic and isoplethic maps as well as alternative formats.
- Simple binary categories in thematic maps may also mask more than they reveal. Facile dichotomies such as forest and nonforest can lead to maps that distort the distribution of tree biodiversity, tree cover, and tree products in the landscape. In the case of Zambrana-Chacuey (see the case study later in this chapter), the highest number of forest tree species occurred in patio gardens (a woman's domain usually mapped as nonforest), and cocoa and coffee stands also sustained a diverse community of wild and domestic trees in combination.
- Land-use and land-cover designations in two-dimensional space, presented in either-or terms, also preclude the adequate and equitable representation of multiple and simultaneous uses, values, and claims by different groups based on gender, class, age, and other axes of identity and difference. The politics of affinity, or of contingent coalitions, are not readily represented in terms of mutually exclusive categories of land cover, land uses, and land users (see case study regarding gendered resource mapping).

  For example, some researchers have found that "mapping techniques that fix and simplify fluid and complex associations can become prescriptive. The lines on the map became the guideline for management and resource access between social groups, be they villages or households. In areas where formal land tenure is not yet recognized but is being negotiated, it is the static Cartesian map which frames future possibilities" (Roth 2003).

The resurgence of ethnic identity related to land and resource claims can serve multiple local or outside aims, and may develop in unpredictable ways, as noted in Thailand by Vandergeest (2003). In examples from Kenya, the politically promoted and manipulated ethnic clashes over land in the Rift Valley pitted pastoralists against farmers.[4] The recourse to historical precedent and ethnic identity also supported a politically motivated redistricting of parliamentary seats to serve the political ends of powerful rulers at that time. Ironically, the current land hunger and destitution of many Kenyan Maasai can be attributed to group ranching schemes hastily implemented in the 1970s and 1980s. The demarcation and titling of large group holdings ignored age, gender, and wealth differences as well as local norms of governance. Discord and dissent over inequitable and unsustainable land management led to subsequent subdivision and sale of private individual (household) plots. This left many people, particularly women, effectively homeless. Current efforts to map Maasai village land claims in Tanzania are encountering distinct but parallel problems and may result in containment and displacement rather than empowerment (Hodgson and Schroeder 2002).

Maps make seemingly simple statements that mask complex narratives of "where." To get our bearings and situate any given map and mapping project beyond the narrow confines of the flat-earth paradigm, we must ask a set of careful questions about the "why" of where, the "how" of where, and the "who" of where. Countermapping efforts can promote critical inventories of the multiple axes of identity and difference that variously join and separate people and shape their relations with landscapes and ecologies. If conducted internally these inventories could locally reposition the mapping practice as well as the issues and items on the map. By questioning categories such as ethnicity, race, class, gender locality, and organizational affiliation and using them to situate multiple maps, we can avoid the trap of an oversimplified map (whether it is an official map or counter-map) that can see only one thing at a time in a given place, from a single standpoint (Rocheleau 1997; Roth 2003).

MAPPING AND THE VARIETIES OF PARTICIPATION

The experiences and reflections of the various contributors to this volume pose several questions about our options and responsibilities in the practice of participatory mapping. Perhaps the most significant development in this field in the last decade has been the recognition that community-based mapping can be done well or poorly and that it matters (Mohamed and Ventura 2000; Poole 1995; McKinnon 2001). Beyond the mere presence or absence of participatory methods, the character and quality of participatory mapping can affect the well-being, even the survival, of people and ecosystems. There can be serious social, economic, and ecological consequences of badly done participatory research and mapping. Even good participatory process does not guarantee successful production, conservation, and empowerment outcomes. Just as with the choice of research designs within a more traditional set of options, the wrong approach—otherwise well implemented—can also lead to problems. Participatory mapping approaches are social technologies, and should be treated with all the ethical concern and care that we already urge for GIS, mapping-as-usual, mechanization, agrochemicals, and other technologies that can benefit or threaten the livelihoods and landscapes of rural people.

Researchers often try to resolve this by having people make the maps themselves. The participatory research and mapping literature is replete with examples of people making their own maps their own way or according to a suite of introduced methods, from sand paintings to clay models. However, the physical construction of maps and models by the people in the place being mapped will not necessarily circumvent the traps in the maps previously noted.

As one who has made maps with, about, and for people and has asked people to make sketches or felt-board maps in various contexts, I can recall several instances where people tried to replicate the official maps that they had already seen. When our jointly constructed pictorial sketch maps or their felt-board scenes were developed in what-if land-use games, they often provided more insights both to them and to me about questions of land use, property, ecology, and landscape change than did their more independent efforts to replicate conventional maps. In cases where people learn to do formal land surveys and maps with standard equipment for topographic and cadastral maps, that they do the labor does not inherently constitute a participatory mapping process.

Whether in official and formal mapping projects or in informal approaches, the mapping itself is part of a larger process, in which someone chooses from an array of possible processes and products to use specific methods and to produce particular kinds of maps. Whatever kind of mapping methods and agendas we bring to people, there is a real need to go beyond skills training to a broader education about maps, their meanings, and their consequences. We need to make clear the potential for using multiple methods and producing a diverse array of maps for different users, different purposes, and internal as well as external applications. The participants need a voice, if not controlling interest, in the choices of what purpose, what kind of map, what process, and what products in mapping initiatives.

Full participation requires clarity of purpose and meaning, the transparency of process in mapping, and the democratic negotiation of mapping process, categories, content, and outcomes among those affected. This still leaves us with the problem of which people constitute legitimate participants and the terms of their involvement.

VARIETIES OF PARTICIPATION IN MAPPING

Process

- Outside mappers enlist local people (communally or individually) as laborers or guides.

- Outside mappers enlist local people (communally or individually) as informants about the location and character of specific features already selected for mapping.
- Mappers from NGOs, governments, corporations, and international agencies consult with local people about the boundaries of particular types of territories and their importance to people.
- Social movements or local groups seek technical assistance with mapping for a specific purpose or to support broad claims of sovereignty, autonomy, or security of tenure.
- Mappers from various groups coordinate with social movements or local organizations to provide maps of features and categories specified by local groups but using standard maps.
- Mappers and local groups convene broad discussions with people-in-place to derive the categories and to design the structure for GIS. The two groups discuss the nature of communities, territories, resources, and the types of claims, values, and meanings that structure people's connections to each other, to other species, and to their physical environments.
- Mappers (or experts on land, land use, ecologies, rules of use, and practice) from the communities and the areas concerned confer with mappers from NGOs to consider the potential uses of maps in a given case and to develop a strategy of mapping, including a repertoire of mapping methods, and a way to derive and choose the relevant categories and formats for various sets of maps.

ORIGINS: WHO IS IN CHARGE? WHOSE IDEA?

- Outside initiatives to map for specialized outside interests (biodiversity maps to define parks, reserves, or genetic-prospecting areas; tourism-potential maps; or mineral-prospecting maps)
- Outside initiatives to map in the national interest (mapping for roads, ports, and other public infrastructure; cadastral maps of property; administrative maps of ethnic and political territories)
- Outside initiatives to map in the interest of local and regional people (cadastral maps and thematic maps of communal or individual property; mapping of sacred sites, ancestral claims, or cultural heritage sites; mapping of resource endowments used and needed by people in the region)
- Coordinated initiatives from outside and within a given region to survey and map particular properties, such as the mapping and monitoring of biodiversity in forests within extractive reserves in the Brazilian Amazon, conducted by national and international scientists from NGOs in

collaboration with national government agencies, grassroots social movements, and local communities
- Locally generated campaigns to map specific resources of intrinsic or strategic importance for maintaining the autonomy, integrity, or viability of particular communities, ethnic groups, or other associations connected to particular territories, landscapes, and ecologies

The key question here is whose objectives and visions are inscribed into whose worlds? And the corollary is how are these to be inscribed?

These questions of participation matter for countermapping, and suggest potential changes in process in territorial-mapping cases. For example, in the Upper Mazaruni land-claim map project, Marcus Colchester (1997, 25; this volume) notes that "intensive training workshops were held. . . . Trainees were taught about . . . compass points, . . . the meaning of grids." This very important and pioneering project still presents me with a persistent stream of questions. Did they really learn "the meaning of grids"? Why not include a serious discussion of the limitations of the two-dimensional, reductionist maps being prepared for the legal case? Can we question this paradigm and justify using it as one strategic tool, rather than stop at teaching them how to really make maps? Can such projects also explore other ways to make maps that protect the region and serve diverse local interests? Why not take advantage of prior work on indigenous cartographies in North America, Australia, and elsewhere that discusses the meanings embedded in spaces and places and the standing of other beings and place itself, beyond our usual understandings of community?

In cases where land claims rest on history, precedent, and ethnic identity (Colchester 1997, this volume; Herlihy and Knapp 2003), selectively participatory mapping may leave out competing claims by other (arguably legitimate) residents and resource users. It may also ignore the ambiguities of ethnic territory designations and the pitfalls of subdividing whole regions into private (community or individual) plots, with freehold title.

Land-claim and biodiversity projects could complement both simple property and biological inventory maps with more complex images, stories, and inventories to better represent the multiple claims within, and to better serve justice and equity objectives over the long-term. In the end, people will have to live with what is inside the boundary. They can neither inhabit nor defend an empty shell.

MULTIMAPS, ALTERNATIVE MAPS, AND ALTERNATIVES TO MAPS

Having reviewed the traps and potential for participatory mapping, there are many options for making counter-maps, alternative maps, and alternatives or complements to maps. To construct alternative maps that reflect the diversity of real people in real places, rather than the simple mirage of state and (sur)real estates, I suggest that mapping practice needs to work through a people's archive of experience, knowledge, and information (Rundstrom 1995; Brody 1981; Roth 2003). Ultimately, the maps produced should be situated within the multiple and overlapping realities of the people and places mapped and not vice versa.

It is possible to map the past, as many already do, and it is often at least as important to map the future. Likewise, we are often mapping what is there but it may be even more important to map what is desired, what is needed, what is missing, and what is possible (both good and bad). In many cases people are already excluded from important hunting, gathering, and agricultural areas and they may need to make the case for compensation (monetary or in-kind) if not restoration of the same lost areas and resources. Mapping what-if scenarios can also provide a sense of current trends and a range of alternative options. Creating scenarios of possible futures often begins and ends with maps of some sort, and the combination of topographic and cadastral maps, thematic maps, sketch maps, photographs, computer-generated maps, and stories can help to create the conditions for negotiations grounded in concrete imagery of people's livelihoods and landscapes.

Mapping plant and animal communities can be crucial to setting the terms for land use and management in any shared lands or in boundary zones where plants and animals may be affected by surrounding land users. People in any given place may value plant and animal species or assemblages as intrinsically important or as instrumentally significant for their products. Maps can reflect the composition as well as the condition of current flora and fauna (wild and domesticated) based on local classifications. For example, if people view a particular forest area as important and potentially rich in wildlife but currently degraded, each of those elements may have a bearing on land claims, access rights, custodial agreements with conservation interests, or claims against other users for damages inflicted. The combination of ecological biodiversity inventories with maps may also carry high strategic value, as local and regional communities seek to ally themselves with national and international conservation interests to limit or resist commercial development initiatives that threaten the cultural and ecological integrity of their area.

To demonstrate the complex realities of cohabitation between various elements of local communities, it may be useful to map the network of people, plants, animals, artifacts, physical features, and technologies and the way they are combined in a given place. This is crucial in cases with conditional or contingent rights of use and residency, such as those granted in extractive reserves in several rubber-tapping and forest-farming communities in the Amazon. Long-term leases are contingent on maintenance of a viable, healthy forest. Accurate and realistic maps of baseline conditions as well as desirable or acceptable future conditions can be crucial to develop fair and measurable criteria for monitoring and compliance. In the absence of clear criteria and illustrative maps, all signs of mechanization or progress in such places could be viewed by some as transgressions or all deviations from the ethnographic past might be read as betrayals of ecological stewardship. For example, Maasai people who live near the Ngorongoro Crater in Tanzania have been frequently arrested for farming, violating reserve rules, even when those farms are for subsistence purposes and confined to former cattle corrals, in effect a kind of intensive maize garden in a small patch within a broad expanse of parkland or savanna (Parkipuny, Ole, and Berger 1993, 113–31). The definition and mapping of baseline conditions and performance criteria for specific places could help to clarify the terms of multiple use in this and similar circumstances, where mapping of broad zones with inflexible rules has created unnecessary conflicts between conservationists and resident people.

Mapping can also focus on networks and flows, getting beyond the "edges and containers" bias, to highlight process and connectivity rather than separation and exclusion. Cadastral maps and political-administrative maps focus on the edges of the container and an insular entity within, when in fact the support processes and livelihoods of people depend more on the structure and function of complex combinations and exchanges, and flows and circulations within and between these units. Complex social networks link people to each other and to land. A legal framework that links households to land exclusively via title deeds in the name of one person—as a single point of control—is not necessarily meaningful or viable divorced from the broader social context. Functional territories of use, access, and management all need to be part of mapping to reconcile what goes on within and between mapped units, to give as much clarity to that as to the containers (shells) and categories of people, plants, animals, products, and uses associated with particular areas.

Mapping the separate realities of the many people and organizations with an interest in a given place can take two very different approaches. We can record multiple perspectives on the same place, in the same terms (i.e., make separate maps of the most and least important areas of the forest for each of three ethnic groups, or for men and women, and then overlay and note zones of convergence or conflict of value and competition or complementarity of use). Alternatively, we can use different media and categories to convey the distinct visions of a specific group or of several groups. For example, some of the figures in the next section put people, their homes, or other species at the center of maps and pictures of ecological networks. These kinds of images could provide a point of departure for negotiations over land and resource ownership and management.

MAPPING THE MULTIPLE POLITICAL ECOLOGIES OF HOME

When we speak of home and homeland, we often refer to some seamless, organic entity that flows naturally from a long association between a particular group of people, a place (as a sort of natural container), and the other species there. It is as if they were all there by some act of mutual destiny. Likewise, we often invoke specific ecological units as the natural home of a particular species or assemblage of species. However, home is perhaps more properly a verb, not a noun, because it is created through practice. It is embedded in relations between humans and other beings, within and across places in complex networks[5] that encompass humans and other beings and their things (technologies, artifacts) in relation to each other.

Social and ecological relations shape the landscape, both literally and metaphorically, and trace the territories of home, habitat, workplace, and marketplace within local space. They influence the making of local places and the places of people in local natures. Home is created and maintained by individuals, households, groups, cultures, states, and a host of plants and animals, as well as by biophysical elements (land, water, wind, fire) and technologies. These homes, in turn, form the centers of a multitude of nested and overlapping human ecologies, influenced by gender, class, age, occupation, locality, and political affiliations.

Two sets of maps from contrasting cultures, economies, and landscapes illustrate the importance and utility of careful attention to the nature of home, including internal differences in land and resource use and tenure. Figures 13.1 and 13.2 illustrate a number of options for gendered access to land and vegetation. In both cases it was necessary to map differences even within individual farms to accurately define widespread, common categories of nested resource use, control, and access. It is crucial to note that because these differences occur within farm and household lands they do not constitute mere details but rather form a foundational pattern repeated throughout the landscape. The same cases demonstrate that the map alone, with no background or interpretation, could be quite deceiving. For example, the gendered distribution of land, labor, and products, as well as responsibility, must be understood in terms of the ethics and logic that have created these arrangements and the extent to which these represent accommodations of institutions imposed from above. In both cases the plot now serves as the major legal instrument of attachment to land.

The farm sketch map of an Akamba family farm in Machakos District, Kenya, uses individual plots of private property, legally owned by the male head of household, as the focal unit for mapping gendered patterns of resource use and access (figures 13.3 and 13.4). The Akamba resisted legal demarcation of household lands as a process of displacement initiated from

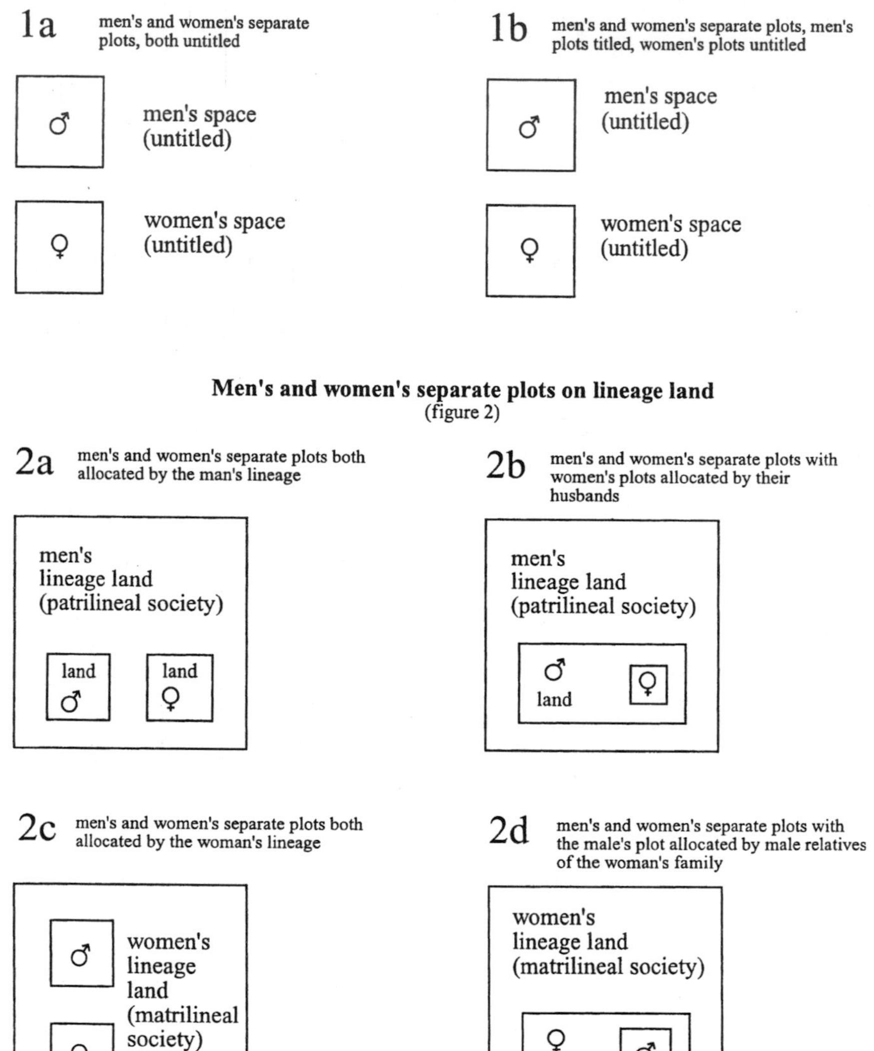

Figure 13.1 Gendered and Shared Use of Space in the Landscape

a women's access to products from a man's tree on individual plots

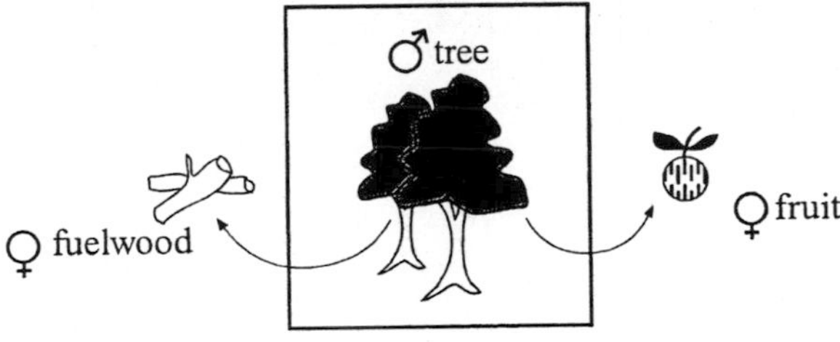

b women's access to products from a man's tree on common lands

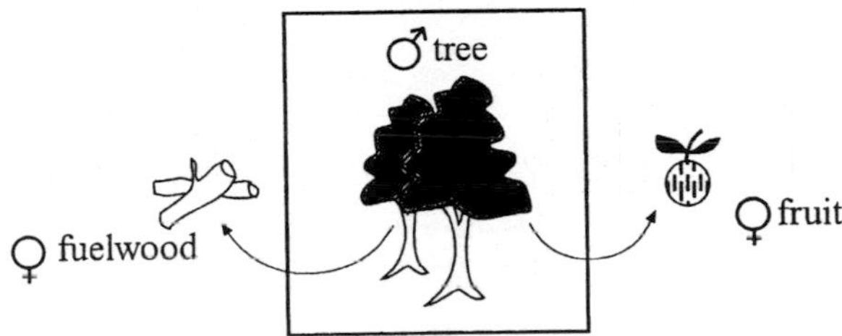

c men's and women's access to different products from common resources on common lands

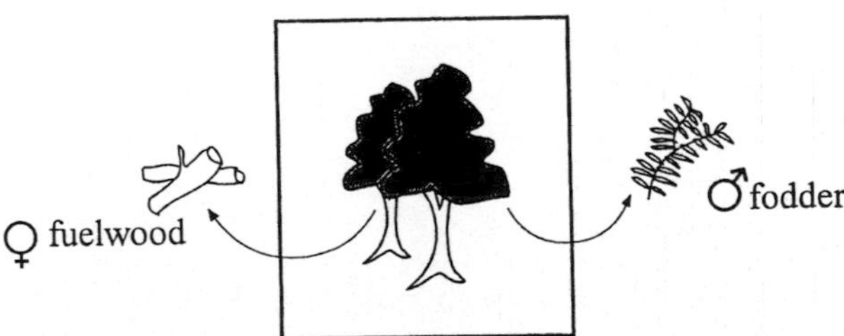

Figure 13.2 Gendered and Shared Access to Particular Products from Specific Resources

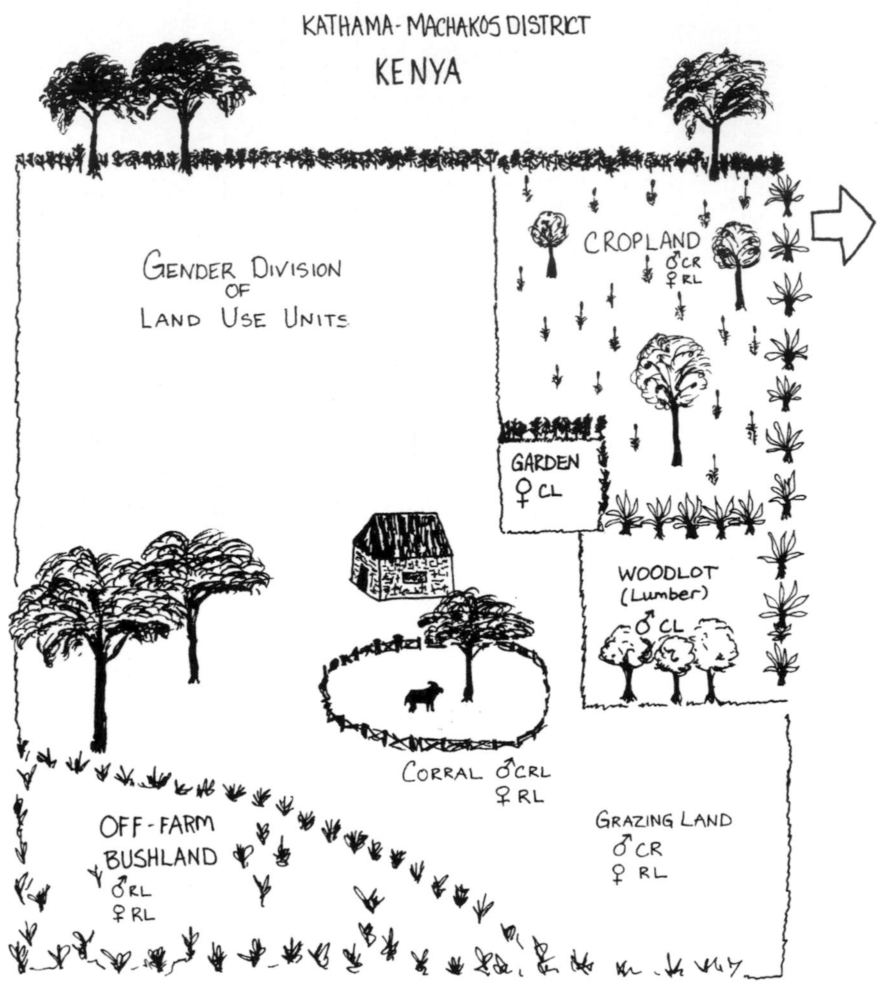

Figure 13.3 Gendered Domains in a Farm in Machakos District, Kenya—Land Use Units

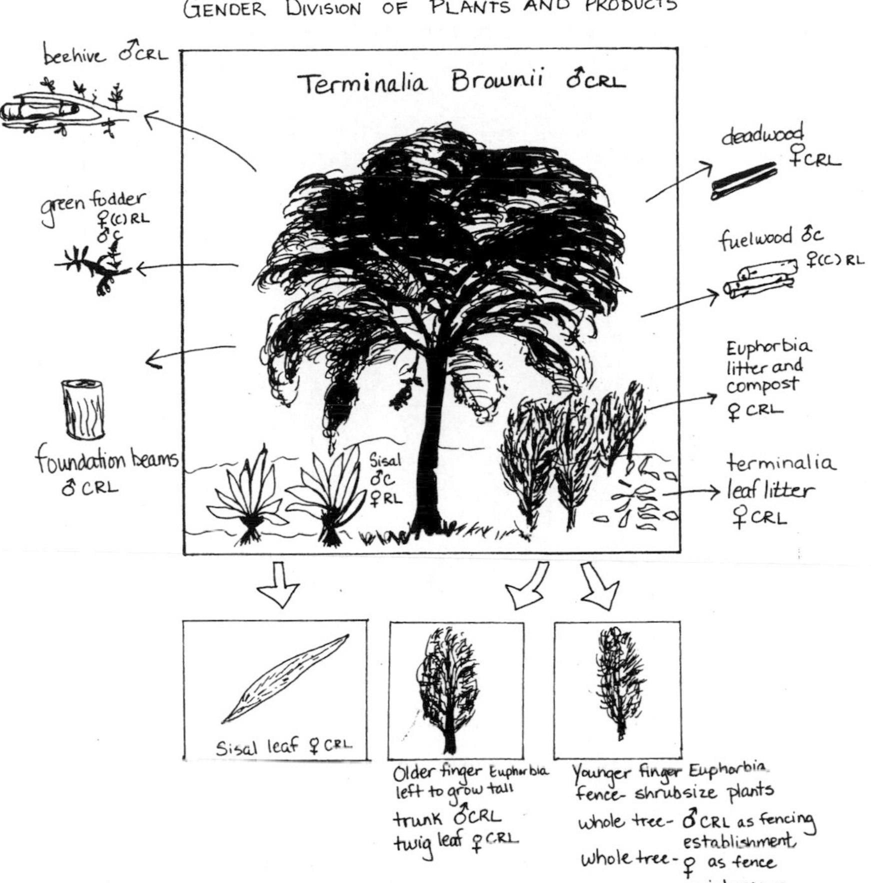

Figure 13.4 Gendered Domains in a Farm in Machakos District, Kenya—Plants and Products

above. A long-standing relationship to the locality and the region held people in place with each other and the land, but since the 1950s the primary legal instrument of attachment has been the set of lines that contains, literally, the household lands legally attributed to a male head of household. Throughout the dry lands of Machakos in the 1970s and 1980s, women as a group chose to ignore maps or to work around, over, and under the lines of existing official property maps, to remap terrains of access, production, and daily practice. They used women's self-help groups to re-create the commons through labor and resource exchange, quilting together a patchwork of shared resources from private plots imposed by the colonial and national governments and registered primarily in the names of individual men.

The gender map in figure 13.3 represents men and women as distinct land-user groups and thereby clarifies the intrahousehold division of control (C), responsibility (R), and labor (L) with respect to land, plant and animal resources, and their products on a farm in Machakos District, Kenya. The objective of this style of image is to present the rural landscape as a gendered domain of conflict, complementarity, and cooperation in resource use and management. In this case, the images are broken out into three scales, to depict the gender division and sharing of lands at household or farm scale; to illustrate the gendered use, access, and control of individual plants within a given plot; and to demonstrate the gendered subdivision of products from particular plants. In this case, the control over most land is vested in men, with the exception of the garden. However, the labor and the provision of products for the household are finely subdivided by gender at all scales, and control is allocated in far more complex ways when we consider plant and animal species and specific products.

In the case of Zambrana, in the Dominican Republic, the farm maps depict what constitutes a farm; what plants, animals, and artifacts are integral to different people's ecologies; which species occur in what patterns; and which species are used, managed, protected, and reproduced by whom (figures 13.5, 13.6, and 13.7). For the smallholder farmers of Zambrana, the land-tenure-reform process was a locus of liberation, leveraged from below. A large proportion of the smallholder farmers in the region gained their lands through a land-struggle campaign within a rural people's federation. People of this region purposely put themselves on the land-tenure-reform map and the forestry map in the terms of the state and the dominant legal framework. They bought time and created more space for themselves with new maps that made their own lives, landscapes, and claims visible and explicit in conventional maps through participation in tree and biodiversity surveys and mapping.

In Zambrana, the boundaries of the enabling regional community that fostered the very rich and diverse ecology of an agroforest were entirely outside the legal framework, whereas the household plots constituted the primary legal instrument to secure people's place in the world. On the other hand, for many women it was their marriage contract that secured their attachment to the land through these household plots.

In both places, putting women's and farm families' places, products, species, and ecologies on the landscape and biodiversity map can increase their legitimacy as environmental, economic, and political actors. In Kathama (Machakos District) the women's group leaders noted the presence of their planted (and mature) trees in the landscape as visible proof of women's contributions to conservation and development at local, regional, and national levels. Maps and photographs of their achievements as resource managers and agroforesters could carry this evidence beyond local communities into

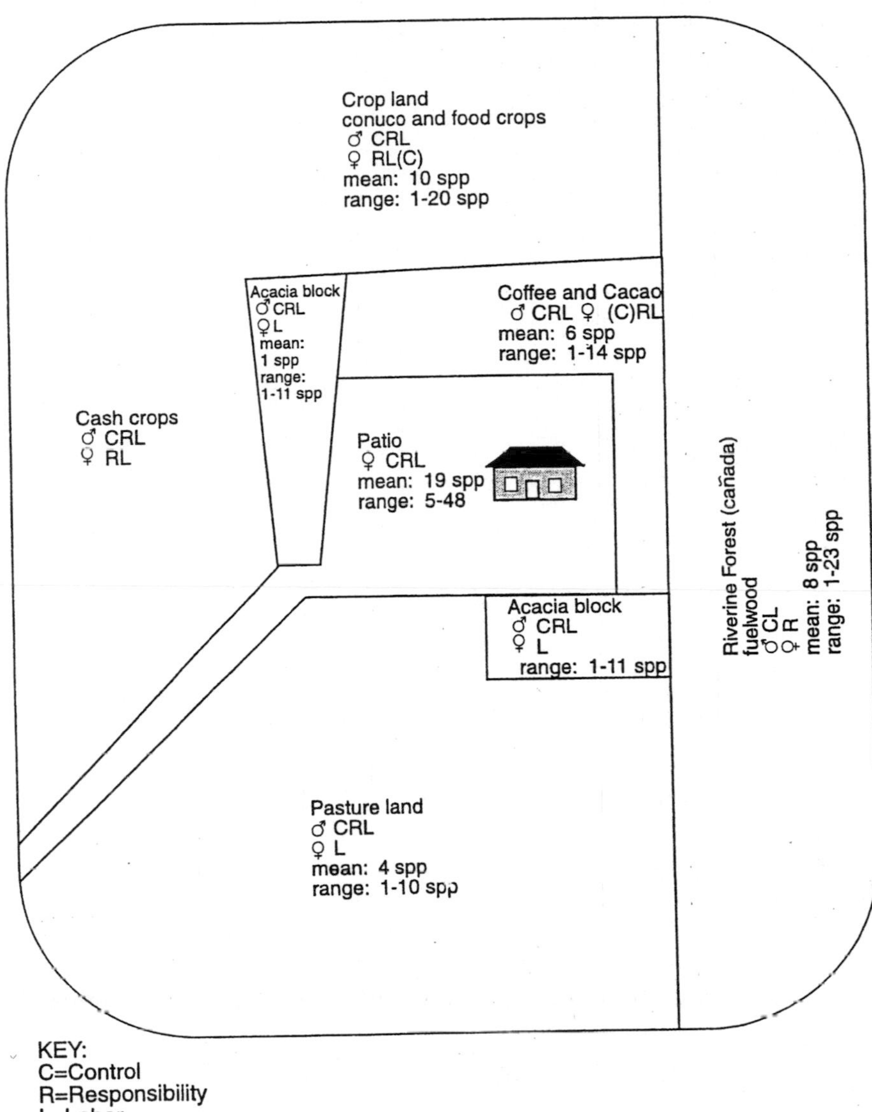

Figure 13.5 Sketch-Map of Crop and Tree Biodiversity in Gendered Domains on the Farm

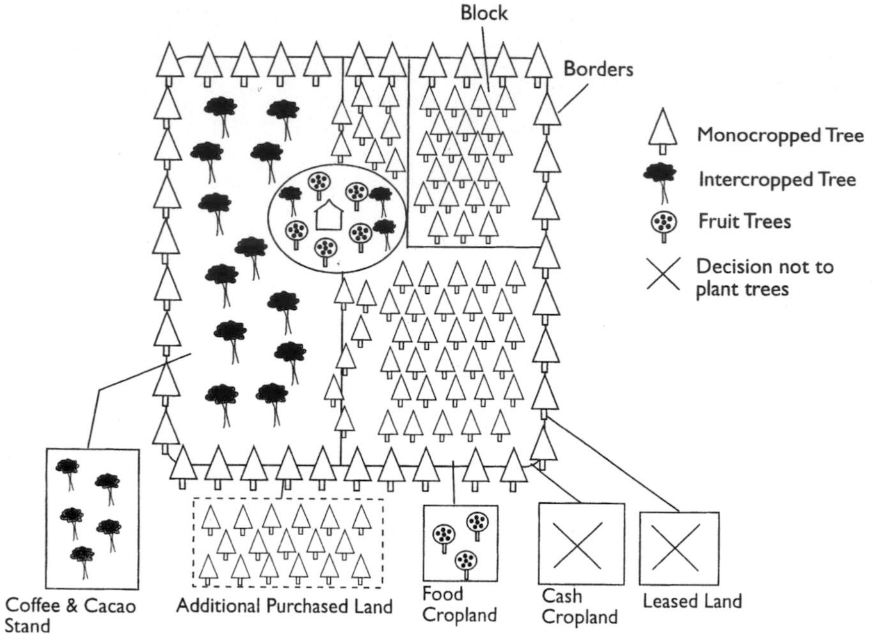

Figure 13.6 Spatial Planting Niches in Rafael and Maria's Farm: 50 Tareas

regional and national policy deliberations. In the case of Zambrana, the maps of on-farm biodiversity reinforced women's participation, decision making, and access to benefits in a commercial timber enterprise as well as a biodiversity project. The maps and diagrams also served to legitimate entire rural communities as resource stewards rather than agents of deforestation, as they had previously been portrayed by the forestry department.

Whether in forest, pastoral, or farming communities, people's access to land and resources previously depended on their ability to thrive on the land, to use or to take and defend their space or resources. Now people depend increasingly on their ability to earn, to pay for food, for land, and for transportation. Future land and resource access may also depend on people's ability to stage a continual, cascading retreat into whatever is left that is unwanted and unaffected (directly) by current extractive enterprises. Alternatively—and more optimistically—rural people and the popular social movements that represent and support them may succeed by getting grid smart from local to planetary scales. They may put themselves on the map of powerful interests as allies, often by playing the culture or environment cards across the fields of geopolitical strategy (Brosius 1999). However, the use of strategic environmental and cultural maps does not preclude the little tactics of habitat. The success of the broad-brush maps still depends heavily

Figure 13.7 Hernando and Marta's Farm

on the careful negotiation of daily practice and social relations within the boundaries and between the lines of zonal and cadastral maps.

In some cases bounded properties on the grid can serve primarily as a protective fortification from external intervention and alienation of land or resources. To balance the local effects of two-dimensional property maps we can then make multiple maps and contingent summary maps, viewed as negotiated settlements with clear conditions, caveats, and identifiable constituencies as signatories.

Grid-smart action could take the form of embracing land-tenure reform to get back a larger turf, one grid square at a time (as in the farming communities of Zambrana). However, the boundary lines of private plots can provide the fissures for future alienation of land. Grid-smart responses can also take the form of resisting privatization and embracing ethnic territories (as described by Poole and Colchester, this volume) or extractive reserves, as in Amazonia. In the dry lands of Machakos in the 1980s, the women simply rewove the commons over and under the property lines in the cadastral maps, through daily practices of connection and reciprocity in social networks embedded in landscapes. The little tactics of grid-locked habitat can take people in several directions. All of these examples bring us back to multimapping and the potential of GIS and other new technologies, as well as expanded imagination, to broaden the scope of community-based mapping beyond our current repertoire of counter-maps, sketch maps, and property claims.

NEW FRONTIERS IN MULTIMAPPING: ALTERNATIVE MAPS AND ALTERNATIVES TO MAPS

New technologies have often been decried by community-based groups and social movements as oppressive because they are unevenly available or because they are not able to convey the full ranges of information, knowledge, and meanings, especially in cross-cultural contexts. However, many media-savvy activists have found new digital sound- and video-recording devices, wireless technologies, and satellite-linked broadcast and computer networks to be powerful instruments of connection and liberation, as embodied by the Zapatista movement in Chiapas (Castells 1997) and the local-to-global connections of women on the Internet (Harcourt 1999). Likewise, GIS and remote-sensing technologies can be very effectively coupled with community-based resource management, land-rights struggles, and cultural survival and environmental defense efforts, as illustrated in the special issues of *Cultural Survival Quarterly* (Poole 1995) on geomatics and by Peter Poole and Marcus Colchester in this volume. Yet the achievements reported are based largely on a transfer of technology, including standard land-survey and cadastral mapping techniques as well as expertise in the interpretation of remotely sensed images (satellite images or aerial photographs). GIS has also been used, primarily to store, analyze, and present fairly standard data on location, especially in cases of territorial demarcation, land-rights claims, identification of special features and sites on the landscape, and evidence of territorial violations and land degradation by outsiders.

What is less obvious but potentially even more significant is that the use of GIS can extend well beyond the transfer of the technology as currently used in most state and commercial applications. There is ample scope to expand the repertoire of data sets that can be entered into and linked within a GIS (Liverman, Moran, and Stern 1998). It is possible to scan and enter sketch maps and photographs into the GIS to illustrate the range of categories, conditions, and features represented within mapped units, whether the units are areas within the boundaries of specific territories or categories displayed as pixels of a given color, as in a land-use map.

GIS can, if artfully mobilized, enable a creative encounter between the social, the ecological, and the cartographic imagination, through the kaleidoscope of multimapping. The kaleidoscope provides perhaps the best metaphor for the possibilities inherent in GIS. Latour describes the transformative power of maps as immutable mobiles, as ways of carrying mobile and permanent visions of routes for journeys of trade and exploration (and ultimately global exploitation). GIS offers the opportunity to create an infinitely mutable mobile memory that stores enough data to produce an unlimited set of specific maps, as needed, for specific purposes. Any given map is a contingent product, devised to suit a particular purpose, yet a map can be fixed, carried, and reproduced, retaining and going beyond Latour's criteria for the map as immutably mobile. The whole system can also produce a multiplicity of maps that represent one of several particular situations, positions, or perspectives within or about a specific set of topics in a particular place or across places in a network.

A well-designed GIS can enable multimapping yet retain the ability to represent the various standpoints in a standard, and thus comparable, format.[6] One obvious advantage of this technology is that it is capable of producing rapid and multiple overlays of various maps and of noting areas or points of difference, conflict, complementarity, competition, or convergence in the identification, location, interpretation, value, authority claims, and use of land, water, plants and animals, and artifacts. Although these overlays are most often used to note simple conflict or convergence or to derive single composite images to guide policy, legal agreements, location decisions, or best land-use practice, there is scope to use these to create multiple scenarios for negotiations. This would be a radical departure from mapping as usual and would take us beyond the duel between maps and counter-maps and on to the use of mutually intelligible maps, numbers, pictures, and stories to seek mutually acceptable solutions. Even better than multiple positions in the same language (or format) is the multilingual and multimedia potential of GIS when it is imaginatively applied.

It is possible to collect and combine photographs (of people, plants, animals, physical features, landscapes, practices, processes, and specific events tied to places and land uses), remotely sensed images (from space or from airplanes), official and standard maps of all kinds, sketch maps, diagrams, illustrations, stories, video footage, and quantitative survey data sets from field surveys of demography, ecology, social organization, and land-use practices. Video and audio recordings in digital form can enrich the GIS with offerings that range from illustrative materials to formal testimony in land claims, to presentations and archives of local expert knowledge on ecology, culture, and livelihood.

The same principle of multimedia, multiperspective, and diversified mapping and information archives can apply even without computer capabilities. Many cultural traditions do include multiple modes of memory, as in oral histories, monuments, or sacred spaces in the landscape, theater, ritual, artifacts, and other means of storing and communicating knowledge about ecology, landscape, culture, politics, and power.

CONCLUSION

The work of community-based mapping may best be described as an arranged encounter between a global positioning system and a local repositioning system. We can choose to focus on mapping people, mapping places, mapping precedents, mapping presence, mapping practices, mapping beings in their place, or mapping beings in relation to each other and to place.

Community-based mapping implies more than mapping as usual by different actors. It brings us to unmapping, remapping, and I hope, multimapping. It also incorporates both map as noun and map as verb. This can encompass mapping (and property claims) as home making, place making, and peace making, as well as the more familiar modes of mapping as place taking, conquest, and war making. To make maps that help to strengthen and define place-based struggles beyond competing claims over blood and soil is to map home, habitat, workplace, marketplace and sacred space from multiple perspectives.

The process of multimapping—in multiple media and from a diversity of perspectives—can help people to rediscover, appreciate, define, document, and defend the historical and current meanings of their lands and to map their dreams for the future. Multimedia data sets can facilitate negotiation and planning within and across groups with common and conflicting dreams. Multimapping, whether with GIS or more conventional and traditional methods, can serve to both express and expand the social, ecological, and cartographic imagination of all participants. In the end, it is crucial for people to make maps, numbers, pictures, and stories for themselves not simply as finely honed paper weapons against a superior power of impoverished imagination.

NOTES

1. A thematic map shows the spatial distribution of one or more specific data themes for standard geographic areas. The map may be qualitative in nature (e.g., predominant farm types) or quantitative (e.g., percentage population change).

2. The current LCC includes eight classes of land, I–VIII. The first four classes are arable land—suitable for cropland—in which the limitations on their use and necessity of conservation measures and careful management increase from I through IV. The criteria for placing a given area in a particular class involve the landscape location, slope of the field, and the depth, texture, and reaction of the soil. The remaining four classes, V–VIII, are not to be used for cropland but may have uses for pasture,

range, woodland, grazing, wildlife, recreation, and esthetic purposes. Within the broad classes are subclasses that signify special limitations such as erosion (e), excess wetness (w), problems in the rooting zone (s), and climatic limitations (c). Within the subclasses are the capability units that give some prediction of expected agricultural yields and indicate treatment needs. The capability units are groupings of soils that have common responses to pasture and crop plants under similar systems of farming.

3. Robin Roth (2003) documents a situation regarding watershed classification in Thailand, where slope, soil, and forest cover on a one-square-kilometer grid determined watershed classifications. Classification 1A is considered unsuitable for agriculture, and thus lands in this zone are legislated not suitable for human habitation. However, the coarse grid misses many areas of apparently sustainable irrigated rice. Peter Vandergeest (1996, 2003) points out that elevation played a central role in demarcating cadastral space in Thailand that was available for ownership (in the lowlands) from forest space allocated to state ownership (in the highlands).

4. In one instance, smallholder Gikuyu farmers were killed in 1992, ostensibly by Maasai pastoralists, in regions where wealthy members of both groups owned extensive wheat farms. Yet a powerful Maasai member of parliament commented on an international radio program that the Maasai were protecting the land against despoliation by the plows of the Gikuyu farmers.

5. See Natalie Stein 2000 for a definition and discussion of actor networks.

6. A note of caution: this can create an illusion of commensurability that may not exist.

REFERENCES

Brody, Hugh. 1981. *Maps and Dreams: Indians and the British Columbia Frontier.* Prospect Heights, Ill.: Waveland.

Brosius, J. Peter. 1999. Analyses and Interventions: Anthropological Engagements with Environmentalism. *Current Anthropology* 40(3): 277–309.

Castells, Manuel. 1997. *The Power of Identity: The Information Age—Economy, Society and Culture.* Oxford: Blackwell Publishers.

Colchester, M. 1997. Mapping against Power: The Upper Mazaruni Land Claim in Guyana Nodal. Paper presented at the conference Representing Communities: Histories and Politics of Community-Based Natural Resource Management, Univ. of Georgia, Athens, 1–3 June.

Dana, Peter H. 1998. Nicaragua's GPSistas: Mapping Their Lands on the Caribbean Coast. *GPS World*, September.

Demeritt, D. 2001a. Islands of Truth, Spaces of Contact and the Genealogy of the Imperial Archive. *Antipode* 33(4).

———. 2001b. Scientific Forest Conservation and the Statistical Picturing of Nature's Limits in the Progressive-Era United States. *Environment and Planning D: Society and Space* 19(4): 431–59.

Eghenter, Cristina. 2000. *Mapping Peoples' Forests: The Role of Mapping in Planning Community-Based Management of Conservation Areas in Indonesia.* Washington, D.C.: Biodiversity Support Program.

Foucault, Michel. 1980. *Power/Knowledge: Selected Interviews and Other Writings, 1972–1977*. Colin Gordon, ed. and trans. New York: Pantheon.

Harcourt, Wendy, ed. 1999. *Women @ Internet: Creating New Cultures in Cyberspace*. London: Zed Books.

Helms, Douglas. 1992. *Readings in the History of the Soil Conservation Service*. Washington, D.C.: Soil Conservation Service.

Herlihy, Peter H., and Gregory Knapp. 2003. Maps of, by, and for the Peoples of Latin America. *Human Organization* 62(4): 303–14.

Hodgson, Dorothy L., and Richard A. Schroeder. 2002. Dilemmas of Counter-Mapping Community Resources in Tanzania. *Development and Change* 33: 79–100.

Kaplan, Robert D. 1994. The Coming Anarchy: How Scarcity, Crime, Overpopulation, Tribalism and Disease Are Rapidly Destroying the Social Fabric of Our Planet. *Atlantic Monthly* 273(2): 44–76.

Karrow, Robert W., Jr. 1997. *Concise Bibliography of the History of Cartography: A Selected, Annotated List of Works on Old Maps and Their Makers, and on Their Collection, Cataloging, Care, and Use*. N.p.

Latour, Bruno. 1987. *Science in Action: How to Follow Scientists and Engineers through Society*. Cambridge, Mass.: Harvard University Press.

Liverman, D. E., R. Rindfuss Moran, and P. Stern. 1998. *People and Pixels: Linking Remote Sensing and Social Science*. Washington, D.C.: National Academy Press.

Lorde, Audre. 1984. *Sister Outsider: Essays and Speeches*. Trumansburg, N.Y.: Crossing Press.

Lynch, Barbara Deutsch. 1996. Marking Territory and Mapping Development: Protected Area Designation in the Dominican Republic. Paper presented at Voices from the Commons, Sixth Annual Conference of the International Association for the Study of Common Property, Berkeley, Calif., 5–8 June.

Lynch, Owen, and J. Kirk Talbott. 1995. *Balancing Acts: Community Based Forestry Management and National Law in Asia and the Pacific*. Washington, D.C.: World Resources Institute.

McKinnon, J. 2001. Mobile Interactive GIS: Bringing Indigenous Knowledge and Scientific Information Together. A Narrative Account. Paper presented at the International Workshop Participatory Technology Development and Local Knowledge for Sustainable Land Use in South East Asia, Chiang Mai, Thailand, 6–7 June.

Mohamed, M., and S. Ventura. 2000. Use of Geomatics for Mapping and Documenting Indigenous Tenure Systems. *Society and Natural Resources* 13: 223–36.

Myers, Norman. 1979. *The Sinking Ark: A New Look at the Problems of Disappearing Species*. New York: Pergamon.

Neumann, Roderick P. 1995. Local Challenges to Global Agendas: Conservation, Economic Liberalization, and the Pastoralists' Rights Movement in Tanzania. *Antipode* 27(4): 363–82.

Neumann, Roderick P., and Richard A. Schroeder. 1995. Manifest Ecological Destinies: Local Rights and Global Environmental Agendas. *Antipode* 27(4): 321–24.

Parkipuny, Moringe, S. Ole, and Dhyani J. Berger. 1993. Maasai Rangelands. In *Voices from Africa: Local Perspectives on Conservation*, ed. Dale Lewis and Nick Carter. Washington, D.C.: World Wildlife Fund.

Peluso, Nancy Lee. 1992. *Rich Forests, Poor People: Resource Control and Resistance in Java*. Berkeley and Los Angeles: University of California Press.

———. 1995. Whose Woods Are These? Counter-Mapping Forest Territories in Kalimantan, Indonesia. *Antipode* 27(4): 383–406.

Poole, P. 1995. *Indigenous Peoples, Mapping and Biodiversity Conservation: An Analysis of Current Activities and Opportunities for Applying Geomatics Technologies.* Washington, D.C.: Biodiversity Support Program.

———, ed. 1995a. *Geomatics: Who Needs It?* Special issue of *Cultural Survival Quarterly* 18(4).

Rangan, Haripriya. 1995. Contested Boundaries: State Policies, Forest Classifications, and Deforestation in the Garhwal Himalayas. *Antipode* 27(4): 342–62.

Rocheleau, D. 1997. Shared Spaces and Sub-Divided Interests in the Uncommons: Gendered Forests, Tree Farms, and Gardens in the Agroforests of Zambrana-Chacuey. *The Common Property Resource Digest* 40: 1–6.

Rocheleau, D., and D. Edmunds. 1997. Women, Men and Trees: Gender, Power and Property in Forest and Agrarian Landscapes. *World Development* 25(8): 1351–71.

Rocheleau, D., and L. Ross. 1995. Trees as Tools, Trees as Text: Struggles over Resources in Zambrana-Chacuey, Dominican Republic. *Antipode* 24(4): 407–28.

Rocheleau, D., K. Wachira, L. Malaret, and B. Wanjohi. 1989. Local Knowledge of Agroforestry and Native Plants. In *Farmer First: Farmer Innovation and Agricultural Research*, ed. R. Chambers, A. Pacey, and L. Thrupp. London: Intermediate Technology Publications.

Rocheleau, D., B. Thomas-Slayter, and D. Edmunds. 1995. Gendered Resource Mapping. *Cultural Survival Quarterly* 18(4): 62–68.

Roc, Emery. 1999. *Except Africa: Re-making Development, Re-thinking Power.* New Brunswick, N.J.: Transaction Books.

Roth, R. 2002. The Fault of Two-Dimensional Spatial Logic: The Re-Organisation of Inhabited Forest Landscapes in Northern Thailand. Paper presented at the Society for Conservation Biology Annual Meeting, Canterbury, U.K., 14–19 July.

———. 2003. Fixed in Space: Two-Dimensional Maps in Multi-Dimensional Worlds. Unpublished Ms.

Rundstrom, Robert A. 1995. AGIS, Indigenous Peoples, and Epistemological Diversity. *Cartography and Geographic Information Systems* 22(1): 45–57.

Schroeder, Richard A. 1993. Shady Practice: Gender and the Political Ecology of Resource Stabilization in Gambian Garden/Orchards. *Economic Geography* 69(4): 349–65.

Slocum, R., L. Wichart, D. Rocheleau, and B. Thomas-Slayter. 1995. *Power, Process and Participation: Tools for Change*. London: Intermediate Technology.

Thompson, John. 1997. Untitled PhD diss., Graduate School of Geography, Clark Univ., Worcester, Mass.

Vandergeest, Peter. 1996. Real Villages: National Narratives of Development. In *Creating the Countryside: The Politics of Rural and Environmental Discourse*, ed E. Melanie DePuis and Peter Vandergeest. Philadelphia: Temple Univ. Press.

———. 2003. Racialization and Citizenship in Thai Forest Politics. *Society and Natural Resources* 16: 19–37.

Walker, P., and P. Peters. 2001. Maps, Metaphors, and Meanings: Boundary Struggles and Village Forest Use on Private and State Land in Malawi. *Society and Natural Resources* 14: 411–24.

Wood, Denis. 1992. *The Power of Maps*. New York: Guilford Press.

Woodward, D., and G. M. Lewis, eds. 1998. *Cartography in the Traditional African, American, Arctic, Australian, and Pacific Societies*. Chicago: University of Chicago Press.

14

Mapping as a Tool for Community Organizing against Power: A Moluccas Experience

Roem Topatimasang

In April 1992 twenty-six representatives of indigenous people from Maluku (the Moluccas) and Irian Jaya (West New Guinea) attended a meeting in Ambon, the provincial town of the Moluccas, in Indonesia, to share information about problems in their respective areas. During the four-day meeting they realized that they faced a common problem: the appropriation of their traditional territories by both the Indonesian government and private companies. Together they formulated a plan of action consisting of an alliance network, an agenda, and a set of methods for pursuing that agenda. There was a heated debate within the group regarding methods: some advocated foregrounding peaceful approaches such as negotiation and consensus seeking, whereas others said they had lost faith in such methods, which they said were "too soft." In the end it was agreed to include the following in their statement: "When peaceful ways are no longer effective, then we should (1) form genuine people's organizations with the goal of defending our land and waterways, (2) disseminate information about our plight to all concerned parties so as to gather support, and (3) if necessary, mobilize ourselves to resist those stealing our land and waters through demonstrations, blockades, etc."[1]

This recommendation was too general, and the statement as a whole conveyed an impression of deep confusion and frustration. All of the participants had experienced alienation of their territories and some of them had been struggling for years to defend their traditional rights. However, as in so many places, they had always been defeated by more powerful forces. These were traditional villagers—nearly all were farmers and fisherfolk with no education beyond secondary high school, and they had little access to information outside their local areas. For some, this was the first time they had left their villages or islands. It is therefore easy to understand why their statement might have appeared simplistic, if determined. Nonetheless, within two years they had demonstrated that their efforts were more than just talk. When a reunion meeting was held in November 1993, more than half of them had successfully formed broad-based organizations in their respective areas, and within those local organizations they were becoming more systematic in their efforts to defend their traditional rights over ancestral domains.

Among other techniques, they were employing mapping as a tool in their struggle. This chapter will explain how and why these groups used mapping techniques and describe the results of these efforts. The chapter is a record of practical experience—I was directly involved as an organizer and facilitator within the affected communities. The chapter is written in straightforward language and draws on narrative cases to provide background and context for readers unfamiliar with the Moluccas. I will begin with a brief description of traditional concepts of territorial ownership and resource management and then present an overview of the history and politics of land and water alienation in the archipelago.

BACKGROUND: THE CONCEPT OF TRADITIONAL TERRITORY

The Moluccas are a group of 1,027 islands, large and small, inhabited and not, situated in eastern Indonesia in the zone from 125° west longitude to 135° east longitude and 5° north latitude to 10° south latitude. Of the total area of 851,000 square kilometers, only 85,728 (10.1 percent) is land. The rest is ocean and includes the deepest water (30,000 feet) in Indonesia: the Banda Sea. A 1990 census counted 1.8 million people, the majority of them fisherfolk living along the shorelines (64.4 percent of Moluccan villages are coastal). Relative to other Indonesian provinces, its population density is low, averaging only two people per square kilometer. However, the land does not need to be fallowed and land shortages are not a major problem. In any case, our interest here is not in statistics but rather in the Moluccan people's concept of land and sea ownership and the historical facts that have generated that concept and influenced its development.

Like indigenous people everywhere, Moluccans are tightly bonded with their places of origin. After love ballads, the dominant form of Moluccan

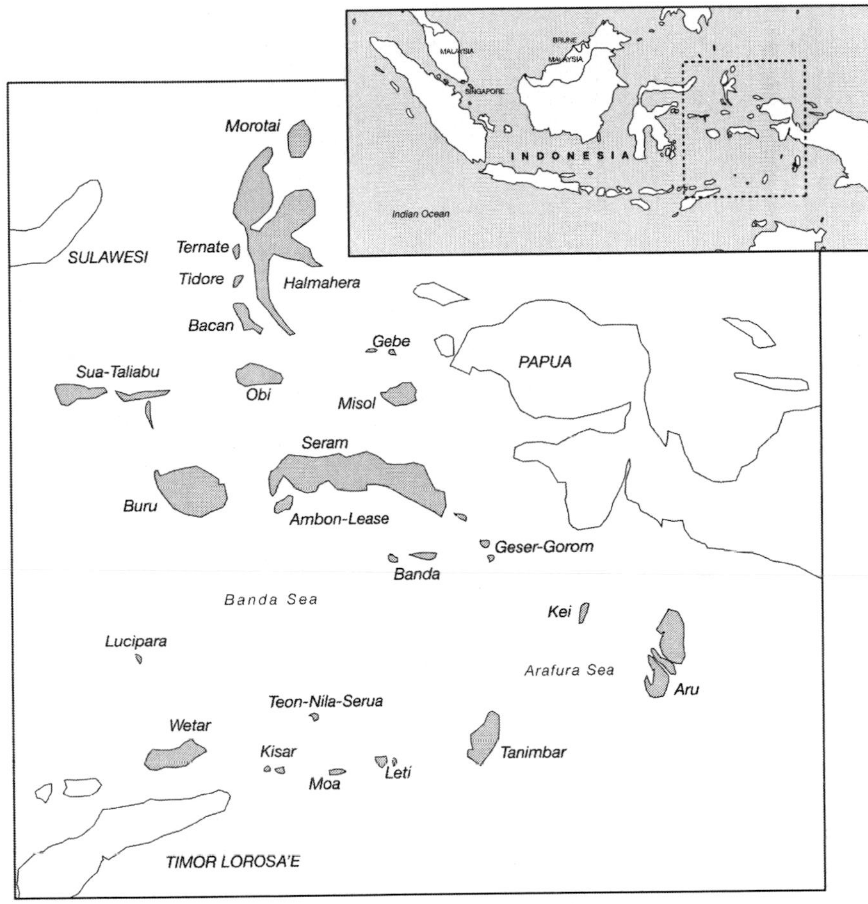

Map 14.1 Maluku Islands

folksong is the ode to the homeland. One's homeland is not merely the place where one is born, grows up, and dies—it is also a focal point of one's cultural identity, historical roots, and spiritual values. And old poem of Kei Island, in the southeastern Moluccas, expressed this in typical fashion.

> We are living in our homeland where we get our food from the land
> We occupy our place and always protect our share
> We carry all the burdens of our village with its customs
> We live as honestly as possible and walk straight ahead
> In this way our customary laws will save us
> So our ancestors will protect us
> And God will bless us[2]

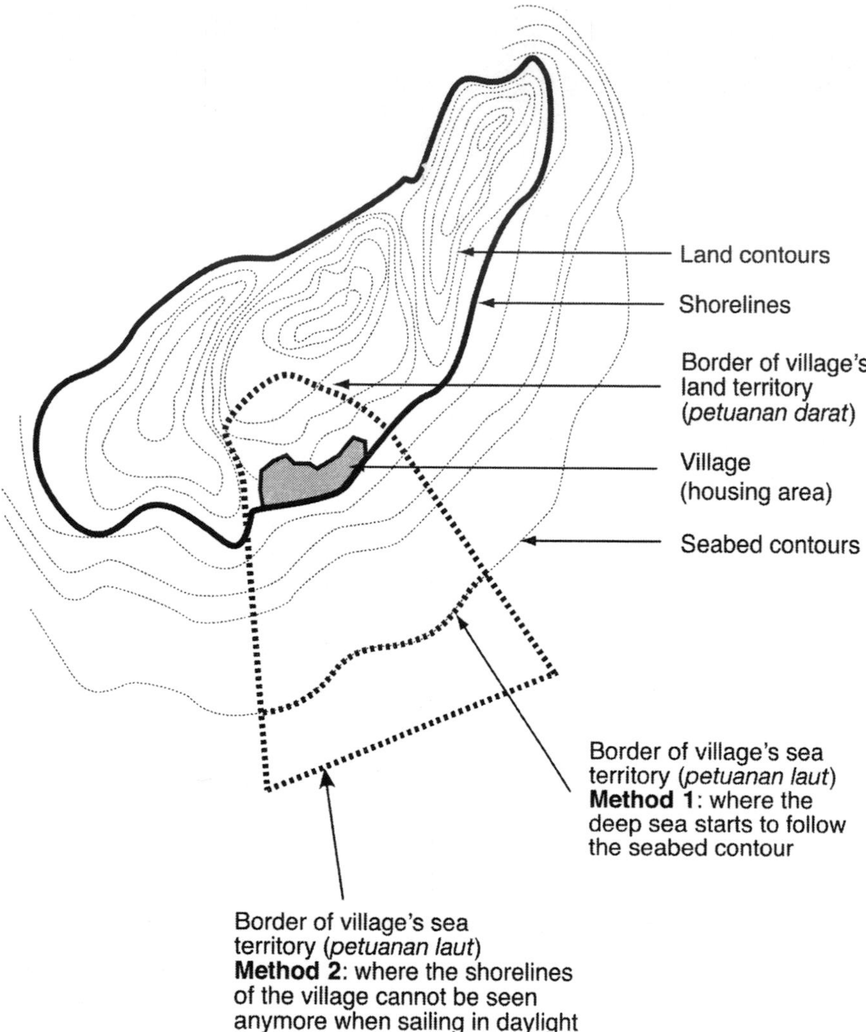

Map 14.2 ***Petuanan negeri*: Illustration of Moluccan Village Territory with Common Property on Both Land and Sea**

For these islanders, the homeland is not only housing lots, yards, or fields, it also includes forests, hills, rivers, and of course, surrounding seas. All one's territories are called *petuanan* (from *tuan*, the owner), and this word is always mentioned with the name of the owner. For instance, *petuanan negeri Ihamahu* means a territory belonging to all the people of the village (*negeri*) of Ihamahu (in Saparua Island, central Moluccas). *Negeri* (literally, country) indicates that a *petuanan*—both the land and the water—is the common property of all the people of that village. Within a *petuanan* of a *negeri* some plots of land belong to certain clans (*marga*). These are called *tanah marga* (clan's land) and are usually housing lots, yards, and cultivated fields. The lands that do not belong to any specific clans belong by default to all people of all the village's clans and are called *tanah negeri*. This is usually primary forest (*ewang*) or secondary forest used as common hunting and gathering grounds (*dusun*). So *negeri* always carries a communal meaning; *petuanan*, too, indicates communal ownership of a territory.

In the Lease Islands in the central Moluccas, for example, a clan's land is called *tanah dati* or *tanah pusaka* (literally, heritage land). A clan's land is an aggregation of all lands and thus a collectively held land: it belongs to individual households (nuclear families) that are part of the extended family of the clan.

However, every nuclear family also has rights to use and harvest from lands of other households of their clan, under certain conditions agreed to and regulated by a council of the clan's elders. To some extent people may also use the land of other clans in their village, as long as this is agreed to and regulated by customary law, or elders, councils of all the clans of that village. These councils are called *saniri* or *seniri*. After two or three generations of the children and the grandchildren of the initial owner using the land, ownership automatically changes and the land becomes the common property of the extended family. In other words, there is no private ownership of land in any absolute sense, and individual ownership of *tanah dati* or *tanah pusaka* is essentially relative in nature.

Local legends give varying accounts of how *petuanan* ownership came about in different places or islands, but there is a common pattern. Usually the process began when someone cleared a plot of land for housing and gardening and then cleared an area of forest for swiddens and for hunting and gathering grounds. They are said to have put a mark at points in each of the different directions that they can reach from the heart of the village, and if no other people have put marks before on those places, they become border points of that territory, or *petuanan*. By extending lines connecting all these points, a complete boundary of a *petuanan darat* (land territory) of a *negeri* is established. The boundaries of *petuanan laut* (sea territory) are formed in a similar manner, with a straight line simply stretched from the two edge points of the land territory at the shoreline into the open sea.

In Watlaar Village, Kei Besar Island, territorial boundaries at sea are set at the points where, when sailing in the daytime, one can no longer see the shoreline of one's village. In other places, for example, in the coastal villages of Halmahera Island, north Moluccas, people determined boundaries in a simpler way: they are where the black water (deep sea) begins. Thus in the Watlaar and Kei islands the outer boundaries of sea territory are generally seen as straight lines, while in Halmahera they are seen as arced lines that follow the contour of the seabed. However sea territory is conceived, throughout the Moluccas it is an integral part of the *petuanan negeri.* Yet it is different from land territories that are owned by certain clans, because sea territory is completely and absolutely communal territory and belongs fully to all the people of a village. No clans, let alone any nuclear family or individual, can claim a particular part of communal sea territory. This applies also to *meti,* the beach land exposed at low tide, where houses may be situated.

Land and sea ownership in the Moluccas is based essentially on the concept of property held in common by local people. If we talk about traditional territorial rights of indigenous Moluccan people, especially in cases of territorial disputes with outsiders, the communal concept of *petuanan negeri* must be a central theme. Historically, there have been disputes over land between clans in the same village or different villages, and sometimes these have led to bloodshed. But in cases where outsiders have tried to appropriate a clan's land, other clans of the same village have always helped to defend their neighbor. In such cases, a clan's land is no longer treated as clan property, but rather as community land, land of the *petuanan negeri* as a whole.

For this reason, when Moluccans cite their communal or collective identities, they do not refer to their clan identity or even that of the association of clans of their village—*anak-anak marga* or *soa* (the children of the clan or association of clans). Instead, they call themselves *anak-anak negeri* (the children of the village). Only when referring to individual or personal identities do they ask, "What is his *marga* or *soa*?"

On the basis of this concept of communal ownership, the indigenous people of the Moluccas have developed a system of managing their common natural resources through varying forms and structures of local social and kinship relationships. In the central Moluccas, social structures are relatively egalitarian, and traditionally, leaders were found at no higher level than the village, a single *negeri.* Here the systems of managing natural resources, too, were relatively simple. Decisions were made through a brief procedure in which representatives of all of a *negeri*'s *soa* voiced their opinions.

Traditional resource management was quite different in the north Moluccas, where social and kinship relations were dominated by the feudal structures of the powerful Ternate and Tidore sultanates. In the southeast Moluccas, especially the Kei Islands, another complicated system of social stratification, based on a caste system, was found and continues to predominate. Traditional resource management in these areas was more complicated. It was the affair not only of individual *negeri* but also of the palaces of the two sultanates. In other cases, resource management might involve power structures formed by federations of several *negeri,* called *ratschaap.* Consequently, decision-making processes became more complex and slower, and they sometimes led to internal tensions. Nonetheless, all of these systems shared communal resource-management systems that employed the principles of mutual benefit and reciprocity to maintain social equilibrium and harmony with nature.

One important component of these traditional systems was *sasi* (from *saksi*, literally, witnesses), a strict prohibition during some periods against taking certain species from nature to ensure their sustainability. Examples of species they regulated are *sasi lola* (*Trochus niloticus*, top shell) on Kei Besar Island, *sasi kima* (*Tridacna gigas*, giant clam) on Kei Kecil Island, *sasi teripang* (*Holothuria* spp., sea cucumber) in the Tanimbar and Aru Islands, and *sasi lompa* (*Thrissa baelama*, a small sardine) on Haruku Island. *Sasi* also could be imposed on locations to preserve natural resources. Examples are *sasi meti* (on low-tide zones), *sasi ewang* (on forests), and *sasi dusun sagu* (on sago palm, *Metroxyllin rumphii*, the local staple). In many parts of the archipelago eternal *sasi* could be declared for areas of sacred primary forests—usually ancestral sites—or for certain sacred wild species. An example is *sasi* that were placed on snakes, monitor lizards, and rats in Nuhuta Island of Tanimbar Kei, in the southeast Moluccas.

Written documents do not tell us conclusively when these *sasi* practices began or why they became common practice throughout the Moluccas. In a legend of Haruku, their ancestors initiated this tradition in the fourteenth century. Legends in other places mention both earlier and later periods. What is clear is that *sasi* were an integral part of the customary laws (*adat*) of all Moluccan communities. As a part of customary laws, regulated by the customary council (*seniri*), *sasi* is not only a secular management system but also a sacred tradition received from the ancestors. Because of this sacred dimension, people obey *sasi*. Indeed, the punishments for violating these laws are not heavy: an easily paid fine (about twenty-five hundred to ten thousand Indonesian rupiah, or one to four U.S. dollars) or light physical punishment (for instance, a symbolic beating on the legs with a rattan stick or an hour standing in the hot sun).

The harshest penalty is the embarrassment of being punished in front of the other villagers. Violators and their families may bear a shameful mark as troublemakers or thieves for generations. In one case in point, in 1988 in a small village of Seram Island, in the central Moluccas, a man who had violated a *sasi* was sentenced by the customary council to walk around the village carrying all of the fruits he had taken from the forbidden *sasi* forest area. He had to stop in every house and loudly shout, "Listen to me, what I did was wrong, and I promise you I will not repeat it in the future!" In a village with a strong community life, this kind of social sanction can be truly unbearable, and in many cases violators decide to leave for a period or even forever. Customary laws have implemented a basic universal principle of law toward violators: there is no obligation to serve the rights of those who have violated the law (*in adimplendii non est adimplendum*). This means that their rights to share in or benefit from their group's communal territory and resources are abolished.

CONTEXT: THE HISTORY AND POLITICS OF APPROPRIATION

Like many of the world's indigenous peoples, this is not the first time Moluccans have battled over their traditional territories. Local tales describe many cases of Moluccans disputing among themselves and even fighting wars over territorial claims. There are usually conflicting interests involved in these disputes, but the winner typically claims the territory of the loser. However, an interesting aspect of these Moluccan disputes is that, under certain conditions, the winner may allow the loser to continue managing the conquered territory.

In the thirteenth century, after the Sultan of Ternate had conquered territory of the Tobelo people in the north and central peninsulas of Halmahera Island, he allowed the Tobelonese to continue hunting, gathering, cultivating, and harvesting there. The sultan asked only that they pay an annual tax and support the sultanate's army logistically in times of war. In another case, when migrants from Luang Island near Timor conquered the people of Kei Islands, they established a new ruling class within Kei society (*mel*) as raja (king or chief) and warriors.[3] They took half the land as their own, and the other half remained fully owned by the indigenous people, who formed a middle class (*ren*). The *ren* advised the *mel*—who were called *tuan tanah* (landlords)—regarding management and jurisdiction of the land and sea as their common property. They also acted as *marinyo* (liaisons) between the *mel* and the ordinary people, the lower class (*ri*).

Among the indigenous Moluccans, generosity and willingness to share are fundamental pillars of communal-territory ownership. There are many examples of these islanders granting part of their land or natural resources to outsiders, sometimes for compassionate reasons. There is an exception to the strict prohibitions of *sasi*, that of an obligation to provide travelers with any foods taken from nature within the *sasi*. But the travelers must eat it onsite and not take it away or sell it. During an event called *buka sasi* (opening the *sasi*, the harvesting time) outsiders were always allowed to freely take home the harvest. In an example of compassion, during the seventeenth century, people of Kei Besar Island granted part of their land to refugees from Banda Islands who had escaped from a Dutch massacre. The Bandanese established their own village and new *petuanan* called Banda Eli, Banda Efruan, and Banda Elat. They continue to peacefully coexist with their hosts today. The only condition for their receiving the land was that they respect and obey local customary laws, and the people adopted them as *anak-anak adat* (children of customary laws) with equal rights and obligations. Another example is the village of Haruku-Sameth in the Lease Islands, where we find an association of extended families or clans called Soa Rumalesi, who are migrants from different families or clans. They have been fully adopted by the local people and now have their own permanent representatives in the customary council. They have their own land and also the right to harvest from the *petuanan negeri* of Haruku-Sameth.

From such processes, indigenous Moluccans developed another, unique kinship relationship in fictive sisterhood and brotherhood pacts called *pela*. *Pela* are sacred pacts in that, as among true sisters and brothers, marriage is strictly prohibited and considered incestuous. When the people of one village become *pela* of the people of another village, both parties have equal rights to benefit from the *petuanan* of the other, as well as equal obligations to protect and defend it. What is interesting is that in many cases *pela* emerged as a form of peace treaty between warring villages.

For centuries, then, Moluccans had had institutionalized ways of resolving territorial conflicts and disputes. This helps explain how many outsiders have managed to live peacefully with the local people. Today, in many parts of the islands, one can find descendants of Buginese or Butonese sailors from Sulawesi and of Chinese and Arab traders, living as fully integrated members of local communities.

This may also help explain why Moluccans do not consider their different races, ethnicities, and religions important. *Pela* that are made up of migrants and indigenous people or villages that are both Christian and Muslim are common throughout the Moluccas. Until recently, this was the only province in Indonesia that had never experienced mass riots based on racial or sectarian sentiments[4]—in other provinces these are practically an annual occurrence.[5] One of the failures of RMS (Republik Maluku Selatan, or the South Moluccan Republic) in the 1950s was the inability of its leaders—a few elite Christian intellectuals and an exclusive group of former Dutch colonial soldiers—to grasp the nature of the *pela* tradition. They provoked local people with anti-Java and anti-Muslim sentiments, which were diametrically opposed to the genuine spirit of *pela*. They did not understand that although there is a strong base of Indonesian Christian communities in this area, more than half its population is Muslim. RMS became an unpopular idea and remains so today even in the center of the revolt in the Lease Islands, in the central Moluccas.

Traditional patterns of territorial appropriation in the Moluccas were quite adaptive, and they continued to be effective means of resolving disputes and conflicts in shifting contexts. But this tradition was drastically changed when, under European colonialism, the Moluccas were brought into the international economic regime. The islands became the world's primary producer of several spices, especially nutmeg (*Myristica fragrans*) and cloves

(*Eugenia aromatica*). The Portuguese and Spaniards began their conquest in the north Moluccas and Banda Islands in the sixteenth century. The British and Dutch came later and, after a long fight with each other, they expelled the Iberian conquistadors. Finally, in the second half of the seventeenth century, the Dutch became the single and absolute rulers of the spice islands. From that moment, the more benign traditional patterns of territorial appropriation described above were changed. Under the Dutch, territorial appropriation meant a total annihilation of local ownership over lands and waters. When people resisted, the colonial bureaucracy and legal system, and in many cases military force, were imposed.

An extreme example is the Hongi Expedition at the beginning of the eighteenth century. Hundreds of thousands of clove trees belonging to people of Ambon Island—the main harbor of the Vereenigde Oostindische Compagnie (VOC, or the Dutch East India Company)—were burned by Dutch troops to maintain a high market price and their monopoly of the world spice trade. In another case, in 1621, fifteen thousand Bandenese were massacred by Dutch soldiers for refusing to move from their homeland, thus hampering a VOC plan to convert the Banda Islands into a huge nutmeg plantation. By the mid-twentieth century colonialism was ending, but its greedy territorial appropriation continued. In 1968 the Indonesian government and Japan's National Federation of Fishery Cooperatives signed the Banda Sea Agreement, under which hundreds of tuna-fishing fleets invaded the traditional water territories of Moluccan communities. Later, in 1975, a state-owned company, PT.Aneka Tambang, evicted hundreds of indigenous people of Gebe Island from their homeland to clear the way for nickel mining. In 1982 a presidential decree (No. 85/1982) that allowed large private companies to use destructive nets of up to ten meters in depth in waters of western Indonesia (Java and Sumatra; east of 130° east longitude) followed an earlier one (No. 39/1980) banning seabed trawling nets in those waters. One of these companies was PT.Daya Guna Samudera (DGS) of the Jayanti Group. Because the small islands in the specified area are almost all islets or are formed from uplifted coral reefs with steep slopes, the traditional fishing grounds of local communities are largely deep water where the ten-meter nets can be used. In 1986 PT.Prima Lirang Mining, a joint-venture Indonesian, Australian, and Dutch gold mining company, occupied the traditional land of people of Wetar Island. In 1988 a logging company belonging to the largest conglomerate in Indonesia, the Salim Group, began operating on Yamdena Island in the ancestral forests of eighteen villages. In 1990 an oil exploration project by Texas Union claimed traditional land of the people of Kei Besar Island. In 1996 copper and gold mining exploration by PT.Aneka Tambang and PT.Ingold, a joint-venture company of Indonesia and Canada, occupied traditional land of the people of Haruku Island. These are merely a few of the better-known cases, and there have been many others involving logging, mining, and fishing concessions in Halmahera, Obi, Sula, Buru, Seram, Aru, and the southernmost islands. They have various names and locations, but all of these *la nueva conquestadors* employ the same method: they do not bother with announcements, permissions, or agreements with the local people, and when the people protest, the government and companies respond by sending military force to intimidate them.

Physical conflicts can no longer be avoided, and they are sometimes bloody. On Yamdena Island, for example, one person died, fourteen were injured, and forty-two were imprisoned without trial. Today, especially in the Aru Islands, it is common to see military or police personnel guarding project sites, or escorting owners or executives. They resemble nothing so much as a group of mercenaries. Just a few years ago, in August 1996, the people of Tanimbar on Kei Island rejected the presence of a cyanide fishing company in their territory, and a military officer took them from their own village and tortured them in another. Humiliation is another weapon: In April 1997 a local government officer, guarded by military and police, came to Haruku village on a Sunday morning when the villagers were attending Mass in their church. Before the last prayer, the officer suddenly interrupted with a long speech blaming the villagers of being stupid, antigovernment, and antidevelopment, and accused these devout Christians of being communists, inside their own church!

The issue of territorial appropriation in the Moluccas, and in Indonesia in general, reflects the conflicting interests of the people vis-à-vis the state. Historical records reveal that, since the colonial period, appropriation of traditional territories by the state has been routine, as those with political and economic power move to control local natural resources. The prime mover of this process has always been capital interests. Once the resources are controlled, domination has to be maintained by repressive instruments, including the legal system.

The Dutch colonial administration introduced a legal principle called *beschickingsrecht*, replacing that of *domeinrecht*. This meant that all the lands and waters within their colonial territories belonged to the state. The people merely had the right to use them, not to own them. When the state needed the land for so-called public purposes, the government compensated them for their products from that land but did not give them payment for the land itself. In some cases this meant people received no compensation at all. Under this system, communal land is essentially state-owned land. This colonial principle has since become part of the legal system of the nation of Indonesia. According to Article 33 of the 1945 Constitution, "All land, waters and skies are under the authority of the state for the maximum benefit of the people." There has been a long debate over the semantics of "under the authority." Some parties say it does not mean that the state owns the land but only that it has a mandate to use all natural resources inside the national territory for the benefit and welfare of the people. This debate has become meaningless in the face of the reality that, whatever observers and analysts may say, the government has the ultimate power to interpret legal matters according to its own interests.

Indeed, the key legal instruments within the authoritarian Indonesian state today are not the Constitution but rather lower-level tools such as presidential and ministerial decrees and provincial regulations. For example, the National Agrarian Act No. 5/1960 was supposed to bring about recognition of the customary land rights of traditional communities. But in fact the act amounts to mere lip service to the issue because government regulations provide no procedures for making that recognition into law. In reality, customary lands of many traditional communities across Indonesia have been converted to huge logging concessions, plantation estates, and mining sites. The famous case of the appropriation and conversion of customary lands of the Amungme and Komoro tribes for the Freeport copper mine in Irian Jaya by a joint-venture company of Indonesia and the United States, PT. Freeport Indonesia, is merely one among many.

Legal instruments are just the first step in providing a de jure basis of legitimation so that the people will have no legal counterarguments to defend their rights. Throughout the history of territorial disputes in Indonesia, the people have never won any land court cases. This is why they have resorted to other actions outside the courtroom, including in many cases mass protests and uprisings. Here again we find the government has produced many legal instruments to suppress such activities. The Dutch colonial administration produced repressive regulations (SOB, *hatzaai artikelen*, *exorbitante rechten*, etc.) that allowed them to charge those involved in mass protests against government policies with contempt of the state's sovereignty. The Indonesian government today continues to use these regulations. Further, the government produced many later regulations for its so-called depoliticization, or floating-mass, policy. These included the controversial Paket Lima Undang-undang Politik (Package of Five Political Acts), intended to place all political parties, mass organizations, and legislative and judicial branches under tight control of a monolithic government bureaucracy and the military forces.

To implement these political regulations more effectively at the community level, the government produced the notorious Act No. 5/1969, on village administration. This did away with autonomous local institutions such as traditional customary councils and village committees and forced them into a single institution called the Lembaga Masyarakat Desa, or LMD (village community institution). They were led by a *lurah* or *kepala desa* (head of village) under direct supervision of a *camat* (head of subdistrict) and a *bupati* (head of district, the regent). Although the village heads were elected by the people for eight-year terms, the candidates were to be selected and approved by the *camat* and *bupati* before the election. The heads were responsible to them, not to the people who had elected them. The act directed that the village heads had the prerogative to select and appoint all members of the LMD, and so they became potentates of the villages. A member of the military, usually a sergeant, was appointed as *bintara pembina desa* (petty officer for village supervision), or *Babinsa*, to watch over each village head. In practice, this military officer is the true ruler of the village and, in many cases of territorial appropriation, he is also the main agent in charge of intimidating or harassing villagers.

In the Moluccas this highly structured machinery of control was effective in keeping autonomous local institutions from functioning. In a meeting in Ambon in September 1996, a group of *tetua* (elders) and *kepala adat* (chiefs) of customary councils from southeast and central Moluccas testified that "the Act No. 5/1969 is like a deadly hammer for us, undermining our traditional institutions so that our people have no independent organizations anymore to speak out freely in defending our rights or to simply manage our daily lives and activities according to our customary laws. The Government's talk of respecting traditions is just rhetoric, empty promises!"[6]

BASIC STRATEGIES: REORGANIZING THE COMMUNITY

"If one catches a shark and wants to disable it, one does not care about its frightening teeth—just grip tightly and break the pectoral fins precisely under its flank!" Thus said a traditional shark hunter of Tarwa Island, southeast Moluccas. That is precisely what the government has done since colonial times to prevent local communities from standing against government policies and from resisting state appropriation of their traditional territories. The government has been well aware that mass movements can take place only if people are well organized. The collective life of traditional communities provides the necessary conditions for such organization, sometimes with incredible staying power. For this reason the government sought to disable these vital, autonomous institutions—to disorganize the people.

Recognizing this, a group of community workers in the Moluccas decided to *re*organize them. They started their work in 1988 in a small village called Evu in the Kei Kecil Islands and established regular weekly meetings with villagers. They began with a focus on daily issues and allowed the people to generate their own themes until, one day, they came up with a problem of conflict between the villagers and the local government. The problem was a dispute over a piece of land they had granted to the local government to build a twenty-three-kilometer-long clean-water piping installation. The pipe ran from a natural spring in the village to Tual, the capital town of the southeast Moluccas District. The government violated the agreement by overstepping the project boundaries that had been agreed to. In response, the villagers forbade all government employees from entering the area and proposed three additional conditions on the project: the government should sign an official statement on agreed boundaries, build a plant to treat the residual waste of lubricating oil from the pump, and allow the villagers to extend pipes to their own houses free of charge. After negotiations, the government finally gave in. This small victory has convinced the villagers and the local organizers of the power of organized action.

The weekly meetings continue, and they have produced many ideas and activities. In 1990 the villagers established a foundation, Nen Masil, named after the woman who created the spring, according to a local tale. They granted a piece of land on which to build an office, meeting hall, workshop, demonstration plots, and cottages. These facilities later became the main information and training center of the communities of Kei Kecil, Kei Besar, Aru, and the Tanimbar Islands. Thus was born a true community-based organization, one founded, managed, and controlled by villagers themselves.

In the same year, a logging concession started operating on Yamdena, the main island of Tanimbar. Two community workers went there and spent a year organizing the people against the concession. This battle became a central focus for them because it involved the number-one tycoon of Indonesia, Liem Swie Liong, and also a huge area of sixty-four thousand hectares of primary forests. The strategy and methods used in Yamdena were those used before in Kei Kecil, and they successfully mobilized the eighteen villages surrounding the concession area. Each village established their own action committees that were directly responsible to their own customary councils. The councils, in turn, gave a mandate to all Yamdena migrants living outside the islands, especially in big cities in Java, to establish a national network named Ikatan Cendekiawan Tanimbar Indonesi (Association of Tanimbar Intellectuals of Indonesia), or ICTI, based in Jakarta. Assisted by a nongovernmental-organization (NGO) network on forest conservation (SKEPHI), they organized protest rallies. In cooperation with several international groups, such as the World Rainforest Movement (WRM) and Down to Earth (DTE), they launched an international campaign and lobbied against the logging. In Yamdena itself, local organizers mobilized boycotts and blockades. Finally, in 1993, the minister of Forestry announced a halt to the logging. The minister and ICTI agreed to a three-year moratorium on logging, during which future plans for the forests of Yamdena would be made. The minister also agreed to consider all of the conditions proposed by the people through ICTI.

After the moratorium period ended, in 1996, the government initiated a new plan for the Yamdena forests. This took the form of establishing timber estates (not logging) under the authority of the state-owned forestry company, INHUTANI, working with a private company, PT Mohtra Agung. As written, the plan appeared to have a sound environmental approach. Because of the nature of the limestone soils and the forests of Yamdena, they selected teakwood rather than vulnerable exotic species like eucalyptus, used for producing pulp. Moreover, the plan would involve local people in a socioagroforestry scheme and would compensate the communities with a 2 percent equity share of the company.

Unfortunately, monolithic structures of bureaucracy have once again manipulated procedures for implementing the scheme. One problem is that of representation. Using standard protocols of Act No. 5/1969, the government appointed the official administration apparatus, rather than the local customary councils, to represent the communities. ICTI then filed a legal complaint in the Administrative Court of Ambon against the local government. The judges refused the complaint, and a complicated negotiation is still going on, but the complaint has prevented the scheme from being implemented effectively. The communities and organizers have continued their work at the community level and to support the work of ICTI at the national and international levels. Among other successes, a petition to the European Parliament was granted in March 1997. Nevertheless, the communities and organizers have for the time being decided to maintain the status quo as the best among the poor choices available, at least until the government fulfills all the original conditions.

This struggle has not yet been won, but by bringing the logging to a halt these people became the first in Indonesia to win a battle against a powerful logging company. In this way, Yamdena is a success story that has confirmed for local organizers their basic assumptions regarding the principles, strategies, and methods of organization. From the experience they gained new lessons on how to work undercover, mediate internal dynamics and conflicts, mobilize support systems, deal with local politics, and very importantly, interlink local actions with extensive campaigns at national and international levels. The Yamdena case further gave the lie to many stereotypes about the inability of traditional communities to establish, manage, and develop complex organizations sustaining activities at multiple levels. They proved themselves capable of mobilizing their own movement, funded through voluntary works and collective savings.

The communities even paid the expensive research costs and professional fees of five senior scientists from the prestigious Gajah Mada University and the Bogor Institute of Agricultural Sciences to conduct an environmental impact assessment in the concession area countering the findings of previous assessments. Their findings were presented in a public seminar in Jakarta, hosted by the Indonesian Institute of Sciences (LIPI), and were decisive in influencing the public opinion that eventually forced the minister to terminate the logging. This is an impressive and unprecedented achievement, unequalled even by the many NGOs of Indonesia that depend, partly or completely, on external funding. Their success inspired organizers to work in similar ways elsewhere in the Moluccas, and their story encouraged other communities to reorganize themselves after having been disorganized by external forces for so long. This began simultaneously in Aru, Seram, Haruku, and the Kei Besar Islands. These areas have yet to achieve results as impressive as Yamdena, but their experiences—especially those of Haruku and the Kei Besar Islands—are nevertheless providing valuable lessons in how traditional institutions, by reviving indigenous practices and systems of knowledge, can build workable frameworks for reorganization and self-empowerment.

In Haruku, one of the traditional bodies under the village customary council is called the Kewang, from *kapala ewang*, meaning "the head of the forests." It is responsible mainly for supervising the implementation of customary laws, particularly those intended to protect the environment and natural resources. The Haruku have developed many creative ways of doing this by combining their traditions with modern and scientific perspectives. They have cooperated closely with local NGOs, universities, and research institutions in developing more systematic efforts toward environmental conservation and education. Among other projects, they have worked to rehabilitate the mangrove and estuary ecosystem, to protect coral reefs, to develop a sanctuary for *maleo* (*Eulopia wallacei*, an endangered megapode bird), and to experiment with sustainable aquaculture techniques. All of these voluntary activities have been coordinated by the local foundation Learissa Kayeli, named after a legendary crocodile said to have brought the *lompa* fish to Haruku. Involved are not only Kewang members (forty persons representing five associations of village clans) but entire communities. In the last five years, action committees have been established among women and youth; even children have formed a group named Kewang Kecil (Little Kewang) to work in a mangrove nursery project as part of their environmental education. The Baileo Kewang (the Kewang hall), on the outskirts of the villages, now functions as a real community center, one more active and effective than the official Baileo Negeri (village hall) at the village center. This is most evident every Friday afternoon when the Kewang members hold their weekly meeting to discuss problems and plans of actions.

A recent struggle of the Haruku people against a plan for gold mining on their traditional territory was initiated from this center. By November 1996, the center's importance had grown to where it was now the venue for meetings of the Kewang and customary councils of more than twenty villages of the Lease Islands (Ambon, Haruku, Saparua, and Nusa Laut). There they formulated a plan to reactivate the Latupatti, a federation of customary councils from several villages or islands. There had been no Latupatti in the twenty-five years since the government's 1971 implementation of Act No. 5/

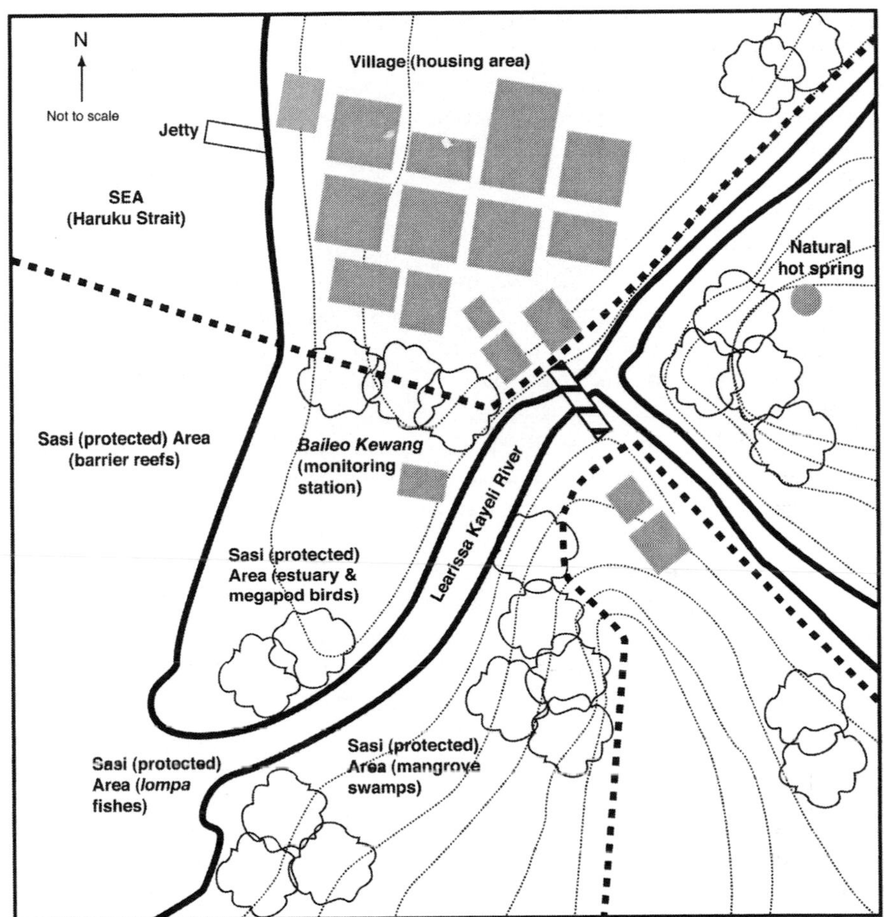

Map 14.3 Haruku Village, Showing *Sasi* Areas

1969. Only time will tell whether this event will be remembered as a historic turning point in the revival of the area's indigenous people.

A similar reorganization has taken place in Kei Besar. In the traditional territory of Maur Ohoiwut, a federation has been established of ten villages encompassing forty-six hamlets and more than fourteen thousand people. In 1992 a series of intensive discussions began with the local customary councils, and in 1994 all of them agreed to ask their supreme chief (the raja) to resign as *kepala desa*. Although this was his office according to the Act No. 5/1969, in fact he had continued to function as the raja. In terms of local and national politics this decision was a rebellion, an act of disobedience against the state. This is the first time in the Moluccas that an official *kepala desa* has openly declared his resignation to the public in such a way, "because I feel that, only as the Raja can, I freely and fully serve the real needs and interests of my people according to our customary laws, something I have proved unable to do during my long term as an official *kepala desa* for the last twenty years."[7] Surprisingly, there were no reactions from his official supervisors, the local *camat* and *bupati*. Subsequently, the customary councils stepped forward to draw up a detailed five-year strategy. Again, a traditional institution was proving itself capable of adopting a modern management approach to serve its needs.

This work was coordinated under a local foundation called *Maur Ohoiwut*—named after the territory itself—which was established in 1993. The foundation was required to report annually to the customary councils in their General Assembly. The assembly has since become better organized and pursues a well-planned thematic agenda. Every year the assembly is attended by more than four hundred participants representing all segments of the communities (e.g., the elderly, women, and youth groups) of every village, and open debate is common during the sessions. In 1995 the assembly agreed to establish a permanent slate of women delegates and to provide them with special sessions, held two days before, to formulate their own presentations to the assembly plenary sessions. One result has been a plan of activities to improve the skills and capacities of local women to take part in the process of managing natural resources, particularly in areas where these are directly related to the women's concerns. Examples are *ruhan met soin* and *met*, low-tide zones where women gather nonfish reef products, and *ohoi murin* and *rok*, the outskirts of fields where women collect daily vegetables, fruits, and herbal plants. This is a historic achievement in a male-dominated traditional community, perhaps unprecedented among the indigenous people of Indonesia. In 1996 the assembly had already formulated a basic draft, the Integrated Community Based Resource Management Plan, to develop a systematic approach to management and control of natural resources. Again, their approach combined their traditional system with modern scientific methods. The plan was designed to counter a controversial protected-forests plan put forward by the government, and a plan for oil exploration of the area devised by Texas Union. Lack of funds, information, and expertise have meant that this initiative is still in its initial stages, and a team is in the process of preparing a detailed technical plan.

These cases are further evidence that it is crucial to form strong organizations that are locally founded, managed, and controlled. This is virtually a precondition for successful community-based resource management and for retaining local rights to those resources. The absence of such an organizational and institutional base will make it difficult to empower communities and leave their institutions artificial and vulnerable to manipulating or cooptation by powerful external forces. This conclusion is confirmed by events in the Aru and Seram Islands, which have unfolded very differently from those on Tanimbar, Kei Besar, and Haruku.

Organizational work on Aru took place among traditional communities in Wokam and Kola Islands, the center of the pearl-cultivation industry for centuries and of modern trawling operations for the last two decades. Almost all of the traditional territories in this area had already been leased or purchased by big pearl companies. In Seram, organization took place among migrants whom the government had involuntarily resettled in 1978 from three tiny volcanic islands (Teon, Nila, and Serua) in the middle of the Banda Sea. The communities in both areas had lost all of their own *petuanan negeri*, their traditional ways of life had mostly disintegrated, and their traditional institutions had virtually disappeared.[8] After five years of trial and error, a true locally based organization was established in 1996, some four years after those in Tanimbar, Kei Besar, and Haruku. During that difficult preparation period, only ten new local organizers were recruited in Aru and six in Seram, compared with no less than twenty each in Tanimbar, Kei Besar, and Haruku during the first two years alone. Although the customary councils in the latter three places have stepped forward with more and more initiatives and new plans, the local organizations in Aru and Seram have managed to begin only the elementary task of reactivating their customary councils.

In 1994 all the local organizers held their first Annual Coordination Meeting in Ambon. They agreed to establish a small office in that provincial town as a clearinghouse and program-coordination center. The office is also responsible for building external networks outside the Moluccas, especially for developing information, expertise, and legal and financial support systems. The office is called Baileo Maluku (Baileo for short), a term that literally means "sacred house" but in everyday life means a community hall or a public place where all villagers can meet, discuss problems, and plan common activities. Every Moluccan village has its own *baileo*, usually an open building with a distinctive architecture, a village landmark beside the church or mosque. The Baileo office in Ambon is responsible for organizing the Annual Coordination Meeting of its constituent local organizations and for reporting to them. The office also facilitates the development of new institutions to develop a support system for all of the organizations. In recent years, Baileo has helped establish a housing cooperative based on Kei Kecil Island, an interinsular trading house in Tual town, and a local credit union based in Dobo town of Aru Island. As part of its advocacy role, it has also founded a legal resources center in Ambon town. This center was established in cooperation with the Law School of Pattimura University of Ambon. All the other new institutions are owned through an equity- or production-sharing scheme. They are managed on a daily basis by local people who have been trained in internship and other programs outside the Moluccas. In sum, the elementary process of organization that started at the grassroots level a few years ago is now entering a more advanced stage.

PROMISING TECHNIQUE: MAPPING

There is, of course, no instant recipe for organizational work that can be applied in every place. The specific circumstances of each community must always be considered. In the organizational work just described, the local organizers have used a variety of methods and techniques that reflect the diverse needs of different communities—no single blueprint or master plan was used. Each local organization presented their goals and needs to the Baileo, which searched for resources to help address them. Through this mechanism the technique of mapping was introduced to Moluccan communities.

The need for mapping was first articulated in early 1993 at a meeting of organizers of Kei Islands. They were beginning to encounter disputes over the boundaries of traditional territories, both between neighboring villages and between the local government and private parties. An opportunity presented itself when the Baileo received information about a community mapping workshop for indigenous people of Southeast Asia, to be held in northern Thailand. The eldest member of the customary council of Evu Village participated in the workshop in January 1994, and afterward he invited the facilitator, a Canadian geographer, to conduct a similar workshop the following June in the Moluccas on Kei Kecil and Kei Besar Islands. The twenty-eight participants in this nine-day workshop were organizers and members of customary councils of communities from the central and southeast Moluccas, Irian Jaya, and Timor Islands. The main focus was basic training in mapping—how to understand, read, interpret, and make standard maps using basic equipment such as a compass, tape meter, and ruler. Because of the boundary disputes, the workshop focused on how to map boundaries. A team from the Baileo acted as cofacilitators and recorded the entire workshop. They subsequently produced an illustrated handbook and a short video, which acted as a training manual. The participants took the manual home and used it to train villagers. Since then, many Moluccan communities have produced boundary maps for their villages and *petuanan negeri*, most of them at a 1:10,000 scale. Some have used these maps to settle boundary disputes, but they have also used them to develop thematic maps for various purposes. These include maps relating to local land-use and tenure management, housing development, and village sanitation plans and clean-water supplies. Some have been developed toward very specific objectives, such as one made to monitor the pristine mangrove belts within the communal territory of ten villages along the west coast of the Kei Kecil

Islands in the Gulf of Hoat Varang. In 1995 Baileo received information about tribal groups in northern Thailand that have used a landscaping model employing three-dimensional mapping techniques. In cooperation with the Popular Communication Program of the South East Asia Regional Institute for Community Education (PCP-SEARICE) based in Kuala Lumpur, Malaysia, Baileo invited two Thai community organizers to conduct a workshop in the Moluccas that May. Most of the participants had also attended the first workshop, and so they were able to further develop their basic skills. The workshop focused on how to read topographic maps and how to build three-dimensional models in an enlarged scale of up to 1:5,000. Because of their vivid features, these maps make excellent tools for facilitating discussions in community meetings, and the meeting focused on how to use them in this way. The model proved an excellent visual kit for community education at grassroots levels. For example, one housewife in Ad Village, Kei Besar Island, after following the entire process of modeling her *petuanan negeri*, said, "Only now can I see the whole of my *negeri*, and realize that we have been harmed by the actions of outsiders for a long time."[9]

Some local organizers went on to creatively develop this modeling technique for use as a medium for many regular activities. Some have combined it with participatory rural appraisal techniques that they had learned previously. For example, they used the model as a simulation kit before carrying out real transects in the field. In October 1994 a group of local fishermen along the north and west coasts of the Kei Kecil Islands employed the same techniques in a reconnaissance survey to monitor the status of coral reefs within their traditional territories. They found that only 40 to 60 percent of these reefs were still intact.[10] They then formulated an action plan to protect the area against further destructive practices such as dynamite and cyanide fishing. In another case in November 1995, two women marine biologists of the Center for Environmental Studies of Pattimura University helped a group of local women carry out a simple transect analysis of the low-tide zones on the west coast of Kei Besar Island. The results led to suggestions to the local customary council that they implement strict regulations on mooring practices and on collecting bait fish and shells and that they prohibit the use of *tuba* (a poison tuber plant traditionally used to paralyze and catch fish).[11] Unfortunately, for technical reasons only the third recommendation was finally adopted by their General Assembly, the following year.[12]

Another creative development is the work of the supreme chief (the raja) of Maur Ohoiwut. He has taken a step forward by using the above techniques to mark off traditional sea and land boundaries of Kei society using a zoning system. Further, he has written down the basic concepts of local customary laws and the history behind these laws. This is the first such document produced by a traditional leader in the Moluccas, perhaps in all of Indonesia. It is an elaborate description of traditional knowledge, focused on a particular theme. It includes an insightful analysis of recent changes, challenges, and prospects.[13]

The document was published with an introduction by Indonesia's minister of Environment. Earlier another chief, of the Kewang of Haruku, had published a document describing the *sasi* of his traditional territory, using a simple sketch-mapping technique.[14] This too was introduced by the minister. From these publications emerged the idea that community mapping projects should not only produce maps but also documents that can be used as historical evidence of traditional territorial ownership. This will allow communities to record and copyright this information on their own behalf, independently of foreign researchers. The results will become a significant contribution to the promotion and advocacy of the indigenous intellectual property rights and the rejection of the existing hegemonic intellectual property rights regime.

Mapping is not really a new undertaking for traditional communities. Sketched lines, shapes, or dots have been used for centuries to demarcate specific areas. In Ohoidertawun Village on the northwest coast of the Kei Kecil Islands, ancient paintings along a two-kilometer granite wall include simple maps. Maps have also been found in stone caves along the mangrove swamps of the northern coast of central Seram near Sawai Village. Mapping activities in the Moluccas in recent years show that traditional communities can employ modern cartographic techniques and even use advanced technology such as global positioning system (GPS) technology and computers. In 1996 with the help of a geography student from the University of Hawaii working in the Kei Islands, both GPS and computer technologies were introduced to local organizers. They were able to use these to revise village boundary maps that they had made before using compasses.

In the Moluccas, as I have described, the emphasis is still on using mapping for organizational purposes at the community level. So far, other than the cases of Evu and Yamdena, mapping techniques have been used only twice as a tool to advocate the territorial rights of traditional communities in conflict with the power centers. The first case was a boundary dispute between the people of Dumar hamlet, Kei Dullah Island, and the local District Office of Fisheries (DOF). In November 1996 some local facilitators helped the Dumar people to map the boundaries of their traditional territories by using compasses, GPS, and a computer. They produced a 1:5,000 map that showed their territorial boundaries, including the boundaries of a piece of land where the DOF had been granted permission to build a fishing pier and auction complex. Not surprisingly, the DOF violated the agreement and constructed an additional road that violated the agreed-upon lines. The people produced the map they had made, and the DOF personnel were quite surprised. Though they had lost the dispute, the DOF officers tried to use their official powers to win through a legal trick. The people contacted the local organizers, and two senior lawyers from the legal resources center in Ambon came to Tual town to provide legal assistance. In the end, the DOF quit the dispute and the people won.

The second case was that of Rhun, a tiny island near Banda. Here the people were helped by an agroforestry student of the Technical University in Berlin who had carried out his dissertation research on the island. The customary council of Rhun had carried out intensive participatory rural appraisal and mapping activities that generated a well-written proposal to the local government and the house of representatives of the central Moluccas District. Supported by excellent maps, the proposal described a comprehensive plan to manage the island's land by combining traditional practices and modern scientific methods. The proposal made legal and political arguments that emphasized the need to recognize traditional land rights and the central role of local people in managing local natural resources. The Rhun people submitted the proposal to the local house of representatives to gain legal recognition through an official decree, a precondition for successfully implementing the plan.[15] A complicated legal and political process is ongoing, and the proposal has yet to be officially recognized. Given Indonesia's bureaucracy and the country's market-oriented economic policies, it may never be.

CONCLUSION

These are just two local cases and do not by themselves prove that community mapping can be an effective tool against Indonesia's political and economic establishment. It is important to note that mapping is an effective tool only at lower political levels. At higher levels of conflict, elites resort to force, against which maps are ineffective, and in such cases communities must turn to other legal and political weapons. In an overcentralized political system like Indonesia's, if communities have no significant legal assistance and lack clear political agendas, maps will merely be maps. The Yamdena case teaches us that community territorial rights can be defended only through well-integrated, multifaceted approaches. Community resource management and organization must take place at multiple levels, ranging from on-the-ground efforts in local villages to the frontlines of political action at the regional, national, and global levels.

POSTCRIPT

In mid-1997, of the regional economic crises that spread through East and Southeast Asian countries, Indonesia's was the worst. The crisis came at the same time as domestic political turbulence, with massive political rallies of students, NGO activists, farmers, workers, indigenous peoples, and women's groups taking place in most big cities. This culminated in May 1998 when more than thirty thousand students blockaded and occupied the huge complex of the National Parliament House in Jakarta. In the end, President Suharto resigned, ending thirty-two years of corrupt military dictatorship.

The first democratic election since 1955 was held in April 1999. The political and legal systems changed, among many others closely related to issues of natural-resource management, local autonomy, and the rights of indigenous peoples. Before the election, in January, the new House of Representatives passed two new national bills—Nos. 22 and 25/1999—on local autonomy and village self-governance. These replaced the notorious Act No. 5/1969. In 2000 the new National Assembly passed the Third Amendment of National Constitution and in 2001 Decree of National Assembly No. IX/2001 recognizing the rights of local communities to own and manage their local natural resources based on their local customs.

All of these new policies provide new challenges and opportunities for Indonesian NGOs to step forward in advocating the rights of the country's local communities and indigenous peoples. The local communities of the Baileo Maluku Network actively participated in establishing the National Alliance of Indigenous Peoples (Aliansi Masyarakat Adat Nusantara, AMAN) and the patron of the network, the supreme chief of Maur Ohoiwut, J. P. Rahail (who died in November 2001), became the chairperson of AMAN's first national congress in Jakarta in 1999. AMAN is now working actively with the national network of NGOs to advocate proper implementation of the Third Amendment of National Constitution and the Decree of National Assembly No. IX/2001.

However, corrupt politicians and military officers are trying to regain power. They have created chaotic situations in many places. One example is the involvement of hundreds of soldiers who deserted the army, police, and an organized criminal militia (*preman*) in a civil war in Aceh and in the ethnic and religious conflicts in west and central Kalimantan, central Sulawesi, and the Molucca islands. The first riots erupted in Ambon town in January 1999, and quickly spread to the islands of Lease, Seram, Banda, Buru, Ternate, Halmahera, Kei, Aru, and Tanimbar.

This has sowed confusion among many local communities in the Moluccas but not those who have been systematically reorganizing themselves for many years. While many still do not know how to respond to all of these major changes, the groups of organized local communities of the Baileo Maluku Network in Kei Islands, led by J. P. Rahail, immediately took the initiative to organize a genuine reconciliation process in the islands, based on their customary laws (*larwul ngabal*) and wisdom (*ken sa vak*). Hundreds of local organizers of the Baileo Maluku Network took part in this voluntary humanitarian and peace-building work. By the end of 2000, they had successfully established a lasting peace in the islands. This was the first success story for a community-based reconciliation process in the Moluccas, or even in Indonesia—one truly initiated by the local people themselves without intervention from the government, security forces, or even outside NGOs.[16] Similar actions were taken by the local community organizers and volunteers of the Baileo Maluku Network in Aru, Tanimbar, Seram, and the Buru islands. They will also be able to establish peace in those islands and the remaining Lease and Ambon islands. The latter are still dealing with corrupt government and military officers and are now isolated as the sole area of conflict in the Moluccas today.

Soon after the peace was established, the local communities of the Baileo Maluku Network began to respond with new policies on natural-resource management, local autonomy, and village self-governance. Again, the best-organized local communities of the Kei Islands were on the front lines. In the beginning of 2002, for example, the people of Evu Village in the Kei Kecil Islands continued their struggle to claim a natural spring in their village (described earlier). Finally, the local district government and the House of Representatives (DPRD) of southeast Moluccas issued an official order to the district's Company of Water Supply (PDAM) to pay the Customary Council of Evu compensation of 100 million rupiah (about U.S. $12,000) and an annual rental payment.

Their neighbor village, Debut, achieved a still more substantive result. Led by senior local community organizers of the Nen Masil Foundation of the Baileo Maluku Network and Alo Jamlean, who was elected as the new chief of the village at the end of 2000, the villagers have creatively implemented the new national bill No. 22/1999. They have been transforming their own traditional structures (*seniri*, the customary council) into a village council of representatives (Badan Perwakilan Desa, BPD) according to the new bill's basic principles of public accountability and subsidiarity (i.e., taking decisions to the lowest possible level of society). In addition to the traditional representatives of all clans, they have added to the council new representatives of women and youth groups, of all religious organizations (Islam, Christianity, and indigenous faiths of Kei), and of migrants (because of the 1999 riots, hundreds of refugees now live in Debut). The chief now directly reports to and is responsible to the council, in an open forum of the annual village assembly attended by all villagers. His report includes the financial management and accounting of village administration. The Nen Masil Foundation of the Baileo Maluku Network is assisting them in an external public auditing process and, on the basis of community mapping from years before, in systematically drafting twenty-four new village regulations (Peraturan Desa, PERDES) on the management of local resources. Particular attention is given to the land-use and tenure system of the village, internal taxes and fines, and developing transparent standard operation procedures for a village planning, budgeting, and accounting system. A mere two years after implementation, the real income of Debut radically increased from only 6 million rupiah before 2001 (solely from the central and district government annual subsidies) to 94 million rupiah in 2001 and to 126 million rupiah in 2002, all without any government subsidies. At the beginning of 2003, the people of Debut went so far as to tell the district government to stop the subsidy, thus avoiding corruption or intervention in their autonomous village governance system due to bill No. 22/1999.[17] There are eight other villages nearby along the west coast of the Kei Kecil Islands that are now trying to replicate Debut's successful model. Even the district government is now encouraging them, and the Office of the Maluku Recovery Program of the United Nations Development Program (UNDP) is suggesting a massive dissemination of Debut's model throughout the Moluccas' four hundred villages.[18]

It has been proven, once again, that a well-organized community is also well prepared to face changes, resolve conflicts that result from them, and even to creatively change itself.

NOTES

1. Translated from *Pertemuan Informal Arafura: Rekoleksi Aktivis se Maluku & Irian Selatan* (Arafura Informal Meeting: Recollection of the Activists of Moluccas Islands and Southern Irian), unpublished report, Ambon, 22–26 April 1992.

2. Translated from J. P. Rahail, *Bat Batang Fitroa Fitnangan: Tata Guna Tanah and Laut Tradisional Kei* (Bat Batang Fitroa Fitnangan: Traditional Land and Marine Systems of the Kei Islands), Sejati, Jakarta, 1995.

3. Some local sources mention that these migrants came from Bali Island and that is why they implemented a caste system. However, no written document mentions precisely when the conquest occurred. Some older people in Letvuan Village in Kei Kecil Island—the conqueror's first settlement—mention "one hundred years ago." The Seram and Banda people migrated to the Kei and Aru Islands in great numbers from the fourteenth through the sixteenth centuries.

4. In Indonesian political terminology, this very sensitive set of issues is referred to as SARA (*suku*, *agama*, and *ras*, or ethnicity, religion, and race) and is easily exploited by government and the military forces as an excuse for taking repressive measures against local people.

5. The first three months of 1997, for example, saw a bloody ethnic riot between local Dayaks and Madurese migrants in west Kalimantan and religious conflicts between Muslims and Christians in west and east Java. For private lands—recognized by a formal certificate registered in the court and the land authority office and with an obligation to pay an annual land tax—government will compensate owners the price of the land, but in many cases the amount is very small. For example, in 1983, when the government wanted to build the multimillion-dollar Kedung Ombo Dam, financed by the World Bank, they paid fifty Indonesian rupiah (about two U.S. cents), or enough to purchase a single cigarette, per square meter. Similar cases

occurred all across the country during that decade, making land issues a major concern. Eventually, the government was forced to increase the compensation rate and improve its procedures of land conversion. Nonetheless, the *beschickingsrecht* principle (discussed later) remains in force, giving the government absolute authority to take over any lands, communal or private, wherever and whenever it wishes. Ten years after the scandalous Kedung Ombo case, land was still being seized in many places, sometimes involving bloody military intervention, as in the case of Nipah, Madura Island, in 1993.

6. Translated from *Permberdayaan Hukum Masyarakat Adat* (Legal Empowerment of Indigenous People), unpublished workshop document, Ambon, 4–6 September 1996. The statement can be read in three papers of the report presented by Supreme Chief J. P. Rahail (of Maur Ohoiwut Territory, Kei Besar Island), retired Chief Bert Ririmasse (of Haruku Village, Lease Island), and Chief Lodewijk Remiassa (of Woitai Village, Seram Island).

7. Translated from an unwritten speech given by the Raja of Maur Ohoiwut J. P. Rahail when he resigned as *kepala desa* of Watlaar Village. It was delivered in the Madiwun Matan Maur Ohoiwut, or MUMMO (General Assembly of the People of Maur Ohoiwut), held in St. Anthonius Church of Watlaar, Kei Besar, 14 November 1994.

8. An elaborated description of the cases of these two places, together with eight others, can be found in the unpublished preliminary survey report of a team of local organizers of Moluccans, *Potret Orang-orang Kalah: Kumpulan Kasus Penyingkiran Orang-orang Asli Kepulauan Maluku* (Portrait of the Losers: Cases of Peripheralization of Indigenous People of the Moluccas), Sejati, Jakarta, 1994, later published by Baileo Maluku and Sejati Foundation. The report describes the basic concept of community organizing addressed in this paper and is the first document to emerge from this community work.

9. *Peragaan Bentang Alam untuk Pengorganisasian Masyarakat* (Landscape Modeling for Community Organizing), workshop report, Ambon, 12–18 May 1995.

10. *Laporan Lokakarya Pengelolaan Sumberdaya Laut* (Report of the Workshop on the Management of Marine Resources), unpub. MS, Ambon, October 1994. Also see "Poisoning the Future," in *Fish-Info*, Ambon, November 1994. This is from a fact-sheet campaign of the Fisheries Working Group of the Moluccas (FWGM), an informal group of researchers of Baileo Maluku.

11. *Laporan Lokakarya Pengelolaan Sumberdaya Pantai oleh Kelompok Perempuan* (Report—Workshop on Management of the Coastal Resources by Women's Groups), unpub. MS, Ambon, November 1995.

12. *Laporan Hasil MUMMO-IV* (Report of the Fourth General Assembly of Maur Ohoiwut), unpub. MS, Watlaar, November 1995.

13. See note 2.

14. Eliza Kissya, *Sasi Aman Haru-ukui: Tradisi Kelola Lingkungan Lestari di Haruku* (*Sasi Aman Haru-ukui*: Tradition of Sustainable Environmental Management in Haruku), Sejati, Jakarta, 1994.

15. For more details see *Masyarakat Pulau Rhun* (The People of Rhun Island), *Tata Guna Tanah Kesepakatan (TGDK) Pulau Rhun: Usulan untuk Pemerintah Daerah Tingkat II Kabupaten Maluku Tengah mengenai Pengembangan dengan*

Keberlanjutan dan Kelestarian Lingkungan Hidup (Agreed Land Use of Rhun Island: Proposal to the Government of Central Moluccas District on a Sustainable Development and Environment), unpub. MS, October 1996. I thank Stefan Stubenvoll, the facilitator of the people of Rhun, and the editor of the proposal, for providing this document and allowing me to cite it.

16. Reports have already been written on this impressive achievement. See, among others, P. M. Laksono, "We Are All One: How Custom Overcame Religious Rivalry in Southeast Maluku," *Inside Indonesia*, April–June 2002. (http://insideindonesia.org). See also Craig C. Thorburn, "Musibah: Entitlement, Violence and Reinventing Tradition in Kei Islands, Southeast Maluku," a paper from the 9th Biennial Conference of the International Association for the Study of Common Property, Victoria Falls, Zimbabwe, 2002. The Baileo Maluku Network itself is now preparing to publish a book about the successful reconciliation process, written by the effort's main actors (local chiefs, community leaders, organizers, and volunteers). It is expected to appear at the end of 2003, to celebrate two years of peace in the Kei Islands.

17. For one report on the impressive achievements of Debut, see Craig C. Thorburn, "Kei Islands Peace Building Programme: Challenge and Opportunities for Programme Development," Evaluation Report to United Nations Development Program (UNDP), Jakarta, 2001.

18. From January to April 2003, UNDP and INSIST (Institute for Social Transformation), based in Yogyakarta, conducted an intensive field assessment study throughout central and southeast Moluccas, and came up with their findings, conclusions, and recommendations based on Debut's model. See INSIST and Partners, "Conflict Analysis and Local Capacity Assessment for Maluku Remaking Program," Report to UNDP, Yogyakarta, 2003. UNDP plans to publish the report, together with a sixteen-minute video documentary, "Village Autonomy: Story from Debut," produced by the Audio-visual Studio of the Nen Masil and the Baileo Maluku Network.

15

Concepts and Strategies for Promoting Legal Recognition of Community-Based Property Rights: Insights from the Philippines and Other Nations

Owen J. Lynch

> Justice denies that the loss of freedom for some is made right by a greater good shared by others. It does not allow that the sacrifices imposed on a few are outweighed by the larger sum of advantages enjoyed by many.
>
> —John Rawls, *Theory of Justice*, 1971

> We live for the time when we see law not as the reflection of the perspectives of the dominant simply because of their dominance but rather a mirror of those who have become powerful because of the eloquence of their wisdom.
>
> —Marvic Leonen, *Engaging the Rhetoric*, 1998

In light of several recent trends regarding conservation and sustainable development, it is important to explore historical and political challenges related to the legal recognition of community-based property rights (CBPR), especially those of indigenous peoples. In this essay I reflect on the sometimes complementary, sometimes uncomplementary roles that scholars and activists play in the promotion of environmental justice and sustainable development.

In this volume, our goal is to confront a problem and a challenge. The problem is that our efforts to promote more just and sustainable societies are largely failing. Our challenge is to address the problem through more effective support for environmental justice by way of sustainable community-based natural resource management (CBNRM). My task is to share insights and experiences related to the use of law and legal strategies for promoting community-based property rights (CBPR) and sustainable CBNRM.

The chapter is organized into two major sections. The first provides a brief overview of my professional background and some institution-building and policy research strategies used in the Philippines to promote the legal recognition of CBPR, especially those held by indigenous peoples. This nascent effort at autobiography represents an attempt to identify and unpack strategies that unfolded day by day, largely as my knowledge base expanded. It is interwoven with a summary of official developments, culminating with the passage of the Indigenous Peoples Rights Act (IPRA) of 1997 and the decisions of the Philippine Supreme Court in December 2000 and October 2001 upholding the constitutionality of the IPRA.

Legal strategies that hold promise for promoting legal recognition of CBPR and sustainable CBNRM in the Philippines may not always be appropriate in other nations. Nevertheless, more than two decades of learning and professional experience convince me that the patterns by which political and economic elites use law to marginalize and oppress rural resource users are largely generic. I am likewise certain that the most effective legal concepts and strategies for promoting justice and sustainable CBNRM are also fundamentally generic. Specific strategies, of course, vary and depend on national and local conditions. Yet our quest to promote human dignity and sustainable development is transcendent, and basic legal principles and concepts for effectively promoting these goals are essentially the same regardless of who we are and where we are located on Earth.

The second section of the chapter manifests this conviction. It comprises a synthesis of theoretical insights and conclusions that began taking shape more than two decades ago in the Philippines and that have since been deepened and refined by research and experience elsewhere in the Global South. Simply stated, most prevailing property rights concepts remain hostile to legal recognition of CBPR and are poorly suited to, or inappropriate for, the widespread promotion of sustainable CBNRM. Therefore, once again, I propose the use of alternative concepts and practical steps.

PART I—PHILIPPINE PRECEDENTS AND EXPERIENCE

Beginnings of a Career

I arrived in the Philippines on 28 August 1980 fresh out of law school and having just taken the Minnesota bar examination. I had been developing expertise in public housing law for the Legal Services Corporation and knew nothing about CBPR or CBNRM. Earlier that year, U.S. Peace Corps–Philippines had recruited me as a volunteer attorney for a two-year tour as part of their innovative and short-lived Upland Community Development Program.

Unlike most Peace Corps programs, which originate in Washington, D.C., or other capital cities, the Upland Program was a product of successful lobbying by volunteers living among so-called ethnic minorities in larger islands' mountainous interiors of the Philippines. The volunteers believed that the problems and potentials of un-Hispanicized, indigenous peoples were unique and merited special attention. The basic problem was the nonrecognition of CBPR over natural resources. The volunteers persuaded the Peace Corps to recruit an attorney volunteer who would try to help upland communities secure legal recognition of their undocumented indigenous property rights and, if possible, make sense out of national laws concerning those rights. To my father's enduring chagrin, I was the recruit.[1]

By August 1982 I had left the Peace Corps, but I remained in the Philippines much longer. In December 1981, I was invited to join the faculty of the University of the Philippines College of Law, where I began to research issues related to national law and CBPR. While at the university I belatedly realized, with considerable surprise, that I had become a mentor for a brilliant and committed group of Filipino law students. Today, many of these lawyers are leading advocates of the environment and human rights in the Philippines, and they deserve much, much more credit than I for the development of effective legal and political strategies in the Philippines. These strategies have had remarkably positive effects on the recognition of indigenous CBPR and the promotion of sustainable CBNRM. But the battle is far from over and much more remains to be done.

Catalyzing the Formation of Public Interest Law NGOs

When I first arrived in the Philippines, public interest law was largely limited to a group of urban-based lawyers. These lawyers worked on behalf of political detainees and other Filipinos who had been subjected to torture and other injustices by the Philippine military and police, often under the protection of officials in the authoritarian government of then-President Ferdinand Marcos. Led by a remarkable man named Jose Diokno, these lawyers waged a valiant struggle for a noble cause. Their focus, however, was almost exclusively on what is considered to be in the realm of civil and political rights. Legal issues related to economic, social, cultural, and environmental rights were largely outside their ambit of concerns.

My task was different. I began an inquiry into the relationship between Philippine national law and what was then referred to as *ancestral land*. I affiliated myself with the Bureau of Forest Development in what was then called the Ministry of Natural Resources, and I hiked to many upland communities throughout Luzon, Mindanao, Palawan, and Mindoro. I soon realized that working within the government's forestry bureaucracy would be not only frustrating but also likely unproductive in terms of promoting legal recognition of the property rights and well-being of indigenous peoples living on so-called public forestland. Hence, when the invitation came in 1981 to join the faculty at the University of the Philippines College of Law, I accepted without hesitation.

The many students who enrolled in my course on Philippine indigenous law soon broadened the ambit of my concerns to include the environment, sustainable development, and Philippine legal history. Several students conducted important research and wrote course papers that helped me better understand various top-down and bottom-up legal perspectives. Others are still pursuing professional careers in ways that have kept me inspired and searching for solutions to a growing array of problems—legal and otherwise—that are related to national self-identity, rural disenfranchisement, human rights, and cultural and environmental degradation.

Mentoring public interest-oriented law students was probably my most important contribution to the development of legal strategies to promote CBPR and CBNRM in the Philippines. The best example of this was the founding of the Legal Rights and Natural Resources Center–*Kasama sa Kalikasan* (LRC-KSK) in 1987 by four former students. I am generally reluctant—by inclination and experience—to promote or otherwise contribute to the creation of new institutions, especially in a country such as the Philippines where there are already so many nongovernmental organizations (NGOs). New institutions, however, are sometimes necessary, and LRC-KSK was created to fill one of those needs. In the span of ten years it became the leading human rights and environmental law research and advocacy NGO in the Philippines.

LRC-KSK has many accomplishments and initiatives to its credit, and I highly recommend their preeminent publication, the *Philippine Natural Resources Law Journal*.[2] Its main goal is "to empower the marginalized and disenfranchised peoples directly dependent on Philippine natural resources."[3] It is organized into teams, including Direct Legal Services, Research and Policy Development, and Campaign Support and Linkages, and it has a Mindanao branch office.

I want to stress that LRC-KSK was not my idea but that of its four founders, including Gus Gatmaytan (this volume). I simply believed in them, their integrity, and their commitment and dared, encouraged, and helped them to develop innovative, alternative legal careers.[4] I would add that most of LRC-KSK's accomplishments were achieved after I moved back to the United States at the end of 1988.

Other Philippine public interest environmental law NGOs have been created since the mid-1980s. Celso Roque, a founder of the Philippine environmental movement, and I conceived of Tanggol Kalikasan (Defend Nature) soon after LRC-KSK's birth. Tanggol Kalikasan was envisioned as an NGO that would focus on litigation as a means to prompt the Philippine judiciary to heed and enforce environmental laws. It has since diffused its outreach activities into legal advocacy, community organizing, and paralegal training efforts. Another NGO, PANLIPI, was organized to provide paralegal training, especially to indigenous and other rural constituencies. Among its major accomplishments has been the development of a nationwide network of lawyers based in provincial cities who provide legal assistance to local communities. The Environmental Legal Assistance Center (ELAC) was established in 1990 by young Visayan lawyers who drew inspiration from the Manila-based environmental law NGOs but wanted to target legal resources on regions in the central Philippines. ELAC now focuses much of its activities on paralegal training, popular legal education, and providing direct legal assistance to local communities. Established lawyers in Davao City created the Mindanao-based Paglilingkod Batas Pangkapatiran (Solidarity in Legal Service) Foundation in 1990 to promote public interest law in general. By 1992 this organization was concentrating on environmental problems, and by 1996 its emphasis on providing legal assistance to ethnically distinct indigenous and Muslim communities was set.

These and other public interest environmental groups coordinate their activities through Environmental Legal Defense (EnDefense). Manila-based public interest law groups, including development and human rights organizations, coordinate their activities through the Alternative Law Group.

Policy Research

The other major prong of the overall legal strategy that developed to promote legal recognition of CBPR and sustainable CBNRM in the Philippines that I have learned to use was collaborative policy research. A crucial goal of this research has been to demythologize and weaken Philippine national laws hostile to CBPR and to promote supportive, alternative legal perspectives. Three research topics have proved most important: the Regalian Doctrine, the Maura Law of 1894, and a 1909 U.S. Supreme Court decision—*Cariño v. Insular Government*. This research has proved to be an essential—and surprisingly successful—part of legal strategy for recognition of indigenous CBPR throughout the Philippines. In the next section I summarize these three research foci to demonstrate how important it is to deconstruct and understand the legal origins of national laws related to CBPR and CBNRM. Research involving the historical deconstruction of the Philippine state that began in the early 1980s continues to contribute to the development of a more just and culturally appropriate legal vision for the Philippines. It is my hope that the research summaries may provide a model for similar in-depth inquiries in other nations.[5]

Mythical Regalian Doctrine

I learned soon after I arrived in the Philippines that the foremost legal obstacle to recognition of ancestral-domain rights was symbolically rooted in the so-called Regalian Doctrine, a concept I have since found in various guises in many other developing countries. The Regalian Doctrine is the original sin of Philippine law and jurisprudence. Conceptually, it highlights the undemocratic (or perhaps more accurately, the misbegotten) origins of the Philippine state. Although evidence of human beings in the Philippine archipelago stretches back at least twenty thousand years, the legal origins of the embryonic Philippine state, by contrast, are rooted in documents signed in 1493 by the Spanish Borgia Pope Alexander VI. The documents, cumulatively known as the Declaration of Alexander, provided the legal basis for the Regalian Doctrine.

According to the doctrine, at some unspecified moment during March 1521, ostensibly after the soon-to-be-killed Ferdinand Magellan "discovered" the archipelago[6] and planted a cross on the island of Limasawa (in what is now known as the Visayas), the sovereign rights of the Philippine people's forebears were unilaterally usurped by, and simultaneously vested in, the Crowns of Castille and Aragón.[7] At the exact same time, every native in the politically undefined and still largely unexplored (not to mention unconquered) archipelago ostensibly became a squatter, bereft of any legal rights to land or other natural resources. The only way they could reacquire sovereignty legally was to get it back from the colonial usurpers. The sole means of removing the squatter label was by procuring a documented property right from the Spanish regime or its state successors. Predictably, procuring a documented property right was—and remains—an exceptionally difficult if not impossible task for most rural resource users.

Despite its arbitrary, mythical, and unjust usurpation of sovereignty and community-based customary property rights and the enactment of the IPRA of 1997, the Regalian Doctrine still theoretically undergirds the legal foundations of the Philippine state. It continues to provide the theoretical bedrock upon which all recognized private property rights in the Philippines—individual or communal—are based.

The Regalian Doctrine is a perfect marginalization tool. On a concrete level, it provides an exceptionally convenient pretext for the state to ignore property rights based on original long-term occupancy and possession. On a more abstract plane, it serves as a conceptual starting point, one so simple and historically befuddled that it continues to hamper thorough analysis of the undemocratic origins, evolution, and ongoing impact of Philippine colonial laws and of the misbegotten nature of the Philippine Republic (see Lynch 1992).

Perhaps most troubling is that continued reliance on the Regalian Doctrine parallels the Philippine state's long-standing negation of the nation's indigenous cultures and values. This has not only contributed to political instability but it exacerbates a chronic identity crisis that has confounded the Philippine Republic (and many other former colonial states) since its inception. The identity crisis is evident in an unbalanced disdain of indigenous Philippine cultures that permeates the perceptions of most (although certainly not all) Filipino elites. This contempt originated in the ethnocentrism of the Spanish and North American colonists. Unfortunately, the estrangement of Philippine elites from their indigenous heritage, and of the Philippine state from its marginalized rural majority, largely continues.

Nowhere is this more evident than in the ways the Philippine state, whether in its colonial or independent guise, has allocated and guaranteed legal rights to land and other natural resources. A recurrent theme in Philippine land law over the last century has been the failure of the state to recognize and protect the CBPR of original long-term occupants. The end result has been the ongoing legal marginalization and displacement of many rural peoples and the empowerment of a small elite with access to and control over state power.

Maura Law of 1894

Contrary to what promoters of the Regalian Doctrine assert, the legal usurpation of indigenous property rights in the Philippines actually dates back only to 1894. Sixteenth-century debates over the legal bases of Spanish sovereignty in its far-flung empire influenced official attitudes concerning the Crown's ownership of land and other natural resources. The uncertainty was exacerbated by reports of greed and brutality being inflicted by Spanish colonists on indigenous peoples in the Americas. After some initial hesitancy, King Philip II resolved that a similar fate would not befall the Philippine natives. To that end, an "irrevocable commitment of the Spanish colonial policy" was that the "natives as 'new Christians,' merited some effective guarantees of their property rights" (Phelan 1959, 94). These guarantees endured for more than three centuries, and various laws were promulgated in Spain to promote them, including many laws that also applied to non-Christians.[8]

In 1894 most indigenous CBPR in the Philippine colony remained undocumented. The vast majority of people in the colony presumably never knew about colonial legislation pertaining to registration of land and other natural resource rights. The uneven Spanish impact, abuses by colonial officials, illiteracy, a dearth of newspapers with wide circulation, lack of money to pay for transportation fares and legal prerequisites (e.g., filing fees, attorney fees, survey costs) all presumably kept most people unaware of and without access to legal processes for documenting and registering their customary property rights.

As a result, attempts to promote the registration and documentation of customary property rights were largely unsuccessful, and those rights that were registered were largely in disarray. In a last attempt to address confusion over property rights in its distant colony, Spain imposed a unilateral registration deadline by way of the Royal Decree of 13 February 1894, better known as the Maura Law. The decree was published and became effective in the Philippine Islands on 17 April of that year. The Maura Law was the last important land law enacted by Spain for its distant Philippine colony (Francisco 1950, 7). Its preamble averred that the decree was enacted to "insure to the natives, in the future, whenever it may be possible, the necessary land for cultivation, in accordance with traditional usages." Article 4, however, revealed a much different purpose. It provided that "title to all agricultural lands which were capable of adjustment under the Royal Decree of . . . 1880, but the adjustment of which has not been sought at the time of promulgation of this decree, . . . will revert to the State. Any claim to such lands by those who might have applied for adjustment of the same but have not done so at the above-mentioned date, will not avail themselves in any way nor at any time."[9] Those whose applications for possessory information titles were pending were given one year to secure their documentation. No extensions were made, and any paper titles issued after 17 April 1895 were deemed to have no force and effect.[10]

The decree's primary author and namesake, the Minister of Colonies, Antonio Maura y Montaner, hailed his creation and gloated that "it must be looked upon as one of our most important legal works" (Malcolm 1916, 55). The Minister's rhetoric was not excessive, but from the perspective of the masses, the importance of the Maura Law did not emanate from any benefits received. Instead, the Maura Law theoretically empowered the colonial regime to deny, for the first time ever, legal recognition of customary property rights. The immediate symbolic effect was to disenfranchise several million rural farmers. "In many cases peasants who had felt secure in their possession of their land and had not known or cared about [documentary] titles were suddenly confronted with the fact that a wealthy person, with the [colonial] law behind him, was claiming their land. These peasants were then driven from it or forced to become tenants" (Pelzer 1945, 90).

Enactment of the Maura Law demonstrated the insular regime's longstanding insensitivity to the plight and potentials of the vast majority of people in the Philippine colony. There was nothing new in this, as colonial regimes were inherently exploitative and unjust. The decree's novelty lay in the fact that the government in Madrid, during the twilight of Spain's Pacific empire, reneged on its centuries-old commitment to respect indigenous CBPR. This virtually unnoticed betrayal of Spain's self-imposed historic role had repercussions that have endured long after Spanish sovereignty over the Philippine Islands was relinquished. The Maura Law provided the legal basis by which the U.S. colonial regime denied any effective recognition of ancestral property rights. More significantly, the philosophy behind the Maura Law provided the legal foundation for the prevailing twentieth-century version of the Regalian Doctrine.

Native Title and *Cariño v. Insular Government*

The most authoritative exposé of the Regalian Doctrine's historical fallaciousness is found in a remarkable decision, *Cariño v. Insular Government*, which was unanimously rendered by the U.S. Supreme Court on 23 February 1909. The *Cariño* decision laid out a legal foundation for a Philippine doctrine of native title (U.S. Supreme Court, volume 212 of *United States Reports*).

In the unanimous decision written by Oliver Wendell Holmes, the court went along with those who argued that Spain, in its early decrees, "embodied the universal feudal theory that all lands were held from the Crown,"[11] but Holmes dismissed these laws as "theory and discourse." The simple fact was, Holmes wrote, "that titles were admitted to exist that owed nothing to the powers of Spain." As for the 1894 Maura Law, Holmes admonished that the decree "should not be construed as confiscation, but as the withdrawal of a privilege to obtain recognition of ownership rights and register title." Holmes went on to emphasize that even if Spain refused to recognize the undocumented property rights of an indigene, it did "not follow that, in the view of the United States, he had lost all rights and was a mere trespasser." Holmes considered such a perspective to be repugnant. In his words, "The argument to that effect seems to amount to a denial of native titles . . . for the want of ceremonies which the Spaniards would not have permitted and had not the power to enforce." Holmes stressed that, being a new sovereign, the United States was not bound by Spanish laws and was free to discard them whenever they clashed with U.S. objectives. "No one, we suppose, would deny," Holmes wrote, that "the first object in the internal administration of the islands, so far as is consistent with paramount necessities, is to do justice to the natives, not to exploit their country for private gain."

In Holmes' opinion, justice was to be meted out in compliance with the Philippine Organic Act, which the U.S. Congress had passed in 1902. He quoted, in particular, the first provision in the act's Philippine Bill of Rights, which mimicked the Fifth Amendment to the U.S. Constitution. It provided that "no law shall be enacted which shall deprive any person of life, liberty, or property without due process of law, or to deny any person the equal protection of the laws." Holmes seemed aghast that the U.S. government "was ready to declare that 'any person' did not embrace the inhabitants of Benguet [where the petitioner, an Ibaloi chieftain, was from], or that it meant by 'property' only that which had become such by ceremonies of which presumably a large part of the inhabitants never had heard, and that it proposed to treat as public land what they, by native custom and by long association—one of the profoundest factors in human thought—regarded as their own."

In the *Cariño* decision, Holmes formulated the holding that provided that "when as far back as testimony or memory goes, the land has been held . . . under a claim of private ownership, it will be presumed to have been held in the same way from before the Spanish conquest, and never to have been public land." The Court went on to rule that any ambiguities or doubts as to the applicability of Spanish laws were, henceforth, to be resolved in favor of applicants for recognition of native title.[12]

The Manila-based U.S. colonial government was not pleased with the holding. It had dreams of establishing large-scale, commercial sugarcane plantations, and recognizing community-based, customary property rights would hamper the implementation of that dream.[13] Cariño's efforts to secure documentary recognition of his ancestral ownership were, ironically, crowned with success.[14] It would have been an act of brazen defiance for the insular regime to refuse to issue his paper title. Except for recognizing Cariño's rights, however, the decision had no effect on the colonial government. Millions of indigenes within the so-called public domain, which at the time encompassed nearly 90 percent of the colony's total landmass, continued to be grossly underestimated. Even more objectionable, in view of the *Cariño* decision, they continued to be labeled as squatters.[15]

Leading Philippine colonial officials repeatedly and publicly expressed the opinion that, once Congress was persuaded to lift the size limitations on corporate holdings in the Philippine Bill of 1902, extensive investments could be drawn into the colony. If their plan was to ever bear fruit, it was important to keep the so-called public domain from becoming officially encumbered with legally recognizable property rights, especially undocumented rights held by poorly regarded tribal and peasant cultivators. Recognizing that undocumented customary rights existed and acknowledging that millions of people in 1909 resided on so-called public lands, would have created another legal obstacle to the colonial regime's efforts to provide wealthy North American investors and collaborating Filipino elites with unencumbered legal access to the colony's natural resources. The creation of new rights would have had a similar effect.[16]

U.S. officials responsible for the Philippine colony, therefore, surreptitiously conceptualized and implemented a scheme that, contrary to official rhetoric and the mandate of the U.S. Congress, ignored and undermined the rights of small-scale owner-cultivators and communities. The key elements of their hidden agenda were to keep estimates of "public" land occupants low and ensure that the processes for recognizing and allocating legal rights to land and other natural resources were inefficient and bureaucratically cumbersome. For its part the insular U.S. regime systematically and successfully blocked any wider application of the *Cariño* precedent and thereby precluded the recognition of native titles and the legal attachment of any other customary, community-based private property rights.

After 1913 the colonial government was rapidly Filipinized—staffed by Filipinos who perpetuated the natural resource laws and policies enacted early on by the new U.S. colonial government. Filipino elites learned to manipulate the system to their advantage and many acquired individual private property rights over large areas of fertile, arable land. All the while, the *Cariño* doctrine of native title continued to be overlooked. Making matters worse for promoters of CBNRM, during the martial law years of President Marcos (1972–1981), Philippine national laws concerning natural resources were made even more hostile to the rights and aspirations of most rural resource users. Most of these martial law refinements have not yet been repealed.

Enduring Legacies of Colonial Laws

The underlying durability of Philippine colonial laws concerning rights to natural resources, including the Regalian Doctrine, cannot be attributed to any equitable or environmentally sustainable outcomes. Recognized individual private property rights in the Philippines include lands where about one-third of the national population lives and works as tenants and day laborers or are their offspring. Within the recognized, that is, documentarily titled, private domain, the Republic of the Philippines is burdened by one of the highest proportions of nonlandowning farm families 25 to 35 percent—found anywhere in the world.[17]

Tenurial problems are equally severe within the so-called public domain—on land over which the state still claims ownership. Pursuant to the Regalian Doctrine, this area in 1997 covered nearly 60 percent of the nation's total landmass. The "public" domain is home to approximately one-third of the national population, or more than twenty-five million people. Most citizens within the "public" domain, including indigenous occupants estimated at more than ten million people, are still officially and indiscriminately labeled as squatters.

The Philippine government, through the Department of Environment and Natural Resources (DENR), claims almost exclusive power to allocate legal rights to use and manage public forest resources. Its policy accords fully with that of its colonial predecessors, which since the 1894 Maura Law was enacted has insisted that all occupants of classified "public" forest lands and coastal zones are squatters, regardless of their length of occupancy. In 1997 the Philippine government claimed ownership to nearly 60 percent of the nation's total land area of 30 million hectares. Almost half of that total is either formally classified as "public" forest or is unclassified and legally presumed to be forested. Most of these areas are in the mountainous interiors of the nation's twelve largest islands, especially Luzon and Mindanao.

The government's ongoing assertion of public ownership over classified forestland has long benefited political and economic elites interested in large-scale commercial extraction and exploitation of forest resources. It has likewise promoted a multitude of conflicts with forest-dependent communities. Rampant and unsustainable commercial logging reached its peak during the decade after martial law was declared in 1972 and often resulted in the arbitrary, forced, and sometimes brutal displacement of forest communities. Since the mid-1980s, the number of timber concessions, however, has steadily declined as the amount of available timber has dramatically diminished. Today the Philippines has less than a half million hectares of primary forest left, and (depending on definitions) three to six million hectares of secondary and residual forests.

Ironically, state-sanctioned usurpation and profiteering by Philippine elites has all too often been legitimated in the name of Philippine nationalism, the unstated rationale being that rampant exploitation by co-citizens is a desirable alternative to rampant exploitation by foreigners. The distinction is, of course, difficult for the exploited to appreciate. One outcome is that the Philippines has been home to the most enduring rural-based rebel insurgency in all of Asia.

Philippine citizens living within the "public" domain have long been invisible peoples, like rural resource users similarly situated in other developing countries. Tens of thousands have been arbitrarily displaced from their ancestral homes, often with state sanction; millions more have long lived under a serious threat of such displacement. Their tenurial predicaments exacerbate a growing array of serious environmental and demographic problems, which the DENR in the past decade has finally begun to address.

Emerging Pro-CBNRM Developments

Popular and official support for sustainable CBNRM, meanwhile, has been steadily increasing over the past decade. The reasons for this are varied and not clearly identified. Some may be rooted in Philippine history, particularly the fostering of public education and a comparatively free press during the U.S. colonial era. Other more recent explanations are rooted in growing public awareness of the severity and importance of the nation's environmental degradation and of the long-overlooked role of indigenous communities in conserving what remains of forest resources.

Political and social activism contributed to the people-power revolution of 1986 that toppled Ferdinand Marcos. That outcome, in turn, fostered a political climate where NGOs and citizen's initiatives were acknowledged as legitimate and important and allowed to flourish. Pressures from international funding institutions—in particular the World Bank, the Asian Development Bank, and the U.S. Agency for International Development (USAID)—to decentralize natural resource management have also been focused and sustained and have contributed to pro-CBNRM policies and programs.

As the twenty-first century commenced, the Philippines continued to be accurately described as an NGO superpower. The NGO and research communities, as well as many community-based people's organizations, are among the most diverse, creative, and effective in the world. Recent Philippine laws and policies reflect the growing influence of civil society and its increasing concern over the degradation of the Philippine environment. Their support for recognition of ancestral-domain rights and government-sponsored CBNRM as important responses to the growing environmental challenges confronting the nation has been crucial. Yet implementation of the new laws, policies, and programs lags, and political will and financial support is still lacking within many government institutions. In addition, many Philippine laws, policies, and programs are more than superficially contradictory, and I sometimes wonder if the internal inconsistencies are intentional.

Despite the generally weak political leverage of forest-dependent communities in the Philippines, most remaining forests are located within indigenous territories. Various strategies are being promoted to enhance the bargaining power of forest-dependent communities so that they can effectively promote their rights and claims and obtain the technical and financial assistance they need to manage natural resources sustainably. The most promising efforts have involved innovative legal and policy research, lobbying of legislators and other government officials, and on-the-ground initiatives by NGOs to disseminate information to forest and fishing communities about their legal rights to natural resources. Perhaps most important have been direct actions by local communities to defend and assert their rights, including the delineation and mapping of their territorial and coastal perimeters and ancestral waters.

Judicial and Legislative Developments

Besides the *Cariño* doctrine of native title, other laws that buttress efforts to promote recognition of CBPR, especially those of indigenous occupants, have also been identified. The Bill of Rights in the 1987 Philippine Constitution, for example, provides that "no person shall be deprived of . . . property without due process of law." Unlike a subsequent section, which prohibits state taking of "private property" for public use without just compensation, the due process provision refers to property in a broader sense. Article 446 of the Philippine Civil Code, meanwhile, provides that "every possessor has a right to be respected in his possession."

For many occupants of the "public" forest zone, the right of possession is bolstered by a stronger right of ownership based on the *Cariño* decision of 1909. In addition, the Philippine Supreme Court has invoked Section 48 of the Public Land Act and affirmed that land occupied for thirty years or more by members of un-Hispanicized ethnic groups is not only ancestral, it is also private.[18]

Existing Philippine laws concerning native title, private rights, and possession provide the legal foundation for a policy of recognition of indigenous CBPR, including those that overlap with forests and potentially even coastal areas. Areas within the classified forest zone, or unclassified "public" land, that have been in original possession for more than thirty years, at least by members of un-Hispanicized ethnic groups, that is, indigenous cultural communities, should not be considered as ever having been public. Instead, the land should be seen as privately owned. This view has increasingly influenced policy making within the Philippine government, even within the Congress. Bills providing for the establishment of legal processes for recognizing, delineating, and protecting ancestral-domain rights have been introduced in the Senate and House of Representatives for more than a decade.

Indigenous Peoples Rights Act of 1997

Surprisingly, the best and most promising bill, the IPRA, passed both chambers and became law on 29 October 1997 (Republic Act No. 8371). IPRA provides for legal recognition of ancestral-domain rights as private community-based property and pursuant to indigenous concepts of ownership.

Perhaps even more remarkable, the Philippine Supreme Court upheld the constitutionality of the IPRA. The decision, released on 6 December 2000, is believed to mark the first time in Asia that a national government has legally recognized indigenous people's territorial rights. Lawyers from LRC-KSK and *Tanggol Kalikasan* (Defend Nature) intervened in support of the IPRA before the Philippine high court. LRC-KSK's petition was on behalf of nearly a hundred representatives of indigenous communities from throughout the nation.

Many provisions in IPRA are potentially troublesome. For example, authority to recognize ancestral-domain rights rests with a National Commission on Indigenous Peoples (NCIP) that requires both strong leaders with integrity and vision and an adequate budget, neither of which have yet been forthcoming. Nevertheless, IPRA represents a remarkable, possibly historic, turnaround for the Philippine state. If interpreted and applied fairly, IPRA can provide indigenous communities in most of the nation's remaining forested areas with national legal incentives for sustainable management. It might also come to represent a repudiation of the Regalian Doctrine and the possible beginning of a new vision for the Philippine nation. Whether these benefits will emerge remains to be seen. In large measure, much still depends on the commitment, strength, and vigilance of Philippine civil society.

National Integrated Protected Areas System Act of 1991

Another significant legislative advance on behalf of some resource-dependent communities is found in the National Integrated Protected Areas System (NIPAS) Act of 1991. The NIPAS law was enacted after the World Bank and Philippine environmental groups exerted strong pressures on the Philippine government to get serious about conserving what remains of the nation's biodiversity and some of its most important ecosystems. Concurrent pressures were brought to bear to ensure that indigenous communities within protected areas were not summarily evicted. Section 13 of the act provides that, within designated protected areas, "Ancestral land and customary rights and interest arising shall be accorded due recognition." Standing alone, this provision could be easily ignored. However, a later sentence in Section 13 is clear and definitive—it establishes that within protected areas the DENR "shall have no power to evict indigenous communities from their present occupancy nor resettle them to another area without their consent."

The NIPAS implementing rules and regulations build on Section 13. Chapter VII of the regulations establishes procedures for the mandatory identification of indigenous communities, the delineation and demarcation of ancestral-domain rights and the participatory formulation and implementation of plans and rules for managing natural resources within ancestral domains. Section 10 of the regulations likewise provides that "the zoning of a protected area and its buffer zones shall not restrict the rights of indigenous communities to pursue traditional and sustainable means of livelihood within their ancestral domain." Unfortunately, as with the IPRA, implementation of the NIPAS laws has been uneven at best. Indigenous Mangyan communities in one part of Mindoro Island became so afraid of and hostile toward NIPAS that plans to establish a protected area were indefinitely postponed (see Erni 1993).

Executive Branch Programs

Before enactment of IPRA, the most promising efforts to promote sustainable CBNRM were found within the Philippine executive branch. In July 1995 President Fidel Ramos issued Executive Order No. 263, which proclaims that "community-based forest management shall be the national strategy to achieve sustainable forestry and social justice." The order mandates the integration of previously separate DENR programs and projects. Well over a thousand rural communities are now participating in various DENR-sponsored CBNRM programs and projects, many of which were established before Executive Order No. 263 was issued.

The evolution of official support for CBNRM in the DENR has been ongoing since the mid-1970s. Over the past two and a half decades, the DENR has developed an often-confusing array of policies and programs for granting tenurial rights to public forest-zone occupants. All of these are based on government grants and fall short of recognizing private CBPR. Pursuant to Executive Order 263, various DENR programs are now integrated under the auspices of a Community-Based Forest Management Office (CBFMO).[19] A standardized model community-based forest-management agreement (CBFMA) is also now in use.

Before IPRA's enactment, the other major DENR initiative was based on DENR Department Administrative Order No. 2 of 1993. The order was issued in response to effective resistance and organizing by indigenous communities, good research, and effective lobbying by NGO allies. It implicitly acknowledged the enduring legal validity of the *Cariño* decision, but it was largely rendered moot by IPRA.

The order established a procedure for delineating and provisionally recognizing the ancestral-domain claims of indigenous forest-dependent communities. Once their areas were delineated, indigenous communities received Certificates of Ancestral Domain Claim (CADCs), which were issued to individuals. Both tenure instruments provide documentary evidence of indigenous property rights, but they recognize only claims. By mid-1998 nearly 2.7 million hectares were covered by CADCs, or nearly 10 percent of the nation's total land mass. Under IPRA, the CADCs are to be converted into Certificates of Ancestral Domain Titles, a process that remains excruciating slow as of 2003.

As with the IPRA, the content of Department Administrative Order No. 2 and its implementation were problematic, a fact that highlights the widespread impacts of these legal reforms. However, despite these problems (some of which should have been anticipated and could have been avoided), in my opinion both the IPRA and the order represent modest but important steps toward full recognition of indigenous people's private CBPR.

Any government-sponsored local natural resource management initiative is likely to be beset with implementation problems, especially in the midst of a profound paradigm shift. Many communities do not know or fully understand their legal rights and options vis-à-vis IPRA and DENR's CBNRM programs. Likewise, at many DENR project sites there is inadequate technical support and assistance. Many projects do not respond to the needs, problems, potentials, and perspectives of local communities. Most funding for the programs has come from foreign donors, especially by way of large loans from the Asian Development Bank and the World Bank, and grants from the Japanese Overseas Economic Cooperation Development fund and USAID. In addition, many DENR regional and field officials still struggle to let go of their previous role as policemen and regulators and adapt to their evolving role as service providers. Nevertheless, Executive Order No. 263, Department Administrative Order No. 2, and IPRA demonstrate the Philippine government's willingness to support the empowerment of natural resource-dependent communities and help them strengthen their position vis-à-vis outside interests.

Meanwhile, as the DENR touts CBNRM with one hand, the other has been promoting Industrial Forest Management Agreements. These agreements provide for continued corporate, commercial logging in residual forests. According to DENR administrative orders, prospective parties to these agreements must identify communities living within the target areas and give them notice of the application, and applicants must enter into mutually agreeable benefit-sharing agreements with local residents. The requirements have been further bolstered by enactment of another administrative order in 1997 providing for the establishment of Socialized Industrial Forest Management Agreements, which are to be held by local communities.

Unfortunately, many timber concessions were converted to Industrial Forest Management Agreements before the DENR issued the new orders that require benefit sharing. The result has been that many forest communities, especially in the large southern island of Mindanao, remain legally marginalized in their ancestral domains. In addition, many agreements are not in compliance with the new orders, a fact that reflects the tenacity of conventional foresters and their resistance to change. But the new administrative orders do provide some potential legal leverage to communities included in Industrial Forest Management Agreement areas after 1993.

Power of Information and Networking

It is evident that good laws and policies, and improvement of bad ones, are not by themselves enough to promote legal recognition of CBPR and sustainable CBNRM, let alone to provide for the well-being of natural resource-dependent communities. Local communities need to know the nature and full extent of their legal rights before government officials and commercial entrepreneurs establish any overlapping rights. When communities do not know their legal rights, they are ill equipped to respond to external pressures. Current laws and policies in the Philippines related to CBPR and CBNRM provide tools for effectively promoting local participation and benefit sharing, as well as for conservation and sustainable development. Communities, therefore, need information on what these legal tools are, how they might choose to use them, and the short- and long-term implications of their decisions. The process of information sharing, however, should not be unidirectional; supporters of community forestry have a lot to share, as well as to learn (Leonen 1998).

Some NGOs are providing natural resource-dependent communities with legal information and paralegal training. Others are establishing and servicing networks for disseminating relevant and timely information to local communities. Successful and effective networks are organized in ways that ensure respect for local cultures and sensitivities and are readily accessible and promptly responsive to the informational needs and requests of the rural communities they serve.

Along with Tanggol Kalikasan and public interest environmental lawyers from various other institutions, I am currently involved in a USAID-Philippines-funded project that is providing direct legal assistance to more than fifty local communities involved in various CBNRM initiatives. The anticipated outcomes of the project are important and fairly modest. A small number of communities participating in DENR-sponsored CBNRM projects are becoming better informed of and able to assert their legal rights and options. The DENR is expected to be better informed of local-level legal concerns, problems, and opportunities, and DENR policies and regulations are more relevant and responsive to local aspirations and conditions. Nevertheless, the goals of the project, and the broader and more important effort to promote sustainable CBNRM in the Philippines, are still part of a vision. Official rhetoric notwithstanding, on-the-ground realities in many locales are still harsh and unfriendly to local communities.

PART II—COMPARATIVE PERSPECTIVES AND SYNTHESES

National Law and CBNRM

In many respects, the Philippines is like other developing countries. Few nation-states, including most in the Global South, broadly recognize either CBPR or local people's contributions to conservation and sustainable management. Likewise, few countries seriously involve local communities in decisions concerning conservation and local resource management. Increasing official rhetoric on the virtues of CBNRM and a steady growth in the number of programs, projects, and in some instances, even pro-CBNRM national laws and policies are welcome developments. They are insufficient by themselves, however, to ensure the success, let alone widespread official and substantive support for sustainable CBNRM.

Disdain and indifference toward rural cultures and peoples persist in many guises. Prejudices are deeply rooted in the history of natural resource policy development and the legal systems upon which most current national laws and policies are based. From a legal perspective, the transition from colonies to modern nation-states in Asia, Africa, and Latin America produced few changes in state laws, policies, and practices for allocating power and wealth among the national citizenries. Meanwhile, although international legal protections are becoming more defined, their impact on local communities and sustainable development remains minimal (Maggio and Lynch 1996).

The bottom line is that most developing countries largely continue to mirror the basic policies and designs of former colonial governments, especially regarding laws concerning the management of and rights to natural resources, including forests and coastal areas. Despite a number of positive legal developments, national laws concerning the use and management of forest resources in at least six Asian countries as of 1995 (Indonesia, Thailand, the Philippines, India, Nepal, and Sri Lanka) were actually more hostile toward local people and communities than was the case during the colonial era (Lynch and Talbott 1995).[20]

Demographic information on forest- and coastal-dependent peoples is sketchy at best, but they clearly have even less political influence than rural farmers living within agricultural areas. The weak bargaining leverage of rural natural resource-dependent communities makes it extraordinarily difficult—and in some cases almost impossible—to promote legal reforms and ensure that local communities are able to participate effectively and substantively in the management of local natural resources.

Research concerning local knowledge and CBNRM is rather recent. Related studies by political scientists, historians, and other social scientists have only just begun to penetrate the prevailing ideology of national laws and legal systems governing the use and ownership of forests and other natural resources. As a result, national laws and policies that create local disincentives for sustainable natural resource management, which are perpetrated by centralized regulatory agencies and legal frameworks, have largely remained unexposed and unchallenged.

The ongoing political and economic disenfranchisement of most rural natural resource users in developing countries and the weak bargaining leverage of indigenous and other local communities are reflected in existing and past laws and policies. Political and economic elites still exercise democratically disproportionate control over national and state governments and international institutions. About 10 percent of the developing world's population, for example, controls one-half to three-quarters of the world's arable areas, whereas 50 percent of people eke out an existence on 3 to 4 percent of the agricultural land base (Cabarle and Heiner 1994).

Lawyers, meanwhile, tend to focus (often for good reasons) on national and international laws and urban issues, especially in capital cities where wealth and power are concentrated. There is little thought and even less research devoted to rural issues, particularly as they relate to local incentives for sustainable development. Creative efforts and solutions that balance prevailing national legal tendencies by giving greater emphasis to problems and contributions of rural peoples and environmental issues, particularly those pertaining to local incentives for sustainable CBNRM, are urgently needed. This is especially important where local people are directly dependent on important and threatened environmental resources, such as forests, rangelands, and coastal areas, and possess local knowledge about how to manage those resources sustainably.

The failure of most governments to recognize the important role of local communities in sustainable CBNRM, of course, has not necessarily terminated communities' management of, and local tenure over, natural resources. Despite expansive claims of ownership, many national governments exercise relatively little control over large areas of forest and coastal resources. Few can pay, train, or maintain the staff needed to survey, patrol, and effectively manage vast areas classified as state owned.

From a legal perspective, the challenge is to surmount legislative and judicial obstacles to CBNRM and to promote the design and implementation of solutions. More specifically, local disincentives for sustainable CBNRM that are established and supported by national laws need to be removed and replaced by incentives that create and foster appropriate legal, regulatory, and economic relationships between local communities; formal governmental institutions on state, local, and international levels; and in some instances, commercial enterprises. These efforts should include policy research, education, advocacy, and institution building and strengthening within governments and civil society. From a legal perspective, there is an especially urgent need in many countries to foster development of public interest environmental law, which includes support for rural resource-dependent communities.

To establish mutually enforceable, appropriate, secure, and enduring legal relationships that promote sustainable CBNRM, local communities should understand what their options, rights, and concomitant duties are in regard to national laws. The national legal framework must also provide support for all claimants. Pilot projects have been known to establish legal precedents that provide an important impetus for establishing new community-oriented policies and programs (Lynch and Talbott 1995; Seymour and Rutherford 1993; Perl et al. 1995; Poffenberger 1990). An adequate legal regime that recognizes the role of and supports grassroots institutions to define, preside over, and redefine the rules of resource use can help provide a fertile environment in which pilot projects can flourish.

On an even more profound level, the substantive continuity between the colonial and politically independent nation-states of Asia, Africa, and Latin America—especially in terms of laws and policies concerning natural resources—remains strong. This raises a host of questions regarding the nature of each nation's social contract. Perhaps foremost is the question of when, if ever, was there any substantive democratic reconstitution of the colonial states that genuinely considered and reflected the aspirations, rights, and potentials of the entire citizenry, especially the poor rural majority.[21]

Ironically, since attainment of political independence by many developing nations, instead of using law to democratize access to natural resources, state assertions of ownership have been broadened and legally reinforced. Ostensibly, this has usually been done in the name of nationalism and the public interest. The public interest, unfortunately, has too often been narrowly defined as the interests of domestic political and economic elites who control their respective states (and are often allied with international interests). Rural peoples, who in many nations of the Global South constitute the vast majority of national citizenries, remain largely unheard and are simplistically stereotyped as ignorant and incapable of managing the natural resources that they rely on for their lives and livelihoods.

A growing body of field research is contradicting this view, demonstrating that many rural peoples throughout the majority world (so-called developing countries) are guardians and stewards of natural resources, including biodiversity reservoirs and carbon sinks. This research, moreover, indicates that many rural peoples possess important local knowledge for managing these resources sustainably. Of course, local conditions and cultures vary and not all local people, including indigenous occupants, respect and protect their natural environments. But all of them are human beings and on that basis alone should have a fundamental right to participate in decisions that directly impact their lives and livelihoods. What right could be more democratic?

Legal Recognition of CBPR

One way to ensure that local voices are heard and respected is by legal recognition of CBPR.[22] Governments can promote and support local incentives for conservation and sustainable management by legally recognizing existing CBPR wherever supported by locally appropriate forms of evidence such as farm fallows, orchards, and gravesites. Government recognition need not necessarily be contingent on or require formal codification or the issuance of any specific documents. More important is the government's fulfillment of its responsibility to help resource-dependent communities defend and benefit from sustainably managed natural resources, whether public or private.

Legal recognition of CBPR would provide state assurance that local people will be better able to profit from investments of their time and labor. It would provide local communities with state-sanctioned authority to prevent migration into their territories, which are often environmentally fragile and overlap with protected areas. It would likewise help local communities better maintain their resources by enforcement of management regulations.

Property rights by themselves, of course, do not provide adequate incentives and conditions for sustainable management; they are a necessary, but insufficient, condition. Technical and other forms of assistance to develop and strengthen local organizational capacities and to support sustainable management and conservation, along with appropriate credit programs that provide economic alternatives to sale or overextraction of resources are also essential.

Concept of CBPR

CBPR are not predicated on any assumption of state ownership, grant, or recognition. Nor are they necessarily contingent on formal documentation. Rather, CBPR refers to a ubiquitous local-level dynamic in which people establish, respect, and enforce community-based management rules regarding natural resource use and development, often with no state involvement or sanction. Typically, longer-established communities, especially indigenous ones, have more-developed understandings of their CBPR, many of which have come into being in response to local environmental conditions.[23]

CBPR *by definition* emanate from and are enforced by communities. Like human rights, which derive their authority from and are recognized by international law as well as natural law concepts, CBPR are not granted by nation-states. The *distinguishing feature* of CBPR is that *they derive their authority from the community in which they operate, not from the state where they are located.* Formal legal recognition of CBPR by the state, however, is generally desirable and can help ensure that CBPR are respected and used in pursuit of the public interest.

Legal recognition of CBPR by majority world governments should be understood to be an aspirational goal that would reflect an ideal outcome for many local communities that are or will be negotiating management agreements with government. Although full legal recognition may not be the final outcome of a particular negotiation with a nation-state, it is important that local communities and advocates on their behalf know of and pursue an ideal outcome. This is fundamental in any credible and fair negotiation process.

References to CBNRM and CBPR should be used only in regard to initiatives that are primarily controlled and legitimated from within a community.

Externally initiated activities with varying degrees of community participation should not be referred to as community-based, at least not until the community exercises primary decision-making authority. Unfortunately, the term *community-based* is loosely used and all too often applied to initiatives with only the limited involvement and support of local communities.

Throughout the majority world, CBPR are often distinguishable from Western property concepts. Western concepts are based largely on state-created and protected private individual rights or on ambiguous socialist concepts that theoretically vest the state with ownership of all land and other natural resources, ostensibly to best promote the public interest.

By contrast with these more familiar, uniform Western concepts, CBPR within a given local community typically encompass a complex bundle of rights that are understood and respected by a self-defined group of local people. As with common property, CBPR are not equivalent or even similar to open-access regimes that by definition are subject to no management rules and are therefore nonexclusionary.

CBPR *often include but are not limited to common property*. They can also encompass various kinds of individual rights and kinship rights, such as inherited rights to agricultural fields and fallows, gardens, and planted or tended trees or rattan clusters. CBPR likewise can include rights to land, wildlife, water, forest products, fish, marine products, intellectual property, and so forth. CBPR may vary in time and place to include rights to seasonally available resources such as fruit, game, fish, water, or grazing areas. They often specify under what circumstances and to what extent certain resources are available to individuals and communities to inhabit, harvest, inherit, hunt, and gather from.

In many, if not most, cases legal documents that provide evidence of CBPR do not yet exist. Locally appropriate forms of evidence—for example, fallow fields, gravesites, orchards, and oral histories—should be accepted as evidence of indigenous ownership. Other admissible evidence could include census reports, tax receipts, and student rosters at local schools, as well as field research and other reports that substantiate assertions of original, long-term occupancy.

Locally appropriate evidence of indigenous ownership should create a legal presumption that the area is covered by CBPR. This is fundamental. Without a legal presumption that areas known to be occupied by indigenous people belong to them, state institutions responsible for issuing tenure instruments will be able to make unilateral and arbitrary determinations that might be detrimental to local communities.

In short, CBPR encompass any rights that are derived from relationships, especially long-term ones, established between local peoples and the natural resources that sustain them. Regardless of whether CBPR cover private or public land and other natural resources, community members—not government officials or employees of NGOs, development institutions, or commercial enterprises—are the primary allocators and enforcers of such rights.

Rethinking Property Rights

An important strategy for using law to promote better and more just environmental governance involves rethinking prevailing theories of property rights in ways that can be constructively applied to benefit local people. Most property-rights theorists and students continue to rely on a four-part typology of property: private (which is a misnomer because it really means individual), commons, state, and open access (which refers to a situation where no defined property rights exist). This typology has been useful in distinguishing common property from open access (see Ostrom 1991; Bromley 1992). It has also, perhaps, been the most important component of ongoing efforts to challenge the impacts of Garnett Hardin's influential article "The Tragedy of the Commons" (1968), which is really about the tragedy of open access and not any tragedy of "the commons."

The continued and largely uncritical reliance on this four-part typology undermines legal pluralism and hampers the development of effective legal and policy tools for helping local people gain recognition of their CBPR. The prevailing typology simply does not work well in law and policy making or in project-design processes. It overlooks the spatially and temporally dynamic nature of CBPR systems. It also promotes the abrupt and often arbitrary disaggregation of individual rights from the community-based systems in which they exist and are legitimated. The World Bank and most other financial lending institutions, as well as most nation-states, promote the disaggregation in the belief that individual property rights are superior to group-based rights because they can be bought and sold—that is, marketed—more easily and that this enhances productivity. While perhaps applicable in some areas in regard to arable land, the prevailing approach overlooks important ecological, cultural, and equity considerations.

Another problem with the prevailing four-part typology is that it implies the presence of a distinct and separable commons within CBPR systems. It is almost impossible, however, to isolate the commons within a CBPR system with any precision. There are usually many different and often overlapping types of commons within a CBPR system. Neighboring villages often share access to natural resources, and subgroups within a community may limit access of other community members to an orchard or a fallow field. Because of this, more practical and applied ways to think about property concepts and rights are needed.

Alternative Typology

An alternative property-rights typology would be to think in terms of two conceptual and interrelated spectra. The first spectrum has public property on one end and private property on the other. Public means owned by the state and private means not owned by the state. The degrees of private and public ownership vary, of course, with some private rights being heavily encumbered by state conditionalities such as easements and zoning restrictions and some public rights being largely unregulated. Private titles, therefore, are not necessarily always the strongest type of property right, although generally they are. It depends on what is in the bundle. To know what a specific property right entails, whether it is a private title or a public lease, ultimately requires that the bundle be deconstructed and defined.[24]

The other spectrum has individual rights on one end and group rights on the other. The group end basically refers to CBPR regimes, most of which typically include individual rights as well as common properties. As already stated, the fundamental characteristic of CBPR is that their primary legitimacy is drawn from the community in which they exist, not from the nation-state in which they are located. The concept of CBPR, therefore, is more focused on the authoritative basis for the property rights rather than on their specific characteristics.

Cross-referencing the two spectra allows the identification of four types of property rights: private individual, public individual, public group, and private group. As will be explained, the last category provides the best (although the most rare and difficult to acquire) outcome for legally protecting CBPR, especially for original long-term occupants of a specific area.

Private CBPR

The ideal state–local community arrangement from the perspective of most indigenous communities would result in legal recognition by the state of private CBPR. Legal recognition of private CBPR would not imply exclusive local community authority. Private property rights are subject to state regulation and monitoring of the use of natural resources. The legal recognition of some communities as holding private CBPR, however, would provide them with much more bargaining leverage with outside interests, including the government, than if their CBPR were considered public. In rural areas the state could still enact some zoning laws, as it often does in urban areas, without violating ownership rights and privileges.

Private rights are typically stronger than public property rights and more difficult to expropriate or allocate to other uses or users without due process and just compensation. While private property is subject to state regulation and can be seized by the state through eminent domain, this can occur only to serve the public interest and when due process requirements are followed. In Papua New Guinea and other Pacific Island nations, for example, where undocumented private CBPR cover vast areas of the terrestrial landmass, local communities can legally oblige the government to consult them and win their cooperation before starting conservation or development initiatives. As private rights holders, they are also better positioned to ensure that the government provides notice and due process, as well as just compensation before their community-based rights are expropriated for any public purpose.[25]

Western-oriented financial institutions, including the World Bank and Asian Development Bank, determinedly promote private individual property rights and direct financial resources to support cadastral surveys and other means to disaggregate individual rights from CBPR. They do this in the belief that lack of cognizable collateral restricts access to credit, which in turn restricts economic opportunity (Soto 2001). The prevailing single-minded approach is based on a religious-like conviction that private individual property rights are preferable in most respects to public rights. This conviction, however, has not yet been extended to private group rights. This is because private group rights are not as easily commoditized, as marketable, as are private individual rights. An increasing amount of research, however, demonstrates that some natural resources are not environmentally best managed under individual property rights (see Ellsworth 2002). This raises the question as to why there is still so little acknowledgment that common property and other forms of group-based property rights may be better suited for managing some natural resources such as watersheds, forests, and coastal areas.

Under the prevailing perspective, it is widely believed that if all natural resources are owned pursuant to private individual titles, the resulting security of tenure will unleash pent-up entrepreneurial energy or greed. Moreover, if all rights to land and other natural resources are freely traded based on their own comparative advantage, people will end up better off than they were before trading. And it is further believed that a system of free trading leads to the most productive and efficient use of natural resources, which is to the benefit of overall society (see Ellsworth 2002).[26]

Legal recognition of private CBPR would not necessarily preclude the eventual disaggregation of individual property rights if a particular local community wants to retain them. It would, however, provide at least a temporary restraint on alienation and thereby give community members more time to adjust to market pressures. As land reform programs around the world have shown again and again, when a poor farmer acquires a private individual property right, it is often sold. Crop failures or family problems frequently force such sales, and the farmer reverts to the very situation that land reform was meant to address—landlessness.

Usufruct agreements such as certificates, leases, or other restrictive tenurial instruments where the property rights remain public, are not so easily traded. They may nevertheless be appropriate in some circumstances, particularly with migrant groups whose rights and claims to natural resources are weaker and whose local knowledge of natural resource management is less developed. In general, however, public-tenure instruments are usually time specific and often are not as conducive to the promotion of long-term sustainable objectives. They are vulnerable to arbitrary state cancellation and thus may fail to provide leaseholders with adequate incentives to make the costly investments required to realize long-term gains (see Bromley 1998).

The simple fact is that private property rights—whether individual or community-based—are less easily cancelled and less easily controlled by government, an important consideration in most majority world countries, where state law is often hostile toward local communities directly dependent on natural resources. Private property rights also provide more leverage when negotiating with governments and wily outsiders such as commercial interests, and this is a benefit many poor rural communities surely could use.

Those who have a visceral, negative reaction to the concept of private community-based rights should remember that *no property rights are absolute*, including private individual ones. No property rights are, or presumably ever were, completely free from some degree of governmental regulation in the public interest. Rather, all property rights within national boundaries, whether public or private, are subject to some degree of state regulation. Furthermore, whether public or private, natural resource rights typically encompass a bundle of rights. Terms such as "ownership," "title," and "leasehold"—often used by outsiders to describe community-based tenurial rights—imply a Western concept of ownership that is often at odds with the principles and practices of community-based tenure. However, the element of ownership implicit in the concept of CBPR should not be interpreted as an alien Western construct being imposed on local communities. Rather, it accommodates the diversity of indigenous resource-management systems and is intended to provide a strategic conceptual tool for helping ensure that the property rights of indigenous and other local communities are legally and appropriately recognized.

Regardless of whether CBPR are considered to be public or private, governments should work to help indigenous and other local communities promote sustainable management and environmental justice and should intervene when they do not. Equitable zoning laws best exemplify this traditional governmental prerogative. Even in urban centers where private individual property rights (fee simple absolute) are commonplace, the state retains power to proscribe certain types of land use and development. Similar restraints could be established for the use of natural resources in rural areas—provided, of course, that they are in the public interest as broadly defined. Some legitimate concerns that would possibly merit zoning restrictions include seasonal migration, endangered species habitat, and watershed protection for downstream hydrology control.

Legal Personalities

Recognizing CBPR will, in most instances, require that local communities be defined in ways that are cognizable to national legal systems. This will probably require that some type of documentary evidence be drafted. The task of defining local communities is best left to the communities themselves, although technical assistance is sometimes needed. Many local communities overlap. Some include conflicting factions and lack internal cohesion. To resolve boundary conflicts with other communities, transparent dispute management processes need to be supported. Training in mediation should be provided to local governments and NGO actors.

Local communities wishing to gain formal legal recognition of their CBPR will need to acquire some form of recognized legal personality. This is typically done in the guise of cooperatives, village assemblies, or nonstock nonprofit corporations—all of which are contingent on state sanction and can be dissolved by the state. The ideal approach would be for the legal personality of a community to be based on a census of all its adult members, not on legal documents that merely acknowledge the existence of a "people" or a formal state entity. In other words, any legal register of CBPR should belong to the members of a community, not to an ethnic group or formal state entity such as a corporation or cooperative.[27] If nothing else, a dual personality should be created so that if the state-sanctioned entity is dissolved, the CBPR would not be deemed to have reverted to the state. In any event, all local institutions involved in any CBNRM initiative should be transparent, accountable, and representative of a significant percentage of the affected community.

Promoting Enterprise Development

The issuance of any tenure instruments recognizing CBPR should not be preconditioned on enterprise development nor should it preclude such development. Experience in the Philippines with forest cooperatives indicates that developing countries would be wise to pursue an approach that accommodates local cultural and ecological variations. Whenever possible, and as desired by communities themselves, people's organizations involved in community-based management projects should be based on preexisting local institutions, including indigenous institutions and leadership systems. The most successful people's organizations identified in a Philippine study funded by USAID were built on indigenous institutions representative of and respected by participating local communities (Luna, Lynch, and Mercado 2004).

In addition, legal and financial mechanisms for supporting enterprise development should be separate from those used to recognize and secure

CBPR. Otherwise, if a cooperative fails financially and is legally shut down, there is no legal personality left to hold the recognized CBPR. Thus the recognized CBPR could be deemed as having reverted to the state, a problem discussed in the preceding section.

Decentralization and CBPR

This paper defines and uses a concept of CBPR that is comprehensive and flexible and is also distinct from the decentralization currently under way in many majority world nations. Decentralization can help foster, create, and support CBNRM initiatives, but decentralization to local government units does not necessarily lead to CBNRM or the legal recognition of private CBPR. In some countries, decentralization or devolution can even preclude CBNRM, and purposely so, because local government officials assume and maintain legal control of valuable resources to fund local government costs.

Throughout the Global South there are literally tens of thousands of local leaders and their constituencies outside the formal bureaucracy who may not benefit from decentralization. The smallest state-created local (district) government units often encompass vast areas that include many local (indigenous or migrant) communities. Admittedly, any concept and definition of village, local community, and CBPR is enormously heterogeneous and dynamic. But the key point is that many local communities and CBPR in developing nations exist outside official government structures, even at the most local level.

One conceptual tool useful for clarifying these issues is to distinguish between the *grant of legal rights* by the state and the *legal recognition of CBPR*. As discussed above, legal rights do not emanate solely from nation-states. There are various theories of law and jurisprudence that acknowledge as much (see, for example, Reisman and Schreiber 1987). When national governments own land and other natural resources, they can decentralize authority to local government units or local officials, who then grant management or property rights (or privileges, as for example, in the case of India's Joint Forest Management Program) to local communities located within their jurisdiction. But when CBPR already cover an area, the state may (and often should) be obliged to recognize these rights, especially when the area is an ancestral domain or indigenous territory that preexists the state and its natural resource classifications.

CONCLUSION

During nearly two decades of trying to identify and develop legal strategies for promoting CBPR and sustainable CBNRM, I have often been asked about my work and what I do. My stock reply is that I light candles to curse the darkness. Despite some hopeful developments, the undemocratic origins, evolution, and effects of contemporary laws and legal concepts hamper efforts in many nations. The legal underpinnings of many nation-states, especially those that originated as colonial states, are generally not known or understood by lawyers and other policy makers. It is no exaggeration, therefore, to characterize national laws in many nations—including those related to CBNRM—as being permeated by a political economy of ignorance that masks the conservative and undemocratic nature of national legal systems. In most (if not virtually all) nations, national laws are still obstacles that undermine efforts to recognize CBPR and promote sustainable CBNRM.

The ignorance has tended to preclude serious debate as to why many existing national laws originated during colonial eras and have become even more undemocratic since political independence. In a more profound sense, ignorance blinds people in many developing countries to the need for broad-based inquiries into how colonially constructed (and inspired) nation-states can develop the conceptual and structural capacity, as well as the grandness of vision, to encompass their rights and aspirations of their materially impoverished majorities and foster conditions that promote sustainable development and social justice.

The use of law as a strategy to promote sustainable CBNRM is just one part of this common agenda. I hope the foregoing narrative helps you to understand and to use law and sociolegal processes more effectively in the nations where you are from and where you work.

NOTES

1. Tragically, my father died within hours of driving me to the airport in Minneapolis on 7 September 1989 to begin, in his words, my first "real job" at the World Resources Institute in Washington, D.C. The following year I earned more than four figures (US$9,999) for the first time ever in a twelve-month span since becoming a lawyer a decade earlier.

2. Annual subscriptions can be obtained by writing LRC-KSK, No. 7 Marunong St., Central East District, Quezon City, Philippines, Tel.: 632-928-1372 / 632-436-1101; Fax: 632-920-7172. Email: lrcksk@info.com.ph.

3. LRC-KSK website, www.lrcksk.org/who_we_are.htm.

4. I learned mentoring skills from great mentors. Foremost in regard to the legal recognition of CBPR and the promotion of sustainable CBNRM were Yale professors Harold Conklin (anthropology) and W. Michael Reisman (law). In the Philippines Jose Diokno was a source of great inspiration. Diokno was perceived by many to be one of the Philippines' leading anti-American politicians (despite his grandfather having been a U.S. citizen). As early as 1981, he took an interest in my research, and quietly and consistently encouraged me to persevere. It was a sad day for the

Philippine public interest law movement when he died soon after the overthrow of Ferdinand Marcos in 1986.

5. An example of much more modest, collaborative historical inquiries in six other countries is synthesized in *Balancing Acts: Community-Based Forest Management in Asia and the Pacific* (Lynch and Talbott 1995).

6. Magellan could hardly have discovered a place that was his destination. In other words, he had a good idea about where he was headed. When Magellan reached the equator, "he strangely did not veer west in search of the Moluccas he knew to be on that line, rather he changed course when he reached the latitude of Luzon and headed straight for the Philippines." Although largely overlooked in historical accounts of the voyage, Magellan's change in course was intentional. Reports concerning East Asian topography had been filtering back to Europe for several decades before the historic trip. The conduits were often Spanish-speaking, Muslim trading merchants whose forebears had been driven out of Spain during the fifteenth-century Christian reconquest. These merchants "interacted with, among others, natives from the still 'undiscovered' Philippine Islands." They also conversed with Portuguese sailors and merchants who, in turn, relayed the information back home (Scott 1987).

7. The planting of a wooden cross symbolized the papal right to proselytize, but the nature and extent of this right in the Philippine colony would not be determined until the end of the sixteenth century. Contrary to the Regalian Doctrine, however, neither the pope, the Spanish king, nor Magellan purported to usurp unilaterally all of the customary property rights, or even the sovereign rights, of the natives. This fact was highlighted during the first week of April when Magellan and his men arrived in Cebu. The local chief asked Magellan's emissaries, including the fleet's lawyer, if the natives were expected to pay tribute to the Spanish Crown. The lawyer replied that there was no such demand; Magellan merely wanted exclusive trade rights.

Still, it was evident that Magellan and his men wanted, and needed, more. During the sixteenth century, Spanish soldiers received no pay; while in foreign lands they often had no alternative but to extract their means of sustenance from peoples they met. Fortunately for Magellan and his men, many of the natives they encountered in the archipelago appeared eager to become Spanish vassals, particularly after they saw the power of the king's cannons.

Of course, not everyone was so easily cowed, a fact soon confirmed on 27 April when Magellan lost his life on the north shore of Mactan Island during a fight with native warriors led by Lapu-Lapu, a local village chieftain. Shortly thereafter, the remaining crewmembers departed the archipelago.

8. As early as 1529, the Emperor Don Carlos ordered that all "laws which are in favor of the Indians should be executed notwithstanding appeal" (Laws of the Indies 2:1:5). Included among these laws was Ordinance 8 of 1523, which prohibited the taking of native "properties, farms, livestock, and fruits unless the sales and ransoms are done *voluntarily and entirely free* [my emphasis]" (Laws of the Indies 4:4:8).

9. An English translation of the Maura Law can be found in a 1901 publication prepared by the colonial Forestry Bureau and titled *Spanish Public Land Laws in the Philippine Islands and Their History to August 13, 1898.* Washington, D.C.: Government Printing Office, 9–17. For an English translation of the implementing regulations, see pp. 19–36.

10. See *Baltazar v. Government, Philippine Reports* 40: 267, 271 (1919).

11. Although technically correct, Holmes was presumably unaware that, unlike in the Spanish American colonies, King Philip II had invoked a novel theory of "consent" to justify his sovereign claims over the Philippines (see Lynch 1989).

12. The following year Holmes penned a decision that recognized customary rights to extract from mineral veins. See *Reavis v. Fianza, United States Reports*, Vol. 215. It was likewise suppressed and still remains largely unknown to most Filipino lawyers and law students. Significantly, these decisions were in accord with prevailing international precedents. In 1926 the leading legal scholar on colonial states and CBPR wrote that "it is improbable that today any colonial power would dispute the proposition that native tribes under its sovereignty who have held lands in common or collective ownership, are entitled to be secured in possession of a sufficient quantity of land to enable them to obtain adequate subsistence in the circumstances of their condition as modified by the presence of a white population." Furthermore, if the presence of Europeans or their progeny created the basis for modifying native land rights, the basis was almost nonexistent in the Philippine Islands because there were relatively few Spaniards or European Americans who migrated and lived there permanently (Lindley 1926, 350).

13. For a superb history of the U.S. sugarcane industry's desire for the acquisition of the Philippines and the role it played in that acquisition, see Francisco and Fast 1985. To my knowledge, the book has yet to be published in the United States.

14. It has been noted that Cariño petitioned for an individual title, even though his CBPR were not individually held. Cariño's living descendants are sensitive to this fact, and are probably correct in believing that he had no option but to use westernized property concepts in his court pleadings. It is also likely that U.S. Supreme Court justices at the turn of the century had little, if any, awareness or understanding of concepts related to common property and CBNRM.

15. The U.S. colonial regime's failure to implement the Cariño decision in a widespread, systemic manner was in violation of constitutional jurisprudence in the United States. See, for example, *Marbury v. Madison*, Cranch 1:137 (1803), which declared at 177 that "it is emphatically the province and duty of the judicial department to say what the law is." This precept has ever since been a hallmark of U.S. constitutional jurisprudence. In 1958 the U.S. tribunal called it "a permanent and indispensable feature of our constitutional system" (*Cooper v. Aaron, United States Reports*, Vol. 358, at 18). See also *Weigall v. Schuster, Philippine Reports*, Vol. 11 (1908) in which the Philippine Supreme Court held, pursuant to Section 9 of the Organic Act, that the commission could add to but not diminish the jurisdiction of the Philippine courts.

16. This estimate is admittedly speculative, but it is not unreasonable. Nor does it likely err on the high side. It merely assumes that about one-third of the population lived on the more than 90 percent of the colonial landmass that was legally considered to be public.

17. These figures are based on information provided by University of Washington law professor Roy Prosterman in 1986. Prosterman is an internationally recognized land reform consultant. In a memorandum prepared with his University of Washington colleague Jeff Riedinger for the Minister of Agriculture, dated 31 March 1986 and

entitled "Preliminary Observations on Status and Needs for a Possible Philippine Land Reform," Prosterman was numerically more specific. In the memo Prosterman and Riedinger estimated that there were "at least" 4.5 million people, and more likely 6 million, living as tenants on rice and corn land and 1.2 to 1.5 million tenants on coconut, hemp, and other "private" land. They also estimated that there were 6 to 7.5 million landless laborers who periodically worked within the "private" domain. Despite increasing demographic pressures, some improvements have been made during the past decade, but they are not believed to be widespread.

18. "Director of Lands and Intermediate Appellate Court v. Acme Plywood & Veneer Co.," *Supreme Courts Reports Annotated*, Vol. 146 (1986).

19. DENR Administrative Order No. 96-229 Establishing Rules and Regulations for the Implementation of Executive Order No. 263, Otherwise Known as the "Community-Based Forest Management Strategy."

20. Although Thailand was never colonized, laws in the kingdom undermining CBPR bear striking similarity to similar laws enacted at similar times in neighboring colonial states. Some problems were addressed in the Thai community forestry law enacted in 1996.

21. The most important contemporary restatement of the social contract theory has probably been made by John Rawls. He incorporates social contract concepts into his overall theory of justice. In Rawls's view, justice is a matter of fairness, whereby "men are to decide in advance how they are to regulate their claims against one another and what is to be the foundation charter of their society." Inequalities are acceptable provided they "result in compensating advantages for everyone, and in particular the least advantaged members of society." Rawls adds that "the merit of the contract terminology is that it conveys the idea that principles of justice may be conceived as principles that would be chosen by rational persons, and that in this way conceptions of justice may be explained and justified." Rawls holds that in "the original position," that is, when the social contract is drafted and the republic is justly constituted, the drafters of the contract should operate behind a "veil of ignorance." This meant that "they do not know how the various alternatives will affect their own particular case and they are obliged to evaluate principles solely on the basis of general considerations" (Rawls 1971, 11, 14–15, 136–37).

22. Although the reference may seem esoteric, it merits emphasis that legal "rights" cannot exist unless there is also a corresponding "duty." Contrary to widespread belief, this duty is not inherent in the rights holder. Rather, to possess a legal right, someone or some institution (typically the government) has a duty to respect that right. In addition, there is no such thing as a legal right between a person and a thing. Rather, all legal rights are between persons. See Hohfeld 1913 and 1917. For example, people do not actually own land. Rather, they can own legal rights to land that other people and institutions have a duty to respect.

23. This does not, however, imply that such norms are uncontested or static. For a more detailed discussion of CBPR, see chapter 1 of *Whose Natural Resources? Whose Common Good? Towards a New Paradigm of Environmental Justice and the National Interest in Indonesia.* Center for International Environmental Law (2002) at www.ciel.org/Law and Communities.

24. The content and nature of the bundle typically varies in all property rights.

One typology identifies control (access), use, indirect economic gain, transfer, residual, and symbolic rights. See Crocombe 1971.

25. The concept of group rights at one end of the spectrum lacks precision because it is more expansive than just common property and can include individual rights. It does, however, facilitate the practical identification of the four prevailing types of legally cognizable property rights.

26. Ellsworth noted that promoters of "individual, private, tradable titles [believe they] are a precondition to economic growth and development. Moreover, property systems anchored in individual, tradable titles are in their view the best option around for managing all property." She added that the classic statement of this position is in Demsetz 1967. For the case of forests, a similar kind of argument is found in Mendelsohn 1994. See also Sjaastad and Bromley 2000.

27. The census of the local community can be periodically updated if necessary. Another option would be to rely on traditional local institutions for ascertaining what rights children and other heirs inherit when listed community members die.

REFERENCES

Bromley, Daniel. 1992. *Making the Commons Work: Theory, Practice, and Policy*. Oakland, Calif.: ICS Press.

———. 1998. Property Regimes in Economic Development: Lessons and Policy Implications. In *Agriculture and the Environment: Perspectives on Sustainable Agricultural Development*, ed. Ernst Lutz. Washington, D.C.: World Bank.

Cabarle, Bruce, and Howard Heiner. 1994. The Role of Non-Governmental Organizations in Forestry. *Journal of Forestry* 92(6).

Crocombe, Ron. 1971. An Approach to the Analysis of Land Tenure Systems. In *Land Tenure in the Pacific*, ed. Ron Crocombe. Melbourne, Australia: Oxford Univ. Press.

Demsetz, Harold. 1967. Toward a Theory of Property Rights. *American Economic Review* 57(2): 347–59.

"Director of Lands v. Intermediate Appellate Court and Acme Plywood & Veneer." *Philippine Supreme Court Reports Annotated.* Vol. 146, 1986.

Ellsworth, Lynn. 2002. *The Link between Tenure Security and Community Livelihoods: A Review of the Theory, Evidence and Implications*. Washington, D.C.: Forest Trends.

Erni, Christian. 1993. Mangyans Reject National Park: What Went Wrong with IPAS on Mindoro. *International Working Group on Indigenous Affairs Newsletter* (third quarter).

Francisco, Luzviminda B., and Jonathan S. Fast. 1985. *Conspiracy for Empire: Big Business, Corruption and the Politics of Imperialism in America, 1876–1907.* Quezon City, Philippines: Foundation for Nationalist Studies.

Francisco, Vicente J. 1950. *Commentaries on the Land Registration Act.* Manila: East Publishing.

Hardin, Garrett. 1968. The Tragedy of the Commons. *Science* 162: 1243–48.

Hohfeld, Wesley N. 1913 and 1917. Fundamental Legal Conceptions as Applied in Judicial Reasoning. *Yale Law Journal* 23 and 26.

Leonen, Marvic M. V. F. 1998. Engaging the Rhetoric: Law and Its Interface with Community Action. In *Local People and Lawyers: Building Alliances for Policy Change: Cases From Africa, Asia and the Americas Presented at a Conference on 12 April 1994*. Washington, D.C.: Johns Hopkins Univ., School of Advanced International Studies, Program on Social Change and Development. Also published in 1995 as an issues paper by the Legal Rights and Natural Resources Center—Kasama sa Kalikasan, Quezon City, Philippines.

Lindley, Mark F. 1926. *The Acquisition and Government of Backward Territory in International Law Being a Treatise on the Law and Practice Relating to Colonial Expansion*. London: Longmans, Green.

Luna, Ipat, Owen J. Lynch, and Caroline Mercado, eds. 2004. *Rural Communities and Philippine Forests: Cases and Insights on Law and Natural Resources*. Manila: Tanggol Kalikasan and Center for International Environmental Law.

Lynch, Owen J. 1989. The Legal Bases for Sovereignty in the Philippine Colony. *Philippine Law Journal* 62(3).

———. 1992. Colonial Legacies in a Fragile Republic: A History of Philippine Natural Resource Laws and State Formation with an Emphasis on the Early U.S. Colonial Regime (1898–1913). PhD diss., Yale Law School, Newhaven, Conn.

Lynch, Owen J., and Kirk Talbott. 1995. *Balancing Acts: Community-Based Forest Management and National Law in Asia and the Pacific*. Washington, D.C.: World Resources Institute.

Maggio, Gregory, and Owen J. Lynch. 1996. Human Rights, Environment, and Economic Development: Existing and Emerging Trends in International Law and Global Society. Paper prepared for the Earth Council by the World Resources Institute. Mimeograph.

Malcolm, George A. 1916. *The Government of the Philippine Islands*. Rochester, N.Y.: Lawyers' Cooperative.

Mendelsohn, Robert. 1994. Property Rights and Tropical Deforestation. *Oxford Economic Papers* 46(5): 750–56.

Ostrom, Elinor. 1991. *Governing the Commons: The Evolution of Institutions for Collective Action*. Cambridge, U.K.: Cambridge Univ. Press.

Pelzer, Karl J. 1945. *Pioneer Settlement in the Asiatic Tropics: Studies in Land Utilization and Agricultural Colonization in Southeast Asia*. New York: American Geographical Society.

Perl, Matthew A., Michael J. Kiernan, Dennis McCaffrey, Robert J. Buschbacher, and Garo Batmanian. 1995. Views from the Forest: Natural Forest Management Initiatives in Latin America. Washington, D.C.: Tropical Forestry Program, World Wildlife Fund. Mimeograph.

Phelan, John L. 1959. *The Hispanization of the Philippines: Spanish Aims and Filipino Responses*. Madison: Univ. of Wisconsin.

Poffenberger, M. 1990. *Keepers of the Forest: Land Management Alternatives in Southeast Asia*. West Hartford, Conn.: Kumarian Press.

Rawls, John. 1971. *A Theory of Justice*. Cambridge, Mass.: Harvard Univ. Press.

Reisman, W. Michael, and Aaron M. Schreiber. 1987. *Jurisprudence: Understanding and Shaping Law*. New Haven, Conn.: New Haven Press.

Republic of the Philippines. 1997. *The President's 1996 Socio-Economic Report*. Manila: National Economic Development Authority.

Scott, William H. 1987. Dymythologizing the Papal Bull "Inter Caetera." *Philippine Studies* 35: 348–56.

Seymour, Francis J., and Danilyn Rutherford. 1993. Contractual Agreements for Community-Based Social Forestry Programs in Asia. In *Legal Frameworks for Forest Management in Asia: Case Studies of Community-State Relations*, ed. Jefferson Fox. Honolulu: East-West Center.

Sjaastad, Espen, and Daniel W. Bromley. 2000. The Prejudices of Property Rights: Of Individualism, Specificity and Security in Property Rights. *Development Policy Review* 18(4): 365–89.

Soto, Hernando de. 2001. *The Mystery of Capital: Why Capitalism Triumphs in the West and Fails Everywhere Else*. New York: Basic Books.

16

Engaging Simplifications: Community-Based Natural Resource Management, Market Processes, and State Agendas in Upland Southeast Asia

Tania Li

The manifest failure of state and market mechanisms to promote sustainable and equitable natural resource management in the developing world has stimulated a search for community-based alternatives (Agrawal and Gibson 1999). Advocates argue that community-based natural-resource management (CBNRM) offers the best prospect for meeting conservation objectives while improving the position of impoverished rural communities who have been denied the fundamental right to substantive participation in decisions that impact their well-being and livelihoods. Arguments in favor of CBNRM thus combine concerns about environmental sustainability, social justice, and development efficiency with assertions about practicality and "good sense" (Lynch and Talbott 1995, 6).

The founding assumption of CBNRM is that people who live close to a resource and whose livelihoods directly depend on it have more interest in

An earlier version of this chapter was presented at the workshop "Representing Communities: Histories and Politics of Community-Based Natural Resource Management" organized by Peter J. Brosius, Anna Tsing, and Charles Zerner, held at Helen, Georgia, 1–3 June 1997. It was previously published under the same title, in *World Development* 30:265–83 (2002), and is reprinted with permission from Elsevier. My research has been supported since 1989 by Canada's Social Science and Humanities Research Council and Dalhousie University, Halifax.

sustainable use and management than do state authorities or distant corporations (see Brosius, Tsing, and Zerner 1998). Advocates acknowledge that there may be exceptions and recognize that rural people are strategic, rational actors rather than "ecologically noble savages" (Lynch and Talbott 1995, 24).[1] They also recognize that communities are often internally heterogeneous and unequal. But they argue (Lynch and Talbott 1995, pp. 43–76) that none of these cautions or caveats significantly undermine the basic premise of CBNRM (Colchester 1994; Lynch and Talbott 1995).[2] By promoting CBNRM, advocates aim to return to communities the right to control their resources and their futures.

YES, BUT, BUT, BUT . . .

Scholars endorsing the aims of CBNRM have considered it important, nonetheless, to offer critical feedback.[3] Indeed, there has been some tension between advocates promoting the CBNRM agenda and scholars who highlight issues such as class and gender inequities, or the mutability of identities and traditions, thus calling concepts such as community, custom, local knowledge, and indigeneity into question (Brosius, Tsing, and Zerner 1998). Advocates worry that scholarly investigations along these lines will detract from, and potentially jeopardize, the CBNRM platform.

Recognizing advocates' concerns, I argued in earlier work that there is a strategic value in CBNRM's simplifications, because a bold and resolute insistence upon a few clear axioms is crucial for making headway in the policy arena (Li 1996). Making use of a loaded phrase like CBNRM to capture the commitment to justice for rural people and, simultaneously, indicate the broad outline of a significant mechanism by which it can be achieved has been an effective strategy for gaining attention and support in the policy arena. The language of community, participation, empowerment, and sustainability is now widely used in conservation, donor, and government circles, even though the meanings ascribed to these terms and the ways they are translated into action vary.[4] Yet the very success of CBNRM's simplifications in engaging a broad constituency highlights the continued need for critical scrutiny, as broad policy goals are translated into specific laws, programs, and projects in different arenas of implementation. Success in creating a more just world is measured not by the effectiveness with which a policy idea is sold, or the passing of legislation or regulations that pertain to it, but in the effects it has on people's lives.

Any legal mechanism, policy, or broadly based program will encounter a range of local conditions and unique dilemmas in its implementation. Detailed studies of the effects of laws and policies on particular places inevitably indicate that local realities are more complex than policy models suggest. In the case of CBNRM, studies highlight the problems of patronage, class, and gender inequities about which advocates have been reminded often enough. My focus in this chapter is not on the general assumptions and principles of CBNRM. Nor do I offer a case study that shows, for example, how CBNRM assumptions and practices work out in the Sulawesi hills where I have conducted field research (see Li 2002). Instead, I offer an intermediate level of analysis, which seeks to explore the fit between CBNRM assumptions and the underlying processes and dilemmas encountered in a particular regional context for which CBNRM has been vigorously promoted: the uplands or mountainous interiors of Indonesia and the Philippines. For these areas, are CBNRM's policy-oriented simplifications, and the legal mechanisms CBNRM promotes, broadly on target?

In the first section, I examine prominent characterizations of the upland groups or communities that CBNRM (as it has been promoted in Asia) is intended to benefit. I then subject these characterizations to empirical scrutiny, focusing not so much on the internal sociopolitical dynamics of upland communities but rather on their changing cultural and economic location in, and engagement with, the broad processes transforming the areas where they live and work. By presenting a more complex and differentiated account of the upland scene, I show that the indigenous, forest-dependent, conservation-oriented communities envisaged as the subjects of CBNRM are more difficult to encounter in the uplands than the rhetoric would suggest. I conclude that, although some people would benefit from CBNRM provisions, others would find themselves reassigned to a marginal economic niche that corresponds poorly to the futures they imagine for themselves.

Second, I examine changing state projects regarding the upland terrains in which candidates for CBNRM are located. I argue that CBNRM, rather than rolling back the state and reducing official interference in local affairs, is a vehicle for realigning the relationship between the state and upland citizens. Contrary to the goal of its proponents, there is increasing evidence that CBNRM has the effect of intensifying state control over upland resources, lives, and livelihoods. For this reason, some upland citizens may resist programs promoted in the name of CBNRM. For others, better integration into the legal and administrative systems of the state is a desirable outcome. The CBNRM simplification that assumes an inherent separation between community and state, and posits community as a natural entity outside or opposed to state processes, fits poorly with the historical and contemporary processes of state and community formation in Southeast Asia's upland regions.

Overall, I will argue that the CBNRM approach advocated for this region, which anchors legal rights in specific practices and identities, locates them in fixed territorial units (communities, ancestral domains), and makes them conditional on sustainability outcomes, is at best a partial response to the need of upland people to secure the benefits of a fuller citizenship.

LOCATING CBNRM IN THE UPLANDS: COMMUNITIES, LIVELIHOODS, AND CONSERVATION AGENDAS

Representing Upland Communities: CBNRM Simplifications

Prominent CBNRM advocates Owen Lynch and Kirk Talbott (1995) and Marcus Colchester (1994) use three main sets of terms to characterize the subjects of their concern. One set emphasizes the impoverishment and political-economic subordination of upland people, victims of the greed and neglect of state and capital. The main mechanism of this subordination has been the definition of the areas they occupy as public domain, or state land, mostly classified as forest. Their legal status is that of squatters, subject to expulsion and displacement by other users, including timber concessionaires and large-scale agricultural or other enterprises with state-granted rights. In the Philippines, this so-called public domain, which covers 60 percent of the national territory, is home to roughly twenty-four million people, or one-third of the nation's population, of whom six to ten million are classified as indigenous (Lynch, this volume; Lynch and Talbott 1995, 22). In Indonesia, about 75 percent of the nation's territory is designated state forestland, and occupied by forty to sixty-five million people (Lynch and Talbott 1995, 22, 55).[5]

A second set of terms emphasizes the distinction between indigenous and nonindigenous people resident in the uplands. In the Philippines, indigenous groups are legally recognized as indigenous cultural communities. In Indonesia some upland people and their supporters have mobilized around the term *masyarakat adat* (people who live in customary ways), but there is very limited legal recognition of this status (Moniaga 1993, 131–50), and social boundaries are hard to draw (Li 2000, 2001a).

The third set of terms refers to the pursuit of specific sorts of livelihoods and resource-management practices. In particular, the subjects of CBNRM are described as "forest-dependent communities," "natural resource dependent communities," and pursuers of "subsistence-level," "traditional and sustainable means of livelihood" (Lynch and Talbott 1995).

Arrayed in this fashion, these three sets of terms can be seen to range from the most to the least inclusive. The first set incorporates all uplanders with insecure tenure; the second focuses on that component of the upland population that is indigenous; the third specifies that the subjects of special concern are those whose livelihoods are tied to particular resources and highlights most of all those who use resources in sustainable ways.

Here I have separated out various elements in the characterization of the subjects of CBNRM. A key part of the CBNRM strategy in the policy arena depends upon eliding them. The founding assumption of CBNRM is that upland people, by virtue of being natural-resource dependent or indigenous, either already have, or could be encouraged to adopt, sustainable resource-management practices. "Conservation and sustainable development," "sustainable natural resource management," "sustainable forestry," "community-based forestry," and especially, "sustainable CBNRM" (Lynch, this volume) insistently convey an *association* between upland resource users and environmental protection, while glossing over whether upland communities already have these characteristics or whether they are instead goals or ideals that could be encouraged or promoted through program initiatives and appropriate incentives.[6]

CBNRM uses an environmental hook to tie rights to particular forms of identity, social organization, livelihood, and resource management. Uplanders are said to deserve resource rights because they are or could be good resource managers. Through these elisions and simplifications, CBNRM is offered to policy makers as an especially powerful tool, capable of addressing both environmental and justice issues as a single package. But is this simplification, and the policy position to which it relates, adequate to the changing character of upland societies and landscapes? I will argue that the forest-dwelling, resource-conserving, traditional indigenous uplanders who serve as exemplars or embodiments of CBNRM are relatively rare on the upland scene. No doubt they do exist, and their interests should be protected, but we should consider whether the simplification that makes this group the icon of CBNRM helps us (or helps policy makers) understand or address the situation unfolding in Southeast Asia's upland regions.

Identifying the Subjects of CBNRM: Mobility, Indigenousness, and Commitment to Place

By separating out the various features that are taken to characterize the subjects of CBNRM, a more complex and differentiated picture of upland lifestyles and resource uses comes into view. The factor that all (or almost all) uplanders have in common is that they occupy land defined as public domain to which they have no legally recognized title. Their common problem is indeed a legal one; beyond this, their circumstances, needs, and interests in conservation vary greatly.

Despite the emphasis on indigenous people in the rhetoric surrounding CBNRM, it is important to recall that at least half of the people inhabiting the Philippine uplands are migrants of lowland origin. The Indonesian census does not report on ethnic origins, but there is no doubt about the massive scale of planned and spontaneous migration to the uplands in the past few decades (Hardjono 1986; Li 1999c, 2002; Peluso 1995). People have moved to the uplands in search of land and livelihoods, and they have varying degrees of commitment to the places in which they currently reside. Some migrants have established small holdings and formed stable neighborhoods (Acciaioli 1998; Hidayati 1994). Others are working as farm laborers or tenants, loggers, miners, road builders, or general laborers with corresponding patterns of mobility. Not all are impoverished. People have moved to the uplands not only because of a push from below but also because of the pull from above, where there are or have been many good opportunities both on and off farm. Migrants are, however, especially vulnerable to sudden declines in the resources on which they depend: if ejected from lucrative logging jobs or failed plantations, for example, they are set adrift. In Indonesia researchers have argued that it is people in this category who are the most deprived, exploited, and vulnerable of all upland inhabitants (Brookfield, Potter, and Byron 1995, 235; Ruiter 1999, 279–310).

The extent to which diverse and sometimes mobile uplanders form communities coherent enough to have, or to develop, systems of natural-resource management and allocation (let alone sustainable and equitable ones) is varied. There are reports of rapacious, short-term use of land by migrants working their way along logging roads or other points of access (Lopez 1987, 213–29; McCarthy 2000a, 112; Vayda and Sahur 1985). There are also reports of migrants developing sustainable resource systems by emulating indigenous practices or inventing new ones suited to their new environments. In one case in the Philippines, migrants made use of the short-term boom-bust profits from logging and open access to frontier land to establish sustainable, mixed agroforestry—a system that migrants often do not have sufficient time and space to develop but one, in this case, they selected because of its favorable returns (Fujisaka and Wollenberg 1991). Several researchers now argue that there is a "continuum of farming systems" practiced by both indigenes and migrants, making sharp distinctions unhelpful (McCarthy 2000a, 112).

Reports of frontier settlement in the Philippines observe that migrants tend to refer to indigenous land as state land and generally treat it as open access, while having recourse to "official" mechanisms such as tax payment to bolster their claims (Anderson 1987, 249–68; Lopez 1987, 213–29). Thus for migrant groups, unsurprisingly, the reference point for rights and obligations in relation to natural resources is more the idea of "the state," and more specifically, the state system at its various levels (from the Philippine *barangay* or Indonesian *desa* on up), than "the community" conceived, as Lynch and Talbott propose, in terms of autonomous rule making (1995, 25, 117).

Even among the indigenous population, however, the existence of communities as natural units for CBNRM is not guaranteed. In Indonesia indigenous people are not necessarily formed into bounded groups, with a clear sense of territorial possession of the type implied by the Philippine category "ancestral domain" (Li 2000; Tsing 1993). State agencies have long refused to acknowledge that some Indonesians are more indigenous than others, although this position is softening (Li 2001a). In the Philippines the colonially imposed separation of Hispanicized and un-Hispanicized groups makes for sharper distinctions (McDermott 2001, 36). Nevertheless, in both countries, indigenous people have often been mobile, sometimes voluntarily as they seek better opportunities, other times because of demographic shifts or one or more episodes of displacement (Brookfield, Potter, and Byron 1995; McDermott 2001, 32–62). Many no longer live on the land of their ancestors, and new and old migrants are often interspersed among them. For years the World Bank in Jakarta has been sponsoring efforts by scholars and nongovernmental organizations (NGOs) to map indigenous groups and territories, but neat, well-defined units have yet to materialize and the issue of definitions remains unresolved (Evers 1995). Identifying on the ground indigenous communities that fit the model presupposed by CBNRM is more difficult in practice than the simplified model would indicate.

Upland Livelihoods, Natural Resources, and Market Involvements

Even when indigenous people have been identified, it is not self-evident that their livelihoods will be any more natural-resource based than those of other upland dwellers. They too work as wage laborers in extractive industries, large farms, or in the lowlands and cities, either seasonally or for long periods.[7] The characterization of indigenous people as forest-resource dependent is even more problematic. There are less than a million hectares of old growth forest left in the Philippines, and less than six million hectares contain any significant tree cover (Lynch and Talbott 1995, 58). Thus most of the officially classified forest land in the Philippine uplands is not forested. Although the remaining Philippine forests are primarily within indigenous territories, most uplanders, even indigenous ones, do not live in forested areas. Similarly in Indonesia, a large proportion of officially classified forestland is denuded of trees, although there remains significant forest cover in inaccessible areas of Kalimantan and West Papua.

Indigenous people who do live in or near forests do not necessarily wish to sustain them as forests. Small-scale logging, rattan collection, and most importantly, temporary or permanent conversions of forest to agricultural uses have long been part of the livelihood repertoire of indigenous uplanders as well as migrants (Brookfield, Potter, and Byron 1995, 112–42; Brown 1994). Sustainable swidden cycles are rare now in the Philippines (Brown 1994, 45), although they are still viable in some places in Indonesia. Population growth, land expropriations, and settler influx have reduced the areas available to indigenous farmers. In some cases these pressures have forced them into a pernicious, destructive form of agriculture (Brown 1994, 45), whereas in other cases they have successfully intensified their farming systems (Brookfield, Potter, and Byron 1995; Brown 1994; Lopez 1987, 213–29;

Padoch and Peluso 1996, 1–12). There are two points to make here: First, the squeeze on swidden and other extensive farming systems has already occurred and will not be reversed; to describe uplanders as forest-dependent does not help us to address this, even if the forms of intensification adopted happen to involve tree crops (rubber, cocoa, fruit, etc.).[8] Second, even without these pressures, many would still have elected to intensify or, where conditions permit, extensify agriculture to increase their access to cash.

Market involvement has long been characteristic of Indonesia's indigenous population. Smallholder tree crops, many of them grown by indigenous people, contributed 12 percent to agricultural gross domestic product (GDP) in 1992, whereas the plantation sector (still the focus of most government attention) contributed only 5 percent (Barlow 1996, 8). In some places with relatively low resource pressure, such as the areas of Kalimantan described by Dove (1993b) and Peluso (1996), rubber or fruit tree groves integrated with swiddens and sometimes *sawah* probably meet the criteria of sustainable agroforestry. Other celebrated examples of resource-management systems that produce commercial crops in a sustainable manner using traditional practices are the Damar gardens of Krui in Sumatra (Michon et al. 2000, 159–203) and rattan plantations of Bentian (Fried 2000, 204–33). Elsewhere, under conditions of land shortage and the need and desire for increased cash incomes, commercial tree groves displace both forest and, sometimes, annual crop production, including food crops (Li 2002; Suryanata 1999).[9] In both Indonesia and the Philippines, production of temperate fruit and vegetables for urban markets has become very important (Brown 1994, 46, 57; Hardjono 1991; Hefner 1990).

Agricultural intensification has led to social and economic changes somewhat akin to those experienced in the lowland green revolution, with the critical difference that the "agrarian transformation" of the uplands has been largely the result of local smallholder initiatives rather than state-sponsored programs (Hart, Turton, and White 1989; Li 1999b, 1–44). Much of this intensification has occurred, moreover, on "state lands" officially classified as forests (Vayda and Sahur 1985). Insecure tenure has sometimes been a problem, as when smallholders are displaced by large-scale agribusiness ventures seeking to exploit the same lands and market opportunities that smallholders have pioneered and developed with remarkable efficiency (White 1999, 231–56). Nevertheless, upland smallholders continue to invest labor and capital to retain their place as the most persistent, numerous, and productive contributors to commercially oriented agriculture, much of it tree-crop based (Potter and Lee 1998, 7).

The boom in smallholder tree-crop production is unmistakable. A survey conducted in Indonesia during the recent economic crisis, a period during which observers expected food security to be a priority, showed instead that the clearing of land for food production decreased both relatively and absolutely, although land dedicated to commercial tree-crop holdings expanded (Sunderlin et al. 2000, 34–36). High export prices pegged to the U.S. dollar and the attempt to use trees as a mechanism to consolidate land claims at a time when political uncertainty weakened forest-boundary enforcement account for Indonesia's tree-crop fever, but these factors only accentuate a preexisting trend (Sunderlin et al. 2000, 42–43). No doubt there are people who will lose from this transition: indigenous smallholders have often been displaced as their land is taken over by local elites or migrants whose capital and connections enable them to better withstand market and ecological adversities (Brookfield, Potter, and Byron 1995, 30; Elson 1997, 90, 99, 102, 240; Hefner 1990; Hirsch 1993, 105; Suryanata 1999). I doubt, however, that processes of agrarian differentiation of this scale can be reversed by CBNRM, especially when migrants and indigenes alike opt for new crops and intensified market involvement in the expectation that their lives and livelihoods will thereby improve (Li 2002; Suryanata 1999).

Conservation Agendas: Marginality Reconfirmed?

In the context of these intensifying market involvements, what are the implications of the 1991 Philippines Integrated Protected Areas Act and its attendant regulations, according to which "the zoning of a protected area and its buffer zones shall not restrict the rights of indigenous communities to pursue traditional and sustainable means of livelihood within their ancestral domain" (Lynch and Talbott 1995, 90)? What is the legal position of these indigenous communities should they elect to cut forest and expand commercial agriculture? What happens if they fail to live up to the ecological standards expected of them as "traditional and indigenous people"? Are they well served by outsider images and expectations, especially when translated into requirements and obligations under new national laws? As Brown observes, "tribal peoples are not being asked if or how they want to manage these forests" (Brown 1994, 95). For Lynch and Talbott, a resource-management system qualifies as "community-based" only if the rules for resource allocation and "management" are set primarily (though not exclusively) by communities themselves (1995, 25). But there is a tension between this position and the assertion that the outcome of that management—sustainability—should be monitored and indeed enforced by the state (Lynch and Talbott 1995, 121), whether or not this fits with local priorities and "imagined futures." Hence Lynch and Talbott's difficult "balancing acts." "Sustainable" is potentially incompatible with "community-based" when the agenda for upland development is set by government officials, NGOs, or donors preoccupied by environmental concerns and convinced of the necessity and wisdom of trees (Rocheleau and Ross 1995). Brown (1994) raises these concerns specifically in regard to the Philippines, but the same issues have arisen in many contexts where imposed environmental agendas framed in participatory rhetorics have reduced the political and economic security of rural populations (Fairhead and Leach 1996; McKinnon 1997, 117–31; Rangan 1993, 155–81; Ribot 1996).

As others have noted, the politics of the environment are such that a new willingness on the part of national elites and resource bureaucracies to recognize the existence and address the needs of upland people does not necessarily mean that long-standing inequalities in resource access have been reversed (Barber 1989; Gauld 2000; McDermott 2001, 32–62). The timing of new forest policies and programs is an indicator: in both the Philippines and Indonesia, uplanders were offered new forms of tenure in the national forest estate only after the best and most lucrative opportunity in the uplands, namely timber extraction, had run its course and elites had found better investments. The natural resources left in the uplands are, increasingly, marginal rather than central to the national economy.[10] The time when community-based natural-resource control would *really* have paid off, during the timber boom of the 1970s and 1980s, has passed. Uplanders are now being offered more control over land and natural resources but only on condition that in the interests of sustainability, biodiversity, and the needs of future generations, they take on responsibility for conserving the little forest that is left and limit their economic aspirations accordingly. What are the implications for justice?

Without denying the populist commitments of innovative legislators and advocates, it is necessary to consider the possibility that the rural people designated as appropriate subjects for CBNRM are expected to conserve trees and soil rather than exploit them for profit because they are poor and marginal and can therefore be asked to bear a burden from which more powerful players are exempt. Michael Dove has drawn attention to the power relations embedded in the conservationist agenda that proposes that "minor forest products" be promoted to meet the (apparently limited) income needs of forest-dwelling people, while the truly profitable resource, timber, is allocated to others. In criticizing this logic, which he dubs "rainforest crunch," he points out that whenever poor people stumble on or develop lucrative opportunities, these are quickly removed from them. Therefore, according to Dove, the "search for 'new' sources of income for 'poor forest dwellers' is often, in reality, a search for opportunities that have no other claimants—a search for unsuccessful development alternatives" (1993a, 18). Poverty, powerlessness, and exclusion from valuable resources are integrally related. Such economic and political linkages are obscured when forest communities are viewed through a lens that stresses tradition, sustainability, or subsistence, and implies that marginality is an elected way of life.

In agriculture as in forest protection, unexamined assumptions about the subsistence-and-conservation priorities of farmers, and the overwhelming conservation preoccupations of outsiders, have resulted in the promotion of agricultural innovations whose economic potential is unproven.[11] If adopted, they have the potential to impoverish upland people. In Thailand, for example, adopters of alley cropping did not experience the increases in production that were promised. They found instead that their fields were invaded by grasses or ravaged by wild animals seeking easy forage. Those determined to resist imposed conservation measures limited their participation to a "token line" designed to please outsiders or avoid sanctions (Enters 1995). Similarly in the Philippines, Brown (1994, 56) describes the vigor with which NGOs and government agencies have promoted "sloping agricultural land technology" (SALT) and the reluctance of uplanders to adopt it, presumably because they have recognized that it does not benefit them.[12]

Even when agricultural improvement programs are successful in economic terms they may still fail to meet the conservation objectives of their proponents if the implications of market engagement are misunderstood. An agroforestry program in Indonesia was designed on the assumption that increased profitability of tree crops (through improved seed stock and marketing) would relieve pressure on neighboring forests. However, instead of sitting back when their (supposedly limited) needs were met, farmers responded to the new opportunities by *expanding* their production into the forests, and migrants (not necessarily poor ones) were also attracted into the area (Angelsen 1995; Tomich and van Noordwijk 1995).

Oil palm plantations are the current focus of Indonesian government initiatives to boost export earnings, and vast areas of logged land have been designated for this purpose in Sumatra, Kalimantan, and West Papua. Much of this land is subject to customary claims, and supporters of CBNRM and indigenous land rights have launched a campaign calling for a moratorium on oil palm on the combined grounds of environment, livelihoods, and social justice (Ruwindrijarto et al. 2000). A closer look at the oil palm question reveals, as usual, more complexity. In some cases, land has been grabbed from communities using coercive tactics, backed by the military, and villagers have been imprisoned for resisting (Ruwindrijarto et al. 2000). In other cases, however, villagers have welcomed oil palm when the conditions have been favorable to them (Potter and Lee 1998, 7, 26, 37). Key to their satisfaction are the terms of the contract linking their land, labor, and production to the nucleus estate with its processing and marketing facilities. As Ben White has argued (1999, 231–56), contract farming need not be disadvantageous to farmers: everything depends on the relative power of the parties to negotiate a fair deal and the surrounding political climate (intimidation and patronage or democracy and the rule of law).

According to a field study conducted in 1997–1998 (Potter and Lee 1998), issues of concern to villagers whose land is zoned for oil palm include the relative proportions of the land they must give up to the estate versus the portion they retain, ready planted with oil-palm; the rate of compensation for land acquired; the extent of the debt they incur for land development and transparency in its administration; the returns for their product (often lower than was promised); the availability of work and rates of pay; the degree of autonomy over current and future land uses; and the opportunity cost of commitment to a monocrop with an uncertain market future. Facilities such as roads and schools are also highly prized, because they enable households to diversify both on and off farm, by educating children for better jobs, engaging in trade, and seeking seasonal or urban employment. Through their participation in this new economic sector they seek, in short, both enhanced livelihoods and social justice. The same study found that conservation, biodiversity, and the communitarian social values associated with CBNRM have played a very limited role in villagers' assessments of oil palm (Potter and Lee 1998, 28).

The component of the CBNRM platform of very high relevance to smallholders faced with oil palm is recognition of their land rights: only when these rights are recognized, whether de facto or de jure, can they enter into a bargaining posture with oil palm estates (Potter and Lee 1998). Without such recognition, they are vulnerable to brutal treatment and expropriation. Plantation companies sometimes ignore customary resource rights on the grounds that their official lease trumps any locally recognized entitlements (Ruwindrijarto et al. 2000, 14). However, since the end of Suharto's New Order, villagers and their NGO supporters have become more vocal and persistent in their claims, and plantation and timber companies recognize that they must negotiate or face expensive delays, blockades, and sabotage (McCarthy 2000a, 107; 2000b). In the face of oil palm's inexorable advance, Potter and Lee (1998) argue that improving the terms on which villagers deal with plantations would have more impact on their future well-being than the many donor-driven conservation programs attempting to restore and intensify indigenous agroforestry systems.[13]

Conservation agendas that assume that upland farmers have (or should have) subsistence goals often run counter to the long-term futures that they imagine and toward which they strive. These futures may include participation, together with lowlanders and city folk, in increasingly generic, nationwide, middle-class consumption styles. Eder (1994) observes that Batak people in the Philippines see themselves, simultaneously, as a deprived underclass lacking the resources (but not the desire) to pursue lowland Filipino lifeways as well as proud bearers of a tribal identity. In the Tengger highlands of Java, Hefner (1990) found that farmers did not anticipate a future in the hills. They were counting on the profits from intensive (and destructive) vegetable production to educate their children and launch them on nonagrarian careers, preferably in the bureaucracy. These are not exceptional situations, and it is not clear that they can be rectified by better technologies and program incentives. They are the predictable outcomes of changing patterns of production and the dynamics of culture and class in contemporary upland settings. They tend to be ignored, overlooked, or explained away to protect the strategic simplifications embedded in CBNRM.

Unless outsider-driven efforts to design better resource-management institutions are clearly rooted in local priorities, they will fail to find the active, concerned local constituency that the notion of sustainable CBNRM seems to guarantee. Meanwhile urban, industrial, agroindustrial, and other large-scale resource users, as well as chemical-dependent lowland farmers, their profit motives unquestioned, are subjected to conservation standards that are very much less rigorous than those expected of communities, especially upland or indigenous ones (Brown 1994, 55).

The Philippines 1995 presidential Executive Order that proclaims "community-based forest management shall be the national strategy to achieve sustainable forestry and social justice" (Lynch, this volume; McDermott 2001, 32) looks rather less promising in light of the foregoing analysis. It pertains specifically to forests, presumably those remote and inaccessible forest remnants with which indigenous people are associated, but not the millions of hectares of official forest land that indigenous and other uplanders continue to cultivate without secure rights. Its limitations as a "national strategy to achieve social justice" have already been pointed out. In effect, the decree allocates marginal resources to marginal people, to be used in limited ways that are only marginally productive for those people but have rather significant benefits to the nation (especially its national image and access to donor funds), the globe (concerned with biodiversity, forest cover), and future generations of ecotourists (both Filipino and foreign) who will be able to contemplate nature and natives preserved in place. There clearly are major issues of justice at stake in the distribution of upland resources and the allocation of responsibilities for their management. However, sustainable CBNRM, by fusing the issue of resource entitlements with that of conservation, may compound rather than resolve problems. Divergent interests are mis-recognized when conservation by communities is presented as simple common sense.

STATE AND LOCAL AGENDAS IN THE UPLANDS: RECONFIGURING LANDSCAPES AND RELATIONSHIPS

In this section, I examine changing state projects regarding the upland terrains in which candidates for CBNRM are located. I argue that, contrary to the goal of its proponents, CBNRM may serve as a vehicle for intensifying state control over upland communities. I also suggest that, for some upland citizens at least, a closer relationship to the state and a fuller incorporation in state projects may be a desirable outcome. Rather than strengthening rural citizens against the state, CBNRM serves as a vehicle for renegotiating the responsibilities and rights of citizenship. It is not, however, the only possible vehicle, and its strengths and weaknesses need, therefore, to be evaluated in relation to the alternatives.

State Agendas and Mechanisms for Rule

Of particular relevance in the contemporary uplands is the process of territorialization through which "all modern states divide their territories into complex and overlapping political and economic zones, rearrange people and resources within these units, and create regulations delineating how and by whom these areas can be used" (Vandergeest and Peluso 1995, 387). Such measures have been undertaken by both colonial and postcolonial regimes, seeking profits for favored elites, tax revenues to support administrative systems, or the assertion of state authority in areas not fully enmeshed in state-defined institutions and processes. Always ongoing and incomplete, territorializing initiatives are commonly contested by the populace. Moreover, they involve many government departments, each with different and possibly conflicting approaches. Strategies for increased control may include privatizing natural resources (within state-defined frameworks) or direct state management; encouraging settlement in unpopulated areas or forbidding settlement; centralizing administrative authority or devolving authority to lower levels. The making of maps, the conduct of censuses, the drawing up of village boundaries and lists, classification and staking forests can all be seen as mechanisms to define, regulate, and assert control over the relationship between population and resources.

Territorializing initiatives in the uplands of the Philippines and Indonesia, as well as Thailand—the focus of Vandergeest and Peluso's analysis—have historically been less intense than those in the lowlands, but their importance is increasing. Nominal control over the Philippine uplands was obtained at the end of the nineteenth century by the U.S. colonial power when it devised and promoted the Regalian Doctrine, proclaiming state prerogative over upland territory, on the (disputed) grounds that the previous Spanish regime had assumed full sovereignty over land and resources (Lynch and Talbott 1995, 41–46; McDermott, 2001, 34). Under Marcos, this doctrine was strengthened by various legal instruments to permit state allies to conduct large-scale resource extraction, leaving people living on state forestland vulnerable to eviction (Brown 1994; Lynch and Talbott 1995, 60). In Indonesia a clause in the 1945 Constitution assigns the government responsibility for managing forestland for the benefit of the population. Under Suharto's

New Order regime, this clause was interpreted to mean total state control, providing the mandate for the 1967 Basic Forest Law that declared about 75 percent of Indonesia's territory (mostly in the uplands) to be forestland under the control of the Ministry of Forestry, and defined the populations living there as squatters (McCarthy 2000a; Moniaga 1993, 131–50). As in the Philippines, the 1967 law ushered in an era of massive state-backed logging of the forests, especially in the uplands and interiors of the so-called outer islands (off Java). Post-Suharto, a new forest law passed in 1999 under Habibie's interim regime incorporated some populist language and made provisions for various forms of community participation in forest management, but it did not fundamentally change the status of national forestland.

Beginning in the 1990s, territorialization initiatives have taken the form of increased recognition of the existence of upland populations. Throughout the period of rapacious logging, it was convenient for government authorities in both the Philippines and Indonesia to undercount, ignore, or deny the existence of the sizable populations living and deriving their livelihoods from this state forestland. A forest department can ignore a few squatters in state forests, but to acknowledge that there are millions of people on this land is to acknowledge that it is not really in control, that the government cannot implement its own laws. During this period, uplanders were people whom neither the forest agency nor any other government department had a structural interest in seeing, at least officially.[14] Advocates for CBNRM point out the negative effects of this invisibility on upland people: namely, their insecure resource tenure and vulnerability to expulsion.[15] But the time came when invisibility also posed problems for the ruling regimes: it made it difficult—or downright contradictory—to set about developing administrative procedures to engage with upland citizens, count them, locate them, list them, and enmesh them in the cultural and political rituals of citizenship. Moreover, state-mandated programs planned on the basis of an unpopulated terrain were always contested. Except when state agencies were able or willing to enforce them coercively, the attempt to implement such programs drew government officials into all kinds of uneasy compromises (Li 1999a; Peluso 1995). Rules that are contradictory, designed not to work, or not enforced outlaw much of the population and render their loyalties ambivalent.[16]

The increasing appeal of CBNRM to government authorities over the past decade can be interpreted in terms of a shift in territorializing strategies and state priorities regarding the uplands. The logging boom over, direct state control over natural resources is less important. What has become urgent in both countries, but especially the Philippines with its ongoing insurgency (McDermott 2001, 35), is the establishment of control over upland populations by pinning them in place, regularizing their resource use according to state-defined rules and procedures and, through the extension of institutions and bureaucratic processes, enmeshing them more firmly as state clients.

CBNRM and the Intensification of Rule in the Philippines and Indonesia

One impulse behind high-level support for the array of community-focused programs adopted in the Philippine uplands is, undoubtedly, the imperative to intensify government control over people. There are also more particular, departmental concerns. Through its various community forestry initiatives, Department of Environment and Natural Resources (DENR) regularizes the position of smallholders who are already present on what it views as its land. The delineation of ancestral domains, similarly, helps to pin indigenous populations in place, and produces the requisite lists, maps, agreements, and lines of authority (McDermott 2001, 32–62). Having laid claim to its population, and provided for their welfare and development, DENR is better able to defend its land from poaching by other state agencies, for example, mining or agriculture. In this transaction DENR gets, according to a recent study, "quite a bargain." It allocates to communities only land that is already denuded of trees and extracts from them cheap labor in reforestation and protection (McDermott 2001, 35). At the same time, DENR retains the powers assumed under the Regalian Doctrine to allocate timber concessions (now called Industrial Forest Management Agreements) on residual forestlands when it is profitable or politically expedient to do so. A study of the DENR observed that this department continues to be dominated by professional, technically trained foresters who are very dubious of community capacity to undertake "scientific forest management" and meet timber-production targets, although they welcome donor funds for community forestry, which have provided a welcome boost to the department's prestige and resources (Gauld 2000).[17]

My argument is not that DENR's community forestry programs are a screen for Machiavellian plans to manipulate citizens, nor are they the seamless product of social engineering. They have been a response, in part at least, to popular pressure, to policy advocacy for CBNRM, and to the environmental preoccupations of donors (Gauld 2000; McDermott 2001, 32–62). Their effects, like their origins, have been complex and contradictory. Giving rights to participants in social or community forestry and recognizing ancestral domains both incorporates these populations in state projects and empowers them to contest and frustrate those projects in ways they could not previously, from their status as squatters or invisible people. Thus state power and people's power, both of which were previously rather diffuse in the uplands where many rules were not enforced and therefore not contested (Brown 1994, 47), have become concentrated in such matters as the identification of appropriate program beneficiaries, boundary delineations, and the interpretation of terms such as *traditional* or *sustainable*. Community forestry and the recognition of ancestral domains are fertile grounds for both co-optation and dissent, in ways that continue to evolve. The significant number of applications for the Certificate of Ancestral Domain Claim (CADC) in the Philippines (seventy-nine claims covering more than a million hectares by 1997), together with the moratorium on CADC approvals declared by the incoming Estrada administration in 1998 (Bryant 2000, 693), indicates that whatever the limitations of the program important material and symbolic resources are indeed at stake.[18]

If community forestry provides one framework for renegotiating the relations between government and people, the Philippine 1991 Local Government Code provides another. The code is intended to devolve control over natural resources and numerous other aspects of government to local levels. This measure would appear to address one of the initial concerns of CBNRM: the problem with decisions being made by distant states. It brings government programs closer to the local level, where presumably they are to be tailored according to local needs and conditions. Whether the more intensive presence and visibility of the state at local levels will increase accountability is an open question. According to a recent study, paternalistic power structures remain entrenched in rural areas (Guevara 2000) and intensified patterns of patronage and land-grabbing by newly empowered local officials have been observed (Brown 1994, 64–65). At any rate, this legal strategy is clearly different from, and possibly counter to, the logic of CBNRM as a system in which "property rights *by definition* emanate from communities" (Lynch and Talbott 1995, 117). The Local Government Code locates control firmly in the hands of state-derived administrative units and encourages people to look toward and work with the state, rather than extrastate community-based structures and practices, to strengthen their hold over resources and improve livelihoods.

In 2001, a decade after the Philippine initiative, Indonesia commenced a comparable program of decentralization that devolves considerable powers to the regency level of government and invites a revival of traditional terminologies and practices for local governance. Despite the populist rhetoric, village-level governance structures are hardly mentioned in the legislation, and it is unclear, for the moment, whether villagers will be able to strengthen their control over the natural resources on which they depend or be subjected to intensified appropriation and exploitation by regency and provincial authorities seeking revenue and "development" (Potter and Lee 1999, 12). Evidently, bringing government closer to the people is not simply a matter of spatial arrangements, and the meaning of terms such as *local* and *community* is hotly contested.[19]

Besides the conflicting claims of various levels of government, different departments continue to vie for access to upland resources. In Indonesia, as in the Philippines, the Department of Forestry has had to defend its position vis-à-vis other departments that eye forestlands for other uses and suggest alternative ways to bring order and development to the huge land areas and populations under Forestry control. As noted earlier, the Department of Agriculture covets the massive logged lands of Kalimantan and Sumatra for conversion to oil palm plantations (Potter and Lee 1999). Community forestry programs can be seen, in part at least, as an attempt to forestall more clearly agricultural alternatives that would remove territory from Department of Forestry control. Under the banner of development, environment, and participation, these programs promise to address the needs of the people by permitting limited livelihoods to be gained from forests under the control and guidance of the Forestry Department (Barber 1989, 410–11). Long-time opponents, forest villagers are now to become allies of the Forestry Department in its project to retain control over its domain. At the same time, coercive removal of those practicing unregulated smallholder agriculture within forest zones continues to be a government policy.

The flurry of forest legislation in post-Suharto Indonesia reveals the limits of community forestry as a basis for legal rights to forestland. Like its 1967 predecessor, the 1999 Forest Law recognizes the category customary forest (*hutan adat*) but continues to subsume it within the national forest estate (*hutan negara*), subject to the control of the Department of Forestry. Like village forests (*hutan desa*) and community forests (*hutan kemasyarakatan*), *hutan adat* is treated as a unit of forest management that must be officially identified, licensed, and monitored by the department, conforming to detailed regulations about use. In customary forest (slated for indigenous folk), rights extend only to forest-product collection, although in community forests some logging is allowed (McCarthy 2000a, 121). In both cases clearing land for agricultural purposes is forbidden, unless it has been designated for conversion to large-scale plantations. Thus shifting cultivation and smallholder tree-crop production are still criminalized. Forest villagers are enjoined to participate in guarding and reforestation, but they have no role in decision making and are assumed to need continuing education and top-down guidance from the department. A Ministerial Decree on Community Forestry (Hutan Kemasyarakatan SK 677/Kpts-II/1998) similarly confirms that community forestry is about the granting of permits for forest use to community groups constituted for the purpose, not about government recognition of preexisting rights that stem from people's long-term residence within, or dependence upon, the forest estate. According to the matrix prepared by Diah Raharjo (1999), its implementation will require a host of information-gathering and registration measures, the effect of which will be to intensify government control over community activity in forests.

From the perspective of the Indonesian Department of Forestry, it matters little whether the operation of fixing people in place and delimiting their boundaries and rights is accomplished under the rules for customary forests, village forests, or community forests. Regardless of their label, the *effect* of these programs is the same: to recognize people's presence in forested areas while conceding nothing on the issue of rights and enmeshing them more securely in state regulatory regimes. Of course, to move from a list of schemes for forest allocation to their imposition on people and landscapes requires a huge administrative effort in mapping, listing, regulating, and excluding that the current government is not equipped to undertake. Moreover, the authority of the government to define such programs is itself contested: many Indonesian NGOs, as well as prominent parliamentarians, protested the new forest law on the grounds that it failed to acknowledge customary rights. They continue to advocate the recognition of rights that are, in Lynch and Talbott's terms, community based, that is, deriving from within the community, as opposed to being granted by the state. Activists are currently debating how to move forward on community forestry: some argue that anything short of government recognition of existing customary land rights and uses (including agrarian ones) is unworthy of the label community-based, whereas others argue that top-down, government-style community forestry offers a significant opening to secure local access rights, the limits on which can later be revised. Thus the "state simplifications" (Scott 1998) embodied in the new forest law do not in fact simplify nor do they necessarily prevail, rather they open up a new arena within which state-society relations can be reworked.

Processes of State and Community Formation

In its approach to communities, CBNRM misses an important step. It takes community as an essence or starting point (for identities, rules, and notions of justice) rather than as the (provisional) result of community-forming processes. It ignores the deep and subtle ways in which communities, states, and NGOs are mutually implicated in relations laced with power. It also underestimates the significance of local initiatives intended to intensify, rather than withdraw from, engagements with state institutions.

In Indonesia, CBNRM rhetoric tends to locate the essence of community in a precolonial past, and then truncate the time frame such that autonomous communities are assumed to have persisted throughout the colonial and postcolonial period, up to the time of intensified logging beginning in the 1960s (Peluso 1995, 399). The nature of that precolonial past is, of course, difficult to research. No doubt there was significant variation in the degree of community coherence and autonomy experienced by local groups across the archipelago. For the colonial and postcolonial period, historical and ethnographic studies of some remote locations in Indonesia's indigenous, upland interior have shown that communities were not natural units, but rather were formed, or at least re-formed, by or in interaction with the programs and initiatives of governing regimes (Henley forthcoming; Li 2001b; Tsing 1993). Certainly today there are few geographical locations, if any, in which communities could be said to have an autonomous existence outside the structures of state control. Similarly, the state system is instantiated in upland communities. As Hirsch (1989, 35) observes for rural Thailand, it is misleading to assume "an extra-village or urban location of the state." Rather than intensified state territorial control arising as a preformed center moves outward to colonize and incorporate preformed communities on the peripheries, the historical record suggests that state formation and community formation have proceeded simultaneously as part of a single process (Agrawal 2001; Li 1999b, 1–44; Sundar 2000, 257).

Under favorable conditions, migrants and indigenous uplanders alike have sought opportunities to realign their relationship to the state system and thereby legitimate their presence and consolidate their hold over resources. They want and need to be enmeshed in administrative structures and processes to claim their place as citizens and clients. Thus they begin to form themselves, or strengthen their formation, as communities as they engage with state institutions, procedures, and personnel (Li 1996; Tsing 1999, 159–202). The irony is that, through intensified interactions with state institutions and NGOs, communities can be simultaneously formed, transformed, co-opted, and constituted as possible loci of demand for, or opposition to, state projects (Agrawal 2001; McDermott 2001, 32–62).

Just as state power is not absolute, it must be stressed that it is not necessarily malevolent: territorialization is a normal state activity, not one peculiar to oppressive regimes. Environmentalists and supporters of peasant struggles who assume that traditional communities are inclined to oppose the state to preserve their own institutions and practices underestimate the extent to which uplanders seek the benefits of a fuller citizenship. Their demands commonly include access to roads, education, and health facilities. The oppositional characterization of "virtuous peasants" and "vicious states" (Bernstein 1990, 71) fails to do justice to the complexities of state–local relations and associated class-structuring processes (Hart 1989; Nugent 1994). It neglects the claims upon the state system for *access* to modernity that characterize many peasant and indigenous people's movements (Rigg 1997; Schurman 1993, 1–48), just as others reject and resist state imperatives. In the Kalimantan case discussed by Tsing (1999, 159–202), Meratus Dayaks did not oppose state territorial strategies of mapping and road building; rather, they wanted to ensure that their community was *on* official maps and roads, a regularized and recognized component of the national framework. In many instances, uplanders are not rejecting development but particular, localized experiences with a development that removes sources of livelihood without providing viable alternatives, fails to bring promised benefits, or distributes resources unevenly (Li 1999b, 1–44).

CONCLUSION

CBNRM has been an important strand in a broader advocacy agenda intended to draw attention to the number of people living in the uplands, to highlight the ways they are marginalized and disadvantaged, to show that many of the negative stereotypes about them have been misplaced, and to propose alternatives. The attention-getting agenda has been well served by the simplification that inverts negative stereotypes, replacing the image of the uplander as a backward peasant wantonly destroying state resources with the image of the coherent, stable, and environmentally responsible upland community. As a result of this advocacy work, something of a paradigm shift has occurred, at least in the ways uplanders are viewed, if not in the ways they are treated. Coercive official conservation that insists on removing people from parks, for example, must now contend with a competing paradigm (Bryant 2000; Peluso 1993). A problem arises, however, in the attempt to turn the simplified counterimage into a reality and treat it as a basis for legal strategies and the search for justice. At this level, it is my view that CBNRM serves upland people less well. Of course, advocates do not claim that CBNRM is the solution to all problems, nor will it fit all groups and situations with their local idiosyncrasies. It is for that reason that I have focused upon underlying processes and tried to assess whether CBNRM and its attendant simplifications are *broadly* on target for an extensive population potentially affected by them. My conclusion is that, as a legal strategy, CBNRM in the form it is currently being promoted in Asia is most compatible with the interests of those who are its icons: unusually isolated, forest-dependent, resource-conserving, traditional indigenous communities so prominent in the uplands as an "imagined country" (Short 1991) but rare in its actual configurations.

As a legal strategy for the majority of upland people, sustainable CBNRM imposes some severe limitations. It makes legal entitlements to resources conditional upon discriminatory and probably unenforceable environmental prerequisites (Brown 1994, 55; McDermott 2001, 39). Although the environmental hook has been useful in gaining allies, support, and donor funds, I am not convinced that this limitation is a necessary one—that it is *only* on this basis that uplanders can gain secure rights to the resources on which they depend. For this reason I believe it is important to keep questioning the hegemonic claims of environmentalism, the ways it threatens to delimit discursive frameworks, define the boundaries of what is possible, and make simple common sense out of some partial truths, thereby legitimating continuing inequalities in power and well-being.

More generally, for reasons I have explored elsewhere in more detail (Li 2001a), I find the attempt to anchor legal rights in specific identities or sets of practices, and the effort to make these conform to territorial units (communities, ancestral domains), a problematic basis for justice. It segments the social and physical terrain and allocates rights and obligations on a differential basis. It runs the risk of replicating old patterns of discrimination in new, environmental garb. The search must therefore continue for legal strategies that secure for uplanders the benefits of a fuller citizenship and offer them, and expect from them, no more and no less than other citizens. To tease out what these strategies might be, it will be necessary to go beyond the simplifications of the CBNRM model and locate its assumptions more precisely within the changing political economy and ecology of upland settings.

A core concern of CBNRM has been to strengthen the capacity of communities to protect their natural resource base from the more destructive and rapacious activities of ruling regimes, among others. The model envisages a shift in power from states to communities, conceived as separate entities. Instead, as I have argued, states and communities are mutually constitutive. CBNRM offers governing regimes an opportunity to rearrange the ways rule is accomplished, while also offering communities an opportunity to realign their position within (but not outside) the state system. Where citizens are indeed up against vicious states, the potential of CBNRM to empower them is very limited.[20] Older vocabularies about peasant struggles, class conflict, and democracy are better able to name the problem and to indicate the forms of collective action through which it might be addressed.

A vision of citizenship adequate to the political, economic, and ecological dilemmas of the new century will need to draw on a "concept of community, seen not as a given society or culture outside of history but as a political association formed through processes of political and cultural creation and imagination—the generation of meaning in contexts of unequal power" (Roseberry 1989, 14). Scholars, activists, donors, government officials, and upland villagers all participate in the processes of cultural creation and imagination surrounding the concept of community and are implicated in the attendant power relations. If scholars decide to refrain from critical engagement, they are party to a political economy of ignorance and complacency, questions unasked, issues not raised, data not collected, and processes ignored—the scenario that has long operated to the detriment of upland people and that many advocates of CBNRM have worked hard to expose and critique. It is not easy to determine when "strategic simplifications" should be subject to scrutiny and when left alone (Brosius 1999). In setting out my arguments, I have been guided by my experience of the vibrant, self-reflexive character of the CBNRM movement in Asia and my impression that it is more than capable of continuing a debate with scholars interested in tracking its progress and considering alternative means to reach common goals.

NOTES

1. The risks to indigenous people that stem from unrealistic assumptions conservationists hold about them have become increasingly apparent in Amazonia and elsewhere (Baviskar 1997; Conklin and Graham 1995; Ellen 1986, 131–58; Fisher 1996; Lohmann 1993; Ramos 1998; Slater 1996, 114–31; Stearman 1994).

2. Lynch and Talbott (1995, 8) acknowledge that evidence for the efficacy of CBNRM in achieving combined livelihood and conservation goals is "anecdotal" and "for now, inconclusive"—although a reader could easily forget this caution in the light of their simplifying style. Colchester (1994, 87) is careful to point out the dangers of "lairdism": the co-optation, corruption, and undemocratic tendency of many indigenous leaders, not least when their communities are granted (or restored) the power to negotiate with timber concessionaires and other commercial interests. He anticipates that new, democratic, community institutions will be needed to control such excesses.

3. For a critical review of CBNRM, especially its dependence on a "mythical" or "enchanted" concept of community, see Agrawal and Gibson 1999. Mosse 1999 describes the emergence of CBNRM constructs in both colonial and contemporary development settings in India. For a discussion that highlights mistaken assumptions about harmony and stasis in both communities and environments, see Leach et al. 1999. On contestations around the meaning of community provoked, in part, by a conservation initiative, see Moore 1998. Gender issues are discussed by Agarwal 1997. Case studies of CBNRM initiatives that founder on local inequalities and other constraints include Belsky 1999 and Wainright and Wehrmeyer 1998. For studies that highlight the limited empowerment achieved by communities in view of the powers retained by government and other stakeholders, see Gauld 2000, Twyman 2000, and McDermott 2001.

4. Pieterse (1998) argues that the idea of development "alternatives" is increasingly incoherent in the light of converging populist paradigms shared by governments, donors, and nongovernmental organizations (NGOs).

5. See Fox and Atok 1997 for an attempt to address the discrepancy between low official numbers and the much higher numbers estimated by advocates.

6. There is a deep but unacknowledged tension between the assertion that sustainable resource-managing communities have existed since eternity (thus proving their effectiveness and viability) and the idea that communities or groups need to be created, their social capital developed by outside stimulation and investment. See, for example, Pretty and Ward (2001). In the Philippines, according to Gauld (2000, 244–47), the Department of Environment and Natural Resources (DENR)—heralded by donors for its progressive community-oriented programs—is convinced that community organization requires external intervention, a job contracted to NGOs at so much per hectare of forest land. The goal of this organizing is to form "communi-

ties" as legal-bureaucratic structures, which can be assigned leases and monitored like corporations.

7. According to Brown (1994, 59) the significance of off-farm income sources and the need to expand them have been neglected as a result of the natural-resource fixation of outsiders.

8. The definition of forests, their anthropogenic or natural character, and the point at which a particular land-use regime is defined as forest management rather than farming is another issue I do not pursue here (see Ellen 1999; Peluso 1996). I tend to emphasize that upland people are farmers to balance the simplification that classifies their activities as forestry or forest management, making their farming, especially commercially oriented farming, relatively invisible.

9. A study of indigenous agroforestry in Amazonia showed that larger landholders could maintain diverse and sustainable systems, whereas households with less land depleted their resource base, highlighting the significance of differentiation within indigenous communities and the problem with assumptions that indigenous systems are intrinsically stable, equitable, and sustainable (Coomes and Burt 1997).

10. The Philippines was a net importer of timber by 1988 (McDermott 2001, 34). Indonesia still has significant timber stocks, enough to fuel patronage systems and entice major commercial interests (McCarthy 2000a, 120).

11. Crasswell et al. 1998 assess a range of agroforestry techniques.

12. For cautions about agroforestry, see Fujisaka 1989. Some successful interventions are described in Current, Lutz, and Scherr 1995. Sato 2000 (p. 164) highlights the "late developers trap," in which candidates for agroforestry cannot return to their traditional practices, but neither are they permitted to "move forward in the same way that 'modern' farmers have done."

13. Note that increased recognition of customary land rights and the attendant capacity to negotiate does not guarantee sustainability: in two case studies of logging, recognition enabled communities to cut into logging profits from which they were previously excluded, but the logging continues. In East Kalimantan, leaders claiming to represent customary communities have been busy selling the rights to newly recognized traditional (*adat*) forests, making use of maps prepared by NGOs for the opposite purpose: to strengthen customary land claims and traditional, sustainable, resource-management systems (Obidzinski 2001). *Adat* leaders have also been active participants in illegal logging networks in Sumatra, where—unable to prevent logging on their lands—they have interpreted their customary rights as an entitlement to levy fees (McCarthy 2000b, 9). No doubt the political and economic pressures on these communities are intense, and they are not necessarily to be faulted, but if this is indeed a trend, it needs to be exposed and addressed.

14. See Sato 2000 for a discussion of the way state simplification projects in Thailand make certain people invisible (as when state forest mapping ignores resident populations) or catch them between competing state agendas (beneficiaries of land allocations under land reform and, simultaneously, forest encroachers). Illegibility is sustained because of its strategic uses to particular state agencies (Sato 2000, 172). James Scott's (1998) argument that modernizing states seek legibility needs to be nuanced by the examination of selective vision at particular conjunctures.

15. Invisibility has been especially problematic for many uplanders in Thailand

who are deemed noncitizens, and there have been fewer programs aimed at incorporating them within state-mandated frameworks. They continue to face statelessness and the possibility of expulsion across national borders (Ganjanapan 1998).

16. As shown in the Indonesian forest sector, for example, by McCarthy (2000b).

17. Forest leases transfer management rights to communities, subject to a host of detailed regulations equivalent to those imposed (though not necessarily enforced) on commercial timber concessions (Gauld 2000, 239).

18. McDermott 2001 provides a critique of the assumptions embedded in the ancestral domain program, a case study of how these match with on-the-ground realities in Palawan, and an assessment of both the limits of this program and the gains it provides to the communities she has studied.

19. McCarthy (2000a, 2000b) argues that Indonesia's centralized forest department has never had effective control over the vast national forest estate. In practice, order has been provided by the long-standing accommodations between local district officials, large and small entrepreneurs, village heads and forest laborers, which systematize illegal logging in the remaining forests, including protected areas and national parks. Thus the state is both distant (Jakarta and its law making) and already intensely localized, a scenario that makes the concept of transferring power from the center to local government quite problematic (McCarthy 2000b, 18). At most, as McCarthy's Sumatran case studies show, logging networks are disrupted by new regulations, only to reconfigure. Similar findings pertain to east Kalimantan (Obidzinski 2001).

20. Sundar argues that donor emphasis on village-based "participatory committees" has helped to create a discourse that diverts attention from the "real issues": in India, she argues, these concern undemocratic, centralized party structures (2000). For west Africa, Ribot also stresses the fatal flaws in donor-led "participation" without democracy (1996).

REFERENCES

Acciaioli, G. 1998. Kinship and Debt: The Social Organisation of Bugis Migration and Fish Marketing at Lake Lindu, Central Sulawesi. In *Authority and Enterprise: Transactions and Texts among the Bugis, Makasarese, and Selayarese*, ed. G. Acciaioli, K. van Dijk, and R. Tol, Leiden, Netherlands: KITLV Press.

Agarwal, B. 1997. Re-Sounding the Alert: Gender, Resources and Community. *World Development* 25: 1373–80.

Agrawal, A. 2001. State Formation in Community Spaces? Decentralization of Control over Forests in the Kumaon Himalaya, India. *Journal of Asian Studies* 60(1): 9–40.

Agrawal, Arun, and C. C. Gibson. 1999. Enchantment and Disenchantment: The Role of Community in Natural Resource Conservation. *World Development* 27(4): 629–49.

Anderson, J. N. 1987. Lands at Risk, People at Risk: Perspectives on Tropical Forest Transformation in the Philippines. In *Lands at Risk in the Third World: Local*

Level Perspectives, ed. P. D. Little, M. M. Horowitz, and A. E. Nyerges. Boulder, Colo.: Westview.

Angelsen, A. 1995. Shifting Cultivation and "Deforestation": A Study from Indonesia. *World Development* 23(10): 1713–29.

Barber, C. V. 1989. The State, the Environment, and Development: The Genesis and Transformation of Social Forestry Policy in New Order Indonesia. PhD diss., Univ. of California, Berkeley.

Barlow, C. 1996. Introduction to *Indonesia Assessment 1995*, ed. C. Barlow and J. Hardjono. Singapore and Canberra: Institute of Southeast Asian Studies.

Baviskar, A. 1997. *In the Belly of the River: Tribal Conflicts over Development in the Narmada Valley*. Oxford and New Delhi: Oxford India Paperbacks.

Belsky, J. 1999. Misrepresenting Communities: The Politics of Community-Based Rural Ecotourism in Gales Point Manatee, Belize. *Rural Sociology* 64(4): 641–66.

Bernstein, H. 1990. Taking the Part of Peasants? In *The Food Question: Profit Versus People?* ed. H. Bernstein, B. Crow, M. Mackintosh, and C. Martin. New York: Monthly Review Press.

Brookfield, H., L. Potter, and Y. Byron. 1995. *In Place of the Forest: Environmental and Socio-economic Transformation in Borneo and the Eastern Malay Peninsula*. Tokyo: United Nations Univ. Press.

Brosius, J. P. 1999. Analyses and Interventions: Anthropological Engagements with Environmentalism. *Current Anthropology* 40(3): 277–309.

Brosius, J. P., A. L. Tsing, and C. Zerner. 1998. Representing Communities: Histories and Politics of Community-Based Natural Resource Management. *Society and Natural Resources* 11(2): 157–68.

Brown, E. C. 1994. Grounds at Stake in Ancestral Domains. In *Patterns of Power and Politics in the Philippines—Implications for Development*, ed. J. F. Eder and R. L. Youngblood. Tempe: Arizona State Univ., 43–76.

Bryant, R. L. 2000. Politicized Moral Geographies: Debating Biodiversity Conservation and Ancestral Domain in the Philippines. *Political Geography* 19: 673–705.

Colchester, M. 1994. Sustaining the Forests: The Community-Based Approach in South and South-East Asia. *Development and Change* 25: 69–100.

Conklin, B., and L. Graham. 1995. The Shifting Middle Ground: Amazonian Indians and Eco-Politics. *American Anthropologist* 97(4): 695–710.

Coomes, O. T., and G. J. Burt. 1997. Indigenous Market-Oriented Agroforestry: Dissecting Local Diversity in Western Amazonia. *Agroforestry Systems* 37: 27–44.

Crasswell, E. T., A. Sajjapongse, D. J. B. Howlett, and A. J. Dowling. 1998. Agroforestry and the Management of Sloping Lands in Asia and the Pacific. *Agroforestry Systems* 38: 121–37.

Current, D., E. Lutz, and S. Scherr. 1995. The Costs and Benefits of Agroforestry to Farmers. *World Bank Research Observer* 10(2): 151–80.

Dove, M. R. 1993a. A Revisionist View of Tropical Deforestation and Development. *Environmental Conservation* 20(1): 17–25.

———. 1993b. Smallholder Rubber and Swidden Agriculture in Borneo: A Sustainable Adaptation to the Ecology and Economy of the Tropical Rainforest. *Economic Botany* 47(2): 136–47.

Eder, J. F. 1994. State-Sponsored "Participatory Development" and Tribal Filipino Ethnic Identity. *Social Analysis* 35: 28–38.

Ellen, R. 1986. What Black Elk Left Unsaid: On the Illusory Images of Green Primitivism. *Anthropology Today* 2(6): 8–12.

———. 1999. Forest Knowledge, Forest Transformation: Political Contingency, Historical Ecology and the Renegotiation of Nature in Central Seram. In *Transforming the Indonesian Uplands: Marginality, Power and Production*, ed. T. M. Li. London: Routledge.

Elson, R. E. 1997. *The End of the Peasantry in Southeast Asia: A Social and Economic History of Peasant Livelihood.* London: Macmillan.

Enters, T. 1995. The Token Line: Adoption and Non-Adoption of Soil Conservation Practices in the Highlands of Northern Thailand. Paper presented at the International Workshop on Soil Conservation Extension, Chiang Mai, Thailand, 4–11 June.

Evers, P. J. 1995. Preliminary Policy and Legal Questions about Recognizing Traditional Land Rights in Indonesia. *Ekonesia* 3:1–23.

Fairhead, J., and M. Leach. 1996. *Misreading the African Landscape: Society and Ecology in a Forest-Savanna Mosaic.* Cambridge, U.K.: Cambridge Univ. Press.

Fisher, W. H. 1996. Native Amazonians and the Making of the Amazon Wilderness: From Discourse of Riches and Sloth to Underdevelopment. In *Creating the Countryside: The Politics of Rural and Environmental Discourse*, ed. E. M. DuPuis and P. Vandergeest. Philadelphia: Temple Univ. Press.

Fox, J., and K. Atok. 1997. Forest-Dweller Demographics in West Kalimantan, Indonesia. *Environmental Conservation* 24(1): 31–37.

Fried, S. G. 2000. Tropical Forests Forever? A Contextual Ecology of Bentian Rattan Agroforestry Systems. In *People, Plants and Justice: The Politics of Nature Conservation*, ed. C. Zerner. New York: Columbia Univ. Press.

Fujisaka, S. 1989. The Need to Build upon Farmer Practice and Knowledge: Reminders from Selected Upland Conservation Projects and Policies. *Agroforestry Systems* 9:141–53.

Fujisaka, S., and E. Wollenberg. 1991. From Forest to Agroforest and Logger to Agroforester: A Case Study. *Agroforestry Systems* 14: 113–29.

Ganjanapan, A. 1998. The Politics of Conservation and the Complexity of Local Control over Forests in the Northern Thai Highlands. *Mountain Research and Development* 18(1): 71–82.

Gauld, R. 2000. Maintaining Centralized Control in Community-Based Forestry: Policy Construction in the Philippines. *Development and Change* 31: 229–54.

Guevara, M. 2000. Decentralization and Economic Development: The Philippine Experience. *Hitotosubashi Journal of Economics* 41(2): 97–109.

Hardjono, J. 1986. Transmigration: Looking to the Future. *Bulletin of Indonesian Economic Studies* 22(2): 28–53.

———. ed. 1991. *Indonesia: Resources, Ecology, and Environment.* Singapore: Oxford Univ. Press.

Hart, G. 1989. Agrarian Change in the Context of State Patronage. In *Agrarian Transformations: Local Processes and the State in Southeast Asia*, ed. G. Hart, A. Turton, and B. White. Berkeley: Univ. of California Press.

Hart, G., A. Turton, and B. White, eds. 1989. *Agrarian Transformations: Local Processes and the State in Southeast Asia.* Berkeley: Univ. of California Press.

Hefner, R. 1990. *The Political Economy of Mountain Java: An Interpretive History*. Berkeley: Univ. of California.

Henley, D. Forthcoming. *Fertility, Food, and Fever: Population, Economy, and Environment in North and Central Sulawesi, 1600–1930*. Leiden, Netherlands: KITLV Press.

Hidayati, D. 1994. Adoption of Indigenous Practice: Survival Strategies of Javanese Transmigrants in South-East Kalimantan. *ASSESS Journal* 1: 56–69.

Hirsch, P. 1989. The State and the Village: Interpreting Rural Development in Thailand. *Development and Change* 20: 35–56.

———. 1993. *Political Economy of Environment in Thailand*. Manila: Journal of Contemporary Asia Publishers.

Leach, M., R. Mearns, and I. Scoones. 1999. Environmental Entitlements: Dynamics and Institutions in Community-Based Natural Resource Management. *World Development* 27: 225–47.

Li, T. M. 1996. Images of Community: Discourse and Strategy in Property Relations. *Development and Change* 27: 501–27.

———. 1999a. Compromising Power: Development, Culture and Rule in Indonesia. *Cultural Anthropology* 14(3): 1–28.

———. 1999b. Marginality, Power and Production: Analysing Upland Transformations. In *Transforming the Indonesian Uplands: Marginality, Power and Production*, ed. T. M. Li. London: Routledge.

———, ed. 1999c. *Transforming the Indonesian Uplands; Marginality, Power and Production*. London: Routledge.

———. 2000. Articulating Indigenous Identity in Indonesia: Resource Politics and the Tribal Slot. *Comparative Studies in Society and History* 42(1): 149–79.

———. 2001a. Masyarakat Adat, Difference, and the Limits of Recognition in Indonesia's Forest Zone. *Modern Asian Studies* 35 (3): 645–76.

———. 2001b. Relational Histories and the Production of Difference on Sulawesi's Upland Frontier. *Journal of Asian Studies* 60(1): 41–66.

———. 2002. Local Histories, Global Markets: Cocoa and Class in Upland Sulawesi. *Development and Change* 30(3): 414–37.

Lohmann, L. 1993. Green Orientalism. *The Ecologist* 23(6): 202–4.

Lopez, M. E. 1987. The Politics of Lands at Risk in a Philippine Frontier. In *Lands at Risk in the Third World: Local Level Perspectives*, ed. P. D. Little, M. M. Horowitz, and A. E. Nyerges. Boulder, Colo.: Westview.

Lynch, O. 1997. Legal Strategies for Community-Based Resource Management in Asia. Paper presented at the workshop Representing Communities: Histories and Politics of Community-Based Natural Resource Management, Univ. of Georgia, 1–3 June.

Lynch, Owen J., and Kirk Talbott. 1995. *Balancing Acts: Community-Based Forest Management and National Law in Asia and the Pacific*. Washington, D.C.: World Resources Institute.

McCarthy, J. 2000a. The Changing Regime: Forest Property and *Reformasi* in Indonesia. *Development and Change* 31:91–129.

———. 2000b. "Wild Logging": The Rise and Fall of Logging Networks and Biodiversity Conservation Projects on Sumatra's Rainforest Frontier. Occasional Paper No. 31. Bogor, Indonesia: Center for International Forestry Research.

McDermott, M. H. 2001. Invoking Community: Indigenous People and Ancestral Domain in Palawan, the Philippines. In *Communities and the Environment: Ethnicity, Gender, and the State in Community-Based Conservation*, ed. A. Agrawal and C. Gibson. New Brunswick: Rutgers Univ. Press.

McKinnon, J. 1997. The Forest of Thailand: Strike Up the Ban? In *Development or Domestication? Indigenous Peoples of Southeast Asia*, ed. D. McCaskill and K. Kempe. Chiang Mai, Thailand: Silkworm / Trasvin.

Michon, G., H. Foresta, D. Kusworo, and P. Levang. 2000. The Damar Agroforests of Krui, Indonesia: Justice for Forest Farmers. In *People, Plants and Justice: The Politics of Nature Conservation*, ed. C. Zerner. New York: Columbia Univ. Press.

Moniaga, S. 1993. Toward Community-Based Forestry and Recognition of *Adat* Property Rights in the Outer Islands of Indonesia. In *Legal Frameworks for Forest Management in Asia: Case Studies of Community/State Relations*, ed. J. Fox. Honolulu: East-West Center Program on Environment.

Moore, D. S. 1998. Clear Waters and Muddied Histories: Environmental History and the Politics of Community in Zimbabwe's Eastern Highlands. *Journal of Southern African Studies* 24(2): 377–403.

Mosse, D. 1999. Colonial and Contemporary Ideologies of "Community Management": The Case of Tank Irrigation Development in South India. *Modern Asian Studies* 33(2): 303–38.

Nugent, D. 1994. Building the State, Making the Nation: The Bases and Limits of State Centralization in "Modern" Peru. *American Anthropologist* 96(2): 333–69.

Obidzinski, K. 2001. *Operational Nature of Illegal Logging in Indonesia and Its Intensification in Recent Times*. Amsterdam: Amsterdam School for Social Science Research, Univ. of Amsterdam.

Padoch, C., and N. L. Peluso. 1996. Borneo People and Forests in Transition: An Introduction. In *Borneo in Transition: People, Forests, Conservation, and Development*, ed. C. Padoch and N. L. Peluso. Kuala Lumpur: Oxford University Press.

Peluso, N. 1993. Coercing Conservation? The Politics of State Resource Control. *Global Environmental Change* 3: 199–217.

———. 1995. Whose Woods Are These? Counter-Mapping Forest Territories in Kalimantan, Indonesia. *Antipode* 27(4): 383–406.

———. 1996. Fruit Trees and Family Trees in an Anthropogenic Forest: Ethics of Access, Property Zones, and Environmental Change in Indonesia. *Comparative Studies in Society and History* 38(3): 510–48.

Pieterse, J. N. 1998. My Paradigm or Yours? Alternative Development, Post-Development, Reflexive Development. *Development and Change* 29(2): 343–73.

Potter, L., and J. Lee. 1998. *Tree Planting in Indonesia: Trends, Impacts and Directions*. Bogor, Indonesia: Center for International Forestry Research.

———. 1999. *Oil-Palm in Indonesia: Its Role in Forest Conversion and the Fires of 1997/98*. Jakarta: World Wildlife Fund.

Pretty, J., and H. Ward. 2001. Social Capital and the Environment. *World Development* 29(2): 209–27.

Raharjo, D. 1999. Matriks Turunan Kebijakan HKM (SK 677). fkkm@egroups.com, 30 September.

Ramos, A. R. 1998. *Indigenism: Ethnic Politics in Brazil*. Madison: Univ. of Wisconsin Press.

Rangan, H. 1993. Romancing the Environment: Popular Environmental Action in the Garhwal Himalayas. In *In Defense of Livelihood: Comparative Studies on Environmental Action*, ed. J. Freidmann and H. Rangan. West Hartford, Conn.: Kumarian Press.

Ribot, J. C. 1996. Participation without Representation: Chiefs, Councils and Forestry Law in the West African Sahel. *Cultural Survival Quarterly* 20(3): 40–44.

Rigg, J. 1997. *Southeast Asia: The Human Landscape of Modernization and Development*. London and New York: Routledge.

Rocheleau, D., and L. Ross. 1995. Trees as Tools, Trees as Text: Struggles over Resources in Zambrana-Chacuey, Dominican Republic. *Antipode* 24(4): 407–28.

Roseberry, W. 1989. *Anthropologies and Histories: Essays in Culture, History, and Political Economy*. New Brunswick, N.J., and London: Rutgers Univ. Press.

Ruiter, T. 1999. Agrarian Transformation in the Uplands of Langkat: Survival of Independent Karo Batak Rubber Smallholders. In *Transforming the Indonesian Uplands: Marginality, Power and Production*, ed. T. M. Li. London: Routledge.

Ruwindrijarto, A., et al. 2000. *Planting Disaster: Indonesia's Large-Scale Oil Palm Plantations*. Bogor, Indonesia: Telepak Indonesia.

Sato, J. 2000. People in Between: Conversion and Conservation of Forest Lands in Thailand. *Development and Change* 31:155–77.

Schuurman, F. J. 1993. Introduction: Development Theory in the 1990s. In *Beyond the Impasse: New Directions in Development Theory*, ed. F. J. Schuurman. London: Zed Books.

Scott, J. C. 1998. *Seeing Like a State: How Certain Schemes to Improve the Human Condition Have Failed*. New Haven, Conn.: Yale Univ. Press.

Short, J. R. 1991. *Imagined Country: Environment, Culture and Society*. London: Routledge.

Slater, C. 1996. Amazonia as Edenic Narrative. In *Uncommon Ground*, ed. W. Cronon. New York: W.W. Norton.

Stearman, A. M. 1994. Revisiting the Myth of the Ecologically Noble Savage in Amazonia: Implications for Indigenous Land Rights. *Culture and Agriculture* 49:2–6.

Sundar, N. 2000. Unpacking the "Joint" in Joint Forest Management. *Development and Change* 31:255–79.

Sunderlin, W. D., I. A. P. Resosudarmo, E. Rianto, and A. Anglesen. 2000. *The Effects of Indonesia's Economic Crisis on Small Farmers and Natural Forest Cover in the Outer Islands*. Bogor, Indonesia: Center for International Forestry Research.

Suryanata, K. 1999. From Home Gardens to Fruit Gardens: Resource Stabilization and Rural Differentiation in Upland Java. In *Transforming the Indonesian Uplands: Marginality, Power and Production*, ed. T. M. Li. London: Routledge.

Tomich, T. P., and M. van Noordwijk. 1995. What Drives Deforestation in Sumatra? Paper presented at the Regional Symposium on Montane Mainland Southeast Asia in Transition, Chiang Mai, Thailand.

Tsing, A. L. 1993. *In the Realm of the Diamond Queen: Marginality in an Out-of-the-Way Place*. Princeton, N.J.: Princeton Univ. Press.

———. 1999. Becoming a Tribal Elder, and Other Green Development Fantasies. In *Transforming the Indonesian Uplands: Marginality, Power and Production*, ed. T. M. Li. London: Routledge.

Twyman, C. 2000. Participatory Conservation? Community-Based Natural Resource Management in Botswana. *Geographical Journal* 166: 323–35.

Vandergeest, P., and N. L. Peluso. 1995. Territorialization and State Power in Thailand. *Theory and Society* 24: 385–426.

Vayda, A. P., and A. Sahur. 1985. Forest Clearing and Pepper Farming by Bugis Migrants in East Kalimantan: Antecedents and Impact. *Indonesia* 39: 93–113.

Wainwright, C., and W. Wehrmeyer. 1998. Success in Integrating Conservation and Development? A Study from Zambia. *World Development* 26(6): 933–44.

White, B. 1999. Nucleus and Plasma: Contract Farming and the Exercise of Power in Upland West Java. In *Transforming the Indonesian Uplands: Marginality, Power and Production*, ed. T. M. Li. London: Routledge.

17

Advocacy as Translation: Notes on the Philippine Experience

Augusto B. Gatmaytan[a]

A few years ago, I assisted a Manobo community in Agusan del Sur province in Mindanaw (Mindanao) in their application for a Certificate of Ancestral Domain Claim (CADC). This document required us to collect anthropological, historical, economic, and political data to support the community's claim that the land they occupy is, in fact, their ancestral territory.

In close consultation and coordination with the community, we undertook the research, had the entire thirteen hundred hectares of the claim surveyed, took photographs and conducted interviews, and finally submitted the collected data to the Department of Environment and Natural Resources (DENR) for evaluation. Having seen the strength of the evidence, we were unqualified in our declaration that the Manobo community owned its ancestral territory (Gatmaytan 1995).

Shortly after submitting the documents, we met with the *datus* (leaders) of that community to discuss follow-up activities. When I asked what steps needed to be taken, the eldest *datu* declared that a ritual must be held. I somewhat blithely assumed that it was a thanksgiving ritual, until it emerged that he was speaking of a *pang-hugas*, a cleansing ritual. When I asked him why we needed a cleansing ritual, he replied that we had committed a *sala*

a. I wish to thank the Legal Rights and Natural Resources Center. Some of the data used in this chapter was derived from previous research projects funded by the Rockefeller Brothers Fund, the Biodiversity Support Program, the Ford Foundation, and the International Center for Research in Agroforestry. Their generous assistance is gratefully acknowledged.

(sin). Nervous now, I asked him what sin we had committed. He said that, in the papers we submitted to the DENR, we had stated a lie.

By this time, of course, I was quietly going out of my mind with worry because a falsehood in the documents we submitted was grounds for rejection of the application, not to mention my disbarment from the practice of law. I asked him what lie we had stated in the application.

The *datu* answered that it was a lie that they, the Manobo, owned the land. With that, my worst fears seemed to have been realized: it seemed to me that we had filed an application for ownership for land that did not belong to the community. I had become, I thought, a party to land grabbing.

Then I asked the *datu* who the true owner of the land was, and he answered that *Magbabaya*, the Manobo Creator, was the owner of the land. Only then did it become clear that, for the *datu*, we had lied because we had claimed that the Manobos owned the land, when in fact, it belonged to God.

In due course, the ritual was held, and we paid a ritual fine of a large pig and an *agong* (brass gong).

UNSHARED MEANINGS

As the tale recounted above suggests, the Manobo have a different perception of ownership as a concept than does the law. In civil law, "ownership" consists of a "bundle of rights," including the right to occupy or possess, use, enjoy or receive the fruits of what is owned, dispose of, recover, abuse, exclude, and enclose (Gatmaytan 2001b).

For the Manobo, a landowner is understood to have the first of these two rights, in the sense that they do indeed exercise acts of possession or occupation of their lands. The landowner may also cede these rights on a temporary basis, as when they lend a portion of land to another for farming purposes. They have limited rights to the fruits of the land, however. Fruits from trees they planted as well as crops belong to the farmer, but wild fruits and edibles, medicinal material, game and fish are all open-access resources. Originally, commercially valuable trees and rattan were once also open-access resources, but beginning in the 1980s, the trend has been toward linking ownership of these resources to land ownership. They also have a notion of recovery or vindication of property rights, through council meetings presided over by the *datu* where disputes are resolved. On the other hand, the Manobo have no traditional concept of disposition or abuse of land, nor of enclosure. They do have an idea of exclusion, but it is limited to the restraint (*dagpon*) of those who would farm, log, or cut rattan in an area without prior permission from the landowner concerned.

Manobo concepts of ownership go beyond the level of merely defining the elements of their "bundle of rights." Theirs is a system that allows for multiple, overlapping ownerships (Gatmaytan 1998). Thus in a single area, the land may actually belong to one Manobo, the farm site on it to another, and the fallow areas surrounding it to still another. At the same time, local spirits (*tagbanwa*) are also thought of as owners of the land, for which reason the agricultural practices specifically include consultation of these spirits. And finally, the land is also owned by *Magbabaya*, the creator, who created the land, "planted" the *tagbanwa* spirits there, and allowed the Manobo to cultivate it and make it "a place" (Gatmaytan 1996).

Another problematic term is the government's insistence on distinguishing between "ancestral land" and "ancestral domains," as provided in DENR Administrative Order No. 2 (1993), the administrative regulations for delineating ancestral lands and domains. Legally, "ancestral lands" cover only the surface of the land. By contrast, the "ancestral domain" is formed by subsurface and all other resources, *along with the land* (DENR 1993; Republic of the Philippines 1997). For most indigenous peoples—and indeed for most people in the Philippines—there is no such distinction between the land and the resources found there. The notion of land (Manobo *pasak*, Banwaon *bugta*) encompasses the land or earth itself, as well as the waters, subsurface minerals, air space, trees and other flora, wildlife, and other local resources. To own the land, then, is to own everything that is found there.

The same failure to share meanings, to grasp local notions or cultural ideas, is found in discussions of other key concepts. *Forest*, for example, legally refers to lands of a certain slope, irrespective of the actual use or vegetative cover. On the other hand, most people in the Philippines think of the forest as a wild, wooded area. *Community*, as well, has different meanings. The government treats the idea of the community as unproblematic, referring to government units of *sitio*, *purok*, and *barangay* or to community organizations operating at these levels. The Manobo and other indigenous groups, however, have a more fluid notion of community, its meaning varying, for example, with context: religious or ritual, land ownership, community territory, or the jurisdiction of local leaders. Even defining community leaders may be problematic, particularly in Agusan del Sur province. Here, the government has an official list of *datus*, who are given papers to that effect. Unfortunately, many of these *datus* are not based in the communities they pretend to represent or speak for, having become registered as official *datu* through connections with government or corporate agencies. This gives rise to a tension between these official *datus* and the actual, village-based *datu*. Moreover, a *datu* may lose his following as age blunts his skills or errors he commits erode his integrity, so that he is a *datu* only in name and no one goes to him for assistance. On the other hand, he may recover his fortunes through some feat of representation or assertion. Leadership thus has a dynamic, waxing and waning with the *datu's* performance and the critical appraisal of the political community (*sakup*).

Beside such key concepts, variances in meanings may also exist at the less abstract, operational level. Examples are the land-use categories currently in use by the government in its various programs and projects. These include such terms as *burial grounds*, *sacred areas*, *agricultural lands*, *residential land*, *hunting and fishing grounds*, and *forest area or reserve* (Gatmaytan 1996).

To illustrate, most people would imagine a burial ground as a cemetery or graveyard where the dead are buried. In many local communities, however, there is no such common graveyard, but rather scattered plots where individuals were buried. How much land is covered by each of these isolated "burial grounds"? Does it refer to the actual gravesite only? Or perhaps to a five-meter radius around it? Ten? Twenty? This attempt at an areal definition has no meaning for the Manobo or the neighboring indigenous groups; what is important is only the fact that someone is buried there.

Another example is agricultural land. For most people, this would mean a clearly defined piece of land where farming is conducted regularly. Among the indigenous groups of Agusan del Sur province, however, an area's status as agricultural land depends on whether it is actually being farmed at a given time. What is thus agricultural in character in one year may not be so in the next. If it is left fallow is it still agricultural in character? If the secondary growth is allowed to mature to its climax growth, is it still agricultural? Or is it now forest area or a hunting ground? Different cultures and communities within those cultures will have different answers. At the same time, there will be no consciousness of the actual areal limits of a farm beyond describing it as wide or small. In fact, the Banwaon and the Manobo do not have any traditional concept of areal measurement. When asked how large their farms are, they answer in terms of the volume of the seeds planted in the area, for example, so many sardine cans, or liter-size milk cans, or sacks of seeds. An area is agricultural because it is planted to a crop, and its size is beside the point.

A third example is the idea of *sacred grounds*. What exactly is meant by this term? Is this an area where entry or use is prohibited? If so, then the Manobo, whose religious and spiritual beliefs are quite complex (Garvan 1929), would have no sacred grounds because to them an area's sacredness is not incompatible with human use or exploitation. If we mean an area where spirits are believed to reside, then the opposite result is achieved, because for the Manobo all aspects of the environment—from rivers and hills to holes in the ground formed by uprooted trees and banks of fallen leaves—are believed to be the residences of members of a bewilderingly large host of *tagbanwa*, elemental spirits of the place. Or by *sacred ground* do we mean an area where people pray, as in a church or chapel? If so, then again all Manobo land is sacred, because rituals may be held anywhere depending on the need. In a sense, *sacred ground* as a distinct land-use category may be meaningless in certain cultures because the sense of the sacred is not divorced from daily activities like farming or hunting. In all of this, there is no specific delineation of how much land precisely is covered by these sacred areas.

Clearly, these examples show the different—focal vis-à-vis periphery-oriented—sense of space of the Manobo and the neighboring Banwaon of Agusan del Sur province. In other words, they tend to describe land by its actual, current use rather than its boundaries. By contrast, the legal system is periphery-oriented, in that it imagines the land as subdivided into discrete zones, each dedicated to specific uses, and describes land by referring to its metes and bounds.

In sum, the indigenous notions of land use are focal in character rather than peripheral, are dynamic or shifting rather than static or fixed, and are based on actual use rather than a preset classification system. In addition, it may be said that indigenous systems allow for multiple use at different levels at any given time. By contrast, the tendency of the legal system is to restrict use to certain identified levels or types, as exemplified by the constitutional land-classification system and the zoning regulations in the National Integrated Protected Areas system (Republic of the Philippines 1991; DENR 1992).

It is thus not surprising that the results of a DENR plan to map the territory of a Banwaon community in Agusan del Sur angered the very people who were supposed to be the project's beneficiaries. The map simply failed to represent reality as the Banwaon villagers knew it. A significant factor was the DENR's insistence on the grid system in mapping, resulting in its failure to refer to local geographic features. As a result, titles were issued for a row of residential lots located on what is in reality a cliff. Another residential lot covers a depression in the ground where many villagers deposit their bodily wastes. Surveyors who could not be bothered to map the twists and turns of creeks in effect ignored local property boundaries. The map thus represents an idealized grid of neatly defined farm and home lots that, though having a very tenuous basis in day-to-day tenure praxis, now has a very real legal existence (Gatmaytan 2000b, 64–107).

HISTORY, ADVOCACY, AND MEANINGS

As the Banwaon discovered, their meanings or cultural ideas are not reflected well, if at all, within the legal system or its implementation. This observation holds true when viewing the history of advocacy for indigenous people's rights to land and resources in the Philippines generally.

The first concrete step toward providing some legal protection for indigenous rights to land and resources came in the form of the Community Stewardship Agreements issued under the DENR's Integrated Social Forestry

Program (Office of the President 1982; Ministry of Natural Resources 1982; DENR 1991). This program was initiated in the 1970s, more as a concession to the demands of international funding agencies than a realization of the need to address social justice issues in the uplands.

The agreements are designed as lease or usufructuary contracts that run for a contract term of fifty years. As such, they clash with the idea of indigenous ownership of land, as opposed to mere stewardship. To indigenous people, they are the owners of the lands and resources they inherited from their ancestors; to enter into a contract of lease or usufruct is to admit that they do not own the land. Secondly, a person or group's relationship with its land has no expiration period; it survives for as long as their people survive. A contract that has a fifty-year limit, after which the community no longer has a legal right to the land, does not reflect the indigenous understanding of their relationship with the land.

In other words, the Social Forestry program was not designed to translate their notions of land and resource rights into law, but merely to provide what for indigenous communities is a short-term form of tenure security (Gibbs, Payuan, and Castillo 1990). This failure to translate local or community aspirations and perspectives explains in part why many communities resisted entering the Social Forestry program, as well as the program's limited success.

This rather feeble attempt to address local community claims or rights to lands and resources—though it admittedly laid the foundation for future people-oriented government programs (DENR 1996a, 1996b; Office of the President 1996)—contributed to the gradual swelling of opposition to the abusive and justly condemned Marcos regime throughout the 1970s and 1980s. During this time, many indigenous people's communities were organized for political action, and they developed the political demand for self-determination, as well as for recognition of their right to ancestral lands and domains.

After the 1986 coup against the Marcos dictatorship, the Constitution was changed so that it contained express provisions protecting indigenous people's rights to ancestral lands and domains. At that point, there was no longer any question that the indigenous peoples had legal claims or rights to ancestral territories. The only question would be how these rights would be defined and apportioned.

In 1993 after the post-Marcos government was finally stabilized, the government issued DENR Administrative Order No. 2 (1993) (DENR 1993), which aimed to document ancestral land and domain claims. These regulations were clearly the result of continuing efforts of indigenous rights advocates and activism by local communities (Leonen 2000).

In theory, the regulations offered an opportunity not only to identify the actual land and rights holders but also to document the underlying cultural practices and social relations (Gatmaytan 1996). The (unproblematized) communities would then be issued Certificates of Ancestral Domain Claims (CADC), evidencing their claim to a specified area.

In practice, however, the effect of the delineation process was to simplify the actual tenure practices and configuration rather than to actually or accurately reflect it. The complexity of indigenous resource-use systems is well attested in the anthropological literature, but an initial survey of the results of the documentation process has been discouraging in terms of reflecting such complexities. Many of the CADCs issued covered areas that were not even surveyed (see DENR 1998). In fact, the best documented of the various applications under DENR Administrative Order No. 2 is that of a coalition of seven Manobo and Mamanwa communities in Surigao del Sur province, and it is known for a fact that the resource use information submitted in it was not as good as it could be.

Moreover, the regulations did not allow communities to contest the rights of companies that had previously secured government contracts to exploit resources in areas now claimed as ancestral territories. Instead, communities must await the expiry of these contracts. This weakness underscored the regulations' unfortunate inability to engage the issue of land and resource ownership by indigenous peoples and communities. This alone already represents a substantial inability to reflect local notions of community rights to land and resources (Gatmaytan 1996).

Weak as the regulations were, there was the expected opposition from logging and other companies worried about their access to local resources and from local government units threatened by loss of jurisdiction or control of territory. Thus a CADC application, despite documentation that was the most thorough and persuasive of all then submitted, according to various sources within DENR, languished for more than two years because the DENR was admittedly afraid of antagonizing two logging firms whose concession areas overlapped the application's area. Still other applications were not approved at all and were left pending at various levels of the DENR bureaucracy.

One interesting development, however, was the use by some companies of these same regulations (Gatmaytan 1996). In exchange for guaranteed access to local resources, a number of companies such as the Australian Western Mining Company have agreed to finance and undertake ancestral domain documentation for communities within their concession areas.

The weakness of the ancestral domains delineation program as a tool for recognition is apparent also from the handful of Ancestral Domain Management Plans (ADMPs) submitted by the CADC areas so far legally registered. Under existing regulations, a CADC holder must file a management plan outlining its resource-tenure system and its economic program (DENR

1996c). Again, the potentials for surfacing local cultural ideas and notions of rights are clear. However, the results have been largely disappointing.

For example, one such ADMP reads like an operations plan for a logging firm rather than a description of an indigenous community's resource-management system (Kalihukang Naghi-usang Minorya n.d.). There are token references to the local Higa-onon culture, but in operational terms these have little significance. In another CADC area, the proposed ADMP shows little emphasis on actual tenure practices and instead appears to be a program for shifting the economic base of the community toward greater integration with the market economy (Indicative Ancestral Domain Management Plan n.d.).

Still, the CADCs—where these were actually approved—did extend to communities rights to local resources that were legally unprecedented. Moreover, the procedure did provide a number of them with some degree of tenure security.

In 1997, as a result of continuing pressure from advocates and indigenous communities, the Philippine legislature promulgated the Indigenous Peoples Rights Act (IPRA) (Republic of the Philippines 1997). The statute actually provides a mechanism for issuing documents of title to (still unproblematized) indigenous peoples or communities, an even more radical step beyond what was provided by the ancestral domains delineation regulations (Leonen 1998; Pavia 1998).

Unfortunately, the constitutionality of the IPRA was quickly challenged before the Supreme Court of the Philippines, and as a result the law was not implemented. Only after the Court finally ruled that the IPRA was constitutional, in September 2001, did the Philippine government begin to implement it. To date, the agency charged with the implementation of the statute has encountered resistance from foreign and local corporate interests, government agencies and officials, insurgent forces, and even from a number of indigenous communities.

ADVOCACY AS TRANSLATION

One metaphor by which we may describe the character of advocacy of community-based resource management systems in general, and ancestral land rights in particular, is the process of translation from one language to another. The operating premise is that indigenous peoples and other resource-dependent rural communities have a "language" made up of its cultural ideas, its sense of space, and the social relations within which they are made operational, and the government and its political and legal system have another.

The advocate's role, then, is to "translate," to render understandable, one language or system to the other. The advocate tries to explain the meaning of the government's policies, laws, and regulations to the communities, who are thus better able to make informed decisions in addressing the various questions confronting them. This effort usually takes the form of various training seminars and workshops at community, institutional, local government, and coalition levels where laws and regulations are discussed, as well as development of appropriate resource materials on such issues.

At the same time, there is a corresponding effort to make the various tenure and management systems lived and practiced by rural communities cognizable to the government, principally by attempting to give them a legal status or character. This process of vesting a legal or official character to existing resource-management or tenure systems is what is meant here by cognizable. This should be understood as state acknowledgment of the existing or actual tenure and other cultural systems used by indigenous peoples and other rural communities, which is then provided legal color or character.

This attempt at translation through advocacy is best exemplified by the very struggle to seek legal recognition for indigenous people's rights to lands and resources. Unfortunately, it appears that the advocates' efforts have resulted in many of the nuances and meanings inscribed in the indigenous languages of space being lost in translation.

I would argue that indigenous peoples have for decades now been demanding state recognition of their rights of self-determination and autonomy, which includes their land and resource rights, as they define them. The indigenous people's historical focus on land rights was only a metaphor for the larger struggle for autonomy and self-determination; that is, for a place within the national political and cultural community. In the process of mediating between indigenous peoples and the state, however, this political demand was translated by advocates as a call for legal mechanisms for tenure security. The ancestral domain delineation regulations of 1993 and, latterly, the IPRA, may be seen to be the results of these advocates' efforts. The IPRA finally translated the indigenous people's demands as a call for titling procedures for indigenous peoples, communities, and individuals. Hence the original political and ideological demand for self-determination for indigenous peoples has been, through the mediation of advocates, reduced to a mechanistic legal procedure for determining who owns what lands. Advocates, in other words, mistook the metaphor for the essence of the struggle, thereby misrepresenting the demands of the indigenous peoples and the issues involved.

It is evident from the text of the statute itself that it embodies a number of contradictions. First, while it is possible to view the IPRA as the product of a decades-long movement for legal protection of indigenous people's rights, the IPRA also represents an ideological victory for the Philippine state (following Giddens 1985). True, the statute represents a successful attempt to wrest rights from the state by forcing it to live up to its own liberal-democratic rhetoric, as set down in the 1987 Constitution. However, by the same agency, the state can now impose its own notions of such key issues as who indigenous peoples are, what their rights are, and what constitute their territories.

Hence the translation of the indigenous people's demands to a tenure program has allowed the state to reiterate its political and administrative power by emplacing a system of surveillance of land ownership and resource transactions (Foucault 1980), the homogenization of space by the simplification and standardization of tenure and tenure-rights (Merry 1992; Alonso 1994), and the commodification of land and resources by the homogenization of rights and the establishment of a system of rights and procedures controlled by the state (Merry 1992). Although the IPRA does extend the right to secure titles to indigenous peoples, at the same time it accomplishes the colonization of its political and economic frontier through the same statute (following Giddens 1985). The irony then is that instead of assuring self-determination and autonomy for indigenous peoples, the IPRA actually subsumes their land and resource claims under the political power of the Philippine state and the global capitalist system to which it is wedded.

Second, the IPRA has, perhaps inevitably, adopted a single, universalizing notion of what indigenous people's rights to land and resources are (Republic of the Philippines 1997). As a necessary result, it has in fact ignored the local "languages" and instead imposed its own understanding of tenure and tenure rights. The irony here is that the IPRA was supposed to be the state's answer to the indigenous people's demands for respect of their cultures. Instead, the state, by selecting a legislative response that demands uniformity in the face of indigenous tenure complexity, mutability, and contingency, actually transgresses local cultures.

Third, the imposition by the state of a single set of meanings may result in militant opposition to the statute itself, such that we are presented with the irony of local resistance to a law that is supposed to protect indigenous people's rights.

The example posed by the IPRA underscores the intrinsic problems of translation, especially when advocacy of indigenous cultural ideas is channeled into the state's mechanisms for policy formulation, legislation, and administrative regulation, which have their own histories, and political and cultural ideas and connotations (Arce, Villareal, and Vries 1994). A legislative response to the demands of indigenous peoples can only result in the imposition of a single, universalizing notion of "ancestral land and domain" rights, in the face of the heterogeneity, complexity, fluidity, and contingent character of indigenous tenure praxis.

In the same way, the process of translation must also contend with the state's economic and political imperatives (Giddens 1985). As we have seen, the state's interest in reiterating its hegemony by installing a system of surveillance and homogenizing and commodifying frontier spaces has found expression in legislation that was supposed to address the demands of indigenous peoples for self-determination and autonomy. The result is the misrepresentation of indigenous people's cultural ideas, political demands, and economic or tenure rights and the ideological capture of key cultural and political concepts.

The example of the IPRA also emphasizes the importance of the identity, interests, and political and cultural assumptions of advocates themselves, that is, those who undertake the task of translation (Gatmaytan 2000a, 37–44; 2001b). It is possible to argue that the statute's strong emphasis on community ownership of resources—which incidentally runs counter to the Manobo and Banwaon notions of land and resource ownership (Gatmaytan 2001b; see also Gatmaytan forthcoming)—was a result of the efforts of advocates who themselves labored under the received or unquestioned assumption that all indigenous peoples in the Philippines practiced communal ownership. There is thus the constant and high risk that crucial meanings or nuances are lost *or imposed* in advocacy, during the process of translation.

Advocates have thus interposed themselves between a state with little institutional cultural sensitivity and indigenous peoples and communities who are still developing their own links to the state, media, and other sources of power and arrogated to themselves the task of translation. With so much power—specifically that of representing the indigenous peoples before the state and its agencies—there is actually little in the way of accountability.

In any case, the role of advocates has implications in any genuine attempt to legally recognize Manobo or other tenure systems. Recognition should not be limited to the level of only a formal association of a specific parcel of land with a specific person or group of persons. It should properly recognize the existence and validity of indigenous tenure systems (Ingold 1987). Otherwise, what is recognized or legally protected will be only the end effect of local tenure systems—the designation of certain individuals or groups as owners or managers but not the system itself that so designated these same individuals or managers on the basis of local cultural ideas. To fail in recognizing the underlying cultural ideas and social relations that constituted these individuals and groups as owners is to uproot local notions of ownership from its context and transplant it into the state's legal system, with negative consequences for its coherence, stability, and continuity. It is unfortunate that there is little evidence that advocates understand and can translate these local, lived systems for the state.

IMPLICATIONS

It is necessary to go beyond the level of whether there is a law or regulation whose rubric describes it as fostering community-based management. It is time to move away from the shallow legalism that assumes that if laws or regulations have been promulgated or issued, the problem has been addressed. In part, this may be due to the political culture of the Philippines, which has an unduly, unhealthily high regard for laws and regulations but not for their implementation.

Others have warned us against focusing too much on "black letter law." Paradoxically, however, the response from certain quarters has been to produce even more black letters, to promulgate even more laws and regulations. The preceding discussion should at the very least suggest that the mere existence of laws and regulations do not necessarily mean an improvement in the lives of people. Simply put, one cannot legislate development (following von Benda-Beckmann 1993).

It is necessary, as well, to move beyond asking whether a community possesses or has been awarded a tenure instrument or other document of title. It is much more productive to focus on how well these instruments reflect or embody local community notions of land and resource rights (Ingold 1987). Only by doing so can we guarantee the fulfillment of the indigenous people's political demands for self-determination, autonomy, and ownership of their lands and resources.

Of course, the state may balk at this, suspecting rightly how inherently subversive the entire discourse of indigenous people's rights can be (Nagengast 1994), at least in the context of the Philippine nation-state. But we will eventually have to address ourselves to the question posed by the struggle of indigenous peoples: What does it mean to be an indigenous people within the political framework of the state? How do we reconcile the demands for self-determination and autonomy, to land and resource control with the political, cultural, and economic imperatives and interests of the state (Gatmaytan 2001a)?

For the present, at least, we cannot do away with the political reality and presence of the state, and by extension, its legal system. We are forced therefore to relate local "languages" of space, concepts and rights, and social relations to the legal system, and this should shift the attention of those involved in addressing indigenous people's issues to determining the terms at which the relationship should be set. More study, negotiations, and "translations" lie ahead of indigenous peoples, and their advocates.

Focusing on how well these instruments translate local notions of land and resource rights would also help assure the substantive development of traditional or local resource management systems. By this standard, the results so far are not encouraging in the Philippines, despite the potential that ancestral domain delineation and other community-oriented programs offer.

Certainly, there may well be identifiable cases of local resource knowledge and management systems being translated beautifully into legal language. These successes, however, are probably due more to the initiative and perseverance of the community and its supporters rather than to the government's management of its programs. At most, the government's mechanisms and programs have provided a window of opportunity for such successes. But the government's role should extend beyond this, to actually taking concrete measures to develop community management, for example, support for organizing efforts, education at various levels, allocation of budgetary and other resources, serious study and appreciation of indigenous and other resource management systems, regulation of the entry of commercial operations that may adversely affect communities, and thorough implementation of its own laws and regulations.

The IPRA does offer the possibility of greater local control of land and resources. This in itself is double-edged in its consequences, however. On one hand, it allows communities the opportunity to limit exploitation of their resources by outsiders and to lay claim to a just portion of the returns from such operations. On the other, it may result in only the intensified exploitation of local resources if communities are (understandably) interested in making money (Resurreccion and Sajor 1998). If this is undertaken at a scale or with an approach indistinguishable from that of any other commercial company, then problems may arise. There is little ecological difference between clear-cutting by communities or by companies. In short, that a community has legal control of the land does not in itself guarantee the sustainability that advocates seek in community-based systems (Van Den Top and Persoon 2000; Vayda 1992; Gatmaytan forthcoming).

Parenthetically, I cannot help remarking that the struggle of indigenous peoples has historically been for political and economic rights and not for the opportunity to display whatever skills they have in terms of sustainable resource management. I am alarmed by some advocates' conflation of the struggle for self-determination and political and cultural autonomy with the struggle for the environment and the possibility that the latter movement captures the former. These are two agendas that, while not necessarily incompatible, are not necessarily compatible, either. The conflation may be a result of advocates' well-meaning but risky strategy of aligning the two agendas with each other (see, for example, Bennagen and Fernan 1996). This approach suggests, however, a fundamental mistranslation of the interests of indigenous peoples, who—to repeat—have historically acted to protect their lives and ways of life rather than an abstracted notion of the environment or biodiversity.

Legal strategies for promoting community-based resource management must locate themselves in the context of these realities. Mentoring of interested lawyers, institution building, policy research, lobbying, legislation and rule promulgation, community training, mapping, and other identified strategies, if geared only toward the development of more regulations, instruments, or programs will have limited impact. What is critical then is to ensure that local "languages" of tenure rights are properly translated into the legal system, retaining their substantive content while receiving legal acknowledgment from the government. This requires advocates in particular to be more reflexive, to take critical notice of the cultural assumptions underlying their own analyses, strategies, and recommendations. If this is not assured, the output of these strategies will—like the IPRA itself—be as much an alien, alienating imposition on indigenous and other rural communities as are other government programs and projects that have spelled disaster for all too many of the indigenous peoples of the Philippines.

This task is continually increasing in urgency, given the intensifying pace of cultural disintegration; environmental degradation; political, economic, and tenure pressures; and misinformation or disinformation by certain quarters. I hope the implementation of the IPRA will reflect an awareness of the colonial character of the IPRA—its surveillance, homogenizing, and commodifying aspects—otherwise the entire struggle of indigenous peoples will have been in vain. This would mean the loss of alternative political and resource management models, continued environmental problems, intensified ethnic disparities and conflicts, economic and cultural poverty, and the violation of indigenous people's fundamental rights to life and a way of life of their choosing.

It is necessary, finally, to give more attention to the economics of recognition, as opposed to its merely formal or legal aspects. In theory, all the laws, rules, and regulations existing today are unnecessary to achieve the promotion of community-based resource management because a legal basis therefore can be established using only the due process clause. That laws or regulations have become necessary is an indicator not of government interest but of its resistance to an idea that is inherently subversive, not so much of the legal system as of the interests of those controlling political and economic power.

CONCLUSION

The task of advocacy may be understood as the translation of existing indigenous and other community resource management systems into terms cognizable by the law.

Several factors affect how well attempts at translations work, given that local communities and the legal system may each have differing definitions, meanings, and frames of reference. Among these is the state's awareness of its own political, economic, and cultural imperatives, and how these affect its understanding of indigenous notions of tenure rights. Another is the dialectical relation between any attempts at translation embodied in laws or regulations and the interests and machinations of large economic or commercial interests. Still another is the identity, interests, cultural, and other assumptions—the very competence—of the advocates themselves. Finally, there are the inherent difficulties of the process of translation itself; the channeling of efforts at advocacy and translation into policy, legislative, or administrative formulation necessarily means a simplification of the heterogeneous, complex, dynamic, and contingent character of local notions of tenure rights.

All these factors figure in the intertwined histories of advocacy of indigenous people's rights, state responses to their demands, and of the IPRA itself. The Philippines today has the IPRA as well as a large number of what the government calls "people-oriented" tenure programs or projects. These do provide opportunities for translation and recognition. Unfortunately, the state itself—and even most of its critics—seems unaware of the economic and political imperatives of the state, and how these affect its understanding of indigenous people's issues and its implementation of the IPRA.

Legal strategies for advancing indigenous people's rights and community-based research-management systems must consider these realities. While these still have a role to play in advancing the rights of indigenous peoples, it is necessary that advocates begin to act with a greater sense of consequence, of responsibility or accountability. This necessarily means the exercise of reflexivity and a greater consciousness of one's own cultural frame of reference. To fail in this is to risk continuing to make the same cultural mistranslations that have been inscribed into the law and, ironically, to defeat the very struggle they set themselves to support.

REFERENCES

Government Materials[b]

DENR. 1991. *Administrative Order No. 4.* (Amended Implementing Regulations for the Integrated Social Forestry Program).

———. 1992. *Administrative Order No. 25.* (Implementing Regulations for the National Integrated Protected Areas Act).

b. Copies of statutes are available at the libraries of the Philippine Senate or Congress, in Quezon City. Presidential issuances are available at the Office of the President, in Manila. Administrative regulations cited in this article are available at the Department of the Environment and Natural Resources main office in Quezon City. Brief descriptions of the contents of the various statutes and regulations cited are provided.

———. 1993. *Administrative Order No. 2.* (Regulations for the Delineation of Ancestral Lands and Domains).

———. 1996a. *Administrative Order No. 29.* (Implementing Regulations for Executive Order No. 263).

———. 1996b. *Administrative Order No. 30.* (Integrating Community Based Forest Management and People Oriented Forestry Programs into DENR's Regular Structure).

———. 1996c. *Administrative Order No. 34.* (Guidelines for the Management of Ancestral Domain Areas).

———. 1998. List of Certificate of Ancestral Domain Claims (CADC) Issued (as of 6 June 1998). Mimeograph.

Ministry of Natural Resources. 1982. *Administrative Order No. 48.* (Implementing Regulations for the Social Forestry Program).

Office of the President. 1982. *Letter of Instructions No. 1260.* (Launching the Social Forestry Program).

———. 1996. *Executive Order No. 263.* (Adopting Community-Based Forest Management as the National Resource Strategy).

Republic of the Philippines. 1991. *Republic Act No. 7586 (An Act for the Establishment and Management of National Integrated Protected Areas System, Defining Its Scope and Coverage, and for Other Purposes).*

———. 1997. *Republic Act No. 8371 (An Act to Recognize, Protect and Promote the Rights of Indigenous Cultural Communities/Indigenous Peoples, Creating a National Commission on Indigenous Peoples, Establishing Implementing Mechanisms, Appropriating Funds Therefor, and for Other Purposes).*

Published Materials

Alonso, Ana Maria. 1994. The Politics of Space, Time and Substance: State Formation, Nationalism and Ethnicity. *Annual Review of Anthropology* 23: 379–405.

Anonymous, N.D. *Indicative Ancestral Domain Management Plan of the T'boli-Ubo Community in Lake Sebu, South Cotabato (for CADC No. 3).* Lake Sebu, South Cotabato Province.

Arce, Alberto, Magdalena Villareal, and Peter De Vries. 1994. The Social Construction of Rural Development. In *Rethinking Social Development: Theory, Research And Practice*, ed. David Booth. London: Longman.

Bennagen, Ponciano L., and Ma. Luisa Lucas-Fernan, eds. 1996. *Consulting the Spirits, Working with Nature, Sharing with Others: Indigenous Research Management in the Philippines.* Quezon City, Philippines: Sentro para sa Ganap na Pamayanan.

Foucault, Michel. 1980. *Power/Knowledge: Selected Interviews and Other Writings, 1972–1977.* Colin Gordon, ed. and trans. New York: Pantheon.

Garvan, John M. 1929. *The Manobos of Mindanao.* Washington, D.C.: National Academy of Sciences.

Gatmaytan, Augusto B. 1995. *Manobo Customs and Traditions: Focus on Land Resource Use.* Unpublished documentation submitted to the Department of Environment and Natural Resources in support for the Certificate of Ancestral Domain Claim application of the Manobo community of Sitio Manguicao, Brgy. Lydia, La Paz, Agusan del Sur province.

———. 1996. Lines across the Land: The State, Ancestral Domains Delineation and the Manobos of Agusan del Sur. *Philippine Natural Resources Law Journal* 7(1): 5–34.

———. 1998. Traditional Manobo Agriculture: Upland Rice Cultivation in the Upper Adgawan River. *Kinaadman* 20(1–4): 1–52.

———. 2000a. Change and the Divided Community: Cautionary Notes on the Documentation of Indigenous Law. In *Lawyering for the Public Interest (Proceedings of the First Alternative Law Conference, 8–12 November 1999, U.P. College of Law, Diliman, Quezon City*, ed. Marvic Leonen. Quezon City, Philippines: Alternative Law Groups.

———. 2000b. Mapmaker: Mythmaker. In *Mapping The Earth, Mapping Life*, ed. Ponciano Bennagen and Antoinette Royo. Quezon City, Philippines: Legal Rights and Natural Resources Center—Kasama Sa Kalikasan.

———. 2001a. The Political Implications of Banwaon Indigenous Law. Paper presented at the Symposium on the Indigenous Peoples Rights Act of 1997, 24–26 October 2001, Univ. of the Philippines, Quezon City.

———. 2001b. Constructions in Conflict: Manobo Tenure as Critique of Law. Paper presented at the 23rd National Conference of the Ugnayang Agham-Tao (Anthropological Association of the Philippines), 22–23 October 2001, Univ. of the Philippines, Quezon City.

———. Forthcoming Issues in Community Resource Management in Northern Mindanaw. Paper prepared for the International Center for Research in Agro-Forestry.

Gibbs, Christopher, Edwin Payuan, and Romulo del Castillo. 1990. The Growth of the Philippine Social Forestry Program. In *Keepers of the Forest: Land Management Alternatives in Southeast Asia*, ed. Mark Poffenberger. Quezon City, Philippines: Ateneo de Manila Univ.

Giddens, Anthony. 1985. *The Nation-State and Violence*. Cambridge: Polity Press.

Ingold, Tim. 1987. *The Appropriation of Nature: Essays on Human Ecology and Social Relations*. Iowa City: Univ. of Iowa Press.

Kalihukang Nagkahi-usang Minorya. N.d. *Ancestral Domain Management Plan (for CADC No. 18)*. Las Nieves, Agusan del Norte province

Leonen, Marvic M. V. F. 1998. Indigenous Peoples Rights Act of 1997 (R.A. 8371): Will This Legal Reality Bring Us to a More Progressive Level of Political Discourse? *Philippine Natural Resources Law Journal* 9(1): 7–45.

———. 2000. NGO Influence on Environmental Policy. In *Forest Policy and Politics in the Philippines: The Dynamics of Participatory Conservation*, ed. Peter Utting. Quezon City, Philippines: United Nations Research Institute for Social Development / Ateneo de Manila Univ.

Merry, Sally Engle. 1992. Anthropology, Law and Transnational Processes. *Annual Review Anthropology* 21: 357–79.

Nagengast, Carole. 1994. Violence, Terror and the Crisis of the State. *Annual Review of Anthropology* 23: 109–36.

Pavia, Antonio, ed. 1998. *A Word, a Comma, Millions of Lives: Perspectives on Senate Bill 1728*. Quezon City, Philippines: UNAC and Katutubong Samahan ng Pilipinas.

Resurreccion, Babette P., and Edsel E. Sajor. 1998. *People, Power and Resources in*

Everyday Life: Critical Essays on the Politics of Environment in the Philippines. Quezon City, Philippines: Institute for Popular Democracy.

Van Den Top, Gerhard, and Gerard Persoon. 2000. Dissolving State Responsibilities to Forests in Northeast Luzon. In *Old Ties, New Solidarities: Studies on Philippine Communities*, ed. Charles J. H. Macdonald and Guillermo M. Pesigan. Quezon City, Philippines: Ateneo de Manila Univ.

Vayda, Andrew P. 1992. Studying Human Actions and Their Environmental Consequences. In *Forestry for People and Nature: Field Research and Theory on Environment and Development in the Cagayan Valley, Philippines*, ed. Cagayan Valley Programme on Environment and Development (CVPED). Isabela, Philippines: Isabela State Univ.

von Benda-Beckmann, Franz. 1993. Scapegoat and Magic Charm: Law in Development Theory and Practice. In *An Anthropological Critique of Development*, ed. Mark Hobart. London and New York: Routledge.

Index

About the Contributors

Janis B. Alcorn is community conservation manager at the Center for Cultural Understanding and Change of the Field Museum and biodiversity advisor to the Garfield Foundation since 2002. She began her career as a village development Peace Corps volunteer in central India. In 1982 she received her doctorate in botany with a minor in anthropology from the University of Texas at Austin. After teaching for three years at Tulane University, she moved to Washington, D.C., to serve as an AAAS Diplomacy Fellow in the U.S. Agency for International Development (USAID) from 1988 to 1990. From 1991 to 2001 she served as director for the Asia program and the Global Peoples, Forests and Reefs program of the Biodiversity Support Program at the World Wildlife Fund (WWF-US). She has carried out research and applied fieldwork in Mexico, Peru, Bolivia, Panama, Namibia, Tanzania, India, Nepal, Bangladesh, Thailand, Indonesia, Philippines, Papua New Guinea, and North America. She has published five books and more than eighty articles on ecology, conservation, ethnobotany, resource management, democratic governance, indigenous peoples, nongovernmental organizations (NGOs), donor best practices, and public policy. She is currently supporting Garfield's program in the Gran Chaco and the Upper Amazon and leading Field's collaborative conservation work in the biodiverse region of Pando, Bolivia, involving municipal governments, communities, NGOs, and the University of the Amazon of Pando.

Grazia Borrini-Feyerabend works on social concerns in conservation both as a volunteer and a consultant. She is vice chair of the CEESP and WCPA Commissions of the IUCN–The World Conservation Union, author of ten books (including *The Wealth of Communities, Beyond Fences—Seeking Social Sustainability in Conservation*, and *Co-management of Natural*

Resources—Organising, Negotiating and Learning by Doing) and cofounder of the NGO Keyke Mate (*solidarity* in the Kotoko language).

J. Peter Brosius is an associate professor in the Department of Anthropology at the University of Georgia, and president of the Anthropology and Environment Section of the American Anthropological Association. He is an associate editor of the journal *Human Ecology* and is on the editorial board of the *American Anthropologist*. His early research explored the historical ecology of deforestation on Mt. Pinatubo, Philippines, but his more recent work has focused on international environmental politics in Sarawak, East Malaysia. Brosius has published widely on ecological and environmental issues and has published extensively in journals such as *American Anthropologist, Current Anthropology, Ambio, Society and Natural Resources, Comparative Studies in Society and History*, and *Identities and Human Ecology*. He is currently completing a book, *Arresting Images: The Sarawak Rainforest Campaign and Transnational Environmental Politics*.

Marcus Colchester received his doctorate in anthropology at the University of Oxford in 1982, on the "Economy, Ecology and Ethnobiology of the Sanema Indians of South Venezuela." He then worked as a consultant in Venezuela studying the impact of development projects on Indians and as a regional coordinator of the national Indigenous Census. As projects director of Survival International, his work focused on the effects of imposed development schemes on human rights, especially in Amazonia, south Asia, and Southeast Asia. He sat on the International Labour Organization's expert committee on the revision of Convention 107. He is a founder member of the World Rainforest Movement, an international network of activists concerned about rainforest destruction. In 1990 he set up the Forest Peoples Programme, which has developed into a well-known NGO active in the field of indigenous rights and the environment. He is currently director. His advocacy work has focused on standard setting and compliance on indigenous rights by United Nations agencies and multilateral and bilateral aid agencies. He has also strongly advocated reforms in conservation policies to respect indigenous peoples' rights. In 1994 he was awarded a Few Conservation Fellowship in recognition of his work in this field. He has acted as a consultant for the International Commission on International Humanitarian Issues, the United Nations Research Institute on Social Development, the World Bank, the World Commission on Dams, the International Centre for Research in Agroforestry, the Centre for International Forestry Research, the World Wide Fund for Nature, the Food and Agriculture Organisation (FAO), the UN Office of the High Commissioner for Human Rights, the Indonesian Environment Forum (WALHI) and the Biodiversity Support Program. He has published extensively in academic and NGO journals and is the author and editor of numerous books, including *The Struggle for Land and the Fate of the Forests* (1993) with Larry Lohmann, and *Guyana: Fragile Frontier—Loggers, Miners and Forest Peoples* (1997). In 2001 he was awarded the Royal Anthropological Institute's Lucy Mair Medal for Applied Anthropology. He is married with two children and lives in the Cotswolds in England.

E. Walter Coward, at the time this chapter was prepared, was a senior director at the Ford Foundation, where he worked for nearly a decade. Before that he was professor of Rural Sociology and Asian Studies at Cornell University, and there he also served as chair of the Department of Rural Sociology, and director of the International Agricultural Program. Now retired, his current interests are with the problems of environment and development in mountainous regions. His most recent publication is "The Kulu Valleys in Motion" (*Himalayan Research Bulletin* 21 [2001]: 5–14), dealing with these issues in the western Himalayas.

Louise Fortmann is a professor of natural resource sociology in the Department of Environmental Science, Policy and Management, University of California at Berkeley. She holds the Rudy Grah Chair in Forestry and Sustainable Development. Her research concerns gender, property, poverty, and the democratization of science. Her inability to milk a cow is the source of much hilarity in her Zimbabwe field site.

Augusto B. Gatmaytan is a lawyer, community organizer, and anthropologist in the Philippines. He began working on issues of indigenous peoples in 1987 and has since focused on assisting Manobo, Banwaon, and other indigenous communities in northern Mindanaw Island.

Emmy Hafild currently serves as secretary general of Transparency International-Indonesia, a coalition of organizations dedicated to promoting government accountability and fighting corruption. Prior to this she was director of WALHI, the Indonesian Forum for Environment/Friends of the Earth.

Tania Li is professor in the Department of Anthropology, University of Toronto. Her work on urban cultural politics resulted in her book *Malays in Singapore* (1989). Since 1990 her research has focused on questions of culture, economy, environment, and development in Indonesia's upland regions. She edited the collection *Transforming the Indonesian Uplands* (1999). Her articles on Indonesia's indigenous peoples' movement, on the formation of communities, on agrarian transformations, and on state-organized resettlement have appeared in journals such as *Development and*

Change, *Cultural Anthropology*, *Comparative Studies in Society and History*, and *World Development*. Her current research concerns governmentality in its colonial and contemporary iterations.

Owen J. Lynch is a senior attorney and director of the Law and Communities Program at the Center for International Environmental Law (CIEL) in Washington, D.C. He has been engaged for more than two decades in fostering public interest law careers in Asia and more recently Africa, the Pacific, and Latin America. His focus is issues related to human rights and sustainable development, and his special expertise is in community-based property rights (CBPR) and their legal recognition in national and international laws. Owen has authored many scholarly articles on rural peoples, legal history, and CBPR and policy advocacy reports. He has coauthored *Whose Resources? Whose Common Good? Towards a New Paradigm of Environmental Justice and the National Interest in Indonesia* (2002) and *Balancing Acts: Community-Based Forest Management and National Law in Asia and the Pacific* (1995).

Marshall W. Murphree was born in Zimbabwe. He was educated at universities in the United States and the United Kingdom, and holds a doctorate in social anthropology from the London School of Economics and Political Science. From 1970 to 1996 he was director of the Centre for Applied Social Sciences at the University of Zimbabwe, and he has been visiting professor at the Universities of Oxford, North Carolina, Duke, and California (at Berkeley). Since retirement in 1996, he has been professor emeritus at the University of Zimbabwe. He is the author of more than seventy publications on rural development and natural resource management, among the most recent being *African Wildlife and Livelihoods: The Promise and Performance of Community Conservation* (2001, edited with D. Hulme), "Protected Areas and the Commons" (2002, *Common Property Resource Digest*), and "Control and the Holy Grail" (2003, in *The Trade in Wildlife*, ed. S. Oldfield). Professor Murphree was chairman of Zimbabwe's Parks and Wildlife Board from 1992–1995 and chairman of IUCN's Sustainable Use Specialist Group from 1994 to 2000. He has been the recipient of a number of conservation awards, the latest being IUCN's Sir Peter Scott Medal for Conservation.

Roderick P. Neumann is associate professor of geography in the Department of International Relations at Florida International University, in Miami. His research interests include the political ecology of Africa and the critical analysis of British colonial conservation geography. He is the author of *Imposing Wilderness: Struggles over Livelihoods and Nature Preservation in Africa*. His newest book, *Making Political Ecology*, is forthcoming.

Peter Poole received his doctorate in geography at McGill University. For the last ten years he has been training community-based teams in mapmaking in the Amazon basin, Southeast Asia and Russia—all of which were used to address tenure issues. In the previous ten years, he worked mostly with Arctic communities on resource-related projects. With a colleague in the Netherlands, he recently formed an Amsterdam-based NGO, Local Earth Observation. Their objective is to provide training and technical support to community-based resource-management groups to maximize their capacity to gather, analyze, and apply the environmental information that they need to manage their lands and negotiate with rival resource interests. In cooperation with the First Nations Aviation Flying School, Tyendinaga Mohawk Territory, he is currently engaged in training projects with Saramaka in Suriname and Inuit in Nunavut, that combine aerial and ground data gathering.

Dianne Rocheleau is an associate professor of geography at Clark University, where she also teaches in the Women's Studies Program, the Global Environmental Studies Program, and the International Development, Community and Environment Program. Before joining the Clark faculty in 1989, she was a senior scientist at the International Center for Research in Agroforestry (ICRAF) and a program officer at the Ford Foundation, Nairobi. She has worked with community-based organizations on land use and conservation research for the past twenty-five years on questions of applied ecology, political ecology, landscape change, and environmental justice, primarily in Kenya, the Dominican Republic, and the United States. She has served on several boards, including the Land Tenure Center, the Center for International Forestry Research (CIFOR), and the International Association for the Study of Common Property (IASCP), and on panels with the National Science Foundation and the National Academy of Sciences, as well as the editorial boards of *Forests, Trees and Livelihoods*; *Gender, Place and Culture* and the *Geographical Journal*. She is coeditor of *Feminist Political Ecology* (1996) and a volume on methodology, *Power, Process and Participation* (1995). She has also coauthored two books: *Agroforestry in Dryland Africa* (1988) and *Gender, Environment and Development in Kenya* (1995). She received a fellowship at Radcliffe Institute for Advanced Study at Harvard University in 2002–2003 to work on a book in progress: *The Invisible Ecologies of Machakos: Landscapes and Life Stories, 1900–2000.*

Richard Schroeder is graduate director and associate professor of geography at Rutgers University. He is the author of *Shady Practices: Agroforestry and Gender Politics in The Gambia* (1999) and coeditor of *Producing Nature and Poverty in Africa* (2000). He is currently conducting research on environmental justice concerns related to wildlife tourism in Tanzania and the political ecology of mushroom harvesting on public lands in two national parks in the Washington, D.C., area.

Richard Chase Smith is an anthropologist who has carried out research and worked among indigenous and nonindigenous residents of the Andean Amazon in Ecuador, Peru, and Bolivia since the late 1960s. His research interests have included the historical links between Andean and Amazonian peoples and cultures; the music, cosmology, and oral history of the Amuesha people (Peru); the politics of land and resource tenure for Amazonian peoples; natural-resource management in Amazonian communities; and the application of geographic information system (GIS) technology to resource and tenure issues. He is a founder and current director of the Instituto del Bien Común in Lima, Peru. He has been a postdoctoral Fellow at Harvard University, and a visiting senior scientist at the Woods Hole Research Center and teaches in the Social Science Graduate Program at San Marcos University, in Lima. He earned his doctorate in anthropology and linguistics at Cornell University.

Christopher B. Tarnowski is a visiting assistant professor of anthropology at Franklin and Marshall College. His research and teaching interests range from the politics of resource management and conservation, nature, development, and ethnic minority policies in Nepal and Southeast Asia to environmentalism and grassroots environmental movements in the United States.

Roem Topatimasang has been a senior facilitator of Indonesian NGOs since the 1980s. He is a founder of Baileo Maluku, a network of organizations of local people's and indigenous people's organizations of the Moluccas, initiated in 1993. He spends most of his time in remote local communities in Indonesia, Malaysia, Cambodia, Vietnam, Thailand, and Timor Lorosa'e. He continues to work as a senior consultant to Maluku's Institutional Capacity and Resources Development Consultants (MICROS) based in Tual, Kei Islands, southeast Moluccas; and to Resources Management and Development Consultants (REMDEC) based in Jakarta. He is a senior facilitator of the Jogyakarta-based Institute for Social Transformation (INSIST), and the Popular Communication Program of the South East Asia Regional Institute for Community Education (PCP-SEARICE) based in Kuala Lumpur. He has written books, monographs, and training manuals on popular education, community organizing, local autonomy, natural-resources management, and the rights of indigenous peoples in Indonesia and Southeast Asian countries. A brief description of his activism, beginning when he was a student of the Teachers' College of the Institute of Educational Sciences in Bandung, West Java, can be found in Dan La Botz's *Made in Indonesia: Indonesian Workers since Suharto* (2001, 2–7).

Anna Lowenhaupt Tsing teaches anthropology at the University of California, Santa Cruz. She is the author of *Friction: An Ethnography of Global Connection* and *In the Realm of the Diamond Queen*. She coedited *Nature in the Global South* (with Paul Greenough) and *Uncertain Terms: Negotiating Gender in American Culture* (with Faye Ginsburg). Her current research focuses on transnational environmental movements in and beyond Indonesia.

Kenneth Wilson was born and raised in Malawi and was involved particularly in Zimbabwe during the 1980s, where he researched his doctorate in ecological anthropology. He was engaged in rural Mozambique from 1989 to 2000, first as a research officer for the Refugee Studies Programme at the University of Oxford and then as the Ford Foundation's program officer responsible for grant making in environment and development, culture and higher education. Following two years with the Ford Foundation in New York as the deputy to the vice president for Education, Media, Arts and Culture, he relocated to California as executive director at The Christensen Fund, developing grant making internationally in arts and culture and environment within a biocultural diversity framework. He holds degrees from the University of Oxford and University College London, and, more importantly, has two daughters.

Charles Zerner is Barbara B. and Bertram Cohn Professor of Environmental Studies at Sarah Lawrence College, codirector of the Environmental Studies/Science, Technology and Society Colloquium Series. He is a contributing editor of *People, Plants, and Justice: The Politics of Nature Conservation* (2000) and *Culture and the Question of Rights: Forests, Coasts and Seas in Southeast Asia* (2002). He is coeditor of *Making Threats: Biofears and Environmental Anxieties* (with Elizabeth Hartmann and Banu Subramania; in press). Zerner has published widely on the history of community-based common property institutions in the Moluccas of Eastern Indonesia. A former botanical artist and trained as a lawyer, Zerner has conducted fieldwork on environmental, legal, and cultural issues in Indonesia as a consultant for the FAO, the World Bank, the Asian Development Bank, and USAID.